P9-EMH-974

JIHAD INCORPORATED

JIHAD INCORPORATED

A Guide to
Militant Islam
in the US

STEVEN EMERSON
and the
Investigative Project
on Terrorism

Prometheus Books
59 John Glenn Drive
Amherst, New York 14228-2197

Published 2006 by Prometheus Books

Inquiries should be addressed to
Prometheus Books
59 John Glenn Drive
Amherst, New York 14228–2197
VOICE: 716–691–0133, ext. 207
FAX: 716–564–2711
WWW.PROMETHEUSBOOKS.COM

10 09 08 07 06 5 4 3 2 1

Library of Congress Cataloging-in-Publication Data

Emerson, Steven.
Jihad incorporated : a guide to militant Islam in the US / by Steven Emerson.
p. cm.
ISBN 13: 978-1-59102-453-8 (hardcover : alk. paper)
ISBN 10: 1-59102-453-6 (hardcover : alk. paper)
1. Terrorists—United States. 2. Terrorism—Religious aspects—Islam. 3. Muslims—United States. 4. Jihad. 5. Islamic fundamentalism. 6. Qaida (Organization) I. Title.

HV6432.E46 2006
363.3250973—dc22 2006020265

Printed in the United States on acid-free paper

This report is dedicated to Jason Scott Korsower, a man of exquisite patience, drive, and intellect whose work is reflected in this report in the core material on terror financing. May he rest in the peace he loved and sought for all people.

CONTENTS

FOREWORD

On September 11, 2001, Americans felt the full fury of al Qaeda as it came to our shores, killing some three thousand people in attacks on the World Trade Center in New York and the Pentagon outside Washington, DC.

As I write this, the United States has managed to go five full years without another tragic attack occurring on its soil. Yet, it would surprise and shock most Americans to learn of the extent to which al Qaeda and other radical Islamic groups have implanted themselves in the United States. From nonprofit "charities" operating under false cover to actual al Qaeda cells to "homegrown" terrorist cells, jihadist groups have been active on American soil for years. Moreover, they continue to stay active: besides al Qaeda being here, Hizballah, Hamas, Islamic Jihad, Lashkar e Tayba, and numerous other groups have recruited supporters, raised funds, disseminated propaganda, planned operations, or carried out paramilitary training. Although the government has done an excellent job in tracking and prosecuting many of these groups, the freedoms of our open society have also afforded protection to others in the radical Islamic orbit.

The government relies on an arsenal of legal weapons to track and prosecute jihadist groups. However, at the same time, organizations in the nongovernmental arena can and do play a pivotal role in shining a light on the activities of those same groups. Often, these public interest organizations—groups like Steven Emerson's Investigative Project on Terrorism—can expose the activities of the radical Islamists in ways that the government cannot.

The governmental role in the War on Terror, in uncovering and fighting the terrorists wherever they may appear, falls both to the executive branch headed by the president and to the US Congress, where I have been privileged to play a role as chairman of the House Intelligence Committee.

As I said on the floor of the House when we considered—and decisively approved—the Global War on Terror resolution in June, the war we find ourselves in with radical Islamists was not of our choosing, but it is the central struggle of our time, the first major conflict of the Information Age.

That war, I noted, did not begin on 9/11. Though that was the occasion that brought the issue squarely to public concern, the battle had begun to come into focus as far back as "2/26"—February 26, 1993, the date of the first, less utterly disastrous, attack on the World Trade Center. Then came the intervening attacks on the Khobar Towers in June 1996, the strikes on our embassies in Kenya and Tanzania in August 1998, and the attack on the USS *Cole* in October 2000.

While those terrorist forays carried overseas datelines, it is vital to recognize the threat of homegrown terrorism—a strain of the terror virus that has already been experienced in Spain, the United Kingdom, Australia, the Netherlands, and, most recently, Canada—and that is unquestionably in the planning stages in our own country as well.

It is in drawing public attention to the dangerous reality of those threats that groups such as terrorist investigator Steven Emerson's Investigative Project on Terrorism come into play. The Investigative Project on Terrorism is a public interest organization that tracks, monitors, and exposes the activities of jihadist groups operating on American soil. Emerson founded the organization in 1995, shortly after broadcast of his pioneering documentary *Jihad in America* on public television in November 1994. Today, it is considered one of the largest repositories of intelligence in the world on the activities, funding, and operations of radical Islamic groups here in the United States and their ties to overseas groups.

Independently supported by contributions from US donors only, the Investigative Project on Terrorism has been in the forefront in the war against militant Islam. The organization works closely with law enforcement and intelligence agencies as well as with members of Congress. I have often received invaluable information from Emerson and his team of investigators, sometimes better than the intelligence I get from official US governmental briefings.

In *Jihad Incorporated*, Emerson and his staff have chronicled the history and operations of militant Islam in the United States. Impeccably sourced, the book lays out in shocking detail the operations of the entire spectrum of radical Islamic groups operating here. Based on court records, law enforcement sources, open-source intelligence, and internal Islamic organization documents, *Jihad Incorporated* is a veritable encyclopedia as well as a definitive chronology of the history of jihadist groups that have been active in the United States. The Investigative Project on Terrorism has performed a true public service in compiling this material. It makes for unsettling reading but it is indispensable to anyone interesting in the nation's security and in knowing more about al Qaeda, Hamas, Hizballah, and virtually every other radical Islamic group in the United States.

The global war against radical Islam will be long, and it will require the patience and perseverance of the American people. That, in turn, will require broad awareness of just the sort of detailed, carefully researched, and substantiated information that this volume provides.

Congressman Peter Hoekstra
Chairman of the House Permanent Select Committee
on Intelligence, July 2006

THE INVESTIGATIVE PROJECT

The Investigative Project was founded in late 1995 by Steven Emerson, who now serves as the project's executive director. The project's foundation lay in the knowledge and research materials used for the documentary *Jihad in America*, broadcast on November 21, 1994. Today, the project maintains the largest nongovernmental data and intelligence library in the world on militant Islam. Project archives contain more than four million documents; thousands of hours of clandestine video- and audiotapes of militant Islamic training, fund-raising, and recruitment gatherings; and tens of thousands of original terrorist manuals, telephone books, and periodicals. The project has in its employ analysts, translators, audio and visual specialists, and undercover operatives.

The project assists the White House, the FBI, the Justice Department, DHS border security agencies, the Secret Service, the Pentagon and its Office of Special Operations, and the Treasury Department in its counterterrorism activities. On numerous specific occasions, the work of the project has enabled law enforcement to successfully intervene in terrorist activity when evidence was otherwise lacking. Key prosecutions against terrorist financiers and leaders operating in the United States have come about, in many instances, because of the singular initial investigations conducted by the project, many of which have been undertaken since 9/11.

INTRODUCTION

Since September 11, 2001, the United States has been engaged in a conflict that surpasses any past conflict in scope and measure. The war on terrorism has demanded, but not exhausted, American efforts, attentions, and national power in every corner of the globe. This conflict is unprecedented because it is waged against a tactic employed by a cruel and repressive ideology that exhorts its adherents to violently oppose that which Western civilization relies upon—namely, natural rights, plurality, and the individual empowerment bestowed by liberty. The terrorists rely on asymmetrical tactics and victimize the civilians among us, often not discriminating between man and woman or between adult and child. They see only the infidel. They see only the *kafir*.

The oft-spoken wisdom is that the 9/11 attacks changed everything. However, reality reveals a different picture. While 9/11 served to clarify and refocus the strategic landscape after the era of strategic uncertainty that followed the end of the Cold War, and while the attacks may have reverberated deep into our national psyche, five years after the attacks we live our lives much as we did on September 10, 2001, aside from longer lines at airports. The American public and the West at large seem to have settled into a dangerous complacency, still unaware of the nature of the diffuse threat that faces our society and way of life. Despite the media's extensive coverage of the subject of terrorism, the public still lacks a substantive understanding of Islamic radicalism, the danger it poses, and the extent to which it operates in the United States—in our cities and even in our halls of government. Societal factors, cultural tendencies, and various groups perpetuate what has become an almost willful ignorance in America. Chief among these factors are extremist groups serving as proxies for our enemies, seeking to block public awareness and render our country ineffective and impotent against our enemies. They conspire to subvert the exercise of public discourse through intimidation and flimsy accusations of racism and exclusion from behind false masks of moderation. These self-styled "advocacy groups" undermine genuine moderate and patriotic Muslim Americans whom they claim to speak for by subverting America's efforts to combat those whose agenda they advance—the Muslim Brotherhood, Hamas, and the Palestinian Islamic Jihad.

These "advocacy groups" have insinuated themselves into the efforts of our government to reach out to Muslim Americans. One may think that productive cooperation between authorities and truly moderate Muslim American leaders would not be difficult to accomplish, but groups that operate in the United States and ascribe to the ideology of the Muslim Brotherhood have assumed control over this outreach and rendered it ineffectual. The true moderates are sidelined by the better-organized and better-funded Islamists who monopolize the discussion with authorities and policymakers.

Radical Islamists have insinuated themselves in the structure of American society to the degree that they have been able to advance their violent and radical cause, often with impunity, through advocacy groups, an array of disingenuous charities and foundations, corporate financing networks, and the halls of academia. Before 9/11, Islamist extremists took advantage of US tax laws and the large Muslim population by setting up charities that operated as terrorist front groups for fund-raising and propaganda purposes. These charities arose as a favored method of terrorist fund-raising among Muslim communities, because charitable giving, or *zakat*, is an obligation for practicing Muslims. While many in the Muslim American community may have been unaware of the true nature of these charities, others undoubtedly were. Extremists in America and elsewhere have exploited this religious goodwill with relative ease, deceiving Muslims who thought they were donating money to help the needy, orphans, or victims of natural disasters. After 9/11, the US government shut down most of the charities with ties to radical Islamic groups, but others have sprung up in their place, with the same individuals and directors as the shuttered charities.

A prominent example of the infiltration of an academic institution is the case of former University of South Florida computer science professor Sami al-Arian, who finally stands convicted, having pled guilty to supporting the Palestinian Islamic Jihad and, as of the writing of this book, faces eighteen more months in prison followed by deportation. In addition to attaining status in the community as a university professor, al-Arian used his position at the university to set up a "think tank," which provided the university with Arabic and Middle Eastern studies professors. Among those he vouched for is the current Secretary-General of the

Palestinian Islamic Jihad, Ramadan Abdullah Shallah, who taught Middle Eastern studies at the University of South Florida until he left in 1995 to assume leadership of the terrorist group. Al-Arian, Shallah, and their colleagues set up annual conferences in the United States in the late eighties and early nineties at which they openly hosted terrorist leaders, including the notorious Egyptian blind shiekh, Omar Abdel Rahman, for the purposes of raising money for the Palestinian Islamic Jihad and spreading *jihadist* propaganda.

An interesting example of corporate infiltration can be found in Virginia, where authorities are still in the midst of exploring the full extent of what has been alleged to be a vast financing network composed of over one hundred corporations, charities, and foundations, most of which are registered at the same nondescript address in Herndon, with interlocking boards of directors. The men who led this vast syndicate, known as the SAAR Network, have documented ties to Islamic extremists and to an overseas financial institution, Bank Al Taqwa. Authorities have alleged that Al Taqwa served Osama bin Laden and the Muslim Brotherhood. Vast amounts of money were shuttled back and forth among the different elements of the SAAR Network and to overseas bank accounts in a pattern that has aroused deep suspicion within several federal agencies and led to a series of raids and seizures.

In the operational behavior of these organizations in the United States and abroad, a clear strategy is evident. Since 9/11, the overarching structure of militant Islam in the world has taken on the characteristics of a worldwide conglomerate. The headquarters of this conglomerate controls the ideology, mission, message, and direction of the entire organization, but bestows considerable operational autonomy on its subsidiaries, which take the form of terrorist cells, charities, companies, advocacy groups, theological organizations, and think tanks. In the United States, we find these subsidiaries working largely in a public relations and financing capacity, but, as this book also demonstrates, American-based subsidiaries of Jihad Inc. have not shied away from pursuing violent goals on our soil.

Five years into the war on terrorism, Osama bin Laden and his al Qaeda associates remain the leading threat to US security despite the neutralization of much of al Qaeda's core leadership through a campaign of apprehension and elimination that began with the infiltration by US Special Forces into Taliban-controlled Afghanistan in 2001. Al Qaeda survived this campaign by radically transforming its modus operandi and structure. Bin Laden, who acts as both guide and ideological leader to al Qaeda operatives, remains isolated, reportedly somewhere on the Afghanistan-Pakistan border, and has grown increasingly dependent on other, more loosely knit affiliated groups to wage jihad. Terrorist groups and provisional cells that share al Qaeda's ideology and commitment to global jihad born out of Algeria, Pakistan, Indonesia, the Philippines, Europe, and elsewhere now represent the primary threat, having assumed frontline responsibility from the core al Qaeda organization. Meanwhile, Iraq has replaced Afghanistan as the new battleground in the war on terrorism. Militant Islamists from the Middle East, Europe, and elsewhere have made Iraq their destination, where they have waged a brutal terrorist campaign in order to drive Iraq into a full-blown civil war along sectarian lines.

On the home front, Zacarias Moussaoui was sentenced to life in prison for his role in the 9/11 attacks in May 2006. The Moussaoui trial provides valuable insight into the difficulties of obtaining tactical intelligence on terrorist attacks today. Despite the belief that the information Moussaoui withheld could have prevented the 9/11 attacks, evidence and testimony from the trial raise questions about the extent of his knowledge of and involvement in the 9/11 plot. Perhaps it is not enough to rely on intelligence and diplomacy to stop the threat of modern terrorism. Terrorist organizations are proficient at utilizing the resources and weaknesses of the United States and other Western countries to further their agendas, including open financial systems, wider access to modern technology, and the basic freedoms of movement and religion. Open societies are inherently and necessarily at a disadvantage in providing a secure environment. The exploitation of these aspects of open societies is what allows the transnational network of terrorists to thrive while remaining hidden. At the Investigative Project on Terrorism (IPT), we have taken on the task of monitoring and investigating terrorist and extremist networks in the United States in order to compensate for the vulnerabilities of our society. This book represents a part of our contribution to the war on terrorism and the national effort to keep our homeland secure.

In *American Jihad*, Steven Emerson told the tale of the infiltration of radical Islamism into American society. This book revisits the same themes, but serves as a broader reference for the public. The Investigative Project on Terrorism staff was responsible for the extensive research in this report. Each analyst at the IPT was given multiple assignments;

some contributed their expertise by topic area while others concentrated on a particular terrorist organization. The overall purpose of the research was to provide a solid factual foundation for answering the question: What is the structure of al Qaeda and radical Islamic activity in the United States today and how has it evolved since 9/11?

At the IPT, we decided that to make a determination about the full panoply of enterprises that support terrorist organizations, we had to address a question that affects every American: To what extent does radical Islamic activity in the United States today pose a threat to US national security at home and abroad? Although no answer can be definitive, the IPT's goal is to set forth sufficient facts so that the American people, policy-makers, and law enforcement officers have the authoritative information needed to engage in a meaningful debate about the government's allocation of its limited resources and its future policy on homeland security.

PART ONE

AL QAEDA TARGETS THE UNITED STATES

-1-

AL QAEDA PRE-9/11: AMERICA FOREWARNED

The 9/11 attack . . . was carried out by a tiny group of people, not enough to man a full platoon. Measured on a governmental scale, the resources behind it were trivial. The group itself was dispatched by an organization based in one of the poorest, most remote, and least industrialized countries on earth. This organization recruited a mixture of young fanatics and highly educated zealots who could not find suitable places in their home societies or were driven from them.

—*The 9/11 Commission Report*

OVERVIEW

It has become accepted wisdom that the 9/11 attacks on America were carried out by a small group of selectively trained individuals operating on a marginal budget that somehow was capable of defeating the security systems of the world's greatest power. The shock at the vulnerability of America to this kind of assault has prompted significant and deserved reflection on a variety of security-related issues not the least of which include immigration policies, airline security, and intelligence sharing.

While all of these reviews are important, it is also illustrative to examine how it came to be that the nineteen terrorists acted as they did in carrying out their attacks. Their actions were not spontaneous or uncalculated. To the contrary, the terrorist attacks of September 11, 2001, were literally the products of lessons learned by al Qaeda over a previous decade of attacks and from a network of senior al Qaeda leaders within America itself.

Al Qaeda is much more than a scattered group of fanatical killers who appear on the world stage every few years through an act of violence and terror. It is an enterprise of terror defined by its meticulous planning, complex fund-raising, and ongoing recruitment through extremist interpretations of Islam. Only by understanding its past actions can we properly assess its current and future intentions. This is the place to start.

THE PRE-9/11 ATTACKS: PLANNING, EXECUTION, AND LEARNING

Al Qaeda began to plan attacks against American targets as early as 1992, when the group's Shura Council issued a fatwa calling for a holy war against the Western "occupation" of Islamic lands.[1] Initially, as al Qaeda was still a small group in its developing phase, most of the attacks were carried out by individuals and groups whose affiliations with bin Laden's organization were mostly ideological. While they cannot be properly characterized as al Qaeda operatives, these operations played a very significant role in the formation of today's al Qaeda. It was thanks to the alliances formed and cultivated in the 1990s and to the skills it acquired through this symbiosis that al Qaeda became increasingly capable of carrying out terrorist attacks throughout the world. Al Qaeda's leadership patiently learned from the successes and the mistakes of its own operations as well as those of its affiliates', improving in efficiency and sophistication with time. This learning experience culminated in the attacks of 9/11, which represented the peak of its operational abilities.

This chapter looks at the Islamist terrorist attacks prior to 9/11, both planned and executed, in chronological order. The 1993 World Trade Center bombing is explored at greatest length, because the details of this (partially) successful operation have provided a template for terrorists seeking to operate inside the United States.

World Trade Center 1993

On February 26, 1993, a few minutes after noon, an explosive device went off beneath the two towers of New York City's World Trade Center. Six people died as a result of the explosion, while more than one thousand had to be treated for injuries. Given the power of the device, authorities were relieved that the number of victims was so relatively small, and an FBI agent subsequently described it as a "miracle."[2] In fact, the structural damage caused by the bomb, which had been placed in a van parked in the underground garage, was significant. The explosion tore a seven-story gash through the structure and almost toppled the Vista Hotel, located on top of the garage where the bomb was detonated. The evacuation of the thousands of panicked office workers was made more difficult by the fact that firefighters had to cut off electric power, because the two million gallons of water pouring from broken pipes to the lower levels of the parking garage could dangerously come in contact with damaged electric systems and cause electrocution.[3]

In the hours following the attack, a claim of responsibility was left on the *New York Daily News* tip line. The message claimed that the "Liberation Army" was responsible for the blast and announced that a list of demands would be sent by mail. A letter containing an ominous message was later received by the *New York Times*:

> We are, the fifth battalion in the Liberation Army, declare our responsibility for the explosion on the mentioned building. This action was done in response for the American political, economical, and military support to Israel the state of terrorism and to the rest of the dictator countries in the region.
>
> Our Demands Are:
>
> 1. Stop all military, economical, and political aid to Israel.
> 2. All diplomatic relations with Israel must stop.
> 3. Not to interfere with any of the Middle East countries interior affairs.
>
> If our demands are not met, all of our functional groups in the army will continue to execute our missions against the military and civilian targets in and out of the United States. For your own information, our army has more than hundred and fifty suicidal soldiers ready to go ahead. The terrorism that Israel practices (Which is supported by America) must be faced with a similar one. The dictatorship and terrorism (also supported by America) that some countries are practicing against their own people must also be faced with terrorism.
>
> The American people must know that their civilians who got killed are not better than those who are getting killed by the American weapons and support.
>
> The American people are responsible for the actions of their government and they must question all for the crimes that their government is committing against other people. Or they—Americans—will be the targets of our operations that could diminish them.[4]

The hunt for the perpetrators began immediately after the attacks. Investigators obtained an important lead while combing through the debris in the garage of the World Trade Center. In this debris, they managed to find the vehicle identification number (VIN) of the van in which the bomb had been placed. Authorities immediately linked the Ford Econoline cargo van to a Ryder rental agency in New Jersey. Three days before the attack the van had been rented by a New Jersey man, Mohammed Salameh, who had reported it stolen in Jersey City the day before the bombing.[5] On March 4, Salameh walked into the Ryder agency, with the intention of reclaiming the $400 deposit fee he had paid for the van. This clumsy move led the FBI to make its first arrest in the case and to uncover a treasure trove of information.[6]

Investigators followed new leads connected to Salameh's arrest and conducted searches in various locations throughout the Greater New York area. As more information began to surface, it had become clear that the bombing had been carried out by a group of foreign-based Islamic fundamentalists with the help of local sympathizers. Although authorities were able to arrest most of the local cohorts, the masterminds of the plot had managed to escape. Mahmoud Abouhalima, one of the bomb makers involved in the attack, had left the country before Salameh's arrest, making his way to Sudan. He was arrested after a few weeks in Egypt and flown back to the United States.[7] More important, Ramzi Yousef, the mastermind of the attack, had left the country a few hours after the bombing, flying from New York's John F. Kennedy International Airport to Pakistan. He would be arrested in Islamabad by local intelligence agencies working in cooperation with the United States only two years later.[8]

The immigration history of Ramzi Yousef represents a quintessential case study in the failures of the US immigration system and its consequences on the country's security. Yousef, a Pakistani who grew up in Kuwait, flew to the United States in September 1992 along with Ahmad Ajaj, a Palestinian from the West Bank. Upon landing at JFK airport, Ajaj was detained by immigration authorities, as he presented a blatantly counterfeit Swedish passport. Inspecting Ajaj's luggage, immigration officers discovered that he was carrying bomb-making manuals and decided to hold him in Immigration and Naturalization Service (INS) detention until shortly after the World Trade Center bombing.[9] Yousef, who claimed to be Iraqi, immediately asked for political asylum and was also briefly detained. Yet, since the INS's holding cells were overcrowded, Yousef was released pending an asylum hearing. As soon as he was released, Yousef made contact with the New York–based militants who helped him execute his plan. He also continued to communicate with Ajaj, who managed to participate in the planning while in detention. A few days after his release by the INS, Ajaj was rearrested, this time for his role in the World Trade Center attack.[10]

More details about the plot have emerged since the day of the attacks. Abdul Rahman Yasin, a native of Bloomington, Indiana, and one of the alleged bomb makers, was arrested in Jersey City shortly after the attacks. Yasin cooperated with investigators, providing the FBI with key names and addresses. As a result, Yasin was curiously released. He left the United States, ending up in Iraq, where he lived as a free man until 1994, when he was arrested by Iraqi police. He was released by Saddam Hussein's regime on the eve of the 2003 Iraqi war, as part of an amnesty program the Iraqi dictator attempted to implement to garner support for his regime. In 2002, while still incarcerated in Iraq, Yasin was interviewed by CBS News's Lesley Stahl, and revealed new details about the 1993 attacks.[11] According to Yasin, Ramzi Yousef's original goal was to detonate several explosive devices in various Jewish neighborhoods in Brooklyn. Yousef ultimately changed targets to a single larger explosion at the World Trade Center, since "the majority of people who work in the World Trade Center are Jews."[12]

Even though they had managed to kill six people, cause damages totaling millions of dollars, and carry out the first terrorist attack by an Islamist group on American soil, the group did not consider the operation a success. Proof of their dissatisfaction comes from a file found on a computer disk belonging to another conspirator, Nidal Ayyad, a chemical company employee who had purchased most of the chemicals used to fabricate the bomb. While expressing disappointment that the explosion had failed to cause the substantial damage sought, the letter warned that the World Trade Center would continue to be a target, and that the calculations for future attacks should be more precise. Both the disappointment for the failed destruction of the buildings and the desire to try a second time were expressed also by the plan's mastermind, Ramzi Yousef, who told interrogators that he had intended to topple one building and have it crash into the other, hoping to kill 250,000 people.[13]

In March 1994, relying on more than one thousand exhibits and the testimony of more than two hundred witnesses, federal prosecutors obtained the conviction of Salameh, Ajaj, Abouhalima, and Ayyad. All the accused were convicted and sentenced to 240 years in prison each, but in

1999 these sentences were reduced to 116 years for Salameh, 114 years for Ajaj, 108 years for Abouhalima, and 117 years for Ayyad.[14] In 1995, Eyad Ismoil, the man who physically drove the truck into the garage of the World Trade Center, was arrested in Jordan.[15] Three years later he received a 240-year sentence.[16]

The Landmarks Plot

In a related development, later in 1993, a total of ten conspirators, including the World Trade Center defendants, were arrested for their involvement in the New York landmarks plot. This involved an elaborate scheme to simultaneously bomb the Holland and Lincoln tunnels, the United Nations building, and FBI headquarters in New York City in the early summer of 1993.[17]

The spiritual leader of the plan was Sheikh Omar Abdel Rahman, a blind, extremist cleric who had moved to the United States from Egypt in 1990. Although in 1998 the FBI dubbed the plot as one of "loosely affiliated groups of like-minded extremists,"[18] today the "Blind Sheikh" is considered a key figure in the development of the Egyptian Islamic Jihad in the United States, helping to infuse the radicals he preached to in New York and New Jersey with spiritual and political resolve. Interestingly, one of the Blind Sheikh's character witnesses at trial was a well-known imam from south Florida, the Galshair Muhammad el-Shukrijumah, whose son, Adnan el-Shukrijumah, is a top al Qaeda operative wanted by the FBI.

In 2004, an FBI special agent described the various participants in the landmarks case:

> [I]n 1993, a plot to bomb the landmarks, tunnels and the FBI building was carried out by a group of conspirators from different jihadist groups including the Egyptian Islamic Jihad, the Sudanese National Islamic Front, Al Fuqra and Hamas. The collaboration of these conspirators from seemingly independent radical Islamic groups represented a hitherto unknown collaboration between jihadist groups, a pattern of collaboration that has been observed since then by Al Qaeda in using the personnel of other groups to collect intelligence in the field.[19]

The conspirators were convicted in October 1995.

The so-called Liberation Army and the landmarks bombing group would not necessarily have identified themselves as members of al Qaeda. Notwithstanding this, the linkages to bin Laden's newly formed group are obvious. The conspiracy's mastermind, Ramzi Yousef, and his accomplice Ahmad Ajaj had trained and studied bomb making in Afghan camps committed to furthering "global jihad." In addition, Yousef's uncle Khalid Sheikh Mohammed ("KSM," discussed in detail in chapter 3), who had first met bin Laden in 1989 while bin Laden was constructing his al Qaeda organization,[20] sent Yousef money to help execute the plot.

Ramzi Yousef's chilling expression of how he had intended to cause the towers to topple foreshadowed al Qaeda's next involvement with New York City. The lesson learned from his nephew's failure was not lost on KSM, who would become the mastermind of the 9/11 attacks that ultimately toppled the Twin Towers eight years later.[21]

The "Bojinka" Plot

The next al Qaeda operation to serve as a lesson for 9/11 unraveled in an almost accidental way and, once again, involved Ramzi Yousef. On January 6, 1995, a Manila police station received a late-night call regarding a suspected minor explosion and fire in an apartment building. The first officers dispatched were told that it was an accident caused by people playing with fireworks. The apartment building, the Dona Josefa, was close to an intended site of a pending papal tour, which led the local police commander to probe further.

The police found an abandoned apartment with hot plates, wiring, and stores of chemicals. Upon returning downstairs, the police encountered the doorman, who identified one of the persons who had rushed from the apartment. The man identified himself as Ahmed Saeed and claimed to be a pilot. The doorman pointed to another man across the street smoking a pipe and talking on a cell phone and identified him as another apartment occupant. Saeed suddenly bolted and in the confusion before he was recaptured, the second man disappeared. The second man was Ramzi Yousef.

Saeed, who was actually Abdul Hakim Murad, provided investigators with a gold mine of information and a shocking glimpse into what was intended. Fingerprints found in the apartment confirmed that one of the other occupants was indeed the 1993 World Trade Center bombing leader, Ramzi Yousef. Materials found in the apartment confirmed that an assassination attempt on the pope was also in the making. Further details laid out on Yousef's laptops and computer disks described diabolical plans, code-named "Bojinka" (slang for explosion), to detonate time-delayed bombs on eleven US long-haul flights over the Pacific.

The presence of Casio watches and references to timers caused investigators to press further. They learned that Yousef had been responsible for an earlier explosion on a December 11, 1994, flight from the Philippines to Tokyo in which a Japanese man was killed when an explosive device planted by Yousef detonated under his seat.[22]

Investigators learned that Yousef's plans extended beyond remote detonation of bombs aboard planes. Murad had received extensive pilot training in the United States. He attended training in New York, Texas, and North Carolina in preparation for suicide attacks against specific US targets. What was missing, Murad explained, were trained pilots.

The third man in the Bojinka plot, Wali Khan, was arrested a few days later but escaped. He was an operative of the Indonesian-based Jemaah Islamiyah and the Filipino Abu Sayyaf terrorist organizations. Khan was recaptured in Malaysia in December 1995 and returned to the United States. He was convicted along with Yousef in 1996 and sentenced to life imprisonment.

Ramzi Yousef, no doubt using one of his twenty-plus aliases, escaped back to Pakistan. It was later learned at Yousef's trial that Murad's capture occurred because Yousef had sent him back to get the laptop with its incriminating evidence. Yousef himself had followed, at a distance, when Murad failed to return.[23]

Murad was returned to the United States in April 1995 where he testified against Ramzi Yousef in 1996. Yousef received a life sentence for his terrorist crimes. Murad was convicted for his terrorism-related activities on May 16, 1998, and also received a life sentence.

US Embassy Bombings in East Africa—An al Qaeda-Conceived Conspiracy

Osama bin Laden and al Qaeda came to the world's attention with the simultaneous bombings of the US embassies in Nairobi, Kenya, and Dar es Salaam, Tanzania, on August 7, 1998. The coordinated attacks resulted in the deaths of 224 people—213 in Nairobi and 11 in Dar es Salaam—and thousands of injuries.[24] Of the 224 fatalities, 12 were Americans. The overwhelming majority of victims of this attack were African Muslims.

The conspiracy aimed at the US embassies in East Africa was carefully planned and executed by al Qaeda, following directives set out by the organization's uppermost ranks.[25] Under bin Laden's direction, al Qaeda operatives had been originally sent to Somalia in 1993 both to attack US forces stationed there and to help train local fighters.[26] To facilitate planning for the future operations, al Qaeda sent operatives Khalid al-Fawwaz and Wadih el-Hage to neighboring Nairobi, where they maintained frequent satellite telephone communication with top al Qaeda leaders in Afghanistan such as Mohammed Atef.[27] While there, the two men set up set up false businesses to serve as a cover for their activities in support of the planning of the embassy attacks. [28]

As investigations following the attacks would show, several of the al Qaeda operatives had one remarkable thing in common: a direct connection to America.

Building al Qaeda in the United States: Wadih el-Hage and Ali Mohamed

While heading al Qaeda's Nairobi cell, Wadih el-Hage (aka Abdus Sabuur, aka Abd al-Sabbur, aka Norman, aka Wa'da Norman) came under grand jury investigation in 1997 for his previous activities while in the United States. He had an interesting history to say the least.

El-Hage came to the United States in the 1980s and acquired legal permanent residence status by marrying an American in 1986. During this time, he began traveling to Afghanistan and later moved to Sudan. It is believed that even during this first stint in America, el-Hage was a part of al Qaeda's US operations. In the late 1980s, el-Hage returned from Afghanistan and relocated to Tucson, Arizona, by then the home of the radical Islamic Center of Tucson and the first United States–based Al Kifah Refugee Center (both discussed in chapter 11).[29]

In early 1990, el-Hage is reported to have had a guest in his home described only as a "tall man" who may have been involved in the subsequent murder of visiting moderate imam Rashad Khalifa.[30]

El-Hage admitted that a man from New York made contact and visited him, but claimed that he did not know of the murderous plot. In the same year, el-Hage was found to have participated in the plot to murder Rabbi Meir Kahane. According to US Attorney Patrick Fitzgerald, el-Hage admitted that he provided Mahmoud Abouhalima with a weapon that was used in the November 1990 murder of Kahane.[31] As noted earlier, Abouhalima was also later convicted for his role in the 1993 World Trade Center conspiracy.

In early 1991, el-Hage left Arizona for Brooklyn's Al Kifah Refugee

Center to help manage its operations. On the same day that el-Hage arrived, then manager Mustafa Shalabi disappeared. His mutilated body was later found in the apartment that he and Abouhalima shared, apparently killed over some kind of a "business" dispute.

Following al Qaeda's move to Sudan around 1991, bin Laden established his headquarters in the Riyadh section of Khartoum. Bin Laden also started businesses in the country in order to generate money, facilitate the travel of his operatives, and acquire explosives, weapons, and chemicals. In early 1992, el-Hage moved his family to Sudan, where he began working directly for bin Laden as personal assistant and fundraiser, setting up various front organizations on behalf of al Qaeda. Around 1994, el-Hage moved to Nairobi to establish businesses and other organizations. While in Kenya, he met repeatedly with one of al Qaeda's top military commanders, Abu Ubaidah al-Banshiri.[32]

El-Hage eventually returned to the United States from Kenya in September 1997.[33] Upon his arrival in New York, el-Hage was stopped by the US government and served a subpoena to testify before a grand jury. According to his indictment, el-Hage lied extensively about his contacts with bin Laden, al-Banshiri, and Khalid al-Fawwaz.

Following the US embassy bombings in Nairobi and Dar es Sallam, el-Hage was subpoenaed again to testify in New York. Again, el-Hage persisted in lying to the grand jury investigating the attacks, saying that he did not work in Kenya on behalf of bin Laden and that he had no contact with him from 1994 to 1998, other than through an aide. He also claimed that his group was not funded in any way by bin Laden.[34]

El-Hage was eventually convicted for his roles in the attack on US military personnel in Somalia and the 1998 US embassy bombings in Kenya and Tanzania. Osama bin Laden and Mohammed Atef were also named in the indictment.[35]

Ali Mohamed

In May 1999, Ali Mohamed was added as a defendant in the 1998 embassy bombings case and the details of this mysterious member of al Qaeda began to emerge. Born in Egypt, Mohamed served in the Egyptian military—mainly in Special Forces and intelligence—in the 1970s and early 1980s. He then worked in counterterrorism security for Egypt Airlines before moving to the United States and marrying an American woman whom he had met on a flight to the United States in 1985.

In 1986, Mohamed enlisted in the US Army and was eventually stationed at Fort Bragg, North Carolina, where he was assigned to the John F. Kennedy Special Warfare Center and given access to sensitive military information. Similar information was later found in El Sayyid Nosair's apartment after Nosair was arrested holding the weapon that had murdered Rabbi Kahane.

In 1991, Mohamed traveled to Afghanistan to escort bin Laden to Sudan. While in Khartoum, Mohamed began training al Qaeda recruits, and by 1994 he was teaching military tactics to bin Laden's personal bodyguards. A confidential source ("CS-2") who testified to the grand jury stated that he personally witnessed Ali Mohamed in Khowst, Afghanistan, training al Qaeda commanders in September 1992.[36]

Choosing the Targets

The planning for the actual embassy attacks appears to have begun in 1993 when Ali Mohamed began scoping out possible targets in Nairobi. In a 2000 plea agreement, Mohamed described his association with al Qaeda and his role in the East Africa attacks:

> In the early 1990s, I was introduced to Al Qaeda—Al Qaeda is the organization headed by Osama Bin Laden—through my involvement with the Egyptian Islamic Jihad. In 1992, I conducted military and basic explosives training for Al Qaeda in Afghanistan. . . . In 1991, I helped transport Osama Bin Laden from Afghanistan to the Sudan. . . .
>
> I assisted Al Qaeda in creating a presence in Nairobi, Kenya, and worked with several others on this project. Abu Ubaidah was in charge of Al Qaeda in Nairobi until he drowned. Khalid Al Fawwaz set up Al Qaeda's office in Nairobi. A car business was set up to create income. Wadih El Hage created a charity organization that would help provide Al Qaeda members with identity documents. I personally helped El Hage by making labels in his home in Nairobi. I personally met Abu Ubaidah and Abu Hafs at Wadih's house in Nairobi.
>
> In late 1993, I was asked by Bin Laden to conduct surveillance of American, British, French and Israeli targets in Nairobi. Among the targets I did surveillance for was the American Embassy in Nairobi, the United States AID Building in Nairobi, the United States Agricultural Office in Nairobi, the French Cultural Center, and French Embassy in Nairobi. These targets were selected to retaliate against the United States for its involvement in Somalia. I took pictures, drew diagrams, and wrote a report.

> I later went to Khartoum, where my surveillance files and photographs were reviewed by Osama Bin Laden, Abu Hafs, Abu Ubaidah, and others. Bin Laden looked at the picture of the American Embassy and pointed to where a truck could go as a suicide bomber.[37]

By January 1994, bin Laden and his senior advisers—including the head of his military committee, Abu Ubaidah al-Banshiri, and Mohammed Atef (aka Abu Hafs)—had agreed that the US embassy in Nairobi would make an "easy" target for an attack.[38] Wadih el-Hage, described in court documents as bin Laden's personal secretary based in Kenya,

> maintained a close operational working relationship with the East African cell . . . that would carry out the bombings of the embassies in Nairobi and Dar Es Salaam [and] arranged for the facilitation and delivery of false travel documents of other Al Qaeda members [and] communicated in code and passed on messages to others in Al Qaeda [and] maintained a close working relationship with others in the East African cell, such as the defendant, Mohamed Odeh.[39]

El-Hage traveled to Afghanistan twice in 1997 to meet personally with bin Laden and Abu Hafs. According to the prosecution, it was after concluding these meetings that el-Hage "brought back with him a new policy, a policy to militarize, to militarize the cell that in 16 or 18 months thereafter would carry out the bombings in East Africa."[40]

Announcing Their Intentions and Claiming Responsibility

On February 23, 1998, on the five-year anniversary of the first World Trade Center bombing, the *Al Quds Al Arabi* newspaper in London printed a communiqué signed jointly by bin Laden and Ayman al-Zawahiri. At that time Zawahiri was the leader of Egyptian Islamic Jihad (EIJ), an organization that was later merged into al Qaeda. It would prove to be one of history's deadliest mergers.

Khalid al-Fawwaz, mediating between *Al Quds Al Arabi*'s London offices and al Qaeda's headquarters in Kandahar, Afghanistan, by satellite telephone, brokered the publication arrangement for the dissemination of the fatwa. One sentence of the fatwa in particular stands out: "The ruling to kill the Americans and their allies—civilians and military—is an individual duty for every Muslim who can do it in any country."[41]

After the fatwa was issued, bin Laden sent a personal letter of thanks to the owner of *Al Quds*, Abdel Bari Atwan:

> I take pleasure in congratulating you for your strong journalistic views towards the truth, and the steadfastness of your newspaper to serve the struggle, and the use of the pen to defend the nation's causes and its holy places, and the carrying out of its task to inform, truly without being touched by elements of temptation and seduction.
>
> As we congratulate you on this great achievement, the efforts to defend the nation's causes and support her defenders, I would like to thank you personally for your interest on the news in the Arab Peninsula and the country Al Haramin [Saudi Arabia], as well as your deep understanding of the ongoing struggle between the good and bad in the area, siding with truth, and supporting it, is a situation which will not be forgotten by the people in the area.[42]

Bin Laden's Communication Procurement Team

In March 2001, during the trial of al Qaeda members involved in the East African embassy bombings, more details of the American al Qaeda connection emerged. Evidence revealed that an employee of a telecommunications firm testified that her company had sold a satellite phone to a man named Ziyad Khaleel. The employee also identified an invoice for additional accessories for the telephone, including a battery pack. Though Khaleel purchased those accessories himself, he instructed the firm to send the equipment to a Mr. Tarik Hamdi.[43]

Hamdi also surfaced later during the trial, in connection both with the satellite telephone and with a letter from *ABC News World News Tonight*, dated May 13, 1998. The letter, addressed to Mohammed Atef, was a follow-up request for a personal interview with bin Laden himself. It referred to previous communications conducted through "Mr. Tarik Hamdi in Washington," whom Atef apparently knew quite well. When the details of that interview were finally arranged, Hamdi traveled alongside an ABC News crew to Afghanistan. On May 17, 1998, when he arrived in Pakistan, Hamdi sent a message via fax to bin Laden's London-based aide, Khalid al-Fawwaz: "Brother Khalid: Peace be upon you. We arrived safely and now we are in the Marriott Hotel."[44]

During this trip, Hamdi delivered the battery pack purchased by Khaleel to bin Laden. The telephone was subsequently employed by bin Laden to confer with his followers across the world. It is believed that this phone was specifically used to deliver the orders to launch the bombing of the American embassies in East Africa.[45]

According to *Newsweek*, Jordanian police arrested Ziyad Khaleel in 1999. The magazine quoted an internal FBI memo that describes Ziyad Khaleel's role as to "procure computers, satellite telephones and covert surveillance equipment" in the United States for al Qaeda.[46] Additionally, in the late 1990s, Khaleel, using the alias Ziyad Sidaqa,[47] registered as the administrative and billing contact of the Palestine Information Center (http://www.palestine-info.com), a Hamas-run Web site.[48] (For more information on terrorists' use of the Internet, see chapter 12.)

Other Implicated Individuals in the Embassies Bombing Plot

Fazul Abdullah Mohammed (aka Harun Fazhl, "Harun") lived with el-Hage and acted as his deputy in Nairobi and as the East Africa "communications" contact. His role was to relay messages between bin Laden at al Qaeda headquarters and local operatives in Africa.[49] He also rented the factory that was used to prepare the explosives, and later removed the bomb-making materials from it before fleeing to Afghanistan.[50]

Mohamed Rashed Daoud Al 'Owhali, who carried out the actual attack in Nairobi, had received training in al Qaeda camps in Afghanistan.[51]

Khalfan Khamis Mohamed, the Dar es Salaam bomber who rented the house in which the explosives used were fashioned, also had trained at al Qaeda camps in Afghanistan.[52]

Mohammed Saddiq Odeh is believed to have joined al Qaeda as early as 1992. According to US prosecutors, he "took training in small arms and he took training in map reading and he took training in basic explosives which included TNT" at various training camps in Afghanistan.[53] He became a key planner of the attacks and technical adviser to the East African cell at the behest of Mohammed Atef, the former al Qaeda military commander who was killed by American forces in Afghanistan in 2001 and who set Odeh up in a fishing business to serve as a cover for his al Qaeda–related activities.

Thus situated, Odeh "worked with [those who] carried out the bombings and he carried them out with them [and] attended several meetings in the spring and the summer of 1998, with the very same people who carried out the bombing, and . . . [was] the technical advisor to those who carried out the bombing in Nairobi."[54]

Abdullah Ahmed Abdullah (aka "Saleh") was the ringleader of both the Nairobi and the Dar es Salaam cells. He communicated messages from bin Laden to the conspirators in East Africa and is alleged to have personally conducted surveillance of the US embassy in Nairobi.[55]

In February 2001, the US government proceeded to trial against four defendants in connection with the East African attacks over whom the United States had obtained jurisdiction: Mohamed Rashed Daoud Al 'Owhali (a Saudi), Khalfan Khamis Mohamed (a Tanzanian), Mohammed Saddiq Odeh (a Palestinian Jordanian), and Wadih el-Hage (a naturalized US citizen born in Lebanon).[56] In October 2001, each was convicted and sentenced to life in prison without the possibility of parole.[57]

Al Qaeda's Lessons Learned

The interrogation of Mohammed Saddiq Odeh gave some indication of al Qaeda's reaction to the mission's result. This prosecution summary of Odeh's statements is revealing:

> Odeh stated that nobody, even Bin Laden himself, could be happy with the results of the bombing. Odeh stated that the operation conducted against Khobar was 100 times better than Nairobi. . . .
>
> Odeh stated that if the cab of the pickup was between the explosives and the embassy, at least 60 percent of the shock wave would be diverted. Odeh stated that the errant shock wave hit the wrong building. Odeh stated that he accepts responsibility for the bomb because he is part of the group and that it was a big mistake and Saleh blundered. . . .
>
> Odeh is in a room with an FBI agent and with people from the Kenyan police, and he understands what the plan was supposed to be because it's reflected in a sketch in his house. The truck was supposed to back up into the embassy, and judging by what he believes happened, because of the incredible number of Kenyans who passed away, who died in that bombing, he believes that the people who carried out the plan that he was a part of made a mistake and that the truck must not have backed up into the embassy and that more Kenyans were killed than he wanted to be killed.[58]

Al Qaeda would digest the "payload delivery" lessons of the embassy bombings.

USS Cole—*An Attack at Sea*

Two years elapsed between the embassy bombings and al Qaeda's next major attack against the United States. On October 12, 2000, the USS *Cole,* a navy missile destroyer, arrived in Aden Harbor, Yemen, for refueling. Roughly two hours after the *Cole* had stopped at the fueling dock, a small white vessel pulled up next to it. The two al Qaeda operatives piloting the vessel then detonated a bomb, killing seventeen sailors and wounding thirty-nine others. Although the explosion left a forty-foot-wide hole in the *Cole,* it did not sink the ship.[59]

This successful attack was actually the bombers' second attempt against a US destroyer in Aden Harbor. Abd al-Rahim al-Nashiri, the local bin Laden lieutenant who oversaw the *Cole* bombing, had first targeted the USS *The Sullivans.* On January 3, 2000, *The Sullivans* had stopped to refuel in Aden Harbor when al-Nashiri and others launched a boat from the beach filled with explosives toward it. The boat was so overloaded with explosives that it sank, forcing al-Nashiri to recover the boat and the explosives the next night.[60]

It is now known that bin Laden and al-Nashiri met several times in the months prior to the *Cole* attack. As a result of those meetings, al-Nashiri was directed to select a target, assemble the personnel, and arrange all financing and operational details. Al-Nashiri apparently suggested attacking an oil tanker but was overruled by bin Laden himself, who wanted to attack a symbol of American power.[61]

Learning from the failed attack against *The Sullivans,* al-Nashiri strengthened the hull of the salvaged boat and added fuel tanks. The resulting improvements to the craft permitted the attack to be carried out, and the vulnerability of even a US warship was demonstrated as intended.

The Los Angeles Airport Millennium Bombing Plot

By the end of 1999, intelligence agencies had gathered a significant amount of information indicating that al Qaeda was planning to carry out terrorist attacks to coincide with the millennium celebrations. As law enforcement agencies were put on high alert, the clumsiness of an al Qaeda operative and the sixth sense of an immigration inspector prevented what could have been a massive attack inside the United States. On December 14, 1999, in Port Angeles, Washington, US Customs Agent Diana Dean decided to stop the last car leaving the ferry that connects Victoria, British Columbia, with the coast of Washington State. As soon as she asked him some basic questions, Agent Dean noticed that the driver was extremely nervous, sweating profusely, and rummaging around the vehicle's console. When asked for identification, the man presented her with what turned out to be fake documents in the name of Benni Antoine Noris.[62]

Agent Dean, now joined by two other inspectors, instructed the man to step out of his vehicle. The men opened the trunk of the car and found several bags filled with a white powder and some suspicious liquids. As one of the inspectors started to frisk him, he slipped out of his jacket and fled. Local police joined the chase, and a short time later the nervous suspect was caught and handcuffed after trying to get away in another car. As they placed him in detention, inspectors thoroughly searched his car, finding more chemicals and timing devices hidden in the tire well. A subsequent laboratory analysis revealed that the chemicals were a highly unstable relative of nitroglycerin.[63]

The man, who spoke only French with a strong North African accent, was kept in detention for a few days while authorities tried to discover his real identity. The FBI received help from the Royal Canadian Mounted Police (RCMP), which revealed that Noris, whose real name was Ahmed Ressam, was an Algerian who had illegally resided in Montreal. Moreover, the Canadians also revealed that they had received a warning about Ressam from French counterterrorism authorities.[64] For reasons that are unclear to this day, Canadian intelligence officials and the RCMP did not act upon the French request and refused to monitor Ressam. With the confirmation that Ressam had attempted to enter the country using false documents, US authorities could keep him in detention and gain time, while investigating the nature of Ressam's intentions. The authorities' initial suspicion was that Ressam was planning to attack the celebration for the millennium at Seattle's Space Needle, which was consequently canceled. But after a series of interviews with the Algerian, they determined that the target was Los Angeles International Airport (LAX), which he planned to attack on the first day of the new year.[65]

Many more details of the plot became clear after Ressam began cooperating with investigators in May 2001.[66] His detailed information provided investigators worldwide with insights into one of the most violent and experienced terrorist groups, the Armed Islamic Group, or Groupes Islamiques Armés (GIA), and its splinter group to which Ressam belonged, the Salafist Group for Preaching and Combat, known by its

French acronym, GSPC, and addressed in detail in chapter 4. Ressam also turned out to be a treasure trove of information on training camps in Afghanistan, transit routes, terrorist presence in the West, and the interconnectivity of Algerian militants and al Qaeda.

Ahmed Ressam was born in Algeria in 1967 but left for France in 1992 when civil war erupted and he chose not to join the radical Islamist movement. In 1994, after living illegally in France for over a year, Ressam avoided forced removal by securing a forged French passport and traveling to Canada.[67]

Remarkably, although Ressam's false identity was discovered at the Montreal airport, he was still permitted entry into Canada after claiming refugee status. Ressam quickly became part of the large Algerian and French African community in Montreal, meeting members of the GIA, including Fateh Kamel, whom French authorities believed was part of a terrorist "cell" in Montreal, and who French authorities subsequently warned the Canadian Security Intelligence Service (CSIS) about.[68]

Within weeks Ressam had launched a life of petty crime, specializing in pickpocketing and luggage theft from which identity documents were obtained. Ressam's new friends introduced him to a local mosque where jihadi recruiting was a regular feature, and soon thereafter he expressed an interest in going to bin Laden's camps for training after friends returned to Montreal with stories about Osama bin Laden's training camps in Afghanistan. As Ressam related during his trial, "My friends talked to me about the training that they have received, the learning that they have gotten about jihad, and encouraged me, so I got interested."[69] Ressam was inspired to follow the same path.

Abderauof Hannachi, another Afghan-trained member of the Montreal group, made contact with Abu Zubaydah, an al Qaeda recruiter in Peshawar, Pakistan, to advise that another recruit was on his way. Before leaving his Canadian haven, Ressam used a stolen baptismal certificate to apply for a valid Canadian passport in the false identity of Benni Norris. Notwithstanding the supposed surveillance that included Ressam, the passport was issued.

Ressam was sent to train in Afghanistan at the Khalden camp shortly after he met with Zubaydah in Pakistan in April 1998. He testified at the New York trial of coconspirator Mokhtar Haouari that it was at Khalden where he was trained to use "light weapons, handguns, small machine guns, large one, Rocket Propelled Grenades (supplied by the Taliban), how to make an explosive charge, the types of explosives, TNT, C4, and urban warfare [which included] how to carry out operations in cities, how to block roads, how to assault buildings, and the strategies used in these operations."[70] Zubaydah himself was sufficiently impressed with Ressam's passport-manipulation abilities to have apparently asked him to acquire additional Canadian passports for distribution to al Qaeda fighters.[71]

Ressam ensconced himself with other Algerians attending Khalden. He planned to meet up with some of them in Canada to rob banks in order to finance "an operation in America . . . before the end of 1999."[72] Also at the Khalden camp, he came under the tutelage of Abu Doha, a highly placed GSPC leader who oversaw the planning for the attack and is addressed further in chapter 4. In mid-1998, Abu Doha, Ressam, and others at the camp began to plan a bombing operation in the United States that would target a large visible facility, such as an airport.[73] Abu Doha pledged to Ressam that he would provide him with money and a way back to Algeria after the attack.[74] In September 1998, Ressam completed his training at Khalden and moved on to another training camp in Toronta, Afghanistan, where he spent a month and a half learning explosives manufacturing. Ressam described the instruction as "how to put chemical substances together to form explosives [and] how to make electronic circuits."[75]

In February 1999, Ressam made his way back to Canada by way of Pakistan and Los Angeles before, notwithstanding being denied refugee status, reentering Canada through Vancouver and then settling illegally in Montreal.[76] In the summer of 1999, Ressam began active pursuit of his preparations for targeting LAX. By September, according to Ressam, "I started buying electronic equipment and electronic components, small electronic components that will be used in putting together electronic circuits" and then in November in Vancouver, "I started collecting chemical materials [to concoct] an explosive substance similar to TNT."[77]

In November 1999, Ressam and Abu Doha spoke once more on the telephone and Doha reiterated his pledge to provide for Ressam's financial needs and travel arrangements back to Algeria.[78] With preparations in order by the end of 1999, Ressam set out for Los Angeles. Along with an accomplice, he drove a rental car packed with their explosives onto a car ferry that traveled from Vancouver to Victoria and then on to Port Angeles in Washington State. Once inside the United States, their plan was to take a train to Los Angeles, scope out LAX, and carry out the operation. They hoped to then return to Montreal and escape to Europe and eventually Algeria.[79]

Having pled guilty to the terrorism charges brought against him, Ressam was sentenced to twenty-two years in prison in July 2005.[80]

The Foiled Jordan Millennium Bombing Plot

In late November 1999, Jordanian intelligence agents arrested sixteen individuals suspected of preparing a terrorist attack timed to coincide with January 1, 2000. The intended targets, according to Jordanian officials, "included the fully booked 400-room Radisson Hotel in downtown Amman, two Christian holy sites and two border crossings into Israel."[81]

Furthermore, the *New York Times* reported, investigators "found out that the group had planned a second wave of bombings against landmarks in Amman, including an airport in Marka and the Citadel, the popular tourist site that includes the Temple of Hercules, the Omayyad Palace and a celebrated Byzantine church." Subsequent police raids at the suspects' safehouses uncovered fake passports, remote control devices, and seventy-one containers of nitric and sulfuric acid. It was enough "to make the equivalent of 16 tons of TNT," according to "Kamel Al Naj, an explosives expert who accompanied the police that night and testified at the trial."[82]

Abu Zubaydah (aka Zain al-Abidin Muhammad Hussain Abu Zubaydah), a Palestinian born in Saudi Arabia and raised in Gaza refugee camps, was soon named as the leader of the plot and as having "served as the link between an al Qaeda cell in Jordan and the group's leadership in Afghanistan."[83] His connections to terrorism were long-standing, with early involvement with Hamas and subsequent affiliation with al-Zawahiri's Egyptian Islamic Jihad, which brought him to al Qaeda and bin Laden.

As noted above with respect to Ahmed Ressam, Abu Zubaydah ran al Qaeda recruitment and jihadi training camps in eastern Afghanistan. He is believed to have started this at the young age of twenty-five and developed into an influential person with proficiency in language and technology in Osama bin Laden's network. One Gulf intelligence official described Abu Zubaydah as having "skills and knowledge and an ability to work all over the world that the older men simply don't have. He is worldly and able to fit in and work anywhere. That has only been enhanced by the amount of traveling he has done. . . . And it makes him very dangerous."[84] Following the death of Mohammed Atef in a US air strike in the fall of 2001, Abu Zubaydah became one of al Qaeda's top-ranking members, in charge of coordinating operatives scattered throughout the world.[85] This Jordanian plot coordinated by him offers a "template [for] the modern face of global Islamic terrorism and how it functions," according to former national counterterrorism coordinator Richard A. Clarke.[86]

As the link between al Qaeda's leadership in Afghanistan and the cell members in Jordan, Abu Zubaydah arranged for cell members to be trained in explosives at an al Qaeda camp in Afghanistan. One of those who had previously trained at Abu Zubaydah's Khalden camp was a Palestinian named Raed Hijazi, who became affiliated with al Qaeda through his association with another Palestinian, Khadar Abu Hoshar. Born in California but raised in Jordan and Saudi Arabia, Hijazi told prosecutors that he was first drawn to the Islamic cause by a fellow Muslim he had met at the Islamic Assistance Organization, a Sacramento mosque and cultural group he joined while studying business at California State University. Later, Hijazi met Abu Hoshar at the Yarmuk Palestinian refugee camp in Syria in 1996. According to a Jordanian prosecutor's statement, the two planned "to carry out terrorist attacks against the Jews and American interests in Jordan."[87] Abu Hoshar's connections would eventually lead them to Abu Zubaydah, to whom they sent reports of their surveillance of their intended targets.[88]

By November 1999, Hijazi had sworn *bayat* (pledged allegiance) to bin Laden, thereby committing himself to do anything bin Laden ordered. According to the Jordanian prosecutors, Hijazi would go on to gather the necessary materials to carry out the attacks, including purchasing remote control devices in London and chemicals in Jordan.[89]

While listening to a tapped telephone line on November 30, 1999, Jordanian intelligence overheard Abu Zubaydah saying "The time for training is over" and instructing Abu Hoshar to carry out the attack on "*al yom alfieh*" (the day of the millennium). Jordanian police raided the suspects' houses that day and made their arrests.[90]

In September 2000, Raed Hijazi was convicted in absentia of being one of the two men who planned the attacks. He was arrested in Syria one month later and was subsequently sent to Jordan where, after trial by a military court in February 2002, he was convicted of targeting American and Israeli interests in Jordan and sentenced to death. [91]

Khadar Abu Hoshar was one of the sixteen individuals detained in the first sweep by Jordanian police on November 30, 1999. He, too, was sentenced to death in 2000 by the Jordanian State Security Court, which upheld his conviction in June 2004.[92]

The Jordanian court also sentenced Abu Zubaydah to death in absentia. He continued to engage in terrorist plots and is believed to have aided the would-be shoe bomber, Richard Reid.[93] Zubaydah's murderous career came to an end on March 28, 2002, when he was captured in a joint Pakistani, CIA, and FBI raid near Faisalabad, Pakistan.[94] Abu Zubaydah remains in US custody at an undisclosed location.

SEPTEMBER 11, 2001: AL QAEDA'S SUPREME PLAN EXECUTED

The attacks of 9/11 represent the finalization and culmination of what al Qaeda had learned in almost ten years of successful and attempted attacks on the United States. The horrific multiple attacks symbolized the organization's supreme operation, meticulously planned and carefully executed, reaching an unprecedented level of sophistication.

Al Qaeda wanted to fulfill the threat of the letter the "Liberation Army" had sent to the *New York Times* in 1993. This time the role of mastermind was played by Yousef's uncle, Khalid Sheikh Mohammed, who had been marginally involved in the 1993 plot, having sent money to his nephew while in New York.

Moreover, al Qaeda learned from its mistakes. In the past, operatives had been arrested and entire operations had failed because counterfeited documents had been used to enter the country. This time, al Qaeda decided not to take the chance again, and all nineteen operatives entered the United States under their own identities, with their own passports, and proper visas.

Once in the United States, the future hijackers were extremely careful in avoiding detection from authorities. Even though some mistakes were made, they did not make the same blunders that characterized other operations. With a few notable exceptions, the operatives avoided mosques and Islamic centers, places where they could be associated with Islamic fundamentalism. Most of them closely respected immigration laws, making sure they did not overstay their visas. They were quick in procuring American driver's licenses (albeit, in some cases, forged ones). When they had casual contacts with US law enforcement they maintained their calm, as instructed by al Qaeda trainers. The core hijackers spoke English well, and some of them were described as quite personable by American neighbors and acquaintances. They blended into American society, acting casually while repeatedly flying from coast to coast. All the while they were studying and mentally rehearsing their murderous plan.

While keeping a low profile in the United States, the future hijackers managed to keep in close contact with Khalid Sheikh Mohammed, Ramzi Binalshibh, and the other overseas planners of the operation. The fact that all these movements and communications happened undetected by authorities can be widely blamed on deficiencies of the pre-9/11 US intelligence community. It is undeniable, however, that 9/11 was a masterpiece of organizational ability and secrecy. It was the fruit of ten years of learning experience.

That Fateful Morning

On the morning of 9/11, three airplanes full of passengers and crew, each carrying a US-trained al Qaeda pilot and four "muscle" hijackers, were seized after their American and United Airlines pilots had established their scheduled course. Mohamed Atta, the leader of the operatives in the United States, was also the leader in the air, telling the passengers to stay quiet while he calmly piloted the first plane—American Airlines Flight 11—toward its target in lower Manhattan. At 8:46 AM, the North Tower of the World Trade Center in New York City was hit.

Marwan al-Shehhi, Atta's flying partner at vocational flight schools in south Florida, guided the second plane—United Airlines Flight 175—into the South Tower at 9:03 AM. By 9:38 AM, US leaders in Washington, DC, knew that their city was also under attack as a third plane—American Airlines Flight 77—piloted by Hani Hanjour, the only hijacker with extensive experience in the United States and a US pilot's license before he entered the United States as an operative, rammed into the west side of the Pentagon.

On a fourth hijacked plane, United Airlines Flight 93, passengers and cabin crew had learned about the hijackings and crashes from cell phone calls, and they heroically charged the three hijackers guarding the cockpit. The hijack pilot, Ziad Jarrah, who had argued with Atta about whether his plane should target the Capitol (Atta's instructions) or the White House (Jarrah's desire), had been taught to abort his mission if the objective could not be reached. Jarrah violently rocked the plane a number of times from side to side and then pitched it up and down trying to impede the passengers' efforts. When it was clear to the hijackers that the unarmed passengers would not permit them to triumph, a voice was recorded at 10:02 AM shouting in Arabic, "Allah is the greatest. Allah is the greatest." Then, a mere twenty minutes of flying time away from Washington, Jarrah aimed the nose of the plane straight into Shanksville, Pennsylvania, farmland. Once more, there were no survivors on the plane.

All told, nearly three thousand people in the planes, in the towers, on the streets of Lower Manhattan, in the Pentagon, and on that Pennsylvania field died. The attacks would forever change the way Americans viewed their security, something previously taken for granted.

A Well-Executed Plan

The simultaneous 9/11 operations represented a major advancement in al Qaeda's operational tactics. The terrorists had learned from their previous mistakes and largely avoided the circumstances that led to them. Ironically, the major exception to this was when three of the four pilots (Atta, Jarrah, and Hanjour) either violated immigration laws or acquired speeding tickets. Atta was clearly inadmissible when he reentered the United States in January 2001, and both Atta and Jarrah received speeding tickets which they failed to pay, and for which Atta received a warrant for his arrest.[95] In the seemingly secure pre-9/11 days, these kinds of incidents were simply not on the radar screen of law enforcement and intelligence agencies, and these chances to unravel the plot slipped away.

Beyond these incidents, however, the plan was very carefully drafted and executed. Mohamed Atta stayed in control of his men following their arrival in the United States as they readied themselves for the operation. It was Atta who traveled abroad when necessary to communicate directly with key associates like Ramzi Binalshibh. Additionally, Atta appears to have had contact within the United States with Adnan el-Shukrijumah (discussed in more detail in chapter 3), a trusted al Qaeda member who had spent many years in south Florida where his father was an imam.[96]

As a permanent legal resident fluent in English, el-Shukrijumah was more familiar than Atta with American rules and culture. An immigration inspector later identified el-Shukrijumah as the man accompanying Atta on May 2, 2001, when Atta brazenly attempted to acquire a longer length of stay for a colleague (believed to be Ziad Jarrah).[97]

Although reports of Atta's behavior in Germany in the late 1990s indicate that he could be belligerent and abrasive, in the United States he was quiet and circumspect. He tended to avoid social situations and mosques. Al Qaeda realized this could be dangerous for operatives due to the infiltration by an FBI informant of the Al Farouq Mosque in Brooklyn, which had helped to uncover the plot to blow up landmarks and tunnels in New York City, including the United Nations Building and the Lincoln and Holland tunnels in 1993.

Atta was adamant that while the overall planning continued, the pilots did what was necessary to gain the necessary instruction and flying hours to acquire legitimate US-issued pilot's licenses. He also paid specific (although inadequate) attention to ensuring that he and al-Shehhi maintained legal immigration status until the execution of the plot. Atta arranged for staff at Huffman Aviation, where they were enrolled, to submit applications to the INS on their behalf so that each could be legally deemed a student until September 8, 2001. His own illegal status, therefore, is all the more ironic.

All but three of the so-called muscle hijackers entered the United States easily as tourists in the early spring and summer of 2001, thereby automatically securing a six-month length of stay. Atta knew that this would provide ample time to train and prepare for the hijackings without risking apprehension and/or deportation for an illegal overstay. As far as federal investigators can tell, these remaining muscle hijackers were not aware of the details of the plan at the time of their arrival.

Unlike the plots of the 1990s, the 9/11 operation minimized the risk of US law enforcement detection of the attack by not using any US residents in executing the scheme itself. In fact, for the first time in an al Qaeda-related plot within the United States, all of the hijackers were members of al Qaeda. Most of them had trained in al Qaeda camps and sworn personal allegiance to bin Laden. According to the head of one of the training camps in Afghanistan, some muscle hijackers were chosen by unnamed Saudi sheikhs who had contacts with al Qaeda.[98] The three key figures in the plot—Atta, Ramzi Binalshibh in Germany, and KSM in Pakistan and Afghanistan—were all members of al Qaeda, acting under the direct supervision and with the direct support of Osama bin Laden.[99]

CONCLUSION

The attacks that followed the 1993 World Trade Center bombing were characterized by an increasing degree of sophistication and closer direct involvement by al Qaeda's top leadership. When the first attack by Islamic radicals in the United States took place in 1993, al Qaeda barely existed as an organization. The mastermind of that operation, Ramzi Yousef, was a man whose affiliation with al Qaeda and bin Laden is debatable. In fact, in a 1997 CNN interview, bin Laden said that he did not know Yousef.[100] Nevertheless, Yousef trained in camps in Afghanistan that were funded by bin Laden and was "at a minimum part of a loose network of Sunni extremists/Islamists who, like Bin Laden, began to focus their rage on the United States."[101] While most of the individuals involved in the first bombing of the World Trade Center and in the 1993 landmarks plot seem to have been unaffiliated with any particular group, one of the spiritual leaders of the men in both plots, Sheikh Omar Abdel Rahman, was also the spiritual leader of the Egyptian Islamic Jihad.

Yousef's plots lacked the necessary sophistication to be highly effective, as exemplified by his mistake in calculating the effects of the explosives used and the level of amateurism displayed in the conspirators' treatment of evidence, their getaway plans, and the letters of responsibility sent after the attack. But more was learned with each attack and foiled plot. Careful surveillance was conducted, tightly managed cells with local managers were put in place, and operatives were carefully vetted at high levels of al Qaeda leadership. The operations were managed by individuals brought from abroad who then used well-established local support networks. Perhaps of greatest importance is the fact that plots failed when al Qaeda's leadership did not directly participate in their formation (the two millennium plots, for example). However, for the cases in which bin Laden was directly involved, such as the East African embassy and USS *Cole* bombings, the attacks were a success. Command and control were obviously central to success—as would be shown again on 9/11.

While the prosecutions that stemmed from the two 1993 plots were effective, the intelligence community did not achieve similar success. Indeed, as the 9/11 Commission noted, "The successful use of the legal system to address the first World Trade Center bombing had the side effect of obscuring the need to examine the character and extent of the new threat facing the United States. The trials did not bring the Bin Laden network to the attention of the public and policymakers."[102]

The FBI assembled some evidence showing that the men convicted in the 1993 World Trade Center bombing were not the only plotters. Materials taken from Ahmad Ajaj indicated that the plot was hatched at or near the Khaldan camp, where Ajaj had gone from Texas in April 1992 to learn how to construct bombs. He had met Ramzi Yousef in Pakistan, where they discussed bombing targets in the United States and assembled a "terrorist kit" that included bomb-making manuals, operations guidance, videotapes advocating terrorist action against the United States, and false identification documents.[103] Nevertheless, no comprehensive investigation of the network and its branches overseas was conducted by the government. If it had been, the US government might have begun to understand that the jihad taking place in Afghanistan was in the process of turning its sights to America.

With operatives already embedded in the United States and a number of willing US citizen converts who can move easily in and out of the country, it would have been naive to think that al Qaeda was not continuing to plan for further attacks within the United States. Following 9/11, American intelligence and law enforcement went into action as never before. As the invaluable work of the 9/11 Commission showed, al Qaeda clearly had institutional supports in place which were available to help when needed . . . including *after* 9/11. This terrorism infrastructure has become the subject of intense scrutiny and prosecution, and continues to pose a threat to the security of the United States and its people.

NOTES

1. National Commission on Terrorist Attacks upon the United States, *The 9/11 Commission Report: Final Report of the National Commission on Terrorist Attacks upon the United States* (New York: Norton, 2004), p. 59.

2. Ibid., p. 71.

3. J. Gilmore Childers and Henry J. DePippo, testimony, Senate Judiciary Subcommittee on Technology, Terrorism, and Government Information, *Foreign Terrorist Activities in America Five Years after the World Trade Center*, 105th Cong., 2nd sess., February 24, 1998.

4. Ibid.

5. *USA v. Rahman*, 93-CR-181, trial transcript, p. 20146 (SD NY September 21, 1995).

6. *USA v. Salameh*, 93-CR-180, trial transcript, pp. 3593–3602 (SD NY December 1, 1993).

7. *USA v. Yousef*, 93-CR-180, trial transcript, pp. 2635–36 (SD NY September 16, 1997).

8. *USA v. Yousef*, 93-CR-180, trial transcript, pp. 5260, 5267 (SD NY November 3, 1997).

9. *USA v. Salameh*, 93-CR-180, trial transcript, pp. 2382–88, 2419–20, 2423–24 (SD NY November 9, 1993).

10. National Commission on Terrorist Attacks upon the United States, *9/11 and Terrorist Travel: Staff Report of the National Commission on Terrorist Attacks upon the United States* (New York: Norton, 2004), pp. 50–51.

11. Abdul Rahman Yasin, interview by Leslie Stahl, *60 Minutes*, CBS, June 2, 2002.

12. Ibid.

13. *USA v. Yousef*, 93-CR-180, trial transcript, pp. 2647, 2664–65 (SD NY September 16, 1997); *USA v. Yousef*, 93-CR-180, trial transcript, p. 4721 (SD NY October 22, 1997).

14. *USA v. Salameh*, 93-CR-180, trial transcript, pp. 9274–80 (SD NY March 4, 1994); Larry Neumeister, "Trade Center Bombers Resentenced to Life Terms," Associated Press, October 14, 1999.

15. "U.S. Attorney General Touts Arrest of Palestinian Bomb Suspect," Agence France Presse, August 3, 1995.

16. *USA v. Salameh, et al.*, 93-CR-180, appeal, p. 165 (SD NY April 6, 1998).

17. *USA v. Rahman*, 93-CR-181, trial transcript, pp. 20657–64 (SD NY October 1995). Omar Abdel-Rahman, charged with leading the conspiracy; El Sayyid Nosair, charged with murdering radical rabbi Meir Kahane; Ibrahim el-Gabrowny, charged with organizing a terrorist training camp; Clement Hampton El (Sheik Rahman), charged with weapons possession; Amir Abdelgani, charged with the construction of bombs; Victor Alvarez provided firearms; Mohammed Saleh agreed to provide money and fuel oil for bombs; Fadil Abdelgani; Tarig Elhassan; and Fares Khallafalla. Nosair and one other defendant were found innocent of transporting explosives.

18. Dale Watson, testimony, Senate Judiciary Subcommittee on Technology, Terrorism, and Government Information, *Foreign Terrorist Activities in America Five Years after the World Trade Center*, 105th Cong., 2nd sess., February 24, 1998.

19. "Affidavit of Shawn S. Devroude in Support of Search Warrant" (ED VA August 20, 2004).

20. 9/11 Commission, *The 9/11 Commission Report*, p. 148.

21. Ibid., p. 73.

22. *USA v. Yousef*, 93-CR-180, trial transcript, pp. 7–11, 13–14, 17–18 (SD NY May 29, 1996).

23. Ibid., pp. 18–20; *USA v. Yousef*, 93-CR-180, trial transcript, pp. 5120–24 (SD NY August 26, 1996).

24. *USA v. Osama bin Laden, et al.*, S(7) 98-CR-1023, trial transcript, pp. 22–24 (SD NY February 5, 2001).

25. *USA v. Osama bin Laden, et al.*, S(7) 98-CR-1023, trial transcript, p. 5230 (SD NY May 1, 2001).

26. Ibid., p. 5255.

27. Ibid., pp. 5288, 5296. This telephone number is also attributed to bin Laden as well as Ayman al-Zawahiri.

28. Ibid., pp. 5261, 5270–71.

29. Kevin Peraino and Evan Thomas, "Odyssey into Jihad: April Ray's Husband Became Bin Laden's Secretary, *Newsweek*, January 14, 2002, p. 40.

30. *USA v. Osama bin Laden, et al.*, 98-CR-1023, bail hearing (SD NY February 8, 1999), p. 15.

31. Mary Jo White, letter to Assistant US Attorney Patrick J. Fitzgerald regarding *United States v. Bin Laden, et al.*, S(2) 98-CR-1023, November 13, 1998.

32. *USA v. Osama bin Laden, et al.*, S(7) 98-CR-1023, trial transcript, pp. 774–76 (SD NY February 15, 2001).

33. *USA v. Osama bin Laden, et al.*, 98-CR-1023, bail hearing, p. 21 (SD NY February 8, 1999).

34. *USA v. Osama bin Laden, et al.*, 98-CR-1023, affirmation, pp. 32–33 (SD NY December 30, 1999).

35. *USA v. Osama bin Laden, et al.*, 98-CR-1023, indictment, pp. 1, 11 (SD NY November 4, 1998).

36. *USA v. Al Mohamed, et al.*, 98-CR-1023, plea, pp. 26–27 (SD NY October 20, 2000).

37. *USA v. Ali Mohamed*, S(7) 98-CR-1023 (LBS), trial transcript, pp. 25–27 (SD NY October 20, 2000).

38. 9/11 Commission, *The 9/11 Commission Report*, p. 68.

39. *USA v. Osama bin Laden, et al.*, S(7) 98-CR-1023, trial transcript, pp. 5224–25 (SD NY May 1, 2001).

40. Ibid., p. 5225.

41. Ibid., pp. 5370–86.

42. Ibid., p. 5385.

43. Ibid., pp. 3028–29, 3033–34, 5292–94.

44. Ibid., pp. 3480–81, 5287–90, 5292–98.

45. Ibid.

46. Donatella Lorch and Daniel Klaidman, "The Plot Thickens," *Newsweek*, February 7, 2000, pp. 44–45.

47. Mark Morris, "Help for bin Laden Linked to Midwest; Saudi Student in Missouri Bought $7,500 Telephone," *Kansas City Star*, September 20, 2001, p. B1.

48. Allwhois Record of Palestine Information Center, http://www.palestineinfo.org.

49. *USA v. Osama bin Laden, et al.*, S(7) 98-CR-1023, trial transcript, pp. 5364–66 (SD NY May 1, 2001).

50. Ibid., p. 5457.

51. Ibid., p. 5298.

52. Ibid., p. 5229.

53. Ibid., p. 5242.

54. Ibid., pp. 5226–27.

55. Ibid., pp. 2013–14, 5482–83; Benjamin Weiser, "Government Says Attack on Guard Was Part of Escape Plan," *New York Times*, December 21, 2000, p. B3.

56. *USA v. Osama bin Laden, et al.*, S(7) 98-CR-1023, trial transcript, p. 7 (SD NY February 5, 2001).

57. Ibid., pp. 104–107, 119–120, 149.

58. Ibid., pp. 5497–98.

59. *USA v. Al Badawi*, 98-CR-1023, indictment, pp. 12–16 (SD NY May 15, 2003); Robert Burns, "Navy Revises Cole Timeline of Events Preceding the Cole Attack," Associated Press, October 21, 2000.

60. Ibid.

61. 9/11 Commission, *The 9/11 Commission Report*, p. 190.

62. *USA v. Ahmed Ressam*, 99-CR-666C, complaint, pp. 2–3 (WD WA December 17, 1999).

63. Hal Bernton et al., "The Crossing: Chapter 12: Ahmed Ressam Fails to Take into Account the Diligence of U.S. Customs Officials When Taking His Explosives across the Border from British Columbia," *Gazette*, August 25, 2002, p. A8.

64. Hal Bernton et al., "Puzzle Pieces: In Chapter 15, U.S. Officials Wonder If the Ressam Case Might Portend Things to Come," *Gazette*, August 28, 2002, p. A15.

65. 9/11 Commission, *The 9/11 Commission Report*, p. 179.

66. Ibid.

67. *USA v. Mokhtar Haouri*, S4 00-CR-17, trial transcript, pp. 536–37 (SD NY July 3, 2001).

68. Hal Bernton et al., "The Terrorist Within: Chapter 7: Joining Jihad," *Seattle Times*, June 23–July 7, 2002.

69. "Trail of a Terrorist: Introduction," *Frontline*, PBS, October 25, 2001.

70. *USA v. Mokhtar Haouari*, S4 00-CR-15, trial transcript, pp. 549–51 (SD NY July 3, 2001).

71. Oriana Zill, "Trail of a Terrorist: Crossing Borders: How Terrorists Use Fake Passports, Visas, and Other Identity Documents," *Frontline*, PBS, October 25, 2001.

72. *USA v. Mokhtar Haouri*, S4 00-CR-17, trial transcript, pp. 554–55 (SD NY July 3, 2001).

73. *USA v. Abu Doha*, 01-CR-00832-RWS, indictment, p. 3 (SD NY August 27, 2001).

74. Ibid.

75. *USA v. Mokhtar Haouri*, S4 00-CR-17, trial transcript, pp. 554–55 (SD NY July 3, 2001).

76. Ibid., p. 560.

77. Ibid., p. 576.

78. *USA v. Abu Doha*, 01-CR-00832-RWS, indictment, pp. 3–4 (SD NY August 27, 2001).

79. *USA v. Mokhtar Haouari, et al.*, S4 00 Cr. 15, trial transcript, pp. 605–608 (SD NY, Cross-examination of Ahmed Ressam, July 3, 2001).

80. *USA v. Ahmed Ressam*, 99-CR-666C, judgement, p. 3 (WDWA July 27, 2005).

81. Judith Miller, "Holy Warriors: Dissecting a Terror Plot from Boston to Amman," *New York Times*, January 15, 2001, p. A1.

82. Ibid.

83. John Walcott, "Pakistani Officials Capture Al Qaida's Top Terrorist Planner," Knight Ridder Washington Bureau, April 2, 2002.

84. Jason Burke, "Jihad Mastermind: How the Perfect Terrorist Plotted the Ultimate Crime," *Observer*, April 7, 2002, p. 18.

85. Walcott, "Pakistani Officials Capture Al Qaida's Top Terrorist Planner."

86. Miller, "Holy Warriors."

87. Ibid.

88. 9/11 Commission, *The 9/11 Commission Report*, p. 175.

89. Miller, "Holy Warriors."

90. Ibid.

91. Ghassan Joha, "Raed Hijazi's Death Conviction Upheld, Room for Appeal," *Star* (Jordan), January 15, 2003; Jamal Halaby, "Military Court Upholds Death Penalty for Jordanian-American Terror Convict," Associated Press, December 8, 2003.

92. "Jordan: Court Upholds Verdicts in Millennium Plot Case," Financial Times Information, Global News Wire—Asia Africa Intelligence Wire, June 24, 2004.

93. Mark Hosenball and Colin Soloway, "The Mouthpiece of Terror," *Newsweek*, June 3, 2002, p. 24.

94. Jerry Seper, "Pakistan Hands Over Al Qaeda Recruiter," *Washington Times*, April 2, 2002, p. A01.

95. 9/11 Commission, *The 9/11 Commission Report*, p. 253.

96. Dana Canedy and Eric Lichtblau, "Family Members Defend Man Sought as 'Imminent Threat' by F.B.I.," *New York Times*, March 22, 2003, p. B12.

97. 9/11 Commission, *9/11 and Terrorist Travel*, p. 216 n. 114.

98. 9/11 Commission, *The 9/11 Commission Report*, p. 233.

99. Ibid., p. 250.

100. "Bombing Trial Witness Describes Nairobi Surveillance Mission," State Department Press Release, February, 22, 2001.

101. Ibid.

102. 9/11 Commission, *The 9/11 Commission Report*, p. 72.

103. Ibid., p. 73.

-2-

AL QAEDA POST-9/11: AMERICAN PLOTS AND VULNERABILITIES DISCOVERED

Finding and rooting out Al Qaeda members once [they are] in the United States is the most serious intelligence and law enforcement challenge.

—FBI director Robert Mueller, February 11, 2003, presentation to US Senate Select Intelligence Committee

OVERVIEW

Since 9/11, al Qaeda has engaged in a variety of plans specifically targeting American civilians within the United States. These plots were hatched primarily by Khalid Sheikh Mohammed (KSM) until his capture by Pakistani authorities outside of Islamabad in March 2003. Each one has displayed his particularly violent approach combined with a malevolent creativity. In this chapter, the various al Qaeda schemes to attack relatively "soft targets" such as multiple apartment buildings, shopping malls, major landmark bridges and railways, and New York buildings, housing some of the country's major financial firms, are examined.

A distinguishing feature of the individual plots as they unfolded was the activation of al Qaeda cell members who were in place within the United States prior to 9/11. While some operatives were given mission-specific assignments, others continued to serve as facilitators in a support network, assisting in such tasks as procuring explosives, money, night-vision goggles, sleeping bags, radios, camouflage suits, global positioning equipment, and identification and travel documents. Each case displayed considerably careful planning, including surveillance.

As is characteristic of al Qaeda's inconspicuous style, these operatives were strategically positioned throughout the United States—often in places not previously associated with terrorist activity, such as Peoria; Chicago; Columbus, Ohio; Baltimore and its suburbs; Seattle; Portland, Oregon; Minneapolis; and upstate New York. While the operatives were distributed throughout the country, all of the plots they served originated in Afghanistan as did all aspects of training, and spiritual and tactical guidance.

The plots were conceived with multiple objectives: to achieve mass casualties, economic damage, destruction of infrastructure, and to create terror within the general population. Some plots never progressed beyond discussion, while others reached operational stages. In some cases, details remain classified or otherwise unavailable. However, it is clear that in every instance KSM failed to bring the plots to fruition.

CRITICAL INFRASTRUCTURE PLOTS

It is now known, albeit in varying degrees of detail, that al Qaeda has pursued multiple plots involving critical infrastructure since 9/11.[1] Its primary objective was to cause significant economic harm to the United States, but always with a dual feature of inflicting maximum casualties. Two extensive plans focused on either federal buildings or significant financial institutions, while the remaining plans were aimed at attacking the US transportation system.

Cargo planes, trucks, trains, buses, bridges, subways, ferries, and tunnels were all considered as either the tool or the target of terror. Also contemplated were mass forest fires. Other planned attacks were aimed at the US energy infrastructure—one at domestic oil refineries and another at nuclear power plants (an interest of the 9/11 hijackers). Still other plots involved poisoning supply chains of food, water, and medicine.

Federal Buildings

Only days after 9/11, American intelligence officers found detailed al Qaeda plans in Hamburg, Germany, for a truck bombing of the US Federal Court House and Post Office in Pittsburgh, Pennsylvania. Interrogations abroad revealed that the federal buildings had been under surveillance with a specific security weakness identified: there was only a single guard stationed at the rear of each building. The plot entailed a car and a tractor-trailer working in tandem. The first vehicle would approach the loading dock adjacent to the guard. After claiming that his car was suffering from mechanical problems, the driver would kill the guard. Then the tractor-trailer would enter the loading dock and detonate its explosives in an effort to replicate the devastation of the 1995 Oklahoma City bombing.

US intelligence also uncovered surveillance information on Pittsburgh in Saudi Arabia and in a cave in Afghanistan. Ken McCabe, former head of the FBI's Pittsburgh Field Office, explained at the time news broke of the foiled plot, "We know that there are Al Qaida representatives overseas who have communicated with individuals from the western Pennsylvania and West Virginia area. We know that from some of the investigations that have been conducted overseas, from some of the military operations that have taken place in Pakistan, Afghanistan, and Iraq."[2]

Transportation

Iyman Faris, a naturalized US citizen born in Kashmir who lived in Ohio, pled guilty in May 2003 to surveilling the Brooklyn Bridge on behalf of al Qaeda, as well as researching and providing information to al Qaeda regarding the tools necessary for possible attacks on US targets.[3] In October 2003, Faris was sentenced to twenty years in prison for providing material support or resources to, and conspiring with, al Qaeda.[4]

Earlier that year, he had been apprehended by federal law enforcement officials based on information that remains classified.[5] It has since been determined that Faris was involved with plots that included cargo planes, the Brooklyn Bridge, and trains, and that he conspired with Nuradin Abdi to bomb a Columbus shopping mall (discussed below).[6]

During questioning subsequent to his arrest, Faris admitted traveling to Afghanistan in 2000 where he met with bin Laden at an al Qaeda training camp. He described how, in a meeting later that year, one of bin Laden's men asked him about ultralight airplanes and said al Qaeda was looking to "procure an escape airplane."[7]

Faris also admitted to federal agents that during a visit to Karachi, Pakistan, in early 2002, he was introduced to KSM. As the two discussed Faris's work as a truck driver in the United States, Faris told KSM that some of his deliveries were made to air cargo planes. KSM was interested in Faris's access to these planes, and the two discussed how cargo planes held "more weight and more fuel, and thus had excellent potential to be converted into weapons."[8] Faris's employer, Yowell Transportation, confirmed that Faris regularly delivered to an air cargo company at the Columbus airport.[9]

According to Faris, KSM told him that al Qaeda was planning two simultaneous attacks in New York City and Washington, DC. The two then discussed destroying the Brooklyn Bridge by severing its suspension cables. Faris was tasked with obtaining the necessary equipment.[10]

In April 2002, Faris returned to the United States and researched "gas cutters" and the Brooklyn Bridge on the Internet. He also traveled to New York City in late 2002 to examine the bridge. He decided the plan was too difficult because of the security and the structure of the bridge. Faris then sent a coded message communicating this to al Qaeda leadership.[11]

Faris was known to be a person of interest to the FBI before 9/11, and he was interviewed by them shortly after the attacks. When he returned to the United States and traveled to New York City, he did so under the watchful eye of the FBI.[12]

Commercial Driver's Licenses

Poor information sharing plagued the pre-9/11 system. The Commercial Motor Vehicle Safety Acts of 1986 and 1999 required a nationwide system to gather information on commercial driver's license (CDL) holders from the various states. This system—the Commercial Driver's License Information System (CDLIS)—was maintained by a subsidiary of the American Association of Motor Vehicles Administration. Its purpose was to ensure that information regarding moving traffic violations of CDL holders was properly maintained in the license-issuing state, regardless of where the infraction occurred. Such information is critical to guarantee that truckers are safe drivers, since certain convictions, such as operating a commercial vehicle under the influence of alcohol, lead to automatic and immediate CDL disqualification.

A 2000 audit by the Department of Transportation revealed pervasive problems in the CDLIS system. Auditors visited ten jurisdictions (nine states plus the District of Columbia) and found that in five, state officials had access to CDLIS but did not disqualify commercial drivers with severe traffic violations. Also during the audit period, 17 percent of the out-of-state convictions sent to CDLIS were not passed on to the licensing state of the violator within ninety days. If the licensing state did not receive this information, it had no reason to disqualify the CDL holder. Moreover, six of the jurisdictions visited and twenty other states that gave the auditors information have masking programs that keep traffic convictions out of commercial drivers' records.[13]

These problems were identified as a terrorism vulnerability thanks to a comprehensive audit designed to prevent improper issuance or retention of CDLs given the potential for harm and the nagging concern that al Qaeda would try and use such vehicles.

A Plan to Explode a Fuel Truck in a New York City Tunnel

Following 9/11, FBI and local police moved quickly to arrest Nabil al-Marabh in Chicago on September 19, 2001. At the time of his arrest, he had a chauffeur's driver's license, a commercial driver's license, and a hazardous materials license.[14] He was once number 27 on the FBI's Most Wanted Terrorists list.[15]

Nabil al-Marabh had fought in Afghanistan and had connections to Raed Hijazi, who had been convicted in Jordan for his role in the Jordanian millennium conspiracy that targeted American and Israeli tourists.[16] According to a Jordanian informant, al-Marabh had planned to martyr himself by "driving a gasoline truck into a New York City tunnel, turning it sideways, opening its fuel valves and having an al Qaeda operative shoot a flare to ignite a massive explosion." The informant explained that al-Marabh and Hijazi were going to obtain the fuel truck by stealing it "from a rest stop in New York and New Jersey" and then targeting either the "Lincoln or Holland tunnels."[17]

The Case of the Alleged Detroit Cell

While police were searching for al-Marabh, they stumbled on a group of men living in an apartment where he had once lived. These men—Karim Koubriti, Ahmed Hannan, and Farouk Ali Haimoud—are alleged to have constituted an al Qaeda sleeper cell.[18] Koubriti and another associate, Abdel Ilah Elmardoudi, were convicted in June 2003 on charges of providing material support to terrorists and document fraud. Youssef Hmimssa, who was also connected to the men, was detained in Iowa but became the main witness for the prosecution and had no charges filed against him.[19]

Hmimssa gave evidence that Koubriti wanted a commercial driver's license with a hazardous materials endorsement to "drive a truck into a crowd coming out of a Detroit baseball stadium, presumably Comerica Park where the Detroit Tigers play."[20] This chilling evidence seemed to give an air of reality to some of the worst fears of America's vulnerability to mass population–inspired terrorist attacks.

In September 2004, the terrorism-related convictions were overturned when a judge in a Michigan district court ruled that the prosecution had withheld information from the defense that was "clearly and materially exculpatory of the Defendants as to the charges against them."[21] The evidence pertained to Hmimssa's reliability as a witness, because the prosecution had not disclosed a letter it had from a fellow inmate, Milton Jones, who said Hmimssa claimed to have lied to the FBI and the Secret Service regarding the Detroit terror case.[22]

License Obtained Despite FBI Watchlisting

Before the 9/11 attacks, the FBI identified Mohammad Kamal Elzahabi as a suspected terrorist. Despite this, in early 2002, Elzahabi received a commercial driver's license to operate a school bus and transport hazardous materials. According to the Minnesota Department of Public Safety's Division of Driver Vehicle and Licensing, the FBI "ran his name through a database and cleared him." In June 2004, Elzahabi's license for transporting toxic materials was still valid, though his school bus driver's license had been canceled in February for unspecified reasons. The Minnesota Department of Public Safety claims that today a person on a terrorism watchlist would be flagged in the computer system as ineligible for the specialized toxic materials license.[23]

License Scheme

A license examiner in Pennsylvania was discovered to have provided hazardous materials permits to roughly twenty people without having them take the required writing and driving tests. All were arrested for lying about their identities on their license applications.[24]

The middleman between the corrupt license examiner and the fraudulent license holders was Abdul Mohamman, also known as Elmeliani Benmoumen. Mohamman received $350 from each applicant, and he paid the license examiner $50 to $100 for each license.[25]

In October 2001, the twenty men were indicted for obtaining the fraudulent licenses, eighteen for obtaining commercial driver's licenses with permission to carry hazardous materials and two for obtaining commercial driver's licenses without a hazardous materials endorsement. Most of the suspects were soon released on bond; none was charged with terrorism-related offenses.[26]

It is important to note that both Elzahabi and al-Marabh obtained their commercial/chauffeur/hazardous materials licenses legally, and not through the fraudulent racket run by Mohamman. Again, while no specific terrorism intentions were discerned, the incidents revealed a systemic vulnerability that clearly needed correction.

New Security Measures

In May 2003, the Transportation Security Administration (TSA) began requiring commercial drivers with hazardous materials specifications to undergo background checks. To date, 3.5 million commercial driver's licenses with hazardous materials endorsements have been checked against "criminal, immigration, and FBI records."[27] Of the 2.7 million truck drivers licensed to carry hazardous materials whose background had been examined by June 2004, twenty-nine were found to have possible relationships with terrorist organizations.[28] These refocused efforts enhanced security.

Subways, Trains, and Buses

Khalid Sheikh Mohammed has reportedly told interrogators that al Qaeda planned to target Washington, DC's Metro subway system, a plot that may have involved using a firebomb. Other interrogations have revealed similar intentions for systems in New York City and elsewhere.[29] One of the New York plots purportedly involved the use of poison gas[30] and, in June 2004, two Iranian security guards who worked for the Iranian mission to the United Nations were expelled after repeatedly videotaping the New York City subways.[31]

In May 2004, a string of suspicious empty suitcases left at New York's Penn Station led to concerns that terrorists were conducting a dry run before launching a Madrid-style attack. Furthermore, authorities in Canada and Great Britain have acted on concerns regarding subway attacks in their jurisdictions as well.[32]

As is evident from the bombing of commuter trains in Madrid, Spain, passenger trains are also in al Qaeda's sights. An October 2002 FBI press release warned that "information from debriefings of Al Qa'ida detainees . . . indicates that the group has considered directly targeting U.S. passenger trains, possibly using operatives who have a Western appearance."[33] Moreover, the FBI stated, "Recently captured Al Qa'ida photographs of U.S. railroad engines, cars, and crossings heighten the intelligence community's concern of this threat."[34]

Specifically, al Qaeda hoped "to derail a train in the industrial corridor of northeast Washington, hoping to smash the cars into tanks of hazardous chemicals stored near the tracks."[35] In his meetings with Iyman Faris, KSM had explained that al Qaeda was planning to derail trains and asked Faris to "obtain" the tools for that plot as well.[36]

In addition, a Department of Homeland Security (DHS) Suspicious Incidents Report from April 2004 expressed concerns that terrorists might be plotting to bomb buses and trains in major American or Canadian cities over the summer.[37] One of the factors that prompted the warning was the chilling discovery, made by Spanish police, of sketches of New York City's Grand Central Terminal in the apartment of Mouhannad Almallah, one of the alleged masterminds of the March 2004 Madrid train bombings.

PATH Tunnel Plot

On July 7, 2006, the FBI announced that it had disrupted an al Qaeda plot targeting the public transit system of Manhattan and New Jersey. In a press release, the FBI stated, "Working closely with the Intelligence/ Information Directorate within the Internal Security Forces of Lebanon and with other foreign law enforcement and intelligence partners, we have disrupted a terrorist network that was in the planning stages of an attack against the transportation system in the New York–New Jersey area. A significant development in this investigation was the arrest of a key suspect by Lebanese authorities."[38]

That suspect, Assem Hammoud, a college professor in computer studies, had been arrested by Lebanese officials in his Beirut apartment in April.[39] According to the FBI, Hammoud, along with seven coconspirators, was planning to infiltrate the United States, via the Canadian border, and board commuter trains while carrying backpacks full of explosives, likely targeting the Port Authority Trans-Hudson, or PATH, tunnel connecting New Jersey to Manhattan.[40]

Lebanese General Security spokesman Elie Baradei said that the FBI and Lebanese officials started investigating Hammoud in mid-2005, after a discussion concerning the tunnel plot appeared over the Internet in e-mails and chat rooms. Baradei also stated that Hammoud was recruited into al Qaeda in 2003 by a Syrian national and that Hammoud received his weapons training in the Palestinian refugee camp Ain Helwah in Lebanon.[41]

Passenger Ferries

For a number of years, al Qaeda has remained interested in targeting the US ferry system. The *Seattle Times* reported in October 2004 that there had been nineteen incidents of terrorist surveillance of the Washington State ferry system.[42] According to law enforcement agencies and the DHS Suspicious Incidents Report, surveillance of ferries may also have taken place in California, Texas, Louisiana, and New York.[43]

As the FBI noted in a July 2003 memo, ferries are attractive to terrorists because "many . . . operate in close proximity to oil terminals, tourist facilities and places of commerce."[44] Authorities suspect that al Qaeda may try and use scuba divers to launch attacks on ferries.[45] An August 2003 DHS bulletin stated that there "has been law enforcement reporting of suspicious individuals having queried marine shops and schools concerning equipment and training."[46] This DHS warning expanded on a May 2002 FBI alert that "various terrorist elements have sought to develop an offensive scuba diver capability."[47] One reason for the alert was that scuba diving manuals were discovered in an al Qaeda safehouse in Afghanistan.[48] In May 2002, the FBI queried dive shops around the United States to determine whether al Qaeda operatives had taken scuba lessons.[49]

Al Qaeda is also believed to be interested in using a suicide bomber to destroy a ferry, as its affiliate, Abu Sayyaf, did in a February 26, 2004, attack that killed 116 in the Philippines.[50]

Financial Center Plots

Al Qaeda has long sought to target institutions symbolizing US economic power. On April 19, 2002, the FBI issued a press release reporting that al Qaeda was considering attacks against US financial institutions in the Northeast, particularly banks, as part of its campaign against US financial interests.[51]

In July 2004, the US government intercepted phone calls and Internet communications that suggested Wall Street had been under operational surveillance in advance of an attack.[52] By late July, authorities in Pakistan had uncovered substantial al Qaeda records on three laptop computers and fifty-one disks that showed surveillance activity dating back to 2000 and 2001, and updated again in 2004.[53] The computers contained five hundred photographs of potential targets inside the United States, including the International Monetary Fund and the World Bank in Washington, DC; Prudential Financial in northern New Jersey; and the Citigroup and the New York Stock Exchange buildings in New York.[54] The American Stock Exchange and NASDAQ were also targeted.[55] Extensive analyses accompanied these photographs, describing in detail the buildings' vulnerabilities to various kinds of terrorist attacks.[56] According to a senior intelligence official, the records contained full descriptions of the types of human populations at these targets, including

> the types of security procedures at some specific buildings; the security checks that are required; the types of security personnel [*sic*] at different posts; whether or not these individuals are armed or not; the presence of security officers at these posts at different times of the day; the types of uniforms that they wear; the number of pedestrians in the area, the number of employees in buildings; information regarding potential escape routes for perpetrators of attacks; different points of reconnaissance in order to ensure that they have the full breadth of information regarding the targets; different types of shops that are nearby.[57]

Information on the physical infrastructure of the buildings and surrounding area covered

> the other facilities in the area . . . the different access measures, as far as whether or not there's a physical desk or intercom systems; types of surveillance activities or counter-surveillance activities such as cameras; good places to go to meet employees; good places to go to acquire additional information . . . the different types of vehicles that in fact can enter different types of parking facilities . . . whether or not certain materials can, if detonated, cause, in fact, buildings to collapse; the placement of such devices and bombs to maximize the damage to the architecture of the building.[58]

And, finally, potential operational strategies were fully assessed in light of the human and physical infrastructure described, including

> the disadvantages of certain types of plans in terms of the possible dissipation of the force in terms of the size, the height of the building, the height of a ceiling where in fact a vehicle might in fact be detonated[;] . . . different means of ingress and egress; how one can get in side buildings[;] . . . configurations of parking lots[;] . . . whether or not the parking garages and facilities are close [to] the core of the buildings and near certain offices[;] . . . the different types of shops nearby that can provide cover for additional types of acquisition of information[;] . . . the many types of procedures that employees themselves have to use for access to buildings.[59]

Al Qaeda gathered much of this information from publicly available sites, but it also clearly and meticulously conducted on-site reconnaissance.[60] Investigators have also speculated that individuals inside the Prudential and Citibank buildings helped al Qaeda with the surveillance. In July 2003, DHS issued a bulletin warning that al Qaeda operatives may attempt to find jobs inside US financial institutions. DHS spokesman Commander David Wray said, "There is new intelligence that indicates specific interest in financial services and indirect indication . . . that led us to believe . . . that threats could come from within as well as without."[61]

Officials believe that Adnan el-Shukrijumah was one of the operatives who conducted the surveillance.[62] They further assert that Issa al-Britani (aka Dhiren Barot, aka Abu Eisa al-Hindi, aka Abu Musa), an al Qaeda operative arrested in London in August 2004, came to the United States posing as a student in order to surveil the Prudential Building in Newark, New Jersey.[63]

Furthermore, Martin Mubanga, a British Muslim convert currently detained at Guantanamo Bay, was apparently "tasked to look into a list of 33 largely New York–based Jewish organizations as targets" and "he received instructions to carry out violence against one, if not all, of the groups listed in the aforementioned list."[64]

According to the 9/11 Commission's *Final Report,* KSM has claimed that, "at Bin Laden's direction in early 2001, he sent Britani to the United States to case potential economic and 'Jewish' targets in New York City."[65] Previously, KSM had sent Britani to visit Riduan Isamuddin (better known as Hambali) in Malaysia. Britani "provided Hambali with two addresses—one in the United States ('possibly in California') and one in South Africa—and told Hambali he could contact 'people in those locations' if he 'needed help.'"[66]

Records in Pakistan also suggested that al Qaeda considered launching the attacks using hijacked tourist helicopters,[67] limousines packed with explosives, or large trucks.[68] Upon discovering this information, DHS raised the threat level to Code Orange for the financial services sector in New York City, northern New Jersey, and Washington, DC.[69]

In December 2004, DHS and the FBI issued a joint "Lessons Learned" Report from the Terrorists Casing of Financial Centers that quotes from the surveillance reports of the terrorists. If anyone needed convincing that the al Qaeda threat to America preexisted and continued past 9/11, this was it.

In the instructions to the agents conducting surveillance, the al Qaeda manual directs that

> the individual who gathers information about a desired location should, in addition to drawing a diagram, describe it and all its details.
>
> The Drawing: The brother should draw a diagram of the area, the street, and the location which is the target of the information-gathering. He should describe its shape and characteristics. The drawing should be realistic so that someone who never saw the location could visualize it. It is preferable to also put on the drawing the directions of traffic, police stations, and security centers.
>
> It is preferable to photograph the area as a whole first, then the street of the [desired] location. If possible, panoramic pictures should be taken. That is, collection of views should be continuous in such a way that all pictures are taken from one location and that the ending of one picture is the beginning of the next.
>
> The Description: It is necessary to gather as much information about the location as possible. For instance: 1) Traffic directions and how wide the streets are, 2) Transportation leading to the location, 3) The area, appearance, and setting of the place, 4) Traffic signals and pedestrian areas, 5) Security personnel centers and government agencies, 6) Embassies and consulates, 7) The economic characteristics of the area and traffic congestion times, 8) Public parks, 9) Amount and location of lighting.[70]

Notes from the actual persons conducting surveillance make clear the deadly intent of al Qaeda:

> Cameras: In the . . . corners of the {facility}, at each there is a round opaque (black) tinted camera in the ceiling. This is the kind that can rotate inside and look in any direction whilst the person that it is focused on is unaware that "all eyes are on him." Apparently, they are not the long-range type and are obviously looking mostly at what may be coming in and out. More importantly, with regards to cameras upstairs in the higher office floors themselves, there are none that can be visually seen; hence either they are simply not there or alternatively they are very well concealed. Indeed, this corporation has no shortage of finance should they wish to do so! Outside there is only one visible one . . . facing completely downwards, peering at what appears to be a staff entrance.
>
> Regarding the columns on this sight, on each corner. . . . On each projection there is a thin metal column that is slightly inside away from the main edge . . . small ones on each corner, plus . . . big central ones . . . in total on

> each face (side). That is not to say that this building is extraordinarily fortified, actually the corner edge columns are quite thin and do not appear to be relatively that strong.
>
> Underground Car Park: On the . . . flank there is an underground car park that runs in a downward slope into the building. (It is located on the side that is nearer to the front entrance.) This car park has . . . entrances . . . for incoming vehicles and . . . for outgoing ones. Between these . . . entrances there is a single bar barrier partition that separates them. The car park is usually manned by 1–2 members of security (usually of African origin). They are equipped with wireless radio communication sets. It is an open car park, i.e. there are no shutters that need to be lifted for entry/exit.
>
> Security: There are about . . . security personnel upstairs (male)—but only . . . that visibly carries a weapon and wears uniform (appears to be a Colt-45 pistol). Outside on the street at the main visitors entrance there are . . . guards—no weapons visible.
>
> For security reasons, visitors are required to have their parcels and baggage X-rayed as soon as they enter the building.[71]

Impersonating a private security guard to penetrate a target was one proposal made by the author when considering an attack.

> The guards are a combination of male and female, usually of African-American descent. Their uniform is that of a . . . blazer, white shirt and dark trousers. They all carry wireless radio sets for communication. Impersonating one of them by means of appearance would not be difficult . . . but it would be very hard to fool other security guards that would well be wary of any strangers.[72]

These are deadly intentions indeed.

Forest Fires Plot

In July 2003, the *Arizona Republic* reported that a high-ranking al Qaeda detainee had plotted to set forest fires in Colorado, Montana, Utah, and Wyoming, citing an FBI memo as its authority:

> The Al Qaida detainee told investigators that his plan called for three or four operatives to travel to the United States and set timed explosive

> devices in forests and grasslands. The devices would be set to detonate after the operatives had left the country. The detainee believed that significant damage to the U.S. economy would result and once it was realized that the fires were terrorist acts, U.S. citizens would put pressure on the U.S. government to change its policies.[73]

Nuclear Power Plants

Al Qaeda is also interested in targeting US nuclear power plants. Diagrams of nuclear power plants have been found in Afghanistan,[74] and in his original vision of using commercial aircraft as weapons, KSM planned that some would crash into power plants.[75] Mohamed Atta also considered targeting a nuclear power plant near New York that he had seen during flights familiarizing himself with the approach to Manhattan.[76] Additionally, a number of times people believed to have ties to Middle Eastern terrorist groups have engaged in what officials suspect to be "pre-operational surveillance" of nuclear power plants.[77]

In November 2003, DHS warned that al Qaeda planned to hijack a cargo jet in Canada, Mexico, or the Caribbean and fly it into a nuclear plant or other critical piece of infrastructure.[78] Representative Curt Weldon of Pennsylvania, who claimed to have two high-level reliable sources inside the Iranian regime, likewise began warning US intelligence in February 2003 that Iranian-linked terrorists planned to hijack Canadian planes and fly them into a nuclear reactor, possibly in New Hampshire.[79]

In a similar plot, terrorists linked to al Qaeda were reported to be planning to hijack a commercial plane and crash it into nuclear-powered submarines and ships based at Pearl Harbor, Hawaii.[80]

Oil Infrastructure Plots

Al Qaeda has demonstrated a sustained interest in targeting the oil infrastructure.[81] The FBI and DHS have repeatedly issued warnings about plans to target Texas oil refineries, most notably in Houston.[82] A number of instances of possible surveillance have further heightened concern. In Washington State[83] as well as in Texas, Maurice McBride, security director for the National Petrochemical and Refiners Association, commented, "Since 9/11 we have had numerous reports of what are apparently surveillance activities. Some of these have been explained away and some have not been."[84]

In December 2003, DHS issued an alert stating that al Qaeda intended to strike Valdez, Alaska, where tankers load oil from the Trans-Alaska pipeline.[85]

Nearly a year earlier, an FBI press release noted that

> Al Qa'ida plans to weaken the petroleum industry by conducting additional sea based attacks against large oil tankers and . . . such attacks may be a part of more extensive operations against port facilities and other energy-related targets including oil facilities and nuclear power plants.[86]

Food, Water, and Drug Contamination Plots

In June 2002, an al Qaeda Web site Jehad.net carried an e-Handbook with chemical and biological weapon recipes, including ricin (a deadly toxin derived from castor beans).[87] Also in June 2002, al Qaeda's spokesman, Suleiman Abu Gheith, used the organization's Web site Alneda.com to make the following statement: "We have the right to kill four million Americans, including one million children," and "we have the right to fight them by chemical and biological weapons so they catch the fatal and unusual diseases Muslims have caught due to U.S. chemical and biological weapons."[88]

While the United States was engaged in military action in Afghanistan, information gained from a high-ranking al Qaeda operative suggested that Wornick, a McAllen, Texas–based company that holds a $67 million contract to provide packaged meals (Meals Ready to Eat—MREs) for the US military, was "a possible terrorist target."[89] According to Michael Shelby, US Attorney for the Southern District of Texas, "U.S. forces on the ground received specific information that links McAllen, Texas, by name and the Wornick facility by name to information within Al Qaida's possession. . . . There had to be an investigation into the possibility that Al Qaida had the intention of infiltrating the Wornick Company for the purposes of contaminating—possibly—the MREs produced by the company."[90] Although no evidence of sabotage has been uncovered, ten temporary employees at Remedy Intelligent Staffing, which referred employees to Wornick, were convicted of Social Security fraud.[91] In addition, Remedy has been charged with falsifying work documents and lying to the FBI's Joint Terrorism Task Force (JTTF).[92]

This is not the only sign that al Qaeda is targeting the food supply. Most notably, in January 2003, officials uncovered a plan to use ricin to poison the food supply of at least one British military base.[93] Hundreds of pages of US agricultural documents were discovered in al Qaeda's caves in Afghanistan,[94] and US forces in Afghanistan also found diagrams of public water facilities.[95]

Moreover, a May 2002 CIA report confirmed that some of the 9/11 hijackers expressed interest in crop-dusting aircraft, which would offer an effective and simple way to spread biological agents, including plant and animal diseases, over large areas.[96] These fears resurfaced in November 2004 after three men stole a crop duster south of San Diego.[97] A TSA advisory issued in response stated, "Past information indicates that members of Al Qai'da may have planned—or may still be planning—to disperse biological or chemical agents from crop dusting aircraft. . . . Law enforcement agencies continue to investigate suspicious incidents and inquiries involving crop dusters and spray equipment."[98]

In January 2003, the World Health Organization warned of a "real and current" threat by terrorists to contaminate food supplies.[99] And, after announcing his resignation in December 2004, Department of Health and Human Services secretary Tommy Thompson commented, "For the life of me, I cannot understand why the terrorists have not attacked our food supply because it is so easy to do. We are importing a lot of food from the Middle East, and it would be easy to tamper with that." He added that only "a very minute amount of food" imports are inspected and that he fears an attack on the food supply "every single night."[100]

Al Qaeda has expressed interest in poisoning medicines as well. In August 2004, Food and Drug Administration commissioner Lester Crawford said that "clues from chatter" (intelligence collected by various types of technical monitoring) and information gleaned from recent arrests and raids suggested that terrorists may try to attack the pharmaceutical supply.[101]

CIVILIAN CASUALTY PLOTS

Plots with the simple objective of creating chaos and mass casualties usually involved so-called soft targets. Terrorists have schemed to attack shopping malls and apartment buildings and to detonate dirty bombs in urban areas. Novel plans to destroy civilian airliners also continue to be devised.

Columbus Shopping Mall Plot

On June 14, 2004, Nuradin Abdi was indicted in Columbus, Ohio, on four criminal counts, including conspiracy to provide material support to al Qaeda.[102] Abdi was allegedly involved in a plot with admitted al Qaeda member Iyman Faris[103] to blow up a Columbus shopping mall. In addition, Abdi allegedly received bomb-making instructions from a coconspirator and had intended to travel to Ethiopia to receive training in guns, guerrilla warfare, and bombs at a military-style training camp.[104]

Federal investigators believe that the plot may have involved as many as five people. The three other men, unnamed, were truck drivers with Faris.[105]

Following Abdi's indictment, Senator Charles Schumer of New York issued a press release detailing a new plan to equip high-risk malls with high-tech radiation detectors; to vastly expand research on devices to detect explosive, biological, and chemical material in public buildings; and to create evacuation plans for shopping centers.[106]

Apartment Building and Dirty Bomb Plots

Jose Padilla, a former Chicago gang member who converted to Islam in Sunrise, Florida, in 1994, worked personally with top al Qaeda leadership on plans to bomb US apartment buildings and detonate a dirty bomb in the United States.[107]

Padilla's path to al Qaeda began in 1998 when he traveled from Miami to Cairo, Egypt, where he would spend the next year and a half. In March 2000, while participating in the hajj (religious pilgrimage) in Saudi Arabia, he met an al Qaeda recruiter. This encounter and subsequent introductions led Padilla to receive admittance to al Qaeda's notorious Al Farouq terrorist training camp in Afghanistan, which he attended in September and October 2000. There, according to Padilla's subsequent interrogation, he received weapons instruction on the "AK-47, G-3, M-16, Uzi, and other machine guns" and training in "topography; communications; camouflage; clandestine surveillance; explosives, including C-4 plastic explosives, dynamite and mines; as well as physical fitness and religious training."[108]

While in Afghanistan, Padilla met Mohammed Atef (Abu Hafs), then al Qaeda's military commander. In early 2001, following a sojourn in Egypt to be with his wife (Atef supplied him with the funds to do so),

Padilla traveled to Karachi, Pakistan, where he lied to American consular officials about losing his passport in order to obtain a clean passport without stamps that indicated his past travel experiences.

In June 2001, Padilla returned to Afghanistan to meet with Atef, who had become a mentor to the American convert. Atef presented him with a specific mission: return to America and blow up apartment buildings using natural gas. Padilla accepted and went on to train with an explosives expert at a site near the Kandahar airport where he learned the basics of "switches, circuits, and timers . . . how to seal an apartment to trap the natural gas, prepare to use that gas, and thereby cause an explosion that would destroy an entire apartment building."[109]

However, the apartment buildings plot soon stumbled because of the irreconcilable differences between Padilla and his training partner, Adnan el-Shukrijumah who, ironically, Padilla had known from his days in Florida. Before the dispute in Afghanistan could be resolved, Atef was killed in a US air strike. Padilla barely escaped with his life.

The apartment buildings plot, along with a new plot to explode a dirty bomb in the United States, gained new impetus when Abu Zubaydah referred Padilla to Khalid Sheikh Mohammed in Pakistan. Interestingly, Padilla's original idea was a "nuclear improvised bomb that they had learned to make from research on the Internet." Skeptical of the plan's chances for success, Zubaydah instead recommended a supposedly more feasible device—"uranium wrapped with explosives to create a dirty bomb"—but sent Padilla to confer further with KSM, who, though more in favor of the apartment bombings plan, gave his blessing to both.[110]

As a result, Padilla would receive training directly from Ramzi bin al-Shibh "in using telephones securely and in al Qaeda's e-mail protocol [while KSM himself] gave $5,000 cash to Padilla [and] Ammar Al Baluchi, who is [KSM's] right-hand man, gave Padilla another $10,000 in cash, travel documents, a cell phone, an e-mail address to be used to notify Al Baluchi when . . . Padilla, reached the United States."[111]

Padilla left Pakistan in April 2002 and, after spending a month in Egypt, arrived at Chicago's O'Hare International Airport on May 8, 2002, where, in circumstances still shrouded in secrecy, he was immediately arrested by the FBI.[112] Padilla was detained by the Department of Defense as an enemy combatant.[113]

On November 17, 2005, a federal grand jury in Miami returned a superseding indictment charging Jose Padilla and four other defendants with conspiracy to murder, kidnap, and maim individuals in a foreign country and provide material support to terrorists as part of a North American terrorist cell that supported violent jihad overseas.[114]

The Fourth Circuit Court of Appeals denied the government's request to transfer Padilla from military to civilian law enforcement custody, pending a final review and decision on the matter by the US Supreme Court.[115] On April 3, 2006, the Court declined to review Padilla's petition for a writ of certiorari.[116]

Another Nuclear Plot

In late 2004, intelligence officials learned of another al Qaeda plot involving nuclear weapons. Sharif al-Masri, a high-ranking al Qaeda operative captured in Pakistan, spoke with interrogators regarding "al Qaeda's interest in moving nuclear materials from Europe to either the U.S. or Mexico." In one plan, al Qaeda would "smuggle nuclear materials to Mexico, then operatives would carry material into the U.S."[117]

In November 2004, Michael Scheuer, the former head of the CIA's bin Laden unit, called bin Laden's acquisition of a nuclear weapon "probably a near thing." He also said that in May 2003, bin Laden "secured from a Saudi sheikh named Hamid Bin Fahd a rather long treatise on the possibility of using nuclear weapons against the Americans, specifically nuclear weapons. And the treatise found that he was perfectly within his rights to use them."[118]

Miami-Based Group

On June 23, 2006, seven suspected homegrown al Qaeda sympathizers were indicted by a federal grand jury in Miami on charges of conspiring to support al Qaeda by plotting attacks on targets that included the Sears Tower in Chicago, the FBI building in North Miami Beach, Florida, and other government buildings in Miami-Dade County.[119] While the men allegedly sought to take part in the militant Islamist war against the United States, they were not Islamists in any traditional sense, but followers of a sect called the Seas of David, which reportedly drew on elements of Christianity and Judaism as well as Islam, and is supposedly related to the beliefs of the Moorish Science Temple of America,[120] "an early 20th century religion founded by the Noble Drew Ali, a wandering African-American circus magician who claimed to have been raised by Cherokee Indians and to have learnt 'high magic' in Egypt. Ali went on to style himself an 'angel' and prophet of Allah."[121] The defendants were identified as Narseal Batiste, Patrick Abraham, Stanley Grant Phanor, Naudimar Herrera, Burson Augustin, Lyblenson Lemorin, and Rothschild Augustine.[122]

According to the indictment, the group's ringleader, Narseal Batiste, voiced the urge to wage a "full ground war" against the United States. The indictment further alleged that the individuals stated the desire to "kill all the devils we can" in planned attacks they hoped would "be just as good or greater than 9/11."[123]

The group came to the attention of authorities when Batiste sought to recruit an individual who was traveling to the Middle East to assist him in locating foreign Islamic extremists to fund his mission. Unknown to Batiste, this individual alerted the FBI, who arranged a meeting between Batiste and an informant of Arab descent who purported to be an al Qaeda operative. In the course of several meetings with the informant in December 2005, Batiste asked for boots, uniforms, guns, radios, vehicles, and $50,000 in cash to help build an "Islamic Army" to wage jihad.[124] During a March 2006 meeting, each member of the group swore an oath of loyalty to al Qaeda. Just prior to the oath taking, which was covertly recorded by law enforcement, Batiste told the informant that he was "grateful" for bin Laden's support and that he "admired the work bin Laden was doing."[125]

PADILLA'S MOSQUE: MASJID AL-IMAN

Adham Hassoun and Jose Padilla

For much of the 1990s, both Adham Hassoun (who was indicted in September 2004 for providing material support to terrorist activities overseas)[126] and Jose Padilla attended Masjid Al-Iman, which is located in a low-income neighborhood of Fort Lauderdale. According to the mosque's imam, Hassoun spoke at the mosque "once every five or six weeks" and delivered "emotional speeches." In 1998, Padilla traveled to Cairo to study Arabic, a trip for which the imam and members of Masjid Al-Iman raised money.[127]

Raed Awad

According to the *Miami Herald*, Hassoun and Padilla "both were close" to Raed Awad, a Palestinian who served as the imam of Masjid Al-Iman from 1994 to 2000. Awad described Hassoun as "a firebrand" and saw parallels between their beliefs: "He was critical of the U.S. government, and I am critical of the U.S. government. I see American policy as one-sided with the Israelis. I see a double standard." Awad acknowledged providing marital counseling to Padilla and his wife.[128]

In the 1990s, Awad was the Holy Land Foundation's chief fund-raiser in Florida,[129] and he raised money in the Caribbean and Latin America as well.[130] As an article in a local newspaper notes, "Although he refuses to estimate how much he collected, he doesn't deny it was in the hundreds of thousands of dollars."[131] After the government shut down the foundation and seized its assets in December 2001, Awad said: "We were collecting money for the orphans and victims in Palestine. The government, under pressure, froze our assets." He added, "That money should go to the families in Palestine. It should not be kept here by the government, it is most distressing."[132] (The foundation is discussed in detail in chapter 9.)

Awad is also the registered agent of Golden Arch Travel (examined further in chapter 12). Golden Arch is linked to Ahmad Ajaj, who was convicted for his role in the 1993 World Trade Center bombing.[133] The travel company scheduled his flight from Houston to Pakistan, where he obtained manuals on explosives and a letter for the travel agent at Golden Arch who booked his ticket.[134]

Rafiq Mahdi

In 2000, Awad asked his friend Rafiq Mahdi, who had previously served as the spiritual leader at the Miami Gardens Mosque, to become the imam at Masjid al-Iman. An African American born in Knoxville, Tennessee, Mahdi had converted to Islam in 1978 at the age of twenty-four and later studied Islam in Saudi Arabia. In an August 2002 interview, Mahdi stated that he was not convinced that al Qaeda masterminded 9/11. He wanted "to hear his (Bin Laden's) side of the story" and criticized the attacks because they did not "benefit" Islam. According to the reporter, "Mahdi . . . implicitly defends the Taliban, saying pointedly that he can't understand why America bombed Afghanistan when 15 of the 19 hijackers were from Saudi Arabia."[135]

When asked about Hamas, Mahdi replied, "[I]n regard to freeing the occupied territories, I support their goal." After commenting that "most Muslims would not view Hamas as a terrorist organization," he added, "Not being under the everyday pressure or reality of living in the occupied territories, I find it difficult to blanketly condemn [suicide bombings], although personally I don't see that it will bring about the desired goal."[136]

Civilian Airliners

Despite the significant increase in airline security since 2001, al Qaeda continues to plot against commercial airliners.[137]

Most notably, according to KSM, al Qaeda envisioned a second wave of attacks in the months after 9/11: hijacked airliners would be flown into the Sears Tower in Chicago and the US Bank Tower in Los Angeles.[138] KSM declared, "We were looking for symbols of economic might."[139]

In December 2001, Richard Reid attempted to blow up a Miami-bound American Airlines flight from Paris by igniting explosives in his shoes.[140] Saajid Mohammed Badat has also been indicted for conspiring with Reid and others in the planned attack.[141]

In July 2003, DHS issued an information circular alerting airlines and airports to the possibility that terrorists in teams of five might hijack commercial airliners on the East Coast, Europe, or Australia: "The plan may involve the use of five-man teams, each of which would attempt to seize control of a commercial aircraft either shortly after takeoff or shortly before landing at a chosen airport. This type of operation would preclude the need for flight-trained hijackers."[142] The information on which this circular was based came from interrogations of senior al Qaeda operatives and electronic intercepts.[143]

In August 2003, DHS warned that "al Qaeda is attempting to create a chemical called nitrocellulose to fashion explosive devices that could be smuggled aboard jetliners." Because nitrocellulose cannot be detected by airport x-ray machines, screeners were directed to pay particular attention to pillows, coats, and stuffed animals.[144] Raids and interrogations also indicated that al Qaeda had attempted to modify camera flash attachments in order to turn them into stun guns or explosive devices.[145]

A further concern of DHS was that al Qaeda hijackers planned to exploit air travel programs that allowed travelers to land in the United States without a visa if they were merely catching a connecting flight to another destination in or out of the country. To address this vulnerability, DHS temporarily suspended the programs.[146]

An FBI memo claimed that terrorists planned to smuggle "ready to build" bomb kits past security and assemble them in airplane bathrooms. It continued: "Terrorist operatives are more confident that they can successfully smuggle [bomb] components, rather than fully assembled bombs past airport security."[147] Over the 2004 New Year's holiday, security concerns led authorities to cancel a number of US-bound flights from

England, France, and Mexico.[148] Similarly, authorities canceled a number of international flights in February 2004 because of fears of a chemical or biological attack aboard an airliner.[149]

In addition to planning how to smuggle weapons and explosives onto airplanes, al Qaeda has studied the use of fake identification to gain access to sensitive airport locations. In an al Qaeda cave in Afghanistan, US forces discovered a congressional study detailing investigators' success in penetrating two commercial airports, as well as a number of federal buildings, by showing fake IDs created with downloadable software.[150] A consistent stream of reporting on the theft of official airport identity cards, trucks, and uniforms has also heightened concern. As Homeland Security officials noted: "Al Qaeda and other terrorist groups likely view the theft or other illegal acquisition of official identification, uniforms or vehicles as an effective way to increase access and decrease scrutiny in furtherance of planning operations."[151]

In a number of instances, suspicious Middle Eastern men appeared to have carried out test runs aboard airplanes—congregating by the lavatories, communicating with people they pretended not to know, and passing packages between them.[152] In one incident, an air marshal broke into the forward lavatory after observing suspicious activity and found a Middle Eastern man who had removed the mirror and was trying to enter the cockpit through the wall. As one air marshal told the *Washington Times*, "No doubt these are dry runs for a terrorist attack."[153]

Al Qaeda continues to seek creative methods of attack. A December 2004 FBI and DHS memo warned that terrorists might use lasers to blind pilots and cause them to crash: "Although lasers are not proven methods of attack like improvised explosive devices [IEDs] and hijackings, terrorist groups overseas have expressed interest in using these devices against human sight."[154] The government warning came in the wake of a number of incidents in which unknown individuals shone laser beams into airline cockpits. A spate of occurrences in late December 2004 further heightened concern.

MISCELLANEOUS PLOTS

Intelligence officials have received information about a staggering array of other plots, which have often led Homeland Security officials to elevate the threat level in response. For example, on October 30, 2001, DHS secretary Tom Ridge explained that a public alert had been issued because "on the basis of credible information we have received from multiple sources, we believe the United States could very well be targeted this week—this next week or so—with a terrorist attack or attacks."[155]

Though too often the threat information has been vague and its credibility difficult to determine, officials after 9/11 have chosen to exercise caution and publicize these warnings. Thus, the Miami police department warned the public in September 2003 about the possibility of a terrorist attack but noted that the FBI was acting on "non-specific, non-confirmed information."[156] Similarly, officials advised New Mexico and California in July 2004 about the possibility of terrorist activity in their states.[157]

Other intelligence has been more specific. For example, in August 2004 the FBI and DHS warned that al Qaeda might assassinate prominent politicians linked to President George W. Bush.[158] That same year, the FBI told US veteran's hospitals[159] and armed forces recruiting centers that they could be targeted.[160] Threats such as those against New York City landmarks[161] and California's bridges[162] combined with suspicious activity reports on the attempted purchase of emergency-service vehicles and the like[163] have further concerned counterterrorism officials.

Ahmed Omar Abu Ali

A high-profile case involved an alleged al Qaeda–affiliated plot to assassinate the president. In November 2005, a federal jury in Alexandria, Virginia, convicted Ahmed Omar Abu Ali ("Abu Ali") on all charges against him, including those of joining al Qaeda and plotting to assassinate President Bush.[164] According to a February 2005 indictment, Abu Ali had helped formulate the assassination plot while he was pursuing religious studies in Medina in Saudi Arabia.[165]

A new indictment in September 2005 spelled out additional charges and allegations against Abu Ali, including plans to smuggle Saudi al Qaeda members into the United States through Mexico, where they along with Ali would set up an al Qaeda cell dedicated to carrying out terrorist operations within the United States.[166]

An American citizen born in Houston and raised in Virginia, Abu Ali attended high school at the Islamic Saudi Academy in Alexandria. He graduated as valedictorian of his class in 1999 and then briefly attended the University of Maryland and the notorious, Saudi-funded Institute of Islamic and Arabic Sciences in America, in Fairfax, Virginia, before moving to Saudi Arabia to study the Qur'an at the Islamic University of

Medina.[167] He was arrested by Saudi authorities along with several others in connection with the May 2003 bombing of a residential compound in Riyadh, Saudi Arabia, that killed thirty-four people, including nine Americans.[168]

Prosecutors said that Abu Ali admitted to his Saudi jailers that he joined an al Qaeda cell soon after he arrived in Saudi Arabia. He further admitted that he wanted to shoot Bush on the street or blow him up with a car bomb.[169] In a court filing unsealed September 19, 2005, Abu Ali likened himself to Mohamed Atta, who led the terror cell that carried out the 9/11 attacks: "I wanted to be the brain, the planner. . . . My idea was . . . I would walk on the street as the President walked by, and I would get close enough to shoot him, or I would use a car bomb."[170] Defense attorneys alleged that Abu Ali's confession to Saudi authorities was obtained under duress. Federal prosecutors, however, denied the allegations and a Saudi prison warden testified through an interpreter that "he [Abu Ali] was not beaten, not even once, never."[171]

Between September 2002 and June 9, 2003, "Abu Ali offered himself to persons in Saudi Arabia associated with al Qaeda as an individual committed to furthering the objectives of al Qaeda."[172] About the same time, Abu Ali received cash payments from an al Qaeda associate to buy a laptop computer, a cellular phone, and books. He also received training in the use of weapons, including hand grenades and explosives, as well as in document forgery.[173]

The following incriminating items were found in a June 16, 2003, search of Abu Ali's residence in Falls Church, Virginia: a six-page document on different types of surveillance methods used by the government and ways to avoid such surveillance; an undated two-page document commending Taliban leader Mullah Omar and the 9/11 attacks and criticizing US military action in Afghanistan; audiotapes in Arabic supporting "violent jihad, the killing of Jews, and a battle by Muslims against Christians and Jews"; and a book written by al Qaeda's deputy leader Ayman al-Zawahiri that "characterizes democracy as a new religion that must be destroyed by war, describes anyone who supports democracy as an infidel, and condemns the Muslim Brotherhood for renouncing violent *jihad* as a means to establish an Islamic state."[174]

Abu Ali had previously been linked to the "Virginia jihad network," in which a group of men trained for jihad against the United States by playing paintball in the Virginia countryside. The government had also alleged that the men had received paramilitary training in Pakistan in preparation to join the jihad in Kashmir. Nine men were eventually convicted. Abu Ali, however, was not charged in the case (see chapter 8).[175]

Lodi, California

On June 8, 2005, the FBI's Sacramento Field Office announced that the Sacramento Joint Terrorism Task Force was conducting an ongoing investigation in Lodi, California,[176] a small farming town south of Sacramento with a sizable and insular Pakistani community.[177] FBI Special-Agent-in Charge Keith Slotter told reporters that although information had not been uncovered to evidence detailed plans for a terrorist attack against a specific target, the Lodi investigation had nonetheless led the FBI to the general conclusion that "various individuals connected to al Qaeda have been operating in the Lodi area in various capacities."[178]

Hamid and Umer Hayat

The JTTF's announcement concerning its open-ended, terrorism-related investigation in Lodi confirmed the context for the June 5 arrest of two Lodi residents by federal agents.[179]

Hamid Hayat, a US citizen who had lived in Pakistan half his life, and his father, Umer Hayat, a naturalized US citizen of Pakistani origin,[180] were detained without bond following their arrests, upon the determination of Magistrate Judge Peter A. Nowinski that the two were flight risks and posed a danger to the community.[181] The men were each charged, in criminal complaints filed by the United States Attorney's Office, with making false statements in a matter within the jurisdiction of the FBI.[182] The matter at issue concerned "international and domestic terrorism,"[183] as clarified by a three-count indictment returned by a federal grand jury on June 16, 2005.[184]

The indictment charged Hamid Hayat with two counts, for knowingly deceiving federal agents, when he denied attending jihadist terrorist training camps in Pakistan.[185] The indictment also charged Hamid's father, Umer Hayat, with one count, making a false statement to a federal agent, when Umer denied firsthand knowledge about the existence of terrorist training camps in Pakistan and his son Hamid's attendance at a jihadist terrorist camp.[186]

According to court documents filed by government prosecutors R. Steven Lapham and S. Robert Tice-Raskin, Hamid Hayat had traveled to Pakistan from the United States with his father, Umer, in April 2003.[187]

During a series of recorded conversations that took place between Hamid Hayat and a secret witness between March and mid-April 2003, Hamid allegedly attested to his belief in jihad, "and swore that he would go to jihad."[188] In another conversation with the secret witness, recorded while Hamid was in Pakistan, Hamid stated "that he genuinely desired to attend a [jihadi terrorist training] camp and strongly indicated . . . that he had been accepted to 'training' and was going to attend the [terrorist training camp] . . . after Ramadan 2003."[189]

Hamid returned to the United States from Pakistan on or about May 30, 2005.[190] A series of events that took place during Hamid's trip back to the United States aroused government concern about Hamid Hayat. While Hamid was en route to the United States on a flight from Korea, it was determined that he was on the "No Fly" list.[191] His plane was subsequently diverted to Japan, where Hamid was questioned by FBI agents as to his association with terrorism and terrorist activities. After denying any such connections, Hamid was downgraded to the "Selectee List" and allowed to continue his journey to the United States.[192]

Back in the United States, on June 4, 2005, Hamid Hayat underwent a polygraph examination at the request of the FBI, during which the FBI questioned him again about his involvement with terrorist activities.[193] Answers provided by Hamid during the polygraph test in response to questions about his association with terrorism were determined to be deceptive.[194] After further questioning, Hamid admitted to authorities that not only had he attended an al Qaeda–run, jihadist training camp in Pakistan for six months in 2003–2004—where he was trained on how to murder Americans—but he had also specifically requested transfer to the United States in order to fulfill his jihadi mission.[195] Hamid divulged that he was in the United States awaiting his jihadi orders.[196]

Hamid's father, Umer Hayat, was also questioned by the FBI on June 4, 2005, regarding his son's associations and connections to terrorism. Umer initially denied having any knowledge about the existence of terrorist training camps in Pakistan.[197] But, after viewing a videotape of Hamid's confession, Umer admitted that his son had indeed attended a jihadist camp in Pakistan in 2003–2004, during which time he was allowed to leave for home on the weekends.[198] Umer Hayat further acknowledged that he had paid for Hamid's flight to Pakistan and provided him with a monthly allowance, while aware that his son had plans to attend a jihadi training camp.[199]

Umer Hayat's interview with federal agents also revealed Hamid's long-standing interest in jihadi terrorism, stemming from the years he spent at a madrassah (Islamic religious school) in Rawalpindi, Pakistan, as a teenager.[200] The madrassah was headed by Hamid's grandfather, and Umer's father-in-law, Qazi Saeed Ur Rehman. According to Umer Hayat, Rehman regularly sent the madrassah's students to jihadi training camps near Rawalpindi.[201] Umer further divulged that the terrorist training camp Hamid attended was operated by a close friend of Qazi Saeed Ur Rehman and that Umer was invited to visit and tour several terrorist training camps in Pakistan because of these connections.[202] During his tour of the jihadi camps, Umer stated that he observed physical training, weapons and urban warfare training, and classroom instruction.[203]

As the Hayats remained in federal custody awaiting their trial,[204] their attorneys focused much of their energy on persuading the court to rescind its decision not to set bail for the defendants.[205] The defense contested the court's reasoning for prohibiting pretrial release, namely, that the defendants posed a flight risk and a danger to the community. They argued that, indeed, the government had not indicted the Hayats directly and specifically with engagement in terrorism or terrorist activity, and thus no "crime of violence" existed to justify detention.[206]

The government, however, warned the defense not to discount the possibility of charges directly related to terrorism being brought against the Hayats in the future.[207] The prosecution emphasized the unique context and implications of the Hayats' false statement charge:

> This is not some garden variety false statement on a loan application or benefits' application. Defendants Hamid Hayat and Umer Hayat are charged with participating in and/or concealing their knowledge about terrorist training aimed at the conducting of jihad (holy war) against the United States. Defendants' charged conduct, on its face, demonstrates that defendants pose . . . [a] danger.[208]

Sure enough, on September 22, 2005, Hamid Hayat was charged in a new federal indictment with providing material support to terrorists, in addition to the two previous counts of making a false statement.[209] Among its counts, the indictment stated that Hamid had returned to the United States from his jihadi training in Pakistan "to wage jihad in the United States against persons within the United States and against real and personal property within the United States" in violation of 18 U.S.C. § 2332b, titled "Acts of Terrorism Transcending National Boundaries."[210]

The new indictment was the first charge of terrorism put forth by the government in its ongoing investigation of Lodi.

The Two Lodi Clerics

On June 6, 2005, one day after the Hayats were arrested by FBI agents, US Immigration and Customs Enforcement (ICE), the largest investigative arm of the Department of Homeland Security,[211] arrested two Islamic clerics from Lodi.[212] The two Pakistani citizens, Shabbir Ahmed and Mohammad Adil Khan, were held in ICE custody as they awaited the opportunity to appear before an immigration judge to contest the charges alleged against them that they violated the terms of their visas.[213]

Both Khan and Ahmed came to the United States on nonimmigrant R-1[214] religious worker visas.[215] Khan, a trained Muslim cleric, first came to the United States in April 2001 to serve as imam of the Lodi Muslim Mosque.[216] According to ICE attorneys, Khan and Ahmed had both worked at the same madrassah in Rawalpindi, Pakistan.[217] In a news release, ICE stated that Ahmed came to Lodi to establish a similar madrassah to the one at which he and Khan had worked in Pakistan, which had served as a place for the recruitment of individuals to jihad.[218]

On August 15, 2005, US Immigration and Customs Enforcement announced that Shabbir Ahmed agreed during his immigration hearing to be deported to his homeland of Pakistan. It was further revealed that in a previously held custody hearing, ICE attorneys laid out evidence linking Ahmed to the Taliban and al Qaeda.[219]

On August 17, 2005, ICE made another announcement concerning the status of Mohammad Adil Khan's legal battle to remain in the United States. Khan, along with his nineteen-year-old son, Mohammad Hassan Adil Khan, was deported back to his home country of Pakistan after voluntarily abandoning legal proceedings.[220]

No doubt ICE viewed the deportations as a victory in the war on terror, to the extent that they clearly represented the extraction and elimination of potential terrorists or terrorist sympathizers and abettors from the midst of a US community. Upon the news of Shabbir Ahmed's deportation to Pakistan, San Fransisco ICE chief counsel Ronald E. Le Fevre stated:

> ICE is gratified by what happened in immigration court. . . . Once he leaves the United States, Mr. Ahmed will no longer be in a position to advance any doctrine of hate from within our community. Today we are one step closer to that goal.[221]

A Lodi-Area Terrorist Network?

According to the new indictment of September 22, 2005, Hamid Hayat intended to carry out his jihadi mission in the United States "upon receipt of orders from other individuals."[222] Thus, federal authorities raised serious concerns about the existence of a Lodi-area terrorist network.

According to the testimony of an FBI agent, Hamid Hayat was waiting to receive instructions about his jihadi mission from the Lodi imam, Shabbir Ahmed.[223] During Ahmed's custody hearing, ICE attorneys presented a diagram detailing the relationship between the imam and several Lodi-area individuals.[224]

On April 25, the jury found Hamid Hayat guilty of one count of providing material support to terrorists for running an al Qaeda jihadi camp in Pakistan and three counts of lying to the FBI about his activities.[225] After the conviction, the Department of Justice summed up the substance of the jury's findings, stating, "Evidence at trial established that, during a period of months between October 2003 and November 2004, defendant Hamid Hayat attended a jihadi training camp in Pakistan and ultimately returned to the United States with the intent to wage jihad upon receipt of orders. According to evidence adduced at trial, between March 2003 and August 2003, defendant Hamid Hayat, during the course of numerous recorded conversations with a cooperating witness, pledged his belief in violent jihad, pledged to go to a jihadi training camp and indicated that he, in fact, was going to jihadi training."[226]

Hamid Hayat is facing a maximum of thirty-nine years in prison. According to the jury foreman, the case of Hamid's guilt was not a close question, as reported in the *Los Angeles Times*:

> The systematic way the jurors moved through the charges during nine days of deliberation was detailed Wednesday by jury foreman Joe Cote, a 64-year-old retired medical equipment salesman from Folsom.
>
> "We scored the entire evidence and testimony," Cote said the day after the conviction, "and it was overwhelmingly in favor of guilt."
>
> Key to the jury's decision, Cote said, were Hayat's own words on an FBI videotape that he had attended a camp, his comments secretly recorded by an undercover informant that indicated Hayat's "willingness" to go for training and a handwritten warrior's prayer in Arabic found in his wallet.
>
> "He got himself in pretty deep. He buried himself," said juror Starr

> Scaccia, 53, an administrative assistant from Roseville, in describing the five-hour videotaped interrogation.[227]

Umer Hayat's jury came to a different conclusion. Earlier in the morning on the same day, the jurors in Umer's case wrote a note to the judge saying that their discussions were "decisively deadlocked" on the question of whether Umer Hayat lied to federal investigators about his son.[228]

Then, on May 31, 2006, the government announced that Umer Hayat had entered a guilty plea as part of a plea agreement. According to the agreement, Hayat pled guilty to making a false statement to the FBI and US Customs and Border Protection (CBP) in violation of 18 U.S.C. §1001,[229] when, in April 2003, upon being detained with his family, including son Hamid Hayat, by FBI and CBP en route from California to Pakistan, Umer Hayat falsely declared to a CBP inspector that he and his family were carrying only $10,000 when they were actually carrying more than $28,000. According to law, individuals carrying currency in excess of $10,000 out of the United States must declare such funds to US Customs.[230]

It was on this very trip to Pakistan that Hamid Hayat attended the jihadi training camp, for which he was convicted of providing "material support to terrorists" on April 25, 2006.[231]

Under the stipulations of the plea agreement, the government recommended that Umer Hayat receive a time-served sentence and a term of three years' supervised release.[232]

Umer Hayat faces a maximum penalty of five years' imprisonment for all charges against him.[233]

The Toledo Jihad Cell

In late 2004, twenty-six-year-old Mohammad Amawi (a dual Jordanian and US citizen) and Wassim Mazloum, a twenty-four-year-old student at the University of Toledo (and a legal permanent resident of the United States), met with Darren "Bilal" Griffin, a man with a US military background who worked as a trainer, to plan for training "for violent Jihad." Unbeknownst to them, Griffin was a paid FBI operative who had been watching their friend Marwan el-Hindi (a naturalized US citizen born in Amman, Jordan). According to a US government indictment, Marwan el-Hindi solicited Griffin in 2002 "to assist in providing security and bodyguard training."[234]

Training Camp Overseas

Soon after the meeting with Mazloum and Amawi, Marwan el-Hindi asked Griffin for help setting up a training camp for aspiring jihadists. This involved traveling together to the Middle East. According to the indictment, el-Hindi told Griffin that he was in contact with individuals who were setting up the training camp facility.

Instruction in Toledo

In November 2004, Amawi and the trainer engaged in lessons on construction of timing devices and IEDs. Amawi stated in part that his aim was to target US military assets.[235] These sessions stretched on into January 2005 when Amawi allegedly showed the trainer a video that demonstrated how to make explosives. A little over a week later there was target-shooting practice with others at an indoor shooting range in Toledo.[236]

According to the US government, by the end of January 2005, Amawi was communicating via computer with some "brothers" in the Middle East who were preparing to cross into Iraq. Amawi downloaded a video called *Martyrdom Operation Vest Preparation* on how to construct a "suicide vest" for use in jihad training. Amawi passed this along to the trainer on a computer disk.[237]

Activities appeared to have sped up in early February 2005. According to the indictment: Marwan el-Hindi and the trainer discussed the use of plastic explosives; Amawi outlined a plan to smuggle a firearm into a Middle Eastern country; and el-Hindi proposed to Griffin that jihad training materials be downloaded onto disks to be shown to two training recruits in Chicago. On February 16, Mazloum, el-Hindi, Amawi, and the trainer met at el-Hindi's residence to coordinate jihad training exercises and discussed how to conceal their training activities.[238]

By April 2005, according to the indictment, Amawi asked to meet the trainer in person instead of communicating by phone. Face-to-face, Amawi asked Griffin if he had a contact overseas who could obtain a chemical explosive on behalf of a "brother" in the Middle East with whom Amawi had been communicating via the Internet, using code to avoid detection. Using the word "pillows" for the chemical explosive, Amawi and his overseas contact continued to discuss acquisition and delivery of the chemical. As April progressed, so did training exercises by members of the Toledo group. This arrangement continued through the summer with talk of using July 4 as a good time to train with explosives, since the sounds of explosions would not raise suspicion. At the end of August 2005, Amawi and Griffin boarded a plane for Jordan. They took five laptops, which, according to the grand jury, were to be delivered to the mujahideen "brothers."[239]

Before the Toledo Cell

This does not appear to be Amawi's first flirtation with jihad. Amawi traveled to Jordan from October 2003 to March 2004. During that time he tried, unsuccessfully, to enter Iraq to wage jihad against the US and coalition forces.[240]

El-Hindi, for his part, was a volunteer at the Salafist Al Qur'an was-Sunnah Society.[241] This society has been on the periphery of numerous terrorism probes over the last several years. El-Hindi also had a business venture with Rafil Dhafir, a Syracuse oncologist serving a twenty-two-year sentence for channeling money to Iraq. Furthermore, Dhafir's charity, Help the Needy, sent money to Benevolence International Foundation (BIF) and Global Relief Foundation (GRF),[242] both shuttered by the US government for terrorism funding on behalf of Hamas and al Qaeda.[243] Additionally, el-Hindi worked as an imam at the Toledo correctional facility for three months in 2003.

Folsom State Prison, California

On August 31, 2005, a federal grand jury in San Ana, California, indicted four men for their alleged roles in a conspiracy to levy war against the US government through terrorism.[244] The conspiracy allegedly involved a terrorist plot to attack US military facilities and Israeli government and Jewish facilities in the Los Angeles area.[245]

The terrorist conspiracy was hatched in California's Folsom State Prison by an inmate who founded a clandestine, radical Islamic organization—Jam'iyyat Ul Islam Is Saheeh (JIS)—and preached the duty of JIS members to target the infidel enemies of Islam for violent attack.[246] Coconspirator Levar Washington, who joined JIS while in prison, allegedly "pledged his loyalty" to defendant and JIS leader Kevin James "until death by martyrdom."[247] Under the "instructions, spiritual and tactical guidance, and support"[248] of JIS leader James, coconspirators Gregory Patterson and Hammad Samana allegedly joined Levar Washington in a terrorist plot "to kill, with premeditation and malice aforethought, members of the United States Government uniformed services . . . [and] foreign officials, namely, officials of the Government of Israel."[249]

The indictment further alleges that members of the conspiracy committed armed robberies of gas stations in order to finance their terrorist operation[250] (see chapter 9, "Charities, Foundations, and Post 9/11 Trends of Terror Financing," for more on such nontraditional terrorist financing schemes).

If convicted of all charges, the defendants face a maximum sentence of life in prison.[251]

CONCLUSION

The many al Qaeda conspiracies conceived and operationalized after 9/11 highlight the terror network's extensive reach inside the United States and the extensive planning that goes into its operations. Also evident, however, is al Qaeda's hesitation in carrying out its various schemes, especially its careful attempts to evade law enforcement. The organization spends years planning in exacting detail, including the thorough analysis of extensive surveillance, as the extensive material connected with the scheme to attack New York's financial district demonstrates. As noted above, casing for the plot began in 2000, and was still being updated in 2004. Similarly, although al Qaeda did not bomb the American embassies in Kenya and Tanzania until August 1998, operatives began casing targets in Nairobi with state-of-the-art video cameras as early as December 1993. The surveillance team even set up a makeshift laboratory to develop their surveillance photographs in an apartment in Nairobi.[252]

Overall, these cases demonstrate al Qaeda's unwavering commitment to striking America at home. Whether its targets are malls, bridges, railways, gas stations, apartment buildings, or sites key to financial markets, al Qaeda has continued to seek out ways to terrorize and demoralize the American public. As it devises schemes that employ truck bombs, dirty bombs, helicopters, and limousines packed with explosives and takes aim at a variety of critical infrastructures hitherto not specifically secured against deliberate attack, al Qaeda will continue to test the ability of US agencies to capture its members and block its efforts.

NOTES

1. Because many of the plots discussed have not yet resulted in indictments, news accounts are relied on when necessary in this chapter.

2. "Team 4: Details of Prior Terrorist Plot Surface," *Pittsburgh Channel,* November 4, 2004.

3. *USA v. Faris,* 03-189-A, plea agreement (ED VA June 19, 2003).

4. "Iyman Faris Sentenced for Providing Material Support to Al Qaeda," US Department of Justice Press Release, October 28, 2003.

5. John Ashcroft, "Remarks of Attorney General Ashcroft Announcing Iyman Faris' Plea Agreement," June 19, 2003, http://www.usdoj.gov/ag/speeches/2003/remarks_061903.htm (accessed January 30, 2005).

6. *USA v. Abdi,* 2-04-CR-88, government's motion to detain defendant and memorandum in support (SD OH June 14, 2004).

7. *USA v. Faris,* 03-189-A, statement of facts, p. 2 (ED VA June 19, 2003).

8. Ibid.

9. R. Jeffrey Smith and Amy DePaul, "'Scout' Had Low Profile," *Washington Post,* June 21, 2003.

10. *USA v. Faris,* 03-189-A, statement of facts, p. 3 (ED VA June 19, 2003).

11. Ibid.

12. Ibid.; Ted Wendling, "Ohio Agents Tailed Terrorist," *Cleveland Plain Dealer,* June 21, 2003.

13. "Disqualifying Commercial Drivers," Audit Report, US Department of Transportation Office of Inspector General, June 30, 2000, p. ii.

14. Kathy Barks Hoffman, "State Records Shed Light on Men Sought in Michigan," Associated Press, September 19, 2001.

15. John Solomon, "Terror Suspect Deport Raises Fuss," Associated Press, June 30, 2004.

16. US Immigration and Customs Enforcement, "Terrorism Investigations Fact Sheet," http://www.ice.gov/graphics/news/factsheets/072704terrorist_fs.htm (accessed August 16, 2005).

17. John Solomon, "Terror Suspect Nabbed, Then Freed," Associated Press, June 2, 2004.

18. *USA v. Koubriti, et al.,* 01-CR-80778, criminal complaint (ED MI September 17, 2001); *USA v. Koubriti, et al.,* 01-CR-80778, second superseding indictment (ED MI August 28, 2002).

19. Richard Serrano and Greg Miller, "Mistakes, Deep Mistrust Doom U.S. Terror Case," *Chicago Tribune,* October 13, 2004.

20. David Runk, "Hmimssa: Defendants in Terror Trial Spoke of Possible Attacks," Associated Press, April 9, 2003.

21. *USA v. Koubriti, et al.*, 01-CR-80778, memorandum and order, p. 8 (ED MI September 2, 2004).

22. Serrano and Miller, "Mistakes, Deep Mistrust Doom U.S. Terror Case."

23. "Terror Suspect Got Hazardous Material OK," Associated Press, July 1, 2004.

24. David Johnston and Neil A. Lewis, "A Nation Challenged: The Investigation," *New York Times*, September 26, 2001.

25. David Shepardson, Ronald J. Hansen, and Norman Sinclair, "FBI Busts 5 in Detroit in Terrorism Manhunt," *Detroit News*, September 27, 2001.

26. Anne Michaud, "16 Middle Eastern Men Indicted in United States," Reuters, October 4, 2001.

27. "Hazardous Materials Truckers to Be Checked," CNN, May 2, 2003.

28. Leslie Miller, "Customs Asked to Look for Terror Signs," Associated Press, June 30, 2004.

29. Allan Lengel and Dan Eggen, "Metro Fire Was Plotted, Al Qaeda Member Says," *Washington Post*, April 9, 2003.

30. "Inside the Kingdom," *Time*, September 15, 2003, p. 38.

31. "Official: U.S. Expels 2 Iranians at the UN," CNN, June 29, 2004; Murray Weiss, "Subway Mystery," *New York Post*, November 18, 2003; Robert McFadden, "Subway Officials Seek Ban on Picture-Taking," *New York Times*, May 21, 2004. A ban on all photography in New York's subway system has been proposed but has not been enacted.

32. Al Guart, "N.Y. Suitcase Scares Spur Terror 'Dry Run' Fear," *New York Post*, May 2, 2004.

33. FBI press release, October 24, 2002, http://www.fbi.gov/pressrel/pressrel02/nlets102402.htm (accessed August 16, 2005).

34. Ibid.

35. Daniel Eisenberg, "The Triple Life of a Qaeda Man," *Time*, June 30, 2003.

36. *USA v. Faris*, 03-189-A, statement of facts, p. 3 (ED VA May 1, 2003).

37. Stewart Bell, "U.S. Warned Canada about Plot to Bomb Transit," *National Post*, May 15, 2004.

38. "Lebanese–US Government Cooperate and Disrupt Plan to NY-NJ Transportation System," FBI press release, July 7, 2006, http://www.fbi.gov/pressrel/pressrel06/transportation_threat070706.htm (accessed July 14, 2006).

39. "FBI: Three Held in New York Tunnel Plot; Suspected Ringleader Posed as Playboy, Professor in Beirut," CNN, July 7, 2006, http://www.cnn.com/2006/US/07/07/tunnel.plot/index.html (accessed July 14, 2006).

40. Ibid.

41. Ibid.

42. Mike Carter, "Why Feds Believe Terrorists Are Probing Ferry System," *Seattle Times*, October 10, 2004.

43. Adam Zagorin, "Suspect Snapshots," *Time*, July 12, 2004.

44. Chris McGann, "Terror 'Chatter' Seems to Target Ferries," *Seattle Post-Intelligencer*, August 1, 2003.

45. Ibid.

46. USCG Captain of the Port Los Angeles-Long Beach in a security bulletin for Port Stakeholders, August 29, 2003.

47. "Possible Use of Scuba Divers to Conduct Terrorist Attack," FBI Counterterrorism Division and the US Coast Guard Directorate of Intelligence, May 24, 2002.

48. Lorenzo Vidino and Erick Stakelbeck, "Dutch Lessons," *Wall Street Journal Europe*, August 8, 2003.

49. Seth Hettena, "Source: Two Sept. 11 Hijackers First Scouted Navy Targets in San Diego," Associated Press, August 21, 2002.

50. James Hookway, "Sinking of Ferry in Philippines Tied to Terrorism," *Wall Street Journal*, May 4, 2004.

51. FBI press release, April 19, 2002, http://www.fbi.gov/pressrel/pressrel02/banks041802.htm (accessed August 16, 2005).

52. Niles Lathem, "Wall St. Targeted," *New York Post*, July 11, 2004.

53. Bill Powell, "Target: America," *Time*, August 8, 2004; David Johnston and David Sanger, "Seized Records Indicate Surveillance of Buildings Was Updated This Spring," *New York Times*, August 13, 2004.

54. Tom Ridge, "Remarks by Secretary of Homeland Security Tom Ridge Regarding Recent Threat Reports," August 1, 2004, http://www.whitehouse.gov/news/releases/2004/08/20040801.html (accessed August 16, 2005).

55. "Sources: More Targets Cited by Al Qaeda," Fox News, August 2, 2004, http://www.foxnews.com/story/0,2933,127830,00.html (accessed August 16, 2005).

56. "Background Briefing by Senior Intelligence Officials," Department of Homeland Security press release, August 1, 2004.

57. Ibid.

58. Ibid.

59. Ibid.

60. Ibid.

61. Bob Sullivan, "Agency Warns Banks of al-Qaida Risk," MSNBC, July 24, 2004, http://www.msnbc.msn.com/id/3072757 (accessed August 16, 2005).

62. Jerry Seper, "Al Qaeda Leader Identified in 'Dirty Bomb' Plot," *Washington Times*, October 5, 2004.

63. Mitchel Maddux, "FBI Says Al-Qaida Scout Used N.J. as Base," *Bergen Record*, October 14, 2004.

64. *Mubanga v. Bush*, 04-CV-1144 RWR, unclassified summary of basis for tribunal decision (DC October 4, 2004).

65. National Commission on Terrorist Attacks upon the United States, *The 9/11 Commission Report: Final Report of the National Commission on Terrorist Attacks upon the United States* (New York: Norton, 2004), p. 150.

66. Ibid., p. 514.

67. David Johnston, "Tourist Copters in New York City a Terror Target," *New York Times*, August 9, 2004.

68. Powell, "Target: America."

69. Ridge, "Remarks by Secretary of Homeland Security Tom Ridge Regarding Recent Threat Reports."

70. *Al Qaeda Training Manual: Twelfth Lesson: Espionage (2) Information Gathering Using Covert Methods*, UK/BM-84 Translation, Department of Justice.

71. "Lessons Learned from New York, New Jersey, and Washington, DC," *DHS-FBI Terrorist Financial Casing Reports*, December 28, 2004.

72. Ibid.

73. Judd Slivka, "Al-Qaida Detainee Targeted Forests, Memo Says," *Arizona Republic*, July 11, 2003.

74. President George W. Bush, State of the Union Address, January 29, 2002.

75. 9/11 Commission, *The 9/11 Commission Report*, p. 154.

76. Ibid., p. 245.

77. Adam Zagorin, "Suspect Snapshots," *Time*, July 12, 2004.

78. Sara Kehaulani Goo, "TSA Pushes for Security in Foreign Cargo," *Washington Post*, November 12, 2003.

79. Eli Lake, "Congressman Warns of Iranian Attack on U.S.," *New York Sun*, December 14, 2004.

80. Bill Gertz, "Terrorists Aim at Pearl Harbor," *Washington Times*, March 3, 2003.

81. "FBI Warns Oil Refineries, Power Plants," Reuters, August 25, 2003.

82. Daniel Klaidman and Mark Hosenball, "A Texas Attack?" *Time*, June 20, 2003; Michael Hedges, "Terrorists Possibly Targeting Texas," *Houston Chronicle*, June 24, 2003; "FBI Warns Texas Oil Refineries of Possible Attack," Reuters, March 25, 2004.

83. Les Blumenthal, "Refinery in Terror Bulletin," *News Tribune*, July 1, 2004.

84. Eli Lake, "Enemy Casing Texas for Attack, U.S. Fears," *New York Sun*, April 30, 2004.

85. "Nation on High Alert Tightens Holiday Security," Fox News, December 23, 2003, http://www.foxnews.com/story/0,2933,106456,00.html (accessed August 16, 2005).

86. FBI press release, October 24, 2002.

87. David Leppard, Gareth Walsh, and Jon Swain, "Terror on the Doorstep," *London Sunday Times*, January 12, 2003.

88. "Al Qaeda Says It'll Use Chem, Bio Weapons," Fox News, June 10, 2002, http://www.foxnews.com/story/0,2933,54868,00.html (accessed August 16, 2005).

89. Mariano Castillo, "Staffing Executive Pleads Not Guilty," *San Antonio Express News*, October 1, 2004.

90. Alma Walzer, "Undocumented Aliens Found at McAllen, Texas, Supplier of Military Meals," *Monitor*, October 1, 2004.

91. Ibid.

92. Castillo, "Staffing Executive Pleads Not Guilty."

93. James Risen and Don Van Natta Jr., "Plot to Poison Food of British Troops Is Suspected," *New York Times*, January 24, 2003.

94. Statement of Senator Susan Collins, Senate Governmental Affairs Committee, "Agroterrorism: The Threat to America's Breadbasket," November 19, 2003.

95. President George W. Bush, State of the Union Address, January 29, 2002.

96. Senator Susan Collins of Maine, speaking about the threat of Agroterrorism, on November 19, 2003, to the Senate Committee on Governmental Affairs, 108th Cong., 1st sess.

97. Adam Zagorin, "Bordering on Nukes?" *Time*, November 14, 2004.

98. "Advisory—Security Information for Aerial Application Operators/Airports," Transportation Security Administration, November 5, 2004.

99. "Terrorist Threats to Food," World Health Organization, January 2003.

100. Jennifer Loven, "Thompson Leaves HHS Warning of Terror Vulnerability," Associated Press, December 3, 2004.

101. "FDA: Al-Qaida Could Poison Medicines," Associated Press, August 12, 2004.

102. *USA v. Abdi*, 2-04-CR-88, indictment (SD OH June 10, 2004).

103. "Iyman Faris Sentenced for Providing Material Support to Al Qaeda," US Department of Justice press release, October 28, 2003.

104. *USA v. Abdi*, 2-04-CR-88, government's motion to detain defendant and memorandum in support, p. 6 (SD OH June 14, 2004).

105. "Investigators: Mall Plot May Have Involved 5 People," NBC Columbus, June 18, 2004, http://www.nbc4columbus.com/news/3434353/detail.html (accessed August 16, 2005).

106. "New Intelligence Shows Terrorists Targeting Shopping Centers," Office of Charles Schumer press release, June 24, 2004.

107. Jodi Wilgoren, "From Chicago Gang to Possible Al Qaeda Ties," *New York Times*, June 11, 2002.

108. James Comey, "Remarks of Deputy Attorney General James Comey Regarding Jose Padilla," June 1, 2004; "Department of Defense Summary of Jose Padilla's Activities with Al Qaeda," June 1, 2004.

109. Ibid.

110. Ibid.

111. Ibid.

112. John Ashcroft, "Statement Regarding the Transfer of Abdullah Al

Muhajir (Born Jose Padilla) to the Department of Defense as an Enemy Combatant," June 10, 2002.

113. John Ashcroft, "Transcript of the Attorney General John Ashcroft Regarding the Transfer of Abdullah Al Muhajir (Born Jose Padilla) to the Department of Defense as an Enemy Combatant," June 10, 2002, http://www.usdoj.gov/ag/speeches/2002/061002agtranscripts.htm (accessed December 14, 2005).

114. *USA v. Adham Amin Hassoun, et al.*, 04-60001-CR-COOKE, superceding indictment (SD FL November 17, 2005).

115. *Jose Padilla v. C. T. Hanft, U.S.N. Commander, Consolidated Naval Brig.*, No. 05-6396 (CA-04-2221-26AJ), order (US Court of Appeals for the 4th Circuit December 21, 2005).

116. *Jose Padilla v. C. T. Hanft, U.S.N. Navy Commander, Consolidated Naval Brig.*, No. 05-533, on petition for writ of certiorari to the United States Court of Appeals for the Fourth Circuit (US Supreme Court, April 3, 2006).

117. Zagorin, "Bordering on Nukes?"

118. "Anonymous Revealed; Michael Scheuer, Former CIA Osama bin Laden Unit Leader, Discusses Early Intelligence Reports and Opportunities to Kill bin Laden," *60 Minutes*, CBS, November 14, 2004.

119. *USA v. Batiste, et al.*, 06-CR-20373, indictment (SD NY June 23, 2006).

120. Frank Main, "Dad: Sears Tower Suspect under Spell of Man," *Chicago Sun-Times*, June 25, 2006; Paul Thompson and Sara Baxter, "Bizarre Cult of Sears Tower 'Plotter,'" *Sunday Times*, June 25, 2006.

121. Thompson and Baxter, "Bizarre Cult of Sears Tower 'Plotter.'"

122. "Seven Florida Men Charged with Conspiring to Support al Qaeda, Attack Targets in the United States," US Department of Justice press release, June 23, 2006.

123. *USA v. Batiste, et al.*, 06-CR-20373, indictment (SD NY June 23, 2006).

124. Ibid.

125. *USA v. Batiste, et al.*, 06-CR-20373, government's motion for pretrial detention (SD NY June 29, 2006).

126. *USA v. Hassoun*, 04-CR-60001, superceding indictment (SD FL March 4, 2004).

127. Wanda DeMarzo, "Ex-Mosque Leader Says Suspect Wasn't Radical in Broward," *Miami Herald*, June 17, 2002; Bob Norman, "A Tale of Two Mosques," *New Times Broward-Palm Beach*, August 1, 2002; David Kidwell, "S. Florida Associate of Padilla Is Arrested," *Miami Herald*, June 15, 2002.

128. Ibid.

129. Ken Thomas, "Man Accused in 'Dirty Bomb' Plot Worshipped at Mosque Once Linked to Terrorist Fund Raising," Associated Press, June 14, 2002.

130. "Floridians Gave $1.9 Million to Alleged Terror Front Groups," Associated Press, December 28, 2001.

131. Norman, "A Tale of Two Mosques."

132. DeMarzo, "Ex-Mosque Leader Says Suspect Wasn't Radical in Broward."

133. "World Trade Center Bombing Suspect Apprehended in Pakistan," US Department of Justice press release, February 8, 1995, http://www.usdoj.gov/opa/pr/Pre_96 /February95/78.txt.html.

134. Michael Fetcher, "Tampa Bay Travel Agent Tied to Terrorist Bomber," *Tampa Tribune*, July 10, 1997.

135. Norman, "A Tale of Two Mosques."

136. Ibid.

137. Leslie Miller, "TSA Head Admits to Airport Security Gaps," Associated Press, September 26, 2003. Significant gaps in airport security remain. For example, in September 2003, TSA chief James Loy admitted that someone could still sneak a blade onto a commercial plane.

138. Richard Winton and Andrew Blankstein, "LAPD: City Was Al Qaeda Target," *Los Angeles Times*, March 31, 2004; 9/11 Commission, *The 9/11 Commission Report*, p. 531.

139. "Al-Qaida Had L.A., Chicago Towers Targeted," United Press International, March 30, 2004.

140. *U.S. v. Reid*, 2-10013-WGY, indictment (D MA January 16, 2002).

141. *U.S. v. Badat*, 04-CR-10223, indictment (D MA October 4, 2004).

142. Sara Kehaulani Goo and Susan Schmidt, "Memo Warns of New Plots to Hijack Jets," *Washington Post*, July 30, 2003.

143. Susan Schmidt, "Al Qaeda Planning More Hijackings, Officials Warn," *Washington Post*, July 29, 2003.

144. Sara Kehaulani Goo and John Mintz, "Pillow Bombs Feared on Planes," *Washington Post*, October 14, 2003.

145. Sara Kehaulani Goo and John Mintz, "Air Travelers Told to Expect Closer Checks on Gadgets," *Washington Post*, August 6, 2003.

146. Sara Kehaulani Goo, "U.S. Suspends No-Visa Air Travel Programs," *Washington Post*, August 3, 2004.

147. Audrey Hudson, "Breaches Seen as Terrorist Tests," *Washington Times*, January 16, 2004.

148. John Mintz and Audrey Burgess, "Suspicious Passengers Questioned in France," *Washington Post*, December 26, 2003; Dana Priest and Sara Kehaulani Goo, "3 Air Routes Focus of Scrutiny," *Washington Post*, January 3, 2004.

149. Sara Kehaulani Goo and Dana Priest, "Flights Cut on Fear of Al Qaeda Attacks," *Washington Post*, February 1, 2004.

150. Leslie Miller, "Lawmakers Push Agency to Develop ID Cards," Associated Press, May 19, 2004.

151. Stewart Bell, "Air Canada Uniform Theft Raises Fear," *National Post*, August 31, 2004.

152. Annie Jacobsen, "Terror in the Skies, Again?" *Wall Street Journal*, July 13, 2004.

153. Audrey Hudson, "Scouting Jetliners for New Attacks," *Washington Times*, July 22, 2004.

154. Curt Anderson, "Government Says Terrorists May Use Lasers," Associated Press, December 9, 2004.

155. Tom Ridge, US Department of Homeland Security press briefing, October 30, 2001.

156. David Cazares and Madeline Baro Diaz, "Miami Alerts Public to Possible Threat," *South Florida Sun*, September 16, 2003.

157. "Calif., N.M. Warned of Possible Terror Threat," Associated Press, July 29, 2004.

158. Zahid Hussain and Daniel McGrory, "Bin Laden's Hit Squads Preparing Wave of Attacks on Politicians," *Times of London*, August 12, 2004.

159. "FBI Bulletin Says Al-Qaida Might Target Veteran Hospitals," Associated Press, August 27, 2004.

160. "FBI Warns Military Recruiters about Terror Threat," Associated Press, August 20, 2004.

161. U.S. Department of the Interior press release, May 21, 2002, http://www.doi.gov/news/020522.html (accessed August 16, 2005).

162. "California Cites 'Credible Threat' against Bridges," CNN, November 1, 2001, http://archives.cnn.com/2001/US/11/01/gen.attack.on.terror/ (accessed August 16, 2005).

163. Al Guart, "'Mideast' Snoops Spurring Ambulance-Bomb Alert," *New York Post*, August 29, 2004; Jeff Rossen, "Ambulance Companies on Alert for Suspiciously Interested Strangers," WABC, August 18, 2004; Richard Danielson and Nora Koch, "Attempts to Buy Vehicles Raise Suspicions," *St. Petersburg Times*, October 22, 2004.

164. *USA v. Ahmed Omar Abu Ali*, 1-05-CR-53, jury verdict (ED VA November 22, 2005).

165. *USA v. Ahmed Omar Abu Ali*, 1-05-CR-53, indictment, p. 8 (ED VA February 3, 2005).

166. *USA v. Ahmed Omar Abu Ali*, 1-05-CR-53, superseding indictment, p. 11 filed February 3, 2005, unsealed February 22, 2005.

167. Jerry Markon and Dana Priest, "Terrorist Plot to Kill Bush Alleged," *Washington Post*, February 23, 2005.

168. *USA v. Ahmed Omar Abu Ali*, 1-05-CR-53, indictment, p. 5 (ED VA February 3, 2005).

169. *USA v. Ahmed Omar Abu Ali*, 05-CR-53, opposition to defendant's motion to suppress, p. 12 (ED VA September 19, 2005).

170. Ibid.

171. Mathew Barakat, "Saudi Warden Says Abu Ali Was Treated Well," Associated Press, November 1, 2005.

172. *USA v. Ahmed Omar Abu Ali*, 1-05-CR-53, indictment, p. 10 (ED VA February 3, 2005).

173. Ibid.

174. Ibid.

175. Jerry Seper, "Suspect in Plot against Bush Linked to 'Paintball Jihadists," *Washington Times*, February 24, 2005.

176. "Investigation Continues in Lodi, California," FBI news release, June 8, 2005, http://sacramento.fbi.gov/pressrel/2005/06082005.htm (accessed August 16, 2005).

177. Andrew Adams, "Lodi, Lackawanna Both Focus of High-Profile Terrorist Investigations by FBI," *Lodi News-Sentinel*, July 12, 2005, http://www.lodinews.com/articles/2005/07/12/terrorism/1_lackawanna_050712.txt (accessed August 16, 2005).

178. "FBI: Al Qaeda Plot Possibly Uncovered," CNN, June 9, 2005, http://www.cnn.com/2005/US/06/09/terror.probe (accessed August 16, 2005).

179. "Investigation Continues in Lodi, California."

180. *USA v. Hamid Hayat and Umer Hayat*, S-05-240 GEB, government's opposition to defendant's motion for reconsideration regarding release on bond, pp. 15–18 (ED CA August 22, 2005).

181. *USA v. Hamid Hayat*, MAG 05-0161-PAN, amended detention order (ED CA June 14, 2005); *USA v. Umer Hayat*, detention order (ED CA June 7, 2005).

182. *USA v. Hamid Hayat*, MAG 05-0161-PAN, criminal complaint (ED CA June 7, 2005); *USA v. Umer Hayat*, MAG 05-1060 PAN, criminal complaint (ED CA June 7, 2005).

183. *USA v. Hamid Hayat and Umer Hayat*, 05-CR-0240, indictment, p. 1 (ED CA June 16, 2005).

184. Ibid.

185. Ibid., pp. 1–2.

186. Ibid., pp. 2–3.

187. *USA v. Hamid Hayat and Umer Hayat*, S-05-240 GEB, government's opposition to defendant's motion for reconsideration regarding release on bond, p. 9 (ED CA August 22, 2005).

188. Ibid.

189. Ibid., pp. 9–10.

190. Ibid., p. 10.

191. *USA v. Hamid Hayat*, MAG 05-1061 PAN, affidavit of Special Agent Pedro Tenoch Aguilar, p. 2 (ED CA June 7, 2005).

192. Ibid.

193. Ibid., p. 3.

194. Ibid.

195. Ibid., pp. 3–4.

196. *USA v. Hamid Hayat and Umer Hayat*, S-05-240 GEB, government's opposition to defendant's motion for reconsideration regarding release on bond, p. 11 (ED CA August 22, 2005).

197. Ibid.

198. *USA v. UmerHayat*, MAG 05-1061 PAN, affidavit of Special Agent Pedro Tenoch Aguilar," p. 5 (ED CA June 7, 2005).

199. Ibid.

200. *USA v. Hamid Hayat and Umer Hayat*, S-05-240 GEB, government's opposition to defendant's motion for reconsideration regarding release on bond, p. 11 (ED CA August 22, 2005).

201. *USA v. Hamid Hayat*, MAG 05-1061 PAN, affidavit of Special Agent Pedro Tenoch Aguilar, p. 6 (ED CA June 7, 2005).

202. Ibid., pp. 5–6.

203. Ibid., 6.

204. "Lodi Father and Son Indicted for Making False Statements to the FBI in Connection with Terrorist Matters," US Department of Justice press release, June 16, 2005.

205. *USA v. Umer Hayat*, S-05-240 GEB, motion for reconsideration regarding release on bond (ED CA August 22, 2005). See also *USA v. Hamid Hayat*, S-05-240 GEB, motion for reconsideration regarding release on bond (ED CA September 19, 2005).

206. *USA v. Hamid Hayat and Umer Hayat*, S-05-240 GEB, defendants' joint reply to government's opposition to defendants' motion for reconsideration regarding release on bond, pp. 5–6 (ED CA August 22, 2005).

207. *USA v. Hamid Hayat and Umer Hayat*, S-05-240 GEB, government's opposition to defendant's motion for reconsideration regarding release on bond, p. 5 (ED CA August 22, 2005).

208. Ibid., p. 8.

209. *USA v. Hamid Hayat and Umer Hayat*, S-05-240 GEB, first superseding indictment (ED CA September 22, 2005).

210. Ibid., pp. 2–3.

211. US Immigration and Customs Enforcement Web site, http://www.ice.gov/graphics/about/index.htm (accessed August 22, 2005).

212. "Investigation Continues in Lodi, California."

213. Ibid.

214. US Citizenship and Immigration Services Web site, http//www.uscis.gov/graphics/services/visas.htm (accessed October 20, 2005).

215. Rone Tempest, "The World; How Visa System Failed to Flag Imam; Shabbir Ahmed's Anti-U.S. Invectives Were Widely Known before He Was Granted Entry," *Los Angeles Times*, July 3, 2005.

216. "Lodi Imam and His Son Are Deported to Pakistan," ICE news release, August 17, 2005.

217. "Former Imam of Lodi Mosque to Be Deported from the United States," ICE news release, August 15, 2005.

218. Ibid.

219. Ibid.

220. "Lodi Imam and His Son Are Deported to Pakistan."

221. "Former Imam of Lodi Mosque to Be Deported from the United States."

222. *USA v. Hamid Hayat and Umer Hayat*, S-05-240 GEB, first superseding indictment, p. 3 (ED CA September 22, 2005).

223. "Former Imam of Lodi Mosque to Be Deported from the United States."

224. Ibid.

225. US Department of Justice press release, "Hamid Hayat Convicted of Terrorism Charges," April 25, 2006, http://releases.usnewswire.com/GetRelease.asp?id=64599.

226. Ibid.

227. Rone Tempest and Eric Bailey, "Lodi Terrorism Conviction Was a Rout, Jury Says," *Los Angeles Times*, April 27, 2005, http://www.latimes.com/news/printedition/california/la-me-lodi27apr27,1,1257005.story?coll=la-headlines-pe-california.

228. Demian Bulwa, "Jury for Lodi Terror Case Deadlocked," *San Francisco Chronicle*, April 25, 2006, http://72.14.203.104/search?q=cache:6BI2D-2aQtIJ:sfgate.com/cgi-bin/article.cgi%3Ff%3D/c/a/2006/04/25/MNGPVIETRT10.DTL+%22decisively+deadlocked%22+umer&hl=en&gl=us&ct=clnk&cd=4.

229. *USA v. Umer Hayat*, S-05-240 GEB, plea agreement (ED CA May 31, 2006).

230. "Umer Hayat Enters Plea to Making False Statement," US Department of Justice press release, May 31, 2006.

231. Ibid.

232. *USA v. Umer Hayat*, S-05-240 GEB, plea agreement (ED CA May 31, 2006).

233. US Department of Justice, "Umer Hayat Enters Plea to Making False Statements."

234. *USA v. Mohammad Zaki Amawi, Marwan Othman El-Hindi and Wassim I. Mazloum*, 06-CR-00719, indictment (NDOH February 16, 2006).

235. Ibid.

236. Ibid.

237. Ibid.

238. Ibid.

239. Ibid.

240. Ibid.

241. "Nickel and Dime Hustler, or Something Worse? Terror Suspect Led Unsettled Life," *Cleveland Plain Dealer*, May 21, 2006.

242. William Kates, "Government Details How Suspect Diverted Charity Funds," Associated Press, March 8, 2003.

243. http://www.treasury.gov/press/releases/po3632.htm and http://www.treasury.gov/press/releases/po3553.htm.

244. *USA v. Kevin James, et al.*, 05-CR-214, indictment (CD CA August 31, 2005).

245. Ibid.

246. Ibid., p. 2.

247. Ibid., p. 7.

248. Ibid., p. 4.

249. Ibid., pp. 11–12.

250. Ibid., pp. 5, 7–10.

251. "Four Men Indicted on Terrorism Charges Related to Conspiracy to Attack Military Facilities, Other Targets," US Department of Justice press release, August 31, 2005.

252. 9/11 Commission, *The 9/11 Commission Report*, p. 68.

-3-

AL QAEDA'S AMERICAN NETWORK

People of America, I remind you of the weighty words of our leaders, Osama Bin Ladin and Dr. Ayman Al Zawahri, that what took place on September 11 was but the opening salvo of the global war on America, and that Allah willing, the magnitude and ferocity of what is coming your way will make you forget about September 11.

—Alleged Al Sahab videotape of "Azzam the American," identified by US intelligence as Adam Gadahn (Aired by ABC News, October 28, 2004)

OVERVIEW

Even before the 9/11 attacks, al Qaeda operations chief Khalid Sheikh Mohammed (KSM) had attained a near legendary status as the "mastermind" for al Qaeda's many conspiracies against the United States. As noted earlier, he was a hands-on manager from the murderous conception of each plot to selection of the operatives, to financing, to training, to developing operational details. Nothing was too big or too small for KSM as long as it involved the death and destruction of Americans and American interests.

The globally transmitted carnage of 9/11 afforded KSM even greater prestige within the al Qaeda movement. As his plots expanded, so did the number of his operatives and the instructions he gave them. Ironically, it was this "success" that ultimately led to his downfall and humiliating capture and confinement.

The capture of KSM in March 2003 at a not-so-safe "safehouse" in Pakistan probably resulted in the elimination of the single most dangerous person intent on inflicting harm and destroying America through attacks launched from within its own borders. As welcome as this is, there is no question that the KSM methodology involved a network of operatives, at different stages of training and preparedness depending on the plots to which they had been assigned. Many have been killed or captured, but at least some remain alive, their whereabouts and intentions unknown. Additionally, new cells acting independently of KSM's network have emerged. This chapter seeks to unveil these nefarious groups at their varying stages of preparedness.

KHALID SHEIKH MOHAMMED

Since 1992, nearly every US-centered al Qaeda plot can be traced directly to KSM. As the *9/11 Commission Report* notes, "KSM applied his imagination, technical aptitude, and managerial skills to hatching and planning an extraordinary array of terrorist schemes. These ideas included conventional car bombing, political assassination, aircraft bombing, hijacking, reservoir poisoning, and, ultimately, the use of aircraft as missiles guided by suicide operatives." Furthermore, "co-workers describe him as an intelligent, efficient, and even-tempered manager who approached his projects with a single-minded dedication that he expected his colleagues to share."[1]

KSM grew up in Kuwait in a religious family and allegedly joined the Muslim Brotherhood at the age of sixteen. In 1983, he came to America where he enrolled first at Chowan College, a Baptist school in Murfreesboro, North Carolina, and then at North Carolina Agricultural and Technical State University in Greensboro. One of his classmates in Greensboro was Ramzi Yousef's brother, who himself later became an al Qaeda member. As noted in chapter 1 Ramzi Yousef was the central planner for the 1993 World Trade Center bombing and the 1995 Bojinka plots against international aircraft in the Philippines aided, of course, by KSM.[2] Not swayed in the least bit by American culture or democratic ideals, he told his captors in 2003 that during his US stay in the 1980s he considered killing the radical Jewish leader Meir Kahane, when Kahane lectured in Greensboro.[3] As described earlier, Kahane was later assassinated, by El Sayyid Nosair, who was also indicted in the 1993 World Trade Center bombing.

After graduating with a mechanical engineering degree in December 1986, KSM traveled to Pakistan, where he was mentored by Abdul Rasul Sayyaf, the head of the Hizbul-Ittihad El-Islami (the Islamic Union Party), and received military training. He put that training to use in Afghanistan, where he fought in the jihad against the Soviets and worked for Abdullah Azzam, bin Laden's mentor and the head of the Mektab Al Khidmat, the precursor organization to al Qaeda.

KSM first began to seriously plot against the United States in 1992 as a result of what he would subsequently describe as his *"violent disagreement with U.S. foreign policy favoring Israel."*[4] During the autumn of that year, KSM and Ramzi Yousef repeatedly discussed the 1993 World Trade Center plot, and, on November 3, 1992, KSM wired $600 to Yousef's coconspirator, Mohammed Salameh. Also in 1992, KSM traveled briefly to Bosnia to fight with the mujahideen there, demonstrating his personal commitment to political and violent jihad.[5]

From Bosnia, KSM moved to Qatar at the personal invitation of Sheikh Abdallah bin Khalid bin Hamad al-Thani, the former minister of Islamic Affairs. Despite working as a project engineer with the Qatari Ministry of Electricity and Water through early 1996, KSM managed to travel extensively in the interests of his terrorist activity.[6] Between 1993 and 1996, he went to China, the Philippines, Bosnia, Brazil, Sudan, and Malaysia.

During his time in the Philippines in 1994, KSM and Yousef developed the Bojinka plot, discovered only after the bomb-making chemicals in their apartment caused a fire. The plot's aim was to bomb twelve American civilian airliners over the Pacific in a two-day span. Another aviation plan emerged as well, this one to "to bomb U.S.-bound cargo carriers by smuggling jackets containing nitrocellulose on board." Dolls wearing clothes containing nitrocellulose were found when Yousef was arrested in February 1995. Also during this time, the two formulated a plan to kill President Clinton on his November 1994 visit to Manila.

In January 1996, as US agents closed in on him, KSM moved to Afghanistan, where he reconnected with Abdul Rasul Sayyaf. That year, he also had his first meeting with bin Laden since 1989 and presented "a menu of ideas for terrorist operations." During this meeting, the plot that would morph into 9/11 was discussed and bin Laden asked KSM to officially join al Qaeda. But KSM turned bin Laden down. As *The 9/11 Commission Report* notes, "He preferred to remain independent and retain the option of working with other *mujahideen* groups still operating in Afghanistan."[7]

Following this, KSM toured India, Iran, Indonesia, and Malaysia, where he met with key Jemaah Islamiyah operative Hambali. He then attempted to enter Chechnya to meet up with the mujahideen leader Ibn al-Khattab but was unable to pass through Azerbaijan. During this time, KSM also claims to have provided assistance (on computer and media projects) to a variety of mujahideen forces, including the Libyan Islamic Fighting Group.[8]

In August 1998, al Qaeda launched simultaneous attacks on the US embassies in Nairobi and Dar es Salaam—bombings that KSM says convinced him of bin Laden's devotion to the cause. Yet despite moving to Kandahar to work with al Qaeda and taking over its media committee, KSM claims that he never formally swore allegiance to bin Laden. Beginning in late 1998, KSM began to work intensely on the 9/11 operation.

As he plotted the details of 9/11, KSM also developed schemes for attacks in Thailand, Singapore, Indonesia, and the Maldives—and more plans for the United States. The latter were efficient, relying on operatives who could easily enter the United States even after the perceived tightening of US border controls after 9/11.[9] Among these was Jose Padilla as well as others with names well known from today's most-wanted lists, such as Adnan el-Shukrijumah, Abderraouf Jdey, and Adam Gadahn.

KSM'S OPERATIVES

Adnan el-Shukrijumah

El-Shukrijumah, aka "Jafar the Pilot," is a Saudi-born[10] permanent US resident alien who has spent fifteen years in the United States (mostly in South Florida) and who speaks fluent English.[11] He was believed to have reentered or sought reentry to the United States using various passports, possibly from Saudi Arabia, Canada, Guyana, and Trinidad.

In the words of a Department of Homeland Security (DHS) document, "KSM has identified Adnan El Shukrijumah, as an operative with standing permission to attack targets in the United States that had been previously approved by Osama Bin Laden."[12] He is a skilled bomb maker and a pilot, and authorities have found a document that ties him (via one of his aliases) to the Oklahoma flight school where Zacarias Moussaoui trained.[13]

FBI director Robert Mueller has referred to el-Shukrijumah as "a trained operative who poses an operational threat to the United States," and warned that el-Shukrijumah has "scouted sites across America that might be vulnerable to terrorist attack."[14]

His suspected activities range from surveillance of high-profile targets in New York's financial district[15] to looking for weaknesses in the Panama Canal,[16] to plotting with Jose Padilla to blow up apartment buildings in the United States.[17] It has also been confirmed that Padilla and el-Shukrijumah attended the same Florida mosque that was also frequented by now-convicted terrorist Imran Mandhai (see below) and Adham Hassoun, who, in 2006, is awaiting trial in the Southern District of Florida on multiple counts of supporting terror and recruiting terrorists carried out over several years.[18]

More ominously, el-Shukrijumah is alleged to have been involved with another Canadian-linked suspect, Ameer el-Maati, in a plan to construct a dirty bomb by attempting to procure radioactive material from McMaster University in Hamilton, Ontario.[19]

His friends included Imran Mandhai, who was convicted in Florida of conspiring to bomb a National Guard armory, power stations, Jewish businesses, and Mount Rushmore.[20] Mandhai was also associated with Hakki Cemal Aksoy, convicted in 2002 for immigration violations[21] but in whose apartment bomb-making manuals and notes were found.

In March 2004, el-Shukrijumah allegedly attended a terrorist summit in Pakistan and met with a number of key al Qaeda members, including Abu Issa al-Hindi, Mohammed Naeem Noor Khan, and Mohammed Babar.[22] Recently he has reportedly been spotted in Mexico[23] and is alleged to have met with members of the Mara Salvatrucha gang (known as MS-13) in Honduras.[24]

Adnan el-Shukrijumah remains a high-priority al Qaeda suspect at large.[25]

Hakki Cemal Aksoy

Aksoy, aka Hasan Yilmaz, was born October 12, 1965, in Turkey. While his early activities are largely unknown, he first came to the attention of US authorities in 2000 when INS agents in Miami received information that he was a fugitive from Turkey, wanted for having unlawfully shot and killed a man.[26]

An INS investigation determined that Aksoy had unsuccessfully filed for political asylum under a false identity. A sealed indictment against Aksoy was obtained on September 22, 2000, and efforts to locate and arrest him ensued.[27]

On November 2, 2000, Aksoy was arrested and the agents immediately obtained a search warrant for his Hollywood, Florida, apartment and executed this search warrant with the assistance of the FBI and other Joint Terrorism Task Force (JTTF) members.[28] Agents discovered a 9 mm semiautomatic pistol and false identity documents in Aksoy's possession.[29]

Aksoy was denied bail. During his pretrial detention at the Miami

Federal Detention Center, he made statements to his cellmate threatening to kill the female INS case agent in his case, claiming he would fashion a homemade knife in jail, hide it on his person, and lunge at the agent in court and stab her to death. Repeated searches and appropriate security measures prevented any such attack.[30]

At the same time, a separate Miami JTTF investigation of Imran Mandhai (mentioned above) revealed a link between him and Aksoy. Mandhai was subsequently convicted in Miami on federal terrorism-related charges and is serving a twelve-year sentence. Mandhai claimed that part of his motivation for engaging in his jihad activities was his desire to free Aksoy, a fellow jihadist, from custody.[31]

Aksoy was convicted in US District Court in Miami on February 13, 2002, on a four-count indictment charging him with making false statements in immigration proceedings, possessing a false alien registration card, and being an illegal alien in possession of a firearm. He is currently serving a ten-year sentence.[32]

Aksoy has denied having any terrorist connections, but he refused to answer questions concerning the materials found in his apartment.

Abderraouf Jdey

Jdey, aka Faruq al-Tunisi, arrived in Canada from his native Tunisia in 1991 and received Canadian citizenship a scant four years later. Four years after that, Jdey received a Canadian passport and departed for Afghanistan.[33]

Evidence presented to the 9/11 Commission has led to the conclusion that while in Afghanistan, Jdey may have trained with Khalid al-Mihdhar and Nawaf al-Hazmi and received instruction from KSM, Mohamed Atta, and Ramzi Binalshibh. After 9/11, a raid on a Pakistani safehouse turned up a letter, possibly written by the al Qaeda leader Saif al-Adil, that indicated Jdey was initially to take part in the 9/11 plot. Moreover, after seizing the house of al Qaeda operations chief Mohammed Atef in Kabul in November 2001, coalition forces found martyrdom videotapes made by Jdey and Binalshibh. KSM himself has claimed that Jdey was not involved in the original 9/11 operation but instead was assigned to a planned second wave of attacks from which he had withdrawn by the summer of 2001.[34]

Contradicting KSM, ironically, is another naturalized Canadian al Qaeda operative, Mohammed Mansour Jabarah, who worked directly for KSM. Jabarrah, originally from St. Catherines, Ontario, told Canadian and American intelligence officials that Jdey downed American Airlines Flight 587 with a shoe bomb on November 12, 2001. A May 2002 Canadian internal government memo characterized this information as coming from a "source of unknown reliability." Jabarah said he was told about Jdey's actions by Abu Abdelrahman, a Saudi al Qaeda member also linked to KSM.[35]

There has been no further public information regarding Jabarah's claims since the startling claim made in 2004. Additionally, Ted Lopatkiewicz, spokesman for the National Transportation Safety Board, refuted the claim when he said, "We have seen no evidence of anything other than an accident here. There has been no evidence found, from what I can tell—at least that's been relayed to us—that there was any criminality involved here. It appears, at least the evidence we have, is that a vertical fin came off, not that there was any kind of event in the cabin."[36]

In 2002, the FBI issued an alert for Jdey and placed him on its wanted list.[37] Subsequently, in May 2004, Attorney General Ashcroft declared him one of seven al Qaeda associates "sought in connection with the possible terrorist threats in the United States."[38] Canadian media have reported that Jdey is believed to have left Canada in November 2001[39] although attribution for that belief is anonymous and may constitute wishful thinking as much as reliable intelligence. What is known is that Jdey remains a person of grave concern to law enforcement authorities while his whereabouts remain a mystery.[40]

Majid Khan

The interrogation of KSM has produced many results, one of which is the arrest of Majid Khan, a former Baltimore resident. Khan, whose relatives own gas stations in Baltimore, was arrested in Pakistan in 2003. KSM has revealed that Khan was tasked to bomb a number of US gas stations by "simultaneously detonating explosives in the stations' underground storage tanks."[41] KSM reportedly wanted to use two or three African American Muslim converts to participate in the plot, and Khan's own interrogation by the FBI confirmed that he saw two African Americans converts when he met with KSM in Pakistan in 2000. Interrogations have also revealed some plans to bring explosives into the United States through a Karachi-based import-export business.[42]

Aafia Siddiqui

Siddiqui, a Pakistani citizen and a US visa holder, studied at Brandeis University and MIT, training in biology and neurology.[43] She is believed to have left Boston in January of 2003.[44] Siddiqui has also spent time in Maryland.[45] Reports have placed Siddiqui in Liberia prior to 9/11, where she allegedly worked to sort out problems between other al Qaeda operatives.[46]

KSM used Siddiqui as a "fixer" to help al Qaeda operatives arriving in the United States.[47] Siddiqui is known, for example, to have rented a post office box to assist Majid Khan in creating a US identity and, according to government sources, Siddiqui was to use her capacity to blend in to American society to similarly aid "other al Qaeda operatives as they entered the United States."[48] In addition, Siddiqui's estranged husband bought body armor, night-vision goggles, and military manuals that were to be sent to Pakistan.[49]

In March 2003, the FBI issued a global alert for Siddiqui. A report of her capture in Pakistan in April 2003 appears to have been false and a month later the FBI issued a BOLO ("be on the lookout") for Siddiqui in connection with current threats against the United States.[50]

Uzair Paracha

Paracha is a Pakistani citizen with lawful permanent resident status in the United States. His most recent entry into the country was in mid-February 2003, when he was staying with relatives in Brooklyn.[51]

After meeting with KSM in Pakistan,[52] Paracha is believed to have agreed to assist al Qaeda by coming to the United States, posing as Majid Khan (a person Paracha knew to be an al Qaeda associate), obtaining immigration documents that would enable Khan to enter the United States, and conducting financial transactions in Khan's name.[53]

It is believed that KSM conspired with Paracha to assist Majid Khan and that Paracha's father, Saifullah, was conscripted to have his import-export firm arrange to smuggle explosives into the United States.[54] Khan and KSM "invested" $200,000 in the firm.[55]

Detained in March 2003 as a material witness, Paracha was charged in August 2003 with conspiring to provide material support and resources to al Qaeda.[56] Paracha's father has also been detained by US authorities and remains in custody in Afghanistan.[57]

Adam Gadahn

Gadahn, a Muslim convert who grew up in California, attended al Qaeda training camps and served as an al Qaeda translator.[58] He is known to have associated with the captured al Qaeda leader Abu Zubaydah and the so-called American Taliban, John Walker Lindh.[59] KSM also allegedly wanted to use Gadahn in his plot to bomb Baltimore gas stations.[60]

In May 2004, the FBI issued a BOLO for Gadahn.[61] In December 2004, Gadahn resurfaced as the likely voice of "Azzam the American" on an al Qaeda videotape threatening attacks against the United States that would far surpass those of 9/11.[62] He also made an appearance in an al Qaeda video released on the first anniversary of the London transit bombings.

Ali al-Marri

Since his capture, the talkative KSM has identified Ali al-Marri as "the point of contact for al Qaeda operatives arriving in the U.S. for September 11 follow-on operations."[63] Attorney General Ashcroft confirmed this claim, stating that al-Marri "was sent by al Qaeda to facilitate another wave of terrorist attacks on Americans."[64] KSM called al-Marri "the perfect sleeper agent because he has studied in the United States, had no criminal record, and had a family with whom he could travel."[65] Phone records have tied al-Marri to a phone number linked to the 9/11 paymaster, Mustafa al-Hawsawi, the 9/11 hijacker Mohamed Atta, and the alleged twentieth hijacker, Zacarias Moussaoui.[66]

Al-Marri reentered the United States on September 10, 2001,[67] in order to enroll in a graduate program at Bradley University in Peoria, Illinois.[68] He was arrested as a material witness on a warrant issued from the Southern District of New York in December 2001,[69] and in May 2003 he was indicted on a number of charges including making false statements to FBI agents during the investigation of the terrorist attacks of September 11, 2001; making false statements to banks in Macomb, Illinois; identity fraud; and access device (credit card number) fraud.[70] In addition to lying about calling the telephone number linked to al-Hawsawi, he told FBI agents that his last visit to the United States before 2001 was in 1991, even though he had entered the country in the summer of 2000.[71] In addition, a search of al-Marri's apartment turned up jihadi material and an almanac bookmarked to locate information on dams, reservoirs, and railroads.[72]

In June 2003, al-Marri was declared an enemy combatant after the US government received, in the words of the Department of Defense, "recent credible information provided by other detainees in the War on Terrorism."[73] One of those detainees alleged that al-Marri was trained in poisons; others said that al-Marri had met with bin Laden at the Al Farouq training camp in Afghanistan and that al-Marri offered to martyr himself.[74] Thanks to KSM, this decidedly big al Qaeda "fish" remains in US custody.

AL QAEDA CELLS

In addition to KSM, other al Qaeda cells have emerged.

The Lackawanna Six

The Lackawanna Six may have been influenced by a lecture given by the extremist imam Juma al-Dosari at a Lackawanna, New York, mosque in 2001. The mosque did not invite al-Dosari to speak again due to his radical beliefs.[75]

In April 2001, the men decided to travel to an al Qaeda guesthouse in Kandahar, Afghanistan, then went to an al Qaeda training camp where they received weapons training. While they were at the camp, bin Laden visited and gave a speech to all of the trainees. One of the men, Sahim Alwan, personally met with bin Laden.[76]

The US government began watching the group when the men returned to upstate New York in June 2001.[77] The FBI arrested five of the men in New York in September 2002. One man was arrested in Bahrain, and then later brought to the United States.[78]

After the six men were arrested, they were indicted on charges of providing material support to a designated foreign terrorist organization. All of the men pleaded guilty to charges of material support and were sentenced to prison terms of seven to ten years.[79] A seventh member of the cell, Jaber Elbaneh, was arrested in Yemen in late 2003,[80] but he is believed to have escaped from a Yemeni prison in February 2006.[81] Kamal Derwish, the cell's alleged ringleader, was killed in a CIA missile strike near Marib, Yemen, in November 2002.[82]

The Portland Seven and Ali Khaled Steitiye

The investigation of Ali Khaled Steitiye, a regular worshiper at the Islamic Center of Portland,[83] led investigators to the Portland, Oregon cell. Skamania County Sheriff's Deputy Mark Mercer, dispatched to a report of gunfire, found Steitiye and five others on September 29, 2001, at a gated gravel pit outside Washougal. Although none of the men were arrested, the sheriff noted their identities and their weapons.[84]

On October 24, 2001, Steitiye was arrested on federal gun and fraud charges. The local sheriff had seen the incident report and contacted the FBI about Steitiye's companions at the gravel pit.[85] The referral was timely because authorities were aware that after the September 11 attacks, Steitiye's "companions" had flown to China in an unsuccessful attempt to gain entry into Pakistan, en route to Afghanistan in the hopes of fighting US troops.[86]

Two of Steitiye's companions, Jeffrey Battle and Patrice Lumumba Battle, pled guilty to conspiracy to levy war against the United States and were sentenced to eighteen years in prison.[87] Jeffrey Battle participated in weapons training in the United States and attempted to travel to Afghanistan to train and fight against the United States and its allies. In a recorded conversation in August 2002, Battle "spoke at length about his disdain for the U.S." According to court documents, "Battle . . . discussed having considered, but ultimately rejected, committing terrorist acts in the U.S.—specifically, mass murder at a Jewish synagogue or school." He preferred to attack the United States abroad. He also discussed "his preference to commit an act of mass murder by staging a raid, as opposed to a suicide mission, because he wanted to be alive to see the damage inflicted." However, he noted that he would be "willing to get caught or die if we could do at least 100 or 1,000, big numbers."[88]

Battle's ex-wife, October Martinique Lewis, who had transferred money to Battle, pled guilty to money-laundering charges.[89] In September 2003, Battle's codefendants Ahmed and Muhammad Bilal pled guilty to conspiracy to contribute services to the Taliban, as well as to federal weapons charges.[90] Another defendant, Maher "Mike" Hawash, pled guilty in August 2003 to conspiracy to supply services to the Taliban.[91]

In June 2002, Steitiye was convicted on the basis of the evidence collected by federal agents at his home and in his car, which included an assault rifle, over one thousand rounds of ammunition, a machete, twenty thousand dollars, a calendar with September 11 circled, and "evidence" suggesting a connection to Hamas. Officials believe Steitiye trained with Hamas.[92]

Steitiye had been convicted in 1984 of felony theft and in 1986 of forging a US Treasury check.[93] An indictment unsealed in June 2004 charged Steitiye with illegally possessing a machine gun and being an ex-convict in possession of a weapon.[94]

The Spanish Cell

In July 2002, Spanish police arrested three men of Syrian descent, two in Madrid and one in Castellón, as part of an investigation on Islamic radicals in Spain code-named "Operation Date."[95] The arrested men were:

- Ghasoub al-Abrash Ghalyoun, aka Abu Musab (already arrested on a different charge in April 2002), who is allegedly a member of the Muslim Brotherhood
- Abdalrahman Alarnaot Abu Aljer, aka Abu Obed
- Mohammed Khair al-Salq

The men were arrested because they possessed suspicious videocassettes made during a 1997 trip to the United States. The judge leading the investigation, Baltasar Garzon, said that the footage al-Abrash had shot of US landmarks "could have been preliminary information for attacks on the World Trade Center towers" and "go beyond the mere curiosity of a tourist."[96] Two of the videotapes were of the Twin Towers, filmed from every angle and at every distance.[97] The other landmarks taped were the Golden Gate Bridge, the Brooklyn Bridge, the Statue of Liberty, a New York airport, the Sears Tower, Disneyland, and Universal Studios in California. Four months after al-Abrash shot the tapes, according to Spanish authorities, another alleged member of the Spanish cell, al-Salq, received a visit from a man identified as Mohammad Bahaiah. He is thought to have been one of Osama bin Laden's couriers between Europe and Afghanistan, and they believe al-Salq may have passed the tapes to him.[98]

OTHER AL QAEDA CONVERTS

Mohammed Babar grew up in Queens and attended St. John's University for a year. On June 3, 2004, he pled guilty to charges of providing material support to al Qaeda and agreed to cooperate with the government.[99]

He admitted sending money, night-vision goggles, sleeping bags, waterproof socks, ponchos, and other equipment to a high-ranking al Qaeda official in South Waziristan from the summer of 2003 to March 2004 for use against US forces in Afghanistan. He also traveled to South Waziristan in January and February 2004 to hand deliver money and supplies to a high-ranking al Qaeda official.[100] In March 2004, he attended a terrorist summit and met with a number of prominent al Qaeda members, including Abu Issa al-Hindi and Adnan el-Shukrijumah.[101]

He also helped set up a terrorist training camp in Pakistan, facilitated terrorist travel, and was involved in a plot to blow up bars, restaurants, and train stations in Britain.[102] Babar, who is affiliated with the London-based Al Muhajiroun,[103] admitted to providing the London cell with bomb-making material.[104]

He first came to investigators' attention after telling a Canadian television show, "I'm willing to kill Americans."[105] He also told a reporter, "I will kill every American that I see. I'm not a New Yorker. I'm a Muslim."[106]

The Babar investigation is part of a larger investigation of what may have been a New York–based sleeper cell plotting attacks before the November 2004 election.[107] While Babar pled guilty in July 2004 and faces up to seventy years in prison, he has yet to be sentenced. Instead, he has become an invaluable resource to US law enforcement and intelligence agents.[108] For example, he has provided information on the July 7, 2005, bombings in London (see chapter 4).[109]

Mohammed Warsame was born in Somalia and sought refugee status in Canada in 1989. He became a naturalized Canadian citizen, but then moved to Minneapolis in 2002.[110]

He was arrested in December 2003 as a material witness in the Zacarias Moussaoui case.[111] At the time of his arrest, he was a student at Minneapolis Community and Technical College.[112] In January 2004, Warsame was indicted and charged with conspiracy to provide material support to al Qaeda.[113]

Warsame has admitted attending an al Qaeda training camp in 2000 and 2001 and receiving military training (weapons, martial arts). He attended lectures given by bin Laden and even sat next to him at a meal.

Moreover, he fought with the Taliban and provided financial assistance to al Qaeda members in Pakistan once he had returned to the United States.[114]

Mohammad Kamal Elzahabi is a Lebanese national who entered the United States in 1984 on a student visa. He paid a woman in Houston, Texas, to marry him and help him obtain legal permanent resident alien status.[115] Elzahabi divorced her in 1988, after he obtained his green card.[116] In June 2004, Elzahabi was charged with two counts of intentionally making "a false material statement and representation" to the FBI in a terrorism-related investigation.[117]

In 1988, he fought in Afghanistan and met with key jihadi figures Abu Musab al-Zarqawi, Raed Hijazi, and Bassam Kanj.[118] He again traveled to Afghanistan in 1991 and remained there for approximately four years. During this time, he was a sniper in combat and served as an instructor in small arms and sniper skills for other jihadists attending the Khalden training camp in Afghanistan. Elzahabi admitted that while he was in Afghanistan, he personally knew al Qaeda training camp aficionado Abu Zubaydah and knew of KSM.[119]

Elzahabi returned to New York City in April 2004 where he ran an axle-repair business. He used this business to help ship to Pakistan portable field radios, which US troops later found in Afghanistan.[120]

From 1997 to 1998 Elzahabi lived in Boston. He worked as a cabdriver and associated with Raed Hijazi, whom he aided in obtaining a Massachusetts driver's license in 1997. Hijazi was later convicted in Jordan for masterminding the failed millennium bombing plot that had targeted American and Israeli tourists in that country. [121] While in Boston, he lived with Bassam Kanj, who helped Hijazi lease a taxi that officials believe was used to fund the Jordan plan.[122]

Elzahabi also traveled to Lebanon, where he provided small arms training to the group of fighters that Bassam Kanj had formed to overthrow the government of Lebanon. Elzahabi stated that he served as a sniper, fighting under the command of Ibn al-Khattab in Chechnya from late 1999 to 2000.[123]

Nabil al-Marabh, another sometime Boston cabdriver, stayed at a terrorist guesthouse in Pakistan known as the House of Martyrs, engaged in weapons training in Afghanistan, and worked for the Muslim World League—then an important source of al Qaeda's funds[124]—in the early 1990s.[125] He then worked at the same Boston cab company as Mohammed Elzahabi, Raed Hijazi, and Bassam Kanj.[126] Al-Marabh maintained a

Boston address from 1989 to 2000.[127] He also lived in Toronto, Detroit, Tampa, and Chicago.[128]

According to al-Marabh, in 1998 Hijazi contacted him from Canada and asked for help in coming to the United States. Al-Marabh transferred $500 to Hijazi for the trip and let Hijazi stay in his home with his wife and stepson. When the FBI interviewed al-Marabh about Hijazi in 1999, he lied and said he did not know him.[129] During his interrogation in Jordan, Hijazi identified al-Marabh as an al Qaeda operative.[130]

On June 27, 2001, al-Marabh tried to illegally enter the United States near Niagara Falls by hiding in the back of a tractor-trailer while in possession of forged identity documents.[131] Moreover, Michigan State records showed al-Marabh receiving five driver's licenses in thirteen months; he had licenses for Massachusetts, Illinois, Ontario, and Florida as well.[132]

Federal investigators have also tied al-Marabh to 9/11 hijackers Ahmed al-Ghamdi and Satam al-Suqami.[133] Additionally, al-Marabh held a commercial driver's license and a permit to haul hazardous materials,[134] including explosives and caustic chemicals.[135]

Al-Marabh was arrested in Chicago in September 2001 on a parole violation related to his stabbing of a man who had lived in his apartment.[136] In 2002, he pled guilty to conspiracy to smuggle an alien into the United States[137] and was ordered deported. At the time, prosecutors said the government had no evidence linking him to terrorism.[138] The judge questioned the government's previous documentation of al-Marabh's ties to terror and also noted his "somewhat sporadic" employment, as well as the $22,000 in cash and $25,000 worth of amber jewels he had in his possession when he was arrested.[139] He was deported to Syria in January 2004. Months later, a press release from Immigration and Customs Enforcement called al-Marabh a "suspected terrorist."[140]

In a related case in September 2001, authorities raided a Detroit residence that had al-Marabh's name on the mailbox; they found three men with fake immigration documents, airport identification badges, and a notebook containing handwritten notes about security at a US military base in Turkey and an airport in Jordan.[141] These men, who may also have been involved in a plot to kill former defense secretary William Cohen during a visit to Turkey,[142] were later charged with being part of an al Qaeda sleeper cell.[143] Although they were convicted in June 2003, the charges were later dismissed in September 2004 by US District Judge Gerald Rosen, following a monthlong investigation by the Justice Department into allegations of prosecutorial misconduct.[144] The Justice Department discovered that there was evidence withheld by the prosecution that they were obligated to turn over to the defense, including an interview with the Tunisian man shown in the videotape of famous landmarks in New York, Las Vegas, and California.[145] According to the Tunisian man, the videotape was actually an amateur video, not surveillance as the prosecution presented in court.[146]

In September 2004, Adham Hassoun was indicted for providing material support to terrorist activities overseas.[147] Previously, Hassoun had been indicted on firearms violations[148] and had been held on immigration violations.[149] In the immigration proceedings, an immigration judge found that Hassoun "was a person engaged in terrorist activity" and ruled that he:

- engaged in a plot to commit an assassination;
- provided material support to terrorist organizations;
- was a member of Al-Gama'a al-Islamiyya (IG), Egypt's largest militant group;
- solicited persons to engage in terrorist activities; and
- recruited Mohammed Yousseff, a "jihad fighter."

In March 2004, federal prosecutors filed a superseding indictment that charged Hassoun with seven criminal charges stemming from a scheme to conceal his activities in recruiting and funding global jihad from federal officials.[150]

In addition, Hassoun is one of the incorporators in Florida of the office of the Benevolence International Foundation,[151] an organization that was designated a financier of terrorism in 2002.[152] Authorities are also investigating his ties to Jose Padilla. Hassoun had contact with Padilla on several occasions, including before Padilla's return to the United States in 2002.[153] According to the *Miami Herald*, "Hassoun even gave Padilla several hundred dollars once as 'an act of charity.'"[154]

Ryan Anderson

In February 2004, National Guardsman Ryan Anderson was arrested at Fort Lewis, a month before he was to be deployed to Iraq. A 2002 graduate of Washington State University and a convert to Islam, Anderson was caught in an Internet sting after he tried to contact al Qaeda operatives on the Web and offer them information about US military capabilities and weaponry.[155] Specifically, he attempted to pass on information about the vulnerabilities of the MIA1 Abrams tank. He also met with undercover agents who he believed were al Qaeda operatives.[156] In September 2004, a court-martial convicted Anderson on all five of the counts he faced[157] and sentenced him to life in prison.[158]

CONCLUSION

The attack of 9/11 was not an isolated instance of al Qaeda infiltration into the United States. In fact, dozens of operatives other than the 9/11 hijackers have managed to enter and embed themselves in the United States, actively carrying out plans to commit terrorist acts against US interests.

These operatives have several characteristics in common: they have (or had) access to al Qaeda leadership, have traveled for training to Afghanistan, are committed to the radical jihad belief system, are willing to use fraud to evade US immigration laws, and choose targets for maximum lethal effect, guided by considerations only of logistics, not ethics.

While the exact number of al Qaeda members awaiting activation in the United States is unknown,[159] it is certain that the operatives associated with KSM achieved a significant presence in this country before September 11. This is corroborated by their arrests by law enforcement, which are occurring more frequently in today's heightened-alert environment.

Even in the post-9/11 era, the cases demonstrate Afghanistan's centrality in the global jihad. Since the Soviet-Afghan war, Afghanistan has been a focal point for jihadis. Attacks ranging from the 1993 World Trade Center bombing[160] to 9/11[161] can be traced to the training camps there.

US intelligence estimates that from 1996 through September 11, 2001, a total of 10,000 to 20,000 fighters underwent instruction in Afghanistan's bin Laden–supported camps (such as Sada, Al Farouq, Khalden, Jihad Wal, Mes Aynak, and Derunta).[162] Former senator Bob Graham, who was involved with the congressional investigation into 9/11, believes that between 70,000 and 120,000 have been trained by al Qaeda.[163]

Ahmed Ressam, the al Qaeda–trained terrorist who sought to blow up Los Angeles International Airport on the eve of January 1, 2000, testified in federal court about the advanced urban warfare skills he was taught at these camps; these varied from "how to blow up the infrastructure of a country . . . [e]lectric plants, gas plants, airports, railroads, large corporations" to "how to mix poisons with other substances . . . designed to be used against intelligence officers and other VIPs."[164]

An overwhelming number of al Qaeda's US-based operatives trained for jihad in Afghanistan: Adnan el-Shukrijumah, Jose Padilla, Iyman Faris, Mohammed Warsame, the Lackawanna Six, Mohammed Elzahabi, Nabil al-Marabh, Raed Hijazi, Adam Gadahn, and Ali al-Marri. Others, like the Portland Seven, attempted to travel to Afghanistan to wage jihad. In Afghanistan, these operatives did more than learn the lethal tools of jihad: they also made valuable contacts that were later activated in the United States.

For example, as discussed above, when Mohammed Elzahabi fought in Afghanistan in 1988, he met Raed Hijazi and Bassam Kanj. They aided one another in Boston in the late 1990s, and Elzahabi also helped Kanj in his efforts to overthrow the government of Lebanon. Similarly, the plot by Jose Padilla and Adnan el-Shukrijumah to simultaneously blow up as many as twenty apartment buildings came together in Afghanistan, as the men strengthened ties initialized in their South Florida mosque. Their relationship later became strained and the two stopped working together.

KSM's choice of operatives to lead US efforts reflects his focus on efficiency: use whatever type of operative can support the cause.[165] Aafia Siddiqui, the well-educated, quiet mother of two, could easily slip in and out of the United States to provide material support. Americans and American residents such as Jose Padilla, Adnan el-Shukrijumah, and Adam Gadahn could blend back into American culture. This demonstrates more than adaptability: these are effective war tactics.

In discussing the summer 2004 terror threat, Attorney General John Ashcroft stressed this point:

> Let me say that the face of Al Qaida may be changing. . . . Al Qaida is a resilient and adaptable organization, known for altering tactics in the face of new security measures. Intelligence sources suggest that ideal Al Qaida operatives may now be in their late 20s or early 30s and may travel with a family to lower their profile.
>
> Our intelligence confirms Al Qaida is seeking recruits who can portray themselves as Europeans. Al Qaida also attracts Muslim extremists among many nationalities and ethnicities, including North Africans and

> South Asians, as well as recruiting young Muslim converts of any nationality inside target countries.[166]

In a court filing, the FBI further underscored al Qaeda's adaptability:

> Al Qaeda, with a disproportionate number of leaders from Palestinian backgrounds, has exhibited a propensity to use others to collect intelligence or conduct reconnaissance. In previous years, Al Qaeda commanders and officials stationed in Western countries, including the United States, have recruited Hamas operatives and volunteers to carry out reconnaissance or serve as couriers. With the increased law enforcement pressure on Al Qaeda since 9-11, there has been a renewed emphasis by Al Qaeda to find confirmed jihadist supporters in the United States by trying to enlist proven members of other groups such as Hamas to make up for the vacuum on the field level.[167]

The geographical distribution of al Qaeda's operatives reflects careful planning, as KSM planted agents in America's heartland (Peoria, Illinois; Columbus, Ohio). As James Turgal, an FBI supervisory special agent in Cincinnati, said, "If you want to assist Al Qaeda, would you live in D.C. or New York . . . ? Why not live in the heartland? This is the perfect place to be."[168] Other al Qaeda members discussed in this volume have operated in Baltimore, Seattle, Portland (Oregon), Miami, Chicago, Detroit, Boston, New York City, Minneapolis, upstate New York, and the Maryland suburbs. Khalid Sheikh Mohammed's legacy remains a dangerous lurking menace to America.

NOTES

1. National Commission on Terrorist Attacks upon the United States, *The 9/11 Commission Report: Final Report of the National Commission on Terrorist Attacks upon the United States* (New York: Norton, 2004), p. 150.
2. Ibid., pp. 145–47.
3. Ibid., p. 488.
4. Ibid., p. 147.
5. Ibid.
6. Ibid.
7. Ibid., p. 149.
8. Ibid., p. 489.
9. Ibid., pp. 149–50.

10. "Tennessee Bureau of Investigations," FBI-JTTF, http://www.tbi.state.tn.us/Fugitives/JTTF/shukrijumah.htm (accessed August 18, 2005).

11. Rober Mueller, "Remarks of FBI Director Robert Mueller on the Summer Terrorist Threat," FBI, May 26, 2004.

12. Evan Thomas, "Al Qaeda in America: The Enemy Within," *Newsweek*, June 23, 2003, p. 40.

13. Jerry Seper, "FBI Steps Up Hunt for Pakistani," *Washington Times*, April 2, 2003; Josh Meyer, Greg Krikorian, and William C. Rempel; "Quiet Investigation Centers on Al Qaeda Aide in New York," *Los Angeles Times*, September 3, 2004.

14. Mueller, "Remarks of FBI Director Robert Mueller on the Summer Terrorist Threat."

15. Jerry Seper, "Al Qaeda Leader Identified in 'Dirty Bomb' Plot," *Washington Times*, October 5, 2004.

16. Evan Thomas, Daniel Klaidman, and Michael Isikoff, "Enemies among Us," *Newsweek*, June 7, 2004, p. 26.

17. James Comey, "Remarks of Deputy Attorney General James Comey Regarding Jose Padilla," June 1, 2004, http://www.usdoj.gov/dag/speech/2004/dag6104.htm (accessed August 19, 2005).

18. Daniel Meron and Barry Sabin, "Department of Justice Joint Statement by Principal Deputy Assistant Attorney General Daniel Meron and Chief, Counterterrorism Section Barry Sabin," US Department of Justice, April 20, 2005.

19. Bill Gertz, "Al Qaeda Pursued a 'Dirty Bomb,'" *Washington Times*, October 17, 2003, p. A01.

20. Timothy J Burger et al., "The Making of the FBI's 'Most Dangerous,'" *Time*, April 7, 2003, p. 71.

21. *USA v. Aksoy*, 00-CR-788-ALL, docket (SD FL January 31, 2003).

22. Elaine Shannon and Tim McGirk, "What Is This Man Plotting?" *Time*, August 23, 2004; Meyer, Krikorian, and Rempel, "Quiet Investigation Centers on Al Qaeda Aide in New York."

23. Seper, "Al Qaeda Leader Identified in 'Dirty Bomb' Plot." Note: A March 21, 2003, *Washington Post* article also placed el-Shukrijumah in Morocco. See Dan Eggen and Manuel Roig-Franzia, "FBI on Global Hunt for Saudi Al Qaeda Suspect," *Washington Post*, March 21, 2003.

24. Jerry Seper, "Al Qaeda Seeks Ties to Local Gangs," *Washington Times*, September 28, 2004. This is not the first report tying Al Qaeda to South American gangs. For example, the same newspaper had claimed in an earlier report that "Al Qaeda members are working with Mexican organized crime groups, such as drug-trafficking organizations, in an attempt to enter the United States covertly." See Bill Gertz, "Terrorists Said to Seek Entry to U.S. Via Mexico," *Washington Times*, April 7, 2003.

25. "Seeking Information on Adnan G. El Shukrijumah," Federal Bureau of Investigation, http://www.fbi.gov/terrorinfo/elshukrijumah.htm (accessed April 26, 2006).

26. Jeff Shields, "Muslim Inmate Cries Foul at U.S.; Émigré Linked to S. Florida Terrorism Plot," *Fort Lauderdale Sun-Sentinel*, January 21, 2003.

27. Ibid.

28. Jeff Shields and Tanya Weinberg, "U.S. Says Plotters Aimed at FPL; Indictment: South Florida Was Terror Target," *Fort Lauderdale Sun-Sentinel*, May 18, 2002.

29. *USA v. Askoy*, 00-788-CR, superseding indictment (SD FL December 15, 2000).

30. Shields and Weinberg, "U.S. Says Plotters Aimed at FPL."

31. Ibid.

32. *USA v. Aksoy*, 00-CR-788-ALL, docket (SD FL January 31, 2003).

33. Stewart Bell, "Montreal Man Downed U.S. Plane, CSIS Told," *National Post*, August 27, 2004.

34. 9/11 Commission, *The 9/11 Commission Report*, p. 527.

35. Bell, "Montreal Man Downed U.S. Plane, CSIS Told."

36. Ibid.

37. FBI Web site, http://www.fbi.gov/terrorinfo/jdey.htm (accessed August 19, 2005). He remains on the list as of August 19, 2005.

38. John Ashcroft, "Remarks of Attorney General John Ashcroft on the Summer Terrorist Threat," May 26, 2004.

39. "Wanted—Again Canadians on an FBI Terror List," CBC News Online, May 27, 2004.

40. Jeremy Loom, "The Key Players: The Global Threat Has Many Faces," *Calgary Sun*, September 11, 2005.

41. Evan Thomas, "Al Qaeda in America."

42. Ibid.

43. Juan Zamarano, "From Islamabad to Panama, Worldwide Search for Terrorism Suspects as U.S. on High Alert," Associated Press, May 27, 2004.

44. Mueller, "Remarks of FBI Director Robert Mueller on the Summer Terrorist Threat."

45. "Terror Suspects Named by U.S. Officials," Associated Press, May 26, 2004.

46. Edward Harris, "Al-Qaida Bought Diamonds Ahead of Sept. 11 Attacks," Associated Press, August 7, 2004.

47. Mueller, "Remarks of FBI Director Robert Mueller on the Summer Terrorist Threat."

48. Thomas, "Al Qaeda in America."

49. Ibid.

50. Federal Bureau of Investigation, "Seeking Information RE: Aafia Siddiqui," http://www.fbi.gov/terrorinfo/siddiqui.htm (accessed August 19, 2005). She remains on the FBI's list of individuals sought for questioning as of August 19, 2005.

51. *USA v. Paracha*, 03-CR-1197, complaint and deposition of Janelle Miller, special agent, Federal Bureau of Investigation, Joint Terrorism Task Force (SD NY August 8, 2003).

52. Greg Smith, "Rag Trade Terror Plot," *New York Daily News*, August 22, 2003.

53. *USA v. Paracha*, 03-CR-1197, complaint and deposition of Janelle Miller.

54. Daniel Klaidman and Mark Hosenball, "Terrorism: Ties to a Qaeda Chief," *Newsweek*, August 18, 2003.

55. *USA v. Paracha*, 03-CR-1197, complaint and deposition of Janelle Miller.

56. Ibid.

57. David Rohde, "In U.S. Web, Pakistani Man Contacts Wife," *New York Times*, September 5, 2003.

58. Mueller, "Remarks of FBI Director Robert Mueller on the Summer Terrorist Threat"; Thomas, Klaidman, and Isikoff, "Enemies among Us."

59. Ibid.

60. Thomas, Klaidman, and Isikoff, "Enemies among Us."

61. "Seeking Information RE: Adam Gadahn," FBI, http://www.fbi.gov/terrorinfo/gadahn.htm (accessed August 19, 2005). He remains on the FBI's list of individuals sought for questioning as of August 19, 2005.

62. Amy Argetsinger, "Muslim Teen Made Conversion to Fury; Intelligence Sources Say Californian Was on Tape," *Washington Post*, December 2, 2004.

63. Thomas, "Al Qaeda in America."

64. John Ashcroft, Senate Judiciary Committee, *The Department of Justice's Efforts to Combat Terrorism*, 108th Cong., 2nd sess., June 8, 2004.

65. Thomas, "Al Qaeda in America." Al-Marri did have a run in with the law—a 1990 DUI charge in Peoria, Illinois.

66. *USA v. Al-Marri*, 03-CR-1044, indictment, p. 6 (CD IL May 22, 2003).

67. Ibid.

68. *USA v. Al-Marri*, 03-CR-1044, complaint, p. 4 (CD IL May 22, 2003).

69. Ibid., p. 11.

70. *USA v. Al-Marri*, 03-CR-1044, indictment, pp. 1–9 (CD IL May 22, 2003).

71. *USA v. Al-Marri*, 03-CR-1044, complaint, pp. 4, 9 (CD IL May 22, 2003).

72. Thomas, "Al Qaeda in America."

73. "Enemy Combatant Taken into Custody," Department of Defense press release, June 23, 2003.

74. "Al Qaeda Suspect Declared 'Enemy Combatant,'" CNN, June 24, 2003.

75. Michael Powell, "No Choice but Guilty," *Washington Post*, July 29, 2003.

76. *U.S. v. Al-Bakri*, 02-M-108, criminal complaint (WD NY September 13, 2002).

77. Ben Dobbin, "U.S. Knew of Terror Cell before 9/11," September 16, 2002.

78. "Sixth Suspect Charged in U.S. Terror Probe," Reuters, September 16, 2002.

79. "Sahim Alwan Sentenced for Providing Material Support to Al Qaeda," Department of Justice press release, December 17, 2003.

80. "Seventh Member of 'Lackawanna Six' in Custody," Associated Press, January 29, 2004.

81. "Man Added to 'Most Wanted Terrorist list," UPI, February 26, 2006.

82. John Lumpkin, "Yemeni-American Killed in Airstrike Was Alleged Leader of Buffalo Cell," Associated Press, November 12, 2002.

83. Mark Larabee, "Man Guilty in Gun, Fraud Case," *Oregonian*, June 18, 2002.

84. Lez Zaitz, "Palestinian Faces Weapons Charges in Portland Terror Case," *Oregonian*, June 10, 2004.

85. Ibid.

86. "Jeffrey Battle, Patrice Lamumba Ford Sentenced to 18 Years in Prison for Seditious Conspiracy," Department of Justice press release, November 24, 2003.

87. Ibid.

88. *USA v. October Martinique Lewis*, CR 02-399-06-JO, government's sentencing memorandum, pp. 13–14 (D OR November 25, 2003).

89. "Jeffrey Battle, Patrice Lamumba Ford Sentenced to 18 Years in Prison for Seditious Conspiracy."

90. Ibid.

91. Ibid.

92. *USA v. Steitiye*, 01-CR-396-BR, indictment (DC OR October 17, 2001); Larabee, "Man Guilty in Gun, Fraud Case."

93. Ibid.

94. Zaitz, "Palestinian Faces Weapons Charges in Portland Terror Case."

95. "Detenidos cuatro supuestos colaboradores de Al Qaeda," Ministerio Del Interior Web site, July 16, 2002, http://www.mir.es/oris/lucha/2002/p071601.htm (accessed August 19, 2005).

96. "Al Qaeda Suspect Videoed WTC," CNN, July 19, 2002.

97. "Spain Arrests Three Suspected Al Qaeda Members," *Christian Science Monitor*, July 17, 2002.

98. "1997 Al Qaeda Tape Shows World Trade Center and Other Landmarks," ABC News, March 3, 2003.

99. William Rashbaum, "Queens Man Admits Ferrying Aid to Al Qaeda in Pakistan," *New York Times*, August 11, 2004.

100. *USA v. Babar*, 04-CR-528, trial transcript (SD NY June 3, 2004).

101. Shannon and McGirk, "What Is This Man Plotting?"

102. *USA v. Babar*, 04-CR-528, trial transcript (SD NY June 3, 2004).

103. David Kaplan et al., "Hundreds of Americans Have Followed the Path to Jihad," *U.S. News & World Report*, June 10, 2002.

104. *USA v. Babar*, 04-CR-528, trial transcript (SD NY June 3, 2004).

105. Meyer, Krikorian, and Rempel, "Quiet Investigation Centers on Al Qaeda Aide in New York."

106. David Kaplan et al., "Hundreds of Americans Have Followed the Path to Jihad."

107. Meyer, Krikorian, and Rempel, "Quiet Investigation Centers on Al Qaeda Aide in New York."

108. Dan Eggen, "Pakistani American Aiding London Probe: Man in U.S. Custody Has Ties to Al Qaeda," *Washington Post*, July 25, 2005.

109. Ibid.

110. *USA v. Warsame*, 04-CR-29, affidavit of Kiann Vandenover in support of pretrial detention (D MN February 6, 2004).

111. Todd Nelson, "Suspect Faces N.Y. Extradition," *Saint Paul Pioneer Press*, December 13, 2003.

112. *USA v. Warsame*, 04-CR-29, affidavit of Kiann Vandenover in support of pretrial detention (D MN February 6, 2004).

113. *USA v. Warsame*, 04-CR-29, indictment (D MN January 20, 2004).

114. Ibid.

115. *USA. v. Elzahabi*, 04-MJ-26, criminal complaint and affidavit of Kiann Vandenover, FBI Special Agent (D MN June 25, 2004).

116. Ibid.

117. Ibid.

118. Ibid. Kanj was killed by Lebanese troops in 2000 while he was leading an attempted violent coup that sought to replace the Lebanese government with a fundamentalist Islamic state.

119. Ibid.

120. Ibid.

121. Ibid.

122. Tim Golden and Judith Miller, "Bin Ladin Operative Is Linked to Suspects," *New York Times*, September 18, 2001.

123. Ibid.

124. *USA v. Arnaout*, 02-CR-892, government's evidentiary proffer supporting the admissibility of coconspirator statements, p. 25 (ND IL January 31, 2003).

125. Steve Fainaru, "Sept. 11 Detainee Is Ordered Deported," *Washington Post*, September 4, 2002.

126. Tom Farmer, "Bin Ladin Operative May Have Lived in Dorchester for More than 10 Years," *Boston Herald*, September 19, 2001; *USA. v. Elzahabi*, 04-MJ-26, criminal complaint and affidavit of Kiann Vandenover, FBI Special Agent (D MN June 25, 2004).

127. Farmer, "Bin Ladin Operative May Have Lived in Dorchester for More than 10 Years."

128. Bill Schiller, "Terrorism Suspect Had Florida Link," *Toronto Star*, October 26, 2001.

129. Fainaru, "Sept. 11 Detainee Is Ordered Deported."

130. Golden and Miller, "Bin Ladin Operative Is Linked to Suspects."

131. Tom Godfrey, "FBI Forms Canuck Link," *Ottawa Sun*, September 23, 2001.

132. Schiller, "Terrorism Suspect Had Florida Link."

133. Golden and Miller, "Bin Ladin Operative Is Linked to Suspects."

134. Philip Shenon and Don Van Natta Jr., "U.S. Says 3 Detainees May Be Tied to Hijackings," *New York Times*, November 1, 2001.

135. Jody Wilgoren and Judith Miller, "Trail of Man Sought in 2 Plots Leads to Chicago and Arrest," *New York Times*, September 21, 2001.

136. "Boston Fugitive Arrested," Federal Bureau of Investigation press release, September 20, 2001; Wilgoren and Miller, "Trail of Man Sought in 2 Plots Leads to Chicago and Arrest."

137. *USA v. Al-Marabh*, 01-CR-244-A, plea agreement (WD NY July 8, 2002).

138. Fainaru, "Sept. 11 Detainee Is Ordered Deported."

139. Anne Marie Owens, "Judge Gets No Answers on Syrian: Former Toronto Suspect Jailed in U.S. for Border Breach," *National Post*, September 4, 2002.

140. "Selected Terrorism Investigations that Involved ICE and ICE Authorities," Immigration & Customs Enforcement press release, July 27, 2004.

141. *USA v. Hannan, et al.*, 01-C-R80778, criminal complaint and affidavit of Robert Pertuso, FBI special agent (ED MI September 18, 2001).

142. "Terror Supporters among Us," Associated Press, November 17, 2001.

143. *USA v. Koubriti, et al.*, 01-C-R80778, indictment (ED MI September 27, 2001).

144. Sarah Karush, "Federal Judge Dismisses Terrorism Charges against Two Men in Detroit, Citing Prosecutors' Zeal," Associated Press, September 3, 2004.

145. "Key Evidence in Terror Case Is Disputed; Feds Admit Troubles," Associated Press, August 12, 2004.

146. Ibid.

147. *USA v. Hassoun*, 04-CR-60001, second superseding indictment (SD FL March 4, 2004).

148. *USA v. Hassoun*, 04-CR-60001, indictment (SD FL January 8, 2004).

149. *USA v. Hassoun*, 04-CR-60001, In re: Adham Amin Hassoun. Adjustment of Status. File No. A74 079 096 (SD FL June 27, 2003).

150. Ibid.

151. "Benevolence International Foundation Articles of Incorporation," Florida Secretary of State, February 12, 1993.

152. "Treasury Designates Benevolence International Foundation and Related Entities as Financiers of Terrorism," Department of Treasury press release, November 19, 2002, http://www.treasury.gov/press/releases/po3632.htm (accessed July 24, 2006).

153. "Al Qaeda Network Operating in U.S," CBS News, June 26, 2002.

154. David Kidwell, "Bomb Suspect, Broward Man Spoke, FBI Says," *Miami Herald*, June 29, 2002.

155. Elizabeth Gillespie, "Accused Soldier Known for Opinions on Islam, Patriotism, and Guns," Associated Press, February 13, 2004.

156. Melanthia Mitchell, "Soldier Arrested in Washington State Wanted to Help al-Qaida," Associated Press, September 2, 2004.

157. Melanthia Mitchell, "Military Jury Convicts Soldier of Trying to Help al-Qaida," Associated Press, September 3, 2004.

158. "US Soldier Sentenced to Life in Prison for Trying to Aid Al-Qaeda," Agence France Presse, September 3, 2004.

159. Evan Thomas, "The Road to September 11," *Newsweek*, October 1, 2001. In October 2001, *Newsweek* reported that the FBI "privately estimated that more than 1,000 individuals—most of them foreign nationals—with suspected terrorist ties are currently living in the United States." *Newsweek* quotes a top US official, who stated, "The American people would be surprised to learn how many of these people there are."

160. 9/11 Commission, *The 9/11 Commission Report*, pp. 72–73.

161. Ibid., p. 164.

162. Ibid., p. 67.

163. *Meet the Press*, NBC, July 13, 2003.

164. *USA v. Haouari*, 00-CR-15, trial transcript, p. 550 (SD NY July 3, 2001); *USA v. Haouari*, 00-CR-15, trial transcript, p. 626 (SD NY July 5, 2001).

165. Martin Chulov, "Agents Finally Come Calling for Jihad Jack," *Australian*, November 19, 2004. In November 2004, Australian authorities arrested another KSM operative, "Jihad" Jack Thomas, who allegedly trained in Afghanistan. He was first identified by John Walker Lindh.

166. Ashcroft, "Remarks of Attorney General John Ashcroft on the Summer Terrorist Threat."

167. *In re Search Warrant of 4502 Whistler Court, Annandale, VA and Infiniti QX4*, affidavit of Special Agent Shawn Devroude (ED VA August 20, 2004).

168. R. Jeffrey Smith and Amy DePaul, "Al Qaeda 'Scout' Had Low Profile," *Washington Post*, June 21, 2003.

-4-

AL QAEDA INTERNATIONAL: ATTACKING US INTERESTS WORLDWIDE

Since [September 11], more than two-thirds of al-Qaida's known leadership have been captured or killed. The rest are on the run—permanently. And we are working with governments around the world to bring to justice al-Qaida's associates—from Jemaah Islamiyah in Indonesia, to Abu Sayef in the Philippines, to Ansar al-Islam in Iraq. Under President Bush's leadership, the United States and our allies have ended terror regimes in Afghanistan and Iraq. All regimes are on notice—supporting terror is not a viable strategy for the long term.

—Remarks by National Security Advisor Condoleezza Rice
at the McConnell Center for Political Leadership,
University of Louisville (March 8, 2004)

OVERVIEW

Al Qaeda affiliates around the world all share common primary objectives, including the amassing of regional political power through broadening the appeal and influence of Islamist fundamentalism and a pervasive hostile rejection of Western—especially American—political and cultural values. This ideology espouses the necessity of attacks against American and other Western interests.

It is important to understand the fundamental structural shift al Qaeda underwent in reaction to the successful US-led invasion of Afghanistan in 2001. Al Qaeda operatives who once trained and fought in Afghanistan were forced to flee, many finding refuge in regions that are considered fertile ground for jihad. Areas of Iraq, Saudi Arabia, the Caucasus, North Africa, and Southeast Asia, where governments exercised little control, became the new bases of operation. Out of necessity for its survival, al Qaeda transformed itself from a centralized network with worldwide connections to a diversified network without a strong central operational hub that relies on those very connections—elements and groups at regional, local, or cell levels—to plan operations and activities. Indeed, the operational center of gravity has shifted.

Today, what formerly was the central command under Osama bin Laden has become less operational and more ideological. Al Qaeda operations are now carried out by two types of groups—the affiliate and the provisional cell. Al Qaeda affiliates are groups that usually were established before their direct association with al Qaeda and retain considerable degrees of autonomy that vary from group to group. Their current leaders include veterans of al Qaeda Afghan training camps and mujahideen who fought against American and American-allied forces in Afghanistan. The provisional cells, some of which are homegrown, include those that carried out the London bombings in July 2005, the Madrid train bombings in March 2004, the Riyadh bombings in May 2003, and others. These cells are established for specific attacks or strategies and are tied more to the worldwide ideology of al Qaeda than to a regional Islamist ideology or cause, like the affiliate groups.[1]

This chapter addresses a selection of the affiliate groups across the globe that support al Qaeda's survival and directly threaten US interests in the areas in which they operate. This is not meant as a comprehensive discussion of all such groups, but instead is a focus on the larger players working actively against US interests. This chapter looks at al Qaeda affiliates, including al Qaeda in Iraq, the Islamist militant network in the Caucasus, the Algerian Salafist Group for Preaching Combat (GSPC), and Jemaah Islamiyah. Also found in this chapter is a treatment of the July 7, 2005, bombings in London, which were executed by an al Qaeda provisional cell.

ABU MUSAB AL-ZARQAWI AND AL QAEDA IN IRAQ

While bin Laden remained the ideological head of al Qaeda and a source of inspiration to thousands of jihadists, Jordanian-born Abu Musab al-Zarqawi, who had an often ambiguous relationship with bin Laden, became the central figure of the worldwide jihad movement until his death in early June 2006. From his base in war-torn Iraq, al-Zarqawi, through his maneuverings, became the fresh new face of an organization forced to splinter following the US invasion of Afghanistan. While bin Laden and the rest of al Qaeda's old guard remained trapped, presumably in the mountainous border region between Pakistan and Afghanistan, al-Zarqawi assumed the lead role of al Qaeda's military front, waging a bloodthirsty war against American interests and the Shiites of Iraq.

Although al-Zarqawi pledged allegiance to Osama bin Laden in October 2004, he commanded a semiautonomous campaign against the United States, its allies, and against fellow Muslims as well. Using brutal tactics such as beheadings, suicide bombings, and assassinations, al-Zarqawi breathed new life into an organization thought to have been marginalized by America's War on Terror. Not surprisingly, according to al-Zarqawi, terrorist acts against the United States are a priority: "Americans as you know, these are the biggest cowards that God has created and the easiest target. And we ask God to allow us to kill, and detain them, so that we can exchange them with our arrested shaykhs and brothers."[2]

Drawing from a pool of veterans from the war in Afghanistan and eager recruits from Islamic countries and Europe, al-Zarqawi founded and cultivated an al Qaeda affiliate in Iraq.[3] After being forced out of Afghanistan by coalition forces like many mujahideen, al-Zarqawi fled to Iran, where he stayed for a few months before heading to Iraq. It is in Iraq that al-Zarqawi teamed up with Kurdish Muslims.

The Creation of Ansar al-Islam

Ansar al-Islam was founded in December 2001 by the Kurdish cleric Mullah Krekar (aka Faraj Ahmad Najmuddin),[4] who then was operating small militant training camps out of northern Iraq. The original mission of this terrorist group was to establish an independent Islamic state in Kurdistan.[5] Its direct opposition was the secular Patriotic Union of Kurdistan (PUK), which controls the eastern part of the territory wrested from Saddam Hussein in 1991.[6] Since the 2003 US-led invasion of Iraq, Ansar al-Islam has played a significant role in the Iraqi insurgency targeting US troops and the evolving infrastructure of the emerging Iraqi state.[7]

To form Ansar al-Islam, Krekar reportedly solicited the help of al Qaeda and bin Laden[8] to fuse together a splinter group of his Islamic

Movement in Kurdistan (IMK) and Jund al-Islam (Soldiers of Islam), a group espousing a strict Wahhabi* lifestyle also descendant from the IMK.[9] This is where al-Zarqawi came into the picture. According to the chief of Kurdish security services in Sulaimaniya, Krekar became the emir of Ansar al-Islam and chose Abu Abdallah al-Shafii as his lieutenant.[10] Krekar gained legal refugee status in Norway in 1991 and he experienced a string of arrests and releases in Norway and the Netherlands beginning in 2002 for allegedly ordering terrorism attacks.[11] He is currently detained in Norway awaiting possible deportation.** In late 2003, al-Shafii, Krekar's Afghan Arab second in command, reportedly replaced Krekar as head of Ansar al-Islam.[12] Other Ansar leaders include the security chief, Ayub Afghani, who has met with bin Laden; Abu Wael;[13] and Husan al-Yamani, a Fallujah cell leader now in US custody.[14]

In 2003, another offshoot of Ansar al-Islam calling itself Ansar al-Sunna formed through the merger of Kurdish Ansar al-Islam operatives, foreign al Qaeda terrorists, and previously unaligned Iraqi Sunnis. Its self-declared leader is Abu Abdullah al-Hassan bin Mahmoud and his deputies are Hemin Bani Shari and Umar Bazynai.[15] The State Department reports that Ansar al-Islam may be giving credit for its attacks to Ansar al-Sunna, suggesting cohesive cooperation.[16]

Al-Zarqawi's followers, who had trained under him at his Herat-based terrorist camp in northwestern Afghanistan, had been dispersed during the 2001 US invasion of Afghanistan and later regrouped in Ansar al-Islam's camps in northern Iraq.[17] Al-Zarqawi had previously found refuge in the groups' camps in northern Iraq, actively recruiting accomplices from among Ansar's ranks for operations in Iraq.[18] He essentially used Ansar al-Islam as a vehicle to establish his own group, Tanzim Qa'idat al-Jihad Fi Bilad al-Rafidayn (al Qaeda Jihad Organization in the Land of the Two Rivers), more popularly known as al Qaeda in Iraq.

---

*Wahhabism, or Salafism, is an austere form of Islam within the Sunni sect that attempts to return to what its adherents believe to be unadulterated Islam as practiced by Muhammad and his companions. In order to achieve this, Salafis strip out what they see as *bida*, or innovations, from the practice of Islam as it has developed over the centuries. Most major Sunni terrorist groups, including Ansar al-Islam and al Qaeda, ascribe to Salafism.

**Krekar has expressed a desire to be deported to Iraq. In June 2006, he stated, "I hope to return to Iraq to fight the American troops" ("Radical Leader Hails bin Laden," *Gulf Daily News*, June 23, 2006). In the same statement, he said, "Osama bin Laden is a good man. I wish him a long life. He is a good Muslim and he is against the Bush administration" (ibid.).

Ansar al-Islam's Operations against the United States

Before the 2003 US invasion of Iraq, Ansar al-Islam limited its operations to attacks on PUK targets, launched from northern Iraq. When US air strikes destroyed Ansar al-Islam's camps at the beginning of the Iraq war, many of its fighters fled to Iran.[19] Since their return to Iraq, Ansar al-Islam followers have been responsible for attacks resulting in the deaths of hundreds of Iraqi civilians and police officers as well as high-profile government officials, including the former Iraqi Governing Council president and the governor of Mosul, Abdel Zahraa Othamn, better known as Izzadine Saleem.[20] Its most high-profile operations include the bombing of the Jordanian embassy in Baghdad on August 7, 2003, the United Nations headquarters in Baghdad on August 19, 2003, and numerous other attacks targeting Shiite mosques, secular Kurds, Iraqi police, and the oil infrastructure.[21] Ansar al-Islam, in tandem with al-Zarqawi, is believed to have supported and perpetuated insurgency attacks against the US military in places such as Fallujah, Tikrit, Bayali, and Baghdad.[22]

In videotaped public confessions, al-Zarqawi and his group claimed responsibility for the abductions and beheadings of civilians such as Nick Berg (American) in May 2004, Eugene Armstrong and Jack Hensley (American) and Kenneth Bigley (British) in September 2004, and Kim Sun-Il (South Korean), Georgi Lazov (Bulgarian), and Murat Yuce (Turkish).[23] Al-Zarqawi was also responsible for attacks on American forces in Iraq and Shiite targets, including religious shrines.[24]

Recruiting and Smuggling into Iraq

The recruitment network developed by al-Zarqawi extends beyond Iraq. Its membership, drawn from across the Middle East, consists of Saudis, Yemenis, Lebanese, Jordanians, Moroccans, Syrians, Palestinians, Afghans, and European Arabs.[25] The existence of a recruiting structure in each of these places is vital to its survival. Support of the terrorist group from both Syria and Iran, with their shared borders with Iraq, is critical for its ability to access what it needs. According to information supplied by Umar Baziyani, a captured lieutenant of al-Zarqawi, this network maintained a strong presence in the Iraqi town of Al Qaim—the site of large-scale US military operations—on the Syrian border, where weapons, cash, and fighters arrived with the help of al-Zarqawi's Syrian-based financiers. Indeed, Baziyani claims that Al Qaim was his entry point into Iraq until the US military pacified it, displacing insurgent operations to other areas.[26]

Iran, too, is thought to be facilitating the movement of al Qaeda in Iraq members as well as matériel to and from Iraq.[27] In August 2004, the commander of the Iranian Revolutionary Guards' Al Quds Corps, Brigadier General Qasem Solaimani, admitted that Iran provided facilities to al-Zarqawi and allowed the free passage of fighters across its border. Despite his hostility to Shiites, al-Zarqawi personally received sanctuary inside Iran after the US assault on Fallujah. According to Solaimani, Iran's support for al-Zarqawi stemmed from its fear of a federal secular Iraq cooperating with the United States.[28] On one occasion inside Iran, al-Zarqawi even reportedly met with Imad Mughniya, the infamous and much-sought-after Lebanese Shiite Hizballah leader. Mughniya (discussed in detail in chapter 6) has himself been active in finding and training fighters for Iraqi Shiite cleric Muqtada al-Sadr's Al Mahdi Army.[29]

Al Qaeda in Iraq has made significant inroads in Europe, drawing recruits from Muslim immigrant populations. Volunteers have traveled from Germany, France, and Italy to Iraq via safe havens in Iran, Turkey, and Syria.[30] A 2003 Italian indictment describes an al Qaeda–allied European support network commanded by al-Zarqawi that is based in northern Italy.[31] The network collected funds and trained volunteers, many from the large Iraqi Kurdish immigrant population scattered throughout Europe. The money and recruits destined for Ansar al-Islam camps in Kurdistan traveled through Turkey, Syria, or Iran. In both Syria and Iran, local secret services aided Ansar al-Islam's efforts.[32] The indictment names Mullah Fuad as al-Zarqawi's key Syria-based operative responsible for providing safehouses and smuggling services for Ansar al-Islam members en route to Iraq.[33]

Similar networks have appeared in Germany, where al-Zarqawi's associate Yasser Hassan, a Jordanian, recruited and sent militants through Iran to Afghanistan.[34] Raids in 2002 uncovered an al Tawhid cell (al Tawhid was the precursor name of al-Zarqawi's organization in Iraq prior to his public affiliation with al Qaeda), yielding hundreds of forged passports from countries including Iran, Iraq, Jordan, and Denmark.[35]

Al-Zarqawi's network has extended its reach into the United States and Europe as well. In August 2004, Ansar al-Islam elements in New York City were identified by the FBI and placed under surveillance.[36]

Al-Zarqawi Attacks US Interests Outside of Iraq

Despite American efforts to contain the violence, al-Zarqawi managed to carry out terrorist operations beyond the borders of Iraq. Like his al Qaeda predecessors, al-Zarqawi spread his network's tentacles to other parts of the globe, including the Middle East, Europe, Russia's North Caucasus, and possibly the United States.

As a native of Jordan, al-Zarqawi took an interest in the destabilization of his homeland. Since the early 1990s, al-Zarqawi, a former convict and soldier in the Jordanian army who later trained for jihad alongside Afghani warlord Gulbuddin Hekmatyar, had been implicated in a number of terrorist attacks on Jordanian soil, primarily against Western and American targets, in an effort to punish the Jordanian government for its alliances with the United States and Israel.

In 2000, Jordan indicted al-Zarqawi in absentia for "his role in the al Qaeda millennial bombing plot targeting the Radisson SAS hotel in Amman as well as other American, Israeli, and Christian religious sites in Jordan."[37] Prior to the Iraq war, he is believed to have ordered the October 2002 assassination of US Agency for International Development officer Laurence Foley in Amman, Jordan.[38]

In April 2004, security officials prevented an attack, which could have been the most devastating strike on Jordanian soil. In a televised confession, al-Zarqawi operative and suspected ringleader Azmi al-Jayyusi described in detail how he along with others planned to carry out a chemical attack against the US embassy and the General Intelligence Department (GID) headquarters in Amman. If successful, the attack could have killed as many as 80,000 people and wounded 120,000. In his confession, al-Jayyusi confessed to receiving $170,000 from al-Zarqawi.[39]

On August 19, 2005, al Qaeda in Iraq claimed responsibility for an attack against the US warship *Ashland* in the Jordanian port city of Aqaba. Terrorists fired three Katyusha rockets at the warship, overshooting it and hitting a military warehouse, killing its Jordanian guard. Although a relatively unknown group calling itself the Brigades of the Martyr Abdullah Azzam initially claimed responsibility, al Qaeda in Iraq issued a statement on its Web site soon thereafter stating, "God has enabled your brothers in the military wing of the al Qaeda in Iraq to plan for the Aqaba invasion a while ago."[40]

Then, on November 9, 2005, terrorists connected to al-Zarqawi struck three hotels in the heart of downtown Amman, Jordan. In a coordinated attack, three suicide bombers detonated explosives nearly simultaneously, killing more than fifty people and wounding over one hundred, including members of a bridal reception. The three attacks specifically targeted Western-affiliated hotel chains, including the Grand Hyatt, the SAS Hotel Radisson, and the Days Inn.[41]

The day after the attack, al-Zarqawi himself, in an audio recorded message, admitted sending the bombers to attack the hotels, claiming that they were sent to "destroy three dens of evil, where Jews, Christians, and others have long been gathering to fight Allah and his messenger." In the same message, al-Zarqawi threatened Jordan's King Abdullah II: "Your star is fading. You will not escape your fate, you descendant of traitors. We will be able to reach your head and chop it off."[42]

It so happened that the SAS Hotel Radisson was the same hotel that al-Zarqawi targeted for attack as part of the so-called millennium plot. Despite setbacks, al-Zarqawi, like bin Laden, remained patient, always keeping the intended target in sight, waiting for the most opportune moment to strike.

Al Qaeda in Iraq after the Death of Abu Musab al-Zarqawi

Al-Zarqawi was killed early in the evening on June 7, 2006, when the US military, acting on information provided by local informants and Jordanian intelligence, dropped two five-hundred-pound bombs in a house northwest of Baghdad.[43] Al-Zarqawi died shortly after he was pulled out of the rubble, despite being provided with medical treatment by US soldiers.[44] Within weeks of his death, he was lauded in video and audio statements from Osama bin Laden, who called him a "lion of jihad,"[45] and Ayman al-Zawahiri, who called him "the prince of martyrs."[46]

After the death of this most infamous terrorist and insurgent leader, the world wondered who would take control of al Qaeda in Iraq and what this one death would mean for the larger insurgency. Via the Internet, al Qaeda in Iraq identified its new leader as Abu Hamza al-Muhajir, a largely unknown figure, who pledged in a statement to persist in the war against "crusaders and Shiites."[47] Since al-Zarqawi's death, the Mujahideen Shura Council, an umbrella organization launched in January 2006 and originally composed of six insurgent groups including al Qaeda in Iraq, has taken a more visible and prominent role in leading the Sunni insurgency. Upon news of al-Zarqawi's death, some experts and pundits predicted the fall of al Qaeda in Iraq. The death of al-Zarqawi was certainly a blow to his terrorist group, but, despite numerous productive raids in the wake of his death, the operational capacity of the group and the insurgency at large has recovered and even gained momentum. The central morgue of Baghdad received 1,595 bodies in June 2006, 16 percent more than were received in the previous month, and twice as many as were received in June 2005.[48] As General George W. Casey, commanding general of the Multinational Force in Iraq, noted in a press conference two weeks after al-Zarqawi's death, "Al Qaeda is hurt in the aftermath of Zarqawi's death. . . . They're hurt, but they're not finished. And they won't be finished for some time."[49]

AL QAEDA IN THE CAUCASUS

Al Qaeda has found a safe haven in the Caucasus, where Chechens and Salafist Arabs, though divergent in their ultimate goals, share logistics, training, and manpower. As al Qaeda operatives were scattering out of Afghanistan in the early months of 2002, al-Zarqawi was restructuring the organization.[50] As noted above, al-Zarqawi moved to Iran[51] and then to northern Iraq,[52] where he coordinated with Ansar al-Islam. There, al-Zarqawi coordinated the movements of his closest lieutenants who had worked for him in the Herat training camp. While some traveled with him and joined Ansar al-Islam, others settled in the Pankisi Gorge,[53] a remote region of Georgia where the central government has little control.

Al Qaeda Moves into the Pankisi Gorge

For these al Qaeda militants, the Pankisi Gorge—mountainous and not patrolled by Georgian authorities—was a logistic windfall. The gorge, just a few miles from the Chechen border, is an ideal refuge for guerrillas who carry out attacks in Chechnya and then retreat and hide in its many caves. Groups of Chechen rebels and foreign terrorists established a presence there when the Russians reinvaded Chechnya in 1999. Subsequent political and military pressure has encouraged many of the rebels to leave.[54] The coexistence of the two groups in the Pankisi Gorge is a microcosm of the relationship between Arab fighters and local mujahideen throughout the Chechen conflict: the Chechens (at least initially) do not share the ideology and the goals of the Arabs, yet accept their help.

A Chechen fighter who had lived in Pankisi Gorge alongside the

Arabs told *Time*: "We are fighting for survival, while they are waging their jihad."[55] Some Chechen commanders did not want to be involved in plans to strike Western targets in Russia, arguing that was not their war.[56] Nevertheless, the al Qaeda Arabs and Chechens became full cooperating partners. Arab charities aided both, and the money they provided to those operating in the gorge region helped ensure their survival. For example, in December 2003 a military court in the former USSR state of Azerbaijan convicted the leaders of a Kuwaiti humanitarian organization (Revival of Islamic Heritage) of recruiting the ethnically Turkish and mostly Muslim Azeris to go to the gorge and then into Chechnya to fight the Russians.[57]

In early 2002, Georgian officials reported that a group of about sixty Arab computer, communications, and financial specialists; military trainers; chemists; and bombers arrived in the area.[58] Using sophisticated satellite-based and encrypted communications, the group focused on supporting both the activities in Chechnya of al Qaeda's Chechen commander, Ibn al-Khattab, and terrorists throughout the world who were planning attacks on US interests.

Al-Khattab was a Saudi from a wealthy family who, according to his older brother, had been given "a scholarship from the Saudi ARAMCO Company and went instead to Afghanistan in 1987 to join the ranks of the mujahidin against the Russians."[59] In 1995, he left Afghanistan to again fight the Russians, this time alongside the Chechens, and was al Qaeda's leader in that region. Al Qaeda recruits fought under al-Khattab's command. Al-Khattab was murdered by a poisoned letter in May 2002, presumably dispatched by the Russians.[60]

In 2002, the "Pankisi Arabs" tried to buy a large amount of explosives. Georgian security officials believe the bombs were intended for a major attack on US or other Western installations in Russia, but together with US authorities they disrupted the plan.[61]

Chemical Weapons Training in Pankisi Gorge

According to US military intelligence, al-Zarqawi dispatched Abu Atiya (Adnan Muhammad Sadik), a former chemical and biological weapons instructor at the Herat camp, to the gorge as his ambassador from the Caucasus.[62] Al-Zarqawi's expertise in this area is well known, and evidence of the testing of such materials has been uncovered in his Ansar al-Islam camps in northern Iraq as well.[63]

In Pankisi Gorge, Abu Atiya, a Palestinian who had lost a leg during the Chechen war, trained militants in the use of toxic gases.[64] Georgian authorities described the trainees as "Middle Eastern chemists skilled in poisons."[65]Abu Atiya was also behind a scheme to ship toxic substances from the camps in Georgia to Turkey.[66] The plot was discovered in July 2002 by the CIA, which warned Turkish authorities that a man (at the time wrongly identified as a Georgian) named Abu Atiya had sent a poisonous biological or chemical substance to an operative in Turkey. The concern was that the substance was to be used against American and Russian targets there.[67]

Abu Atiya then turned his attention to western European targets. Secretary of State Colin Powell told the UN Security Council that Abu Atiya "tasked at least nine North African extremists in 2001 to travel to Europe to conduct poison and explosive attacks."[68] French authorities discovered the first cell in December 2002 with their arrest of four militants who were planning to blow up the Russian embassy in Paris.[69] According to Nicolas Sarkozy, French interior minister, three of the individuals arrested (Merouane Benahmed, Menad Benchellali, and Noureddine Merabet) had received training in toxic substances from high-ranking al Qaeda operatives in training camps in Pankisi Gorge.[70] Moreover, the three were linked to the Algerian terrorist organization Armed Islamic Group, had fought with Afghan and Chechen mujahideen, and were part of a network that had previously planned attacks in Europe.[71] These terrorists claimed they sought to attack the Russian embassy to avenge the death of al-Khattab,[72] an influential figure for Islamic radicals worldwide.

The information gathered by French authorities after the arrests led investigators to another cell in northern London where a January 2003 search found caches of cyanide poisons, toxic gas, and ricin.[73] The discovery of ricin sent shock waves throughout the security agencies of Europe, where governments dreaded the possibility of a chemical or biological attack. The ensuing investigation led to arrests in Spain[74] and to the raid of London's Finsbury Park Mosque.[75] During a connected raid in Manchester, a senior British police officer was stabbed to death by an Algerian terrorist suspect.[76]

The European ricin investigation revealed how Pankisi Gorge and Chechnya played a significant role in al Qaeda's post-9/11 operations. The poison's manufacture was found to be consistent with the process described in al Qaeda manuals and in a notebook found by Russian Special Forces during a raid of a rebel base in Chechnya.[77] The French judge Jean-Louis Bruguière, who has prosecuted dozens of cases involving Islamic terrorism, declared: "There has been a change of sanctuary and a change of strategy. We know that some of the suspects were trained with chemicals in Georgia and Chechnya. The Chechens are experts in chemical warfare. And Chechnya is closer to Europe than Afghanistan."[78] The Russians did not miss the opportunity to reinforce their point that al Qaeda and Chechnya are linked. The Kremlin's spokesman for Chechnya, Sergei Yastrzhembsky, said of the ricin investigation: "The given fact speaks not just of ties, but of the use of Chechnya as a part of the network of international terrorist organizations."[79]

US Counterterrorism Efforts in Pankisi Gorge

In April 2002, the United States created a new plan to provide military training to Georgia.[80] Under the Georgia Train and Equip Program (GTEP), Georgian troops have received extensive training by US Special Forces to "enhance counter-terrorism capabilities and address the situation in the Pankisi Gorge."[81] The program officially ended in April 2004.[82] This military cooperation may have aided some successes. In October 2002, for example, Georgian authorities trumpeted the arrest of fifteen Arab militants linked to al Qaeda who were subsequently turned over to the United States.[83]

While some important arrests have been made, it is unclear whether the situation in Pankisi Gorge has improved. In February 2003, the Georgian State Security Ministry announced that al Qaeda members had fled the gorge.[84] Notwithstanding this, in May 2003, Russian deputy prosecutor general Sergei Fridinsky declared that about seven hundred terrorists were still operating in the region,[85] spurring a frank statement by a former Georgian defense minister who said that "they are out of Pankisi, but they are still moving freely along the border."[86] Given the cuts in Georgia's defense spending caused by the country's economic crisis, al Qaeda will likely continue to operate out of the gorge and cooperate with the Chechens in training and weapons development, raising concerns for US and regional security.

AL QAEDA AFFILIATES

Al Qaeda in the Arabian Peninsula

Not unlike al-Zarqawi's journey from Jordan to the camps of Afghanistan to Iraq, other hardened members of the mujahideen, fresh from battle, returned to their native Saudi Arabia, in an effort to bring the battle home, so to speak. Up until 2003, Saudi Arabia played down the fact that there were extremists living within the kingdom who were targeting not only the royal monarchy, but their American guests living there. Paradoxically, a series of attacks against American targets during 2003–2004 made it clear that a religiously conservative country that supported extremist groups internationally would no longer be immune from terrorist attacks.

The new wave of violence against American targets in Saudi Arabia began on May 12, 2003, when Saudi terrorists struck at three Western apartment complexes in Riyadh, killing thirty-five people, including nine American citizens, and wounding hundreds of others, including another fourteen Americans. In subsequent terror sweeps, Saudi Arabian police cracked down on those connected to the attacks. Among those arrested was Falls Church, Virginia, native Ahmed Omar Abu Ali (discussed in more detail in chapter 2), who was convicted by the United States of conspiring to plot the assassination of President George W. Bush.[87] According to the indictment, Abu Ali, who had been studying at the University of Medina, met with a number of al Qaeda operatives wanted in connection with the Riyadh attack.[88]

Through the course of the investigation, Saudi officials realized that the attack was not necessarily a random act of violence, but, in fact, part of a greater plot devised by bin Laden and al Qaeda to drive Americans out of the kingdom. Among those arrested in connection with the bombing was Ali Abd al-Rahman al-Faqasi al-Ghamdi (aka Abu Bakr al-Azdi). Al-Ghamdi, the accused mastermind of the Riyadh bombing, reportedly turned himself over to the authorities. According to *The 9/11 Commission Report*, al-Ghamdi was an associate of Khalid Sheikh Mohammed and was on the original list of twenty-six potential hijackers for the September 11 attacks, but was taken off at the last minute by bin Laden personally to be used for the future, in a "larger" operation.[89] Following the US strike on Tora Bora, officials believe that al-Ghamdi was among those who escaped to Iran, where officials believe that he may have linked up with al Qaeda commander Saif al-Adil, who is believed to have trained the 9/11 hijackers and helped coordinate the 1998 embassy bombings in Kenya and Tanzania.[90] During the trial of Ahmed Omar Abu Ali, *Newsweek* speculated that al-Ghamdi may have been the mysterious "coconspirator #4," whom the federal indictment claims conspired with Abu Ali to attack the United States.[91]

Another two militants—Turki al-Dandani and Yousif Salih Fahd Ala'yeeri—were also among those suspected in the Riyadh attack. Saudi officials claimed that al-Dandani and Ala'yeeri ran a number of al Qaeda training camps in the desert of the kingdom to prepare Saudis for jihad.[92] According to Saudi police, al-Dandani commanded the attack on the Riyadh compound. Only a week prior to the triple suicide bombing, Saudi police listed al-Dandani as the number one figure on a list of nineteen suspected militants wanted in connection with an arms cache found in Riyadh.[93] Turki al-Dandani worked closely with al Qaeda commanders Abd al-Rahim al-Nashiri and Walid Ba'Attash, both of whom were accused of plotting the attack on the USS *Cole*.[94] Before al-Dandani could be arrested, he blew himself up with a hand grenade.[95]

Ala'yeeri's connection to the greater al Qaeda nexus is rooted in Afghanistan. As a teenager, Ala'yeeri reached Afghanistan to train for jihad and quickly advanced through the ranks, becoming head of the Al Farouq camp, located near Kandahar. Establishing himself as a loyal member of al Qaeda, Ala'yeeri also became Osama bin Laden's bodyguard. In order to assist in al Qaeda's operation overseas, Ala'yeeri was sent to Somalia to assist in terrorist efforts there. Upon his return to Saudi Arabia, Ala'yeeri focused on raising funds for jihadists in Bosnia-Herzegovina, Kosovo, and Chechnya. While in Saudi Arabia, Ala'yeeri was given the responsibility of heading al Qaeda's branch on the Arabian Peninsula.

Following a police chase in Turba Ha'il, Saudi police shot and killed Ala'yeeri. *Al Watan* newspaper (Saudi Arabia) reported that Ala'yeeri was carrying a six-month-old handwritten letter from Osama bin Laden the day he was killed, in which it congratulated an unknown person for "achievements."[96]

Despite efforts to rein in terrorists, violence continued in Saudi Arabia unabated. Nearly six months after the Riyadh attack, terrorists struck again at the Al Muhayya residential compound. A truck laden with explosives entered the compound and detonated, killing seventeen people (including five children). Although the victims of the attack were mostly Saudis, it is possible that the terrorists may have intended to target Westerners who had been previously living there. According to an official working for the Muhayya residential compound, expatriate occupancy had dropped off significantly since the May attacks, from 97 percent to 53 percent.[97]

Following the attack, a group calling itself al Qaeda in the Arabian Peninsula claimed responsibility for the attack. The London-based Saudi newspaper *Al Majallah* reported on an e-mail sent by al Qaeda operative Muhammad al-Ablaj, in which he admitted to the strikes and warned of future attacks. In response to the number of Saudis who were killed in the attack, al-Ablaj referred back to the "unification and jihad" fatwa that called for the killing of Muslims who intermingle with Westerners.[98] This clear admission of guilt was an indication that al Qaeda, despite recent setbacks, found a way to root itself in Saudi Arabia, in an attempt to rid the kingdom of its Western presence.

As quickly as Saudi security forces hunted down and killed those responsible for the recent attacks, al Qaeda found replacements to fill its positions and continue its front. Following Ala'yeeri's death, the command was passed to Khalid al-Hajj, who was subsequently killed in the neighborhood of Al Nissam.[99] Upon al-Hajj's death, power was then transferred to Abdelaziz al-Muqrin, who proved to be a most capable lieutenant, pulling off a string of successful assassinations and attacks against Western targets, including Americans, in 2004.

Like Ala'yeeri, al-Muqrin began his terrorist career as a teenager, training in the camps of Afghanistan. Proving his self-worth, al-Muqrin moved up the al Qaeda ladder, at one point becoming a camp trainer. By the time he was in his midtwenties, he was sent to Algeria to fight alongside the Islamic Liberation Front, and was given the assignment to smuggle weapons from Spain to Algeria, via Morocco. After Algeria, he was sent to Bosnia-Herzegovina, where he both trained and participated in battle. During a brief stint in Somalia, where he was fighting against the Ethiopians, he was captured by Ethiopian authorities and subsequently extradited back to Saudi Arabia. Upon arrival, al-Muqrin was sentenced to four years in prison, but was released early due to good behavior, which included such acts as memorizing the Qur'an.[100]

Under al-Muqrin's leadership, Saudi Arabia witnessed a spike in violence committed by al Qaeda's Saudi branch. On June 8, 2004, American Robert Jacobs was killed by terrorists in Riyadh. Jacobs, who had been working for the Vinnell Corporation, a subsidiary of Northrop-Grumman that assists in the training of Saudi security forces, was ambushed by gunmen outside of his home and shot nine times in the head.[101] A videotape signed by al Qaeda in the Arabian Peninsula released soon after the murder showed an unidentified man, who appeared to be a Westerner, slumped over in his garage, while two men run up to him with guns drawn. The videotape was titled "The Murder of the Jewish American Robert Jacob, Who Worked for the Vinnell Espionage Firm."[102]

Five days after the Jacobs killing, another American, Kenneth Scroggs, who worked for Lockheed Martin, was killed outside his house. Later on that same day, Paul Johnson Jr., a coworker of Scroggs, was kidnapped by terrorists. In a videotaped recording, a gunman reported to be al-Muqrin threatened to kill Johnson in less than seventy-two hours unless Saudi Arabia released al Qaeda prisoners and Westerners left the Arabian Peninsula. Fulfilling their promise, al Qaeda executed Johnson, beheading him in the process and posting his grisly remains on its Web site. The same Web site posted a defiant message, "In answer to what we promised . . . to kill Paul Marshall (Johnson) after the period is over . . . the infidel got his fair treatment. Let him taste something that Muslims have long tasted from Apache helicopter fire and missiles."[103] According to the London newspaper *Al Sharq Al Awsat*, Paul Johnson's severed head would later be found in al Qaeda operative Saleh al-Awfi's refrigerator.[104]

This sudden rash of violence prompted Saudi Arabia to finally take action against what they perceived as a threat to their relative stability. In response to the Johnson beheading, security forces swept down on the al Qaeda cell in Riyadh. In what was later to be considered by Saudi Arabia to be a "major blow" to its al Qaeda presence, al-Muqrin was killed in a shootout between Saudi police and al Qaeda.[105]

Although al-Muqrin's death was arguably a crippling blow to al Qaeda's branch in Saudi Arabia, as always, al Qaeda found somebody to fill the role. A Web site claimed that Saleh al-Awfi, another of Saudi Arabia's most wanted terrorists, had been chosen to succeed al-Muqrin as al Qaeda commander in Saudi Arabia. According to news reports, al-Awfi, like his predecessors, cut his teeth in areas like Afghanistan, Bosnia, and Iraq. A former prison guard in the Saudi army, al-Awfi is also said to have met with bin Laden and Taliban leader Mullah Omar shortly before the attacks on September 11 and is reported to have traveled to Northern Iraq to join Ansar al-Islam.[106]

Under the leadership of al-Awfi, al Qaeda in the Arabian Peninsula continued to target American interests. On December 6, 2004, five terrorists stormed the US consulate in Jeddah. Although ultimately unsuccessful, the militants killed five non-American employees working at the consulate. Al Qaeda in the Arabian Peninsula posted a statement on its Web site claming responsibility for the attack.[107]

Since the attack in Jeddah, fewer attacks have occurred in the kingdom. Successful Saudi terror sweeps have apprehended or killed off a majority of the militants wanted on the original list of terrorists posted in May 2003. On August 18, 2005, al-Awfi was reportedly killed in a raid by security forces in the holy city of Medina.[108] Saudi Arabians would like to believe that the sudden drop in violence is a result of police action.

However, more than investigations, raids, and arrests are required to eliminate the presence of al Qaeda and other like-minded terrorists in Saudi Arabia. Al Qaeda in the Arabian Peninsula may be damaged, but it is far from defeated. On February 24, 2006, al Qaeda operatives drove two cars loaded with explosives to Saudi Arabia's most vital oil and gas facility at Abqaiq. Security guards managed to disable and detonate the vehicles with gunfire before they hit the main entrance. Had the terrorists been successful, they would have eliminated roughly 10 percent of the world's daily oil consumption.[109]

GSPC AND THE ALGERIAN CONNECTION

When the Algerian civil war broke out in 1992, it set in motion a chain of events and circumstances that led to the creation and widespread proliferation of a virulent terrorist group called the Salafist Group for Preaching and Combat, known by its French acronym, GSPC. In 1992, national elections were to take place in Algeria, which had been dominated by one political party, the secular National Liberation Front (FLN), since France granted the country independence in 1962.[110] As the decades passed, the FLN's dominance of political, economic, social, cultural, and religious life in Algeria had left much of the population disaffected. When the Islamic Salvation Front (FIS), a party that advocated Islamist rule, was established in 1989, it offered an alternative to the FLN that was attractive to large segments of the Algerian population. The party promoted a wide spectrum of Islamist beliefs, not all of which were militant in nature, but militants did represent a significant block in the FIS. Two years after its inception, the FIS was the largest political party in Algeria and was all but assured victory in the scheduled national elections; however, the FLN leadership panicked and canceled the elections with the support of the military. In January 1992, violence erupted and quickly spiraled into a bloody civil war defined by attrition, massacres, and militant Islam.[111]

Shortly after civil war engulfed Algeria, the Armed Islamic Group (GIA) was founded by FIS leaders who rejected the idea of a peaceful settlement to the conflict. Many of those who emerged as leaders in the GIA were veterans of the Afghan-Soviet conflict,[112] during which many had developed ties with Osama bin Laden and all had become skilled in guerrilla warfare. The GIA quickly assumed the dominant role in the war against the government and became noted for its proclivity for attacks against civilians, civil servants, and European expatriates. Its preferred techniques included bombings, assassinations, and slitting its victims' throats.

While the war raged, Algerian militants associated with the GIA left Algeria and settled in Europe, especially in Italy, Spain, France, Germany, and the United Kingdom. These immigrants developed networks to funnel arms, funds, and forged documents to support their fellow militants fighting in Algeria.

In 1994, GIA operatives hijacked an Air France flight from Algiers to Paris and three passengers were killed before French antiterrorism police secured the plane.[113] The hijacking was the first significant attack on European soil by Algerian militants connected to the GIA. The next summer and fall brought bombings to the streets of France.[114] Algerian militants connected to the GIA and later to the GSPC have plotted against European targets numerous times. Two of these attacks include the incident in Strasbourg, where a plot to bomb a Christmas market was foiled, and the London ricin threat where militants connected to the Finsbury Park Mosque planned to deploy the poison ricin as explained earlier in this chapter.

In 1997, public opinion in Algeria swayed dramatically against the GIA. The populace had become disenchanted with the Islamist terrorist group because of its bloodthirsty tactics directed toward the civilian populace. As part of its offensive against the government and its supporters, the GIA had massacred entire villages, indiscriminately killing men, women, and children.[115] Other terrorist groups, including Al-Gama'a al-Islamiyya of Egypt and the Libyan Armed Group, condemned the attacks and the GIA.[116] Into this vacuum stepped Hassan Hattab, also known as Abu Hamza. This GIA commander had left the group after the 1996 killing of former GIA leader Djamel Zitouni in 1996[117] and founded the

Salafist Group for Preaching and Combat in 1998.[118] The new terrorist group began with seven hundred in its ranks, but those numbers grew quickly, having reached four thousand by 2002.[119]

The GSPC shortly became the primary Algerian terrorist group and inherited the vast network of Algerian militants in Europe from the dishonored GIA. The GSPC also inherited and strengthened ties to Osama bin Laden's network of training camps, which were thriving in Afghanistan by this time. While the GIA had limited its ties to bin Laden, it has been stated that the GSPC was founded under the influence and direction of Osama bin Laden. This information was originally garnered in 1998 from Mohamed Berrached, a terrorist who worked for Hattab who was on trial for kidnapping and killing six people in Algeria.[120] According to Berrached's claims, which were based on his witnessing of a telephone conversation between bin Laden and Hattab, bin Laden had compelled Hattab to found the group in order to strengthen the image of the Islamist rebels in Algeria after it had been damaged by the GIA massacres.[121] Berrached said that bin Laden chose the group's name.[122] Berrached also claimed that GSPC operatives had trained at Hizballah camps in Lebanon and had connections with militants from Libya and Morocco.[123]

There has been some speculation as to the validity of Berrached's claims supported by suspicions that the Algerian government may have been exaggerating purported ties to guarantee and strengthen support from the West. However, any such skepticism about ties between al Qaeda and the GSPC has been proven hollow by intelligence findings regarding operational ties between the worldwide Islamist terrorist group network and the GSPC. These existent operational ties were present in certain failed GSPC plots against US targets including the 1999 millennium bombing plot against Los Angeles International Airport, the planned 2001 attack against the US embassy in Paris, and the 2002 plot against the US embassy in Rome.

Additionally, intelligence officials in Algeria and Europe have uncovered cooperation between high-level figures in al Qaeda and the GSPC. For ten days in July 2001, Mohamed Atta, the ringleader of the nineteen-member hijacking teams of the 9/11 attacks, was in Spain where he met with a terrorist cell of six Algerian GSPC operatives.[124] The members of this GSPC cell were arrested shortly after the 9/11 attacks in connection with the plot against the US embassy in Paris,[125] which is explored in further detail below. In 2002, Algerian officials reported that Emad Abdelwahid Ahmed Alwan, an al Qaeda leader who operated in northern and western Africa, had been killed in a military raid in Algeria where he was liaising with the GSPC.[126] Later that year, it was reported that three Saudis representing bin Laden had met with a senior GSPC member,[127] perhaps to reestablish operational links after Ahmed Alwan's death.

In November 2005, the Moroccan security services completed an in-depth investigation of militant networks in northern Africa. The investigation uncovered a high degree of interconnectivity among Islamist militants in the Maghreb countries—Morocco, Algeria, Tunisia, and Libya. Many of the findings of the investigation were based on intercepted messages from Khaled Abu Basir al-Jazairi, an al Qaeda liaison to operatives in several European nations who, acting on behalf of Mohamed Raha, a Moroccan who had brought foreign fighters through Syria into Iraq, contacted bin Laden. One of the messages spoke of GSPC plans to formally announce its association with al Qaeda. The messages also spoke of developing plans to unite all militant Islamist movements in North Africa under the GSPC, which would then be reformulated as a new group called Qaedat al-Jihad in the Arab Maghreb Countries.[128]

The investigation also discovered that the GSPC planned on reworking its recruiting efforts and funneling recruits from the Maghreb countries into GSPC training camps. From there, these newly trained terrorists would participate in jihad against the Algerian government and be sent through Syria into Iraq where they would carry out suicide operations on behalf of al Qaeda in Iraq. US officials have echoed this claim.[129] In the summer of 2005, French diplomats in Algeria expressed concerns about the GSPC allying itself with al Qaeda in Iraq out of a desire to contribute further to the global jihad movement.[130] The French have noted that Abu Musab Abdel Wadoud, the current leader of the GSPC, had been in contact with al-Zarqawi via written correspondence. The GSPC has formally professed support for al-Zarqawi, as well as bin Laden and Taliban leader Mullah Mohammed Omar, in the past.[131] The Moroccan investigation and the findings of various French and American services have effectively demonstrated high-level and still growing cooperation and affinity between the GSPC and al Qaeda.[132]

Rachid Boukhalfa, aka Abu Doha, a high-level GSPC figure, is now imprisoned in the city in which he was based: London. He is also under indictment in the United States for his involvement in the millennium bombing plot and has played a large role in planning other attacks against US targets. Details of the millennium bombing plot and the apprehension of Ahmed Ressam are given in chapter 1. As mentioned in that chapter, Abu Doha directed the attack and oversaw the cell that facilitated the plot after having met Ressam at an al Qaeda training camp in Khalden, Afghanistan—a camp that he founded with permission from Osama bin Laden.[133] Doha eventually left the camp and settled in London, where, according to a British judge on the case, Mr. Justice Ouseley, "he had brought cohesion to the Algerian extremists based [in the United Kingdom] and he had strengthened the existing links with individuals associated with the terrorist training facilities in Afghanistan and in Pakistan."[134] Abu Doha was arrested in 2001 in London in connection with the Strasbourg plot mentioned earlier that was to target a Christmas market with bombs. He was planning to flee to Saudi Arabia. A subsequent search of his London home resulted in the seizure of counterfeit identity documents and documents with notations for bomb-making chemicals. Abu Doha was heavily involved in facilitating the transport and training of Algerian militants in Afghanistan and coordinating the efforts of various cells in Europe and Canada.[135]

In 2001, Nizar Trabelsi, a Tunisian former soccer player and recovering drug addict, was arrested in Paris with a machine gun and plans for an attack on the US embassy in Paris.[136] A local restaurant was searched in connection with the arrest and 220 pounds of sulfur and thirteen gallons of acetone were seized along with other bomb-making materials.[137] Earlier that year, an underling of Abu Doha named Djamel Begal had been arrested at the Dubai airport for involvement in the same plot.[138] He had landed in Dubai en route to London from Afghanistan where he had met with Abu Zubaydah, the high-level al Qaeda commander who was captured in 2002.[139] Upon his arrest, Begal readily confessed and gave counterterrorism authorities a treasure trove of information about the operations of the GSPC. It was his confession that led to Trabelsi's arrest. Begal purportedly recruited Zacarias Moussaoui, the alleged twentieth hijacker, and Richard Reid, the shoe bomber.[140] Begal also had ties to Takfir Wal Hijra, a terrorist movement once led by Ayman al-Zawahiri.[141] The next year, Abu Doha set his sights on another US embassy in another major European capital. According to Italian authorities, Doha was behind a GSPC Milan cell that, in 2002, aimed to use cyanide to poison the water supply and ventilation system of the US embassy in Rome.[142] Another report stated that the cell planned to attack the embassy with a van packed with explosives.[143]

In 2003, it was alleged by security forces from Algeria and Mali that there was a GSPC plot to bomb the US embassy in Bamako, Mali. However, the threats did not result in any changes in the security alert level at the embassy. Some have speculated that Malian authorities may have fabricated the threat on their own or manipulated intelligence in order to gain US support for their security services.[144]

Concern in the US intelligence community over the threat posed by the GSPC has steadily grown, cultivated by the close relationship the group has with al Qaeda, and its willingness to directly attack US targets in Europe, North Africa, the Middle East, and in America itself. The development of the GSPC and its pattern of alignment with like-minded North African militant groups and the al Qaeda network clearly delineates this terrorist group as emblematic of the current nature of the al Qaeda affiliate group.

TERROR IN SOUTHEAST ASIA

Jemaah Islamiyah

The Jemaah Islamiyah (JI) organization is the largest radical Islamist terrorist group in Southeast Asia. It has ideological and operational relations to al Qaeda.

Traditionally, Islam in Southeast Asia has been a pluralistic, democratizing force. For example, Indonesia's (and the world's) largest Muslim organization, Nahdlatul Ulama (NU), played a major role in the democratization movement opposing General Suharto's dictatorship. NU members pushed for democratic pluralism, human rights, and interfaith tolerance.[145]

At the same time, Southeast Asia was also experiencing a contradictory global reformist movement that spread through Islam in the twentieth century. The "reformers" promoted strict, fundamentalist interpretations of the Qur'an. Suharto's regime had limited the expression of political Islamic views. As the detailed White Paper presented to Singapore's parliament in January 2003 explains, following Suharto's resignation in 1998, this suppression ended and dozens of new Islamic political parties were formed. During this period, several members of the organization now known as Jemaah Islamiyah returned to Indonesia.[146]

Jemaah Islamiyah, meaning "Islamic Communities," is descended from another organization, Darul Islam ("House of Islam"), whose goal was to expel the Dutch colonial presence from Indonesia and create an Islamic state. Following the end of Dutch rule, Darul Islam continued to fight the Indonesian government until 1962, when it was suppressed; its leaders remained underground in Indonesia. In 1985, many of them fled the Suharto regime and moved to Malaysia. During the next decade, they renamed the organization Jemaah Islamiyah and recruited members in Singapore and Malaysia.[147] As an organization, JI is particularly amorphous. Membership in the organization is informal and largely based on ideological beliefs spawned by Islamic schools throughout certain countries of Southeast Asia.

Mission

JI's mission is spelled out in a short operational and philosophical manual, *Pedoman Umum Perjuangan Jemaah Islamiyah* (PUPJI), or *General Guide to the Struggle of JI*. This document envisions the creation of a Southeast Asian caliphate, or Islamic state. Containing Indonesia, Malaysia, Singapore, Brunei, and the south Philippines, this Sharia state would "guarantee the implementation of Islamic law with integrity." The PUPJI also states JI's ultimate goal of "the return of the caliphate and the sovereignty of Allah's law in the four corners of the earth."[148]

Operations in Concert with al Qaeda

In 1999, JI joined an alliance of at least nine militant Islamic organizations in Southeast Asia known as the Rabitatul Mujahidin, or Mujahideen Coalition. This coalition shared finances, arms, training, and personnel resources. It included the Moro Islamic Liberation Front (MILF), an organization seeking a separate homeland in the southern third of the Philippines for the Islamic Moro ethnic group, and two unnamed Thai and Bangladeshi organizations. The Rabitatul met in 1999 and 2000 in Malaysia to plan attacks within Malaysia against Philippine entities. The Philippines were targeted because of the nation's crackdown against MILF activities in the southern part of the state. In August 2000, a bomb exploded in Jakarta near the Philippine ambassador's home, killing two and injuring twenty. A few months later, JI began its own attacks. On Christmas Eve in 2000, it carried out multiple church bombings in Indonesian cities, leaving nineteen dead and forty-seven wounded. In addition, twenty-two died in a bombing of a passenger train in Manila, also in December 2000.[149]

These attacks pale in comparison to JI's most successful operation—the bombing of a nightclub on the Indonesian island of Bali. In October 2002, a suicide bomb in the nightclub, located in Bali's major tourist district, caused patrons to rush onto the street. Once hundreds of clubgoers were outside, a huge car bomb detonated. The explosion killed 202 people and maimed about 300 more. A concurrent bombing occurred three hundred yards from the US consulate in Indonesia. Interrogations of suspects revealed that the consulate was the target. Though this second attack did not cause any damage, JI's attempt at synchronized attacks is reminiscent of al Qaeda, which has made multiple coordinated strikes its calling card.[150]

Eleven days after the Bali attack, the United States designated JI a terrorist organization.[151] Two days later, the United Nations added JI to its terrorist list.[152]

Indonesian authorities believe that JI also perpetrated the bombing of the Marriott Hotel Jakarta in August 2003. This suicide car bombing outside the hotel's main entrance killed 12 and wounded 150.[153] The bombers used a cell phone to detonate the explosives, the same method employed in the Bali attack. The specific mix of explosives detected in the wreckage of the Marriott attack—RDX and TNT—matched that from Bali as well.[154]

In addition to operational similarities, Indonesian police had intelligence indicating that JI was targeting the area surrounding the Marriott before the bombing occurred, gleaned from documents found a month before when they arrested seven suspected JI members in Jakarta.[155] The strongest evidence connecting JI to the Marriott attack came from a severed head found at the scene. Police reconstructed the head and showed it to two JI members jailed for their alleged involvement in the Christmas Eve church bombings and other attacks; they identified the man as Asmar Latinsani. They also admitted to recruiting him into JI.[156] Police believe Latinsani was the driver of the vehicle containing the explosives.[157]

In another JI operation in August 2004, one year after the Marriott bombing, a car bomb exploded outside the Australian embassy in Jakarta. The attack killed 9 and wounded 173.[158] Forty-five minutes before the bombing, Indonesian police received a mobile phone text message that threatened an attack on a Western embassy unless police released the Islamic cleric Abu Bakar Bashir, whom Indonesian authorities consider the spiritual leader of Jemaah Islamiyah.[159] Bashir's founding role in JI is discussed later in this chapter.

A day after the attack, a statement on a radical Islamic Web site, purportedly from JI, claimed responsibility:

> We decided to settle accounts with Australia, one of the worst enemies of God and Islam. . . . A mujahideen brother succeeded in carrying out a martyr operation with a car bomb against the Australian embassy. . . . We advise Australians in Indonesia to leave this country or else we will transform it into a cemetery for them. We advise the Australian Government to withdraw its troops from Iraq. . . .Our jihad will continue until the liberation of the land of Muslims.

The statement was signed "Jemaah Islamiyah in eastern Asia—department of information—Indonesia."[160]

On October 1, 2005, JI launched another attack, again in Bali at a bar and shopping area. These suicide bombings took the lives of twenty-two victims and the two suicide bombers.[161] Four of the victims, and likely the main targets, were Australian. Indonesian authorities claimed this attack was indicative of a new JI strategy that will implement smaller and easily hidden explosives against even softer targets.[162] Also noteworthy was the use of operatives from outside of the JI network, who may have trained in the Philippines, in preparing the attack, although it is believed by intelligence agencies that Zulkarnaen, currently the military chief of JI, was the ultimate planner behind the attacks and directed two operatives, Noordin Mohamed Top—a Malaysian—and Azahari bin Husin, who remain on the run after an intensive manhunt.[163]

Some JI plans have been thwarted. When Singaporean authorities arrested several JI suspects in December 2001 and September 2002, they gained a gold mine of information about the organization's schemes and methods. Several attacks against the United States in Singapore had been devised, and al Qaeda operatives were often involved in their planning.

One plot focused on coordinated truck bombings on the US and Israeli embassies and US naval facilities. The operation involved the al Qaeda operative "Sammy," a Canadian Arab whose real name is Mohammed Mansour Jabarah, who was to work with JI cell members. JI members suggested the Australian and British high commissions, as well as American corporate buildings, as possible targets. Local JI members conducted extensive video surveillance on the sites. Before the attacks were to occur, the local JI operatives were to leave Singapore and the actual suicide bombers were to be brought into the country. Sammy acted as a main link between al Qaeda and JI.[164]

Another JI plot entailed attacking US servicemen and family members as they rode in a shuttle bus from US naval facilities to a transit station. In 1999, JI conducted detailed surveillance, making videos and drawing maps of the targeted station. The leader of JI in Malaysia, Faiz bin Abu Bakar Bafana, traveled to Afghanistan to share the surveillance and attack plan with one of bin Laden's top associates, Mohammed Atef. Atef ordered Faiz to proceed with the attack.[165] A few months later, the leader of a Singaporean JI cell, Mohamed Khalim bin Jaffar, also traveled to Afghanistan to explain the transit station attack to al Qaeda lieutenants; for unknown reasons, it was never attempted. The surveillance maps and video for the plot were found in Atef's home during the US invasion of Afghanistan in 2001.[166]

A third prospective attack targeted US naval vessels stationed off the northeast shore of Singapore. This operational plan displayed the impressive technical savvy of the Singapore JI cell. A suicide vessel loaded with explosives would ram into a naval ship as it passed through the narrowest part of a channel, where the US ship would be unable to maneuver and evade the suicide vessel. The cell also planned a route that would enable the suicide ship to avoid visual and radar detection until the attack was imminent. JI conducted surveillance of naval vessels from a nearby restaurant, but lacked the resources to execute the plan.[167]

Yet another plot involved attacks against US and Israeli soft targets. Members of a JI cell established in Singapore after the 9/11 attacks reconnoitered the Singapore American School and various American and Israeli businesses. They studied the movements of US guards and obtained photos and maps of the target buildings. But after the wave of arrests of JI suspects in Malaysia in 2001, this particular JI cell became dormant.[168]

JI also conceived plans to attack various Singaporean interests within the country in a way that would throw the blame on Malaysia. This ambitious plot envisioned an ensuing war between the nations that would destabilize both governments, enabling JI to overthrow them and then create an Islamic state spanning Malaysia and Singapore. JI cased public facilities such as airports, water treatment facilities, and transit stations.[169]

Finally, according to Cambodian authorities, JI-affiliated operatives had made plans to bomb the American and British embassies in Phnom Penh in 2002.[170]

Leadership

As mentioned above, JI was created in Malaysia by Darul Islam leaders who fled Singapore. Two of the key figures were the Indonesian clerics Abdullah Sunkgar and Abu Bakar Bashir. Sungkar, who fought in the Afghan war in the 1980s, arranged for at least eleven JI recruits to receive training in al Qaeda's camps in Afghanistan.[171] This cooperation helped foster the operational relationships between JI and al Qaeda.

Abu Bakar Bashir became the spiritual leader of Jemaah Islamiyah following Sungkar's death in 1999. Several JI operatives, including suspects in the Bali and Marriott bombings, attended Bashir's *pesantren* (madrassah) in Indonesia.[172] Information linking Bashir to the Christmas Eve bombings in 2000 led to his arrest by the Indonesian authorities—coincidentally, one week after the Bali bombing.[173]

Prosecutors charged Bashir with being the head of JI and with plotting to overthrow the Megawati government in Indonesia, along with other more minor offenses. Bashir maintained through the trial that Jemaah Islamiyah did not exist. In the end, the court dismissed the major charge that Bashir controlled JI, and no connection between Bashir and the Bali attack was proved. Found guilty of being involved in the plot to kill Megawati and some lesser charges (including forgery), Bashir was sentenced to four years in prison. An appeals court and later the Indonesian Supreme Court cut his sentence first to three years, and then to eighteen months.[174]

Bashir completed his sentence in April 2004, only to be rearrested by Indonesian police on the belief that he had approved the Bali bombing and other attacks. The prosecution attempted to implicate him as the head of JI. At the trial, a former instructor of a JI training camp identified Bashir as the emir, or spiritual leader, of the group. The instructor also claimed that Bashir stayed for a few days at the training camp and spoke at graduation ceremonies for the recruits.[175]

Bashir was convicted in March 2005 of participating in the Bali conspiracy by encouraging the bombers and was sentenced to thirty months in prison, which was upheld by an Indonesian Appeal Court. [176] An Indonesian court then reduced his sentence by four months and fifteen days for "behaving very well."[177]

Bashir was released from prison on June 14, 2006, to the stern objection of the Australian government. In an interview given two weeks after his release, he noted the necessity of enforcing Islamic law and stated, "If the world wants peace, then Islamic leadership is a must. This comes from God and his messengers, not from me."[178]

The current JI leader in the spotlight and elusive alleged architect of the most recent Bali bombing, Zulkarnaen, began his militant career in Pakistan in the 1980s, where he was trained.[179] He became a protégé of Sunkgar, one of the JI founders mentioned above, and later founded the JI special operations unit.[180] While his participation in this recent attack has given Zulkarnaen much attention, his past involvement in JI activities merited him previous notice. He is believed to have taken part in the planning of the first Bali bombing and the Marriott bombing and may have actually prepared the bombs themselves.[181] When the organization's former leader, Hambali (addressed below), was captured in Thailand in August of 2003, Zulkarnaen took over JI operations.[182]

Hambali and al Qaeda

Abdullah Sungkar and Abu Bakar Bashir founded JI and served as its spiritual leaders, but the JI's most effective operational leader was Riduan Isamuddin, better known as Hambali. Thai authorities captured Hambali in August 2003 and handed him over to US authorities. The CIA has since interrogated Hambali, who has revealed information about JI operations as well as its extensive cooperation with al Qaeda.[183]

Born and raised in Indonesia, Hambali went to Malaysia in the 1980s, where Sungkar and other radicals had fled to escape Suharto's repression of political Islam. Hambali met Sungkar and embraced his vision of creating a Southeast Asian caliphate. Sungkar persuaded Hambali to join the Afghan-Soviet battle. After attending a training camp, Hambali went to Afghanistan in 1986 where he fought alongside the mujahideen for eighteen months. Following his return, he maintained contact with Sungkar and eventually became the JI's head of operations for the Malaysia and Singapore region.[184] Southeast Asian intelligence has linked Hambali with many of JI's attacks in recent years. Indonesian intelligence believes that Hambali masterminded the 2002 Bali attack and arranged for the financial resources to carry it out.[185]

In 1996, Khalid Sheikh Mohammed met with Hambali. The two began cooperating and formed the major nexus between al Qaeda and JI. For example, KSM sent the al Qaeda operative Issa al-Britani to Malaysia so that Hambali could tutor him. Al-Britani was later sent to the United States to reconnoiter "potential economic and 'Jewish' targets in New York City."[186]

In 1998, bin Laden asked JI's leaders, Bashir and Sungkar, to ally themselves with al Qaeda to further their common goals. Hambali began working closely with both KSM and Mohammed Atef (Atef's greenlighting of the JI plot to attack a US shuttle bus in Singapore was discussed earlier in this chapter). The relationship between the two organizations was mutually beneficial. For example, at one point al Qaeda needed a new scientist to command its biological weapons program. Hambali obliged by sending a JI member, Yazid Sufaat, to bin Laden's deputy, Ayman al-Zawahiri, in Kandahar. Sufaat tried to culture anthrax for al Qaeda in 2001 in a lab in Afghanistan. Before shifting to al Qaeda's weapons program, Sufaat was involved in JI's Christmas Eve church bombings.[187]

Support to 9/11 Operatives

Perhaps most important, Hambali aided al Qaeda members who were later involved in the USS *Cole* bombing and the 9/11 attacks. In late 1999, KSM had just trained three al Qaeda operatives in Karachi: Nawaf al-Hazmi, Khalid al-Mihdhar, and Tawfiq bin Attash. In 2000, bin Attash aided the USS *Cole* bombing, and al-Hazmi and al-Mihdhar were among the nineteen 9/11 hijackers. Hambali helped the men with travel and lodging costs as they moved through Kuala Lumpur, Malaysia. He even arranged for them to stay at the home of Yazid Sufaat in Kuala Lumpur.[188]

In addition to coordinating operations with Hambali, KSM apparently had a strong philosophical impact on him. Initially, Hambali's focus was attacking the interests of secular Southeast Asian governments. KSM claims he persuaded Hambali to instead concentrate on attacking American interests in Southeast Asia to damage the US economy.[189] The numerous unfulfilled JI plans against American military and economic plans detailed earlier likely reflect KSM's influence.

The travel of JI members to Afghanistan to brief al Qaeda members and Mohammed Atef's approval of the transit station plot shows that in some cases JI was subservient to al Qaeda. JI's three major leaders—Sungkar, Bashir, and Hambali—are either dead or in custody. Hambali, who was most involved in operational activities, is probably the most important catch. Due to his key role in coordinating activities with al Qaeda, his capture has probably weakened not just JI but also al Qaeda's operational ability in Southeast Asia. Yet JI has proved that even without Hambali, it is still capable of major attacks. The Australian embassy bombing in Jakarta and the 2005 Bali bombing show that JI is capable of overcoming arrests of key leaders and replacing its leadership; it is not a static organization.

Despite JI's expressed anger at the coalition's occupation of Iraq, in all likelihood the departure of Western troops would not bring a stop to its attacks; however, the great unpopularity of the Iraq war in Indonesia may aid JI's recruitment of new members. But the 2002 Bali bombings, JI's most deadly attack, occurred well before the invasion of Iraq. The organization's grand goal, a Southeast Asian caliphate, is independent of events outside the region.

Banning Jemaah Islamiyah?

The most recent Bali bombings have stirred contentious debate both within Indonesia and around the world about banning Jemaah Islamiyah. Advocates on both sides of the issue come from all segments of the political and religious spectrum. In the first days after the most recent attacks, when many Western governments called for the banning of JI, Indonesia, the world's most populous Muslim nation, reacted unenthusiastically, claiming the organization was too nebulous for a ban to be effective. The Indonesian government's reluctance may also be due to sympathy for radicals among many influential figures there and a fear of banning an organization whose name translates to "Islamic Communities" in a country where many citizens see the current government as playing the role of minion to the West.[190]

Shortly after the bombings, leading figures in the Australian government, most notably Prime Minister John Howard and Foreign Minister Alexander Downer, said that a ban would be ineffective.[191] However, the Australian Labor Party was successful in pressuring the government to compel Indonesia to ban JI, arguing that if a JI ban is instituted, the numerous schools operated by JI elements could be shut down, thus eliminating an important recruiting venue for the terror group.[192] The Australian government has formally requested through Foreign Minister Downer and South Australian Premier Mike Rann that Indonesia ban JI, and while the Indonesian government is considering new antiterrorism measures, it is still unclear if a formal ban will be instituted.[193]

THE LONDON BOMBINGS

The 2005 London suicide bombings on the metro transit system present an important case study in the fundamental shift in al Qaeda procedures. With most of al Qaeda's pre-9/11 operatives either killed or captured and al-Zarqawi now dead, al Qaeda will increasingly be dependent on home-grown operatives, loyal to the cause of waging Islamic jihad, but who have tenuous ties to the organization itself. Muslims known as "clean skins" with no prior history of terrorist activity, but driven by their rabid hatred for Western culture, will be increasingly utilized for terrorist attacks. More alarmingly, Muslim converts, like Jose Padilla and the Belgian suicide bomber Muriel Degauque, who may illicit little notice from authorities because of their ethnic makeup, will also be used as future operatives.

On July 7, 2005 (7/7), London experienced its most violent day since the Battle of Britain during World War II. In a series of four coordinated suicide bombings, timed to coincide with a G8 conference in Scotland, that targeted London's public transportation, fifty-two people were killed and over seven hundred were injured. Three of the blasts occurred almost simultaneously at 8:50 AM in the underground train system on trains full of commuters on their way to work.[194] The fourth blast occurred approximately an hour later on a bus.[195] The bombers were Mohammad Sidique Khan, Shehzhad Tanweer, Hasib Mir Hussain, and Germaine Lindsay. All of the bombers were native-born Britons of Pakistani descent except for Lindsay, a Jamaican by birth who had moved to Britain.[196]

British authorities reacted and a flurry of activity began. Within five days, six houses had been raided in the Leeds area and there had been many controlled explosions at other sites. At some of these sites, TATP, the explosive used in the attacks, was found and seized or detonated. Police found explosives in the car Germaine Lindsay had driven to meet the other bombers in Luton.[197] Lindsay was connected to a bomb factory in Leeds.[198] Other addresses were later searched in the West Yorkshire area and in Aylesbury. Within ten days, eight hundred witnesses had been interviewed and six thousand CCTV (closed-circuit TV) tapes were in the process of being analyzed.[199] Claims of responsibility from two groups—the Secret Organization of al Qaeda in Europe and Abu Hafs al-Masri Brigade—were quickly discredited.[200]

The three men from Leeds had bonded at a government-funded community center located in the Beeston area of Leeds called Hamara. Khan and Tanweer may have originally met at the Iqra Learning Center, a shadowy bookstore in Leeds where they both volunteered, which may have served as a local center for indoctrination.[201] In 2001, Khan and some of his friends were asked to leave the mosque at which they worshiped for upsetting other worshipers with their strict Wahhabi assertions and beliefs. In the beginning of 2003, Khan went on the Hajj pilgrimage to Mecca. When he returned, he began to be repeatedly delinquent from his duties at the school he worked at and often missed work for weeks. Parents at the school noted that, upon his return from the Hajj, he changed noticeably and was more forceful with the children. Investigators believe that he met Germaine Lindsay through a paintball group in the Leeds area at this point in time.[202]

Another young man of Pakistani origin who was a close confidant of Khan is believed by investigators to have originally been slated to be one of the London bombers. This man was in Pakistan around the same time period as Khan and Tanweer and likely attended a terrorist training camp. It has been reported that Hussain was not one of the original four and took this man's place in the plot.[203]

Al Qaeda Connections

While official British reports claim there is no firm evidence demonstrating any connection between the four bombers and the larger al Qaeda network, it is clear that these ties do exist. Sources in the Pakistani intelligence community are less ambiguous about these ties—they are certain that they exist. All of the bombers went on lengthy trips to Pakistan where authorities allege they met with terrorists connected to al Qaeda. Khan and Tanweer flew to Karachi, Pakistan, a city where al Qaeda is known to have operated, in November 2004 and spent three months in that country. Hussain was in Karachi five months before Khan and Tanweer's arrival.[204] Khan and Tanweer had both previously traveled to Pakistan individually. Germaine Lindsay went to Pakistan and possibly to Afghanistan. All four men later reported that they had lost their passports and British authorities believe that they did so in order to avoid scrutiny of their trips to Pakistan.[205] These trips raised many eyebrows in the worldwide intelligence community. Additionally, Tanweer made several phone calls to a stolen cellular phone in Pakistan up until July 4—three days prior to the attacks.[206]

The main issue of concern regarding the Pakistan trips is the men with whom the 7/7 terrorists met and the organizations those men are associated with. Pakistani authorities told the *Times* in London that their investigations have led them to believe that Khan and Tanweer met with the mastermind of the London attacks in a hotel in Karachi at which the two stayed for a week upon their arrival in Pakistan.[207] After leaving the hotel, they traveled to Lahore, where Tanweer attended a madrassah that has been identified as having ties with militants.[208] Pakistani authorities have claimed that Tanweer was in touch with terrorists from Lashkar e Taiba and Jaish e Mohammed, two terrorist groups tied to al Qaeda that strive for Kashmiri independence.[209] It is also believed that Khan and Tanweer may have attended a training camp in Pakistan or Afghanistan during this trip where they received instruction on explosives.[210]

The British government believes Khan received some sort of terrorist training while in Pakistan[211] and acknowledges that certain meetings in Pakistan "suggest advice or direction may have been provided from individuals there."[212] Pakistani security officials are certain that Khan and Tanweer attended an al Qaeda camp and perhaps were taught by Abu Hamza Rabia, an al Qaeda terrorist killed late in 2005 who was described as the group's number three commander.[213]

While Khan was in Pakistan, he met with Mohammed Junaid Babar, who pleaded guilty in the United States in 2004 to providing material support to al Qaeda. Babar has also admitted to setting up terrorist training camps in Afghanistan and aiding in a failed plot to bomb British pubs, train stations, and restaurants in 2004.[214] He was a main player in the Al Muhajiroun terrorist group's cell in Queens, New York.[215]

Al Muhajiroun was founded and led by Omar Bakri Muhammed in London in the mid-1990s and its leadership has repeatedly expressed solidarity with bin Laden. Omar Bakri Muhammed has claimed to represent bin Laden on occasion. He once referred to the nineteen hijackers from the 9/11 attacks as "the Magnificent 19" and has insisted that the United States is a legitimate target for Muslims to attack with any weapons that may be available.[216]

Khan and Tanweer also met with a Briton named Zeeshan Siddique in Pakistan.[217] Zeeshan Siddique, who was arrested in May 2005 in Peshwar, Pakistan, is also a friend of Mohammed Junaid Babar. They spent two and a half months together in Lahore, Pakistan.[218] Interestingly, Siddique's close friend in college in West London was Asif Hanif, a suicide bomber associated with Al Muhajiroun who carried out the bombing in Tel Aviv in 2003.[219] On Siddique's phone numbers of known al Qaeda terrorists and Islamists in Britain implicated in an August 2004 bombing plot in London were found. His diary also displays knowledge of a nonspecific operation called "wagon" that may have been the London attacks, which some have speculated were scheduled for the spring but postponed until July. This theory meshes with information garnered from Abu Faraj al-Libi, a Libyan who was captured in May 2005 in Pakistan and has been alleged to have been the third-in-command of the al Qaeda network.[220] An unnamed senior Pakistani official cited by the *New York Daily News* has asserted that upon his capture, al-Libi was planning an operation to assassinate both President George W. Bush and President Musharraff of Pakistan.[221] He had already organized plots on Musharraff's life that had failed.[222] Authorities have claimed that al-Libi directed the al Qaeda cells in London. During interrogation, he revealed knowledge of a plot to attack London's transportation system that was to take place in May 2005 that was canceled or postponed.[223]

Another figure of interest in the 7/7 plot is Mohammed Naeem Noor Khan, a Pakistani in his midtwenties who has admitted to administering al Qaeda communication networks and Web sites.[224] Noor Khan admitted to his Pakistani interrogators that he spent twenty-five days training at a terrorist camp in Afghanistan in June 1998.[225] He was also in contact with the brother of the Jemaah Islamiyah figure mentioned in the previous section, Riduan Isamuddin, aka Hambali.[226] Information obtained from his computer files and interrogation were instrumental in the investigation and apprehension of the eight men implicated in the August 2004 London bomb plot[227]—the same men whose phone numbers were found with Zeeshan Siddique.

One of these eight men implicated in the August 2004 London bomb plot was Abu Issa al-Hindi, a highly connected al Qaeda operative until his capture in 2004. At the age of twenty, al-Hindi converted to Islam and found an affinity with extremist beliefs espoused in some London mosques,[228] especially the Finsbury Park Mosque, whose congregation was led by Abu Hamza al-Masri, a radical imam imprisoned in Britain pending extradition to the United States where he is to be charged with being involved in a 1999 plot to set up a terrorist camp in Oregon.[229] Another figure, who some suspect as being the mastermind of the 7/7 attacks, Haroon Rashid Aswat, is also awaiting extradition to the United States from Britain for the same charges.[230]

The Pakistan connections with the London attacks demonstrate al

Qaeda's complicity with the 7/7 attacks. The bombers met with militants and members of al Qaeda affiliate groups, such as Lashkar e Taiba and Jaish e Muhammad, in Pakistan and may have trained at al Qaeda camps in Afghanistan. Some of the men they met with have aided al Qaeda and engaged in al Qaeda operations. These men have their own ties to highly placed al Qaeda figures. A member of the al Qaeda leadership admitted knowledge of an attack based on the 7/7 model that was postponed from the spring of 2005.

Abu Hamza al-Masri, the former imam of the now infamous Finsbury Park mosque, is connected to two key al Qaeda–tied figures in the larger 7/7 plot terrorist nexus. One of the eight men implicated in the August 2004 London bomb plot (referred to above in association with Zeeshan Siddique, Mohammad Junaid Babar, and Mohammed Naeem Noor Khan) was Abu Issa al-Hindi, a highly connected al Qaeda operative until his capture in 2004. Al-Hindi and his coconspirators analyzed and gauged wind pressure on buildings around London in an effort to determine their weakest points.[231] Their plot was incredibly detailed and had it come to fruition, many lives would have been lost. Al-Hindi worshiped at the Finsbury Park Mosque, where he was drawn to the extremist fiery sermons of al-Masri. Haroon Rashid Aswat served as al-Masri's aide at the mosque.[232] The shadowy figure of Haroon Rashid Aswat and the scant information surrounding his potential involvement in the 7/7 attacks have given rise to interesting speculation. Aswat allegedly called the 7/7 bombers approximately twenty times from a location in Britain before leaving the country shortly before 7/7 for Zambia.[233] He was sent back from Zambia to Britain where he was arrested, but he is not being charged with involvement in the 7/7 plot. Aswat is being extradicted to the United States for involvement in the Oregon terrorist training camp plot in which al-Masri is implicated.[234]

Mohammad Sidique Khan's videotaped speech shows al Qaeda's influence in the formulation of the attack. In the video, Khan praises al Qaeda's three main figures, saying:

> I myself, I myself I make *dua* to Allah . . . to raise me amongst those whom I love like the prophets, the messengers, the martyrs, and today's heroes like our beloved Sheikh Osama bin Laden, Dr. Ayman al-Zawahiri, and Abu Musab al-Zarqawi, and all the other brothers and sisters that are fighting.[235]

Bin Laden, al-Zawahiri, and al-Zarqawi, the three top luminaries of the contemporary al Qaeda network, are the only individuals mentioned by name in Khan's short speech. Ayman al-Zawahiri appears in the second segment of the video, praising the attack and claiming it for al Qaeda.

Ayman al-Zawahiri, in a video released by As-Sahab on the first anniversary of the London transportation bombings, claimed that Shehzad Tanweer went to "the bases of Qaeda al-Jihad."[236] Al-Zawahiri claims that Tanweer would speak often of Palestine "about the backing that the British give the Jews and the clear oppression which they commit against the Muslims."[237] Later in the video, a narrator explains over footage of terrorist training in explosives,

> And so, to repel this oppression, Shehzad dedicated himself to training with passion and devotion, and received, along with the martyr Siddique Khan, focused and practical instruction in the manufacture of explosives and their use at the camps of Qaeda al-Jihad, those camps whose inductees don't need to score high averages nor pass entrance exams. All they need is jealousy for their religion and Ummah and love for Jihad and martyrdom in the path of Allah.[238]

The narrator also claims that Tanweer and Khan chose the specific stations and targets they would attack while they were in Pakistan. The targeted stations were supposedly chosen because of the "symbolic meaning and spiritual significance" the names of those stations have for the West.[239]

These claims from al-Zawahiri and the narrator of the video support the possibility that Tanweer did train with terrorists associated with al-Zawahiri and al Qaeda or that he actually met al-Zawahiri—however, the latter is unlikely. It is possible that al-Zawahiri's claims are counterfeit in totality. Regardless of whom Tanweer met in Pakistan, what is certain is that al-Zawahiri felt it important to communicate this message in order to diminish British support for Israel as well as the willingness of the British to maintain their military presence in Iraq and Afghanistan.

CONCLUSION

Al Qaeda affiliates established before US and allied forces invaded Afghanistan in the fall and winter of 2001 have proved critical to the organization's survival. Al Qaeda in Iraq is serving as the latest magnet for Islamist warriors, and the support that al Qaeda needs to continue its terrorism is grounded in its friendships in the Pankisi Gorge region of Georgia, the heavily Muslim-populated countries of Southeast Asia, the harsh deserts of North Africa, and beyond. These regions, with their harsh climates and terrain, serve many purposes: they offer refuge, mental hardening, and further training, whether combat training in the deserts of Iraq or chemical weapons training in the mountainous caves of the former Soviet Union.

NOTES

1. Yoram Schwietzer and Sari Goldstein Ferber, *Al-Qaeda and the Internationalization of Suicide Terrorism* (Tel Aviv: Jaffee Center for Strategic Studies, November 2005), pp. 18–19.

2. "Zarkawi's Cry: A Terrorist's Words of Despair," *National Review Online*, February 12, 2004.

3. Agence France Presse, "Zarqawi Pledges Allegiance to Bin Ladin," October 17, 2004.

4. Council on Foreign Relations Web site, http://www.cfrterrorism.org/groups/ansar.html (accessed August 22, 2005).

5. Indictment of Muhamad Majid and Others, Ordinanza di Applicazione della Misura della Custodia Cautelare in Carcere, Tribunal of Milan, Italy (November 25, 2003).

6. Michael Ware, "Kurdistan: Death in the Afternoon," *Time*, February 26, 2003.

7. Richard Boucher, "Foreign Terrorist Organizations: Designation of Ansar al-Islam (Al), Redesignation of Three Others," US Department of State press statement, March 22, 2004.

8. "Treasury Department Statement Regarding the Designation of Ansar al-Islam," US Department of the Treasury, February 20, 2003.

9. Council on Foreign Relations Web site, http://www.cfrterrorism.org/groups/ansar.html (accessed August 22, 2005).

10. Scott Peterson, "The Rise and Fall of Ansar al-Islam," *Christian Science Monitor*, October 16, 2003; Marco Lombardi, "Anatomy of Ansar al Islam," *Limes Online* (Italy), January 2004. Aso Hawleri was captured in Mosul in August 2003.

11. Peter Ford, "A Suspect Emerges as Key Link in Terror Chain," *Christian Science Monitor*, January 23, 2004.

12. Council on Foreign Relations Web site, http://www.cfrterrorism.org/groups/ansar.html (accessed August 22, 2005); Wurya Hawleri, "Confusion over the Identity of a Killed Ansar al-Islam Leading Figure," *Iraqi Kurdistan Dispatch*, January 5, 2003. Abu Abdallah al-Shafii's aliases include Warba Holiri al-Kurdi.

13. Peterson, "The Rise and Fall of Ansar al-Islam."

14. "Top Al-Qaida, Ansar al-Islam Arrests," Al-Jazeerah, January 24, 2004.

15. Michael Rubin, "Ansar al-Sunna: Iraq's New Terrorist Threat," *Middle East Bulletin*, May 2004.

16. "Chapter 6, Terrorist Groups," *Country Reports on Terrorism*, State Department, April 27, 2005, http://www.state.gov/s/ct/rls/45394.htm (accessed October 25, 2005).

17. Dominik Cziesche and Georg Mascolo, "Departure for the Killing Fields," *Der Speigel*, December 8, 2003; Indictment of Muhamad Majid and others.

18. Ford, "A Suspect Emerges as Key Link in Terror Chain."

19. Associated Press, "Ansar al-Islam's Stronghold Provides Grim Example of Militant Rule," March 8, 2004.

20. Richard Boucher, "Foreign Terrorist Organization: Designation of Jama'at al-Tawhid wa'al-Jihad and Aliases," US Department of State press statement, October 15, 2004.

21. Council on Foreign Relations Web site, http://www.cfrterrorism.org/groups/ansar.html (accessed August 22, 2005); Jonathan Schanzer, "Inside the Zarqawi Network," *Weekly Standard*, August 16, 2004.

22. Dominik Cziesche and Georg Mascolo, "Departure for the Killing Fields," *Der Speigel*, December 8, 2003; Jonathan Schanzer, "Ansar al-Islam: Back in Iraq," *Middle East Quarterly* (Winter 2004).

23. Boucher, "Foreign Terrorist Organization."

24. Associated Press, "Al-Zarqawi Blamed for Spike in Iraq Deaths," June 16, 2005.

25. Schanzer, "Ansar al-Islam: Back in Iraq."

26. Schanzer, "Inside the Zarqawi Network."

27. Schanzer, "Ansar al-Islam: Back in Iraq."

28. "Iranian Guards Leader Reportedly Admits Helping Al-Zarqawi," BBC Worldwide Monitoring, August 12, 2004.

29. Ibid.; Ali Nurizadeh, "Iran's Al-Quds Corps Chief Reportedly Admits Providing Facilities to Al-Zarqawi," *Al Sharq al Awsat* (London), August 11, 2004, p. 2.

30. Cziesche and Mascolo, "Departure for the Killing Fields."

31. Indictment of Muhamad Majid and Others.

32. "Investigations Show Direct Link between Italy, Ansar al-Islam, Al-Qa'ida," *Milan Corriere della Sera* (Italy), October 27, 2003.

33. Indictment of Muhamad Majid and Others; "Italy Terror Suspects Arrested," CNN, November 29, 2003.

34. Yasser Hassan's alias is Abu Ali; Indictment of Muhamad Majid and Others.

35. Matthew Levitt, "USA Ties Terrorist Attacks in Iraq to Extensive Zarqawi Network," *Jane's Intelligence Review*, April 1, 2004.

36. Greg B. Smith, "FBI Fears Qaeda Suspects in City," *New York Daily News*, August 4, 2004.

37. Matthew Levitt, "The Zarqawi Node in the Terror Matrix," *National Review Online*, February 6, 2003, http://www.nationalreview.com/comment/comment-levitt020603.asp (accessed August 22, 2005).

38. Jonathan Schanzer, "Ansar Al-Islam: Iraq's Al-Qaeda Connection: Policy Watch #669," *Washington Institute of Near East Policy*, January 15, 2003.

39. "Jordan Says Major Al Qaeda Plot Disrupted," CNN, April 26, 2005.

40. Associated Press, "Al Qaeda Claims Responsibility for Ship Attack," August 23, 2005.

41. Joel Greenberg, "Al Qaeda Defends Jordan Attack," *Chicago Tribune*, November 11, 2005.

42. "Al Qaeda Explains Amman Bombing Threatens: 'In a few days the infidel leaders will witness an event that will make the Amman bombings look insignificant,'" Middle East Medial and Research Institute, December 8, 2005.

43. "Zarqawi Tried to Flee after Surviving US Air Strike on Hideout, Military Confirms," *Sunday Tribune* (Ireland), June 11, 2006; Dan Murphy and Mark Sappenfield, "A Long Trail to Finding Zarqawi," *Christian Science Monitor*, June 9, 2006.

44. "Zarqawi Tried to Flee after Surviving US Air Strike on Hideout, Military Confirms."

45. Karen DeYoung, "Bin Laden Praises al-Zarqawi as a 'Lion of Jihad,'" *Irish Times*, July 1, 2006.

46. "The World in Brief," *Los Angeles Times*, June 24 2006.

47. Richard A. Oppel and Khalid Al-Ansary, "Dozens Die in Timed Attacks Aimed at Top Kirkuk Officials," *New York Times*, June 14, 2006.

48. Sabrian Tavernis and Sahar Nageeb, "Wave of Bodies in Baghdad's Central Morgue Signals a Stepped-Up Pace of Sectarian Killing," *New York Times*, July 5, 2006.

49. General George W. Casey, Department of Defense news briefing, June 22, 2006.

50. Indictment of Muhamad Majid and Others.

51. Deposition of Shadi Abdallah, Federal High Court, Karlsruhe, Germany (November 18, 2002).

52. Indictment of Muhamad Majid and Others.

53. Ibid.

54. Alex Rodriguez, "Chechen Fighters Lose Stronghold in Georgia Gorge; US Fears Militants Linked to Al Qaeda," *Chicago Tribune*, July 20, 2003.

55. Paul Quinn-Judge, "Inside Al Qaeda's Georgia Refuge," *Time*, October 19, 2002.

56. Ibid.

57. Associated Press, "Azeri Military Court Finds Leaders of Kuwaiti Organization Guilty of Recruiting Volunteers to Fight Russians in Chechnya," December 11, 2003.

58. Quinn-Judge, "Inside Al Qaeda's Georgia Refuge."

59. Mansur al Suwaylim, brother of Chechen rebel commander Khattab,

interviewed by Muwaff Al Qaeda al Nuwaysir, translated from Arabic, May 2, 2002.

60. Ibid.

61. Paul Quinn-Judge, "Inside Al Qaeda's Georgia Refuge."

62. Indictment of Muhamad Majid and Others.

63. Jeffrey Fleishman, "Militants' Crude Camp Leaves Questions Unanswered," *Los Angeles Times*, April 27, 2003.

64. Indictment of Muhamad Majid and Others.

65. Paul Quinn-Judge et al., "A Poisonous Plot," *Time*, January 20, 2003

66. Indictment of Muhamad Majid and Others.

67. "CIA Warns Turkish Police on Poisonous Substance," BBC Monitoring International Reports, July 10, 2002.

68. Colin Powell, "Remarks to the United Nations Security Council by Secretary of State Colin Powell," US Department of State, February 5, 2003.

69. Nicolas Sarkozy (French interior minister), "A propos de l'interpellation de plusieurs par la DST" (In Connection with the Interpollation of Several by the DST), *Le Ministère de l'Intérieur, de la Sécurité Intérieure et des Libertés Locales*, December 27, 2002.

70. Ibid.

71. Quinn-Judge et al., "A Poisonous Plot."

72. Sarkozy, "A propos de l'interpellation de plusieurs par la DST."

73. "Terror Police Find Deadly Poison," BBC, January 7, 2003; Sebastian Rotella, "A Road to Ansar Began in Italy," *Los Angeles Times*, April 28, 2003; Justin Davenport and Keith Dovkants, "Mosque Linked to Key Network Plotting Major Attacks," *London Evening Standard*, January 21, 2003.

74. Agence France Presse, "Spain Arrests and Questions Algerian Militant Suspect," September 12, 2003.

75. Agence France Presse, Robert MacPherson, "Police Questions Detainees after London Mosque Raid," January 21, 2003.

76. "Ricin Raid Victim Was Blair Guard," CNN, January 15, 2003, http://www.cnn.com/2003/WORLD/europe/01/15/britain.terror.police (accessed August 22, 2005).

77. Sebastian Rotella and Janet Stobart, "North African Arraigned in British Slaying," *Los Angeles Times*, January 18, 2003.

78. Sebastian Rotella, "Extremists Find Fertile Soil in Europe," *Los Angeles Times*, March 2, 2003.

79. David Stern, "Detainees Held in France Linked to Chechnya," *Financial Times*, December 21, 2002.

80. "Georgia 'Train and Equip' Program Begins," Department of Defense press release, April 29, 2002.

81. Ibid.

82. "GTEP Program Graduates Last Group of Georgian Soldiers," US Embassy in Georgia press release, April 24, 2004.

83. Peter Baker, "15 Tied to Al Qaeda Turned Over to the US; Arab Militants Caught in Georgian Gorge," *Washington Post*, October 22, 2002.

84. "Georgian Security Minister Says al-Qa'ida Contacts Have Fled Pankisi," ITAR-TASS News Agency, February 6, 2003.

85. "Russia: Deputy Prosecutor Says Up to 700 Rebels May Be in Pankisi Gorge," INTERFAX News Agency, May 19, 2003.

86. Alex Rodriguez, "Chechen Fighters Lose Stronghold in Georgia Gorge; US Fears Militants Linked to Al Qaeda," *Chicago Tribune*, July 20, 2003.

87. *USA v. Ahmed Omar Abu Ali*, 05-CR-53, indictment (ED VA 2005).

88. Ibid, p. 5.

89. National Commission on Terrorist Attacks upon the United States, *The 9/11 Commission Report: Final Report of the National Commission on Terrorist Attacks upon the United States* (New York: Norton, 2004), pp. 235, 525.

90. Associated Press, "Riyadh Bombing Suspect in Custody," June 26, 2003.

91. Michael Isikoff and Mark Hosenball, "Terror Watch: Abu-Ali Tied to Riyadh Bombing Architect," *Newsweek*, March 2, 2005. See also *USA v. Ahmed Omar Abu Ali*, 05-CR-53, indictment (ED VA 2005).

92. Associated Press, "Official: Saudi Authorities Discover Militant Camps," January 15, 2004.

93. "Foiling Plans for Terrorist Attacks and the Seizure of Explosives and Weapons Belonging to a Group Linked with Al Qaeda in Riyadh," *Ain-Al-Yaqeen*, May 9, 2003 http://www.ain-al-yaqeen.com/issues/20030509/feat5en.htm (accessed on February 10, 2006).

94. Elaine Shannon, "Al Qaeda Seeks Canadian Operatives," *Time*, July 8, 2003.

95. "Al Qaida Bombings Kingpin in Suicide," *Birmingham Post*, July 4, 2003.

96. Associated Press, "Suspected Militant Killed by Saudi Police Was Carrying Letter Signed by Osama bin Laden," June 3, 2003.

97. Agence France Presse, "Saudi Authorities Step Up Security at Compounds after Terror Alert," December 3, 2003

98. "Al Qa'ida Claims Responsibility for Saudi Bombings," *Al Majjalah*, November 9, 2003, FBIS Translation GMP20031111000129.

99. "Article Notes Changes in Weakening Al Qaeda Branch in Saudi Arabia," *Al Sharq Al Awsat*, January 1, 2005, FBIS Translation GMP 20050101000062.

100. "London Based Saudi Paper Profiles 'Local Leader' of Al Qaeda in Saudi Arabia," *Al Sharq Al Awsat*, December 10, 2005, FBIS Translation GMP20031210000089.

101. Agence France Presse, "Al Qaeda Video Claims Murder of American in Saudi Arabia," June 13, 2004.

102. Reuters, "American Killed on Tape: Al-Qaida," June 13, 2004.

103. Associated Press, "U.S. Hostage Beheaded," June 18, 2004.

104. "Saudi Arabia: Writer Labels Al Qaeda Danger 'Real and Present,'" *Al Sharq Al Awsat*, December 7, 2004, FBIS Translation GMP20041207000262.

105. "Saudi Official Lauds Major Blow to Al Qaeda," CNN, June 20, 2004.

106. "Report Profiles al-Qa'ida's New Leader in Saudi Arabia Salih Al-Awfi," *Al Sharq Al Awsat*, June 21, 2004, FBIS Translation GMP20040621000041. See also Craig Whitlock, "Saudis Facing Return of Radicals," *Washington Post*, July 11, 2004.

107. "Al Qaeda Declaration on U.S. Consulate Attack," Jamestown Foundation, December 7, 2005, http://www.jamestown.org/news_details.php?news_id=81# (accessed January 4, 2006).

108. "FYI-Saudi Arabia: Al Qaida Leader Salih al-Awfi Killed in Holy Medina," Al Arabiyah Television, August 28, 2005, FBIS 200508181477.1_6d70000c40e42fb4.

109. Hassan M. Fattah, "Suicide Bombers Fail to Enter Saudi Oil Plant," *New York Times*, February 25, 2006.

110. Gerrie Swart and Hussein Solomon, "Algeria: The Politics of Fundamentalism and Extremism," Africa Institute of South Africa, October 17, 2003, http://www.ai.org.za/electronic_monograph.asp?ID=14 (accessed December 28, 2005).

111. Ibid.

112. Jonathan Schanzer, "Algeria's GSPC and America's 'War on Terror,'" PolicyWatch#666, Washington Institute, October 2, 2002, http://www.washingtoninstitute.org/templateC05.php?CID=1544 (accessed December 26, 2005).

113. "Group Profile: Armed Islamic Group," MIPT Terrorism Knowledge Base, http://www.tkb.org/Group.jsp?groupID=27 (accessed December 28, 2005).

114. "Bomb Attacks Suspect Is Facing Extradition," *Glasgow Herald*, September 28, 1996.

115. Lara Marlowe, "Villagers Decapitated and Set Alight in Massacre by Algerian Islamists," *Irish Times*, August 7, 1997; Martin Regg Cohn, "Amid Carnage, Algerians Find Will to Vote," *Toronto Star*, June 1, 1997; "Algerian Militants Massacre 111," *Australian*, August 6, 1997.

116. Kepel Gilles, *Jihad: The Trail of Political Islam*, trans. Anthony F. Roberts (Cambridge, MA: Harvard University Press, 2002), p. 254.

117. Associated Press, Rachid Khiari, "Algerian Rebel Group Names Former Bosnian Fighter as New Leader," December 8, 1996.

118. Schanzer, "Algeria's GSPC and America's 'War on Terror.'"

119. Ibid.

120. Agence France Presse, "Bin Laden Held to Be Behind an Armed Algerian Islamic Movement," February 15, 1999; Swart and Solomon, "Algeria: The Politics of Fundamentalism and Extremism."

121. Agence France Presse, "Bin Laden Held to Be Behind an Armed Algerian Islamic Movement"; "Meet Algeria's 'Salafi Group,'" *Mideast Mirror*, June 17, 1999.

122. "Meet Algeria's 'Salafi Group,'" *Mideast Mirror*, June 17, 1999.

123. Agence France Presse, "Bin Laden Held to Be Behind an Armed Algerian Islamic Movement."

124. John Ungoed-Thomas et al., "How the Horrors Point to Hamburg," *London Sunday Times*, September 30, 2001.

125. Ibid.

126. Hassane Meftahi, "Militant Killed Said to Be al-Qaida," Associated Press, November 25, 2002.

127. Associated Press, "Report: Bin Laden Has Sent Three Saudi Envoys to Algeria," December 27, 2002.

128. Ahmad al-Arqam, "Moroccan Source: Terrorist Cell Reveals Plans for Establishing Al-Qaeda in North African Countries," *Al Sharq Al Awsat*, December 8, 2005.

129. Kevin Whitelaw, "The Mutating Threat," *U.S. News & World Report*, December 26, 2005.

130. Bu-Allam Ghamrasah, "Algerian Salafi Group Said Contacting Zarqawi to Target Franch Nationals," A*l Sharq Al Awsat*, July 2, 2005.

131. BBC Monitoring, "Algerian Islamist Group Backs Al-Qa'ida, Warns Arab Summit," March 23, 2005.

132. Al-Arqam, "Moroccan Source.

133. Sean O'Neill, "Was Ricin the Last Act of a Terrorist Cell?" *Times*, April 15, 2005.

134. Mr. Justice Ouseley, quoted in ibid.

135. *United States v. Abu Doha*, 01-MAG-1242, complaint, pp. 4–7 (SD NY July 2, 2001).

136. Ungoed-Thomas et al., "How the Horrors Point to Hamburg"; Jason Burke, "9/11 Six Months On: Terrorism: Bin Laden's Men Wait to Take Bloody Revenge," *Observer*, March 10, 2002.

137. Ungoed-Thomas et al., "How the Horrors Point to Hamburg."

138. Ibid.; Ian Burrel, John Lichfield, and Robert Verkaik, "Manchester Police Killing: Islamists—Warning Signs of Algerian Terror Cells as Early as 1994," *Independent*, January 16, 2003.

139. Sean O'Neill, "Quiet Lives Hit a Quest to Recruit for Global Jihad," *Daily Telegraph*, April 2, 2003; "Profile: Abu Zubaydah," BBC News, April 2, 2002, http://news.bbc.co.uk/1/hi/world/south_asia/1907462.stm (accessed December 29, 2005).

140. Burke, "9/11 Six Months On."

141. O'Neill, "Quiet Lives Hit a Quest to Recruit for Global Jihad"; Chris Hedges, "A European Dragnet Captures New Clues to bin Laden's Network," *New York Times*, October 12, 2001.

142. Sean O'Neill, "'Architect of Terror' Held in British Jail Cell," *Daily Telegraph*, January 9, 2003; Paul Gallagher, "Algerian Militants the Main Terror Threat to Britain, Experts Warn," *Scotsman*, January 16, 2003.

143. "Italian Daily on Al-Qa'idah's Foiled Attack on Target in Milan," *Milan Corriere della Sera*, October 20, 2001.

144. Alex Belida, "No Proof of Terror Plots against U.S. in Mali, Says Defense Official," Voice of America News, June 10, 2003.

145. Douglas E. Ramage, House Subcommittee on Asia and the Pacific, Committee on International Relations, *Islam in Asia*, 108th Cong., 2nd sess., July 14, 2004.

146. "The Jemaah Islamiyah Arrests and the Threat of Terrorism," White Paper, Presented to Parliament by Command of the President of the Republic of Singapore, January 7, 2003, p. 6.

147. Ibid.

148. Muhklas, "General Guide to the Struggle"; "The Jemaah Islamiyah Arrests and the Threat of Terrorism"; Singapore Ministry of Home Affairs Web site, http://www2.mha.gov.sg/mha/detailed .jsp?artid=675&type=4&root=0 &parent=0&cat=0&mode=arc (accessed August 23, 2003).

149. "The Jemaah Islamiyah Arrests and the Threat of Terrorism."

150. US Department of State, *2003 Patterns of Global Terrorism* (Washington, DC: GPO, April 29, 2004); Colin Powell, "Designation of a Foreign Terrorist Organization," US Department of State, October 23, 2002.

151. Powell, "Designation of a Foreign Terrorist Organization."

152. "1267 Committee Adds Name of an Entity to Its List," United Nations press release, October 25, 2002.

153. US Department of State, *2003 Patterns of Global Terrorism*; Powell, "Designation of a Foreign Terrorist Organization," p. 16.

154. Steven Gutkin, "Indonesian Police Point to Similarities between Marriott Bombing and Bali Attacks," Associated Press, August 7, 2003.

155. Ibid.

156. "Severed Head Clue to Jakarta Bomb," BBC, August 8, 2003.

157. "Police Score Breakthrough in Hotel Bombing Probe," *New Straits Times*, August 9, 2003.

158. Chris Brummitt, "Muslim Militants Explode Car Bomb at Australian Embassy, Killing Nine," Associated Press, September 9, 2004.

159. Marianne Kearney, "Warning of Bomb in Text Message," *Daily Telegraph*, September 11, 2004.

160. Agence France Presse, "Jemaah Islamiyah Claims Jakarta Car Bombing: Internet Site," September 9, 2004.

161. Agence France Presse, "Bali Death Toll Rises as Suspected Mastermind Escapes Police Raid," October 8, 2005; "Bali: Police Made First Arrest," CNN, Ocotber 11, 2005, http://www.cnn.com/2005/WORLD/asiapcf/10/11/bali .arrest.ap/index.html (accessed October 25, 2005).

162. "After Blasts, Indonesia Eyes Tightening Anti-terror Laws," *Orlando Sentinel*, October 15, 2005.

163. Ibid; "Copter in Indonesia Drops Pictures of Two Sought in Bombings on Bali," *Buffalo News*, October 9, 2005; "JI Phone Calls Bombing Clues," *Sydney Daily Telegraph*, October 11, 2005; "Terror Search Sweeps Wider," *Courier Mail*, October 5, 2005; "Indonesian Police Chief Says Malaysian Bali Bombing Suspect 'Lonely Man,'" *Star* (Malaysia), May 24, 2006.

164. "The Jemaah Islamiyah Arrests and the Threat of Terrorism," p. 9.

165. Ibid., pp. 11–12.

166. Ibid., pp. 29–30.

167. Ibid., p. 13.

168. Ibid., pp. 30–31.

169. Ibid.

170. Reuters, "Cambodia Jails JI Suspect for Life, Frees Egyptian," December 29, 2004.

171. "The Jemaah Islamiyah Arrests and the Threat of Terrorism," p. 7.

172. Matthew Moore, "Bashir Jailed for Degree of Treason," *Age* (Australia), September 23, 2003; Agence France Presse, "Jakarta Bomb Suspect Was Graduate of Bashir's School: Report," August 10, 2003.

173. Slobodan Lekic, "Indonesian Cleric Prays for bin Laden and Checks into Hospital, Avoiding Police Questioning," Associated Press, October 18, 2002.

174. Moore, "Bashir Jailed for Degree of Treason"; Associated Press, "Ruling to Bring Early Freedom for Indonesian Militant Cleric," March 9, 2004.

175. "Freed Cleric Re-arrested over Bali Bombing," *Guardian*, April 30, 2004; "Indonesian Court Hears Bashir was Jemaah Chief," Reuters, December 21, 2004.

176. "Indonesia High Court Rejects Bashir Terror Appeal," Voice of America, www.voanews.com/tibetan/2005-05-16-voa14.cfm (accessed August 23, 2005). In August 2005, Indonesia Justice Minister Hamid Awaluddin said Bashir's sentence would be reduced of an uncertain amount. Agence France Presse, "Indonesia to Cut Sentences of Militant Cleric, Bashir, Bali Bombers: Report," August 13, 2005.

177. "Indonesia Cuts Bashir Sentence," *Australian*, August 17, 2005.

178. Achmad Sukarsono and Jerry Norton, "Interview—Anti-Islam 'Crusade' Doomed, Indonesia's Bashir Says," Reuters, June 30, 2006.

179. "Trail of Bali Suspects Leads Back to 2002; Indonesian Police Hunt for Alleged Architect of Previous Attacks on Island," *Washington Post*, October 7, 2005.

180. Ibid.

181. "Indonesian Terrorist Linked to bin Ladin," *Sydney Morning Herald*, November 20, 2003.

182. Ibid.; "Hambali 'Eyed Bankok Embassies,'" BBC, August 22, 2003.

183. "Asia's Most Wanted in US Hands," CNN, August 15, 2003.

184. 9/11 Commission, *The 9/11 Commission Report*, p. 150.

185. "Hambali: 'Asia's Bin Laden,'" BBC News, August 15, 2003.

186. 9/11 Commission, *The 9/11 Commission Report*, p. 150.

187. Ibid., pp. 151, 490.

188. Ibid.

189. Ibid., pp. 151, 159.

190. Shawn Donnan, "Australia to Push Indonesia to Improve Its Security and Ban Jemaah Islamiyah," *Financial Times*, October 11, 2005.

191. "Ban Called Naïve—Bali—Evidence Hunt," *Sydney Daily Telegraph*, October 5, 2005.

192. "Bali Hell, the Investigation; JI Ban 'Could Make Situation Worse,'" *Advertiser*, October 5, 2005.

193. Raymond Bonner, "Indonesia Considers Tougher Anti-Terror Laws," *New York Times*, October 13, 2005; Australian Associated Press, "SA: Rann Urges Indonesia to Outlaw JI," October 17 2005.

194. "Incident Profile, Abu Hafs Al-Masri Brigade and Secret Organization of Al Qaeda in Europe Attacked Transportation Target (July 7, 2005, United Kingdom) Incident 24394," National Memorial Institute for the Prevention of Terrorism—Terrorism Knowledge Base, http://ww.tbk.org/Incident.jsp?incID=24394 (accessed December 14, 2005).

195. Ibid.

196. British Home Office, "Report of the Official Account of the Bombings in London on 7th July 2005," May 11, 2006, pp. 17–18.

197. "London Bombers 'Were All British,'" BBC News, July 12, 2005, http://news.bbc.co.uk/go/pr/fr/-/2/hi/uk_news/4676577.stm (accessed December 14, 2005).

198. David Leppard, "MI5 Judged Bomber 'No Threat,'" *Sunday Times*, July 17, 2005, http://www.timesonlne.co.uk/article/0,,2087-1697562,00.html (accessed December 14, 2005).

199. "Police Investigation Continues into the 7/7 Bombings," Metropolitan Police Services press release, http://cms.met.police.uk/met/layout/set/print/content/view/full/1362 (accessed December 14, 2005).

200. "London Bombers Met on Raft Trip," *Toronto Star*, July 25, 2005.

201. Tara Pepper and Mark Hosenball, "A Deadly Puzzle," *Newsweek*, July 25, 2005; Paul Tumelty, "New Developments Following the London Bombings," *Jamestown Foundation Terrorism Monitor* 3, no. 23 (December 2, 2005).

202. Tumelty, "New Developments Following the London Bombings," p. 7.

203. Zahid Hussain et al., "Police Track Down Suspect Who Lost His Nerve at the Last Minute," *London Times*, July 8, 2006.

204. Daniel McGrory and Zahid Hussain, "Bombers 'Met Chief Plotter' in Karachi," *Times*, July 18, 2005.

205. Alan Cowell, "Al Jazeera Video Links London Bombings to Al Qaeda," *New York Times*, September 2, 2005.

206. Massoud Ansari and Andrew Alderson, "Pakistani Mobile Phone Link to London Bombing," *Sunday Telegraph*, September 11, 2005.

207. Ibid.

208. "2 London bombers visited Pakistan," *CNN*, July 18, 2005, http://www.cnn.com/2005/WORLD/europe/07/18/london.attacks (accessed December 14, 2005); Antony Barnett and Mark Townsend, "World: Al-Qaeda 'Link to 7/7' Found in Iraq: Captured Man 'Had Computer Information' on London Attacks," *Observer*, September 11, 2005.

209. Tara Pepper and Mark Hosenball, "A Deadly Puzzle," *Newsweek*, July 25, 2005.

210. Barnett and Townsend, "World: Al-Qaeda 'Link to 7/7' Found in Iraq."

211. British Home Office, "Report of the Official Account of the Bombings in London on 7th July 2005," p. 20.

212. "Report into the London Terrorist Attacks on 7 July 2005," Intelligence and Security Committee (Great Britain), May 2006.

213. Hussain et al., "Police Track Down Suspect Who Lost His Nerve at the Last Minute"; "Al Qaeda No. 3 Is Dead, but How?" CNN, December 4, 2005, http://www.cnn.com/2005/WORLD/asiapcf/12/03/pakistan.rabia/index.html (accessed July 10, 2005).

214. Leppard, "MI5 Judged Bomber 'No Threat.'"

215. Tumelty, "New Developments Following the London Bombings."

216. Omar Bakri Muhammad, interviewed by Anthony McRoy, *Christianity Today*, February 1, 2005, http://www.christianitytoday.com/ct/2005/105/22.0.html (accessed December 20, 2005).

217. Ibid.

218. McGrory and Hussain, "Bombers 'Met Chief Plotter' in Karachi."

219. David Rohde and Mohammed Khan, "Jihadist's Self-Portrait: Alone and Seething," *International Herald Tribune*, August 9, 2005.

220. McGrory and Hussain, "Bombers 'Met Chief Plotter' in Karachi"; Rohde and Khan, "Jihadist's Self-Portrait."

221. "Key Leader Profile, Al-Libbi, Abu Faraj," MIPT, http://www.tkb.org/KeyLeader.jsp?memID=6097 (accessed December 19, 2005).

222. James Gordon Meek, "Al Qaeda Fiend Targeted Bush," *Daily News*, December 23, 2005.

223. Ibid.

224. JFO McAllister et al., "Hate Around the Corner; in a Stunning Twist, Investigators Blame the London Attacks on Four Homegrown Suicide Bombers—and Look for Global Links to al-Qaeda," *Time*, July 25, 2005.

225. Ibid.; Douglas Jehl and David Rohde, "Captured Qaeda Figure Led Way to Information behind Warning," *New York Times*, August 2, 2004.

226. Jehl and Rohde, "Captured Qaeda Figure Led Way to Information behind Warning."

227. Ibid.

228. JFO McAllister et al., "Hate Around the Corner.

229. Andreas Ulrich et al., "How Widespread Is Terrorism in Europe?" Speigel Online, June 11, 2005, http://service.spiegel.de/cache/international/spiegel/0,1518,364661,00.html (accessed December 20, 2005).

230. Sam Howe Verhovek, "Swede Charged in Plot to Set Up Camp; Oussama Kassir Is Accused of Trying to Start a Terrorist Training Facility in Oregon," *Los Angeles Times*, December 14, 2005.

231. Ibid.

232. Ulrich et al., "How Widespread Is Terrorism in Europe?"

233. Tumelty, "New Developments Following the London Bombings."

234. Ibid.

235. Mohammad Sidique Khan, quoted in "London Bomber: Text in Full," BBC News, September 1, 2005, http://news.bbc.co.uk/go/pr/fr/-/2/hi/uk_news/4206800 (accessed December 14, 2005).

236. Ayman al-Zawahiri, London bombing one-year anniversary video.

237. Ibid.

238. Narrator, London bombing one-year anniversary video.

239. Al- Zawahiri, London bombing one-year anniversary video.

PART TWO

OTHER KEY TERRORIST NETWORKS

-5-

HAMAS, THE ISLAMIC RESISTANCE MOVEMENT

To give your life as jihad. To give your money as jihad. That is an obligation upon every Muslim. It is the principle of Shari'ah, and all of the thinkers and traditionalists agree on this: that if any inch of Muslim land is occupied by others, then Jihad is an obligation.

—Abdullah Azzam, the father of the jihad movement, speaking at an Islamic Association of Palestine (IAP) Convention in Oklahoma in December 1988, as videotaped and distributed by IAP's video production company, Aqsa Vision

OVERVIEW

In 1987, shortly after the outbreak of the first Palestinian Intifada, members of the Muslim Brotherhood decided that to become more involved in the uprising they needed to create a new organization. The Muslim Brotherhood's leader in the Gaza Strip, Sheikh Ahmed Yassin,[1] proceeded to form the Islamic Resistance Movement (Harakat al-Muqawamah al-Islamiyya), otherwise known as Hamas.[2] Though its leaders have occasionally claimed that they are willing to broker a cease-fire with Israel, Hamas's goals since its inception have been the destruction of Israel and the establishment of a Palestinian Islamic state in its place. The Hamas charter, issued on August 18, 1988, and never amended, outlines the movement's jihadist beliefs and rejects any possibility of peace with Israel: "As far as the ideology of the Islamic Resistance Movement is concerned, giving up any part of Palestine is like giving up part of its religion. . . . There is no solution to the Palestinian problem except by Jihad. The initiatives, options, and international conferences are a waste of time and a kind of child's play."[3]

Pursuant to an Executive Order issued by President Clinton designed to "Prohibit Transactions with Terrorists Who Threaten to Disrupt the Middle East Peace Process," Hamas was designated by the US government as a Specially Designated Terrorist (SDT) organization in January

1995.[4] Since 1995, every time the executive and legislative branches of the United States government have developed new means for designating terrorist entities, Hamas has been included in this designation process. Evidence collected since 9/11 suggests that the group may try to conduct terrorist operations against targets in the United States and that it may be collaborating with other terrorist organizations in gathering intelligence for US-based attacks. In its early years, Hamas was involved in training and recruiting operatives on US soil for military operations in Israel.[5] However, since its inception, Hamas's activities in the United States now appear to be largely focused on providing the group with financial and political support in its ongoing jihad against Israel.

When Israel banned Hamas in 1989, the group set up charitable and political organizations in the United States and also began to actively raise funds at radical Islamic conferences on American soil. Two of the organizations, the Holy Land Foundation for Relief and Development (HLF) (discussed mainly in chapter 9) and the Al Aqsa Educational Fund (AAEF), were founded to provide funding for Hamas activities in the West Bank and Gaza Strip. Two others, the Islamic Association for Palestine (IAP) and the United Association for Studies and Research (UASR), became propaganda[6] and political[7] organs.

By the late 1990s, Hamas's fund-raising efforts in the United States had begun to pay huge dividends, thanks to a wider audience and to the sophisticated techniques employed by the radical pro-Palestinian entity IAP.

HAMAS'S INITIAL PRESENCE IN THE UNITED STATES

On September 14, 1993, FBI electronic surveillance captured a conversation among Shukri Abu Bakr, Abdelhaleem al-Ashqar, and Muin Muhammad (aka Muin Shabib). The three were discussing details of a meeting to be held the following month at the Philadelphia Marriott, including who should be invited, who should speak, and who should present position papers.[8] The meeting's overriding goal was to develop a strategy to thwart the framework for peace set out in the Oslo Accords and to bolster Hamas's fund-raising and political activities in the United States.[9]

On October 1–3, 1993, leaders of the Holy Land Foundation for Relief and Development, the Al Aqsa Educational Fund, and the Islamic Association for Palestine met in Philadelphia.[10] Among them were five HLF officials who were indicted along with the organization in July 2004: Executive Director Haitham Maghawri, Chief Executive Officer Shukri Abu Bakr, Treasurer Ghassan Elashi,[11] Chairman of the Board Mohammed el-Mezain,[12] and a fund-raiser, Mufid Abdulqader.[13] Others in attendance included Abdelhaleem al-Ashqar, one of the meeting's organizers and head of the Al Aqsa Educational Fund, who was indicted in August 2004 for his role in providing material support or resources to Hamas;[14] Ismail Elbarasse, an associate and joint bank-account holder of then Hamas leader Musa Abu Marzook; and Omar Ahmad, the president of the IAP.[15]

According to FBI analysis of the meeting, participants "spent much effort hiding their association with the Islamic Resistance Movement, a.k.a. HAMAS. Instead, they referred to HAMAS as 'Samah,' which is HAMAS spelled backwards."[16] Their main concern was to determine how organizations in the United States could support Hamas. They contemplated the merger of HLF and IAP,[17] noting that "the institutions here should be at the service of the Movement over there.... This should include finance, information, political, and everything."[18] Another speaker urged his colleagues to "focus on those people who are directly connected with Jihad."[19] When Shukri Abu Bakr addressed the conference, he emphasized that to be effective, the attendees "ha[d] to behave as an American organization—and take care of the people and not a particular population. Our relation has to be good with everyone . . . but we can give the Islamists 100,000 [dollars] and 5,000 to the others."[20]

In the end, participants decided that most of the funds collected by these groups in the future would be directed toward weakening the peace process and strengthening Hamas.[21] In his presentation, al-Ashqar stressed the need for "charitable" activities, saying, "We need to support the families of the martyrs. This efforts [*sic*] has to continue."[22] He also told his listeners that they should avoid revealing Hamas's true agenda to the American public, and should present it instead as a movement to attain Palestinian human rights.[23]

As part of their support for the jihad in Palestine, the participants discussed the critical importance of domestic lobbying. Stressing the need for deeper engagement with the American Muslim community, one attendee spoke of the groups' "attempting to encourage the Islamic community to be involved in the political life in this country." He commented, "We should assist them in this task. This will be an entrance for us to put, through the Islamic community, pressure on the Congress and the decision makers in America."[24]

In a follow-up meeting in Oxford, Mississippi, in 1994, Musa Abu Marzook and other leaders of Hamas agreed that HLF would henceforth serve as "the primary fundraising entity in the United States" for Hamas.[25] HLF played that role until it was named as a Specially Designated Global Terrorist (SDGT) organization by the US Department of the Treasury in December 2001.

HAMAS TAKES AIM AT THE UNITED STATES

To date, Hamas's attacks in the Middle East have claimed more than a dozen American victims.[26] One of the best-known cases is that of David Boim, a seventeen-year-old American yeshiva student who was gunned down at a bus stop in the West Bank by two Hamas terrorists in 1996. In December 2004, four Islamic organizations, including HLF, IAP, and UASR, and one individual were found liable for Boim's murder and ordered to pay $156 million in damages to the Boim family.[27]

Although Hamas has yet to carry out a terrorist operation within the United States, its operatives participated in the foiled 1993 New York City landmark bombing plot. According to an August 2004 affidavit by an FBI agent, members of Hamas were among the conspirators who, in 1993, plotted "to bomb the landmarks, tunnels and the FBI building."[28]

Moreover, FBI agents have expressed concern that Hamas operatives currently have the capacity to carry out terrorist attacks on American soil.[29] Two incidents in particular have heightened these fears. In December 2003, Israeli authorities arrested Jamal Aqal, a Canadian citizen, and charged him with receiving weapons and explosives training from Hamas to be employed in terrorist operations against Jewish targets in Canada and New York City.[30] And in August 2004, Ismail Elbarasse—a former IAP employee and Hamas activist[31]—was arrested after authorities witnessed his wife videotaping Maryland's Chesapeake Bay Bridge from their SUV as Elbarasse drove. The images captured by Elbarasse's wife included close-ups of cables and other features that, according to an FBI affidavit filed in the case, were "integral to the structural integrity of the bridge."[32] A search of Elbarasse's home turned up an "anarchist cookbook," a document identified as "Spreadsheet of trained pilots 'Law Enforcement Only,'" and a piece of paper containing the address of the Norfolk Naval Station.[33]

The FBI affidavit also noted that al Qaeda has a track record of enlisting Hamas members to conduct surveillance:

> Al Qaeda, with a disproportionate number of leaders from Palestinian backgrounds, has exhibited a propensity to use others to collect intelligence or conduct reconnaissance. In previous years, Al Qaeda commanders and officials stationed in western countries, including the United States, have recruited Hamas operatives and volunteers to carry out reconnaissance or serve as couriers. With the increased law enforcement pressure on Al Qaeda since 9-11, there has been a renewed emphasis by Al Qaeda to find confirmed jihadist supporters in the United States by trying to enlist proven members of other groups such as Hamas to make up for the vacuum on the field level.[34]

In September 2004, following Israel's assassination of a Hamas operative in Damascus, the *Jerusalem Post* reported that Hamas leaders had begun considering whether the group should begin hitting Jewish and Israeli targets throughout the world.[35] Prior to the US invasion of Iraq in March 2003, Hamas leaders in Gaza and the West Bank openly discussed expanding the group's operations to include US targets. In November 2003, Sheikh Ahmed Yassin stated that "it is necessary to fight America in all arenas."[36] Yassin—who was assassinated by Israeli Defense Forces in March 2004—issued a fatwa, or religious decree, ordering Muslims to kill Americans wherever they were found if US troops set foot on Iraqi soil.[37]

In March 2003 another Hamas leader, Dr. Abdel Aziz Rantisi, declared: "As long as there is an American aggression against a Muslim country, Iraqis must defend themselves, using all means." He also said the Iraqis should conduct "martyrdom operations, using explosive belts against the American and British soldiers" in their country.[38] In "Why Shouldn't We Attack the United States?"—an article published on a Hamas Web site in 2003—Rantisi stated that for Hamas, attacking America was not only "a moral and national duty—but above all, a religious one."[39] Immediately before Israeli security forces assassinated Rantisi in April 2004, he took part in a Gaza rally supporting the terrorist insurgency against US forces in Iraq. Amid chants of "Death to America" and the burning of American flags by onlookers, Rantisi called on Iraqis to "strike and burn" US troops, and "teach them the lessons of suicide actions."[40]

Also in April 2004, Hamas's political chief, Khalid Mishaal, declared that the organization's "battle is with two sides. One of them is the strongest power in the world, the United States, and the second is the strongest power in the region [Israel]."[41] A few months later, Mishaal, along with several other prominent radical Islamist leaders, signed a statement calling on Muslims worldwide to join with the Al Mahdi Army of the radical Iraqi cleric Muqtada Al-Sadr in its fight against American forces in Iraq.[42] Al-Sadr himself had already vowed to serve as the "striking arm" on behalf of Hamas in Iraq.[43]

HAMAS LEADERSHIP AND FINANCING FROM THE UNITED STATES

Musa Abu Marzook helped establish charitable and business enterprises—notably the Holy Land Foundation, the high-tech company Infocom, the United Association for Studies and Research, and the Islamic Association of Palestine—that raised millions of dollars for Hamas, and beginning in 1991 he acted as the group's chief operative in the United States.[44] At that time, Marzook was the leader of the Hamas Political Bureau, the leadership grouping of Hamas operating outside Israel, the West Bank, and the Gaza Strip.

Shortly after Hamas was designated a terrorist organization by the US Treasury Department in 1995, Marzook—who had been living in Northern Virginia—was individually named as a Specially Designated Terrorist (SDT) pursuant to Executive Order 12947 on August 29, 1995.[45] Later that year he was arrested at John F. Kennedy International Airport in New York on his return from a trip to the Middle East. He was deported to Jordan in 1997.[46] Today, Marzook operates out of Damascus, Syria, as the deputy chief of Hamas's political bureau.[47]

On August 22, 2003, Marzook was named an SDGT pursuant to Executive Order 13224.[48] A year later, he was indicted in Chicago for "a 15-year federal racketeering conspiracy in the United States and abroad" to illegally fund terrorist activities.[49] In the same indictment filed against Marzook, two other suspected high-level Hamas financiers, Muhammad Salah and Abdelhaleem al-Ashqar, were charged with providing material support to Hamas, racketeering, and money laundering; they were arrested in Chicago and Virginia, respectively.[50] Named as an unindicted coconspirator in the case was Ismail Elbarasse, who had worked for a time as an assistant to Marzook. On January 12, 1990, he and Marzook opened a joint bank account in Arlington, Virginia, in the name of IAP[51] into which $125,000 was deposited between 1990 and 1991.[52] Elbarasse's name also had appeared on a $100,000 check that Marzook had written to HLF in 1992.[53] Moreover, in the months before the 1993 Philadelphia meeting, Elbarasse had wired $735,000 to the Hamas operative Muhammad Salah,[54] who was also held liable for the death of David Boim in the case mentioned above.[55]

HAMAS PROPAGANDA: THE ISLAMIC ASSOCIATION FOR PALESTINE

The Islamic Association for Palestine (IAP) was founded on November 6, 1981, in Illinois.[56] According to the group's incorporation documents, its purpose is "to carry out religious educational, social, charitable, and informational activities for Muslims of Palestinian origin and other Muslims residing in North America."[57] According to former FBI assistant director for investigations Oliver "Buck" Revell, IAP serves as a Hamas front.[58] Moreover, a 2001 INS memo extensively documents IAP's support for Hamas, noting that the "facts strongly suggest" that IAP is "part of Hamas' propaganda apparatus."[59]

The courts have also explicitly tied IAP to Hamas. In August 2002, a federal judge ruled that IAP has "acted in support of Hamas."[60] The November 2004 judgment in the *Boim* case echoed this declaration, as federal magistrate judge Arlander Keys noted that there is "evidence that IAP provided material support to Hamas."[61] Keys pointed to "an abundance of evidence" that "IAP . . . desired to see Hamas' activities succeed, and . . . engaged in some act of helping those activities succeed,"[62] adding that "if IAP has never outrightly cheered on Hamas' terrorist activities, it has come awfully close."[63]

IAP has long been a central player in Hamas's US support network. It has published and distributed official Hamas statements,[64] including the Hamas charter, a fiercely anti-Semitic document. The October 1988 issue of *Ila Filastin,* IAP's flagship Arabic publication, declared that "the IAP will deliver [the] charter of the Hamas movement to all over the American continents."[65]

IAP has also printed Hamas communiqués, such as the following statement in the December 1988 *Ila Filastin:* "The call for Jihad in the name of Allah, is the only way for liberation of Palestine and all the Muslims' lands. We [Hamas] promise Allah, in continuing the Jihad way and with the martyrdom's way."[66] *Ila Filastin,* written in Arabic, was replaced by the Arabic-language *Al Zaitounah* in 1991; the IAP produced and distributed the English-language *Muslim World Monitor.* The Arabic publications frequently praised Hamas terror attacks. An October 1994 *Al Zaitounah* headline captured the magazine's ideological bent: "In Its Greatest Operation, Hamas Takes Credit for the Bombing of an Israeli Bus in the Center of Tel Aviv."

Another key element of IAP's Hamas propaganda machine was its audiovisual wing, Aqsa Vision,[67] which distributed both audio- and videocassettes at reasonable prices. IAP's more notable productions included a three-part video series titled *Al Waad* (*The Promise*).[68] Each part opens with a song in which Muslims are encouraged "to pick up the stone and stone the Jews."[69]

Another video produced by Aqsa Vision, *Palestine Come to Jihad,*[70] states, "Blessed be your right hand O' You hero child that throws the stones at the Israeli occupiers." Additionally, the video quotes the famous hadith regarding the day of judgment, "O' Muslim, O' God's Servant, there is a Jew behind me come and kill him."[71] Several times during the video, IAP requests a donation and instructs the audience to send "tax-deductible donations" to the Occupied Land Funds (or OLF, the predecessor to the HLF).

IAP's annual conferences provided the organization with an additional forum for promoting the Hamas agenda. For example, the October 1988 *Ila Filastin* reported that "the Islamic Association for Palestine held conferences and activities to celebrate [the] one-year anniversary of the blessed Intifada and . . . the inception of the Hamas movement."[72] Hamas members frequently appeared at these events.[73] At the 1989 IAP conference in Kansas City, a masked Hamas commander urged attendees "to take up arms with [Hamas] . . . to take up arms and arms alone!"[74] Standing in front of a massive banner that read "Palestine is Islamic from the River to the Sea," he lauded a string of Hamas attacks—including one in July 1989 in which a Hamas member gained control of a bus and steered it into a ravine, killing fourteen people.[75]

At these conferences, IAP raised significant amounts of money for HLF. In fact, substantial portion of the money IAP raised during its Intifada celebrations in the late 1980s and early 1990s went to HLF (before 1991, to OLF; see below).[76] All the proceeds from IAP's 1996 convention went to HLF as well.[77] In its publications[78] and on its Web site, IAP encouraged people to donate to HLF,[79] and the close relationship between the two organizations was spelled out in a contract.[80] Tellingly,

IAP's president testified in the *Boim* case that IAP worked to "promote [HLF] in every way."[81]

IAP's Leadership

Rafeeq Jaber had been IAP's president from 1999[82] through its demise in late 2004.[83] He also has headed the organization's Chicago chapter since 1993.[84] Jaber also served as board chairman of the Bridgeview Mosque in Illinois[85] and as an incorporator and board member of the Council on American-Islamic Relations (CAIR).[86]

In his capacity as IAP's president, Jaber issued a statement praising the terrorist group Hizballah for its success against Israel:

> I thank ALLAH for this victory which was due to the tremendous efforts of the Islamic resistance movement, Hezbollah. . . . Maybe the PA will take a hard look at the slippery road it is now traveling and join the resistance to Zionist occupation in order to liberate the land of Palestine. I firmly believe that Palestine will never be liberated by any other means.[87]

Yasser Bushnaq (aka Yasser Saleh) also served as president of IAP.[88] During his tenure, IAP printed some of Hamas's most incendiary communiqués. Bushnaq was one of two signatories of the Marzook Legal Defense Fund,[89] which defended Hamas leader Musa Abu Marzook up until his deportation to Jordan.[90] Bushnaq also helped found the American Middle Eastern League for Palestine.[91] AMELP, the parent corporation of, and the tax-exempt vehicle for, the Islamic Association of Palestine, incorporated the "IAP Information Office,"[92] which served as the publisher of all of IAP's publications.

Bushnaq, who attended[93] a February 2001 conference in Beirut, Lebanon, with members of al Qaeda, Hamas, Islamic Jihad, and Hizballah,[94] also ran Solidarity International for Human Rights (SIHR).[95] SIHR offered to pay the legal fees of Agus Budiman, an Indonesian man living in Virginia who pled guilty to identification fraud in Alexandria in March 2001.[96] Federal investigators believed that Budiman was linked to Mohamed Atta and Ziad Jarrah, two of the September 11 hijackers, though the judge sentenced him only to time served and found no link to the hijackings.[97]

Another key IAP figure is Omar Ahmad, who has been the chairman of the board of the Council on American-Islamic Relations (CAIR) since its incorporation in 1994 through May 2005.[98] In 1993 and

1994, Ahmad was the president of IAP.[99] While being deposed in the *Boim* case, he acknowledged that IAP published statements and information from Hamas[100] and he personally admitted bringing Hamas speakers to IAP conferences.[101] At IAP, Ahmad "worked closely"[102] with CAIR executive director Nihad Awad, who was IAP's public relations director in 1993 and 1994,[103] as well as a contributing editor of the *Muslim World Monitor*.[104]

In addition to holding conferences and publishing periodicals that praised the activities of Hamas, IAP also cultivated relationships with local mosques and imams in the United States who were sympathetic to Hamas's goals. One example of such a mosque is the Bridgeview Mosque, also known as the Mosque Foundation, in Bridgeview, Illinois, a suburb of Chicago.

The Mosque Foundation, Bridgeview, Illinois

Evidence shows the imam of the Mosque Foundation, Jamal Sa'id, had ties to the Muslim Brotherhood and has been active in Hamas front organizations. During an interrogation in an Israeli prison, Hamas leader Muhammad Salah said that he "started out with the Muslim Brothers in 1978 with Sheikh Jamal Sa'id, who serves as Sheikh of the Mosque of the Arab Community in Chicago."[105] Mohammad Jarad, another US citizen convicted in Israel of working for Hamas, has also been linked to Sa'id.[106] According to an Israeli indictment, "[I]n December 1992 before his travel to visit family in Ein Yabroud, [Jarad] met with Sheikh Jamal Sa'id, the Imam of a mosque in Chicago, who instructed him to meet with [Mohammad Kathem Suwalha, aka Abu Ubaada], a top Hamas operative in London, to get assignments for operations in the region in the course of his intended visit."[107] In addition to Sa'id's work at the Mosque Foundation, he also served for a time as treasurer of the Al Aqsa Educational Fund.[108] Furthermore, he was a frequent speaker at IAP conferences,[109] and the Mosque Foundation served as a venue for various IAP[110] events. Rafeeq Jaber, former president of IAP, also served on the board of the Mosque Foundation.[111]

Hamas Pays the Price: The Quranic Literacy Institute

The Quranic Literacy Institute (QLI) was an Illinois nonprofit corporation that purported to translate and publish sacred Islamic texts. Evidence suggests, however, that it has also engaged in laundering money for Hamas.[112] In the same November 2004 judgment in the *Boim* case, the judge also concluded that QLI funded Hamas.[113]

QLI also employed another defendant in the *Boim* case, Muhammad Abdul Hamid Khalil Salah (referred to here as Muhammad Salah)—who admitted to being a US leader of Hamas—as a computer analyst, though it denied ever having hired him.[114]

HAMAS FUND-RAISING ACTIVITIES

Abdel Jabbar Hamdan: HLF Fund-Raiser for Hamas

In July 2005, the American Civil Liberties Union (ACLU) filed a seventeen-page petition in a US district court on behalf of Abdel Jabbar Hamdan, who was arrested on immigration charges in July 2004.[115] Born in a Palestinian refugee camp in Jordan, Hamdan had been living in the United States illegally on a student visa issued more than twenty-five years ago. On April 7, 2006, an appeals board ruled that Hamdan should be deported to Jordan.[116]

Hamdan had earlier served as a primary spokesperson and fund-raiser for the Texas-based Islamic charity, the Holy Land Foundation (HLF). The charity was shut down in December 2001 after it was suspected of funneling money to the Palestinian terrorist group Hamas.[117] In July 2004, in a forty-two-count federal indictment seven of the foundation's top officials were charged with conspiracy to provide aid to Hamas and the families of suicide bombers. Hamdan was not charged in that case.[118]

The petition, written by ACLU lawyer Ranjana Natarajan, states that "there is not one shred of evidence in support of the government's argument that Hamdan poses a danger to national security."[119] Natarajan further claims that the charges against Mr. Hamdan are arbitrary and that federal officials "never even attempted to prove Hamdan raised funds with the intent to further terrorist activity."[120]

But Lori Haley, spokesperson for the US Immigration and Customs Enforcement (ICE) in Laguna Niguel, refutes the claim. She said an immigration court ruled that Hamdan "should have known that his activities constituted material support for a terrorist organization."[121] For instance, evidence produced at Hamdan's immigration hearing included a videotape, which showed the forty-four-year-old fund-raising in front of a

Hamas flag. The videotape further called for jihad and praised violence. The judge said that this contradicted Hamdan's defense that he was unaware that the funds were being raised for Hamas.[122]

Because of his past ties to an organization linked to the sponsorship of terrorism, Hamdan's request that he be freed on bail has been declined.[123]

The Holy Land Foundation

From its inception, the Holy Land Foundation for Relief and Development claimed to be a nonprofit, tax-exempt, charitable organization whose main mission was to assist needy individuals in the West Bank and Gaza. However, evidence collected by federal authorities and the Investigative Project on Terrorism indicates that HLF provided financial support to Hamas throughout its existence. This section reviews HLF's beginnings and connections to Hamas. Its methods and means of financing are examined in chapter 9.

The origins of the Holy Land Foundation date back to 1987, when Shukri Abu Bakr, with assistance from Mohammed el-Mezain, Ghassan Elashi, and others, founded the Occupied Land Fund.[124] In 1991, OLF changed its name to the Holy Land Foundation[125] and soon thereafter moved its headquarters from California to Richardson, Texas. HLF eventually established offices throughout the United States (including California, Illinois, Michigan, New Jersey,[126] and Florida[127]) and abroad, in Brazil[128] as well as in Israel, the West Bank, and the Gaza Strip.[129]

Financial records indicate that Abu Bakr had established a financial relationship with the Hamas leader Marzook in April 1988, when HLF sent about $100,000 to Marzook and his associates.[130] In or around 1989, the amount of funds that HLF was providing to Hamas increased dramatically. Between April 1989 and October 1989, the charity wire transferred approximately $725,000 to an account held by the Islamic Center of Gaza, which was founded by the Hamas leader Sheikh Ahmed Yassin and used by him to coordinate and conduct Hamas activities.[131]

HLF Connections to Hamas Leadership

At least two members of HLF's senior leadership are related to Marzook by blood or marriage: Mohammed el-Mezain, a former chairman of the board and director of endowments of HLF, is Marzook's cousin,[132] while

Ghassan Elashi, who served first as HLF's treasurer and later as chairman of its board, is a cousin of Marzook's wife, Nadia Elashi.[133]

But these personal ties to Hamas members do not end with Marzook. Akram Mishal, HLF's project and grants director, is Hamas leader Khalid Mishaal's cousin;[134] and Mufid Abdulqader, Mishaal's half brother, was a top fund-raiser for HLF.[135] The familial links found in HLF are not unusual in terrorist-financing operations.[136]

HLF's leaders in the West Bank and Gaza Strip included Muhammad Anati,[137] who ran the HLF office near Jerusalem; Kamal al-Timimi, who ran an office in Hebron; and Zuhair Barghati, a former head of the organization's Gaza Strip office. Anati told Israeli authorities in an interview that he had been enlisted by Hamas in 1990 and that HLF provided aid to Hamas.[138] Al-Timimi was identified by Israeli authorities as a Hamas member and was deported to Lebanon in 1992 for his ties to the organization.[139]

Around the time of HLF's move to Texas, Marzook donated $210,000 to the organization as a onetime cash donation.[140] Marzook's personal secretary, Nasser al-Khatib,[141] is also listed that year as having given the organization a onetime cash donation of $22,450.[142] According to Special Agent David Kane of the Bureau of Immigration and Customs Enforcement (ICE), "HLF was started in large part with $210,000 from Hamas leader Musa Abu Marzook."[143] Another official source states that "HLF and OLF . . . received significant initial funding from Mousa Abu Marzook."[144]

In 1992, Hamas experienced a serious setback when Israel deported more than four hundred Hamas and Palestinian Islamic Jihad members to the Marj Al Zuhour refugee camp in southern Lebanon. HLF, in turn, quickly rushed to the aid of the deported. According to a 1993 HLF newsletter:

> The *HLF* was the first relief organization to respond to the crisis. In December of 1992, more that 10,000 appeals were sent across the nation, which raised more that $100,000 to provide emergency relief to the exiled men and their families.
>
> The *HLF* has sent more than $60,000 to 397 Palestinian deportees to provide them with daily needs and necessary food and medicine. On the other hand their families back home have received more than $150,000 to help them overcome the hardship the expulsion has created.[145]

Throughout its existence, HLF actively supplied financial aid to the families of Hamas members who were wounded, killed, or deported.[146] In fact, HLF's Jerusalem chairman, Muhammad Anati, told Israeli authorities during an interrogation that the family of Imad Akel—who, before his death, had served as a leader of Hamas's military wing, the Izz Al Din Al Qassam Brigades—was supported by HLF funds.[147]

Al Aqsa Educational Fund

AAEF was incorporated in 1993 by Abdelhaleem al-Ashqar (aka Abu Hassan) and Imad Sarsour at the University of Mississippi in Oxford.[148] According to an advertisement it ran in *Al Zaitounah,* the charity also ran an office in Athens, Ohio.[149] Its purpose was ostensibly to raise money for charities located in the West Bank and Gaza Strip.[150] An FBI report issued in 2001 described AAEF as a Hamas front;[151] and in August 2004, al-Ashqar was indicted in Chicago along with Marzook and Muhammad Salah on charges that he participated in a racketeering conspiracy in the United States to finance Hamas terror abroad.[152]

In its first year of existence, AAEF distributed a $15,000 grant to a group identified as the Society of Islamic Sciences and Culture.[153] This appears to be the same organization as Jerusalem's Association of Islamic Sciences and Cultures, which is run by Jamil Hamami, a Hamas member[154] who during the 1990s traveled to the United States to raise money for HLF and AAEF.[155]

Like HLF, AAEF distributed aid to Hamas-linked individuals and organizations. AAEF advertisements were featured at least thirteen times in IAP's publication *Al Zaitounah* in 1993 and early 1994. Many of the ads led with the English caption: "Educational Institutions in West Bank and Gaza Strip are suffering from Israeli policies. They are in need of your financial support in order to survive."[156]

One AAEF advertisement, published September 17, 1993, in *Al Zaitounah,* said that the fund aimed to "support the [Hamas] deportees in Marj Al Zuhour" in southern Lebanon and "provide the opportunity of education for . . . the children of the martyrs, the prisoners, and the orphans."[157] The ad also explained that AAEF "chooses, indiscriminately, several needy students from the families of martyrs or detainees and provides them with financial support in the form of tuition, registration, and admission to the university."[158]

During the early 1990s, AAEF competed with HLF in raising funds for Hamas in the United States. But in 1994, Marzook and other Hamas leaders decided that US fund-raising efforts should be managed by HLF.[159]

AAEF Leadership

According to *Hamas*, a book by Ronni Shaked and Aviva Shaavi, AAEF's former executive director, Abdelhaleem al-Ashqar was "responsible for transferring funds to the [Palestinian] territories" and served as the head of the Hamas Operations Committee in the United States.[160] In November 1992, the Israeli government advised the United States that al-Ashqar was a Hamas member who was involved in the movement of funds from the United States to Hamas in the West Bank and Gaza.[161]

Sufiyan Abu Samara, who served as the "point man" in Gaza for the transfer of funds for Hamas activities, disclosed in interviews with the Israeli police that al-Ashqar was one of the financial supporters for Hamas military activities:

> Later on in the same manner I received forty thousand Dollars and seventy thousand Dollars and I gave to Abu Anas and his activists and when the checks were finished there was another way to get money. It was through a fellow who is in the U.S. and his name is Abd Al Halim Al Ashki [*sic*], alias Abu Hassan. He called me to my house and told me that he is the mediator between me and Abu Omar [Musa Abu Marzook]. He gave me his phone number in the U.S. to get in touch and also gave me the phone number of someone from the Sajaiyah neighborhood and told me that he had a deposit for me, that is, from Hamas. He asked me to get in touch with the resident of Sajaiyah and to receive the money from him. . . . After that, Abu Anas asked me to get in touch with Abu Hassan in the U.S. and tell him to deposit 300,000 dollars to a bank account number in Egypt. I called and told Abu Hassan the account number and gave him the message. After that Abu Hassan called me twice and told me that the first time he deposited 200 thousand dollars and the second time he added that he deposited 100 thousand and that is in connection with the money and Hamas activity.[162]

According to IRS forms filed by AAEF, Mohammed Jaghlit (aka Mohammed el-Gajhleet) served as president of AAEF between 1993 and 1996.[163] Jaghlit is a key officer of the SAAR network (see chapter 10), which consists of dozens of for-profit companies and charitable entities—located mostly in Virginia—under the control of a group of individuals who federal authorities suspect of providing material support to terrorists, laundering money, and evading taxes.[164] The address Jaghlit provided on AAEF's tax forms is the same address from which the SAAR Foundation operated.[165] On March 20, 2002, federal agents raided many offices and homes of SAAR network organizations and individuals, including the residence of Mohammed Jaghlit.[166]

Muin Mohammad (aka Muin Shabib, Kamel Mohammad Shabib, and Abu Muhammad) is one of the original founders of AAEF and is listed on the group's 1993 IRS Form 990 as the secretary of the AAEF executive committee.[167] According to an FBI Action Memorandum, Muin Kamel Mohammed Shabib attended the October 1993 Hamas conference in Philadelphia along with Abdelhaleem al-Ashqar and others.[168] And documents submitted by the Department of Justice in court proceedings in the District of Columbia regarding HLF show that Shabib was identified by the government of Israel as a senior Hamas operative formerly in charge of Hamas's Central Section (Ramallah-Jerusalem) in the West Bank.[169]

On March 16, 1994, the FBI in Falls Church, Virginia, interviewed Shabib at the home of Yasser Bushnaq, a former president of the IAP. During the interview, Shabib admitted supporting Hamas financially and politically.[170] Shabib "was interviewed under the pretext of gaining information relating to his immigration status" (he had applied for political asylum in December 1993).[171]

Other AAEF leaders include Imam Jamal Sa'id of the Mosque Foundation, who served as AAEF's treasurer, and Fawaz Mushtaha, who was on AAEF's board of trustees.[172] Mushtaha also worked as IAP's Washington, DC, representative.[173] In addition to having been IAP's president,[174] Yasser Bushnaq also served as an officer for AAEF[175] and as director of Solidarity International for Human Rights.[176] SIHR has been under congressional investigation for possible terrorism financing.[177] Furthermore, Muhammad Salah identified another AAEF employee in the United States, Anan el-Karmi—who was listed as secretary of the organization's executive committee in 1995[178]—as a member of the Hamas security committee. [179]

AAEF's Sponsorship of Hamas Members and Activities

In the early part of 1994, Hamas leader Sheikh Jamil Hamami came to the United States to fund-raise in Michigan, Chicago, and Philadelphia on behalf of AAEF.[180]

Al-Ashqar and AAEF were active in the notorious 1993 meeting in Philadelphia of Hamas leaders, and much of the cost of the meeting was paid for by the AAEF.[181] It was al-Ashqar who suggested the objective of the meeting and issued the invitations.

United Association for Studies and Research

The United Association for Studies and Research (UASR), an Islamic think tank based in Springfield, Virginia, was founded in 1989 in Chicago by a number of individuals. Among them were Mousa Abu Marzook, who served as the first president of UASR's board of directors,[182] and Nabil Sadoun.[183] Sadoun also headed the Muslim Arab Youth Association (MAYA),[184] which, according to the confessions of Hamas members in Israel, provided bomb-making and munitions training for Hamas operatives at its annual conferences in the United States.[185] Sadoun currently serves on CAIR's board of directors.[186]

Another member of UASR's inner circle is Ahmed bin Yousef (aka Yousef Saleh), who has served as the organization's executive director since 1992.[187] Bin Yousef published a book that pays tribute to the deceased founder of Hamas, Sheikh Ahmed Yassin. *Ahmed Yassin: The Phenomenon, the Miracle, and the Legend of the Challenge* contains letters extolling the imminent victory of Hamas over the Jews. One such letter, written by a Hamas member in Chicago for Hamas operatives in the Palestinian territories, read: "Greetings to you from here in America, from over the seas, that you may know that we are your sons of the era, the era of Allah, the era of Islam, the era of Palestine, the era of Jihad, the era of Hamas, until complete liberation of all Palestine from the river to the sea!"[188]

While the organizations discussed above are significant for their success in fund-raising and distributing propaganda, UASR's importance is political. According to a 1993 *New York Times* article, Muhammad Salah, a Hamas terrorist convicted by an Israeli court, confessed that "the political command of Hamas in the United States is at the United Association for Studies and Research in Springfield, Virginia. [Salah] identified the Hamas leader in the United States as the head of the institute, Ahmad Yousef, a writer whose code name he said was Abu Ahmed. [Salah] also said that Mousa Abu Marzouk, known as Abu Omar, 51, of Arlington, Virginia, was the political chief."[189]

And in 2004, a document filed by the US government in the case of

Fawaz Damrah, a Cleveland imam, stated that "available public source information, taken as a whole, indicates that UASR through its Executive Director, has demonstrated its sympathies for Hamas and that several of its key associates are, or have been, integrally involved in Hamas activities."[190]

Further proof of UASR and bin Yousef's connections to Hamas can be found in an indictment filed in Florida against various individuals involved in providing material support for the Palestinian Islamic Jihad terrorist organization. According to the indictment, "On or about July 29, 1994, [the leader of the Islamic Jihad group in Florida] sent a facsimile to Ahmed Yousef of a draft proposal to unify Palestinian activities in the Territories, including those of the PIJ and HAMAS."[191] This implied that bin Yousef would remark on the draft from the perspective of Hamas while those in Florida would remark from the perspective of the Islamic Jihad.

InfoCom

Incorporated in Richardson, Texas, in 1992 and run by Ghassan Elashi and his four brothers, Infocom sold computer systems and networking, telecommunications, and Internet services, and also exported computers to the Middle East.[192] According to the US government, in or around July 1992, Marzook, who is married to the Elashis' cousin Nadia, "sent, or caused to be sent, $150,000" to Infocom.[193] The government alleges that in total, Infocom received at least $250,000 in investment capital from accounts controlled by Marzook.[194]

On September 5, 2001, Infocom was informed that two of its bank accounts were being frozen because of a 1993 investment from the wife of a top Hamas political leader.[195] The following day, federal agents raided Infocom's Richardson offices.[196] The investigation into the business dealings of InfoCom culminated in the arrests of four Elashi brothers—Bayan, Ghassan, Basman, and Hazim—on December 17, 2002. The fifth Elashi brother, Ihsan ("Sammy"), was already in custody on an unrelated charge.[197] Marzook and his wife, Nadia Elashi, were also indicted, along with Infocom itself.[198] The two-part trial was comprised of a thirty-three-count indictment that included export violations involving Syria and Libya, money laundering, and conspiracy to deal in the property of a Specially Designated Terrorist.[199]

In July 2004, Bayan Elashi, Ghassan Elashi, Basman Elashi, Hazim Elashi, and Ihsan Elashi along with the Infocom Corporation were "convicted on charges they conspired to violate the Export Administration

Regulations and the Libyan Sanctions Regulations. Specifically, each of the five brothers was also found guilty of conspiracy to file false Shipper's Export Declaration forms. All of the brothers were convicted of the false statements charges and all of the defendants except Ihsan Elashi were also convicted on money laundering charges."[200]

In addition to the Infocom conviction, Ghassan Elashi and his two brothers Basman and Bayan Elashi were each found "guilty of conspiracy to deal in the property of a Specially Designated Terrorist and conspiracy to commit money laundering."[201]

Leadership

As already noted, InfoCom was controlled by the Elashi brothers. Bayan Elashi served as chief executive officer of InfoCom and technical contact for IAP and HLF, as well as hundreds of other Islamic clients in the United States and the Middle East. Basman Elashi was InfoCom's operations manager[202] and was president of IAP-Texas from 1995 to 1998.[203]

Ghassan Elashi, who was InfoCom's vice president for marketing,[204] incorporated an IAP office in California in 1986 and served as the board treasurer[205] and chairman[206] of HLF. He was also on the board of directors of CAIR-Texas.[207]

Radical Islamist and Terrorist Web Sites

In addition to providing the servers for some of the United States' largest radical Islamist organizations, among them the Islamic Society of North America and the Muslim Students Association, InfoCom also hosted the Web sites of the Holy Land Foundation and the Islamic Association for Palestine.[208]

CONCLUSION

Over the past almost two decades, the United States has proven a fertile ground for Hamas fund-raising,[209] and much of this activity was facilitated by Hamas leader Musa Abu Marzook. During the 1980s and 1990s, Hamas set up charitable and political organizations in the United States that funneled money to Hamas terrorists in the West Bank and Gaza. Although the US government has enjoyed a great deal of success in recent years in hampering this illicit fund-raising network—most notably the deportation of Marzook, the shutdown of the Holy Land Foundation for Relief and Development, and the indictments of Abdelhaleem al-Ashqar, Ismail Elbarasse, and Muhammad Salah—much work remains to be done. For instance, several Muslim American groups—like the Islamic Association for Palestine—continue to use the cover of the First Amendment to promote their terrorist activities.

While Hamas's main objective remains the destruction of Israel and the establishment of a Palestinian Islamic state in its place, the group has, in the very least, considered carrying out attacks on American soil. Threatening statements made by Hamas leaders against the United States and its activities in Iraq, combined with the arrests of Jamal Aqal and Ismail Elbarasse, have raised concerns in the American intelligence community that Hamas may be seeking not only to carry out its own attacks on American soil but also to conduct surveillance for other terrorist groups. Given these possibilities and the troubling history of Hamas members who have established operations on US soil, any statements or movements the group makes regarding America warrant the closest scrutiny.

NOTES

1. Action Memorandum, Holy Land Foundation for Relief and Development International Emergency Economic Powers Act, from Dale Watson, assistant director FBI Counterterrorism Division to Richard Newcomb, director of the Office of Foreign Assets Control, Department of Treasury, November 5, 2001, p. 3 (hereinafter "Watson Action Memorandum").

2. Ziad Abu-Amr, "Hamas: A Historical and Political Background," *Journal of Palestine Studies* 22, no. 4 (Summer 1993): 10.

3. Muhammad Maqdisi, "Charter of the Islamic Resistance Movement (Hamas) of Palestine," *Journal of Palestine Studies* 22, no. 4 (Summer 1993): 126.

4. "Annex to Federal Register: Prohibiting Transactions with Terrorists Who Threaten to Disrupt the Middle East Peace Process Executive Order 12947" (January 25, 1995).

5. *State of Israel v. Nasser Issa Gal'al Hayedmi*, ID#23474141, charge sheet (March 6, 1993).

6. *In the matter of Hasan Faisal and Yousef Sabri*, "Notice of Revocation of petition for Amerasian, Widow, or Special. Immigrant (Form I-360), Attachment."

7. Judith Miller, "Israel Says That a Prisoner's Tale Links Arabs in the US to Terrorism," *New York Times*, February 17, 1993.

8. *Holy Land Foundation for Relief and Development v. Ashcroft, et al.*, 02-CV-442, 1930–34 (D DC August 2002).

9. Watson Action Memorandum, p. 12.

10. *Holy Land Foundation for Relief and Development v. Ashcroft, et al.*, 02-CV-442, exhibit 14: FBI memorandum regarding the Philadelphia conference, October 27, 1993, p. 255 (D DC August 2002).

11. *USA v. Holy Land Foundation for Relief and Development, et al.*, 04-CR-240, indictment (ND TX July 26, 2004).

12. *Holy Land Foundation for Relief and Development v. Ashcroft, et al.*, 02-CV-442, exhibit 14: FBI memorandum regarding the Philadelphia conference, October 27, 1993, p. 255 (D DC August 2002).

13. Ibid.

14. Watson Action Memorandum, p. 9.

15. *USA v. Holy Land Foundation for Relief and Development, et al.*, 04-CR-240, indictment (ND TX July 26, 2004); *Holy Land Foundation for Relief and Development v. Ashcroft*, 219 F. Supp. 2d 57, 70 (D DC 2002), and other sources. The senior Hamas leader who was captured by Israeli authorities was Muhammad Salah, who had been active in the United States. He returned to the United States in 1997, after serving a four-year prison sentence in Israel.

16. Watson Action Memorandum, p. 12.

17. *Holy Land Foundation for Relief and Development v. Ashcroft, et al.*, 02-CV-442, exhibit 28: FBI analysis of the Philadelphia conference, October 27, 1993, p. 1439 (D DC August 2002).

18. Ibid., p. 1431.

19. Ibid., p. 1445.

20. Ibid., p. 1434.

21. Watson Action Memorandum, p. 13.

22. *Holy Land Foundation for Relief and Development v. Ashcroft, et al.*, 02-CV-442, Exhibit 28: FBI analysis of the Philadelphia conference, October 27, 1993, p. 1421 (D DC August 2002).

23. Ibid., pp. 1419–20.

24. Ibid., p. 1455.

25. Watson Action Memorandum, p. 14.

26. "American Victims of Mideast Terrorist Attacks," Jewish Virtual Library Web site, http://www.jewishvirtuallibrary.org/jsource/Terrorism/usvictims.html (accessed August 10, 2005).

27. *Boim et al v. QLI, et al.*, 00-CV-2905, judgment (ND IL December 8, 2004).

28. *In re Search Warrant of 4502 Whistler Court, Annandale, VA, et al.*, EDVA, Affidavit in Support of Search Warrant: SA FBI Shawn Devroude, August 20, 2004.

29. "Eli Lake, "Hamas Agents Lurking in U.S., FBI Warns," *New York Sun*, April 29, 2004.

30. "Hamas Trained Terrorist, Canadian National, Arrested by ISA," Israel Ministry of Foreign Affairs, December 8, 2003.

31. *Holy Land Foundation for Relief and Development v. Ashcroft, et al.*, 02-CV-442, memorandum opinion, p. 20 (D DC August 8, 2002).

32. *In re Search Warrant of 4502 Whistler Court, Annandale, VA, et al.*, EDVA, Affidavit in Support of Search Warrant: SA FBI Shawn Devroude, August 20, 2004.

33. Erich Rich and Jerry Markon, "Va. Man Held as Witness in Case Tied to Hamas," *Washington Post*, August 25, 2004.

34. *In re Search Warrant of 4502 Whistler Court, Annandale, VA, et al.*, EDVA, Affidavit in Support of Search Warrant: SA FBI Shawn Devroude, August 20, 2004.

35. Khaled Abu Toameh, "Hamas Split Over Exporting Terror Campaign," *Jerusalem Post*, September 27, 2004.

36. Hassan Abu Hashish, "Founder and Leader of Hamas Sheikh Ahmad Yassin Addresses the Nation in a Comprehensive Dialogue" *Al Haqa'iq*, November 23, 2003, http://www.alhaqaeq.net/defaultch.asp?action=showarticle&secid=7&articleid=14037 (accessed August 10, 2005).

37. "Hamas' Spiritual Leader Declares Possible War on U.S," Fox Special Report with Brit Hume, Fox News Channel, February 17, 2003.

38. James Bennet, "Hamas Urges Iraqis to Make Suicide Attacks on the Invaders," *New York Times*, March 22, 2003.

39. Reuven Pax, "Rantisi vs. the United States: New Policy of a New Leader of Hamas?" Intelligence and Terrorism Information Center, November 2003.

40. Arnon Regular, "Thousands Attend Pro-Iraq Rallies in West Bank and Gaza," *Haaretz*, April 11, 2004.

41. "Arab States to Ask UN to Condemn Rantisi Killing," *Haaretz*, April 19, 2004.

42. *Al Quds Al Arabi* (London), August 23, 2004; "The Muslim Brotherhood Movement in Support of Fighting American Forces in Iraq," Special Dispatch 3, September 2004, http://www.memri.de/uebersetzungen_analysen/themen/islamistische_ideologie/isl_mbrotherhood_03_09_04.html (accessed August 10, 2005).

43. "Maverick Cleric Inspires Uprising," CBS News, April 4, 2004.

44. *Holy Land Foundation for Relief and Development v. Ashcroft, et al.*, 02-CV-442, memorandum opinion, p. 20 (D DC August 8, 2002).

45. "OFAC Recent Actions," US Department of Treasury, Office of Foreign Assets Control, August 21, 2003.

46. Richard Leiby, "Unorthodox Attorney," *Washington Post*, August 8, 2002.

47. "U.S. Interagency Efforts to Combat Terrorist Financing," US Department of State, December 15, 2003.

48. Ibid.

49. "Chicago and Washington, D.C., Area Men among Three Indicted in Racketeering Conspiracy in U.S. to Finance Hamas Terror Abroad," US Department of Justice press release; *USA v. Ashqar, et al.*, 03-CR-978 (ND IL August 20, 2004).

50. *USA v. Ashqar, et al.*, 03-CR-978, second superceding indictment (ND IL August 20, 2004).

51. Watson Action Memorandum, p. 16.

52. Ibid.

53. Ibid., p. 15.

54. Ibid., p. 11.

55. *Boim et al v. Quranic Literacy Institute, et al.*, 00-CV-2905, memorandum and order (ND IL November 10, 2004).

56. "Articles of Incorporation of Islamic Association for Palestine," Illinois Secretary of State, November 6, 1981.

57. Ibid.

58. Oliver Revell, "Protecting America: Law Enforcement Views Radical Islam," *Middle East Forum*, March 1995.

59. *In the matter of Hasan Faisal and Yousef Sabri*, "Notice of Revocation of petition for Amerasian, Widow, or Special. Immigrant (Form I-360), Attachment."

60. *Holy Land Foundation for Relief and Development v. John Ashcroft, et al.*, 02-CV-442, memorandum opinion, p. 21 (D DC August 8 2002).

61. *Boim et al. v. Quranic Literacy Institute, et al.*, 00-CV-2905, memorandum and order, p. 61 (ND IL November 10, 2004).

62. Ibid., p. 62.

63. Ibid., p. 59.

64. Ibid., p. 9.

65. *Ila Filastin*, October 1988, p. 10.

66. Ibid.

67. Web Archive of Islamic Association for Palestine Web site, http://web.archive.org/web/20000301140706/www.iap.org/sounds/songs/songs.html (accessed August 10, 2005). The address and phone number given match those of the IAP Information Office.

68. *The Waad*, video material from the Islamic Association for Palestine, produced by Aqsa Vision, obtained by the Investigative Project.

69. Ibid.

70. *Palestine Come to Jihad*, video material from the Islamic Association for Palestine, produced by Aqsa Vision, obtained by the Investigative Project.

71. Ibid.

72. *Ila Filastin*, October 1988.

73. Khalil al-Qawka, a Hamas leader, appeared at the November 26, 1991, IAP conference in New Jersey, video material from the Islamic Association for Palestine, obtained by the Investigative Project.

74. Transcript, Islamic Association for Palestine, annual conference, Kansas City, Missouri, December 27–30, 1989.

75. Eileen Alt Powell, "Reports Say Assailant Carefully Planned Bus Attack in Israel," Associated Press, July 7, 1989.

76. *Boim et al. v. QLI, et al.*, 00-CV-2905, deposition of Rafeeq Jaber, pp. 77–78 (ND IL April 9, 2003).

77. Ibid., pp. 253–55.

78. *Muslim World Monitor*, July 30, 1993; *Muslim World Monitor*, February 9, 1994; *Muslim World Monitor*, February 2, 1995. For more on IAP's promotion of HLF in its publications, see *Holy Land Foundation for Relief and Development v. Ashcroft*, 02-CV-442, exhibit 28, p. 1443 (D DC 02-442 GK).

79. Ibid.

80. *Boim et al. v. QLI, et al.*, 00-CV-2905, deposition of Rafeeq Jaber, pp. 199, 206 (ND IL April 9, 2003).

81. Ibid., p. 206.

82. Ibid., pp. 10–12.

83. The last update of the Web site of the Islamic Association for Palestine was made November 2004, http://web.archive.org/web/20041105040555/http://www.iap.org/ (accessed December 12, 2005).

84. *Boim et al. v. QLI, et al.*, 00-CV-2905, deposition of Rafeeq Jaber, pp. 10–12 (ND IL April 9, 2003)

85. "1991–1997 Mosque Foundation Annual Reports," Illinois Secretary of State.

86. "1994 and 1995 Council on American-Islamic Relations Form 990," Internal Revenue Service (IRS).

87. "IAP President Statement Regarding Israeli Withdrawal from Southern Lebanon," distributed on the IAP-Net electronic mail list, May 24, 2000.

88. *Ila Filastin*, February 1990, p. 70.

89. "Paper Trail Leads to Hamas," *Dallas Morning News*, April 8, 1996.

90. "Prosecutors Capitalize on Increased Access to Wiretap Evidence," *Wall Street Journal*, January 21, 2003.

91. "American Middle Eastern League for Palestine Form 1023," Internal Revenue Service (IRS), May 9, 1991; "1991 and 1992 American Middle Eastern League for Palestine Form 990," Internal Revenue Service (IRS).

92. "American Middle Eastern League for Palestine Articles of Incorporation," Texas Secretary of State, March 13, 1990; "American Middle Eastern League for Palestine Form 1023," Internal Revenue Service (IRS), May 9, 1991.

93. "Imad-Ad-Dean Ahmad's Address to the First Conference on Jerusalem," Minaret of Freedom Institute, January 29, 2001, http://www.minaret.org/beirutconference.htm (accessed August 10, 2005); "US Evenhanded in Mideast Criticism," CBS News, February 14, 2001.

94. Niles Latham, "Islamic Terror Groups Form Unholy Alliance," *New York Post*, February 12, 2001.

95. Federal News Service, "Press Conference with the American Muslim Society," September 18, 2001.

96. "FBI Once Declared Agus Budiman Clean," *Jakarta Post*, November 26, 2001.

97. "VA Case a Window on Terror Probe," *Washington Post*, November 29, 2001; Tom Jackman, "ID Fraud Case Ends in Va.; Indonesian Sentenced to Time Served; No Sept. 11 Link Found," *Washington Post*, May 11, 2002.

98. "Board Member, A Short Biography of Omar Ahmad," CAIR Web site,

http://www.cair-net.org/default.asp?Page=Board&person=Omar (accessed August 10, 2005).

99. Nihad Awad, "Muslim-Americans in Mainstream America," *Link*, February–March 2000; Omar Yayha, "Letter to IAP Members/Supporters," December 1, 1993; *Al Zaitounah*, August 25, 1994, p. 14.

100. *Boim et al. v. Quranic Literacy Institute, et al.*, 00-CV-2905, deposition of Omar Ahmad, p. 255 (ND IL May 27, 2003).

101. Ibid., p. 123.

102. Nihad Awad, "Muslim-Americans in Mainstream America," *Link*, February–March 2000.

103. Ibid.

104. *Muslim World Monitor*, July 30, 1993, p. 2.

105. *Request for the Extradition of Marzook*, vol. 2, Salah Statements 4E, August 21, 1995.

106. *Efrat Ungar et al. v. The Palestine Liberation Organization et al.*, memorandum and order, p. 45 (DRI July 3, 2003).

107. *Indictment of Mohammad Hilmi Ibrahim Jarad*, Israeli Defense Forces Military Court (March 11, 1993).

108. "Al Aqsa Educational Fund Form 990," State of Mississippi, 1995 and 1996.

109. Imam Jamal Said was listed on the IAP conference programs for 1999, 2000, and 2001.

110. IAP and the Mosque Foundation cosponsored Intifada Day at the Mosque Foundation. "IAP-Net: Chicago: Intifada Day on June 23," IAP Listserv e-mail, June 23, 2001. See also "IAP-Net: IAP Hosts Rallies for Palestine in Several U.S. Cities, IAP President Urges People to Do More," IAP Listserv e-mail, October 5, 2000.

111. "Struggle for the Soul of Islam; The Mosque and Several Noted Islamic Groups," *Chicago Tribune*, February 8, 2004.

112. *Boim et al. v. Quranic Literacy Institute, et al.*, 00-CV-2905, affidavit of Robert Wright, pp. 1, 32 (ND IL June 8, 1998).

113. *Boim et al. v. Quranic Literacy Institute, et al.*, 00-CV-2905, memorandum and order (ND IL November 10, 2004).

114. *Boim et al. v. Quranic Literacy Institute, et al.*, 00-CV-2905, defendants; motion to dismiss, motions for Rule 11 sanctions, p. 8 (ND IL January 10, 2001).

115. *Hamdan v. Alberto Gonzalez, et al.*, 05-CV-5144, petition for writ of habeas corpus (CD CA July 14, 2005).

116. H. G. Reza, "Muslim Should Be Deported, Board Rules," *Los Angeles Times*, April 12, 2006, http://www.latimes.com/news/local/la-me-hamdan 12apr12,1,29877.story?ctrack=1&cset=true (accessed April 13, 2006).

117. "Shutting Down the Terrorist Financial Network," US Treasury Department, December 4, 2001, http://www.ustreas.gov/press/releases/po841.htm (accessed July 5, 2006).

118. *USA v. HLF et al.*, 04-CR-240, indictment (ND TX July 26, 2004).

119. Associated Press, "Civil Rights Lawyers Petition for Deportee's Release," July 15, 2005.

120. Ibid.

121. Ibid.

122. "Former High-Ranking Official for Holy Land Foundation Ordered Removed from the United States," US Department of Justice press release, February 8, 2005.

123. Ibid.

124. "Occupied Land Fund" (advertisement), *Ila Filastin*, October 1988, p. 14.

125. "Holy Land Foundation" (advertisement), *Al Zaitounah*, October 14, 1991, p. 14.

126. *HLF News*, October 1996.

127. Florida Department of State, Division of Corporations, the Holy Land Foundation for Relief and Development, Inc., Document Number: F98000001960, Registered Agent: Raed Awad, 3336 W. Broward Blvd., Ft Lauderdale, FL 33312.

128. HLF Programs and Objectives brochure, in Arabic.

129. Watson Action Memorandum, p. 8.

130. *USA v. Holy Land Foundation for Relief and Development, et al.*, 04-CR-240, indictment, p. 8 (ND TX July 27, 2004).

131. Ibid.

132. Ibid., p. 7.

133. Ibid.

134. Ibid.

135. Ibid.

136. For example, see the discussion of the financing of the Palestinian Islamic Jihad (PIJ) in the United States in chapter 8.

137. *Holy Land Foundation News Letter*, December 1993, p. 6.

138. Ibid. Watson Action Memorandum, pp. 23–24. Anati was arrested and detained by Israel on charges of aiding and abetting a terrorist organization on December 10, 1997.

139. Ibid., p. 25.

140. "1993 Holy Land Foundation for Relief and Development Form 990," Internal Revenue Service (IRS).

141. Nasser al-Khatib was described as Marzook's secretary in an affidavit filed by FBI Special Agent Robert Wright pursuant to a civil forfeiture case presented in Chicago, Illinois, against the property of individuals suspected of providing financial support for the terrorist activities of Hamas within the State of Israel.

142. "1993 Holy Land Foundation for Relief and Development Form 990," Internal Revenue Service (IRS).

143. *USA v. Soliman Biheiri*, 03-365-A, redacted sentencing declaration (ED VA December 11, 2003).

144. Evidentiary Memorandum for R. Richard Newcomb on Redesignation of Holy Land Foundation For Relief and Development, p. 2.

145. "Urgent—Deportees Not Forgotten!" *Holy Land* 1, no. 1 (June 2005).

146. *Holy Land Foundation for Relief and Development v. John Ashcroft, et al.*, 02-CV-442, memorandum opinion, pp. 8–9 (D DC August 8, 2002).

147. Mohammed Anati statement, interviewed by Israeli Police Department, December 17, 1997.

148. "Articles of Incorporation for Al Aqsa Educational Fund," State of Mississippi, January 26, 1993.

149. "Al Aqsa Educational Fund" (advertisement), *Al Zaitounah*, September 3, 1993. Listed as Al-Aqsa Educational Fund, 13 Stewart Street, Athens, OH 45701.

150. Ibid.

151. Watson Action Memorandum, p. 13.

152. US Department of Justice press release, "Chicago and Washington, D.C., Area Men Among Three Indicted in Racketeering Conspiracy in U.S. to Finance Hamas Terror Abroad," August 20, 2004.

153. "Al-Aqsa Educational Fund Tax Form 990," State of Mississippi, 1993, p. 9.

154. Bill Hutman, "Police Close Islamic Center in Jerusalem," *Jerusalem Post*, March 8, 1996.

155. *Holy Land Foundation for Relief and Development v. John Ashcroft, et al.*, exhibit 29, p. 1478 (D DC August 2002).

156. AAEF advertisements found in *Al Zaitounah*, February 19, 1993; March 19, 1993; April 30, 1993; May 14, 1993; May 28, 1993; August 6, 1993; August 20, 1993; September 3, 1993; September 17, 1993; October 15, 1993; December 3, 1993. In 1994: January 20, 1994.

157. Al Aqsa Educational Fund Advertisement, *Al Zaitounah*, September 17, 1993.

158. Ibid.

159. *Holy Land Foundation for Relief and Development v. John Ashcroft, et al.*, exhibit 29, p. 1478 (D DC August 2002).

160. Ronni Shaked and Aviva Shaavi, *Hamas: From the Belief in Allah to the Road to Terrorism* (Jerusalem: Keter Publishing, 1994), p. 164.

161. Watson Action Memorandum, p. 9.

162. *Holy Land Foundation for Relief and Development v. John Ashcroft, et al.*, exhibit 16, pp. 286–88 (D DC August 2002).

163. "Al Aqsa Educational Fund Form 990," State of Mississippi, 1993, 1995, and 1996; "Al Aqsa Educational Fund Form 1023," State of Mississippi, 1994.

164. *Redacted Sworn Affidavit of United States Customs Service Senior Special Agent David Kane in Support of Application for Search Warrant, In the Matter of Searches Involving 555 Grove Street, Herndon, Virginia, and Related Locations*, 02-114-MG, § X, ¶ 111 (ED VA March 2002).

165. Ibid. ; "Al Aqsa Educational Fund Form 990," State of Mississippi, 1996.

166. Douglas Farah and John Mintz, "U.S. Trails VA Muslim Money, Ties," *Washington Post*, October 7, 2002.

167. "Al Aqsa Educational Fund Form 990," State of Mississippi, 1996.

168. Watson Action Memorandum, p. 9.

169. *Holy Land Foundation for Relief and Development v. John Ashcroft, et al.*, exhibit 24, p. 1478 (D DC August 2002).

170. Watson Action Memorandum, p. 11.

171. *Holy Land Foundation for Relief and Development v. John Ashcroft, et al.*, exhibit 22, p. 1478 (D DC August 2002).

172. "Al Aqsa Educational Fund Form 990," State of Mississippi, 1993.

173. Islamic Association for Palestine, Web archive, http://web.archive.org/web/20021003010427/www.iap.org/contactus.htm (accessed August 10, 2005).

174. "From the Activities of the Union," *Ila Filastin*, February 1990, p. 70.

175. "Al Aqsa Educational Fund Form 990," State of Mississippi, 1993.

176. Federal News Service, "Press Conference with the American Muslim Society."

177. "Records Sought about Tax-exempt Organizations for Committee's Terror Finance Probe," US Senate Finance Committee press release, January 14, 2004, http://grassley.senate.gov/releases/2004/p04r01-14a.htm (accessed August 10, 2005).

178. "Al Aqsa Educational Fund Form 990," State of Mississippi, 1995.

179. *Request for the Extradition of Marzook*, vol. 2, Salah Statements 4E, August 21, 1995.

180. *Holy Land Foundation for Relief and Development v. John Ashcroft, et al.*, exhibit 29, p. 1478 (D DC August 2002).

181. As discussed earlier in this chapter.

182. *United Association for Studies and Research: Annual Report* (Springfield: State of Illinois, 1990).

183. *United Association for Studies and Research: Articles of Incorporation* (Springfield: State of Illinois, 1989).

184. "Muslim Arab Youth Association Articles of Incorporation," State of Indiana, 1990; "Muslim Arab Youth Association Form 1023," State of Indiana, 1990.

185. *State of Israel v. Nasser Issa Gal'al Hayedmi*, ID#23474141, verdict (June 23, 1993); videotape, Islamic Association for Palestine/Muslim Arab Youth Association Conference, Kansas City, MO, December 1990.

186. Council on American-Islamic Relations, http://www.cair-net.org/default.asp?Page=Board (accessed August 10, 2005).

187. *United Association for Studies and Research: Annual Report.*

188. Ahmed bin Yousef, *Ahmed Yassin: The Phenomenon, the Miracle, and the Legend of the Challenge* (ICRS, 1990).

189. Miller, "Israel Says That a Prisoner's Tale Links Arabs in the US to Terrorism."

190. *U.S. v. Damra*, 03-CR-484, "United States' Response in Opposition to Defendant Fawaz Damra's Motion for Permission to Travel to Springfield, Virginia (D DC March 24, 2004).

191. *USA v. Sami Amin Al-Arian, et al.*, Case No. 8:03-CR-77-T-30TBM, superseding indictment, p. 50 (MD FL September 21, 2004).

192. *U.S. v. Infocom, et al.*, 02-CR-052-R, superseding indictment (ND TX December 17, 2002).

193. Ibid.

194. Ibid.

195. Steve McGonigle, "Local Firm's Accounts Frozen," *Dallas Morning News*, September 26, 2001.

196. David Koenig, "FBI Raids Dallas-Area Internet Business as Part of Terrorism Investigation," Associated Press, September 6, 2001.

197. Angela K. Brown, "Four Men in Texas Arrested by Anti-terrorism Task Force," Associated Press, December 18, 2002.

198. *U.S. v. Infocom, et al.*, 02-CR-052-R, superseding indictment (ND TX December 17, 2002).

199. Ibid.

200. "More Federal Convictions for Elashi Brothers and Infocom Corporation at Second Trial," US Department of Justice United States Attorney Northern District of Texas, April 14, 2005, http://www.usdoj.gov/usao/txn/PressRel05/elashi_conv_part2.pdf (accessed July 5, 2006).

201. Ibid.

202. McGonigle, "Local Firm's Accounts Frozen."

203. "Islamic Association for Palestine Texas Franchise Tax Public Information Report," Richardson, Texas, 1995–1998.

204. McGonigle, "Local Firm's Accounts Frozen."

205. "Holy Land Foundation for Relief and Development Form 990," State of Texas, 1993 and 1998.

206. "Holy Land Foundation for Relief and Development Form 990," State of Texas, 1999.

207. "Council on American Islamic Relations Articles of Incorporation," State of Texas, 1998.

208. McGonigle, "Local Firm's Accounts Frozen."

209. Lara Jakes Jordan, "Four Arrested for Suspected Terror Ties," Associated Press, January 19, 2005. In a recent example, Hussam Ahmad Khalil, "a Jordanian national, [was] arrested Jan. 6 [2005] at the Los Angeles airport for allegedly violating state trademark regulations regarding impure oil. Authorities suspect he sends up to $40,000 to the Middle East each month and believe he is a member of Hamas. He is also suspected of wire fraud, trademark violations, harboring illegal aliens, narcotic smuggling and visa fraud."

-6-

HIZBALLAH: "THE PARTY OF GOD"

We are often asked: Who are we, the Hizballah, and what is our identity? We are the sons of the umma (Muslim community) – the party of God (Hizb Allah) the vanguard of which was made victorious by God in Iran. There the vanguard succeeded to lay down the bases of a Muslim state which plays a central role in the world. . . . We combat [US] abomination and we shall tear out its very roots, its primary roots, which are the United States. All attempts made to drive us into marginal actions will fail, especially as our determination to fight the U.S. is solid.

—An open letter regarding "The Hizballah Program," *Jerusalem Quarterly* 48 (Fall 1988), originally published in *al Safir* (Beirut), February 16, 1985, and also in a separate brochure

We consider it [America] to be an enemy because it wants to humiliate our governments, our regimes, and our peoples. Because it is the greatest plunder of our treasures, our oil, and our resources, while millions in our nation suffer unemployment, poverty, hunger, unmarriagability, ignorance, darkness, and so on. America. . . . This American administration is an enemy. Our motto, which we are not afraid to repeat year after year, is: "Death to America."

—Hizballah leader Hassan Nasrallah, Middle East Media Research Institute, Special Dispatch Series, no. 867 (February 22, 2005)

OVERVIEW

The Shiite extremist group Hizballah ("Party of God") has a long and bloody history of violence in the Middle East against Israel, its citizens, and the United States. Less known are its continuing public declarations of violent intent against American interests, its covert criminal activity in America to raise funds, and its ominous partnership with al Qaeda. An analysis of these developments is indeed timely because there are those in the West, especially in Europe, who contemplate a future "role" for Hizballah as the political sands of Lebanon shift once again. The war in Iraq, rumblings of a nuclear threat from Iran, withdrawal of Syrian forces from Lebanon, and the renewed warfare that commenced in the summer of 2006 in the Gaza Strip and Lebanon have combined to create a climate where the political future of the region is unclear.

Not surprisingly, existing organized groups like Hamas and Hizballah have achieved active involvement in the newly emerging political process. Accordingly, this chapter will clarify Hizballah's terrorist past and detail its current overt hostile actions against America, including its operational partnership with al Qaeda.

Hizballah's interaction with America began in 1983 with a bloody suicide attack on American peacekeepers who had been dispatched to Lebanon during that country's ruinous civil war. That event was followed by deliberate kidnapping of Americans and unrelenting terrorist attacks against Israeli civilians. Hizballah has also expanded its tactics to include drug running and other criminal enterprises within the United States, for the express purpose of raising US dollars to buy weapons and other technologies that are then sent back to Hizballah in Lebanon.

Hizballah has launched organizational meetings with other terrorist groups that shared its call for an the Islamic caliphate or a global Islamic state, and opened its training facilities to al Qaeda.[1] As the working relationship between Hizballah and al Qaeda grows, so, too, does the concern that the result may be increased attacks on American targets.

Hizballah has never wavered from its overt hostility to America. Examination of statements by Hizballah's secretary-general, Sheikh Hassan Nasrallah, reinforces the group's continued hostility toward the United States. In February 2005, Hizballah's own Al Manar TV aired two speeches by Nasrallah in which he reiterated Hizballah's attitude toward the United States:

> The American administration is behind Israel. I must clarify that when I say "America" I do not mean the American people, most of whom are distant and ignorant of what is going on in the world, and of what its government and army are doing in the world. Nevertheless, we consider the current administration an enemy of our [Islamic] nation and of the peoples of our nation, because it has always taken a position of aggression, of occupation, and of supporting Israel with weapons, airplanes, tanks, money, as well as political support, and unlimited protection.

> We consider it to be an enemy because it wants to humiliate our governments, our regimes, and our peoples. Because it is the greatest plunderer [of] our treasures, our oil, and our resources, while millions in our nation suffer unemployment, poverty, hunger, unmarriageability, ignorance, darkness, and so on. America.... This American administration is an enemy. Our motto, which we are not afraid to repeat year after year, is: "Death to America."[2]

HISTORY OF VIOLENCE

The 1980s: Attacks in Lebanon

Hizballah is primarily known for its terrorist actions against Israel. Since 1999, more than a thousand Israelis have been killed;[3] and many thousands more have been injured by suicide bombings, kidnappings, and mortar and sniper attacks in the lethal campaigns waged by Hizballah and Palestinian terrorist organizations. Hizballah first entered the American consciousness in 1983. US Marines had entered Lebanon in July 1982 as part of an international peacekeeping force to oversee the Palestinian Liberation Organization's departure during a bloody civil war. Although the first American detachment had left in September 1982, war erupted again and US forces returned within a few weeks. On October 23, 1983, terrorists hijacked a water delivery truck and replaced it with their own truck, loaded with explosives, which was then driven into the Marine barracks at the Beirut International Airport.[4] The truck crashed through a barrier and wall of sandbags surrounding the barracks, drove to the center of the American compound, and detonated, killing 241 American servicemen.[5] In some respects, this event is fairly seen as the opening salvo in the Islamist terrorist war on America.

After this attack, US forces pulled out of Lebanon. Through this single act, Hizballah killed more Americans than any other terrorist organization until the 9/11 attacks.[6] Less than a year later, in September 1984, another suicide bombing rocked the American embassy in Beirut. The bomb was powerful enough to demolish the building. It wounded the American ambassador and killed two US military officers and twelve Lebanese civilians.[7]

Hizballah's American Kidnapping Campaign

In addition to the troop withdrawal, the US government issued a State Department travel advisory warning that "the situation in Lebanon remains hazardous" and that "all Americans should avoid travel to Lebanon at this time."[8] Despite this, many Americans stayed in Lebanon for professional reasons. Although those who remained took security precautions—sometimes quite elaborate—a number of them were kidnapped by Hizballah and held hostage for years in deplorable conditions. The circumstances of their kidnappings suggest that Hizballah had intimate knowledge of the kidnapped Americans' daily routines.

The American Kidnap Victims

The most infamous kidnapping from this period is that of Terry Anderson, an American journalist working in Beirut. In March 1985, while dropping off his tennis partner following an early Saturday morning match, Anderson was accosted by a number of young men, forced from his car at gunpoint, and herded into the backseat of his assailants' vehicle. Anderson was held hostage for nearly seven years.[9]

Similarly, Father Lawrence M. Jenco, then Beirut's director of Catholic Relief Services, was kidnapped in early 1985 and held for one and a half years.[10] David Jacobsen, the chief executive officer of the American University of Beirut (AUB) Medical Center, was kidnapped by armed men in a van while walking between the AUB campus and the medical center. He was also held for a year and a half.[11] Frank Reed, who owned and operated two private schools in Beirut, was abducted at gunpoint while on his way to meet his wife for lunch in September 1986. He was held captive for more than three and a half years.[12] Joseph Cicippio, comptroller of AUB and its hospital, who was kidnapped in the early morning of September 1986 while leaving his faculty apartment, was held for five years and three months.[13] Thomas M. Sutherland, AUB's dean of the Faculty of Agricultural and Food Sciences, was kidnapped during the six-mile drive from Beirut's airport to AUB's campus and was held prisoner for more than six years.[14]

The kidnapping of John R. Cronin, then a graduate student at the American University of Beirut, was mercifully short compared to these others. As Cronin was being examined in the emergency room at AUB's hospital because he was suffering from a bowel obstruction, four armed men burst in and forced him out of the hospital, even though the doctor and nurse pleaded with Cronin's captors that his condition was "very serious."[15] Although Cronin was held for only four days, his physical condition deteriorated rapidly because of both his illness and repeated beatings.[16] Robert Polhill, a teacher at Beirut University College, was held in captivity for more than three years despite having diabetes, and his abductors prevented him from receiving regular insulin injections.[17]

Some American hostages died in captivity. William Buckley, the CIA station chief, was kidnapped from his Beirut apartment's underground garage in March 1984. He was held captive for a total of 444 days, during which time he was interrogated, tortured, and denied medical care. Buckley's remains were found with a catheter and a set of intravenous tubes. Dr. Bruce Tefft, a medical examiner and retired CIA officer, testified during a civil trial related to Buckley's death that these instruments could have been used to torture Buckley and cause extreme pain. Ultimately, torture, lack of food, and lack of medical care caused Buckley's death on June 3, 1985, after a period of grave illness.[18]

Hizballah also murdered Peter Kilburn, an AUB librarian and instructor of library sciences. Kilburn was kidnapped from his Beirut apartment in November 1984 and held captive until April 1986. On April 14, 1986, the United States bombed Libya in retaliation for a Libyan-sponsored terrorist attack on a Berlin nightclub frequented by US service members. After Libyan agents in Lebanon stated that they wished to purchase and murder an American hostage in retaliation for the US bombing of Tripoli, Hizballah *sold* Kilburn to a Libyan terrorist group for approximately $3 million. He was found shot in the back of the head near the side of a Beirut road on April 17, 1986.[19]

For sheer vicious brutality, few terrorist groups can match Hizballah, and this should never be forgotten.

The Early 1990s: Hizballah Goes International

Its success at home emboldened Hizballah to expand its actions abroad. In June 1985, a commercial airliner en route from Athens to Rome was hijacked and diverted to Beirut. During the flight, several American servicemen were brutally beaten by the hijackers and one, US Navy Petty Officer Robert Stethem, was executed with a gunshot to the head. The remaining servicemen were held captive for another two weeks before they were released to Syrian military personnel and flown home.[20]

In the 1990s, Hizballah launched attacks on Jewish targets throughout the world and appears to have carried out some killings related to its South American drug-trafficking enterprise used to finance its terrorist operations.[21] For all of this, from approximately 1987 to 1996, little of Hizballah's violence was directed against the United States. It was, however, directed elsewhere.

US and Israeli officials believe that Hizballah carried out two dramatic attacks against Jewish targets in Buenos Aires, Argentina, in the early 1990s. In March 1992, a suicide car bomber blew up the Israeli embassy, killing 29 (including 11 Israelis) and injuring more than 250 people.[22] After the attack, Islamic fundamentalists in Beirut described the attacks as revenge for Israel's killing of the Hizballah leader Sheikh Abbas Musawi.[23] Then on July 18, 1994, Hizballah targeted Jewish civilians in Buenos Aires, bombing a Jewish community center that left ninety-six people dead.[24] On the next day, a passenger plane crashed in Panama; most of the twenty-one who died were Jewish, and again Hizballah is believed to have been responsible.[25] Also in July 1994, two Jewish targets in London were hit; a car bomb outside the Israeli embassy in London that injured fourteen people and another vehicle, packed with explosives, exploded outside a Jewish fund-raising event twelve hours later injuring twenty people.[26]

There is evidence that Hizballah terrorists attempted to bomb Israel's embassy in Bangkok, Thailand, on March 17, 1994.[27] The plot was foiled by luck. After a minor traffic accident between a truck and a motorbike on the morning of March 17, the driver of the truck—who appeared to be Middle Eastern—fled from the scene. In searching the truck, police discovered a huge amount of explosives, including several small C-4 bombs and about a ton of ammonium nitrate.[28]

A newspaper in Singapore, drawing on the findings of Singapore's Internal Security Department (ISD), has reported that Hizballah also planned attacks on US and Israeli ships in Singapore in the 1990s.[29] According to the *Straits Times*, in the early 1990s some Hizballah operatives recruited a group of five Muslims through religious classes in Singapore. Although those men balked when asked to photograph the US and Israeli embassies, other Hizballah operatives carried out surveillance of Singapore's coastline in 1995. The ISD concluded that Hizballah's action during this period showed intent to attack US and Israeli ships either in the Singapore Straits or at the country's docks.[30]

Hizballah operatives have been arrested in Thailand, Singapore, and the Philippines, and the terrorist group has also been active in Malaysia, Indonesia, Taiwan, and South Korea, demonstrating its increasingly international scope from the 1990s onward.[31]

Mid-1990s and Forward: Hizballah and al Qaeda Contacts

The final report of the 9/11 Commission discussed numerous connections between Hizballah and al Qaeda. Their operational contacts began as early as January 1994, when, in preparation for the bombing of the US embassy in Nairobi, top al Qaeda operatives were sent by Osama bin Laden to Hizballah training camps in Lebanon.[32] In addition, while the Khobar Towers bombing was principally carried out by Saudi Hizballah, *The 9/11 Commission Report* notes that "there are also signs that al Qaeda played some role, as yet unknown."[33]

Moreover, there are indications of direct connections between Hizballah and al Qaeda operatives in the months leading up to the September 11 attacks. In October 2000, a number of the future hijackers traveled throughout the Middle East on the same flights as Hizballah operatives. In November 2000, a senior Hizballah operative and Ahmed al-Ghamdi were on the same flight to Beirut. The same month, Wail al-Shehri, Waleed al-Shehri, and Ahmed al-Ghamdi traveled together from Beirut and then to Iran, and an associate of a senior Hizballah operative took the same flight to Iran. Perhaps these were coincidences but the evidence strongly suggests that "the travel of this group was important enough to merit the attention of senior figures in Hizballah."[34]

Khobar Towers

In 1996, Hizballah again gained worldwide attention with the bombing of the Khobar Towers housing compound at the King Abdul Aziz Air Base near Dhahran, Saudi Arabia. The base was being used exclusively to house foreign military personnel who had been stationed in Saudi Arabia since the end of the Gulf War in 1991. Most were Americans.[35]

At around 10:00 PM on the night of June 25, 1996, two cars and a fuel truck pulled up outside the Khobar Towers complex.[36] When Saudi security guards responsible for perimeter defense approached to ask the drivers what the truck was doing there, the men jumped into a getaway car and sped off.[37]

Though the guards tried to warn residents to flee, a bomb exploded less than four minutes later—far too quickly for an evacuation to be completed.[38] Another warning came from Staff Sergeant Alfredo Guerrero, who had been on the roof of one of the buildings when he noticed a white Chevrolet Caprice followed by a large tanker truck pull into a public parking lot adjacent to the compound.[39] When he saw two men leap from the truck's cab into the waiting Caprice and drive away at top speed, he realized that something was seriously wrong. Guerrero radioed a quick report to headquarters, and then he and two lookouts ran down to the residential floors, pounding on doors and telling residents to get out of the building.[40] Although he made it only to the seventh floor before the bomb exploded, his quick reaction has been credited with saving many lives, since many of the evacuees were on the stairwell of the building farthest from the bomb when the blast occurred.[41]

The explosion had enormous force, leaving a blackened crater thirty-five feet deep and eighty-five feet long—more destruction than had been wrought by the Oklahoma City bomb detonated the previous year. At the time, General J. H. Binford Peay, head of US Central Command, told reporters that the bomb appeared to be far more powerful than had been used in any previous terrorist attack on Americans in the Mideast.[42] In all, nineteen American servicemen were killed in the attack and hundreds more were injured.[43]

Perhaps recognizing the harm it would cause its sponsor both within and outside the Arab world, Hizballah did not take credit for the attack. Subsequent investigation by the United States, however, had identified Saudi Hizballah as the likely perpetrators with Iranian sponsorship and assistance from other organizations including al Qaeda.[44]

The Khobar Towers indictment identifies the perpetrators of the attacks as members of Saudi Hizballah, explaining that a number of related terrorist organizations in Saudi Arabia, Lebanon, Kuwait, Bahrain, and elsewhere operate under the name "Hizballah." Their common link is that all are "inspired, supported, and directed by elements of the Iranian government." Saudi Hizballah operated primarily in Saudi Arabia and promoted the use of violence against US nationals and property located in Saudi Arabia.[45]

East African Embassy Bombings

While many observers believed that the theological differences between Hizballah (a Shiite-based organization) and al Qaeda (a Sunni-based organization) would prevent their cooperation, history has proved that theory regrettably unfounded. *The 9/11 Commission Report* indicates tactical cooperation between the groups was important in the preparations for the 1998 East African bombings.[46] Ali Mohamed—the former US Green Beret who pled guilty to conspiring with bin Laden to bomb US embassies in Africa—has described providing security for a meeting in Sudan "between al Qaeda . . . and Iran and Hizballah . . . between Mughniyah, Hizballah's chief, and Bin Laden."[47] Mohamed testified that Hizballah provided al Qaeda with explosives training and that Iran "used Hizballah to supply explosives that were disguised to look like rocks."[48]

Post-9/11 Cooperation with al Qaeda Strengthens

By 2002, the connections between both groups had become clear. A senior US administration official with access to daily intelligence reports commented that there was "no doubt at all" that Hizballah and al Qaeda were communicating on logistical matters. For example, administration and intelligence officials received multiple confirmations of a March 2002 meeting in Lebanon between Hizballah, al Qaeda, and Hamas figures.[49] Moreover, there are reports of an October 2002 meeting in Bosnia at which several terrorist groups, including Hizballah and al Qaeda, "resolved to consolidate various Islamic movements in the fight against the U.S."[50] And in December 2002, Israeli prime minister Ariel Sharon claimed that al Qaeda operatives had entered the Gaza Strip and Lebanon and were collaborating with Hizballah to attack Israeli targets.[51]

Despite denials from both Hizballah and al Qaeda, there is no doubt that, at least since 2002, cooperation between the two groups has included coordination on explosives and tactics training, money laundering, weapons smuggling, and acquiring forged documents.[52]

A Familiar Face in a New Place? Imad Mughniya in Iraq

Experts have attributed Iraq's insurgency against coalition forces to a mix of Baathist remnants from Saddam Hussein's regime and foreign militants, such as Abu Musab al-Zarqawi's al Qaeda–affiliated network. But some Western intelligence officials also believe that a familiar face, Imad Mughniya, has been increasingly involved in various aspects of the insurgency.

Imad Mughniya's Résumé

American officials first came to know Mughniya, a Hizballah commander, in the 1980s and 1990s. He is on the FBI's Most Wanted Terrorists list for his alleged role in a number of attacks on US targets.[53] Indeed, he is believed to have been involved in many of the major terrorist actions: the 1983 bombing of the US Marine Corps barracks in Beirut (241 dead), the US embassy bombing in Beirut (23 dead), and in the Khobar Towers bombing in Saudi Arabia in 1996 (19 dead). He was also involved in the 1994 bombing of the Argentine-Israeli Community Center in Buenos Aires (85 dead).[54] These attacks made Mughniya perhaps the world's most deadly effective terrorist until Osama bin Laden.

Mughniya's Role in the Iraqi Insurgency

Intelligence officials believe Mughniya has been coordinating suicide attacks in southern Iraq. In one such attack in April 2004, five suicide car bombs killed seventy-three people in Basra. Mughniya reportedly met with al-Zarqawi in Iran. Mughniya was integral in forming Iraqi Shiite cleric Muqtada al-Sadr's Al Mahdi Army and the training of its fighters for Iraqi attacks.[55] Moreover, Mughniya has sent his own Hizballah forces to Iraq and continues to train insurgents in camps along the Iranian border.[56]

In turn, al-Sadr has made public statements in support of Hizballah while Hizballah has held rallies in Beirut supporting the Iraqi insurgency.[57] Hizballah has also allowed al-Sadr to use its television station, Al Manar, as a platform.[58] Hizballah members in Iraq are coordinating plans with certain elements of the Iranian Revolutionary Guards, continuing a partnership that developed in the 1980s.[59]

TRAINING

Hizballah has some of the largest and most sophisticated training camps in the world (especially now that al Qaeda's Afghan camps have been destroyed) with centers in Bosnia, Iran, South Africa, Syria, and the tri-border area of Brazil, Argentina, and Paraguay. The most significant camp is located in Lebanon's Bekaa Valley where terrorists from a number of organizations have come to train. Organizations represented at these camps include the Basque separatist group ETA, the Red Brigades, the Kurdistan Workers' Party, and the Irish Republican Army. The Islamic militant groups Hamas and Islamic Jihad have also trained at Hizballah camps in the Bekaa Valley.[60]

The al Qaeda–Hizballah partnership has been noted in the Bekaa Valley camps as well, [61] and American officials have concluded that Syria controls these camps.[62] They cover a considerable area and have access to secure communications. Courses are offered in document forgery, bomb making, and assassination.[63] Additionally, a former Iranian intelligence officer has testified in a German 9/11-related trial that he saw 9/11 pilot Ziad Jarrah at a Hizballah training center near Tehran in 1997. [64]

Some of the instructors at Hizballah's Bekaa Valley camp are drawn from the Iranian Revolutionary Guard Corps and Iran's Ministry of Intelligence.[65] In many cases, Hizballah's training centers exist with the blessings of the government of the country in which they are located, such as in Syria and Iran.[66] Syria provides additional logistical support to Hizballah's training by allowing operatives to move freely through Syria and on into the Bekaa Valley and from the Bekaa Valley into Beirut.[67] Iran also hosts Hizballah training camps. For example, intelligence analysts believe that terrorists who participated in the 1996 Khobar Towers bombing "were recruited in Syria and trained in Hizballah camps in Lebanon and Iran."[68] The US government has also alleged that the Islamist regime in Sudan has provided training for Hizballah.[69]

Other Hizballah training centers operate in areas beyond the control of their host countries. The triborder region of Brazil, Argentina, and Paraguay, which has long been suspected of serving as a training ground for Hizballah and other groups, is one such example.[70] Argentina alleges that a number of farms serve as Hizballah training centers.[71] The lack of law enforcement in this area combined with a sizable and radical Islamic population, who openly celebrated the anniversary of 9/11, enables these training centers to operate with little to no interference from local authorities.

Hizballah has also made inroads in South Africa, as well as in Europe. In 1996, Israel lodged a formal complaint with the South African government regarding the existence of five Hizballah training centers in that country.[72] NATO officers and Western diplomats stationed in Bosnia noted the existence of Hizballah training centers in Muslim-controlled areas.[73]

CRIMINAL ACTIVITIES INSIDE THE UNITED STATES

In the United States, high-level Hizballah operatives have conducted complex, interstate criminal enterprises to raise money, a portion of which was then used to purchase high-technology weaponry and multiuse goods forwarded on to the group in Lebanon. Operatives established criminal networks with clear chains of command that engaged in cigarette smuggling, production of precursors for methamphetamine, counterfeiting, and bank and credit card fraud. It is now known that Hizballah's criminal activities in the United States raised millions of dollars and went undetected for a number of years. The breadth of the activity began to emerge with the first arrests in the various cases in July 2000, for cigarette smuggling originating in Charlotte, North Carolina.

Hizballah's leadership in Lebanon has been implicated in these enterprises—most notably Haj Hassan Hilu Laqis, who was at one time in charge of its North American procurement operations.[74] Another Hizballah leader who was clearly involved in the cigarette-smuggling ring discussed below is Sheikh Abbas Harake, Hizballah's military commander in Lebanon, who liaised directly with the ring's leader, Mohamad Hammoud.[75] Lebanese Hizballah connections to these scams go as high up the chain of command as Ayatollah Mohammed Hussein Fadlallah, Hizballah's spiritual leader.[76]

As the subsequent investigation and prosecution would show, the link between Hammoud and the spiritual and military leadership of Hizballah was direct. US Attorney Bob Conrad, who prosecuted the Charlotte cell, commented: "I believe that the structure was in place to carry out a command [to commit a violent act]."[77]

Cigarette-Smuggling Scams

The Charlotte, North Carolina, smuggling ring was an extremely advanced enterprise with a clear and elaborate structure. The ATF currently has more than three hundred open cases of illicit cigarette trafficking,[78] and ATF assistant director Michael Bouchard has commented, "The deeper we dig into these cases, the more ties to terrorism we're discovering."[79]

Cigarettes were bought in North Carolina and sold in Michigan. Operatives were stationed in Canada and Lebanon. Each operative was assigned specific tasks, including maintaining communications with cell members in Canada,[80] selling cigarettes at convenience stores,[81] driving trucks filled with crates of smuggled cigarettes interstate, and procuring high-tech tools for Hizballah members in Lebanon. While the cell members in North America have largely been identified and apprehended, no arrests have been made on the "receiving" end of the gang in Lebanon.

In the various schemes, large volumes of cigarettes purchased in states with low cigarette taxes (such as Virginia and North Carolina) are transported north along Interstate 95 to states with higher cigarettes taxes (Maryland, New Jersey, New York, and Pennsylvania).[82] Because the smugglers pay no taxes on the cigarettes they resell, they can offer a large discount from the usual local price. As a senior ATF official explained, such smuggling is quite lucrative. For example, a smuggler could buy a carton (ten packs) of cigarettes for around $20 in Virginia (where, until September 2004, the cigarette tax was 2.5 cents per pack), and then resell it in New York City (where the tax is $1.50 per pack) for about $40 a carton. A single truckload of cigarettes can yield a $2 million profit.[83]

In June 2002, a federal jury in Charlotte convicted the brothers Mohamad Hammoud and Chawki Youssef Hammoud of funneling profits from their multimillion-dollar cigarette-smuggling ring to Hizballah in addition to the domestic smuggling crimes.[84] According to the indictment, the members of the cell planned to acquire for Hizballah such items as night-vision devices, global positioning systems, mine and metal detection equipment, stun guns, nitrogen cutters (designed for cutting metal under water), laser range finders, camera equipment, advanced aircraft analysis and design software, military-style lensatic compasses, and mining, drilling, and blasting equipment.[85]

Evidence at Hammoud's trial included a receipt from Fadlallah to Hammoud for $1,300 that Hammoud had wired to Hizballah as well as a photograph of Hammoud holding an assault rifle at a Hizballah camp in Lebanon.[86] In addition to demonstrating the cell's close relationship with Fadlallah, prosecutors showed that profits from the ring were sent to Hizballah leaders and that Hammoud spoke by telephone with Sheikh Abbas Harake, Hizballah's military commander in Lebanon.[87]

Said Mohamad Harb, also based in Charlotte, provided the link between the cigarette-smuggling operation and a Hizballah equipment procurement cell in Canada, where he met and coordinated with a Hizballah "purchasing agent."[88] Harb was a key figure in transferring goods to Hizballah in part because of his expertise with fake credit cards.[89] In particular, Harb would set up credit card and banking scams to purchase dual-use equipment (night-vision devices, mine detection equipment, etc.) for Hizballah.[90]

Others implicated in the Charlotte case included three men in Dearborn, Michigan. One of them, Bassam Youssef Hammoud, was another brother of the ring's leader; in March 2002, he pled guilty to smuggling cigarettes and laundering money as a part of the Charlotte ring.[91] The others, Elias Mohamad Akhdar and Hassan Makki, were convicted of engaging in a separate smuggling ring that transported tax-free cigarettes from the Seneca Nation of Indians' Cattaraugus reservation in New York State to stores in Michigan.[92] They funneled some of the $2 million in illegal profits to Hizballah in Lebanon. Makki specifically admitted using the cigarette ring, in part to financially support Hizballah after the State Department designated it a foreign terrorist organization, and was sentenced to nearly five years in prison. Akhdar was sentenced to nearly six years in prison.[93]

Mohammed Hassan Dbouk and his brother-in-law, Ali Adham Amhaz, ran the Canadian operation.[94] Dbouk and Amhaz reported directly to Haj Hassan Hilu Laqis, Hizballah's chief military procurement officer in Lebanon.[95] Their activities were funded in part with money that Laqis sent from Lebanon and in part by their own criminal activities in Canada, such as credit card and banking scams.[96]

Dbouk was a high-ranking Hizballah member and a reconnaissance and intelligence specialist employed by the Hizballah-run Al Manar television station. As such, he oversaw military equipment acquisitions such as night-vision goggles and global positioning systems.[97] According to the Canadian Security Intelligence Service, at one point, a Charlotte cell member flew to Seattle to deliver a series of forged checks to Dbouk who then used them to purchase equipment for Hizballah.[98]

Further insight into Hizballah's operations in Canada was provided by Mohammed Hussein al-Husseini, an admitted Hizballah member who was arrested in Canada in 1997. Al-Husseini's arrest yielded a great deal of information about Hizballah's inner workings. When asked about the existence of Hizballah in Montreal, he replied, "Hizballah has members in Montreal, Ottawa, Toronto—in all of Canada."[99] The Israelis also have in custody a Hizballah operative from Canada, Fauzi Ayub, whom they claim was sent back to the Middle East to organize attacks on Israel.[100]

Procurement Scams

According to an April 2004 FBI report, "To support Hizballah, these criminal enterprises, primarily based in the Detroit area, are engaged in a wide range of offenses, including credit card fraud, bank fraud, mail fraud, mortgage fraud, wire fraud, bankruptcy fraud, [and] money laundering."[101] An FBI affidavit of May 2003 specifically mentioned a Mohammed Krayem who "sent approximately $200,000 (Canadian) to his brother," and noted that the money was used to "purchase military equipment from United Nations Protection Forces stationed in southern Lebanon."[102] This military equipment, including night-vision goggles, was then passed on to Hizballah. Krayem was indicted in September 2003 in Michigan, but is still at large; he is believed to be in Lebanon.[103]

The same May 2003 FBI affidavit also named Mahmoud Youssef Kourani, who was charged with conspiracy to provide material support or resources to Hizballah. Kourani allegedly sent $40,000 to his brother Haidar Kourani, Hizballah's chief of military security in southern Lebanon. According to the FBI, Kourani sold a home in the Detroit area and channeled the sale's proceeds to Hizballah. A confidential informant told the FBI that Kourani revealed he had been sent to Iran by Hizballah on multiple occasions to get military training. The FBI said that its confidential informant "stated that he/she believes that if Hizballah tasked Kourani to do something in the United States, he would carry out the mission on behalf of the organization."[104] After pleading guilty to conspiring to provide support to Hizballah in March of 2005, Mahmoud Kourani was sentenced to fifty-four months in prison.[105]

In an intriguing side note, the FBI informant also said that Mahmoud and Haidar Kourani were members of the same Hizballah "unit" that took responsibility for the abduction, torture, and murder of US Marine Lieutenant Colonel William Higgins in February 1988.[106]

Fawzi Mustapha Assi's 1998 arrest in Detroit for attempting to procure $120,000 worth of thermal imaging gear for Hizballah revealed another link between Dearborn and Hizballah. In addition, Ali Boumelhem was convicted in 2001 of shipping two shotguns and 750 rounds of ammunition to Hizballah in Lebanon.[107] At Michigan gun shows where background checks were not required, Boumelhem had been able to acquire what one news service called an "arsenal of shotguns, hundreds of rounds of ammunition, flash suppressers, and assault weapon parts."[108]

In June 2004, a Lebanese Canadian "businessman" Naji Antoine Abi Khalil and his alleged coconspirator Mikel M. Mudallal of Torrance, California, were arrested on charges of laundering money and offering to deliver night-vision goggles and infrared aiming devices to Hizballah.[109] A Manhattan federal court later sentenced Khalil to sixty months in prison for attempting to export military night-vision equipment to Hizballah. Khalil also received a prison term of fifty-seven months in a separate money-laundering charge filed in the Eastern District Court of Arkansas.[110]

Last spring, Nemr Ali-Rahal, who became a US citizen in 1999 after arriving from Lebanon on a student visa in 1985, was arrested and charged with bank fraud, credit fraud, and a related conspiracy charge.

In 2004, Rahal drove to Canada with his son. When they were stopped at the border upon their return to the United States, chemical testing on both Rahal's and his son's passports revealed traces of military explosives. This led to a search warrant being executed on his home, where the evidence of the alleged financial frauds was found. Also found was a wide array of materials related to Hizballah, including a photo of Nasrallah, a video of Nasrallah speaking, a video of Hizballah "martyrs," a photo of Rahal burning a torn American flag, a video of Rahal rubbing his feet on an Israeli flag, a photo of Rahal under a poster of Ayatollah Khomeini, and a video of Rahal and his son at a parade and rally for Hizballah's youth group in Lebanon. However, the prosecution has acknowledged that they have no direct evidence of any illegal involvement between Rahal and Hizballah and it is important to remember that he is not being charged with providing material support to Hizballah.[111] Nevertheless, in May 2006, Rahal was convicted on charges of aiding and abetting bank fraud and sentenced to thirty-three months in prison.[112] Rahal and his wife defrauded nine American banks out of more than $500,000 by making false claims on mortgage and loan forms and "inflat[ing] the apparent available balances on his own credit accounts by making bogus electronic 'pay-by-phone' payments against several of his bank accounts."[113]

Intellectual Property Crime

Hizballah supporters have engaged in a wide range of other illegal moneymaking ventures to raise funds for the organization. Carratu International, a leading corporate investigation company, claimed in 2002 that some counterfeit products offered at Internet sites and street markets may be sold to fund terrorist organizations like Hizballah.[114] Fake goods range from power tools to "designer" clothes and pharmaceutical products, such as Viagra, Prozac, and Xenical.[115] Stratfor—a leading private intelligence firm that provides corporations, governments, and individuals with geopolitical analysis and forecasts—reports that Hizballah has even supported past operations by selling knockoff designer products on New York City street corners.[116]

When a Los Angeles County sheriff's lieutenant was booking a man in 2004 for selling knockoff designer items such as Gucci handbags and Prada shoes out of his clothing store, he noticed a large tattoo in Arabic characters on the man's arm. The tattoo turned out to be the symbol for Hizballah. This was one of many similar cases in Southern California in which men have been accused of selling these designer knockoffs and diverting the profits to Hizballah. Hizballah is not the only organization utilizing this method. Law enforcement has reported that Russian, Eurasian, and Asian criminal gangs have also been peddling knockoffs to fund their organizations.[117]

Intellectual property crime is defined as "counterfeited and pirated goods, manufactured and sold for profit without the consent of the patent or trademark holder."[118] Terrorist involvement in intellectual property crime can be either direct or indirect. Criminal activity is deemed *direct* when terrorist group members themselves produce, distribute, and sell counterfeit goods. They then use the money to finance their operations.

Involvement is indirect when sympathizers or other individuals conduct a counterfeiting operation, and then send the funds to what they know is a terrorist group. The money may pass through several layers of middlemen before actually reaching the terrorist entity.[119]

The FBI estimates that counterfeiting costs US businesses $200–250 billion a year.[120]

Tax Evasion

In May 2006, a federal indictment unsealed in the Eastern District Court of Detroit charged Talal Khalil Chahine of Dearborn, Michigan, and the owner of the Middle Eastern "La Shish" restaurant chain, and Elfat el-Aouar, a La Shish financial manager and Chahine's wife, on four counts each of income-tax evasion.[121] According to the indictment, both Talal Chahine and Elfat el-Aouar engaged in a scheme that skimmed over $16 million from the restaurants and funneled it to their native Lebanon.[122] Court records further alleged that in August 2002, el-Aouar and Chahine attended a fund-raising event in Lebanon and the keynote speakers for the event were Talal Chahine and Sheikh Muhammad Hussein Fadlallah. Fadlallah is a key Hizballah leader based in Lebanon, who has been designated a specially designated terrorist by the US Department of Treasury.[123] Further, in a raid of el-Aouar's residence, federal authorities seized a letter, written in Arabic, that thanked Chahine "for sponsoring 40 Lebanese orphans during the years 2000–2001."[124] According to a document filed in court by the prosecution, authorities also found a binder containing pictures of sponsored orphans. The document also claimed "that the sponsorship of orphans is a euphemism used by Hizballah to refer to the orphans of martyrs."[125]

Al Qaeda

Al Qaeda training manuals recommend the sale of counterfeit products to raise funds.[126] Investigators suspect that a New York City counterfeit T-shirt ring helped finance the 1993 World Trade Center bombing.[127] In May 1996, the FBI seized one hundred thousand counterfeit T-shirts that were to be sold during the 1996 Summer Olympics in Atlanta. Subsequent investigation revealed that followers of Sheikh Omar Abdel Rahman ran the operation.[128] Officials in Britain seized six forty-foot trucks filled with counterfeit Nike, Burberry, and Aquascutum apparel that had been made in Pakistan. Officials believe that proceeds from these sales were to be sent to al Qaeda.[129]

In late 2001, Danish customs officials in Copenhagen found cases of undeclared goods, including Vicks Vaporub, Head & Shoulders shampoo, Oil of Olay skin cream, Vaseline, and Chanel No. 5 perfume. The officers noticed that the goods seemed counterfeit, and local corporate offices of the brands confirmed their suspicion. Danish officials seized the shipment, which totaled eight tons, and an investigation revealed the goods were shipped from Dubai by a known member of al Qaeda. An official of the European Commission Customs Coordination Office said the man was a "prominent member of Al Qa'idah." The goods' final destination was Great Britain.[130]

The Recording Industry Association of America has evidence that Dawood Ibrahim,[131] named a "Specially Designated Global Terrorist" by the US Treasury Department in October 2003, financed two illegal CD plants in Pakistan. Treasury officials noted that Ibrahim is "an Indian crime lord, [who] has found common cause with Al Qaida, sharing his smuggling routes with the terror syndicate and funding attacks by Islamic extremists aimed at destabilizing the Indian government."[132]

Hizballah has also made use of counterfeit goods, particularly in the South American triborder region of Paraguay, Brazil, and Argentina. There, in February 2000, Ali Khalil Mehri was arrested for selling millions of dollars' worth of counterfeit Sega, Sony, and Nintendo software and funneling the money to Hizballah.[133] In his home, authorities found videos and CDs of known suicide bombers rallying others to the cause.[134]

In July 2003, while searching the offices of suspected Hizballah financiers in Paraguay, police discovered boxes of counterfeit goods.[135] Hizballah has also manufactured and exported counterfeit pharmaceutical products.[136] In October 2003, authorities in Beirut intercepted counterfeit brake pads and shock absorbers valued at $1.2 million. Interpol Secretary-General Ronald Noble told European and American legislators meeting in Dublin in April 2004 that "subsequent enquiries revealed that profits from these consignments, had they not been intercepted, were destined for supporters of Hizballah."[137]

The terrorist counterfeiting plots that have been uncovered surely constitute only a tiny amount of the total fraud that occurs. Former CIA and State Department counterterrorism officer Larry Johnson posits that if "eight tons of counterfeit goods have been seized, we may rest assured that there are another 80, if not 800, that have got through undetected."[138]

Dual Use: Counterfeiting as a Means of Terrorism?

Another threat is the possible use of counterfeit pharmaceuticals not only as a means of raising money but as a direct conduit for terrorist attacks. Investigators have uncovered several examples of counterfeit drugs. This scenario is especially troubling because terrorist groups could use these methods not just to gain profit but to spread death, simply by adding toxins or infectious agents to them.[139]

Drug Running

In the United States and South America, Hizballah financiers have also been involved in large-scale drug operations involving methamphetamine.[140] The most noteworthy example is a massive drug-trafficking ring that smuggled tractor-trailer loads of pseudoephedrine from Canada to

Detroit, and then from Detroit to California. Once in California, the Mexican-run criminal organizations would use the pseudoephedrine to produce large quantities of methamphetamine.[141]

Organized Crime Drug Enforcement Task Force (OCDETF) investigators from the Drug Enforcement Agency, Customs, the Internal Revenue Service, and the Royal Canadian Mounted Police launched Operation Mountain Express III to unravel the drug ring. In doing so they discovered that the drug traffickers had been funneling profits to Middle Eastern terrorist groups, including Hizballah.[142] Although it is not known how much of the profits went specifically to Hizballah, authorities have tracked $10 million back to the Middle East,[143] at least some of which aided Hizballah, according to then DEA administrator Asa Hutchison.[144]

The Mountain Express III investigation resulted in the arrest of defendants in twelve cities across the United States and Canada, along with the seizure of more than thirty-five tons of pseudoephedrine (which could be used to produce thirty thousand pounds of methamphetamine), 179 pounds of finished methamphetamine, six clandestine drug laboratories, and $4.5 million in US currency.[145]

Independent verification of Hizballah's ties to the drug trade came as well from Operation Green Quest, a multiagency task force on terrorist financing designed to bring the Treasury's expertise to bear in "identifying, disrupting, and dismantling the financial infrastructures and sources of terrorist funding." Though not directly aimed at Hizballah, Green Quest has exposed laundered drug money to the group.[146]

In another case, Ohio resident Mohammad Shabib was involved in a sprawling drug enterprise used to finance Hizballah.[147] Beginning in the early 1990s, Shabib hauled about three tons of pseudoephedrine from Canada to California, where his colleagues sold the medicine to Mexican gangs that would turn it into the street drug methamphetamine. It is unclear exactly how much of this money went to finance terrorism, but Shabib's drug trade did contribute to Hizballah's financing.[148]

CONCLUSION

At a time when American attention is focused on al Qaeda, it is possible that Hizballah might be viewed as a "former" threat to America. Nothing could be further from the truth. While Hizballah has not directly attacked American interests for a number of years, the organization's founding principles are vehemently and violently anti-American. Its continuing, publicly expressed hatred for the United States, its cooperation with al Qaeda, and its well-established operational presence in the United States are all reasons for concern.

Currently, US and international law enforcement agencies are doing important work in investigating and prosecuting Hizballah members who participate in criminal enterprises aimed at fund-raising for Hizballah's continuing campaign of violence in the Middle East. Ongoing intelligence activities directly focused on Hizballah's support for and cooperation with al Qaeda will be essential as America confronts its terrorist foes.

NOTES

1. National Commission on Terrorist Attacks upon the United States, *The 9/11 Commission Report: Final Report of the National Commission on Terrorist Attacks upon the United States* (New York: Norton, 2004), pp. 68, 240–41.

2. "Hassan Nasrallah, 'The American Administration Is Our Enemy . . . Death to America,'" Al Manar Television, February 22, 2005, http://memritv.org/Search.asp?ACT=S9&P1=566 (accessed August 12, 2005).

3. Clive James, "Written in Bad Blood," *Weekend Australian*, April 10, 2004, p. 19.

4. "Beirut Barracks Attack Remembered," CBS News, October 23, 2003.

5. *Peterson, et al. v. Islamic Republic of Iran, et al.*, 01-CV-2094, memorandum opinion (D DC May 30, 2003).

6. "FBI Strategic Plan 2004-2009," FBI, http://www.fbi.gov/publications/strategicplan/stategicplantext.htm (accessed August 2005).

7. *Wagner, et al. v. Islamic Republic of Iran, et al.*, 01-CV-1799, decision and order (D DC November 6, 2001).

8. "Current Actions," *Department of State Bulletin*, April 1984.

9. *Anderson, et al. v. Islamic Republic of Iran, et al.*, 99-CV-0698, decision and order (D DC March 24, 2000).

10. *Jenco, et al., v. Islamic Republic of Iran, et al.*, 00-CV-549, memorandum opinion (D DC August 2, 2001).

11. *Cicippio, et al. v. Islamic Republic of Iran, et al.*, 96-CV-1805, decision and order (D DC August 27, 1998).

12. Ibid.

13. Ibid.

14. *Sutherland, et al. v. Islamic Republic of Iran, et al.*, 99-CV-3279, memorandum opinion (D DC June 25, 2001).

15. *Cronin v. Islamic Republic of Iran, et al.*, 99-CV-2890, memorandum opinion (D DC December 18, 2002).

16. Ibid.

17. *Polhill, et al. v. Islamic Republic of Iran, et al.*, 00-CV-1798, decision and order (D DC August 23, 2001).

18. *Surette v. Islamic Republic of Iran, et al.*, 01-CV-0570, opinion (D DC November 1, 2002).

19. *Kilburn v. Islamic Republic of Iran, et al.*, 01-CV-1301, memorandum opinion (D DC August 8, 2003).

20. *Stethem, et al. v. Islamic Republic of Iran, et al.*, 00-CV-0159, decision and order (D DC April 19, 2002).

21. Lenilson Ferreira, "Hezbollah Suspected in Slaying Lebanese Couple in Brazil," Japan Economic Newswire, March 11, 2002.

22. "Hezbollah's New Threat," *Washington Times*, December 10, 2002, p. A16; Tim Weiner, "Iran and Allies Are Suspected in Bomb Wave," *New York Times*, July 29, 1994, p. A1.

23. "Group: Israeli Embassy Bombed for Revenge," *Chicago Tribune*, March 19, 1992, p. C2.

24. Tracy Wilkinson, "Death Toll in Argentine Blast Rises to 96," *Los Angeles Times*, July 26, 1994, p. A4.

25. "Report: Bomb Caused Panama Crash," *Chicago Tribune*, July 26, 1994, p. C1.

26. Tim Weiner, "Iran and Allies Are Suspected in Bomb Wave," *New York Times*, July 29, 1994, p. A4.

27. Matthew Levitt, "Smeared in Blood, Hizballah Fingerprints All Over Globe," *Australian*, June 9, 2003, p. 11.

28. "Plot to Bomb Israeli Embassy in Thailand Foiled by Luck," Japan Economic Newswire, March 17, 1994.

29. "Singapore Paper Reports on Alleged Hezbollah Activity during 1990s," BBC Worldwide Monitoring, June 9, 2002; Levitt, "Smeared in Blood, Hizballah Fingerprints All Over Globe."

30. BBC Worldwide Monitoring, "Singapore Paper Reports on Alleged Hezbollah Activity during 1990s."

31. Levitt, "Smeared in Blood, Hizballah Fingerprints All Over Globe."

32. 9/11 Commission, *The 9/11 Commission Report*, p. 68.

33. Ibid., p. 60.

34. Ibid., pp. 240–41.

35. Rupert Cornwell, "US Airmen Killed by Truck Bomb Attack in Saudi," *London Independent*, June 26, 1996, p. 1.

36. Philip Shenon, "23 U.S. Troops Die in Truck Bombing at Big Saudi Base," *New York Times*, June 26, 1996, p. A1.

37. Ibid.

38. Ibid.

39. Bruce W. Nelan et al., "The Bomb in Saudi Arabia Raises Two Questions: How Safe Were the Troops? How Safe Is the Regime?" *Time*, July 8, 1996, p. 20.

40. Ibid.

41. Katherine McIntire Peters, "Defending the Troops," *Government Executive*, April 1, 1997, p. 38.

42. Philip Shenon, "Officials Says Size of Bomb Caught Military by Surprise," *New York Times*, June 27, 1996, p. A11.

43. Steven Lee Myers, "At a Saudi Base, U.S. Digs In, Gingerly, for a Longer Stay," *New York Times*, December 29, 1997, p. A1.

44. 9/11 Commission, *The 9/11 Commission Report*, p. 60.

45. *USA v. Al-Mughassil*, 01-CR-228, indictment (ED VA June 21, 2001).

46. 9/11 Commission, *The 9/11 Commission Report*, p. 68.

47. *USA v. Ali Mohamed*, 98-CR-1023, plea, p. 28 (SD NY October 20, 2000).

48. Ibid.

49. Dana Priest and Douglas Farah, "Terror Alliance Has U.S. Worried; Hezbollah, Al Qaeda Seen Joining Forces," *Washington Post*, June 30, 2002, p. A1; "Research Note: Hezbollah in Profile," Department of the Parliamentary Library, June 2, 2003.

50. Department of the Parliamentary Library, "Research Note: Hezbollah in Profile."

51. Associated Press, "Al Qaeda in Gaza and Southern Lebanon, Sharon Says," December 5, 2002.

52. Priest and Farah, "Terror Alliance Has U.S. Worried.

53. "Most Wanted Terrorists," FBI, November 5, 2004.

54. *USA v. Ali Mohamed*, 98-CR-1023, plea, p. 28.

55. Ali Nurizadeh, "Iran's Al-Quds Corps Chief Reportedly Admits Providing Facilities to Al-Zarqawi," *Al Sharq Al Awsat* (London), August 11, 2004, p. P2.

56. Con Coughlin, "Beirut Veteran Blamed Over Basra Attacks," *London Sunday Telegraph*, April 24, 2004, http://www.telegraph.co.uk/news/main.jhtml?xml=/news/2004/04/25/wirq225.xml (accessed April 25, 2004).

57. "Hizbullah Secretary General, Sheikh Hassan Nasrallah, Threatens the US," Al Manar Television, May 18, 2004, http://www.memritv.org/Transcript.asp?P1=74 (accessed January 24, 2005); Hizbullah Chief Nabil Qawuq, "We Support the Iraqi Resistance in Its Right to Oust the Occupier," Al Manar Television, August 23, 2004, http://www.memritv.org/Transcript.asp?P1=216 (accessed January 24, 2005).

58. "Shiite Leader Muqtada Al-Sadr Comments on US Threats, Mediation Efforts," Al Manar Television, April 14, 2004, translated by FBIS; "Muqtada Al-Sadr Calls for 'Jihad' against US Forces," Al Manar Television, August 14, 2004, translated by BBC Monitoring.

59. Ali Nurizadeh, "Iran's Al-Quds Corps Chief Reportedly Admits Providing Facilities to Al-Zarqawi," *Al Sharq Al Awsat* (London), August 11, 2004, p. P2.

60. Douglas Frantz, "More Firepower for Palestinians," *New York Times*, April 7, 2002, Foreign Desk, p. 1.

61. "Signs Point to Al Qaeda Regrouping," Bulletin's Frontrunner, June 12, 2002.

62. Glenn Kessler, "U.S.-Syria Relations Not Quite as Cold; Officials Cite Assad's Anti-Terror Aid," *Washington Post*, June 20, 2002, p. A15.

63. Susan Taylor Martin, "Experts Disagree on Dangers of Syria," *St. Petersburg (FL) Times*, November 3, 2002, p. 1A.

64. Dirk Laabs and Sebastian Rotella, "Witness in September 11 Trial Links Iran with Al Qaeda," *Los Angeles Times*, January 22, 2004, p. A3.

65. Jeffrey Goldberg, "In the Party of God; Are Terrorists in Lebanon Preparing for a Larger War?" *New Yorker*, October 14, 2002, p. 180.

66. Bob Graham, "Collateral Damage: Iraq and the Future of U.S.-Syrian Relations," Council on Foreign Relations, April 24, 2003.

67. Frank R. Wolf, Commerce, Justice, State, and Judiciary Subcommittee, *FY 2005 Securities and Exchange Commission Appropriations*, 108th Cong., 2nd sess., March 31, 2004.

68. Matthew A. Levitt, "Confronting Syrian Support for Terrorist Groups," *Middle East Intelligence Bulletin*, May 2003.

69. Roger Winter, director of US Committee on Refugees, Senate Foreign Relations Committee, African Affairs Subcommittee, 105th Cong., 1st sess., May 15, 1997.

70. Jerry Seper, "Terror Cell on Rise in South America," *Washington Times*, December 18, 2002, p. A6.

71. "The Battle for Lebanon Explodes in Argentina," *Frontline World*, May 2003.

72. Associated Press, "Israel Asks South Africa to Investigate Reports of Hezbollah Camps," April 29, 1996.

73. Douglas Stanglin et al., "Trent Lott's New Senate Phone Pal," *U.S. News & World Report*, September 9, 1996, pp. 16, 18; Matthew A. Levitt, Joint Hearing of the Committee on International Relations, Subcommittee on the Middle East and Central Asia and the Subcommittee on International Terrorism and Nonproliferation, *Iranian State Sponsorship of Terror: Threatening U.S. Security, Global Stability, and Regional Peace*, 109th Cong., 1st sess., February 16, 2005.

74. *USA v. Hammoud, et al.*, 00-CR-147, testimony of Matthew Levitt, pp. 1059–60 (WD NC June 5, 2002).

75. *USA v. Hammoud, et al.*, 00-CR-147, testimony of Matthew Levitt, pp. 1067–68 (WD NC June 5, 2002).

76. *USA v. Hammoud, et al.*, 00-CR-147, testimony of Samir Kalini, p. 1699 (WD NC June 13, 2002).

77. Jeffrey Goldberg, "In the Party of God; Hezbollah Sets Up Operations in South America and the United States," *New Yorker*, October 28, 2005, p. 75.

78. Sari Horwitz, "Cigarette Smuggling Linked to Terrorism," *Washington Post*, June 8, 2004, p. A1.

79. Ibid.

80. *USA v. Hammoud, et al.*, 00-CR-147, affidavit in support of warrants for arrest, searches, and seizure, pp. 35–36 (WD NC July 20, 2000).

81. *USA v. Hammoud, et al.*, 00-CR-147, superseding indictment, pp. 20–21 (WD NC March 28, 2001).

82. Horwitz, "Cigarette Smuggling Linked to Terrorism."

83. Ibid.

84. *USA v. Hammoud, et al.*, 00-CR-147, jury verdict as to Chawki Youssef Hammoud (WD NC June 21, 2002); *USA v. Hammoud, et al.*, 00-CR-147, jury verdict as to Mohamad Youssef Hammoud" (WD NC June 24, 2002).

85. *USA v. Hammoud, et al.*, 00-CR-147, superseding indictment, pp. 42–43 (WD NC March 28, 2001).

86. *USA v. Hammoud, et al.*, 00-CR-147, testimony of Hesham El-Gamiel, pp. 1011–12 (WD NC June 13, 2002); *USA v. Hammoud, et al.*, 00-CR-147, government exhibit no. 266-1 (WD NC).

87. *USA v. Hammoud, et al.*, 00-CR-147, testimony of Matthew Levitt, pp. 1058–59 (WD NC June 5, 2002); Gary L. Wright, "Brothers Found Guilty of Plotting to Aid Terrorists," *Charlotte Observer*, June 22, 2002, p. 1A.

88. *USA v. Hammoud, et al.*, 00-CR-147, testimony of Said Mohamad Harb," pp. 1474–78 (WD NC June 10, 2002).

89. *USA v. Hammoud, et al.*, 00-CR-147, superseding indictment, pp. 41–42 (WD NC March 28, 2001).

90. Ibid., pp. 41–43.

91. *USA v. Hammoud, et al.*, 00-CR-147, plea agreement as to Bassam Youssef Hammoud (WD NC March 11, 2002).

92. "Elias Mohamed Akhdar, 31, of Dearborn, Michigan, Was Sentenced in Federal Court in Detroit to 70 Months," US Department of Justice press release, January 8, 2004.

93. Ibid.

94. *USA v. Hammoud, et al.*, 00-CR-147, affidavit in support of warrants for arrest, searches, and seizure, p. 36 (WD NC July 20, 2000); Matthew Levitt, "Banning Hizballah Activity in Canada," *Policywatch #698*, January 6, 2003.

95. *USA v. Hammoud, et al.*, 00-CR-147, affidavit in support of warrants for arrest, searches, and seizure, p. 36 (WD NC July 20, 2000).

96. *USA v. Hammoud, et al.*, 00-CR-147, superseding indictment, pp. 42–43 (WD NC March 28, 2001).

97. *USA v. Hammoud, et al.*, 00-CR-147, testimony of Said Mohamad Harb, pp. 1477, 1487–88 (WD NC June 10, 2002).

98. *USA v. Hammoud, et al.*, 00-CR-147, affidavit in support of warrants for arrest, searches, and seizure, p. 36 (WD NC July 20, 2000).

99. Steven Emerson, US House Subcommittee on Immigration and Claims, *Terrorism and Immigration Policy*, 106th Cong., 2nd sess., January 25, 2000.

100. Jonathan Kay, "Ayub Case Illustrates the Need for Profiling: Ottawa

Should Stop Lecturing U.S. about Border Policies," *National Post* (Canada), October 31, 2002, p. A10.

101. *Report to the National Commission on Terrorist Attacks upon the United States: The FBI's Counterterrorism Program since September 11th, 2001* (Washington, DC: Department of Justice, April 14, 2004), p. 70.

102. David Shepardson, "FBI Links Two Terror Cases; Court Filing Says Two Men Indicted in Detroit Sent Thousands of Dollars to Hezbollah," *Detroit News*, April 18, 2004, p. 1B.

103. *USA v. Akhdar, et al.*, 03-CR-80079, second superseding indictment (ED MI September 25, 2003).

104. Shepardson, "FBI Links Two Terror Cases."

105. "Lebanese Man Sentenced in Conspiracy to Support a Designated Foreign Terrorist Organization," U.S. Immigration and Customs Enforcement press release, June 15,2005, http://www.ice.gov/graphics/news/newsreleases/articles/050615detroit.htm (accessed December 12, 2005).

106. Ibid.

107. Ronald J. Hansen, "Lebanese in Metro Detroit on Edge: Feelings Mixed about Conspiracy to Help Hezbollah," *Detroit News*, January 2, 2002.

108. Swanee Hunt, "Mothers and Guns," Scripps Howard News Service, May 14, 2003.

109. *USA v. Khalil, et al.*, 04-MJ-1034, indictment, pp. 1–2 (SD NY June 16, 2004).

110. "Naji Antoine Abi Khalil Sentenced to 60 Months' Imprisonment for Attempting to Export Military Night-Vision Equipment to Hizballah," US Department of Justice press release, February 2, 2006.

111. *USA v. Rahal*, 05-CR-80389, order of detention pending trial (ED MI May 4, 2005).

112. *USA v. Rahal*, 05-CR-80476, judgment (ED MI May 12, 2006).

113. *USA v. Rahal*, 05-80476, Rule 11 plea agreement, pp. 2–3 (ED MI January 17, 2006).

114. John Von Radowitz, "Fake Internet Goods; Linked to Terrorists," Press Association, June 25, 2002.

115. Ibid.

116. "Islamist Militants and Organized Crime," Stratfor, June 15, 2004, http://web2.stratfor.com/MORS/Story.neo?storyId=233125 (accessed June 16, 2004).

117. Josh Meyer, "The Nation; Knockoff Dealers Could Have Designs on Terror; A Senate Panel Is Told That Some Traffickers of High-end Counterfeits Have Ties to Hezbollah," *Los Angeles Times*, May 26, 2005, National Desk, p. A1.

118. Ronald K. Noble, Interpol Secretary-General, House Committee on International Relations, *The Links between Intellectual Property Crime and Terrorist Financing*, 108th Cong., 1st sess., July 16, 2003.

119. Ibid.

120. FBI press release, July 17, 2002.

121. *USA v. Chahine, et al.*, 06-CR-20248, indictment (ED MI May 10, 2006).

122. Ibid.

123. *USA v. El Aouar*, 06-CR-20248, government's written proffer in support of its request for detention pending trial (ED MI May 22, 2006).

124. Ibid.

125. Ibid.

126. Isabel Vincent, "Fake, and Dangerous: Women Who Buy Knock-Offs and Counterfeits of Designer Handbags Don't Realize These Harmless Luxury Goods May Be Funding Terrorism," *National Post*, September 27, 2003, p. SP1.

127. John Solomon and Ted Bridis, "Feds Track Sales of Counterfeit Goods, Money to Terror Groups," Associated Press, October 25, 2002.

128. John Mintz and Douglas Farah, "Small Scams Probed for Terror Ties, Muslim, Arab Stores Monitored as Part of Post–September 11 Inquiry," *Washington Post*, August 12, 2002, p. A1.

129. Simon Hughes, "Osama Clothes Racket Is Foiled," *Sun* (UK), May 15, 2004.

130. "Al-Qa'idah Trading in Fake Branded Goods," BBC Monitoring Europe, September 11, 2002.

131. Brooks Boliek, "Interpol IDs Piracy Link to Funding of Terrorism," Reuters, June 10, 2004.

132. "U.S. Designates Dawood Ibrahim as Terrorist Supporter," US Treasury Department press release, October 16, 2003.

133. Noble, *The Lnks between Intellectual Property Crime and Terrorist Financing*.

134. Anthony Faiola, "U.S. Terrorist Search Reaches Paraguay," *Washington Post*, October 13, 2001, p. A21.

135. Agence France Presse, "Document Seized in Cuidad Del Este from Alleged Hezbollah Financier Offices," July 4, 2003.

136. Von Radowitz, "Fake Internet Goods 'Linked to Terrorists.'"

137. Reuters, "'Terror' Groups Cashing in on Fake Goods—Interpol," April 7, 2004.

138. BBC Monitoring Europe, "Al-Qa'idah Trading in Fake Branded Goods."

139. Timothy Trainer, House International Relations Committee, *International/Global Intellectual Property Theft: Links to Terrorism and Terrorist Organizations*, 108th Cong., 2nd sess., July 16, 2003.

140. Josh Lefkowitz and Erick Stakelbeck, "Bin Laden's Hustlers," *Front Page*, September 21, 2004; Lenilson Ferreira, "Hezbollah Suspected in Slaying Lebanese Couple in Brazil," Japan Economic Newswire, March 11, 2002.

141. Office of Management and Budget, "Budget of the United States Government, Fiscal Year 2004—Appendix: Department of Justice," April 19, 2004.

142. Ibid.

143. Mintz and Farah, "Small Scams Probed for Terror Ties; Muslim, Arab Stores Monitored as Part of Post–September 11 Inquiry."

144. Greg Krikorian, "Terrorists Received Drug Money, U.S. Says," *Los Angeles Times*, May 10, 2002, p. 22.

145. Office of Management and Budget, "Budget of the United States Government, Fiscal Year 2004—Appendix: Department of Justice."

146. Sean Holstege, "Drug Probe Links Oakland to Mideast; DEA Seeks Liquor Store Owner, Arrests Laney College Student in National Sting Operation," *Oakland Tribune*, September 22, 2002.

147. Amanda Garrett, "Terrorists' Money Takes Convoluted Path in U.S.," *Cleveland Plain Dealer*, January 18, 2004, p. A1.

148. Ibid.

-7-

PALESTINIAN ISLAMIC JIHAD

We assemble today to stand up and pay our respects to the march of the martyrs, which increases, does not decrease, and to the river of blood that gushes forth and does extinguish. From butchery to butchery and from martyrdom to martyrdom, from Jihad to Jihad.

—Sami al-Arian,
1990 Islamic Committee for Palestine (ICP) Conference
held in Chicago, Illinois[1]

Dear sons of our Palestinian people and the martyrs, we are against this American and Israeli peace. This peace has no benefit to the Arab nation and the Palestinian people. So our blessed uprising will not stop. Only the jihad and the true unity of our nation will terrify the enemy. Death and shame on Israeli agents. Death to all the criminals and to America the enemy of our people. This case is a just one.

—Ghassan Ballut, ICP representative,
1991 ICP Conference held in Chicago, Illinois[2]

OVERVIEW

The Palestinian Islamic Jihad (PIJ), or Harakat al-Jihad al-Islami al-Filastini, has a simple goal: to rid the Islamic world of Western influence, particularly that of the United States and Israel. PIJ, like all other terrorist groups, considers its terrorist activity a justifiable means to a righteous end. PIJ as well as Hamas have as their ultimate aim the destruction of Israel and the creation of an Islamic state from the Jordan River to the Mediterranean Sea. Each, however, has distinct political priorities and conflicting views on the degree of Islamic rule over the Palestinian *ummah* (community).

For Americans, these differences are harder to discern, but in the Middle East they factionalize the Palestinian population as the two groups vie for adherents. Both established branches in the United States in the early 1990s; Hamas eventually became the fund-raising powerhouse, after the US-based PIJ leadership came under intense scrutiny from US law enforcement agencies in the mid-1990s. Both groups have carried out hundreds of attacks in Israel, which have sometimes resulted in American casualties, but neither group has attacked Americans on their own soil.

PIJ's prominence as a designated foreign terrorist organization[3] is due mostly to its alleged US leader, Sami al-Arian. Its position in the United States, therefore, is inextricably linked to his fate. In February 2003, al-Arian was indicted along with eight other codefendants (only three of whom were tried alongside him, the rest were overseas) on charges ranging from providing material support or resources to a designated foreign terrorist organization to engaging in a racketeering enterprise on behalf of PIJ to multiple counts of mail fraud and immigration violations. Al-Arian's codefendants included other individuals associated with two organizations set up by al-Arian in Tampa, Florida, as an infrastructure for PIJ in the United States, namely, the World and Islam Studies Enterprise (WISE) and the Islamic Concern Project, aka the Islamic Committee for Palestine (ICP). In addition, the current secretary-general of PIJ and former colleague of al-Arian in Tampa, Dr. Ramadan Shallah, and the PIJ spiritual leader and cofounder, Sheikh Abd al-Aziz al-Awda were also indicted.[4] Al-Arian was tried along with three US-based codefendants in 2005, and a more detailed discussion of the case appears later in this chapter. Another notable aspect of PIJ's US presence is its intimate connection to other terrorist organizations and their US fronts. One such example was revealed in the investigation of the one hundred Herndon, Virginia, businesses and charities that showed ties between representatives of PIJ, Hamas, and the Muslim Brotherhood.[5]

PIJ OVERSEAS

"PIJ has been involved in terrorist attacks including bombings, suicide bombings (referred to as martyrdom operations), shooting attacks, kidnappings and stabbings. The favored method of attack by the group is suicide bombings, through either explosive belts or car bombs. PIJ has at times carried out double suicide bombing attacks at the same location within a short space of time to target bystanders from the first attack."[6]

On June 5, 2002, at 7:20 AM, sixteen-year-old suicide bomber Hamza Samudi drove his van, packed to the brim with explosives, next to Egged commuter bus no. 830 at the Megiddo Junction in northern Israel. The explosion that followed his self-detonation killed seventeen people and injured another thirty-eight.[7] Ramadan Abdullah Shallah, the secretary-general of the Palestinian Islamic Jihad, claimed responsibility for the attack on behalf of his organization, saying that it was executed to commemorate the Six Days' War.[8]

Financial support for operations such as the one at Megiddo Junction came at least in part from contributions made within the United States. The decadelong investigation into US-based PIJ front groups identified the network as "a criminal organization whose members and associates engaged in acts of violence including murder, extortion, money laundering, fraud and misuse of visas, and operated worldwide."[9] The extent of the US PIJ cell under the supervision of Sami al-Arian will be detailed herein.

The Muslim Brotherhood and the Beginnings of PIJ

The Palestinian Islamic Jihad was formed in 1980 as an offshoot of the original radical Islamic group, the notorious Jamiat Al-Ikhwan Al-Muslimin, more commonly known as the Muslim Brotherhood. The brotherhood was founded in Egypt in 1928[10] by Hassan al-Banna in an attempt to revive the caliphate in response to growing secularism in Egypt. Devoted to returning the Islamic world to what they viewed as the "pure" state of the Qur'an's original precepts, members of the Muslim Brotherhood recognized jihad as central to achieving their ultimate goal. They emphasized the honor and reverence given to those who sacrifice their lives as martyrs in the name of Islam, proclaiming: "Allah is our objective. The Prophet is our leader. Quran is our law. Jihad is our way. Dying in the way of Allah is our highest hope."[11]

The members of the brotherhood who formed the Palestinian Islamic Jihad in 1980 believed that the problems of Muslims were rooted in the Palestinian struggle against Israel, which they viewed as an oppressive Zionist force. Therefore, reforming the Muslim world had to begin with purging Israeli and Western influences from what was considered the Palestinian region. This was their major point of contention with the Muslim Brotherhood school of thought, which focused on a pan-Islamic agenda ahead of the creation of an independent Palestinian state. Hamas, or the Islamic Resistance Movement, which was established a few years after PIJ in 1987, is another example of this trend of emphasizing the

Palestinian issue.[12] Although PIJ and Hamas are the most visible representatives of Palestinian Islamic militancy, they are quite distinct in their manifestations of the old brotherhood line.

PIJ's Leadership

The ousting of Shah Mohammad Reza Pahlavi and his pro-Western regime in the 1979 Iranian revolution sparked a wave of religious fundamentalism and was inspirational for pan-Islamic groups like the Brotherhood. Interest in militant Islam surged throughout the Middle East and many were inspired by Ayatollah Khomeini's call for changes in other regimes.[13] Fathi Shiqaqi and Sheikh Abd al-Aziz al-Awda, two Muslim Brotherhood activists and Palestinian graduates of Zaqaziq University,[14] responded by founding PIJ in 1980 in Egypt, splitting from the Palestinian Muslim Brotherhood in the Gaza Strip.[15]

Shiqaqi and al-Awda were highly influenced by the Islamic revolution in Iran as well as the militancy of Egyptian Islamic student organizations during this period. In 1981, it was discovered that the new organization was closely linked with the assassins of Egyptian president Anwar Sadat and was expelled from Egypt. Following its expulsion, the group, with Shiqaqi and al-Awda at its head, reemerged in the Gaza Strip where it would go on to execute numerous terrorist attacks. At the beginning of the first intifada, or Palestinian uprising, in 1987, PIJ "numbered some 250 militants and several hundred sympathizers in the universities and the young activists around the mosques."[16]

Since its inception, PIJ has been very assertive in securing its role as a militant force in the Palestinian struggle. It continues to thrive as an organization because of its dedication to recruitment and active fundraising. Universities in both the West Bank and Gaza Strip are used as forums for recruitment to the Palestinian Islamic Jihad.[17] Educational institutions have been essential to expanding membership in terrorist organizations and ensuring the emergence of the next generation of *shaheeds* (martyrs).

Israeli jails have also proven to be a fertile source for recruitment. Historically, the Israeli government repeatedly imprisoned Islamic Jihad leaders, only to discover that their effort to contain terrorism was having the opposite effect.[18] Similarly, mosques have been utilized as headquarters for recruitment[19] and sermons were specifically tailored to indoctrinate and minister the jihad mentality to the masses. PIJ's firm priority of procuring new militants and "martyrs" ensures its continued survival as a force within the region and the certainty of continuing civilian victims. It is, by definition, a vicious circle and a conscious PIJ strategy.

The resulting violence carried out by the scores of PIJ members prompted an investigation that eventually resulted in the arrests of al-Awda and Shiqaqi, followed by their deportation from Gaza. PIJ then relocated to Lebanon where it mobilized further support from Iran.[20] After obtaining the necessary financial assistance, Shiqaqi—PIJ's first secretary-general—and al-Awda cofounded PIJ headquarters in 1988 in Beirut.[21] One year later, PIJ headquarters were relocated permanently to Damascus, Syria; smaller branches were also established in Jordan, Algeria, and Libya.[22] There were four mosques in the Gaza Strip that were controlled by Islamic Jihad members, one of which was the Izz Al Din Al Qassam Mosque, which was the headquarters of the jihad's spiritual leader, Sheikh al-Awda, until his deportation abroad by the Israeli military authorities.[23] The organization recruited many members during sermons at the Al Qassam Mosque in the Gaza Strip.

In addition to Shiqaqi and al-Awda, PIJ founders included Ramadan Abdullah Shallah[24] and Bashir Musa Nafi.[25] All four were later associated with the World and Islam Studies Enterprise (WISE) and Islamic Concern Project (ICP) in the United States, both organizations founded by former University of South Florida professor Sami al-Arian.[26] Shallah and Nafi were key PIJ figures in the United Kingdom,[27] where Nafi remains, while Shallah is the current secretary-general of PIJ in Damascus today.[28]

Ramadan Abdullah Shallah

Born Ramadan Abdullah Muhammad Shallah in 1958 in the Gaza Strip, Shallah first became active in the Muslim Brotherhood as a teenager. The brotherhood would eventually cover the costs of his tuition at Zaqaziq University in Egypt, known for its fervent Islamic fundamentalism during the 1970s. While a student in Egypt, Shallah befriended a group of like-minded Palestinians who sought to emulate various Egyptian-based jihadi groups. Returning to Gaza in 1981, Shallah began teaching economics at Islamic University.[29]

In 1986, Ramadan Shallah went to England to pursue a PhD in economics at Durham University.[30] While in England, Shallah worked with Bashir Nafi,[31] who had himself moved to London in 1983[32] to facilitate communications among PIJ operatives and to supply PIJ operations with vital financial support through its London office. Nafi's own associations with PIJ were publicly cited as early as 1990,[33] prior to the official founding of WISE. Together, Shallah and Nafi ran PIJ operations (primarily communications between PIJ leaders and operatives) from London. Ronni Shaked, a former officer in the Israeli General Security Services (the Israeli equivalent of the FBI), describes the PIJ London activities involving Shallah and Nafi:

> Moreover, he [Shiqaqi] had founded a front based in London to ensure easier communication with the Occupied Territories. . . . The main channel of communication between the headquarters in Damascus to the activists in the territories was through the London base of the movement. All activities in London were directed by Dr. Ramadan Shallah, who was born in Gaza. Shallah was one of the first Islamic Jihad members in the territories and was among the people who were most close to Dr. Shiqaqi.
>
> He went to England to continue his studies and was appointed as the head of the London branch. At the end of 1988, he arrived to London, as well as Bashir Nafi from the Kalandia Refugee Camp. After his deportation from the territories, Nafi was sent to assist Dr. Shallah.
>
> From their base in London, they both ran the activities of Islamic Jihad in the territories—the military activity, the information, the advertising, and the distribution of the communiqués. The base in London was responsible for delivering the money to finance the activity and for sending the Islamic Jihad communiqués which were distributed throughout the Occupied Territories. The contact man in Gaza was Omar Shallah, who was Dr. Ramadan Shallah's younger brother, and was a member in one of the PIJ units.
>
> Since they were afraid of someone listening, the Islamic Jihad people used a very sophisticated method of communication: Dr. Ramadan would call his brother from London using codewords which by then Omar meant would have to wait until night for the next operational orders. The base for communication was an industrial business in the center of Israel from which Omar's friend used to work, where he could call London and talk for hours with no disturbances. During these conversations, Nafi used to dictate to Omar the context of the next fliers and to tell him about the next military instructions or to guide him in other issues concerning the movement. The text of the fliers and the instructions were sent by Ramadan Shallah to Dr. Jamil Alyan who was responsible for the distribution of the fliers in the territories.[34]

At the same time that Shallah and Nafi were operating PIJ in London,[35] they were also associated with WISE and ICP—the representative PIJ organizations in the United States. In 1991, Shallah moved to Tampa, Florida, and thereafter WISE was used as a vehicle to distribute Islamic Jihad propaganda and organize fund-raising activities in the United States. ICP became a political front for PIJ activities outside the Middle East.

Shallah worked at the University of South Florida while still executing his duties as a PIJ official.[36] When Fathi Shiqaqi died in October 1995 in Malta, Shallah was appointed to succeed him as PIJ secretary-general.[37] By that time, Shallah had just left his position at WISE, resurfacing in Damascus to attend Shiqaqi's funeral and assume his new role. On November 27, 1995, shortly after his move to Syria, Shallah was named a specially designated terrorist by the United States.[38]

For many years, Sheikh al-Awda, PIJ spiritual leader, was a featured attendee and guest speaker at the Islamic Concern Project conferences. On January 23, 1995, he, too, was designated as a specially designated terrorist.[39]

PIJ SETS UP SHOP IN SOUTH FLORIDA

In 1975, Sami al-Arian, an Egyptian citizen of Palestinian descent who was born in Kuwait, arrived in the United States on a student visa. After graduating from Southern Illinois University in 1978, he attended North Carolina State University and earned both a master's degree in electrical engineering and a doctorate in computer engineering.[40] In 1986, al-Arian moved to Tampa to take up a position as an assistant professor of computer science at the University of South Florida (USF).[41] Acting as a member of the political wing of PIJ, al-Arian proceeded to set up a series of front organizations in order to raise money, spread propaganda, and win recruits for PIJ.

The Islamic Concern Project and the Islamic Committee for Palestine (ICP)

On October 14, 1988, al-Arian and his brother-in-law Mazen al-Najjar, *another* instructor at USF, and others incorporated the Islamic Concern Project.[42] According to its articles of incorporation, its purposes were:

> Charitable, cultural, social, educational and religious in which the concept of brotherhood, freedom, justice, unity, piety, righteousness and peace shall be propagated. In addition the organization shall take human projects of helping the poor, the refugees, the displaced, the orphans, the sick, the handicapped and the homeless.[43]

As a charitable organization, the Islamic Concern Project could avoid revealing its spending records. Such concealment was imperative for an organization whose purpose was to mobilize funds and other resources on behalf of the Palestinian Islamic Jihad, primarily by coordinating radical Islamic conferences and distributing propaganda. According to US law enforcement agents, the Islamic Concern Project used the money raised at conferences to finance and support PIJ endeavors outside the United States.[44] Prosecutors, in the indictment against Sami al-Arian, alleged that "the enterprise members would and did actively solicit and raise monies and funds and support for the PIJ and PIJ goals in various ways."[45]

Under the corporate structure of the Islamic Concern Project, al-Arian created an alias called the Islamic Committee for Palestine (ICP).[46] Whereas the Islamic Concern Project name seemed innocuous, the ICP name was more reflective of the organization's purpose: to provide a venue for the dissemination of PIJ ideology and fund-raising for PIJ endeavors. Throughout its existence, ICP sponsored numerous rallies and conferences showcasing militant Islamists, known for their hateful rhetoric and radical jihadi ideologies. PIJ spiritual leader Sheikh al-Awda was a frequent speaker at these rallies and conferences espousing PIJ ideology. Former PIJ secretary-general Fathi Shiqaqi was also advertised in ICP publications as an invited speaker for at least one of the annual conventions held by ICP.[47] Other invited headliners included Rashid al-Ghannoushi, the leader of the Tunisian Al Nahda movement charged in 1987 with plotting to overthrow the Tunisian government,[48] and Shiekh Omar Abdel Rahman, the Egyptian "blind cleric," spiritual leader of the group that bombed the World Trade Center in 1993 and convicted for his role in a plot to bomb landmarks and tunnels in New York City.[49]

Of particular note, Hassan al-Turabi, the former spiritual leader of the Sudanese National Islamic Front,[50] had been invited to participate in various ICP conferences although he was unable to attend. He did, however, attend a roundtable on May 10, 1992, that was cosponsored by WISE and the University of South Florida as part of their cooperative agreement.[51] The views that were espoused by al-Turabi at this event caused a flurry of media controversy.[52] Flown into the United States for the sole purpose of attending, and in some cases speaking at these ICP events, these radical attendees had an influential presence that created a more militant environment.

The Third Annual ICP conference, "Islam: The Road to Victory" (December 28–31, 1990), lauded terrorist activity and was a clear example of the radical atmosphere mentioned above. Before its close, attendees had passed a resolution urging all Palestinians to reject any negotiations or compromises with Israel about land and to instead pursue the liberation of Palestine exclusively through armed struggle. Sami al-Arian, in his role as "moderator" of the conference, opened the event by declaring:

> We assemble today to stand up and pay our respects to the march of the martyrs, which increases, does not decrease, and to the river of blood that gushes forth and does extinguish. From butchery to butchery and from martyrdom to martyrdom, from Jihad to Jihad. . . .[53]

Likewise, at the Fourth Annual ICP Conference, "Islam, Palestine and the West" (December 27–31, 1991), Sami al-Arian was heard spewing hate-laced rhetoric including, "He [Allah] cursed those who are the son of Israel through David and Jesus, the son of Mary. . . . Those people, God made monkeys and pigs. Jihad is our path. . . . Victory to Islam. Death to Israel."[54]

Transcripts of these inflammatory speeches were reported by *NBC Dateline* as part of a 2001 exposé on al-Arian's activities.[55]

The Fifth Annual ICP Conference, "Islamic Resurgence and the New World" (December 25–28, 1992), featured al-Arian, Shallah, and other members of WISE and ICP. The US government's superseding indictment of al-Arian, Shallah, and others summarized statements made by Shallah to this gathering regarding his feelings about the United States:

> RAMADAN ABDULLAH SHALLAH spoke and said the enemies were the United States, the Zionists and the Arab Governments. He said that Muslims should not be defensive or apologize against charges including charges of terrorism, that Jihad required Muslims to terrorize, devastate, humiliate and degrade enemies because they were enemies of Allah and that the Koran instructed Muslims to fight and kill those people.[56]

Shallah's own words give an accurate picture of ICP's true agenda: the spread of an ideology that promotes hate and violence against Israel, the United States, and secular Arab governments.

In addition to organizing conferences, ICP distributed an Arabic-language monthly newsletter titled *Al Islam wa Filastin* (*Islam and Palestine*). This publication, which gave as its return address al-Arian's Tampa office,[57] provides key evidence of the connection between ICP in Florida and the Palestinian Islamic Jihad. *Al Islam wa Filastin* often included both notices of upcoming ICP conferences and PIJ communiqués that took credit for earlier terrorist attacks.[58] Al-Arian regularly denied any awareness that editorials in the publication mentioned or condoned acts of jihad. In the December 1, 1990, issue, the Islamic Fund for Palestine (IFP), another subsidiary of the Islamic Concern Project, was characterized as being "for the Martyrs, for the injured, for the prisoners and for the Jihad on the land of Palestine."[59] This fund provided subsidies to families whose immediate family members were arrested or "martyred" in a terrorist attack.[60] An article about the IFP in the August 1989 newsletter, which told stories of Palestinians arrested, tortured, and dying through repressive Israeli actions, described how the IFP was structured to distribute its moneys to families of "martyrs" and prisoners as well as to Islamic institutions and mosques.[61] This publication and its advertisements are yet another example of ICP's outward support of terrorism.

A second publication, published by the Islamic Concern Project from the winter of 1992 to the spring of 1994, was titled *Inquiry*. ICP and WISE founder and executive Sami al-Arian was listed as the editor-in-chief and managing editor of this magazine.[62] *Inquiry* contained many editorials that discussed and promoted the activities of the Palestinian Islamic Jihad. An example of such inflammatory content was included in the January 1993 edition:

> We are not claiming that the Intifada is going to liberate Palestine today or tomorrow, but we are saying that it is the beginning of the end of this corrupt existence the West has planted in our homeland.[63]

Yet another ICP publication, even more openly tied to PIJ, was called *Al Mujahid*. The front page of each addition featured the PIJ logo, along with the words: "Publication Produced by the Islamic Jihad Movement in Palestine–Lebanon."[64]

World and Islam Studies Enterprise (WISE)

Aside from his involvement with ICP, Sami al-Arian served as the chairman of the World and Islam Studies Enterprise. Like ICP, WISE was founded in Tampa, and though it was incorporated separately, the two organizations essentially constituted a single entity. In addition to having similar goals and methods of operation, the organizations had overlapping directorships and at one time shared a single mailing address.[65]

Incorporated on January 1, 1991,[66] WISE purportedly operated as a think tank and an academic research center organized entirely for the purpose of education, research, and analysis. Its stated aims also included the promotion of international peace, tolerance, and understanding, particularly in the Muslim world.[67] Ramadan Abdullah Shallah was WISE's director of administration until he left for Damascus in October 1995 to lead PIJ.[68] On March 11, 1992, Shallah entered into a formal partnership on behalf of WISE with the University of South Florida[69] that enabled WISE and the university to cooperate in programming research, conferences, and training and enrichment for graduate students.[70] The arrangement was formalized in writing, and Shallah signed on behalf of WISE.

Regardless of contrary arguments set forth by faculty members at the university who worked with WISE, the University of South Florida through its partnership with WISE and its employment of PIJ leaders Shallah and al-Arian was used as a base for terrorist ends.[71] Pursuant to the agreement, WISE was able to sponsor "conferences" where PIJ fundraising took place and to create and distribute publications saturated with anti-Jewish and anti-Western propaganda.

Al-Arian continues to deny that his enterprises had anything to do with promoting terror. In February 2004, he described WISE as:

> [a] research and academic institute established to foster dialogue between Western academics and Muslim academics and intellectuals. In five years, between 1990 and its closing in 1995, WISE produced over 4000 pages of journals and proceedings. In these journals and proceedings, over 100 professors, academics and intellectuals participated. They were among the top university professors in the country in the areas of Islam, the Middle East, and International Studies.[72]

In 1995, federal agents obtained search warrants for the premises of WISE and ICP, and the office and home of Sami al-Arian. As a result of the searches conducted, both WISE and ICP were shut down.[73] The searches uncovered a wealth of evidence. The documents and communiqués that were confiscated persuaded authorities that ICP and WISE were not the organizations that they claimed to be.

Raising Money for PIJ

ICP and WISE cooperated to raise money for PIJ activities. One of the ICP's methods involved the creation of specific funds, such as the Islamic

Fund for Palestine and the Muslim Women's Society (MWS), and solicited donations for them in its various publications. The IFP directed its funds to orphans and families of martyred soldiers. ICP published an "Informational Guide" pamphlet in English that described its purposes:

> I.C.P. contributes to the support of the Palestinian people's struggle and defiance in their occupied land, and to the alleviation of their humanitarian and economical suffering through contribution to the "Islamic Fund for Palestine" (I.F.P.), which handles the collection and distribution of financial contributions to the people in occupied Palestine.
>
> There exists an extreme shortage of work opportunities and family economical and market turnover. A result of the loss of a great number of martyrs, the incapacitation of the wounded and handicapped, and the administrative arrest, detention and unjust incarceration of thousands. It is incumbent upon us to spend all we can in terms of money and effort from outside Palestine to support the hold-out of this nation.[74]

Another conduit for PIJ financing was the Elehssan Society.[75] Headquartered in Bethlehem with branch offices throughout the West Bank and Gaza Strip, the Elehssan Society defines among its goals "[s]upporting and assisting the martyrs' children and their families,"[76] and functioned essentially as a "charitable society" network tied to PIJ. Implicated in the federal case against Sami al-Arian, the Elehssan Society has been characterized as the "fund-raising arm of the PIJ in Gaza and the West Bank, and solicited, collected, and distributed donations."[77] Ziad Abu Amr, a former Palestinian legislator, university professor, author, and expert on PIJ, submitted a declaration in bond redetermination proceedings for Mazen al-Najjar that identified the Elehssan Society as being a PIJ-backed institution. [78] As a result of its role in financing PIJ activities, the Elehssan Society was designated by the United States as a Specially Designated Global Terrorist (SDGT) entity on May 4, 2005.[79]

Coconspirators involved in the al-Arian case allegedly used this organization as a conduit to further their terror-financing scheme. They did so by promoting the society as being engaged in Palestinian social and health initiatives. The true nature of the fund-raising is captured in a wiretap-recorded telephone conversation between coconspirator Hatem Fariz and PIJ operative Salah Abu Hassanein in Gaza. The intercepted conversation took place on November 10, 2002, where the potential of Fariz transferring $7,000 to Gaza is discussed. The conversation is recounted in the superseding indictment:

> Hatem Fariz said that Salah Abu Hassanein had to change the name of the organization in Gaza because the name "The Elehssan Society" was recognized as an organization that could not receive funds from the United States. They then agreed to change the name of the organization by adding the word "Birr"[80] to "The Elehssan Society" and put that new name on receipts that Salah Abu Hassanein would send to the United States. Hatem Fariz also instructed Salah Abu Hassanein that *he could use the money however he wanted,* [emphasis added] but they needed to create a receipt for the donations so that Fariz could gain the trust of the donors in the United States.[81]

Hatem Fariz pled guilty to conspiracy to make and receive contributions of funds, goods, or services to the Palestinian Islamic Jihad, and on July 25, 2006, he was sentenced to three years and one month in prison.[82]

THE INVESTIGATIONS

The 1994 PBS documentary *Jihad in America,* produced by Steven Emerson, included a segment on the PIJ apparatus set up in Tampa under the tutelage of Sami al-Arian.

In 1995, Michael Fechter, an investigative reporter for the *Tampa Tribune,* wrote a series of stories about al-Arian. His articles pulled no punches and described the double life of Sami al-Arian in terms hard to ignore: "On the University of South Florida campus, Sami Al Arian is an award-winning young engineering professor. In his off hours, he presides over a nonprofit organization that helps raise money in the name of two groups that claim responsibility for bombings that have killed hundreds in Israel and around the world."[83]

The stories, along with other media accounts focusing on al-Arian, caught the interest of federal agencies, and a lengthy investigation by agents from the FBI, the INS, and the US Customs Department into al-Arian's activities in ICP and WISE soon followed. In his November 1995 affidavit seeking a search warrant for the offices of ICP and WISE, along with al-Arian's residence and office, INS supervisory special agent Bill West bluntly noted al-Arian's use of ICP and WISE as fronts to further suspicious and potentially unlawful activities:

> Based upon the facts and information that I have set forth in the instant affidavit, I have probable cause to believe that ICP and WISE were uti-

> lized by Sami Al Arian and Ramadan Abdullah Shallah as "fronts" in order to enable individuals to enter the United States, in an apparent lawful fashion, despite the fact that these individuals were international terrorists. Among the unlawful methods employed by these terrorist organizations are the apparent lawful procurement and use of visas and other documents relating to immigration which enables terrorists and other excludable aliens to [*sic*] gain entry into the United States through false statements, misrepresentations, and other forms of fraud.[84]

The Evolution of the Tampa PIJ Criminal Investigation

The fifty-count federal criminal indictment of Sami al-Arian and seven codefendants filed in February 2003 in Tampa, Florida, is highly informative. It reveals that the US government had begun a confidential intelligence investigation of al-Arian in early 1994. Federal immigration and criminal investigators and prosecutors, however, had little or no knowledge of that ongoing inquiry because of laws and policies that remained in place until the passage of the USA PATRIOT Act immediately following the 9/11 attacks.

The criminal investigation of al-Arian and the alleged PIJ cabal in Tampa effectively began in November 1994 with the airing of *Jihad in America*. Special Agent Bill West, who was the chief of what was then the Special Investigations Unit in the Miami district office of the INS, launched an immigration fraud investigation based on the information contained in the documentary, which led to the subsequent criminal investigation.[85]

West's INS unit was responsible for INS participation in multiagency investigations targeting organized crime and national security cases, including counterterrorism matters involving the FBI. Though his mission generally concentrated on South Florida, the Miami district office of the INS covered the entire state, with suboffices in Tampa, Orlando, and Jacksonville. West possessed experience investigating organized crime and national security cases handled by the INS throughout Florida.

After watching *Jihad in America*, West took note of the segment involving al-Arian and the PIJ connection in Tampa.[86] INS record checks on al-Arian revealed that he was a permanent resident alien who had recently applied at the INS office in Tampa to become a naturalized US citizen. Other record checks conducted on al-Arian revealed that the professor was involved with ICP and WISE as discussed above, something he had omitted on his naturalization application as required by law.[87] That revelation would spell the beginning of the end for Sami al-Arian's PIJ network, ultimately leading to the federal indictment filed against al-Arian and his colleagues nearly a decade later.

Based on this initial indication of wrongdoing, then Miami INS district director, Walter D. "Dan" Cadman, approved the case's assignment as a national security–related investigation of INS fraud, with the INS portion controlled by West's unit. Dan Vara, the INS chief legal officer for the district, was assigned to work closely with West on the case.

As the investigation continued during 1995, the INS, FBI, and US Attorney's Office realized that there was a prima facie case against al-Arian and perhaps others for felony immigration charges—fraud involved in the naturalization process, visa fraud, and aiding and abetting the entrance of certain excludable aliens into the United States. Though the FBI had said nothing about its separate intelligence investigation, the bureau in Tampa quickly agreed that pursuing a criminal case against al-Arian and his associates in a joint effort with the INS was the best way to proceed. As a result, FBI special agent Barry Carmody was assigned as the criminal case agent.[88]

Now vastly more familiar with al-Arian and his PIJ affiliation, investigators jointly agreed that this was far more than an immigration case. It had become a criminal investigation into the more substantial charges of terrorism and supporting terrorism.

After reports that al-Arian's associate Ramadan Abdullah Shallah had surfaced in Damascus as the new leader of PIJ were verified in the fall of 1995, it became clear that the pace of the investigation needed to accelerate. The agents worried that PIJ's operations were about to become more active and violent and, given PIJ's link to South Florida, might even find their way to the United States. The investigators thus came to believe that they were acting not just to pursue evidence for a criminal case but also, to some degree, to prevent a possible attack. These new developments persuaded them to seek search warrants for al-Arian's residence, his office at the University of South Florida, and the office of WISE. As noted above, the existing prima facie evidence of immigration violations was the probable cause given for the search warrants, which were issued and executed in November 1995.

Those searches yielded several thousand items—mostly documents, audio- and videotapes, and computer records, many in Arabic. The review, translation, and analysis of that evidence took several years. In the process, new leads were generated that required further investigation, which in turn produced more evidence to process, review, and analyze.

During this time, additional suspects were identified. Deportation proceedings against al-Arian's brother-in-law and board member of both WISE and ICP Mazen al-Najjar, which were commenced in the mid-1980s but were not pursued due to an INS administrative oversight, were renewed, and in May 1997 the immigration court ordered him deported.[89] Al-Najjar was taken into INS custody shortly thereafter. The government argued that al-Najjar's detention was necessary, based in part on classified evidence released to the INS by the FBI (which by then had disclosed part of its intelligence investigation to certain INS officials, as authorized by federal law). Al-Najjar was imprisoned for three and a half years while he appealed his deportation order. His case drew a great deal of media attention, most of which focused on the propriety of using classified evidence obtained through an intelligence investigation (referred to by opponents of this process by the nefarious name of "secret evidence") in immigration proceedings.

Mazen al-Najjar, Sami al-Arian's brother-in-law, was a cofounder and the executive director of WISE.[90] In addition to serving as editor of WISE's journal, *Qira 'at Siyasiyyah* (*Political Readings*),[91] al-Najjar attended all of the ICP conferences described above.

The 1995 investigation uncovered a web of immigration violations, from al-Najjar's simple overstay of his student visa to his fraudulent marriage to an American woman for the purpose of obtaining permanent resident status. Prior to his deportation, al-Najjar was detained as a threat to US national security.[92]

Special Agent West put the security-driven deportation into context:

> The marriage fraud evidence was not used as a basis for the underlying deportation charge, which was his overstaying his original student visa (F-1) authorized period of admission. We used the evidence of the marriage fraud primarily in the hearings related to the denial of discretionary relief from deportation and in the custody proceedings. It was important, as it demonstrated his propensity to engage in deception and fraud, but it was not the basis for his being found deportable . . . that was a basic overstay nonimmigrant. One of the ironies of the Al Najjar deportation case was just that . . . a "simple" overstay F-1 student case cost millions of dollars, eight years of litigation (1994–2002) and nearly four years of detention in order to effect his removal from the US. All because that overstay student happened to be a Ph.D. terror suspect instead of a dishwasher or bag boy. That in itself says something about the system.[93]

Based on a federal court order, al-Najjar was released from INS custody in December 2000, but was rearrested for his immigration violations in November 2001. Ultimately, al-Najjar exhausted his appeals. Al-Najjar's deportation, which was originally ordered on May 13, 1997, finally took place in 2002.[94] The February 2003 indictment lists al-Najjar as "unindicted coconspirator 12," but with additional evidence gathered, a superseding indictment filed in September of that year included al-Najjar as a defendant, asserting that he was part of the PIJ leadership in the United States.[95]

Mazen al-Najjar was not the only PIJ-affiliated member to be deported from the United States as a result of immigration fraud. Bashir Musa Nafi, one of the original PIJ cofounders with Fathi Shiqaqi, who worked for the Palestinian Islamic Jihad at its UK-based headquarters, eventually suffered the same fate.

In September 1992, al-Arian filed a petition for a temporary worker's visa with the INS on behalf of Nafi to allow him to enter the country as a research director employed by WISE.[96] In fact, Nafi was employed by the International Institute of Islamic Thought (IIIT), and this lie on his INS petition led to Nafi's deportation to London on July 1, 1996, only four days after being apprehended by immigration authorities.[97] IIIT itself was investigated in 2002 as part of an Operation Green Quest raid on SAAR-related business enterprises (see chapter 10).

In addition to his leadership role in London, Nafi attended ICP conferences in the United States in 1988 and 1989, all of which had Islamic extremist agendas and featured anti-Semitic and anti-American incitement as well as patent support of Jihadi violence.[98]

Notwithstanding the INS cases against al-Najjar and Nafi, the investigation into the PIJ command-and-control structure in Tampa continued with growing evidence especially following passage of the USA PATRIOT Act, which permitted the sharing of evidence between intelligence agents in the FBI and those agents within the FBI tasked with law enforcement duties and developing evidence to be used in criminal cases.[99] A grand jury indictment was eventually handed down in February 2003.

Execution of the search warrants in 1995 produced many terrorist-related items, including the PIJ Manifesto, which describes in detail the organization's structure, its goals and principles, and the roles and responsibilities of various offices.[100] One of those declared goals was "the creation of a situation of terror, instability and panic in the souls (minds) of Zionists and especially the groups of settlers, and force them to leave their houses."[101]

The government alleged[102] that the central purpose of both ICP and WISE was to facilitate communication between PIJ's leaders around the world. The November raid uncovered several boxes of documents, including correspondence, facsimiles, and communiqués, which demonstrated how ICP and WISE helped coordinate PIJ activities. For example, a PIJ communiqué dated December 11, 1992, and translated from Arabic, read in part:

> The Islamic Jihad Movement of Palestine
> Oh Our Palestinian people!
> The Saif Al Islam [Sword of Islam] Brigades, the Brigades of Islamic Jihad in Palestine follow the Zionist enemy and fight it, in order to prove that the only way for liberation of Palestine is through armed Jihad, and that the negotiations of surrender between those who claim that they represent our people and the Zionist, serve only the enemies of our [Islamic] Nation. This [*sic*] negotiations will only increase our steadfastness and our determination to continue in our right path Islam and the commitment to protect our people and our land.[103]

The First Annual ICP Conference, "Islam, Intifada and the Future" (December 23–26, 1988),[104] served as a fund-raising venue and hub for PIJ recruitment.[105] Likewise, the Second Annual ICP Conference, "Palestine, Intifada, and the Horizons of the Islamic Renaissance" (December 22–25, 1989), featured Sami al-Arian shouting: "This great intifada is not more than a ring in the big chain of the ongoing jihad against Zionism and the racist resettlement, and it remains the most powerful, effective and dedicated tool."[106]

Fawaz Damrah

The fund-raising efforts of the Ohio-based Imam Fawaz Damrah were central to the achievements of PIJ in the United States. Damrah had been the leader of the Islamic Center of Cleveland,[107] the largest mosque in the state, since 1991.[108] Damrah's leadership role was not solely limited to religious preaching since he was simultaneously spearheading fund-raising efforts for PIJ.

While serving as imam at the Cleveland mosque, Damrah "gained a local reputation as a leader of the interfaith community who strove to bridge the gaps separating the Christian, Jewish, and Muslim faiths."[109] Damrah's fund-raising efforts, however, were directed toward an organization that was anything but tolerant; PIJ advocated jihad against Israel and the West and actively recruited individuals to serve these militant ends.

Damrah's radical activity in the United States began while he was living in Brooklyn, before he became the imam in Cleveland. While residing in Brooklyn, Damrah was affiliated with the Al Kifah Refugee Center,[110] a predecessor organization to al Qaeda.[111] Damrah also served as the spiritual leader of the Al Farouq Mosque in Brooklyn,[112] an institution frequented by conspirators who were implicated in the 1993 World Trade Center bombing;[113] Damrah himself was later implicated as an unindicted coconspirator in this devastating attack.[114]

In addition to being named as an unindicted coconspirator in the 1993 bombing, Damrah is also identified as Unindicted Coconspirator One in the indictment against Sami al-Arian, as a result of fund-raising efforts on behalf of ICP.[115]

Throughout his tenure in Brooklyn and later while working in Cleveland, Damrah attended PIJ events such as ICP conferences in the company of many notable PIJ members. A transcript of the 1989 ICP conference reveals a particular incendiary comment made by Damrah, proudly admitting his involvement in terrorist activity: "But we are terrorists! And that goes for our political level as well!"[116]

At a similar conference held in Chicago in 1991, Damrah encouraged the attendants in the audience to "point their gun toward the enemy, toward the children of pigs and monkeys, the Jews."[117]

A speech made by Damrah during an April 1991 conference reveals the close relationship that al-Arian and Damrah shared:

> He [Sami al-Arian] is the head of the Islamic Committee for Palestine (ICP); and as a brief excerpt about the ICP, it is the active arm (Al Ziraa Al Amil) of the Islamic Jihad Movement in Palestine. We prefer here to call it the ICP for security reasons.[118]

This quote was included in the al-Arian indictment although the identity of the unindicted coconspirator is not revealed; however, a videotape of Damrah's speech was played during the trial.[119] A videotape of the conference released by the INS was also shown at Damrah's trial in 2004.[120]

Finally, on January 13, 2002, Damrah was arrested and charged with the illegitimate procurement of US citizenship. Like the original al-Arian investigation, Damrah's charges dealt with his deliberate failure to include pertinent information and including false statements on his application for naturalization in 1993.[121] Among the crucial information that Damrah failed to disclose was his undeniable involvement with the Al Kifah Refugee Center and his association with PIJ and ICP.[122] The violations continued with Damrah falsely stating on his application that he had never incited or supported the persecution of any individual on the basis of inherent characteristics such as race or religion,[123] which, based on his inflammatory comments during ICP events, was demonstrably false.

Damrah was eventually found guilty by a jury, spent two months in prison, and was released in January 2005.[124] As part of the sentence subsequent to his release, Damrah was required to comply with a four-month period of house arrest.[125] On March 15, 2005, the US Court of Appeals for the Sixth Circuit upheld his conviction,[126] clearing the way for deportation hearings to begin. In January 2006, three years after Damrah's initial arrest, he reached an agreement with the government to be deported to either Qatar, United Arab Emirates, Sudan, Egypt, or the Palestinian territories.[127]

The O'Reilly Factor *Interview and Its Aftermath*

In a September 2001 episode of the Fox News Channel TV show *The O'Reilly Factor*, Sami al-Arian appeared as a guest to discuss the controversy surrounding his relationship with Ramadan Abdullah Shallah. During the broadcast, Bill O'Reilly quoted al-Arian verbatim from transcripts recorded at various ICP rallies and conferences. An exchange between O'Reilly and al-Arian followed:

> O'Reilly: In—in 1988, you did a little speaking engagement in Cleveland, and you were quoted as saying, "Jihad is our path. Victory to Islam. Death to Israel. Revolution. Revolution until victory. Rolling to Jerusalem."
>
> Al Arian: Let me just put it into context. When President Bush talked about crusade, we understand what he meant here. The Muslim world thought he is going to carry a cross and go invade the Muslim world and turn them into Christians. We have to understand the context. When you say "Death to Israel," you mean death to occupation, death to apartheid, death to oppression.[128]

Immediately following this interview, the University of South Florida was inundated with angry calls and complaints from people outraged that the university was employing as a faculty member someone who might be a supporter of terrorists. In September 2001, al-Arian was placed on paid leave, and in December 2001, USF's board of trustees voted 12 to 1 to recommend al-Arian's dismissal from the university.[129] His supporters would later criticize his firing as suppressing free speech and academic freedom.[130]

THE TRIAL

In February 2003, federal authorities arrested Sami al-Arian and charged him, along with six coconspirators, in a fifty-count indictment.[131] The indictment alleges that al-Arian was the leader of a criminal racketeering enterprise known as PIJ in the United States and that all of the defendants knowingly assisted PIJ in the Middle East by providing the organization with financial support and resources. It further states that the defendants "supported Palestinian Islamic Jihad and with conspiracy to kill and maim people abroad, conspiracy to provide material support to the group, extortion, perjury and other charges."[132] Al-Arian was also charged with money laundering, unlawfully attempting to procure naturalization, and obstruction of justice in the deportation case of Mazen al-Najjar. The indictment in part reflected the more aggressive law enforcement policy instituted after 9/11 against terrorist activity in the United States.[133] In September 2003, a 156-page fifty-three count superseding indictment added charges against the seven codefendants, made changes to previous allegations, and added allegations against Mazen al-Najjar as a codefendant rather than as an unindicted coconspirator.

The trial was originally slated to begin in January 2005. Al-Arian's attorneys submitted a series of motions that would delay the start of the trial for several months. They challenged the constitutionality of the classified evidence in the case, gained primarily through wiretap and surveillance search warrants obtained via the Foreign Intelligence Surveillance Act (FISA), which permits surveillance of "agents of a foreign power" acting within the United States. Pursuant to FISA, PIJ qualified as a foreign power, and al-Arian and his codefendants were reasonably believed to be agents of PIJ within the United States. However, in December 2004, the presiding judge ruled in favor of the prosecution in the first of four defense motions, permitting the prosecution to use as evidence wiretaps translated by military personnel.[134]

Al-Arian's request for a change of venue was also denied[135] and, one month prior to the commencement of his trial, the US government designated the Elehssan Society as a Specially Designated Global Terrorist (SDGT) entity for its role as a front for PIJ.[136]

Almost a year and a half after al-Arian and his codefendants were indicted, the trial against the accused North American leader of PIJ and his associates finally commenced. Jury selection began on May 16, 2005, and, after the jury was seated, the lawyers' opening statements began on June 6, 2005.

The prosecution opened the trial, describing al-Arian's and his codefendants' activity on behalf of PIJ in the United States, from organizations and charities set up by the professor to conference and fund-raisers organized by his group, to contacts with PIJ leadership overseas and bank transfers on behalf of PIJ employees. Lead prosecutor Terry Furr gave the opening statement and credited *Jihad in America* as the "triggering event" that started a greater media inquiry ultimately leading to al-Arian's indictment almost a decade later.

The defense painted the case as an attack on al-Arian's First Amendment rights to speech and association, citing the "American tradition" of protecting "unpopular" views and claiming that this case demonstrated the government's intent to stifle pro-Palestinian views, which are considered unpopular in American society.

The trial lasted over six months, and the prosecution put over seventy witnesses on the stand and entered thousands of hours of wiretapped phone conversations into evidence, demonstrating al-Arian's frequent and high-level contacts with the top leadership of PIJ, as well as video evidence demonstrating his fund-raising efforts on behalf of the terrorist organization.

A key piece of evidence was a February 1995 letter written by al-Arian soliciting funds from a Kuwaiti legislator after a PIJ double suicide bombing in Beit Lid, Israel, on January 22, 1995. Al-Arian wrote:

> The latest operation, carried out by the two *mujahideen* who were martyred for the sake of God, is the best guide and witness to what the believing few can do in the face of Arab and Islamic collapse at the heels of the Zionist enemy and in keeping the flame of faith, steadfastness, and defiance glowing. Perhaps few know, while many are unaware, that these *mujahideen* were martyred while owing debt and having big fami-

> lies with no means to support themselves and the head of the household offered his life for God, glory be to He, defending the honor of this nation! The Islamic movement in Palestine is poor, hungry and destitute. The Jihad is in a state of great misfortune and has nothing. The brothers, your neighbors to the north, give very little assistance, which does not diminish the hunger and which proves, day after day, that the principles and slogans which we uphold are one thing and what actually occurs is something else. . . . I call upon you to try to extend true support of the jihad effort in Palestine so that operations such as these can continue, so that people do not lose faith in Islam and its representatives, and so that we can prove to people and to history that Islam properly responded to the circumstances despite a difficult stage in time, and a terrible era.[137]

The defense conceded that al-Arian had written the letter, but contended that there was no proof the letter was ever sent. The letter was written one month after PIJ was designated by President Clinton as a terrorist group, in response to the Beit Lid attack.[138]

The prosecution rested its case on October 27, 2005, at which point al-Arian's attorney, William Moffitt, informed the court that he was not going to put on a defense for his client, shocking most observers.[139] During Moffitt's closing arguments, he conceded that al-Arian, despite a decade's worth of public denials, was in fact affiliated with PIJ. The *St. Petersburg Times* described that portion of the argument as follows:

> Yes, said Moffitt, Al-Arian was affiliated with the cultural, charitable arm of the PIJ, and he lied to the media about it because he was afraid WISE would be shut down. But he was never part of PIJ violence. He simply wanted, said Moffitt, to get money so WISE could keep telling the Palestinian story in the United States.[140]

After closing arguments, the jury received instructions and began deliberations on November 15, 2005.[141]

The jury deliberations were, at times, heated. One juror felt compelled to write a note to the judge, described in the *Miami Herald*:

> "I am sorry to say at this time I can no longer deliberate under the conditions you put forth," the unidentified juror said in a note to U.S. District Judge James S. Moody Jr., one day after Moody urged the jury to seek agreement on all charges. "Being that I am in the minority, I feel I am being whipped to change and I am not alone. . . . My nerves and my conscience are being whipped into submission."[142]

After three weeks of deliberating, and despite Moffitt's admission that his client was connected at a high level to PIJ, the jury returned a verdict on December 6, 2005, acquitting al-Arian of eight of the seventeen charges against him. Al-Arian was found not guilty of several major charges, including conspiracy to murder and maim abroad, providing material support to a designated foreign terrorist organization, and obstruction of justice. The jury deadlocked on the remaining nine charges, including conspiracy to provide material support to a designated foreign terrorist organization, money laundering, and unlawful procurement of naturalization.[143]

Two of al-Arian's codefendants, Sameeh Hammoudeh and Ghassan Ballut, were acquitted on all charges, while the jury found codefendant Hatem Fariz not guilty on twenty-five counts, deadlocking on the eight remaining charges against him.[144]

Upon news of the verdicts, the editorial board of the *St. Petersburg Times* wrote:

> Even though Al-Arian was not convicted of supporting terrorist acts, he stands exposed for what he is—*a carrier of hate.* He is not just an innocent academic with unpopular views about the Israeli-Palestinian conflict, as he has so often claimed, or a "prisoner of conscience." The trial demonstrated that Al-Arian was deeply connected to the PIJ, which is believed responsible for more than 100 deaths in the Middle East. *He was described by his own lawyers as a fundraiser for the "charitable arm of the PIJ."* And Al-Arian was not blind to the group's monstrous tactics, as he was the regular recipient of faxes announcing the group's suicide bombings. . . . As a legal resident, Al-Arian has abused this nation's hospitality and engaged in conduct that may warrant his deportation. The trial has laid bare Al-Arian's involvement in one of the most violent groups in the Middle East. He may now claim an acquittal, but he can never again claim moral innocence.[145] (emphasis added)

And despite the verdict, the Immigration and Customs Enforcement (ICE) remained unconvinced that the trial absolved al-Arian for his connections to PIJ. ICE spokesperson Pam McCullough told the *St. Petersburg Times* that "[w]e believe there is clear and convincing evidence that he had ties to terrorist organizations" and announced the intent to pursue deportation proceedings against al-Arian after the government decided whether or not to retry him on the deadlocked charges.[146]

One juror described the deliberations as "difficult" and "frustrating."

From the Associated Press:

> "It was very difficult at times in the deliberation area," juror 211 said in an interview. "It was hard. We would state the way we felt and vote the way we felt and continually we were asked, 'Where do you come up with this?' We would go over our points and other people couldn't see that. It was frustrating."[147]

The same juror described the situation to the *Tampa Tribune* in an online forum:

> I was one of the jurors that voted Sami Al-Arian and Hatem Fariz guilty on several counts. . . . I can sleep at night knowing I saw all of the evidence and my votes were based upon that evidence.[148]

But juror 211 remained in the minority. The *Tampa Tribune* described the feelings of the other juror who sided with 211:

> Only one other juror agreed with her by the time deliberations ended Dec. 6. The other juror told Moody she felt "whipped into submission" by those favoring acquittal.[149]

On April 14, 2006, after more than a decade of denying any involvement with PIJ, and five months after the conclusion of the jury trial, Sami al-Arian pled guilty to "conspiracy to make or receive contributions of funds, goods or services to or for the benefit of the Palestinian Islamic Jihad, a Specially Designated Terrorist." A condition of al-Arian's guilty plea includes his submission to the Bureau of Immigration and Customs enforcement for deportation proceedings.[150]

As part of the plea agreement, al-Arian admitted that he "performed services for the PIJ in 1995 and thereafter" and that he was "aware that the PIJ achieved its objectives by, among other means, acts of violence."[151] The agreement states that the services al-Arian performed for PIJ "included filing for Immigration benefits for individuals associated with the PIJ, hiding the identities of individuals associated with the PIJ, and providing assistance for an individual (Mazen al-Najjar) associated with the PIJ in an United States Court proceeding."[152]

On May 1, 2006, al-Arian was sentenced to fifty-seven months in prison.[153] Al-Arian will get credit for time served (at the time of sentencing, he had already been imprisoned for thirty-eight months), and will most likely finish out the last year and a half of his sentence at the FCI Coleman Federal Penitentiary north of Tampa, before being deported. Speaking to al-Arian at the sentencing hearing, Judge Moody said, "You are a master manipulator. The evidence is clear in this case. You were a leader of the PIJ."[154] Commenting on al-Arian's level of compliance with PIJ terrorism, Moody continued, "You lifted not one finger. To the contrary, you laughed when you heard of the bombings."[155] Further, Moody knocked down the defense's position that al-Arian was merely working on behalf of pro-Palestinian charities, telling al-Arian: "Your only connection to widows and orphans was that you create them," and he blasted al-Arian's repeated abuses of American hospitality, stating, "Your children attend the finest universities in this country, while you raise money to blow up the children of others."[156]

The plea agreement and the admissions contained therein represent a victory for the government of the United States after the far from perfect result of the jury trial. The Department of Justice, legal analysts, and counterterrorism officials will continue to debate what factors led to the ultimate result of the trial, but at least one commentator blamed a faulty jury instruction which emphasized that mere membership in PIJ, despite its designation as a foreign terrorist organization, was not enough to prove guilt.[157] Ronald Radosh, in the *Weekly Standard*, cites reaction from the Justice Department:

> A source high up in the Department of Justice who is close to the prosecution summed up the outcome this way: "Justice might have been better served by admitting up front that they were not trying to prove he ordered and funded a specific terrorist attack or suicide bombing; only that he engaged in raising money for an illegal terrorist group and arranged for its receipt by them, for which he was ably thanked. By spending much time showing the jury the horror of PIJ attacks upon civilians, the jury was reinforced in its thinking that the government had to prove Al-Arian's support of these specific acts."[158]

THE CASE OF ARWAH JABER

In June 2005, Arwah Jaber, a PhD in chemistry at the University of Arkansas, was arrested by federal agents while attempting to board a plane at the Northwest Arkansas Regional Airport. Jaber had been told by his professors that he would be unable to graduate in May 2005, and, as an alternative, he decided to join PIJ and engage in a holy war against Israel. Jaber, a naturalized US citizen born in the West Bank town of Yamoun, allegedly said to federal authorities that he told his doctoral professor and others at the university he was going to Palestine to "fight for freedom, peace and justice."

The criminal complaint against Jaber details specific e-mails to his professors in which he stated that, due to the fact that he was not going to be able to graduate as planned, he "decided to take an honorable job in Palestine with the Palestinian Islamic Jihad Organization to pursue a more noble cause—freedom, justice and peace for the Palestinians and to fight the Israeli terrorism."[159] He also wrote that "[t]his action will make it impossible for me to come back to the states for dissertation defense—assuming I am still alive. However, I shall do my best finish [*sic*] my degree before I leave."

In August 2005, Jaber was indicted by a federal grand jury on charges of attempting to provide material support to a foreign terrorist organization, failure to disclose an alias on applications for both naturalization and for a passport, as well as using a fake Social Security number on credit card applications.[160]

On June 19, 2006, Jaber was acquitted on the terrorism charge, but was found guilty of two counts of using a false Social Security number on a credit card application, making a false statement on his naturalization application, and making a false statement on his passport application.[161] Jaber admitted during testimony that he made up a Social Security number but said that he did not believe he was doing anything wrong.[162]

The judge in the case has said that no decisions on the revocation of Jaber's citizenship will be made until after he has had the opportunity to appeal his convictions.[163] In addition to the revocation of his citizenship and potential deportation, Jaber is facing a maximum of ten years in prison for each of his guilty charges.[164]

CONCLUSION

PIJ's commitment to violence continues to this day. As outlined in this chapter, there are significant reasons why Americans should be particularly aware of this group. On November 4, 2001, less than two months following September 11, another attack against civilians occurred in Israel resulting in forty-six injuries as well as the death of two civilians aboard a bus, one of whom was an American teenager.[165] The Palestinian Islamic Jihad claimed responsibility with characteristic glee.

More recently, on February 25, 2005, a suicide bomber approached the crowded Tel Aviv Stage Club and detonated the explosive strapped to his body, killing five Israelis and wounding more than fifty others. The Palestinian Islamic Jihad claimed responsibility for this action not long after the attack.

In the wake of the most recent attempt to rekindle the peace process, the Palestinian Islamic Jihad was the first terrorist organization to carry out an attack to undermine Israeli and Palestinian initiatives. Ramadan Abdullah Shallah has been identified as being directly responsible for ordering the attacks via telephone.[166] According to a March 2005 ABC News interview, Secretary of State Condoleezza Rice has stated, "There is firm evidence that Palestinian Islamic Jihad sitting in Damascus not only knew about these attacks, but was involved in the planning."[167]

PIJ also claimed responsibility for a July 12, 2005, suicide bomb attack on a shopping mall in Netanya, killing five Israelis and wounding ninety more. A PIJ suicide bomber attacked the same mall in December 5, 2005, killing five more Israelis and injuring more than fifty people.

PIJ violence and ongoing terrorist activities such as these most recent events that occurred post-9/11 were only possible by the continued funding and support streaming from PIJ's US-based infrastructure. The devastation caused by the hijackings did not deter al-Arian and his codefendants from continuing to back terrorism in the Middle East. Although al-Arian was partially acquitted, his trial did formally illustrate his ties to PIJ, and his firing, arrest, and trial effectively removed the terror-linked professor from his tenured position at an American college campus. Despite the outcome of the case, it will be very difficult for al-Arian or any other operative connected to PIJ to reconstitute US-based operations. Unfortunately, due to the potential public perception that al-Arian was completely innocent and only prosecuted for his "unpopular" beliefs, the possibility remains that future PIJ associates can set up front groups in the United States under cover of an "academic" or "charitable" guise. Al-Arian's future activities are likely to be watched closely by both sides in the war on terror.

NOTES

1. Translation of Islamic Committee for Palestine Conference booklet, "Islam: The Road to Victory," Third Annual ICP Conference, Chicago, IL, December 28–31, 1990.

2. Ghassan Ballut, "Islam, Palestine, and the West," Transcript of Fourth Annual ICP Conference, Chicago, IL, December 27–31, 1991.

3. "62 Federal Register 52650; Designation of Foreign Terrorist Organizations, Part IV," Department of State, October 8, 1997.

4. *USA v. Al Arian, et al.*, 03-CR-77, superceding indictment, p. 1 (MD FL September 21, 2004).

5. Affidavit in Support of Application for Search Warrant, "In the Matter of Searches Involving 555 Grove Street, Herndon, Virginia, and Related Locations," (ED VA), October 2003.

6. "Palestinian Islamic Jihad," Government of Australia, National Security, May 3, 2004 http://www.nationalsecurity.gov.au/agd/WWW/nationalsecurityHome.nsf/Page/Listing_of_Terrorist_Organisations_terrorist_listing_Palestinian_Islamic_Jihad_-_Listed_3_May_2004 (accessed August 12, 2005).

7. Jack Katzenell, "Suicide Attack Kills 17 Passengers in Bus Blast in Israel," Associated Press, June 5, 2002.

8. "Tenet Warns Arafat," *Jerusalem Post*, June 6, 2002.

9. *USA v. Al Arian, et al.*, 03-CR-77, superseding indictment, p. 8 (MD FL September 21, 2004).

10. Ziad Abu Amr, *Islamic Fundamentalism in the West Bank and Gaza Strip – Muslim Brotherhood and Islamic Jihad* (Bloomington: Indiana University Press, 1994), p. 1.

11. Matthew Gutman, "Brothers in Arms," *Jerusalem Post*, November 4, 2004.

12. Harvey W. Kushner, *The Future of Terrorism: Violence in the New Millennium* (Thousand Oaks, CA: Sage Publications, 1998), p. 8.

13. Yehudit Barsky, *Islamic Jihad Movement in Palestine* (American Jewish Committee, 2002), p. 9.

14. Ibid.

15. "Harakat al-Jihad al-Islami al-Filastini," International Policy Institute for Counter-Terrorism (ICT), http://web.archive.org/web/20040603082723/www.ict.org.il/organizations/org_frame.cfm?orgid=14 (accessed July 24, 2006).

16. Ibid.

17. Abu Amr, *Islamic Fundamentalism in the West Bank and Gaza Strip*, p. 96.

18. Ibid., p. 95.

19. Ibid.

20. Aviva Shabi and Ronni Shaked, *Hamas: M'Emunah B'Allah L'Derech Ha-Terror (Hamas: From Belief in Allah to Terror)* (Jerusalem: Keter Publishing House, 1994), p. 207.

21. Barsky, *Islamic Jihad Movement in Palestine*, p. 13.

22. Roni Shaked, "The Orders to Murder Arrive by Fax from Damascus," *Yediot Aharanot*, November 18, 1994.

23. Abu Amr, *Islamic Fundamentalism in the West Bank and Gaza Strip*, p. 96.

24. Ibid., pp. 94–95.

25. *Oxford Dictionary of Islam*, ed. John Esposito (New York: Oxford University Press, 2003), p. 147. Professor Esposito confirms Bashir Musa as a PIJ founder. Musa is an alias used by Nafi. Nafi's role in founding PIJ is also confirmed by Professors Mayer Hatina (Tel Aviv University) and Reuven Paz (Haifa University).

26. "Articles of Incorporation of the Islamic Concern Project, Inc.," Florida Secretary of State, October 14, 1988; "Articles of Incorporation of World and Islam Studies Enterprise, Inc. (WISE)," Florida Secretary of State, January 1, 1991.

27. Thomas Mayer, "Pro-Iranian Fundamentalism in Gaza," in *Religious Radicalism and Politics in the Middle East*, ed. Emmanuel Sivan and Menachem Friedman (Albany: State University of New York Press, 1990), p. 148.

28. "Members of the Palestinian Islamic Jihad Arrested, Charged with Racketeering and Conspiracy to Provide Support to Terrorists," US Department of Justice press release, February 20, 2003.

29. "Special Bulletin Information: Palestinian Islamic Jihad," Intelligence and Terrorism Information Center at the Center for Special Studies (C.S.S), October 2003.

30. Résumé of Ramadan Abdullah Shallah; Cathy Cummins, "USF Was Proliferation of Part-Time Professors," *Tampa Tribune*, November 29, 1996.

31. Mayer, "Pro-Iranian Fundamentalism in Gaza," p. 148; Shabi and Shaked, *Hamas*, p. 207. Fathi Shiqaqi met Bashir Nafi in Egypt and developed a relationship with him in Gaza. Shiqaqi found Nafi to be an "ideological friend." Nafi, while in Egypt, had "given refuge to a suspect in Sadat's assassination."

32. Ramadan Shallah lists on his résumé that he was on the editorial board of the publication *Al Alam* out of London from 1987 to 1989, and Bashir Nafi's résumé shows that he was on the same board from 1985 to 1987. Also note that Nafi took a position as a teaching assistant in London in 1983.

33. Mayer, "Pro-Iranian Fundamentalism in Gaza," p. 148.

34. Shabi and Shaked, *Hamas*, pp. 210–11.

35. "New Jihad Head Was Active in Britain, US," *Jerusalem Post*, October 31, 1995.

36. *USA v. Al Arian, et al.*, 03-CR-77, plea agreement, p. 10 (MD FL April 14, 2006).

37. "Special Bulletin Information: Palestinian Islamic Jihad," Intelligence and Terrorism Information Center at the Center for Special Studies.

38. "Executive Order 12947: Prohibiting Transactions with Terrorists," *Federal Register* 60, no. 16 (January 25, 1995).

39. "Specially Designated Nationals and Blocked Persons," Department of Treasury, Office of Foreign Assets Control, January 10, 1995, p. 13.

40. Résumé of Sami al-Arian; Steve Cavendish et al., "Building a Case: Ties to Terror," *St. Petersburg Times*, February 21, 2003.

41. Ibid.

42. Florida Secretary of State, "Articles of Incorporation of the Islamic Concern Project, Inc."

43. Ibid.

44. *USA v. Al Arian, et al.*, 03-CR-77, indictment, pp. 11–12 (MD FL February 19, 2004).

45. *USA v. Al Arian, et al.*, 03-CR-77, superseding indictment, p. 13 (MD FL September 21, 2004).

46. Articles of Incorporation, Islamic Concern Project, Inc., October 20, 1988; IRS Form, Certification of Lack of Records, Islamic Committee for Palestine, *USA v. Al Arian, et al.*, 03-CR-77, exhibit 37A (MD FL)

47. "Palestine, Intifada and the Horizons of the Islamic Renaissance," Second Annual ICP Conference, Chicago, IL, December 22–25, 1989, listed as "Dr. Fathi Abdulaziz"; see also *USA v. Al Arian, et al.*, 03-CR-77, superseding indictment, p. 3 (MD FL September 21, 2004), listed as "Fathi Shiqaqi a/k/a Fathi Adbul Azeez."

48. Allan Thompson, "Canada Bars Exiled Tunisian Activist Islamist Leader Accused of Links to Terrorism," *Toronto Star*, May 21, 1998, p. A7.

49. *USA v. Rahman et al.*, 93-CR-181, judgment (SD NY February 23, 1996).

50. Sudan has been designated by the Department of State to be a state sponsor of terrorism.

51. Report by William Reece Smith Jr. commissioned by former USF president Betty Castor, regarding USF's affiliation with WISE, March 27, 1996.

52. Michael Fechter, "USF Brass Discuss Think Tank; Jewish Leaders Voice Concern over School's Ties to Islamic Group," *Tampa Tribune*, June 8, 1995.

53. Translation of Islamic Committee for Palestine Conference Booklet, "Islam: The Road to Victory," Third Annual ICP Conference.

54. Sami al-Arian (speech), "Islam, Palestine, and the West," Fourth Annual ICP Conference, Chicago, IL, December 27–31, 1991.

55. "The Enemy Within; University of South Florida Professor Sami Al Arian Claims Despite Evidence, to Not Be Terrorist Fund-Raiser," *Dateline NBC*, October 28, 2001.

56. *USA v. Al Arian, et al.*, 03-CR-77, superseding indictment, pp. 21–22 (MD FL September 21, 2004).

57. ICP, PO Box 82009, Tampa, FL 33682-2009 (*Islam and Palestine*, December 1990).

58. *USA v. Al Arian, et al.*, 03-CR-77, exhibit 42H (MD FL), *Islam and Palestine*, May 1989, with reference to murders by Nidal Zalloum in Jerusalem on May 3, 1989; *USA v. Al Arian, et al.*, 03-CR-77, exhibit 42I (MD FL), *Islam and Palestine*, August 1989, with reference to attack on Bus 405 in July 1989.

59. *Islam and Palestine*, December 1990.

60. *Inquiry* 2, no. 8, June/July 1993.

61. "Islamic Fund for Palestine," *Islam and Palestine*, August 1989.

62. *Inquiry* 1, no. 2, March/April 1992.

63. Izeldin Ibrahim, "The Qur'anic Dimension of Palestine," *Inquiry*, January 1993, pp. 46–48.

64. *USA v. Al Arian, et al.*, 03-CR-77, exhibit 437 (MD FL), ICP Informational Guide.

65. *USA v. Al Arian, et al.*, 03-CR-77, exhibit 301 (MD FL), WISE articles of incorporation filed February 21, 1991. See also *USA v. Al Arian, et al.*, 03-CR-77, exhibit 430 (MD FL); ICP articles of incorporation with letter from Florida Department of State stating they were filed on October 10, 1988.

66. "Articles of Incorporation of World and Islam Studies Enterprise, Inc. (WISE)," Florida Secretary of State, January 1, 1991.

67. Ibid.

68. Ramadan Abdullah Shallah Curriculum Vitae; *USA v. Al Arian, et al.*, 03-CR-77, exhibit 309 (MD FL April 14, 2006).

69. "World and Islam Studies Enterprise (WISE) and University of South Florida (USF) Cooperative Activities," March 11, 1992.

70. Ibid.

71. *USA v. Al Arian, et al.*, 03-CR-77, plea agreement, p. 10 (MD FL April 14, 2006).

72. Sami al-Arian, interview, *Chronicle for Higher Education*, http://www.freesamialarian.com/speaks/speaks8.htm (accessed August 12, 2005). Sami al-Arian gave this response when during a Q&A session organized by the *Chronicle for Higher Education* he was asked, "Was the 'think tank' that you organized at USF in fact a vehicle for the dissemination of terrorist propaganda and activity?"

73. Barsky, *Islamic Jihad Movement in Palestine*, p. 24.

74. *USA v. Al Arian, et al.*, 03-CR-77, exhibit 437 (MD FL), ICP Informational Guide.

75. Jamiya Elehssan Al Khairiya, also known in English as the Elehssan Society, the Elehssan Charitable Society, or the Ihsan Charity.

76. Web archive of the Elehssan Society, http://web.archive.org/web/20030810052412/www.elehssan.com/eng/english.html (accessed August 12, 2005).

77. *USA v. Al Arian, et al.*, 03-CR-77, superceding indictment, Count 1, A, ¶20 (MD FL September 21, 2004).

78. "In the Matter of Mazen Al Najjar in Bond Redetermination Proceedings, Declaration of Ziad Abu Amr," Department of Justice, Executive Office of Immigration Review, Office of the Immigration Judge, October 30, 2000, p. 1.

79. United States Department of the Treasury, "Recent OFAC Actions," May 4, 2005.

80. By adding the word "Birr" to the title, the organization's name changes from the Elehssan Society to the Elesshan Charitable Society. See note 75.

81. *USA v. Al Arian, et al.*, 03-CR-77, superceding indictment, Count 1, E, ¶319A (MD FL September 21, 2004).

82. *USA v. Al Arian, et al.*, 03-CR-77, judgment (MD FL July 25, 2004).

83. Michael Fechter, "Part 1: Ties to Terrorists," *Tampa Tribune*, May 28, 1995.

84. "Affidavit of INS Supervisory Special Agent William West," In re: Search of ICP/WISE Offices, et al., November 17, 1995, pp. 12–13.

85. Bill West, "Tampa PIJ Defendant Sentenced in Separate Fraud Case," Counterterrorism Blog, June 6, 2005, http://counterterrorismblog.org/2005/06/tampa_pij_defendant_sentenced.php (accessed July 11, 2006).

86. Bill West, "Sami into the Sunset," Counterterrorism Blog, http://counterterrorismblog.org/2006/05/Sami_into_the_Sunset.pht (accessed July 28, 2006).

87. *USA v. Al Arian, et al.*, 03-CR-77, exhibit 17-A (MD FL) INS Form N-400, Application for Naturalization for Sami Al-Arian, December 30, 1993.

88. Affidavit of FBI Special Agent M. Barry Carmody, MD FL, December 19, 1997.

89. "In re Mazen Abdel Abdulkarin Al Najjar," in Deportation Proceedings, File No: A26-599-077 (United States Immigation Court, Miami Florida, Sitting in Orlando Florida), May 13, 1997.

90. Mazen A. al-Najjar curriculum vitae; Meghan Clyne, "Concern Mounts over Brandeis Professor's Ties to Islamic Jihad," *New York Sun*, January 17, 2003.

91. "Title Page," *Qira'at Siyasiyyah* 1, no. 1, Winter 1991.

92. "Department of Justice Statement Regarding the Arrest of Mazen Al Najjar," US Department of Justice press release, November 24, 2001; Michael Fetcher, "Al-Najjar to Be Deported to Middle East," *Tampa Tribune*, August 20, 2002.

93. E-mail correspondence with former Special Agent William West, January 18, 2005.

94. "Memorandum Decision of the Immigration Judge," In the Matter of Mazen A. Al Najjar, EOIR Bradenton, FL A26-599-077, June 23, 1997, p. 1.

95. *USA v. Al Arian, et al.*, 03-CR-77, indictment, p. 5 (MD FL February 20, 2003); *USA v. Al Arian, et al.*, 03-CR-77, superseding indictment, p. 5 (MD FL September 21, 2004).

96. *USA v. Al Arian, et al.*, 03-CR-77, superseding indictment, p. 21 (MD FL September 21, 2004).

97. Ibid., p. 4.

98. Sami al-Arian (speech), "Islam, Palestine, and the West," Fourth Annual ICP Conference, Chicago, IL, December 27–31, 1991; *USA v. Al Arian, et al.*, 03-CR-77, superseding indictment, pp. 21–22 (MD FL September 21, 2004); Fawaz Damra (speech), "Palestine, Intifadah, and the Horizons of the Islamic Renaissance," ICP Second Annual Conference, Chicago, IL, December 22–25, 1989.

99. "Terror Financing Case in Florida Puts the Patriot Act to the Test," Associated Press, January 19, 2004, http://www.cnn.com/2004/LAW/01/19/attacks.professor.ap/index.html, which states:

The law at the time didn't allow the agents to share what they knew with fellow FBI agents who later began investigating possible criminal charges against Al-Arian, accused of aiding terrorists.

That all changed in the spring of 2002 when the Patriot Act, the law enacted in the weeks following the September 11, 2001, attacks, gave the government greatly expanded surveillance and search powers. . . .

Former FBI Agent Joe Navarro, who had been assigned to the criminal side of the investigation, recalls the meeting when the scope of the other FBI probe became clear.

"It was 'Holy moley! There's a lot there!" he said.

"It was just one of those awesome moments when you realize how much there is," Navarro added. "When you realize there is literally a room full—not a box full or a filing cabinet full—of evidence. It sort of shocks you." . . .

Former government agents who spent years investigating Al-Arian tell of a frustrating investigation hindered in part by the inability of intelligence agents to share what they knew until the Patriot Act became law.

"Everything changed," said Barry Carmody, who was among the team of agents working the criminal case against Al-Arian. "We needed to be able to gamble with 52 cards, not half the deck," he said.

One agent who knew the full gamut of the government's evidence against Al-Arian and his brother-in-law, Mazen Al-Najjar, was William West, who worked at the time for the U.S. Immigration and Naturalization Service.

West was the lead agent in the effort to deport Al-Najjar, who was held for more than three years on the then-classified evidence linking both him and Al-Arian to the Palestinian Islamic Jihad.

Government agents and attorneys were sharply criticized for holding Al-Najjar, who was eventually deported months before Al-Arian and the others were indicted. Al-Najjar is named as an unindicted coconspirator in court documents.

"It was terribly frustrating because from the perspective of the classified information we could use, we knew all along we were on the right track and we were pursing the right people," West said.

100. *USA v. Al Arian, et al.*, 03-CR-77, superseding indictment, p. 75 (MD FL September 21, 2004).

101. "The Internal Manifest of the Palestinian Islamic Jihad," seized from WISE and ICP offices during the 1995 investigation.

102. *USA v. Al Arian, et al.*, 03-CR-77, superseding indictment, p. 13 (MD FL September 21, 2004).

103. "Palestinian Islamic Jihad Communiqué," December 11, 1992, seized from WISE and ICP offices during the 1995 investigation.

104. "Islam, Intifada and the Future," First Annual ICP Conference, St. Louis, MO, December 23–26, 1988.

105. *USA v. Al Arian, et al.*, 03-CR-77, superseding indictment, p. 16 (MD FL September 21, 2004).

106. Dr. Sami al-Arian, opening statement, "Palestine, Intifada and the Prospects of Islamic Resurgence," 1989 ICP Annual Conference, Chicago, IL, December 1989.

107. *United States v. Damrah*, 03-CR-484, 334 F. Supp. 2d 967 (ND OH September 13, 2004).

108. *United States v. Damrah*, 03-CR-484, memorandum opinion [resolving Doc. No. 164] (ND OH August 30, 2004).

109. Ibid.

110. *USA v. Damrah*, 03-CR-484, indictment (ND OH December 18, 2003).

111. "Additional Background Information on Charities Designated under Executive Order 13224," http://www.treas.gov/offices/enforcement/key-issues/protecting/charities_execorder_13224-i.shtml#m (accessed August 12, 2005).

112. *USA v. Damrah*, 03-CR-484, memorandum opinion, p. 1 (ND OH September 23, 2004).

113. Amanda Garret, "Indictment Tells of Terrorism Link to Cleveland," *Plain Dealer*, February 23, 2003.

114. *USA v. Elgabrowny, et al.*, 93-CR-181, list of 173 possible coconspirators submitted by Mary Jo White (SD NY February 2, 1995).

115. *USA v. Al Arian, et al.*, 03-CR-77, superseding indictment, pp. 17–18 (MD FL September 21, 2004).

116. Fawaz Damra (speech), "Palestine, Intifadah, and the Horizons of the Islamic Renaissance," Second Annual Conference, Chicago, IL, December 22–25, 1989.

117. ICP event commemorating the "Great Intifada" at Currie High School, Chicago, IL, September 29, 1991.

118. "A Round Table Discussion about Jihad and the Intifadah," Islamic Center of Cleveland, Ohio, April 7, 1991.

119. Ibid. Entered into evidence in *USA v. Al Arian, et al.*, 03-CR-77, as exhibit 565.

120. Sabrina Eaton, "Imam Here Is Linked to Terror Suspect," *Plain Dealer*, February 21, 2003.

121. *USA v. Damrah*, 03-CR-484, indictment, p. 2 (ND OH December 18, 2003).

122. Ibid.

123. Ibid.

124. Amanda Garrett and Robert Smith, "Imam Released after Two Months in Prison," *Plain Dealer*, January 21, 2005.

125. Ibid.

126. *USA v. Damrah*, 04-4216, appeal ruling (US 6th Cir. March 15, 2005).

127. Tom Krisher, "Ohio Imam Accused of Terror Ties to Leave U.S.," Associated Press, January 5, 2006.

128. Sami al-Arian, interview by Bill O'Reilly, *O'Reilly Factor*, FOX News, February 20, 2003.

129. Michele Sager and Michael Fecther, "USF Condemns, Fires Al-Arian," *Tampa Tribune*, February 27, 2003.

130. "USF Condemned by the American Association of University Professors," Tampa Bay Coalition for Justice and Peace, June 16, 2003, http://www.freesamialarian.com/pressreleases/press6.htm (accessed August 12, 2005).

131. US Department of Justice press release, "Members of the Palestinian Islamic Jihad Arrested, Charged with Racketeering and Conspiracy to Provide Support to Terrorists."

132. "Feds Bust Alleged Terror Ring," CBS, February 20, 2003, http://www.cbsnews.com/stories/2002/08/22/attack/main519520.shtml (accessed August 12, 2005).

133. In announcing the indictment and the arrests of four members of the North American faction of PIJ, Attorney General John Ashcroft declared: "We make no distinction between those who carry out terrorist attacks and those who knowingly finance, manage or supervise terrorist organizations." US Department of Justice press release, "Members of the Palestinian Islamic Jihad Arrested, Charged with Racketeering and Conspiracy to Provide Support to Terrorists."

134. "Military Translating Wiretap Not Violation, Judge Rules," Tampa Bay Online, December 19, 2004, http://news.tbo.com/news/MGBXKY7CV2E.html (accessed August 12, 2005).

135. *USA v. Al Arian et al.*, 03-CR-77, order denying motions to transfer venue (MD FL May 23, 2005).

136. "Treasury Designates Charity Funneling Money to Palestinian Islamic Jihad," United States Treasury Department press release, May 4, 2005.

137. *USA v. Al Arian, et al.*, 03-CR-77, exhibit 516 (MD FL), copy of letter to Ismail al-Shaati from Sami al-Arian, dated February 10, 1995, requesting funds for PIJ; Meg Laughlin, "Lawyers Present Al-Arian Letter," *St. Petersburg Times*, August 9, 2005.

138. "Executive Order 12947: Prohibiting Transactions with Terrorists."

139. Meg Laughlin, "5-month Prosecution, 8 Words for Defense," *St. Petersburg Times*, October 28, 2005.

140. Meg Laughlin, "Evidence Is Lacking, Al-Arian Defense Says," *St. Petersburg Times*, November 10, 2005.

141. Mitch Stacy, "Jury to Deliberate Ex-professor's Trial," Associated Press, November 14, 2005.

142. Phil Long and Martin Merzer, "Jury Clears Former Florida Professor of Terrorism-Related Charge," *Miami Herald*, December 6, 2005.

143. *USA v. Al Arian, et al.*, 03-CR-77, Al Arian verdict form (MD FL December 6, 2005).

144. *USA v. Al Arian, et al.*, 03-CR-77, Hammoudeh verdict form (MD FL December 6, 2005); *USA v. Al Arian, et al.*, 03-CR-77, Ballut verdict form (MD FL

December 6, 2005); *USA v. Al Arian, et al.*, 03-CR-77, Fariz verdict form (MD FL December 6, 2005).

145. "The Al-Arian Verdict," *St. Petersburg Times*, December 7, 2005.

146. Jennifer Liberto, "Al-Arian Unlikely to Be Set Free," *St. Petersburg Times*, January 2, 2006.

147. Associated Press, "Al-Arian Juror Says Deliberations in Terrorism Case 'Very Difficult,'" December 27, 2005.

148. Michael Fecther, "'I Can Sleep at Night,' Juror Says," *Tampa Tribune*, December 25, 2005.

149. Ibid.

150. *USA v. Al Arian, et al.*, 03-CR-77, plea agreement, p. 1563 (MD FL April 14, 2006).

151. Ibid., p. 11.

152. Ibid.

153. *USA v. Al Arian, et al.*, 03-CR-77, judgment in a criminal case (MD FL May 1, 2006).

154. *USA v. Al Arian, et al.*, 03-CR-77, transcript of sentencing for dates of 05/01/06 held before Judge James Moody (MD FL May 1, 2006).

155. Ibid.

156. Ibid.

157. Ronald Radosh, "Professor of Terror; Why Sami al-Arian Got Off This Time," *Weekly Standard*, January 2, 2006.

158. Ibid.

159. *USA v. Jaber*, 05-M-5022, criminal complaint (WD Ark June 16, 2005).

160. *USA v. Jaber*, 05-CR-50030, indictment, pp. 1–2 (WD AR August 11, 2005).

161. *USA v. Jaber*, 05-CR-50030, verdict form (WD AR June 19, 2006).

162. Sharon C. Fitzgerald, "Fayetteville: Jaber: Fraud, Terrorist or Both?" *Arkansas Democrat-Gazette*, June 18, 2006, http://www.nwanews.com/adg/News/157985/ (accessed July 10, 2006).

163. Associated Press, "Jihad Member to Appeal US Conviction," *Jerusalem Post*, July 1, 2006, http://www.jpost.com/servlet/Satellite?cid=1150885894416&pagename=JPost%2FJPArticle%2FShowFull (accessed July 10, 2006).

164. Associated Press, "Man Acquitted on Terror Charge in Ark.," June 20, 2006, http://www.guardian.co.uk/uslatest/story/0,,-5899762,00.html (accessed July 10, 2006).

165. *USA v. Al Arian, et al.*, 03-CR-77, superseding indictment, p. 88 (MD FL September 21, 2004).

166. "Head of Islamic Jihad Taught Middle East Studies at US University," Arutz Sheva, http://www.israeln.com/news.php3?id=77982 (accessed August 11, 2006).

167. Jonathan Karl and Luis Martinez, "Rice: Syria-Based Terror Group Planned Tel Aviv Attack," ABC News, March 1, 2005.

ARMY OF THE REPUBLIC OF BOSNIA AND HERCEGOVINA
MILITARY UNIT 5080-ZEPCE
Number: 12-592/94
Date: 03 June 1994

LETTER OF GRATITUDE TO

INTERNATIONAL MUSLIM HUMANITARIAN ORGANIZATION

"BIF"

-This humanitarian organization assisted this military unit 5080-Zepce, especially 1/5080-Zepce with food, clothing and footwear.
-The above mentioned humanitarian organization during the period from the end of 1992 to June, 1994 assisted this military unit with the following:

1. Plastic/nylon	2500 square meters
2. Uniforms	2000 pieces
3. Boots	2000 pairs
4. Mass communication resources	10 stations

-With this opportunity, we wish to thank this Muslim humanitarian organization on their noted assistance and collaboration with this military unit and especially with 1/5080-Zepce.
-We hope that the development of this mutual collaboration will continue between 1/5080 and the above mentioned humanitarian Muslim organization and we especially thank them on their past assistance to the families of our fighters like they assisted the families of our clerics and disabled.
-May ALLAH reward all employees of this humanitarian Muslim organization who invest their hard work for the freedom of Bosnia and Hercegovina.
-On behalf of military unit 1/5080 and myself, I send my warmest regards to the above mentioned organization and may ALLAH reward them.
VICTORY IS NEAR FOR THOSE WHO FOLLOW ALLAH'S PATH!

Deputy Commander
(BiH Army seal and signature)

BIF-1B081-02-03716

English translation of a letter from a Bosnian military unit thanking the Benevolence International Foundation (BIF) for contributing military supplies. Exhibit from *USA v. Arnaout*, 02-CR-892 (ND IL).

ARMIJA REPUBLIKE BOSNE I HERCEGOVINE
VOJNA JEDINICA 5080- ŽEPČE
Broj: 12-592/93
Dana, 03. 06. 1994. godine

ZAHVALNICA

MEĐUNARODNOJ MUSLIMANSKOJ HUMANITARNOJ ORGANIZACIJI
"B I F"

- Ova humanitarna organizacija pomogla je ovoj Vojnoj jedinici 5080- Žepče a posebno 1/5080-Žepče u hrani odjeći i obući.
- Navedena humanitarna organizacija je u proteklom periodu od kraja 1992. godine do juna 1994. godine pomogla ovoj Vojnoj jedinici u sledećem:

1. Plastika /najlon/	2500 m^2
2. Uniformi	2000 komada
3. Čizama	2000 komada
4. U sredstvima veze	10 stanica

- Ovom prilikom želimo da se zahvalimo ovoj Muslimanskoj humanitarnoj organizaciji na ukazanoj pomoći i saradnji sa ovom Vojnom jedinicom a posebno sa 1/5080-Žepče.
- Nadamo da će se i dalje razvijati obostrana saradnja između 1/5080 i navedene humanitarne Muslimanske organizacije a posebno im se zahvaljujemo na dosadašnjoj pomoći porodicama naših boraca kao i porodicama šehida i invalida.
- Nek ALLAH nagradi sve radnike ove humanitarne Muslimanske organizacije što ulažu trud za slobodnu Bosnu i Hercegovinu.
U ime Vojne jedinice 1/5080 i usvoje lično ime najtopije se zahvaljujem navedenoj organizaciji i neka ih ALLAH nagradi DŽENETOM.
POBJEDA JE BLIZU ZA ONE KOJI SU NA ALLAHOVOM PUTU!

Zamjenik Komandanta

BIF-1B081-02-03716

Letter from a Bosnian military unit thanking the Benevolence International Foundation (BIF) for contributing military supplies. Exhibit from *USA v. Arnaout*, 02-CR-892 (ND IL).

In the name of Allah, the Compassionate, the Merciful

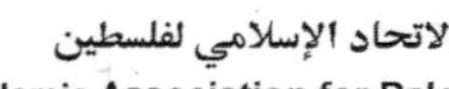

الاتحاد الإسلامي لفلسطين

Islamic Association for Palestine

10661 S. Roberts Rd., Palos Hills, IL. 60465 Tel. (708) 974-3380 Fax (708) 974-3389
E mail: iapinfo@iap.org Website: www.iap.org Fax on Demand: (708) 974-3380

October 25, 2000

Dear Brother Ismail Royer, CAIR Communications Specialist:
Assalamu Alaikum,

I hope that this message reaches you in the best of health. t is indeed our pleasure at the Islamic Association for Palestine (IAP) to invite you to attend and participate in our annual convention that will be held on the 23rd through the 26th of November of this year in the city of Chicago, IL., under the title of "*All Palestine is Sacred*".

Along with its other programs and activities throughout the year, the IAP's goal for this convention is to encourage a comprehensive and balanced role for the American Muslim and Arab communities in serving their local and international concerns. Promoting the Palestinian issue as a central one for the Ummah and empowering our communities and increasing their influence in making the policies that affects their future in America and the future of the Muslims and Arabs around the Globe. The convention will be arranged around main and parallel sessions, seminars, workshops and special youth programs. Distinguished Muslim, Arab and American leaders and scholars from North America and abroad will address the convention in both Arabic and English languages.

The convention's program committee has requested that you participate in one of the main sessions that deals with **Internet Activism** which will be held on Saturday, November 25th 2000. You will have a little over an hour for your presentation, then the floor will be open for questions and comments. Please, supply us with your written speech, so we publicize it in our publications. It is preferable to send it to us before the convention through the fax, regular or electronic mail, or on a computer floppy desk. We heard about your presentation at the CAIR Leadership Conference, and we feel that this would be an appropriate topic.

We are very honored to have you among our guest speakers in this important gathering for our Muslim and Arab community. Thousands of attendees will be looking forward to meeting you and benefiting from your knowledge and experience. Please call us to confirm your presence at the convention. Until we see you at the convention, we leave you with our best greetings. Assalamu Alykum.

Your brother
Rafeeq Jaber

President of the IAP

IAP 02642

* The IAP is the largest national grassroots organization serving the American Muslim, Arab and Palestinian communities and dedicated to advancing a just and comprehensive solution to the cause of Palestine.

Islamic Association for Palestine letter to CAIR Communications Specialist Ismail Royer. Source: *Boim v. QLI, et al.*, 00-C-2905 (ND IL).

In the name of Allah, the Compassionate, the Merciful

الإتحاد الإسلامي لفلسطين

Islamic Association for Palestine
10661 S. Roberts Rd. #202, Palos Hills, IL. 60465. Tel. (708) 974-3380 Fax (708) 974-3389
E mail: iapinfo@iap.org Website: www.iap.org

5/6/1997

"قل بفضل الله وبرحمته فبذلك فليفرحوا ، هو خير مما يجمعون"

After His Release From Prison, the IAP Thanks All Those Who Supported the Case of Dr. Musa Abu Marzouk

On May 5th . Dr. Musa Abu Marzouk, the Chairman of Hamas, Political Office, Was released and deported to Jordan after serving 21 months in New York prison. The deportation took place as the result of an agreement by which Dr. Abu Marzouk gave up his permanent residency status in the United State in exchange for American guarantees that it would not place any pressure upon any country which permitted him the right to reside or work within its borders. The completion of Abu Marzouk issue marks the completion of a very bitter experience for the American Muslim community and the Islamic Association for Palestine (IAP) uses this occasion to stress a number of points:

- **When Israel requested the extradition of Dr. Abu Marzouk to try him as a terrorist it knew that he was innocent of such charges but it wanted to exploit the issue as a means of its comprehensive war against all those who work for -with charitable, social and political ways- the Palestinian and other Islamic causes. To curb Hamas's political activities, Israel targeted it's political leader.**
- **The Zionist lobby in America used the issue to launch a media campaign against the American Muslim community in an attempt to tie the community to terrorism in the minds of the American public and scare the Muslim community away from working for Islamic causes especially Palestine.**
- **The American Muslim community, by the praise of Allah, took a courageous position in the face of great pressures and came to the realization that it must stand up for its rights. Rather than back away from supporting Islamic causes, our community increased its support for organization working for the Palestinian cause, especially the Islamic Association for Palestine whose 1996 convention was a big success.**
- **The empty results of the anti-Muslim media campaign confirmed that American Muslim organizations working for Palestinian causes are legitimate American organizations working within the laws of this country and that they have no ties to terrorism.**
- **The official American position toward the Dr. Abu Marzouk case was unjust and proved that even the American justice system can come under the influence of Israel and its American lobby. When Israel withdrew its extradition request it laid bare the reality that the case was political rather than legal and that Dr. Abu Marzouk's most basic legal rights had been violated. The case Should prove to be a lesson to the American government not to again fall prey to Israeli schemes, and to the American people of the danger the enormous strength of the Israeli lobby presents to some of the most cherished American values and liberties.**
- **The American administration must not rest secure with Israeli admonition that it seeks peace, but must go beyond that and pressure Israel to stop violating international laws as well as the most basic civil and humanitarian rights of the Palestinian people.**

The IAP sends its heartfelt thanks to the entire American Muslim and Arab community for the courageous stand it took in defense of Dr. Abu Marzouk and a special thanks to the "Committee for the Defense of Dr. Abu Marzouk" and its chairman Dr. Abd al-Rahman al-Amoudi. We also call upon those other organizations which did 'lot take such a stand to reevaluate their positions. We call upon everyone to do tile following:

Increase all forms of support to the central Muslim issue of Palestine by way of supporting the leadership of this work in America represented by the Islamic Association for Palestine, with the aim of arriving at a just American position toward the issue and achieving a complete and just solution to the cause of Palestine.

- **Work to strengthen the Arab and Islamic community in America politically and in terms of their representation in the media, and to resist all form of discrimination the community is subjected to.**

Note: Distribute this action alert at your center and address it in your Friday Khutba and other gatherings. Sponsor an action alert with you donation. Each action alert costs around $500, so be generous.

* The IAP is the largest national grassroots organization serving the American Muslim, Arab and Palestinian communities and dedicated to advancing a just and comprehensive solution to the cause of Palestine.

IAP 00041

Islamic Association for Palestine communiqué offering thanks for supporting top Hamas official, Musa Abu Marzook. Source: *Boim* case.

In the name of Allah, the Compassionate, the Merciful

الإتحاد الإسلامي لفلسطين

Islamic Association for Palestine

10661 S. Roberts Rd., Palos Hills, IL. 60465 Tel. (708) 974-3380 Fax (708) 974-3389
E mail: iapinfo@iap.org Website: www.iap.org Fax on Demand: (708) 974-3380

11/3/1999

Dear Dr. Sami Al-Arian,
Assalamu Alaikum,

Following on the earlier communications that took place between us, it is indeed our pleasure at the Islamic Association for Palestine (IAP) to confirm your invitation to attend our annual convention that will be held on the 25th through the 28th of November of this year in the city of Chicago, IL., under the title of "*Century of Empowerment*".

Along with its other programs and activities throughout the year, the IAP's goal for this convention is to encourage a comprehensive and balanced role for the American Muslim and Arab communities to serve their local and international concerns. Promoting the Palestinian issue as a central one for the Ummah, and empowering our communities to increase their influence are only some of the outcomes we hope to achieve. The convention will be arranged around main and parallel sessions, seminars, workshops and special youth programs. A distinguished array of Muslim, Arab and American leaders, as well as scholars from North America and abroad will address the convention in both the Arabic and English languages. The main topics we hope to address at this year's convention include:

- The history of Palestine up to the present day including the history and effects of peace policies and Israeli actions
- The common factors of the Arab and Muslim world: foreign occupation and intervention and the requirements for change towards a universal role in serving humanity
- Muslim and Arab communities in America: challenges and opportunities; developing influence in policy making; mobilizing human and financial resources for reform

Dear Dr. Al-Arian, the convention's programming committee has arranged that you participate in the session entitled "Anti-Terrorist Laws and Their Application". Underlying themes of this broad topic include:

1. A discussion of the definition and impacts of such laws.
2. A deeper understanding of how they can be applied, against whom and under what circumstances.

We would like this session to address cases in which these laws have been used and solutions to cope with them. This lecture will be a joint session given by yourself and Congressman David Bonior, in which both of you will be given the opportunity to share your research and knowledge on this subject. If it is possible for you to supply us with your written speech in advance, we could include it in our publications. We would also like to request from you a brief biography of yourself to be given by the moderator as well as a photo, if possible.

Dear brother, it is our pleasure to cover your registration fees, hotel room, and food cost.

Please fill out the attached registration form and send it to us no later than November 15th, 1999. Your reply is important, as it is necessary we receive your registration form for processing .

Your brother
Rafeeq Jaber

President of the IAP

IAP 02634

* **The IAP is the largest national grassroots organization serving the American Muslim, Arab and Palestinian communities and dedicated to advancing a just and comprehensive solution to the cause of Palestine.**

Letter from Islamic Association for Palestine president Rafeeq Jaber inviting Palestinian Islamic Jihad operative Sami al-Arian to speak at an IAP convention. Source: *Boim* case.

In the name of Allah, the Compassionate, the Merciful

الإتحاد الإسلامي لفلسطين

IAP

Islamic Association for Palestine

10661 S. Roberts Rd., Palos Hills, IL. 60465 Tel. (708) 974-3380 Fax (708) 974-3389
E mail: iapinfo@iap.org Website: www.iap.org Fax on Demand: (708) 974-3380

11/18/1999

Dear Brother Omar Yahya,
Assalamu Alaikum,

Following on the earlier communications that took place between us, it is indeed our pleasure at the Islamic Association for Palestine (IAP) to confirm your invitation to attend our annual convention that will be held on the 25th through the 28th of November of this year in the city of Chicago, IL., under the title of "*Century of Empowerment*".

Along with its other programs and activities throughout the year, the IAP's goal for this convention is to encourage a comprehensive and balanced role for the American Muslim and Arab communities to serve their local and international concerns. Promoting the Palestinian issue as a central one for the Ummah, and empowering our communities to increase their influence are only some of the outcomes we hope to achieve. The convention will be arranged around main and parallel sessions, seminars, workshops and special youth programs. A distinguished array of Muslim, Arab and American leaders, as well as scholars from North America and abroad will address the convention in both the Arabic and English languages. The main topics we hope to address at this year's convention include:

- **The history of Palestine up to the present day including the history and effects of peace policies and Israeli actions**
- **The comm1on factors of the Arab and Muslim world: foreign occupation and intervention and the requirements for change towards a universal role in serving humanity**
- **Muslim and Arab communities in America: challenges and opportunities; developing influence in policy making; mobilizing human and financial resources for reform**

Dear Brother Omar Yahya, the convention's programming committee has arranged that you participate in the :

1. **Session entitled "CAIR Presentation", which will be held Thursday November 25th at 5:30 p.m. in English for the Youth program.**
2. **You will be the Moderator of the session entitled " Anti Terrorism Law " by Dr. Sami Aryan and Abdullah Mitchel. Which will be held Friday November 26th at 10:45 AM .**

We would like this session to address the roles Muslims should be taking and the potential impacts of this. This lecture will be a joint session given by yourself and Brother Shaker Assayed, in which both of you will be given the opportunity to share your research and knowledge on this subject. If it is possible for you to supply us with your written speech in advance, we could include it in our publications. We would also like to request from you a brief biography of yourself to be given by the moderator as well as a photo, if possible.

Dear brother, it is our pleasure to cover your registration fees, hotel room, and food cost.

Your brother/ Rafeeq Jaber

Convention Chairman

IAP 02638

* The IAP is the largest national grassroots organization serving the American Muslim, Arab and Palestinian communities and dedicated to advancing a just and comprehensive solution to the cause of Palestine.

Letter from Islamic Association for Palestine president Rafeeq Jaber inviting Council on Islamic-American Relations (CAIR) founder, and former IAP employee, Omar Yahya (aka Omar Ahmed) to an IAP convention. Source: *Boim* case.

The Secretary of State
of the United States of America
hereby requests all whom it may concern to permit the citizen/
national of the United States named herein to pass
without delay or hindrance and in case of need to
give all lawful aid and protection.

Le Secrétaire d'Etat
des Etats-Unis d'Amérique
prie par les présentes toutes autorités compétentes de laisser passer
le citoyen ou ressortissant des Etats-Unis titulaire du présent passeport,
sans délai ni difficulté et, en cas de besoin, de lui accorder
toute aide et protection légitimes.

Ali Mohamed

SIGNATURE OF BEARER/SIGNATURE DU TITULAIRE

NOT VALID UNTIL SIGNED

UNITED STATES OF AMERICA

PASSPORT
PASSEPORT

Type/Catégorie: P
Code of issuing State / code du pays émetteur: USA
PASSPORT NO./NO. DU PASSEPORT

Surname / Nom
MOHAMED

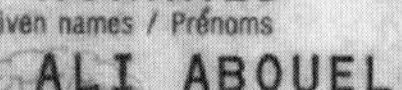

Given names / Prénoms
ALI ABOUELSEOUD

Nationality / Nationalité
UNITED STATES OF AMERICA

Date of birth / Date de naissance
03 JUN/JUN 52

Sex / Sexe
M

Place of birth / Lieu de naissance
EGYPT

Date of issue / Date de délivrance
20 DEC/DEC 89

Date of expiration / Date d'expiration
19 DEC/DEC 99

Authority / Autorité
PASSPORT AGENCY
WASHINGTON, D.C.

Amendments/
Modifications
SEE PAGE
24

P<USAMOHAMED<<ALI<ABOUELSEOUD<<<<<<<<<<<<<<<
<<<<<<<<<<<<<<<<6

Passport of embassy bomber Ali Mohamed, al Qaeda operative and former US Army sergeant who admitted involvement in the embassy bombings. Source: *USA v. Bin Laden, et al.*, 98-CR-1023 (SD NY).

Aftermath of the embassy bombing in Nairobi, Kenya. Source: *USA v. Bin Laden, et al.*

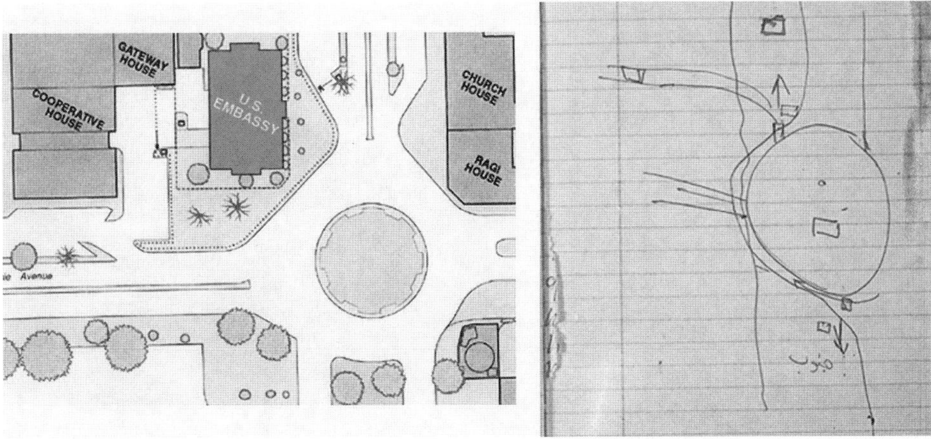

Map and drawing of the US embassy and surrounding area used by the al Qaeda bombers. Source: *USA v. Bin Laden, et al.*

The Secretary of State
of the United States of America
hereby requests all whom it may concern to permit the citizen/
national of the United States named herein to pass
without delay or hindrance and in case of need to
give all lawful aid and protection.

Le Secrétaire d'Etat
des Etats-Unis d'Amérique
prie par les présentes toutes autorités compétentes de laisser passer
le citoyen ou ressortissant des Etats-Unis titulaire du présent passeport,
sans délai ni difficulté et, en cas de besoin, de lui accorder
toute aide et protection légitimes.

Wadih El Hage

SIGNATURE OF BEARER/SIGNATURE DU TITULAIRE

1B1AUG97/EN2-3

UNITED STATES OF AMERICA

PASSPORT
PASSEPORT

Type/Catégorie: P
Code of Issuing State / code du pays émetteur: USA
PASSPORT NO./NO. DU PASSEPORT:

Surname / Nom
EL-HAGE
Given names / Prénoms
WADIH ELIAS
Nationality / Nationalité
UNITED STATES OF AMERICA
Date of birth / Date de naissance
25 JUL/JUI 60
Sex / Sexe: M
Place of birth / Lieu de naissance: LEBANON
Date of issue / Date de délivrance: 23 JAN/JAN 95
Date of expiration / Date d'expiration: 22 JAN/JAN 05
Authority / Autorité: U.S. EMBASSY ROME, ITALY
Amendments/ Modifications SEE PAGE 48

P<USAEL<HAGE<<WADIH<ELIAS<<<<<<<<<<<<<<<<<<<<
<<<<<<<<<<<<<<<<2

Passport of Wadi el-Hage, personal secretary to Osama bin Laden. Source: *USA v. Bin Laden, et al.*

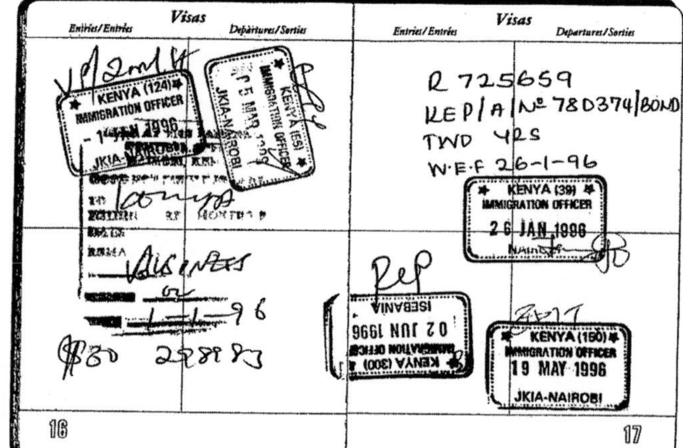

Passport stamps on Wadi el-Hage's passport showing travel into Kenya. Source: *USA v. Bin Laden, et al.*

1B1AUG97/EN2-10

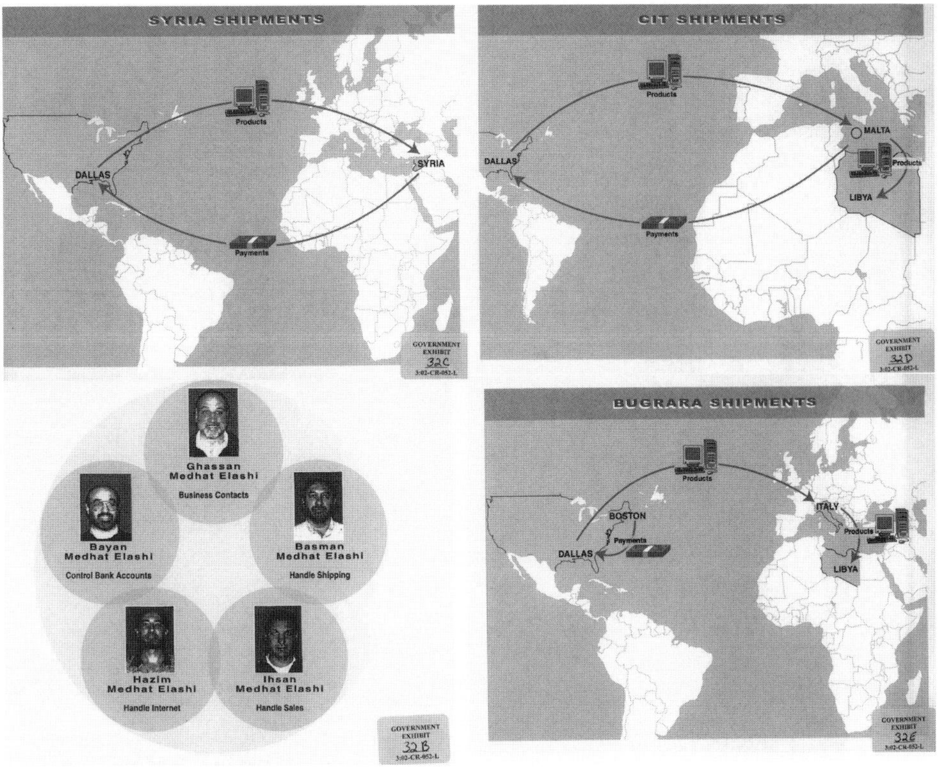

SYRIA SHIPMENTS

Products
DALLAS
SYRIA
Payments
GOVERNMENT EXHIBIT 32C 3:02-CR-052-L

CIT SHIPMENTS

Products
MALTA
DALLAS
Products
LIBYA
Payments
GOVERNMENT EXHIBIT 32D 3:02-CR-052-L

Ghassan Medhat Elashi
Business Contacts
Bayan Medhat Elashi
Control Bank Accounts
Basman Medhat Elashi
Handle Shipping
Hazim Medhat Elashi
Handle Internet
Ihsan Medhat Elashi
Handle Sales
GOVERNMENT EXHIBIT 32B 3:02-CR-052-L

BUGRARA SHIPMENTS

Products
ITALY
BOSTON
Payments
DALLAS
Products
LIBYA
GOVERNMENT EXHIBIT 32E 3:02-CR-052-L

Trial exhibits demonstrating illegal shipments and transactions and a depiction of the roles of the Elashi family in the scheme. Source: *USA v. Infocom*, 02-CR-52 (ND TX).

Khalid Shaikh Mohammed

Omar Abdel Rahman, the "Blind Sheikh," is currently serving a life sentence in Colorado.

Mohamed Atta, ringleader of the 9/11 hijackers.

Source of bottom three photos: *USA v. Moussaoui*, 01-CR-455 (ED VA).

Wallpaper from a Lashkar e Taiba Web site. Source: The Investigative Project on Terrorism.

Mahdi Bray, head of the Muslim American Society Freedom Foundation, raising his arms as Abdurahman Alamoudi, who is serving a twenty-three-year prison sentence, asks the crowd if they support Hamas. At that same rally, Bray raised an arm in support of Hizballah as well. Source: The Investigative Project on Terrorism.

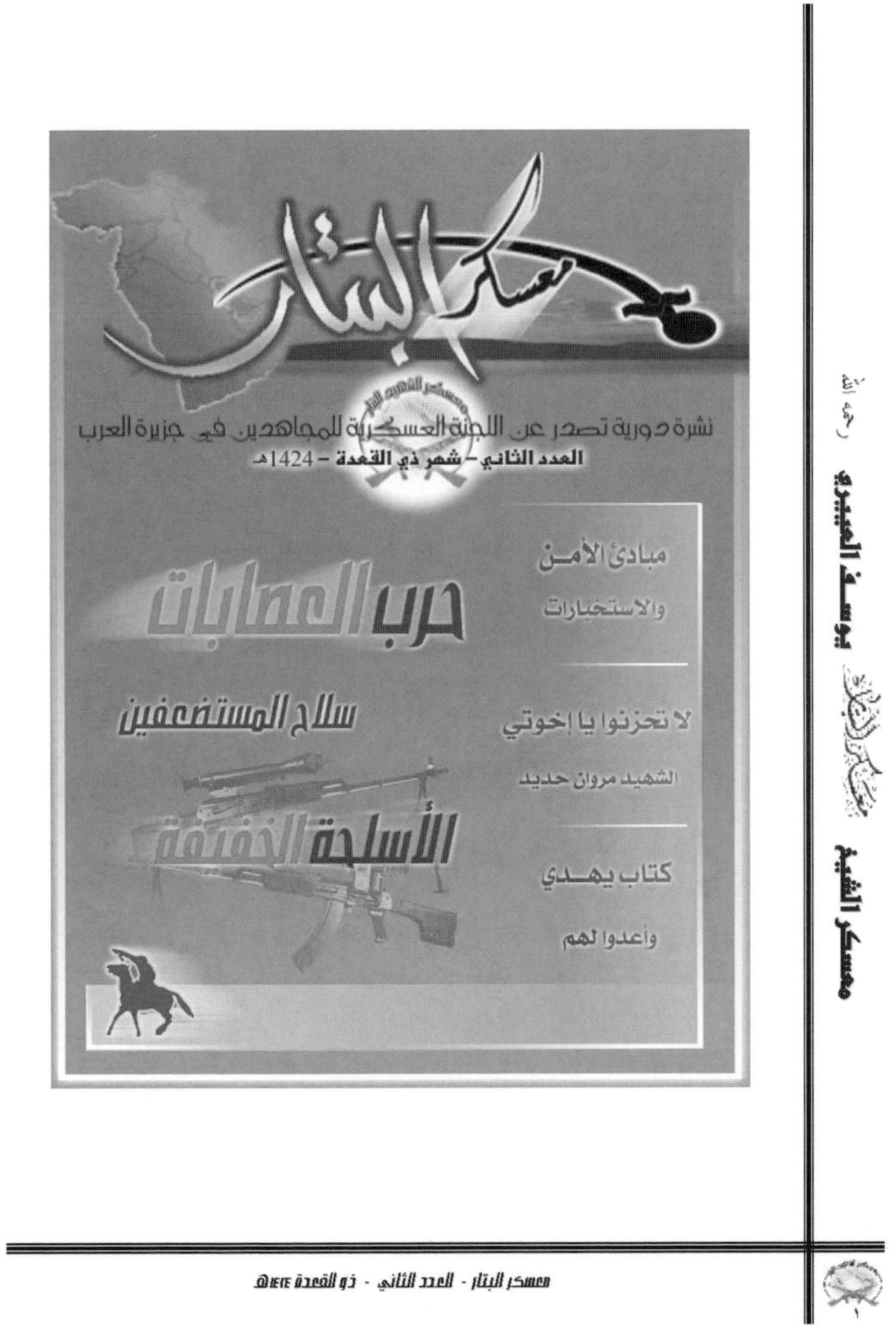

معسكر البتار

نشرة دورية تصدر عن اللجنة العسكرية للمجاهدين في جزيرة العرب

العدد الثاني – شهر ذي القعدة – 1424هـ

مبادئ الأمن والاستخبارات

حرب العصابات

لا تحزنوا يا إخوتي

الشهيد مروان حديد

سلاح المستضعفين

الأسلحة الخفيفة

كتاب يهدي

وأعدوا لهم

معسكر الشيخ يوسف العييري رحمه الله

١

The cover of an al Qaeda military Internet magazine, *Al Batar*. Source: The Investigative Project on Terrorism.

Abu Musab al-Zarqawi, deceased leader of al Qaeda in Iraq. Source: The Investigative Project on Terrorism.

The late Abu Musab al-Zarqawi with his men. Source: The Investigative Project on Terrorism.

BILL OF SALE

This is to validate that:

I, Yong K. Kwon, who reside at:

Have sold a firearm, AK-47 (SAR/RPKY) with Serial #: S1-03371-99, to:

Randy Royer, who resides at:

For the amount of $400 (US Dollars) on the 17th of September, 2000.

Yong K. Kwon

Randy Royer

Witness(es)

Seifullah Chapman

Hammād Abdur-Raheem

The AK-47 Randall Royer bought from Yong Kwon and the bill of sale. Source: *USA v. Royer, et al.*, 03-CR-296 (ED VA).

The nine convicted "Paintball Jihadis" (from left to right, beginning at top: Randall Royer, Yong Kwon, Ibrahim Hamdi, Muhammed Aatique, Seifullah Chapman, Khwaja Mahmood Hasan, Hammad Abdur-Raheem, Donald Surratt, and Masoud Khan). Source: *USA v. Royer, et al.*

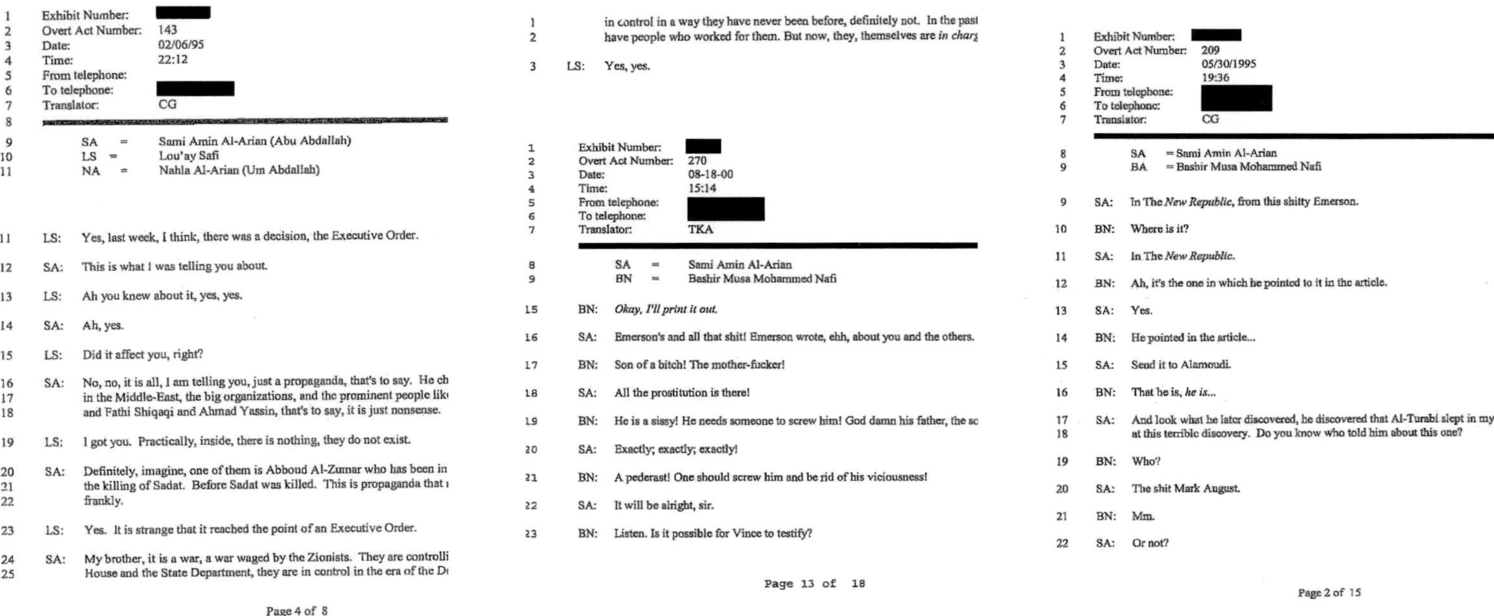

Exhibit Number: [redacted]
Overt Act Number: 143
Date: 02/06/95
Time: 22:12
From telephone:
To telephone: [redacted]
Translator: CG

SA = Sami Amin Al-Arian (Abu Abdallah)
LS = Lou'ay Safi
NA = Nahla Al-Arian (Um Abdallah)

LS: Yes, last week, I think, there was a decision, the Executive Order.

SA: This is what I was telling you about.

LS: Ah you knew about it, yes, yes.

SA: Ah, yes.

LS: Did it affect you, right?

SA: No, no, it is all, I am telling you, just a propaganda, that's to say. He ch in the Middle-East, the big organizations, and the prominent people lik and Fathi Shiqaqi and Ahmad Yassin, that's to say, it is just nonsense.

LS: I got you. Practically, inside, there is nothing, they do not exist.

SA: Definitely, imagine, one of them is Abboud Al-Zumar who has been in the killing of Sadat. Before Sadat was killed. This is propaganda that frankly.

LS: Yes. It is strange that it reached the point of an Executive Order.

SA: My brother, it is a war, a war waged by the Zionists. They are controlli House and the State Department, they are in control in the era of the D

Page 4 of 8

in control in a way they have never been before, definitely not. In the past have people who worked for them. But now, they, themselves are *in charg*

LS: Yes, yes.

Exhibit Number: [redacted]
Overt Act Number: 270
Date: 08-18-00
Time: 15:14
From telephone:
To telephone: [redacted]
Translator: TKA

SA = Sami Amin Al-Arian
BN = Bashir Musa Mohammed Nafi

BN: *Okay, I'll print it out.*

SA: Emerson's and all that shit! Emerson wrote, ehh, about you and the others.

BN: Son of a bitch! The mother-fucker!

SA: All the prostitution is there!

BN: He is a sissy! He needs someone to screw him! God damn his father, the sc

SA: Exactly; exactly; exactly!

BN: A pederast! One should screw him and be rid of his viciousness!

SA: It will be alright, sir.

BN: Listen. Is it possible for Vince to testify?

Page 13 of 18

Exhibit Number: [redacted]
Overt Act Number: 209
Date: 05/30/1995
Time: 19:36
From telephone: [redacted]
To telephone:
Translator: CG

SA = Sami Amin Al-Arian
BA = Bashir Musa Mohammed Nafi

SA: In The *New Republic*, from this shitty Emerson.

BN: Where is it?

SA: In The *New Republic.*

BN: Ah, it's the one in which he pointed to it in the article.

SA: Yes.

BN: He pointed in the article...

SA: Send it to Alamoudi.

BN: That he is, *he is...*

SA: And look what he later discovered, he discovered that Al-Turabi slept in my h at this terrible discovery. Do you know who told him about this one?

BN: Who?

SA: The shit Mark August.

BN: Mm.

SA: Or not?

Page 2 of 15

Translations of wiretap conversations between Sami al-Arian and associates, introduced into evidence during the trial. Source: *USA v. Al Arian, et al.*, 03-CR-77 (MD FL).

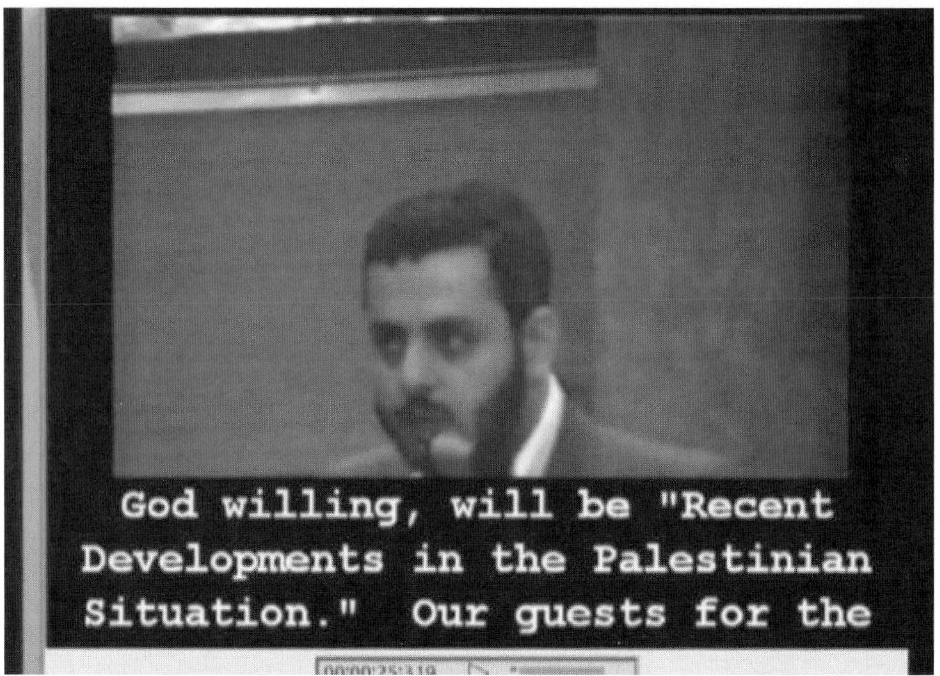
God willing, will be "Recent
Developments in the Palestinian
Situation." Our guests for the

Ramadan Abdullah Shallah, who would leave WISE and the University of South Florida to become the secretary-general of the Palestinian Islamic Jihad (PIJ), speaking at an Islamic Committee for Palestine (ICP) convention. Source: *USA v. Al Arian, et al.*

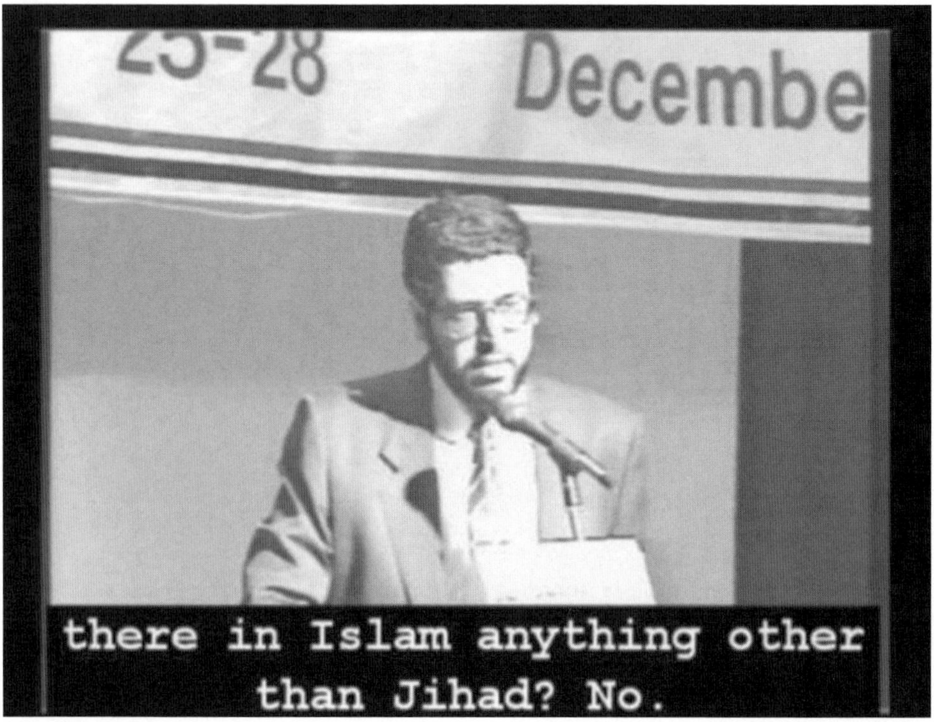

Mazen al-Najjar speaking at an ICP convention. Source: *USA v. Al Arian, et al.*

Sami al-Arian speaking at an ICP convention. Source: *USA v. Al Arian, et al.*

PIJ cofounder and spiritual leader Abdel Aziz al-Awda speaking at an ICP convention. Source: *USA v. Al Arian, et al.*

Exhibit #: T-516
Translator: FG (STIPULATED)

In the name of God, the Compassionate, the Merciful

Dear Brother Dr. Isma'il al-Shatti,

May God protect you.

Peace and God's compassion and blessing be upon you.

May God bring my letter to you and may it find you and your honorable family in good health and best wishes on the occasion of the blessed Ramadan. May God guide you so you can fast, pray and attain goodness during this month.

My dear brother,

I apologize for the loss of contact between us. However, I've been keeping up with your news. I was upset with you for not contacting us during your last visit. In any case, I hope that I will be able to visit you soon once I obtain my American passport. I also hope that the good relationship between us continues.

As a matter of fact, I would like to discuss with you a very important matter concerning the future of work in Palestine and the ability of the Islamic movement to confront the great challenges before it. In short, you are well aware that this movement, represented by its branches, Hamas and the Jihad, is being threatened by the enemy, the neighboring regimes, and even worldwide. Preserving the spirit and flame of jihad against the enemy is a general Islamic responsibility and cannot be left to rest upon the shoulders of the few among our nation. Nevertheless, these few shoulder the responsibility and the nation's honor, even putting their souls in their hands to prove that Islam is capable of responding to oppression, aggression, and desecration of the sacred places and Muslims' dignity.

The latest operation, carried out by the two mujahideen who were martyred for the sake of God, is the best guide and witness to what the believing few can do in the face of Arab and Islamic collapse at the heels of the Zionist enemy and in keeping the flame of faith, steadfastness, and defiance glowing.

Perhaps few know, while many are unaware, that these mujahideen were martyred while owing debt and having big families with no means to support themselves after the head of the household offered his life for God, glory be to He, defending the honor of this nation!

The Islamic movement in Palestine is poor, hungry, and destitute. The Jihad is in a state of great misfortune and has nothing. The brothers, your neighbors to the north, give very little assistance, which does not diminish the hunger and which proves, day after day, that the principles and slogans which we uphold are one thing and what actually occurs is something else.

The movement's financial situation is very difficult and it cannot fulfill its responsibilities toward the martyrs and detainees. Nevertheless, it carries out distinctive operations which the combined Arab armies have failed to do. The relationship with the brothers in Hamas is very good and making steady progress, and there are serious attempts at unification and permanent coordination.

I call upon you to try to extend true support of the jihad effort in Palestine so that operations such as these can continue, so that people do not lose faith in Islam and its representatives, and so that we can prove to people and to history that Islam properly responded to the circumstances despite a difficult stage in time, and a terrible era.

I would like to hear from you concerning the feasibility of assistance from benevolent people and institutions whom you know to the jihad in Palestine. My address and telephone number are attached. May God grant you success . .. Peace and God's compassion and blessing be upon you.

Your brother,

Sami al-Arian

2/10/95

Translation of a letter written by Sami al-Arian to Kuwaiti legislator Ismail al-Shatti, soliciting funds for the PIJ. Source: *USA v. Al Arian, et al.*

-8-

THE PAKISTANI JIHADIST NETWORK

Al Qaeda has been trying to use the organizational infrastructure of the Lashkar e Taiba (LET) in Pakistan, its network in the Islamic world, and its large funds for stepping up acts of terrorism against the USA and Israel.

—B. Raman, South Asia Analysis Group director,
Institute for Topical Studies;
Cabinet Secretariat, Government of India (ret.), (March 5, 2003)

OVERVIEW

The threat posed by radical Pakistani Islamic groups should be considered alongside the activities of international terror groups such as al Qaeda, Hizballah, and Hamas. Today, little analysis exists of the activities of radical Islamic organizations operating in the United States. Since 9/11, US authorities have arrested operatives in Virginia, Colorado, and New York connected to a number of these groups, including Jamaat Al Fuqra, Lashkar e Taiba (LeT), Jaish e Mohammed (JeM), and Harkat ul Mujahideen (HuM). Several of these individuals attended terrorist training camps in Pakistan, fought US troops in Afghanistan after 9/11, and plotted attacks on US soil. In addition, some of them have close ties to prominent Islamist parties in Pakistan—the Jamaat e Islami (JI) and the Jamiat Ulema Islami Fazlur (JUI-F)—known for their virulent anti-American rhetoric and criticism of Pakistan's cooperation with the United States in the war on terror.[1]

Today, there are some indications that terrorists trained in camps run by Pakistani terrorist groups are still traveling to America to form sleeper cells. A February 2004 article in the *Washington Times* reported that "intelligence and law-enforcement officials say dozens of Islamic extremists have already been routed through Europe to Muslim communities in the United States."[2] Moreover, a Department of Homeland Security memo of June 2004 warned immigration inspectors at certain airports to be on the lookout for individuals, particularly of Pakistani origin, who may have trained in Pakistani terror camps and who could be plotting attacks within the United States. The memo further noted that it was not unreasonable "to expect that many of the individuals trained are destined to commit illegal activities in the United States."[3]

Jamaat Al Fuqra is one of the Pakistan-based groups operating in the United States. This group, dominated by African Americans, boasts more than three thousand members and has established enclaves throughout the United States. With links to an array of terrorist acts (including the 1995 New York City landmarks plot), murders, fire bombings on US soil, and fraudulent fund-raising schemes, Al Fuqra has attracted the interest of law enforcement.

JAMAAT AL FUQRA

Jamaat Al Fuqra (Community of the Impoverished) is an international Islamic organization founded by the Pakistani cleric Sheikh Mubarak Ali Jilani Hashemi.[4] Al Fuqra is known to be "a splinter group of the extremist Army of Muhammad, [the] jihadi organization recently banned by Pakistani President Pervez Musharraf [that has] long-standing connections [to] senior ISI [i.e., Pakistani intelligence] officials."[5] The US State Department describes Al Fuqra as a group that "seeks to purify Islam through violence."[6] Though banned in Pakistan, it has made significant inroads in the United States.

Al Fuqra first took root in the United States in 1980 when Jilani traveled to Brooklyn, New York, to recruit followers at local African American mosques. With an ammunition belt around his waist, Jilani urged listeners to join the Afghan jihad against the Soviets.[7] Jilani's self-created persona, which glorifies him for performing medical and psychological miracles for his Islamic followers, had the effect of making Al Fuqra into something of a personality cult.[8]

By the early 1980s, Jilani had incorporated the Muslims of the Americas (MOA), a tax-exempt organization, and the Quranic Open University, MOA's educational arm.[9] During that decade a number of isolated, insulated Al Fuqra–connected communes were founded throughout the United States and Canada.[10] A biographical Web site about Jilani explains, "The majority of Sheikh Jilani's followers purchased land in areas away from the urban metropolis and developed small villages where they could raise their children in a wholesome environment and live a life of pure Islam, free from the decadence of a godless society."[11] Followers set up schools for these children as well, such as the GateWay Academy Public Charter School in California.[12] The group's headquarters were set up in Hancock, New York,[13] with other communities established in Michigan, Oregon,[14] Colorado,[15] California, North Carolina, South Carolina, Georgia, Pennsylvania, Tennessee, and Virginia.[16]

Some segments of Al Fuqra have a long history of both crime and terrorism, but there is no evidence that this can be attributed to all of its members. Addressing a news conference in 2002, Muhammad Haseeb Abdul-Haqq, a spokesman for the MOA settlement in Hancock, New York—also called Islamberg by MOA—disavowed any connections to terrorism and gave assurances that the group had "no sinister or evil designs," and that the group was situated in rural areas to avoid the "decadence and immorality of the inner cities."[17] What is known, however, is that there have been at least seventeen murders, some thirteen bombings and arsons, numerous hate crimes, and various—some high-profile—financial crimes committed by Al Fuqra members throughout the United States.[18]

Residents of MOA keep a low profile, deny the existence of Al Fuqra, and outwardly maintain a very benign image.[19] For example, in June 2004, there was an event in Philadelphia with participants driving in from Islamberg in New York, Islamville in Tennessee, Hoy Islamville in South Carolina, and Mian Mir in Michigan. The event consisted solely of youth singing groups from the aforementioned states performing Islamic songs. There was no mention whatsoever of Al Fuqra anywhere in the literature. The event was put together by the Islamic Naat Group (ING). According to the program:

> Why ING? Under the direction of our perfect Murshid, El Sheikh Sayed Mubarik Ali Shah Jilani, Syeda Gazala Jilani formed the Islamic Naat Group of USA, Canada and Pakistan as an activity and project for our youth who are being consumed by this dunya and its music, which is the instrument of shaitan [Satan]. All the songs glorify and praise Allah, his blessed holy last navi (salla allahu alaihi wassalaam) and the friends of Allah. All the singers are the youth of this Jamaat the lovers of Allah and Rasool Allah (salla allahu alaihi wassalaam), the Muslims of the Americas. They (the youth) competitively compose new songs; some are with the halal drum (duff) while others simply use the instruments of the voice.[20]

The program also advertised the event as Islamic Naat Group LLC in Association with International Quranic Open University and listed the chief executive officer of the Lahore Campus as Syeda Ghazala Jilani. The program also listed the Islamic Naat Group, LLC with a PO Box in Red House, Virginia.[21]

Red House, Virginia, is one of the MOA sites and was featured in a November 2002 PBS television segment called "Gun Land." The segment showed how MOA members in Red House skirted gun laws in order to arm themselves. Former Colorado government investigator Susan Fenger (who led a large investigation into Al Fuqra in Colorado after explosives and weapons were found in a storage locker by Colorado Springs police in 1989) supplied the show with a video of Sheikh Jilani stating:

> We have already established under the auspices of Muslims of America, Incorporated . . . the organization is called Soldiers of Allah. . . . You are most welcome to join one of our, you know, advanced training courses in Islamic Military Warfare.[22]

Background

Al Fuqra first appeared on the national radar screen in 1983 with the arrest of Stephen Paul Paster, an Al Fuqra leader and bomb maker. After being convicted for bombing a Portland, Oregon, hotel owned by an Indian guru, he served four years of a twenty-year sentence. He now lives in Lahore, Pakistan, where US authorities say he trains visiting Al Fuqra members in the use of explosives.[23]

Aside from the Portland bombing, there have been numerous other attacks on various religious institutions, and Al Fuqra members have been arrested, tried, and convicted of an array of crimes.[24] In September of 1989, police in Colorado Springs found a storage locker filled with weapons and explosives which opened up a large-scale investigation into Al Fuqra in the Colorado area. Among the findings:

> Several explosive components—thirty to forty pounds of explosives, three large pipe bombs, a number of smaller improvised explosive devices, shape charges, ten handguns—some with obliterated serial numbers—silencers in various stages of manufacture, military training manuals, reloading equipment, bomb-making instructions, and numerous FUQRA-related publications were located in this storage

> area. Titles of some of the publications included "Guerilla Warfare," "Counter Guerilla Operations," "Understanding Amateur Radio," and "Fair Weather Flying," and "Basic Blueprint Reading and Sketching." Several silhouettes for firearms target practice were also discovered, including one with the words "FBI Anti-terrorist team" written on the target's torso bullseye." There were also "documents concerning potential 'targets' for destruction and murder in the Los Angeles, Tucson, and Denver areas, including surveillance-type photographs, maps with hand-drawn overlays, notes, etc., concerning these targets. In addition, references to Buckley Air National Guard Base, Rocky Mountain Arsenal, the Air Force Academy, and electrical facilities in Colorado, and Warren Air Force Base, and two Wyoming National Guard armories in Wyoming were found. A somewhat detailed description of a fire-bombing attack on what is believed to have been the Hare Krishna Temple in Denver was also discovered. An attack, as described in these writings, did, in fact, take place in Denver in August 1984, causing an estimated $200,000 in damage. Investigation by Denver authorities at that time revealed that a Hare Krishna Temple in Philadelphia, where FUQRA activity also had been noted, was firebombed in a similar fashion.[25]

Among the many documents found in the Colorado Springs storage locker were numerous blank birth certificates; blank Social Security cards; several sets of Colorado driver's licenses, each containing a picture of the same individual, but each with a different identity; and many underground press publications concerning the assembly of phony identification—to be reproduced in a manner to "withstand even close government scrutiny."[26]

In 1991, a Canadian jury convicted Al Fuqra operatives of "conspiracy to commit mischief endangering life" relating to plans to bomb Hindu targets.[27] A raid in October 1992 on a 101-acre compound in Colorado uncovered a weapons cache of military rifles (American M-16s and M-14s as well as Soviet AK-47s).[28]

Sheikh Jilani, the group's leader, also was videotaped participating in a 1993 meeting in the Sudan organized by Hassan al-Turabi. In attendance were members of Hizballah, Palestinian Islamic Jihad, Hamas, the Popular Front for the Liberation of Palestine, the Democratic Front for the Liberation of Palestine, and, possibly, al Qaeda. At the meeting, chants of "Down, down USA! Down, down CIA!" and (in Arabic) "Death to the Jews!" were heard.[29]

Al Fuqra's Connections to al Qaeda?

Beginning in the early 1990s, Al Fuqra appeared to have an interesting overlap with al Qaeda. Operatives of the two organizations have fought jihad together in Afghanistan and Chechnya, and they have cooperated in such high-profile acts of terror as the murder in 1990 of Rashad Khalifa in Tucson and the 1995 New York landmarks case.

A US citizen and convert to Islam, Al Fuqra–linked Clement Rodney Hampton El was sufficiently inspired to take his cause abroad.[30] In 1988, he was recruited by Afghan mujahideen leader Gulbuddin Hekmatyar's Hizb al Islami (Islamic Party) to fight against the Soviet Union in Afghanistan.[31] After he lost a leg in battle, he returned to the United States where he gained renown in his community—where he was known as "Dr. Rashid"—for trying to rid its inner-city streets of crime but also for his ability to acquire weapons for that purpose.[32] In 1995, he was convicted and sentenced to thirty-five years in prison for his involvement in helping obtain explosives for the New York City landmarks plot.[33] Hampton El's case increased the concern of US authorities that Al Fuqra had come under al Qaeda's influence.[34] US authorities believe that other members of Al Fuqra also have fought in Afghanistan, as well as in Chechnya and Kashmir.[35]

In 2001, Al Fuqra's name surfaced during the trial of those involved in the 1998 East African embassy bombings. Wadih el-Hage, an al Qaeda lieutenant and bin Laden's personal secretary, was being tried for his role in the 1998 East African embassy bombings (for which he was convicted). El-Hage confessed that while he was living in Tucson, Arizona, in the late 1980s, he harbored and aided an individual sent to surveil Rashad Khalifa, an imam visiting the Islamic Center of Tucson.[36] He also testified that he considered Khalifa's 1990 assassination to be "a good thing."[37] Two Al Fuqra members, James Donald Williams and Nicolas Edward Laurent Flinton, eventually were tried and convicted of conspiracy in the murder; the actual killer was never identified by prosecutors.[38] As discussed in chapter 11, the Islamic Center of Tucson was a key base for al Qaeda's activities in the late 1980s.

Bilking the Government and Other Financial Crimes

In addition to Al Fuqra members who are in state and federal prisons on murder and/or weapons charges, there are also members who have been convicted on various fraud charges, including credit card, driver's license, welfare, and workers' compensation scams.[39] Al Fuqra prisoners allegedly recruit others in the prison system.[40]

Members of Al Fuqra have been associated with sophisticated fraud, bilking money out of government funds and fraudulently obtaining government contracts. In 1993, James D. Williams, the head of an Al Fuqra cell based at the Trout Creek Ranch near Buena Vista, Colorado, was sentenced "for conspiracy to commit first-degree murder" (of Khalifa) and "two counts of racketeering and second-degree forgery"; the latter charges arose from his submission of bogus workers' compensation claims, which defrauded Colorado taxpayers of $350,000.[41]

Vincente Pierre was convicted of fraud in the same scheme and sentenced to four years of probation.[42] As part of the scam, Al Fuqra, through the MOA, had registered nonexistent entities—"McClean Carpenters," "Professional Security International" (PSI), and the like—which then received checks from the insurance fund (mailed to post office boxes).[43]

According to then chief criminal investigator of the Colorado Department of Labor and Employment Susan M. Fenger, the creation of PSI as a security firm enabled Al Fuqra operatives to obtain the federal licenses needed to purchase automatic weapons.[44] Furthermore, PSI was able to obtain bid packages from numerous federal departments and agencies, including Health and Human Services, the Veterans Administration, and Defense. An investigator for the Colorado State Department of Labor and Employment was able to track a portion of the funds laundered by Al Fuqra to Pakistan.[45]

A second case of financial fraud involved the GateWay Academy Public Charter School, whose founder and superintendent, Khadijah Ghafur, was convicted in July 2006 of defrauding private investors and stealing public funds. Ghafur has continued to insist that the allegations came out of post-9/11 prejudice against Muslims and denied any wrongdoings, but a jury convicted her and two other GateWay employees with Ghafur facing a prison sentence of up to seventeen years.[46]

The school's charter was initially issued by the FUSD (Fresno Unified School District) and was revoked in January 2002 after the school failed to provide a financial audit regarding a deficit of $1.3 million.[47] The jury convicted Ghafur on diverting $75,000 in state school funds in order to repay a loan to an individual who lent the money to Ghafur to buy land for the religious community and $30,000 to a private corporation that authorities claim later channeled money to Khadijah Ghafur's husband.

In addition, Ghafur was convicted for grand theft involving inflated school attendance figures to raise $630,000 from private investors.[48]

Ghafur served as a member of the board of directors of Jilani's Quranic Open University. The school was located on the premises of Baladullah ("City of God")—a one-thousand-acre MOA settlement that she established around 1989 near Fresno, California, which also was GateWay's main headquarters. Baladullah was the immediate destination for at least two of Jilani's followers who arrived in California. Soon after its founding, neighbors began to complain of hearing loud gunfire on the property.[49]

The commune was targeted by local authorities after Ramadan Abdullah, a Jilani follower and Quranic Open University student, was charged with the August 2001 murder of a Fresno County sheriff's deputy.[50]

Another Baladullah resident was James Hobson, who was arrested in 2001 at the GateWay Academy in Fresno for his part in smuggling guns between South Carolina and New York.[51] Thomas D. Win, special agent for the California Department of Justice, told reporters that the Fresno Police Department's investigation of Baladullah and GateWay resulted from information supplied by the "[United States] marshal's service that the group living at the compound were possibly members of a group known as FUQRA, which was involved in several bombings, assassinations and fraud dating back to the 1980s."[52]

LASHKAR E TAIBA (LeT)

Designated a foreign terrorist organization by the US government on December 26, 2001,[53] Lashkar e Taiba (Army of the Righteous) has ties to al Qaeda and, according to the government, "claims to have trained thousands of *mujahideen* to fight in areas including Afghanistan, Kashmir, Bosnia, Chechnya, Kosovo, and the Philippines."[54] LeT also has espoused waging violent jihad against the United States, Britain, Russia, and Israel,[55] and has vowed to "plant Islamic flags in Delhi, Tel Aviv, and Washington."[56]

LeT is an outgrowth of Markaz Dawa Wa'al Irshad (a name that roughly translates as "Center for Invitation [to Islam] and Instructions"), which was founded in 1986 to assist in the Afghan jihad. As it expanded, it established a military wing.[57] Following the Russian retreat from

Afghanistan, Markaz Dawa Wa'al Irshad and LeT turned their attention to fighting the Indian government.[58] Since 1993, LeT has conducted a number of operations against Indian troops and civilian targets in Kashmir. According to a US government media release, in August 2001 alone it is believed to have been responsible for eight separate attacks that killed nearly one hundred people, mostly Hindu Indians.[59] Both LeT and Jaish e Mohammed (discussed below) are suspected of involvement in the December 13, 2001, attack on the Indian parliament complex that killed nine and injured eighteen.[60]

LeT, which is based in Muridke and Muzaffarabad, Pakistan, collects donations from the Pakistani communities in the Persian Gulf and United Kingdom, from Pakistani and Kashmiri businessmen, and from Islamic nongovernmental organizations.[61] According to B. Raman, a former high-ranking Indian government official, "al Qaeda has been trying to use the organizational infrastructure of the LeT in Pakistan, its network in the Islamic world, and its large funds for stepping up acts of terrorism against the USA and Israel."[62]

The Indictment of Ismail "Randall" Royer and the Paintball Jihadis

The June 2003 indictment of eleven men, nine of whom are US citizens, for their involvement with LeT suggests that the organization is playing a role in the global jihad.[63] A superseding indictment against the group, filed on September 23, 2003, listed additional charges—most significantly conspiracy to levy war against the United States and conspiracy to provide material support to al Qaeda.[64]

The most public face of the group was Ismail "Randall" Royer, a convert to Islam who had worked as a communications specialist for the Council on American-Islamic Relations[65] and as the communications director of the Muslim American Society.[66] Both organizations are discussed in greater detail in chapter 12.

Royer, who pled guilty to weapons and explosives charges in January 2004,[67] helped recruit the other men from the suburbs of Washington, DC, to train as mujahideen with LeT. Their training—which included paintball war games intended to simulate combat—began in the United States and was completed at camps in Pakistan.[68] As part of their preparation to go into combat, the organizers and recruits purchased weapons, including AK-47 rifles, to develop familiarity and skill with the arms used by mujahideen around the world. For two years, the group trained at firing ranges in Virginia and Pennsylvania, and seven of the defendants traveled to Pakistan.[69]

After 9/11, members of the Virginia jihad network gathered in Northern Virginia where their spiritual leader, Ali al-Timimi,[70] told them that it was time for them to act. According to al-Timimi's indictment, "on or about September 16, 2001, at the meeting at [future defendant Yong] Kwon's house, Ali Al Timimi told his listeners that American troops soon to be deployed in Afghanistan would be legitimate targets of the violent jihad in which his listeners had a duty to engage." Al-Timimi also advised two of the cell members "how to reach the Lashkar e Taiba camp undetected."[71]

According to a Department of Justice press release, "within a week of the 9/11 attacks, four of the defendants traveled to Pakistan and joined LeT operations there."[72] Yong Kwon and Khwaja Hasan, who have both pled guilty, stated that one reason they traveled to the Lashkar camp was to obtain military training for the purpose of engaging in jihad elsewhere, including Afghanistan.[73]

In October 2001, al-Timimi again discussed fighting jihad in Afghanistan with members of the cell. At that time, the indictment states, he "provided . . . historical examples from Islamic history justifying attacks on civilians" and argued that "mujahideen killed while fighting Americans in Afghanistan would die as martyrs." He then recommended that those listening "obtain jihad training from Lashkar e Taiba because its belief system was good and it focused on combat."[74]

Al-Timimi, the last member of the cell to be indicted (in September 2004), was convicted in April for inciting terrorist activity, for attempting to contribute services to the Taliban, and on explosives and other firearms charges. He subsequently was sentenced to life in prison,[75] but was released on bail pending appeal by the presiding judge, Leonie Brinkma. Of the others in the group, six have pled guilty, three were convicted, and two were acquitted.[76]

The Virginia Network Widens

Expanding on the "Virginia jihad network" case, two US citizens were indicted in May 2005 for conspiring to aid al Qaeda. As a result of a two-year sting operation, Tarik ibn Osman Shah and Rafiq Sabir were arrested after talking to FBI agents about providing assistance to al Qaeda.

Shah, a part-time jazz musician and martial arts instructor from the Bronx, talked about providing martial arts training to willing Muslims to "prepare" for jihad. Although he wanted to travel to Afghanistan in 1998, he was unable to and, instead, settled on the idea of setting up a jihadi training camp in the United States, going as far as inquiring about using a warehouse on Long Island as his base of operations. In the course of the sting operation set up by the FBI, Shah discussed how he would go about recruiting "brothers" for jihad and that it was imperative to find those "willing to press the fight."[77]

Despite the travel restrictions and his inability to wage jihad overseas, Shah was content with and deeply committed to waging jihad within the United States. He discussed his desire to learn how to use chemical weapons, explosives, and firearms. In a chilling example of his duplicity, Shah, commenting on a brief encounter with a young lady on the street, starkly told an undercover FBI agent that he "could be joking around and smiling and then cutting their throats in the next second."[78]

As for Rafiq Sabir, he easily masked his terrorist beliefs by becoming a quiet, seemingly legitimate member of American society. Sabir, a physician who lived in an affluent neighborhood in Boca Raton, Florida, received his medical degree at Columbia University in New York and practiced medicine at several different hospitals in the New York region. Furthermore, unlike Shah, Sabir spent significant time in Saudi Arabia, where he claimed to have worked as a physician on a military base in Riyadh, possibly providing medical assistance to wounded mujahideen.[79]

Although it is unknown how Shah and Sabir became acquainted, it has been reported that they both shared the same address on Adam Clayton Powell Jr. Boulevard in Harlem, New York. Shah used the address as the home for his business, called the Expansion of Knowledge Center, while Sabir used the same address as his home address in the early 1990s.[80]

From then on, the two kept in close contact with each other. Over the course of the two-year investigation, phone records indicate, they had multiple conversations with one another in which they talked about writing and producing a jihadi manual and video for potential jihadi trainees. In demonstration of the strength of their fraternal bond, they decided that they would join al Qaeda together. Shah especially felt a close relationship with Sabir, often referring to Sabir as his "brother" and "partner" and declaring that they should be considered a "package deal."[81] Ultimately, both Shah and Sabir took "bayat" and swore allegiance to Osama bin Laden, thus solidifying their commitment to al Qaeda.[82]

In the wake of the arrests, the civil rights and Muslim communities immediately came to Shah's and Sabir's defense. Khurrum Walid, a former Miami-Dade County public defender and pro bono lawyer for the Council on American-Islamic Relations, showed willingness to represent Sabir, after receiving a phone call from Sabir's wife, Arlene Morgan, requesting his services. Walid described the case as "good" and "very defensible."[83]

The scope of the investigation widened further when police officers, searching through Shah's possessions, found phone numbers including one belonging to an individual involved in the "Virginia jihad network." The number belonged to Seifullah Chapman, a Muslim convert and a coconspirator in the Virginia paintball case, who at his trial admitted to attending a LeT training camp in 2001.[84] Another number found in Shah's possession belonged to Mahmud Faruq Brent, a paramedic living in Maryland, who received martial arts training from Shah. Brent, also known as Mahmud al-Mutazzim, was arrested on August 4, 2005, for also attending a LeT training camp in Pakistan.[85]

Following his arrest, Tarik Shah cooperated with prosecutors by providing information regarding Brent. He told prosecutors that, during the summer of 2001, he and Brent lived together in Beacon, New York. Shah instructed Brent in martial arts and watched movies espousing jihad in Bosnia. Following the September 11 attacks, Brent and Shah were "kicked out" of the local mosque in which they had been occasionally training.[86]

It was within this time period that Brent allegedly traveled to Pakistani camps to train for jihad. Upon his return to the United States, Brent bragged to Shah that he had been at an unspecified camp, presumably in Pakistan, where he trained with the "mujahideen" in the "mountains."[87]

"Abu Adam Jibreel, an American-Born Shaheed"

The men in Virginia were not the first Americans to travel to Pakistan to train and work with Lashkar. According to a number of Islamic Web site postings[88] in 2001, Atlanta resident Abu Adam Jibreel converted to Islam and then came under the influence of former Black Panther H. Rap Brown. Brown, himself a convert, assumed the name Abdullah al-Amin and was the imam at the Atlanta Community Mosque. Brown, or al-

Amin, subsequently was convicted of murdering a police officer and currently is serving a life sentence in prison.[89]

According to the Web site information, Jibreel received military training from a former US Army Ranger, and in 1997 he traveled to Kashmir to further train with LeT. Jibreel is reported to have been killed later that year during an assault on an Indian army station.[90]

Jamia Abi Bakr Madrassah and Lashkar's International Scope

The Jamia Abi Bakr Madrassah (Pakistani religious school) in Karachi with strong ties to LeT also attracted Americans since, according to its own officials, a dozen Americans have "studied" there.[91] LeT's reach also goes beyond North America. Australian authorities allege that a LeT cell in Sydney was planning attacks against a number of targets, including the national power grid.[92] One member of the Virginia jihad network, Ibrahim al-Hamdi, testified from prison against Faheem Lodhi, an alleged Australian LeT operative.[93] Additionally, David Hicks, an Australian convert to Islam currently being held at Guantanamo Bay, trained with LeT before being captured in Afghanistan.[94]

The Shadow Detainees

In the spring and summer of 2002, the *New York Times* reported that a number of men "believed to be American citizens" were captured in Afghanistan. According to the *Times*, officials "believe that the men form a disjointed network of disaffected Westerners who converted to Islam and have been drawn to militant causes, fighting alongside al Qaeda, the Taliban or guerrillas in Kashmir." One man, known as "Ahmed Muhammad" or "Benjamin," is believed to be an associate of Jose Padilla. According to this account, some of the men may have converted to Islam in US prisons and furthered their religious education at a Pakistani madrassah run by Mufti Muhammad Iltimas. Officials have so far declined to provide any further details of the detainees out of concern that the ongoing interrogations could be impeded.[95]

JAISH E MOHAMMED (JeM)

In December 2001, the US government designated Jaish e Mohammed as a foreign terrorist organization.[96] The group was founded by Masood Azhar in early 2000 soon after his release from Indian imprisonment. Azhar's release along with those of Omar Sayed Sheikh and Mushtaq Ahmed Zargar was secured in 1999 in exchange for 155 hostages hijacked on an Indian Airlines flight from Kathmandu.[97] Sheikh, a leading member of the movement,[98] is reported to have been directly involved in wiring money to Mohamed Atta and in the subsequent kidnapping and murder of Daniel Pearl.[99]

JeM's recognized goal is to join Kashmir and Pakistan, and in order to achieve this it has linked itself with the Jamiat Ulema I Islam Fazlur Rehman faction (JUI-F), a radical Pakistani political party. Since its creation, JeM has been responsible for a number of deadly terrorist acts, including a suicide attack on the Kashmir legislative assembly building that killed thirty-one and an attack on the Indian parliament that killed nine.[100]

The US State Department has declared that JeM "has several hundred armed supporters located in Pakistan and in India's southern Kashmir and Doda regions and in the Kashmir valley. . . . Supporters are mostly Pakistanis and Kashmiris and also include Afghans and Arab veterans of the Afghan war." Moreover, JeM, which operated training camps in Afghanistan until the fall of 2001, had ties to the Taliban and allegedly received funding from Osama bin Laden.[101]

Like Al Fuqra and Lashkar e Taiba, Jaish e Mohammed also has had members operating in the United States.

One such individual is Sajjad Nasser, a legal permanent resident, who in August 2001 traveled to Pakistan where he attended a JeM training camp and learned to use rocket launchers.[102] In 2002, after his brother died in Afghanistan while fighting US forces, Nasser traveled there himself to fight against the US-led coalition.[103] Nasser was arrested upon his return to the United States in March 2003 on charges of possessing counterfeit immigration documents and was convicted in December of that year. During the proceedings Nasser also allegedly claimed that he and his cousin were members of a Denver-based sleeper cell, and the presiding judge concluded that Nasser provided "material support" to a terrorist organization. Sajjad Nasser was deported in August 2004.[104]

In September 2004, Imran Khan, who is related to Nasser by marriage, pled guilty to possession of a fake immigration document and agreed not to challenge his deportation.[105] Six of Khan's relatives had been arrested in March 2003 for exaggerating the closeness of his relationship to them in order to facilitate his entry into the United States. One of the indicted men, Abdul Qayyam, and his wife, Chris Marie Warren, stated that Khan was their son, when he actually was Qayyam's nephew. According to the indictment, Irfan Kamran, Qayyum's real son, knew that the claim was a lie, as did Haroon Rashid, Saima Saima, and Sajjad Nasser.[106] In May 2003 they were indicted for conspiring to defraud the government and for making false statements to federal agents.[107]

The FBI believes that Irfan Kamran, Khan's cousin (see above paragraph to keep the complicated family relationships straight), also has terrorist connections, or has expressed interest in carrying out terrorist acts.[108] According to a declassified government document introduced into court proceedings, Kamran expressed his support for the Taliban and al Qaeda after 9/11 and indicated his desire to fight US troops in Afghanistan. He had previously traveled to Pakistan in 1995, 1997, 1998, and 2000.[109] In addition, FBI special agent Michael Castro has testified that Kamran and another JeM member, Haroon Rashid, were waiting for orders to launch attacks in Colorado.[110]

Federal agents have accused Rashid of having trained in a terrorist camp after 9/11, of fighting with the Taliban and al Qaeda,[111] and of boasting about killing US troops in Afghanistan.[112] The Associated Press cites FBI documents in which Rashid claimed to be waiting for instructions to carry out attacks in the United States.[113] A pawnshop owner reported that Rashid, whose computer contained images of bin Laden and Mohamed Atta, had inquired about purchasing a global positioning system and a high-powered rifle with a nightscope.[114] The prosecutor told the judge at a detention hearing, "He poses a threat to everyone in this community and this country."[115]

Several years before Kamran, Rashid, and Nasser were arrested, they had all worked for an airport shuttle company. During this time, they had expressed their interest in waging jihad and their support for the Taliban.[116]

JAMAAT E ISLAMI (JI)

Jamaat e Islami, which the US government has referenced as an "Islamic fundamentalist political party,"[117] was founded in 1941 in the Bangladesh region of British India.[118] It now is Pakistan's largest religious party and is clearly linked to the Muslim Brotherhood. According to a UPI reporter, "Jamaat is dominated by those who studied at secular schools but later became avowed Muslims and are now known as Islamists."[119] The party is led by Qazi Hussain Ahmad, who also serves as leader of the Muttahida Majlis e Amal (MMA)—a coalition of six Islamist opposition parties that holds about 20 percent of Pakistan's national assembly seats.[120] The leadership of JI and the Jamiat Ulema Islami Fazlur (JUI-F), the MMA's two main constituents, is known for its anti-American propaganda and criticism of Pakistan's cooperation with the United States.[121] In his June 2003 delineation of the MMA's objectives, for instance, JI secretary-general Munawar Hasan is quoted as saying: "[T]he Muttahida Majlis-i-Amal (MMA) has a very clear program. The MMA is capable to bring a neat and clean revolution and rid the country of the United States. At present, the United States is on the verge of collapse. It is like an ice block that is constantly melting and one day, it will dissolve."[122]

During the Soviet jihad, JI supported Gulbuddin Hekmatyar,[123] who was named as a Specially Designated Global Terrorist in February 2003. In announcing the designation, the State Department noted "information indicating that Gulbuddin Hekmatyar has participated in and supported terrorist acts committed by al-Qa'ida and the Taliban."[124]

Although JI currently has a significant base of support among Pakistan's educated middle class, it has remained involved in jihadi causes. During the 1990s, JI members, in conjunction with high-ranking al Qaeda operatives, ran training camps that prepared recruits to fight jihad in Kashmir.[125] JI also harbored al Qaeda fighters after the 2001 US military campaign in Afghanistan. Indeed, 9/11 mastermind Khalid Sheikh Mohammed was captured in a house owned by a JI member.[126]

The JI and other Pakistani Islamist political parties have been known to finance and operate madrassahs that have taught anti-Western and anti-American values. Then secretary of state Colin Powell, in fact, described the curriculum taught in these religious schools as "programs that do nothing but prepare youngsters to be fundamentalists and to be terrorists." The more extremist madrassahs have also been known to harbor terrorists. For instance, a number of high-profile terrorists have graduated from the Darul Uloom Islamia Binori madrassah in Karachi, including JeM leader Maulana Azhar and the chief of the Harkat ul Mujahideen, Fazlur Rehman Khalil. Most of the top leadership of the Taliban is also from Binori.[127]

JI voiced its support for Hamas following the decision of Jordan to deport Hamas members so as to keep them from using the kingdom as a base for attacks.

> In our view the deportation step is not a just step and only serves the Zionist interest of weakening the political struggle for liberation and dividing the resistance forces. Jamaa't Islami Pakistan firmly believes that defending the usurped rights and Islamic Holy lands is a duty of all noble Muslims and it therefore urges your highness to: Immediately allow the deported brothers return home to their people and families. Restore for them their right of legitimate political work and information in accordance with the understanding that existed between the "Hamas" Movement and Jordanian government since 1993.[128]

JI has also advanced the usual "9/11 denial" conspiracy theories. In a statement released on September 20, 2001, JI's assistant secretary-general asked:

> Why was one of four thousand Jews employed in Twin Tower not present on the day of calamity? Why did Israeli Prime Minister not join the scheduled function organized by Zionist community in consultation with Israeli Intelligence Agency on that day? When the whole world is stunned into grief in consequence of the sudden tragic incident, why were some Jews making fun of and busy in taking photographs of havoc in a very cool brain? Why has evidence for kidnapping four planes not yet been recovered? Why are Muslims being blamed for the terrific incident in spite of not having any Muslim of four pilots? . . . As part of their design to conceal their misdeeds, was this incident brought about to divert the attention of the world citizenry from Israel's continued heinous persecution on Palestinian Muslims? Was the motive of this attack to foil the recent initiative to build up a cordial relation between the Muslim Ummah and Christian world?[129]

In an interview with BBC's *Hardtalk* program, JI president Qazi Hussain Ahmad claimed that al Qaeda did not have the capability to carry out the 9/11 attacks, adding: "The Zionists must be behind the attacks as they were the only beneficiaries of the September 11 incident."[130]

Following 9/11, Pakistani authorities arrested JI president Qazi Hussain Ahmad,[131] who had organized a number of violent protests after Pakistan refused to support Osama bin Laden and the Taliban. Ahmad was released in February 2002.[132]

More recently, the JI leadership charged that the 7/7 London bombings may have been "engineered" by Western governments.[133] According to Liaqat Baluch, deputy head of JI: "This is very tragic. . . . But this could also be a strategy by Europe and America to line up against Muslims. They are directly saying that Muslim groups or al-Qaida are behind these bombings. Then how can it be ruled out that these are not engineered blasts."[134]

JI in the United States

JI has a significant presence in the United States. Most notably, the Queens, New York–based Islamic Circle of North America (ICNA), which was founded in 1971,[135] has significant ties to JI.[136] According to a pamphlet published and distributed by ICNA, the organization's goal is to "achieve the pleasure of Allah through the establishment of the Islamic system in this land."[137] UPI has reported the claims of US officials that "ISNA [the Islamic Society of North America] and ICNA have been receiving financial assistance from sources in Saudi Arabia and the oil-rich Gulf states. These sources, they say, are already under investigation for their links to Taliban and Al Qaida."[138]

ICNA featured JI's president, Qazi Hussain Ahmad, at its 2000 conference in Baltimore,[139] and sponsored his visit to Florida a year earlier.[140] In an interview that appeared in the August 1999 edition of the *Message*, ICNA's monthly newsmagazine, Ahmad told the publication's editor, Zaheer Uddin, "The West has given a bad name to the Mujahideen and now to Taliban. They are working against both of them. Therefore they must form unity between their own. They must be aware of the coming threat."[141] Also in 1999, Ghulam Azam, the head of Jamaat e Islami, Bangladesh, was a featured speaker at ICNA's convention.[142]

Some individuals in the United States have been more directly linked to JI. In August 2004, Yassin Aref, the imam of the Masjid As Salam Mosque in Albany, New York, and Mohammed Hossain, the mosque's founder, were both indicted in a money-laundering scheme to make profits from the sale of grenade launchers to terrorists.[143] The scheme was part of a yearlong FBI sting operation that began in July 2003 when a Pakistani immigrant who served as an informant convinced Aref and Hossain to take part in a plot involving the sale of a shoulder-fired missile that was used to assassinate a Pakistani diplomat in New York City.[144] According to the complaint, Hossain told an FBI informant that "he was a member of Jamaat e Islami (JI)."[145] A superseding indictment in September 2004 further charged both Aref and Hossain with conspiracy to provide material support to the JeM.[146]

HARKAT UL MUJAHIDEEN (HuM)

The Harkat ul Mujahideen (HuM) was formed in 1985 by a breakaway faction of the Harkat ul Jihad al Islami (HuJI) to wage jihad against Soviet forces in Afghanistan. Following the Soviet withdrawal from Afghanistan in 1989, the group turned to terrorist activity in the Jammu and Kashmir region in India.[147] The group, designated a terrorist organization since 1997, operates out of Kashmir and has links to Osama bin Laden through its leader, Farooq Kashmiri. HuM masterminded the 1999 Indian Airlines hijacking that secured the release of Masood Azhar, Omar Sayed, and Mushtaq Zargar and has carried out numerous attacks on civilian and military targets in Kashmir. Following 9/11, the group's training camps in Afghanistan were destroyed by US air strikes.[148]

Although authorities have yet to identify HuM members in the United States, a number of Americans have been involved with the group overseas. After John Walker Lindh, "the American Taliban," attended a pro-Taliban Pakistani madrassah,[149] he spent months training in a HuM camp. Then, in May or June 2001, Lindh decided he wanted to fight with the Taliban. Carrying a letter of introduction from HuM officials, Lindh presented himself to Taliban recruiters and later attended al Qaeda's infamous Al Faruq training camp, where he learned to use rocket-propelled grenades and other weapons. In November 2001, an exhausted and demoralized Lindh surrendered to Northern Alliance troops.[150]

Lindh is not the only American jihadi linked to HuM. In 2002 a *New York Times* reporter discovered a document at a Harkat safehouse in Kabul bearing Hiram Torres's name, address, and telephone number. Torres, who grew up in Perth Amboy, New Jersey, was a high school valedictorian who studied briefly at Yale[151] and was reportedly obsessed with Adolf Hitler.[152] His friend told the *Times* that Torres's "dream was to be part of a revolution somewhere."[153] His whereabouts remain unknown.

TABLIGHI JAMAAT (TJ)

Tablighi Jamaat, which means "group that propagates the faith" in Arabic, is a Muslim missionary organization founded in India. Its members travel between mosques, madrassahs, and college campuses preaching the need for a return to purist Islamic values and seeking recruits who are frequently disaffected young men in search of an identity.[154] The group operates branches throughout the world, including in Pakistan, Europe, Canada, and the United States. TJ's roots in Pakistan are particularly deep; nearly two million people attend its annual Muslim meeting in Raiwind, Pakistan.[155] Although the group claims that its efforts are purely spiritual in nature and that its aims are apolitical and nonviolent, TJ has figured prominently in a number of high-profile terrorism cases.

In several instances, terrorist operatives pretended to be TJ members in order to escape detection. For example, when al Qaeda tasked Iyman Faris (discussed in chapter 2) to exchange old airline tickets, Faris disguised himself as a member of Tablighi Jamaat.[156] Similarly, the Lackawanna Six told family members they were traveling to Pakistan for TJ training, but instead ended up at an al Qaeda training camp in Afghanistan.[157] Analysts also have argued that TJ has "served as a springboard into militancy" for a number of terrorists, pointing out that it was the organization through which John Walker Lindh, Richard Reid, and Jose Padilla all embarked on their path to jihad.[158] It was a TJ preacher, for example, who helped Lindh enroll in a pro-Taliban madrassah in Pakistan. And Jeffrey Battle of the Portland Seven traveled to Bangladesh in search of TJ members who could help him join the Taliban.[159]

Although these cases do not provide clear-cut evidence of involvement in terrorism, many in the law enforcement community are extremely concerned about TJ, particularly because it controls mosques in at least ten states and has about fifty thousand members in the United States. According to an April 2004 Defense Intelligence Agency (DIA) memo, cited by NBC News, seven US-based TJ leaders are being investigated. The memo further states that a TJ official in the Midwest "has associations with several Al-Qaida supporters" and may be recruiting "converts for nefarious purposes."[160] Michael J. Heimbach, deputy chief of the FBI's international terrorism section, echoes the DIA's concern about TJ's recruitment efforts, noting "we have found that al Qaeda used them for recruiting, now and in the past."[161] Such a connection makes even more disturbing the DIA memo's observation that TJ members "have the capability to conduct a terrorist attack in the U.S.," though there is nothing to suggest such a plan is in the works.[162]

Because of TJ's philosophy of a strict adherence to Islam, its members seek to gather Muslims in separate communities so that they may avoid interacting with non-Muslim communities and institutions.[163] TJ also advocates such fundamentalist ideals as a complete rejection of gender equality/integration as well as democracy itself. This emphasis on disengagement from the Western world around them makes the path of jihad attractive for a young man in search of an "identity." As Khaled Abou Fadl, a UCLA professor, commented, "You teach people to exclude themselves, that they don't fit in, that the modern world is an aberration, an offense, some form of blasphemy. By preparing people in this fashion, you are preparing them to be in a state of warfare against this world." He added, "I think that militants exploit the alienated and withdrawn social attitude created by the Tablighis by fishing in the Tablighi pond."[164]

In addition to advocating disengagement, TJ's leadership preaches that jihad is the duty of all Muslims. At TJ's 2002 annual gathering, TJ speakers said that if "the right time for jihad ever [comes] the followers of TJ would offer the highest number of dead in the battle-field."[165] One TJ member in Queens, New York, interviewed by the *New York Times*, parroted this view, commenting, "Man, I know I'd kill anybody who killed another Muslim."[166]

MOHAJIR QUAMI MOVEMENT-HAQIQI

In January 2005, the Chicago Police Department expelled Patricia Eng-Hussain from its recruit class. Eng-Hussein was fired for not disclosing that her husband, Mohammad Azam Hussain, had been arrested by the Chicago Joint Terrorism Task Force. Hussain was charged with lying on his immigration application after failing to admit that he was what federal prosecutors called "an active and founding member of the Mohajir Quami Movement-Haqiqi, a militant offshoot of the Pakistani political group MQM."[167] Moreover, according to the *Chicago Sun Times*, Hussain told prosecutors that "he took part in a 'death camp' in Pakistan where he learned to use weapons and explosives" and "maintained contact with Afaq Ahmad, head of the Haqiqi faction, while Ahmad was a fugitive.[168] Ahmad recently was charged in Pakistan with murder and kidnapping."[169]

AMERICANS AT ISLAMIST SCHOOLS

A number of Americans have traveled to Pakistan to attend radical Pakistani madrassahs. Some have gone to the Haqqania School, which is located near Peshawar and has produced the majority of the Taliban's senior leadership. According to *U.S. News & World Report*:

> In 1995, seven Arab-Americans enrolled in the school, among them Zaid Bin Tufail of North Carolina, Zahid Al Shafi of Texas, and Ahmed Abi Bakr of Washington, D.C. All received military training and fought with Taliban units. . . . Other students included two African-Americans: a "Dr. Bernard" from New York, who arrived in 1997, and "Abdullah," whose parents . . . settled in Michigan; he, too, joined the Taliban and was reported "martyred" near Mazar e Sharif in 1999 or 2000.[170]

In addition, three Americans studied at the Tajweed Ul Koran Madrassah in Quetta in 1996 and then proceeded to Afghanistan, where they trained with the Taliban. Abu Bakar al-Faisal, a Chicagoan who had previously belonged to the Nation of Islam, studied at the pro-Taliban madrassah Jamiah Hamaddia. He was later killed while fighting with the Taliban in 1999. Finally, it is also important to note that Al Fuqra (discussed above) sent more than one hundred American citizens to Pakistan, supposedly to study Islam.[171]

A Historical Perspective on Americans: Fighting Jihad Overseas

According to Robert Blitzer, a retired FBI terrorism chief, "between 1,000 and 2,000 jihadists left America during the 1990s alone." Blitzer further told *U.S. News & World Report* that, in the reporter's paraphrase, "federal agents monitored some 40 to 50 *jihadists* leaving each year from just two New York mosques during the mid-'90s." Pakistani intelligence officials confirmed Blitzer's claims to *U.S. News & World Report*, estimating that four hundred Americans had trained in Pakistani and Afghan camps since 1989.[172]

Though their numbers before 9/11 may have been sizable, US agencies made no comprehensive effort to monitor Americans training for and waging jihad overseas—in large part because they were not targeting the United States.

As Blitzer told the *Washington Post*, "We didn't understand the magnitude of what was going on here, and there. . . . We only had a few snippets [about these American militants], and we certainly didn't have the records of Al Kifah," the organization with offices across the United States that often helped them make the journey (see chapter 11).[173] Nonetheless, counterterrorism officials and journalists have thoroughly documented some American jihadis fighting overseas. A few examples are considered below.

Abu Malik

During February 2001 testimony when he was on trial for the East African embassy bombings, Wadih el-Hage was shown a series of photos. He identified one of the individuals as "Abu Malik" and noted that he had seen the man in Sudan in 1993 or 1994 at Taba Investments, a company owned by Osama bin Laden.[174] El-Hage further testified that Malik was from New York, had fought the Soviets in Afghanistan, and had been trained in martial arts.[175]

A *U.S. News & World Report* piece added, "Investigators believe he is the most important of a handful of native-born Americans associated with al Qaeda during its Sudan days."[176]

Isa Abdullah Ali (aka Kevin Holt, Abu Abdullah)

Isa Abdullah Ali, a former Army Ranger who fought briefly in Vietnam, converted to Islam in the early 1970s. While living in Washington, DC, he worked at the Iranian embassy and was associated with David Belfield, who, in 1980, killed an anti-Khomeini activist in Bethesda, Maryland.[177] Then, in June 1982, Ali went to Lebanon, where he served as a sniper with a Shiite Muslim militia and claimed to have killed nine Israelis.[178]

Ali eventually moved on to fight in Afghanistan before coming back to the United States. He regularly visited Sheikh Omar Abdel Rahman's mosque in New York,[179] but finally returned to Washington, where he worked at a popular nightspot.[180]

In 1995, Ali could not resist the call of jihad and traveled to Bosnia, where he began to harass US troops in what a reporter called a "beat-up" Humvee.[181] Officials were concerned that Ali, who previously had been arrested for impersonation, could easily pass for a US soldier.[182]After he attempted to gain access to a NATO compound, NATO issued a bulletin warning troops about him.[183] Lieutenant Colonel Arnie Owens, a Pentagon spokesman, commented, "He is regarded as a potential security threat to American personnel."[184]

Mohammad Zaki

In 1993, in San Diego, Mohammad Zaki and Kifah Jayyousi created the American Islamic Group (AIG), American Worldwide Relief, and the Islamic Information Center of the Americas with the avowed purpose of advancing the cause of jihad. AIG served as the political organ for the entities, publishing communiqués and news reports. In one communiqué, AIG requested donations to help defend Sheikh Omar Abdel Rahman, characterizing the case, which was presided over by a "Jewish judge," as the "U.S. Government vs. Islam."[185] In April 1996, AIG's "Islam Report" contained the following item:

> The American Islamic Group is deeply honored and proud to report to all Muslims the Martyrdom (Shahadah) InshaAllah of one of its own faithful people in the land of Chechnya. Brother Mohammad Zaki. Brother Mohammad Zaki was the head of our Chechnya Relief effort which was started in November 1994. He is believed to be the first American Muslim to be killed in Chechnya. May Allah count him as Martyr and accept his Jihad. Brother Mohammad Zaki established contacts and relief routes inside Chechnya along with others, due to his extensive relief experiences in Afghanistan and Bosnia. Brother Mohammad Zaki worked through our sister organization "American Worldwide Relief," based in San Diego with divisions in other states.[186]

Kifah Jayyousi later served as facilities director for both the Washington, DC,[187] and Detroit public schools.[188] Jayyousi has recently been indicted in Florida on criminal charges of conspiracy to provide material support to terrorists, providing material support to terrorists, and conspiracy to murder, kidnap, and maim individuals in a foreign country. He is jointly charged with Adham Amin Hassoun (aka Abu Sayyaf) and Mohammed Hesham Youseff (aka Abu Turab).[189]

Aukai Collins

One of Mohammad Zaki's associates in San Diego was a young convert by the name of Aukai Collins. In his 2002 memoir, *My Jihad*, which he dedicated to Zaki, Collins details his path to jihad and asserts that he fought in Pakistan, Kashmir, Afghanistan, Chechnya, and Kosovo.[190] Collins also claims that while working as an FBI informant in Arizona, he passed along information on the 9/11 hijacker Hani Hanjour. The FBI disputes Collins's story, denying that he provided information about Hani Hanjour prior to September 11.[191]

Khalid Abu al-Dahab

An Islamic Jihad operative who lived in the San Francisco Bay area for twelve years, Khalid Abu al-Dahab fought in both the Balkans and Afghanistan.[192] He was a close associate of Ali Mohammed, and he recruited ten American al Qaeda members and helped bring al Qaeda's second in command, Ayman al-Zawahiri, to California in 1995 to raise roughly $500,000. Al-Dahab was arrested in Egypt in 1998 and currently is incarcerated there.[193]

CONCLUSION

Although their activities and networks in the United States are scarcely recognized, Pakistani terror groups and affiliates such as TJ continue to recruit members here. These individuals are quickly activated, sent first to be educated at Pakistani madrassahs, then to be trained in camps where Pakistani and al Qaeda elements (such as HuM) commingle, and finally to fight for jihad. If they survive to return to the United States, their will and ability to strike pose a significant danger to US national security—as the actions of Al Fuqra's Clement Rodney Hampton El and LeT'S Ismail "Randall" Royer demonstrate.

Deserved attention has been paid to Hamas, Hizballah, and the Palestinian Islamic Jihad, which continue to use the United States to raise money and find recruits for their causes. As the June 2005 arrests in Lodi, California, reveal,[194] equal attention is required for the numerous Pakistani groups here that are prolific, well trained, and highly sympathetic to the goals of the better-known terrorist groups, including al Qaeda. Because they are made up largely—almost entirely, in the case of Al Fuqra—of American citizens, simply barring their members' entry is insufficient. Law enforcement agencies must dismantle these organizations from within the United States, an action that provides both challenge and opportunity.

NOTES

1. K. Alan Kronstadt and Bruce Vaughn, "Terrorism in South Asia," *CRS Report for Congress*, August 31, 2005, p. 24.

2. Jerry Seper, "Islamic Extremists Invade U.S.," *Washington Times*, February 10, 2004.

3. Josh Meyer, "U.S. Steps Up Airport Focus on Pakistan," *Los Angeles Times*, July 1, 2004.

4. "Al-Fuqra: Holy Warriors of Terrorism," Anti-Defamation League, 1993, http://www.adl.org/extremism/moa/al-fuqra.pdf (accessed July 18, 2006).

5. Richard Sale, "Pakistan ISI Link to Pearl Kidnap Probed," United Press International, January 29, 2002.

6. "Patterns of Global Terrorism: 1999; Appendix B: Background Information on Terrorist Groups," US Department of State, April 2000, http://www.usemb.se/terror/rpt1999/appb.html (accessed July 18, 2006).

7. David E Kaplan et al., "Hundreds of Americans Have Followed the Path to Jihad," *U.S. News & World Report*, June 10, 2002.

8. "Imam El-Sheikh Syed Mubarik Ali Shah Jilani El-Hashimi, al-Hasani wal-Husaini: A Guide to the Way of Allahu Ta'ala and His Holy Last Messenger," Umma.com: The Muslim Directory online, http://www.ummah.net/Al_adaab/sheikh/sheikhji.html (accessed February 1, 2005).

9. STRATFOR, "United States: The Jamaat Al-Fuqra Threat," June 3, 2005.

10. Mira L. Boland, "Sheikh Gilani's American Disciples; What to Make of the Islamic Compounds across America Affiliated with the Pakistani Radical Group Jamaat al-Fuqra?" *Weekly Standard*, March 18, 2002.

11. "Imam El-Sheikh Syed Mubarik Ali Shah Jilani El-Hashimi, al-Hasani wal-Husaini.

12. Sean Webby, "Muslim Group, under Scrutiny, Abandons Enclave," *San Jose Mercury News*, June 15, 2002, p. A19.

13. John J. Miller, "A Junior Al Qaeda . . . Right Here at Home: Meet al Fuqra," *National Review Online*, January 31, 2001, http://www.nationalreview.com/flashback/flashback-miller013102.shtml (July 18, 2006).

14. John Kane and April Wall, "Identifying Links between White Collar Crime and Terrorism," National White Collar Crime Center, September 2004.

15. "Al-Fuqra," MIPT Terrorism Knowledge Base, http://www.tkb.org/Group.jsp?groupID=3426 (accessed August 1, 2006).

16. John Machacek, "Muslim Group Decries Bad Rep from Government, Media," Gannett News Service, January 9, 2002.

17. Ibid.

18. "Al-Fuqra," MIPT Terrorism Knowledge Base; STRATFOR, "United States: The Jamaat Al-Fuqra Threat," June 3, 2005.

19. STRATFOR, "United States: The Jamaat Al-Fuqra Threat."

20. Al Mehfil un Nasheed program, June 27, 2004.

21. Ibid.

22. "Gun Land," *NOW* with Bill Moyers, November 15, 2002, http://pbs.org/now/transcript/transcript_gunland.html.

23. Jerry Seper and Steve Miller, "Sniper Suspects May Be Followers; Ties Sought to Militant Muslim Group Jamaat al-Fuqra," *Washington Times*, November 13, 2002, p. A10; Boland, "Sheikh Gilani's American Disciples."

24. "Al Fuqra," MIPT Terrorism Knowledge base.

25. Colorado Department of Law, "Information Regarding Colorado's Investigation and Prosecution of Members of Jamaat ul Fuqra," http://www.ago.state.co.us/reports/fuqra.stm (accessed Junes 29, 2004).

26. Ibid.

27. Boland, "Sheikh Gilani's American Disciples."

28. "Al-Fuqra: Holy Warriors of Terrorism."

29. Pankratz, "September 11 Renews al-Fuqra Focus Colo."

30. Peter Jennings, *World News Tonight*, ABC News, June 29, 1993. See also Francis X. Clines, "Spector of Terror; U.S.-Born Suspect in Bombing Plots: Zealous Causes and Civic Roles," *New York Times*, June 28, 1993, p. B2.

31. Ibid.

32. Mary B. W. Tabor, "9th Held in Bomb Plot as Tie Is Made to a 1991 Murder," *New York Times*, July 1, 1993, p. B3; Craig Wolff, "Police Link Suspect to a Radical Sect," *New York Times*, June 27, 1993, p. 29.

33. *USA v. Omar Ahmad Ali Abdel-Rahman, et al.*, 93-CR-181-KTD, indictment, p. 10 (ED VA March 17, 1993); Jessica Stern, "The Protean Enemy," *Foreign Affairs*, July–August 2003, p. 27.

34. Stern, "The Protean Enemy."

35. Kaplan et al., "Hundreds of Americans Have Followed the Path to Jihad."

36. *USA v. Usama bin Laden, et al.*, trial transcript, p. 790 (SD NY February 15, 2001).

37. Ibid., p. 798.

38. Boland, "Sheikh Gilani's American Disciples."

39. STRATFOR, "United States: The Jamaat Al-Fuqra Threat."

40. Ibid.

41. Howard Pankratz, "69-year Term in Temple Blast Ex-fugitive Led Colo, 'Fuqra'Cell," *Denver Post*, March 17, 2001, p. B1.

42. Rex Bowman, "Man Held as Leader of Terrorist Cell; Hasn't Been Linked to September 11 Attacks," *Richmond Times-Dispatch*, September 29, 2001, p. A1.

43. "Al-Fuqra: Holy Warriors of Terrorism."

44. South Asia Terrorism Portal Web site http://www.satp.org/satporgtp/countries/pakistan/terroristoutfits/jamaat-ul-fuqra.htm (accessed January 2005).

45. Boland, "Sheikh Gilani's American Disciples."

46. Brandon Bailey, "School Founder Found Guilty," *San Jose Mercury News*, July 4, 2006.

47. Organized Crime in California, Annual Report to the California Legislature 2004, Office of the Attorney General; California Department of Justice, Division of Law Enforcement/Criminal Intelligence Bureau.

48. Bailey, "School Founder Found Guilty."

49. Sean Webby and Brandon Baily, "Cleric's Followers Have Hopscotched around California," *San Jose Mercury News*, February 2, 2002, p. A20.

50. Miller, "California Raids Charter School with Ties to Terrorists"; Boland, "Sheikh Gilani's American Disciples."

51. Webby and Baily, "Cleric's Followers Have Hopscotched around California."

52. Javier Erik Olvera and Cyndee Fontana, "Surveillance, Records Led to GateWay Raid," *Fresno Bee*, February 27, 2002, p. A1.

53. "Powell Names Two Groups as Foreign Terrorist Organizations," US Department of State, December 26, 2001.

54. *USA v. Royer, et al.*, 03-CR-296, indictment, p. 3 (ED VA June 25, 2003).

55. "Defendants Convicted in Northern Virginia Jihad Trial," US Department of Justice news release, March 4, 2004.

56. Kaplan et al., "Hundreds of Americans Have Followed the Path to Jihad."

57. *USA v. Royer, et al.*, 03-CR-296, indictment, p. 2 (ED VA June 25, 2003).

58. Ibid., p. 3.

59. "Day 100 of the War on Terrorism: More Steps to Shut Down Terrorist Support Networks," Department of Homeland Security press release, December 20, 2001.

60. K. Alan Kronstadt and Bruce Vaughn, "Terrorism in South Asia," *CRS Report for Congress*, August 31, 2005, p. 38.

61. Ibid.

62. B. Raman, "Al Qaeda & Lashkar-E-Toiba," South Asia Analysis Group, March 5, 2003, http://www.saag.org/papers7/paper678.html (accessed July 18, 2006).

63. *USA v. Royer, et al.*, 03-CR-296, indictment, pp. 1–2 (ED VA June 25, 2003).

64. US Department of Justice news release, September 25, 2003.

65. "Guest CV: Ismail Royer," http://www.islamonline.net/livedialogue/english/Guestcv.asp?hGuestID=605R88 (accessed August 15, 2005).

66. Ismail Royer, "America Must Revise Stance Towards Islamic World," Muslim American Society, December 9, 2002, http://www.masnet.org/articlesand papers.asp?id=33 (accessed July 18, 2006).

67. "Two Defendants in Virginia Jihad Case Plead Guilty to Weapons Charges, Will Cooperate with Ongoing Investigations," US Department of Justice news release, January 16, 2004.

68. "Defendants Convicted in Northern Virginia Jihad Trial," US Department of Justice news release, March 4, 2004, http://www.usdoj.gov/opa/pr/2004/March/04_crm_139.htm.

69. Ibid.

70. Al-Timimi was a highly respected lecturer at the Dar Al Arqam Islamic Center in Falls Church, Virginia, *USA v. Al Timimi*, 04-CR-385, indictment (ED VA September 23, 2004).

71. *USA v. Al Timimi*, 04-CR-385, indictment (ED VA September 23, 2004).

72. "Defendants Convicted in Northern Virginia Jihad Trial."

73. "Two Defendants in Virginia Jihad Case Plead Guilty to Weapons Charges."

74. *USA v. Al Timimi*, 04-CR-385, indictment (ED VA September 23, 2004).

75. *USA v. Al Timimi*, 04-CR-385, judgment (ED VA July 13, 2005).

76. "Defendants Convicted in Northern Virginia Jihad Trial."

77. *USA v. Tarik ibn Osman Shah, et al.*, 05-MJ-00956, complaint, pp. 4–5 (SD NY May 27, 2005).

78. Ibid., pp. 11–12.

79. Ibid., p. 14.

80. John-Thor Dahlburg and Walter Roche, "2 Suspects to Be Arraigned; U.S. Citizens Accused of Planning to Help Al Qaeda, with Training, Medical Care," *Los Angeles Times*, May 31, 2005.

81. *USA v. Tarik ibn Osman Shah, et al.*, 05-MJ-00956, complaint, p. 10 (SD NY May 27, 2005).

82. Ibid., pp. 16–17.

83. Jane Musgrave, "Doctor Hires Ex-Public Defender," *Palm Beach Post*, June 4, 2005.

84. Ibid., p. 4.

85. "U.S. Arrests Maryland Man for Providing Material Support to Foreign Terrorist Organizations," United States Attorney Southern District of New York, August 4, 2005.

86. *USA v. Mahmud Faruq Brent*, 05-MAG-1398, complaint, p. 8 (SD NY August 3, 2005).

87. Ibid., pp. 8–9.

88. Abdur-Raheem As-Siddiqui Web Posting, "Abu Adam Jibreel, An American Born Shaheed," May 20, 2001, http://www.fuckusama.com/forums/viewtopic.php?t=3&view=previous&sid=86faa542753d274d20374ac2bb2eb107 (accessed July 18, 2006).

89. Donna Leinwand, "A U.S. Teen's Journey to Jihad," *USA Today*, June 14, 2002; Mitch Stacy, "Former '60s Radical H. Rap Brown Sentenced to Life in Prison," Associated Press, March 14, 2002.

90. Kaplan et al., "Hundreds of Americans Have Followed the Path to Jihad."

91. Ibid.

92. Agence France Presse, "Suspected Terrorist Planned to Bomb Australia's Electricity Grid: Report," April 23, 2004; Nicholas Rufford and Tony Vermeer, "ASIO Alert on Four Sydney Suspects," *Sunday Telegraph*, April 18, 2004.

93. "FBI Told 'Facts' Based on Dreams: Terror Trial," *Sydney Morning Herald*,

December 16, 2004, http://www.smh.com.au/news/Anti-Terror-Watch/FBI-told-facts-based-on-dreams-terror-trial/2004/12/16/1102787182029.html (accessed July 18, 2006).

94. Josh Lefkowitz and Lorenzo Vidino, "Al Qaeda's New Recruits," *Wall Street Journal Europe*, August 28, 2003.

95. Dexter Filkins, "Traces of Terror: The Dragnet," *New York Times*, June 13, 2002.

96. Kronstadt and Vaughn, "Terrorism in South Asia," p. 38. See also "Foreign Terrorist Organizations (FTOs)," US Department of State fact sheet, October 11, 2005.

97. "Hijack Drama Ends, All Hostages Freed, 3 Militants Released," *Press Trust of India*, December 31, 1999.

98. MIPT Terrorism Knowledge Base Web site, http://www.tkb.org/Group.jsp?groupID=58 (accessed December 20, 2005).

99. Geoffrey Mohan and Tyler Marshall, "'Definitive Signs' Indicate Reporter Is Alive, Police Say," *Los Angeles Times*, February 7, 2002.

100. "Patterns of Global Terrorism, 2003," United States Department of State, June 2004.

101. Ibid.

102. Nasser's wife and nine-month-old son are American citizens who are still in the United States. "Denver Man Deported after Attending Terrorist Training Camp," TheDenverChannel.com, August 26, 2004; Associated Press, "Pakistani Guilty of Having a Fake Document," September 1, 2004.

103. Howard Pankratz and John Ingold, "Pakistani Case Creates Gap of Opinion," *Denver Post*, April 6, 2003.

104. "ICE Deports Two Linked to Terrorist Activity," Immigration & Customs Enforcement (ICE), September 13, 2004; Michael Riley and Jim Hughes, "'Capone' Tactic in Terror Fight Questioned," *Denver Post*, July 27, 2003.

105. Associated Press, "Pakistani Guilty of Having a Fake Document."

106. *USA v. Qayyum*, 03-CR-127, superceding indictment (D CO May 22, 2003); Jon Sarche, "Pakistani Man Detained in Colorado on Alleged Terror Ties," Associated Press, April 1, 2003.

107. *USA v. Qayyum*, 03-CR-127, superceding indictment (D CO May 22, 2003).

108. Pankratz and Ingold, "Pakistani Case Creates Gap of Opinion."

109. Ibid.

110. Associated Press, "Pakistanis Accused of Terror Ties Ordered Released on Bond," April 8, 2003.

111. John Ashcroft, "Prepared Remarks of Attorney General John Ashcroft: Success and Strategies in the Effort to Liberate Iraq," April 17, 2003.

112. Associated Press, "Agent: Suspect Bragged of Killing Troops," April 1, 2003.

113. Ibid.

114. Howard Pankratz, "Lakewood Pakistani Detained," *Denver Post*, April 1, 2003.

115. Associated Press, "Agent: Suspect Bragged of Killing Troops," April 1, 2003.

116. Pankratz and Ingold, "Pakistani Case Creates Gap of Opinion."

117. *USA v. Aref, et al.*, 04-CR-402, criminal complaint, p. 12 (ND NY August 5, 2004).

118. Web archive of Jamaat-e-Islami Web site, "About Jamaat-e-Islami," http://wasearch,loc.gov/sep11/20010926071637/http://www.jamaat-e-islami.org/index.asp?,/overview.htm (accessed February 4, 2005).

119. Anwar Iqbal, "Pakistan May Take on a Religious Giant," United Press International, August 11, 2004.

120. Kronstadt and Vaughn, "Terrorism in South Asia," p. 23.

121. Ibid., pp. 23–24.

122. "JI Secretary General Warns Musharraf, Jamali Against Collusion with US," *Rawalpindi Nawa-i-Waqt* (FBIS Translated Text; AFS Document Number: SAP20030613000095), June 13, 2003.

123. Ibid.

124. "Designation of Gulbuddin Hekmatyar as a Terrorist," US Department of State press release, February 19, 2003.

125. Iqbal, "Pakistan May Take on a Religious Giant."

126. Agence France Press, "Pakistan Asked to Explain Islamic Party Link to al-Qaeda Suspects," March 3, 2003; Anwar Iqbal, "Pakistan Arrests 63 al-Qaida Suspects," United Press International, August 16, 2004.

127. A. B. Mahapatra, "The Killer from Binori," *News Insight*, December 12, 2005.

128. "JI Memorandum to Jordan Monarch through Embassy," http://www.jamaat.org/world/memojordan.html (accessed February 4, 2005).

129. "Web Archive of Jamaat-e-Islami Ameer Challenges U.S. Accusation of Muslim Involvement in Attack on America," http://wasearch,loc.gov/sep11/20010926072318/http://www.jamaat-e-islami.org/index.asp?./news_body/september202001.html (accessed February 4, 2005).

130. "Bin Laden Was Not Capable of Carrying Out 9/11 Attacks," *Geo TV* Web site, http://www.geo.tv/main_files/pakistan.aspx?id=86414 (accessed December 14, 2005).

131. "Qasi Hussain Ahmad," Jamaat-e-Islami Web site, http://www.jamaat.org/leadership/qha.html (accessed February 5, 2005).

132. Associated Press, "Pakistan Frees Top Pro-Taliban Militant Leader on Bail," February 28, 2002.

133. Sadaqat Jan, "Radical Pakistani Lawmaker Says London Attacks May Have Been 'Engineered' by West," Associated Press, July 8, 2005. See also Kronstadt and Vaughn, "Terrorism in South Asia," p. 24.

134. Ibid.

135. "About US," ICNA Web site, http://www.icna.org/ICNA/ (accessed February 4, 2005).

136. Anwar Iqbal, "Sept 11: No Change in Muslim Leadership," United Press International, September 6, 2002.

137. "Islamic Circle of North America: An Introduction," brochure, collected at 22nd ICNA Annual Convention, Pittsburgh, PA, July 4–6, 1997.

138. Anwar Iqbal, "Bush Dinner: U.S. Muslim Groups in Trouble," United Press International, October 29, 2003.

139. "25th Annual Convention: Islamic Circle of North America," audiotape, July 2, 2000.

140. Paul Brinkley-Rogers, "Pakistani Opposition Leader Will Speak to Area Muslims at Meeting on BCC Campus," *Miami Herald*, July 9, 1999.

141. Qazi Hussein Ahmad, interviewed by Zaheer Uddin, *Message International*, August 1999, p. 41.

142. Twenty-fourth National Convention of the Islamic Circle of North America, July 2–4, 1999, event program; Islam in Bangladesh Web site, "Jamaat e Islami Bangladesh," http://www.islam-bd.org/Jamaat/jamaat_home.html (accessed August 12, 2005).

143. *USA v. Aref, et al.*, 04-CR-402, indictment (ND NY August 6, 2004).

144. *USA v. Aref, et al.*, 04-CR-402, criminal complaint (ND NY August 5, 2004).

145. Ibid.

146. *USA v. Aref, et al.*, 04-CR-402, superseding indictment (ND NY September 29, 2005).

147. MIPT Terrorism Knowledge Base Web site, http://www.satp.org/satporgtp/countries/india/states/jandk/terrorist_outfits/harkatul_mujahideen.htm (accessed on December 21, 2005).

148. "Patterns of Global Terrorism, 2003," US Department of State, June 2004.

149. Kaplan et al., "Hundreds of Americans Have Followed the Path to Jihad."

150. *USA v. Lindh*, 02-CR-37A, indictment (ED VA February 5, 2002).

151. David Rohde and James Risen, "Long-Vanished U.S. Student, and a Clue on a Kabul Floor," *New York Times*, February 6, 2002.

152. Kaplan et al., "Hundreds of Americans Have Followed the Path to Jihad."

153. Rohde and Risen, "Long-Vanished U.S. Student."

154. Susan Sachs, "A Muslim Missionary Group Draws New Scrutiny in U.S.," *New York Times*, July 14, 2003.

155. Alex Alexiev, "The Pakistani Time Bomb," *Commentary*, March 2003.

156. *USA v. Faris, et al.*, 03189-A, statement of facts (ED VA May 1, 2003).

157. *USA v. Goba et al.*, 02-CR-214, criminal complaint (WD NY September 3, 2002); Susan Sachs, "A Muslim Missionary Group Draws New Scrutiny in U.S.," *New York Times*, July 14, 2003.

158. Jessica Stern, "The Protean Enemy: Al Qaeda," *Foreign Affairs* 82, no. 4 (July 1, 2003).

159. Sachs, "A Muslim Missionary Group Draws New Scrutiny in U.S."

160. Lisa Myers, "FBI Monitors Islamic Group for Terror Ties," NBC News, January 18, 2005.

161. Sachs, "A Muslim Missionary Group Draws New Scrutiny in U.S."

162. Myers, "FBI Monitors Islamic Group for Terror Ties."

163. Olivier Roy, "EuroIslam: The Jihad Within?" *National Interest*, March 1, 2003.

164. Sachs, "A Muslim Missionary Group Draws New Scrutiny in U.S."

165. "Tablighi Jamaat Must Remain Apolitical," *Daily Times* (Pakistan), July 16, 2003.

166. Sachs, "A Muslim Missionary Group Draws New Scrutiny in U.S."

167. Frank Main, "Recruit Married to Pakistani 'Militant' Fired," *Chicago Sun Times*, January 23, 2005.

168. Ibid.

169. Frank Main, "Recruit Married to Pakistani 'Militant' Fired," *Chicago Sun Times*, January 23, 2005.

170. Kaplan et al., "Hundreds of Americans Have Followed the Path to Jihad."

171. Ibid.

172. Ibid.

173. John Mintz, "For U.S., American 'Holy Warriors' Hard to Track," *Washington Post*, July 16, 2002.

174. *USA v. Bin Laden, et al.*, S(7) 98-CR-1023, testimony of Wadih El-Hage, pp. 742–43 (SD NY February 15, 2001).

175. Ibid., pp. 744–46.

176. Kaplan et al., "Hundreds of Americans Have Followed the Path to Jihad."

177. William Branigin, "U.S. Sniper in Beirut," *Washington Post*, July 29, 1982.

178. Ibid.

179. "Issa Abdullah Ali (Bosnia)," *Indigo Publications Intelligence Newsletter*, no. 282, February 22, 1996.

180. Brian Blomquist, "'Terrorist' Was a Regular in Adams Morgan Bar," *Washington Times*, January 26, 1996.

181. Mark Rice-Oxley, "Islamic Maverick Toying with US Forces in Bosnia: Soldiers," Agence France Presse, February 10, 1996.

182. Ibid.

183. Harry Rosenthal, "Profile of a Fugitive: 'Very, Very Weird Story,'" Associated Press, January 24, 1996.

184. Tim Winer, "NATO Forces Are Warned of U.S. Extremist in Bosnia," *New York Times*, January 24, 1996.

185. Islam@Powergrid,electriciti.com (American Islamic Group), "Islam Report (Just In! $800 Million Spent to Destroy Islam)," December 8, 1994, http://www.isnet.org/archive-milis/dec94/0178.html (accessed August 12, 2005).

186. Islam@Powergrid,electriciti.com (American Islamic Group), "Islam Report (Chechnya Needs You Now! Urgent)," *MSANews*, June 7, 1995, http://

web,archive.org/web/20021231180254/http://www.naqshbandi.net/haqqani/Islam/Shariah/muamalaat/jihad/chechen_news.html (accessed August 12, 2005).

187. Piet Van Lier, "Akron Involves Community in Master Plan," March/April 2001, http://www.catalyst-cleveland.org/04-01/0401update1.htm (accessed February 8, 2005).

188. Ed Finkel, "Dilapidated Schools a National Problem," November 1998, http://www.catalyst-chicago.org/11-98/118else.htm (accessed February 8, 2005).

189. "Kifah Wael Jayyousi Added as a Defendant in Hassoun and Youssef Prosecution," US Department of Justice press release, April 7, 2005.

190. Aukai Collins, *My Jihad* (Guilford, CT: Lyons Press, 2002).

191. Aukai Collins, interviewed by John Gibson, *The Big Story with John Gibson*, Fox News, May 24, 2002.

192. Kaplan et al., "Hundreds of Americans Have Followed the Path to Jihad."

193. Lance Williams, "Bin Laden's Bay Area Recruiter," *San Francisco Chronicle*, November 21, 2001.

194. *USA v. Hayat*, MAG 05-151, criminal complaint (ED CA June 7, 2005).

PART THREE:

UNRAVELING THE SUPPORT NETWORK OF TERRORISTS WITHIN THE UNITED STATES

-9-

CHARITIES, FOUNDATIONS, "ADVOCACY," AND POST-9/11 TRENDS OF TERRORIST FINANCING

"Our presence in North America gives us a unique opportunity to monitor, explore and follow up. . . . We are in the center which leads the conspiracy against our Islamic world. . . . Therefore, we, here can monitor and watch the American policies and the activities of those questionable organizations. . . . Therefore, we have the capability to establish a Center for Studies, Intelligence and Information. . . . Members of the Group should be able to infiltrate the sensitive intelligence agencies or the embassies in order to collect information and build close relationships with the people in charge in these establishments." They should also use every opportunity to "collect information from those relatives and friends who work in sensitive positions in the government, et cetera. . . ."

—Unsigned document seized in a 1995 raid of former University of South Florida professor Sami al-Arian[1]

OVERVIEW

In the fall of 1996, senior representatives from seven US-based Islamic charities met to discuss the creation of an Islamic charity council to strengthen intercharity cooperation. Those charities were: the Holy Land Foundation for Relief and Development (HLF), Global Relief Foundation (GRF), Benevolence International Foundation (BIF), Islamic African Relief Agency (IARA), International Relief Association (IRA/LIFE), Mercy International, and the International Relief Organization (IRO). The meeting resulted in the establishment of the Council of American Muslim Charities (CAMC) on August 9, 1997.[2]

After 9/11, four of these seven organizations were designated terrorist financiers by the US Treasury Department and shut down. Two others have had their offices searched by US authorities on suspicion of financing terrorism. One of those two had two branch offices abroad designated by the US Treasury Department as terrorist financiers in the summer of 2006 for their role in al Qaeda financing. Evidence ties the seventh organization to terrorism as well.

This chapter will briefly explore the backgrounds and cooperative activities of these charities, and then use case studies to examine their methods of fund-raising, the funding sources they exploited, and the techniques they used to transfer funds to terrorist organizations. Additionally, this chapter will address the influence of American Islamic advocacy groups—such as the Council on American-Islamic Relations (CAIR), the Islamic Society of North America (ISNA), the Muslim Public Affairs Council (MPAC), the Muslim American Society (MAS), and the Islamic Circle of North America (ICNA)—that subvert the interests and safety of American and Western interests behind a veil of false moderation. Analyzing these and other related organizations will provide insight into the murky network of Islamist charities, foundations, institutes, and advocacy groups that operate in the United States for the purpose of supporting radical Islamist causes throughout the world.

Finally, recent trends in terrorist financing in the United States through criminal activity and other means will be explored in the context of the post-9/11 environment. Since 9/11, the exploitation of nontraditional methods for moving funds to terrorist groups has increased.

THE "SEVEN"

The Holy Land Foundation for Relief and Development (HLFRD/HLF) was an Islamic charity headquartered in Richardson, Texas, with US and overseas branches (also discussed in chapter 5). Set up in the late 1980s, HLF received a $210,000 cash donation from Hamas leader Musa Abu Marzook in 1992.[3] The US Department of the Treasury Office of Foreign Assets Control (OFAC) froze HLF's assets on December 4, 2001.[4] In July 2004, HLF and seven of its leaders were named in an indictment, which stated that HLF had sent $24 million to people and groups linked to Hamas between 1988 and 1995.[5] Since 1995, HLF and its members illegally sent $12.4 million to support

Hamas and its goal of creating an Islamic Palestinian state by eliminating Israel through violent jihad.[6]

The Global Relief Foundation (GRF) was incorporated as a nonprofit organization in 1992 and headquartered in Bridgeview, Illinois.[7] GRF had overseas "registered" offices in Islamabad, Pakistan; Brussels, Belgium; Sarajevo, Bosnia; Zagreb, Croatia; and Baku, Azerbaijan.[8] The same December 14, 2001, order from the US Treasury Department that froze the assets of HLF was also directed at GRF.[9] Immediately thereafter, the FBI raided GRF's Illinois offices, seizing records and arresting the foundation's CEO, Rabih Haddad. The search warrants were executed on the same day that NATO-led peacekeepers and UN police raided GRF's offices in Yugoslavia.[10] GRF claims it was the second-largest Islamic charity in the United States, raising about $5 million annually.[11]

The Benevolence International Foundation (BIF) began in Saudi Arabia in the late 1980s as Lajnat Al Birr Al Islamiah (LBI).[12] It was renamed when it was incorporated in the United States in 1992 as a nonprofit organization with headquarters in Burbank, Illinois.[13] It was founded by Sheikh Adel Abdul Jalil Batterjee, a wealthy Saudi Arabian, who wished to provide support for the mujahideen fighting the Soviets in Afghanistan, as well as to facilitate the immigration of jihadists into the conflict zone.[14] Evidence indicates that after the war in Afghanistan ended, BIF helped al Qaeda establish its presence in Sudan, Bosnia, and Chechnya, providing similar support for the mujahideen in those conflicts.[15] It is believed that BIF raised more than $17.5 million between 1993 and 2001.[16]

Islamic African Relief Agency (IARA), which also was known both as the Islamic American Relief Agency and the Islamic Relief Agency (ISRA), is a Sudanese-based Islamic charity group headquartered in Khartoum with branches throughout the world.[17] It is thought to have been established by the Sudanese Islamic Da'wa (Call) Organization,[18] which was formed in the 1980s to aid the spread of Islam across Africa. Sudanese students at the University of Missouri founded the US branch of IARA on February 25, 1985, to "assist in the famine crisis in Africa, particularly the Sudan region."[19] IARA-USA's headquarters remain in Columbia, Missouri, and it has regional offices throughout the country.[20] On October 13, 2004, the worldwide network of IARA and five of its senior officials were added to the list of Specially Designated Global Terrorists (SDGTs) by the US Treasury Department for financing Osama bin Laden, al Qaeda, the Taliban, Hamas, and Al Ittihad Al Islami.[21]

The International Relief Association (IRA/LIFE) is a nonprofit organization that provides humanitarian assistance to needy people throughout the world, with a particular focus on Iraq. It was incorporated as IRA in California in December 1992.[22] In 1994, IRA moved its headquarters to Michigan, and in 1998 changed its name to LIFE for Relief and Development (LIFE).[23] LIFE currently is headquartered in Southfield, Michigan, and has branches in California, Iraq, Syria, Pakistan, and Sierra Leone.[24] From 1993 to 2002, LIFE raised more than $47 million and received more than $39 million in grants;[25] it generated more than $11 million in total revenue in 2003.[26] In June 2004, LIFE's Baghdad office was raided by US troops, who seized files and computers.[27]

Mercy International is the current name of Human Concern International (HCI), a charitable organization whose first branch in the United States was established in Denver, Colorado, in 1986.[28] One of HCI's primary projects was to raise funds for the Afghan jihad against the Soviets while also distributing funds to Muslims in Africa and Lebanon and to Palestinians in Jordan.[29] In 1988, HCI incorporated in Garden City, Michigan, and in 1989 it officially changed its name to Mercy International.[30]

Remarks at the 1993 MAYA (Muslim Arab Youth Association) conference left no doubt about the purpose and motivation of HCI or its new incarnation, Mercy International:

> The Jews have conquered every place in Jerusalem, Mosques were violated in Gaza, Quran books have been torn and urinated upon. I ask of you to do something for the rights of your brothers. The HCI is the right place for this case. I speak to you on behalf of Mercy International that operates in the Bosnian arena. These two institutions are the only one who deals with the situation. HCI represents both of these bodies so you can give the money to them.[31]

The International Relief Organization (IRO) is a Virginia nonprofit corporation that serves as a "United States arm" of the Jeddah-based International Islamic Relief Organization (IIRO). It was established in July 1991. IIRO itself is a major financial branch of the Saudi "evangelical charity" organization known as Al Rabita Al Alami Al Islamiya, or the Muslim World League (MWL).[32]

Founded in 1962 to "promote Islamic unity," the MWL is one of the largest of the Saudi Islamic evangelical charities.[33] Around 1993, in conversations with Jamal Ahmed al-Fadl (then a senior al Qaeda lieutenant), bin Laden identified MWL as one of three Muslim charities that were primary sources of al Qaeda's funds.[34] MWL's US office was raided in 2002 as part of the Green Quest terrorism-financing probe.[35]

IRO's mission is to fund institutions, groups, and individuals in sympathy with its parent organizations—IIRO and MWL—in effect promoting the Wahhabi brand of Islam throughout the world. Often this promotion includes funding radical jihadist causes. Western intelligence sources have traced IIRO money transfers to bank accounts in London, England, and in Amman, Jordan. The funds then are channeled through front groups to Palestinian organizations in Gaza and the West Bank tied to Hamas.[36] IRO also has played a role in funding terrorism using business fronts, as discussed below.

The FBI raided IRO's Virginia office in 1997 as part of an investigation into money laundering and terrorism. FBI agent Valerie Donohue declared in an affidavit: "IRO holds itself out to the public as a charitable organization, but has disbursed significant sums of money in ways that do not appear consistent with a charitable mission."[37]

In 2002, Operation Green Quest agents (a multiagency task force on terrorist financing established in October 2001) raided IRO again.[38] In 2004, IRO was also under investigation by the Senate Finance Committee for its possible terrorist ties.[39] In August 2006, the US Treasury Department designated IIRO's branch offices in the Philippines and Indonesia for "fundraising for al Qaeda and affiliated terrorist groups."[40]

Domestic and International Cooperation

In addition to establishing a charity council, these charities and their leadership have cooperated on overseas fund-raising operations. Within the United States, their leaders spoke together at events and "informative" conferences to help raise funds for other charities affiliated with terror organizations. Often these events featured prominent radical Islamic leaders who supported terrorism. The main speaker at an April 1996 LIFE fund-raiser was Sheikh Abdulmunem Abu Zant, a militant Jordanian cleric who has lauded Hamas and called for war against Western "infidels."

In August 1990, Sheikh Abu Zant thundered in a sermon:

> May God attack the Jews and those who stand with them. May God attack the Americans and those who stand with them. May God attack the Soviets and those who stand with them. May God attack the English and French and those who stand with them. May God destroy completely America and enslave the Jews for rejecting the "Islamic way." We call for a people's war."[41]

During the 1991 Gulf War, Abu Zant became famous for his virulent public exhortations of violence against Western "infidels." According to Abu Zant, it was "not a war between Iraq and the U.S., but rather one between Islam and the infidels."[42] In October 1999, Abu Zant gave a fiery series of sermons denouncing the Jordanian government's restrictions on Hamas's activity in the kingdom. The sermons were so militant that Jordanian authorities summarily arrested him.[43]

At Islamic conferences held annually in locations across the United States, leaders of the seven charities would come together on panels primarily to raise funds. Frequently, the host for these gatherings was the Islamic Society of North America (ISNA).

Sami al-Arian, who is discussed in depth in chapter 7, was one of ISNA's cosponsors.[44] Al-Arian was indicted on February 20, 2003, for allegedly serving as the North American leader of Palestinian Islamic Jihad (PIJ), which has been designated as a terrorist organization by the US government and has acknowledged responsibility for the deaths of two Americans and more than a hundred Israelis.[45] Although al-Arian was acquitted of several charges against him, the jury remained deadlocked on most of the charges, including conspiracy to support a terrorist organization.[46] During the trial, al-Arian's lawyers conceded the fact that al-Arian was "affiliated" with PIJ.[47] In a plea deal, al-Arian agreed to plead guilty to the charge of "conspiracy to make or receive contributions of funds, goods, or services to or for the benefit of the Palestinian Islamic Jihad."[48] On May 1, 2006, al-Arian was sentenced to fifty-seven months in prison[49] and will be deported upon completion of his sentence. For a thorough treatment of al-Arian's activities, see chapter 7.

ISNA's radical roots go far beyond al-Arian. In 1986, ISNA gave $170,000 in start-up capital to IARA.[50] In addition, the Holy Land Foundation (then known as the Occupied Land Fund, or OLF), was initially located at the same address as ISNA[51] and, in 1992, ISNA donated at least $14,384 to the Occupied Land Fund.[52] Finally, in a letter published in 1997 by the *Washington Report on Middle East Affairs*, Hamas leader Musa Abu Marzook thanked ISNA for supporting him while he was in prison in the United States awaiting extradition to Israel.[53]

ISNA has defended an array of terrorists and terrorist charities. When HLF was shut down in December 2001, ISNA issued a joint statement with seven other Islamic groups:[54]

> American Muslims support President Bush's effort to cut off funding for terrorism and we call for a peaceful resolution to the Middle East conflict. These goals will not be achieved by taking food out of the mouths of Palestinian orphans or by succumbing to politically-motivated smear campaigns by those who would perpetuate Israel's brutal occupation.[55] . . .
>
> We ask that President Bush reconsider what we believe is an unjust and counterproductive move that can only damage America's credibility with Muslims in this country and around the world and could create the impression that there has been a shift from a war on terrorism to an attack on Islam.[56]

According to the *Washington Post*, ISNA is one of at least two dozen Muslim groups whose financial records were being probed by the Senate Finance Committee "as part of a widening congressional investigation into alleged ties between tax-exempt organizations and terrorist groups."[57]

In late 2005, Senator Grassley announced that the Senate Finance Committee's inquiry regarding these charities was completed. Senator Grassley released a statement on December 6, 2005, which explained that, while the review was complete, "[t]he fact that the Committee has taken no public action based on the review does not mean that these groups have been 'cleared' by the Committee."[58] The statement went on to clarify that the reason for the review was to fulfill oversight obligations and to explore possibilities for legislation, and that these responsibilities would continue to be fulfilled in relation to charities designated by the Treasury Department and "other similar charities that come to the Committee's attention."[59] Certain Islamic groups, notably ISNA, issued releases that falsely claimed that they had been "cleared," and that the committee's actions amounted to a "fishing expedition."[60]

The seven organizations also frequently supported each other financially. For example, IRO gave significant intercharity donations during the 1990s:[61] $10,000 in 1992 to IARA; $21,980 in 1996, $1,800 in 1997, and $300 in 1998 to HLF;[62] $156,768 and $40,060 in 1996 and 1997, respectively, to Mercy International Canada (which may be linked to Mercy USA);[63]

and $10,000 in 1995 and $300 in 1998 to IRA/LIFE.[64] Similarly, HLF donated $10,000 to IRA/LIFE in 1995 and created the "HLF-Iraq Fund" to support their efforts in Iraq.[65]

At least one fund-raiser has been employed by more than one of the seven charities. Abdel Jabbar Hamdan worked first as a top HLF fund-raiser and then for LIFE.[66] On the same day that HLF and seven of its top officials were indicted, Hamdan was arrested on immigration violations.[67] Hamdan has since been ordered deported.

In general, each charity targeted a specific region abroad as the focus of its efforts. HLF's primary interest was Palestine and supporting Hamas, while BIF focused on Bosnia and to a lesser extent Chechnya,[68] supporting jihad fighters in those regions with links to al Qaeda. IRA/LIFE paid special attention to projects in Iraq, while IARA concentrated on Africa and in particular Sudan.

As a lesser priority, these organizations also offered support in unstable regions beyond those areas that were their main concern. For example, HLF worked on projects in the Balkans, in Chechnya, and throughout the Middle East, which may or may not have involved the financing of terrorism, and BIF had a long history of supporting jihad groups around the world.[69] The charity supported terrorist and militant groups, beginning with the Afghan mujahideen (who gave rise to al Qaeda). Later, BIF allegedly lent its support to the fighters in Sudan and assisted Islamic militants and fighters first in Bosnia-Herzegovina and then in Chechnya.[70]

At times, these charities would undertake joint projects and initiatives. LIFE sponsored orphans in Iraq and advertised that they established a sewing training center with Mercy International in the early 2000s.[71] In 1998, BIF coordinated some of its efforts abroad with other charities; it reported "perform[ing] $7,640 worth of Zabiha (feeding the needy) in Afghanistan on behalf of IRA" and "$5,785 worth in Chechnya for IRO."[72] BIF also worked with HLF to "set up medical relief projects for the Palestinians."[73] GRF and IARA conducted joint projects in Somalia.[74] HLF and GRF were listed on the Web site of Interpal,[75] a UK-based charity that was designated in 2003 by the US Treasury for funding Hamas.[76] Donations were collected in the name of GRF, but the bank account information provided was for HLF.[77]

In their cooperative work abroad, these charities often dealt with the same foreign-based organizations. LIFE and HLF both worked closely with the Jordan branch of Human Appeal International (HAI), a charity with ties to Hamas.[78] Forms filed by HLF with the IRS show that it gave HAI-Jordan $31,475 in 1997, $105,236 in 1998, $281,608 in 1999, and $233,377 from January to September 2000. Between January 1997 and April 1999, $34,745 was transferred.[79]

HAI-Jordan and HLF were also connected through overlapping leadership. According to a 2001 FBI memo:

> FBI investigation has determined that Bassam Fares was the HLFRD's Projects and Grants Director, from February 1997 until his voluntary removal from the United States in 2000. Fares held a senior HLF position. From April 1990 through May 1993, Fares was the Deputy Regional Manager for HAI in Jordan. . . . It currently appears that HAI-Jordan could be serving as a conduit through which the HLFRD sends funds to its HLFRD representative in Amman. The HLFRD is not licensed to operate in Jordan, and thus cannot legally have an office or bank account in Amman, Jordan. It is likely that this close relationship with the HAI allows the HLFRD to circumvent this restriction on its activities.[80]

Humanitarian Projects

There is little doubt that charitable organizations that are or may be linked to terrorism financing have also, both independently and jointly, engaged in humanitarian projects aimed at improving the lives and general welfare of people in certain regions. Frequently, however, these selective humanitarian actions were undertaken in conjunction with a campaign to generate momentum and support for radical Islamic causes that continue to use terrorism as a means to accomplish goals.

BIF (discussed later in this chapter) reportedly has done significant amounts of charitable work, albeit on a selective basis.[81] The question is whether, acting under this guise, it also has supplied funds to jihadist fighters linked to al Qaeda and other terrorist organizations. HLF actively worked to relieve the suffering of Palestinian families, but it was selective. Most of the families HLF supported were relatives of known Hamas members who had been wounded, killed, or deported. This kind of "charity," intentional or otherwise, serves to assist Hamas's recruitment and terrorist reward efforts in the West Bank and Gaza.[82]

A large number of individual and corporate donors were unaware that Islamic charities were financing terrorism from the United States. Most were likely duped by a humanitarian veneer and propaganda. BIF, which described itself as "a humanitarian organization dedicated to helping those afflicted by wars,"[83] stated that it provided short-term relief (such as emergency food distribution) and funded long-term projects to bring "education and self-sufficiency to the children, widowed, refugees, injured and staff of vital governmental institutions."[84] Most corporate and other "arms-length" donors, such as those using the English version of BIF's Web site to make contributions, were apparently led to believe that BIF's mission was to support "purely relief" efforts in areas with significant Muslim populations.[85] Indeed, BIF board members were very cautious when considering to what degree, and to whom, they should reveal BIF's agenda to support jihadist endeavors.[86]

Methods and Sources of Funding Terror

US-based charities that are or may be financing terrorism are involved in a variety of fund-raising activities. These include

- sponsoring or speaking at conferences
- staffing booths at conferences
- collecting donations at mosques
- sponsoring radical Islamic speakers and terrorist leaders
- partnering with businesses and Islamic organizations
- publishing newsletters
- advertising in Islamic publications and distributing promotional videos and audiotapes
- maintaining Web sites with donation pages

Fund-raising relies on individual, corporate, and other institutional donations from foreign and domestic sources. Many charities also are involved in profit sharing with businesses, and they generate income by investing in the stock market and elsewhere. They can transfer money to terrorist groups directly through their offices abroad and indirectly through committees, centers affiliated with terrorist organizations, or other charities involved in or suspected of financing terrorism. In short, legitimate means can be deployed for illegitimate purposes.

THE HOLY LAND FOUNDATION

Holy Land Foundation Indicted

In July 2004, the Holy Land Foundation, Mohammed el-Mezain, and six of its other leaders were named in a forty-two-count indictment for providing material support to Hamas, engaging in prohibited financial transactions with a Specially Designated Global Terrorist, money laundering, conspiracy, and filing false tax returns.[87] As noted at the beginning of this chapter, HLF was accused of illegally sending millions of dollars to support Hamas.

In addition to holding a key position with HLF, el-Mezain was one of the founders and the first imam of the Islamic Center of Passaic County (ICPC) in New Jersey.[88] FBI assistant director Dale Watson wrote in a memorandum on November 5, 2001:

> HLFRD-1, an FBI source who has provided reliable information in the past reported that during a speech at the Islamic Center of Passaic County (ICPC) in November, 1994, Mohammad El Mezain, the HLFRD's (Holy Land Foundation for Relief and Development) current Director of Endowments and former Chairman of the HLFRD Board, admitted that some of the money collected by the ICPC and the HLFRD goes to Hamas or Hamas activities in Israel.[89]

On behalf of IAP, at a 1992 MAYA conference, el-Mesain pleaded with audience members to support families of martyrs:

> Do you want to pay money for the sake of Allah? Answer maybe yes or no. If you say yes, say Allahu Akhbar. (Audience repeats Allahu Akhbar)
>
> Do you want to look after the children of the martyrs? Answer maybe yes or no. If you say yes, say Allahu Akhbar. (Audience repeats Allahu Akhbar)
>
> The Prophet Muhammad said those who participate in the preparation for the fighters of Allah as if they fought themselves and those who look after the family of the fighters for Allah as if they fought by themselves. Do you want to do so? Say Allahu Akbar.[90]

The methods and sources of that financing are discussed below and the details of the Holy Land Foundation's origins and connections to Hamas's leadership are described in chapter 5. HLF enjoyed great success as its assets increased significantly over the years. In 1992, HLF raised about $2 million. By 1998, that amount had more than doubled to $5 million, and, by 2000, it reached $13 million.[91]

Methods of Financing

HLF officials used a variety of methods to raise funds. During the late 1980s and early 1990s, HLF openly solicited money for Hamas, and its intentions were widely known or understood within some segments of the Muslim community. An HLF official in Israel described the US Islamic conferences to his Israeli interrogators:

> These conferences would be held in large centers all over the United States, in Islamic centers—in gathering halls. Between hundreds and thousands of Muslim people would attend these conferences and, regarding your question, the advertisements for these conferences was advertised through the newspapers, TV and cable ads, me, myself, I saw ads which appeared also in the newspapers in the English language.
>
> During the conferences, even though there is freedom of speech, it is impossible to talk about everything, even the word Hamas, you cannot say it during these conferences because not all of the people who attend the conference support Hamas and not all of them are Muslims. Of course, regarding your question, the Muslims who attended those conferences knew that the institute—The Holy Land Foundation—supports Hamas.[92]

After the signing of the Oslo Accords between Israel and the Palestinian Liberation Organization (PLO) in 1993, and as the US government moved to designate Hamas a foreign terrorist organization (FTO) (that action was completed in 1997), a crackdown on the Hamas leadership in the United States began. During this time, HLF increased its efforts to disguise its relationship with Hamas. As the indictment against HLF notes:

> After the designation, upon instruction by the HLF, the speakers changed tactics by using inflammatory language which was designed to support HAMAS and its violent activities without openly mentioning HAMAS.[93]

Conferences and Lectures

In the 1990s and after, HLF both hosted fund-raisers and maintained booths at various Islamic conferences throughout the United States. A typical fund-raising event sponsored by the charity, held in Chicago on August 2, 1998, was titled "Fifty Years of Education through Occupation." During these events, the foundation's members would peddle newsletters, videotapes, and other materials, while its leaders, such as Shukri Abu Bakr and Mohammed el-Mezain, would lecture conference attendees on various Islamic topics, including supporting the Islamic resistance in Palestine. At times, HLF representatives performed skits and songs that glorified killing Jews and advocated the destruction of Israel.[94]

At an HLF fund-raiser in Buena Park, California, on September 30, 1997, Shukri Abu Bakr declared that conference participants owed the people fighting for the Islamic state in the West Bank and Gaza Strip their financial support by giving to HLF, and that the goal of Hamas to form an Islamic state could not be thwarted.[95]

HLF promotional materials also were common at the Islamic conferences held by such organizations as the Islamic Association for Palestine (IAP), the Islamic Society of North America (ISNA), the Muslim Arab Youth Association (MAYA), and the Islamic Assembly of North America (IANA).

Video and audio recordings available and often featured at these conferences and events lionized the efforts of Islamic charities and *zakat* committees (i.e., committees for charitable giving), most of which were aligned with Hamas. For instance, promotional videos such as *The Massacres of Lebanon and Our Relief Work* focused on the foundation's aid to and relief work in Muslim countries. Ultimately, these tapes promoted the Islamic resistance in Palestine and elsewhere and helped raise funds for these causes.

During the early 1990s, HLF invited and paid the travel expenses of senior Hamas leaders to speak at Islamic conferences in the United States—notably Jamil Hamami and Sheikh Muhammad Siyam, who addressed fund-raising events between September 1990 and November 1991.[96] This sponsorship of senior Hamas leaders continued through the latter half of 1994.[97]

HLF Publications and Advertisements

From its inception as the Occupied Land Fund (OLF), HLF secured funds through solicitations, advertisements, and official statements in Islamic publications and newsletters, specifically the IAP's publications: *Ila Filastin* (later *Al Zaitounah*) and the *Muslim World Monitor*. One solicitation in *Ila Filastin* solicitation urged readers to send checks to the Occupied Land Fund in Plainfield, Indiana, by praising the intifada: "Allahu Akbar [God is Great] to the continuing Intifada."[98] Similarly, a communiqué from the Islamic Association of Palestine (IAP) Information Office in December 1989 urged donors to give to the Occupied Land Fund and take part in "Jihad for the sake of Allah by donating . . . in support of the Intifada's families." The communiqué declared, "The only way to liberate Palestine, all Palestine, is by way of Jihad," and "The Islamic Resistance Movement (Hamas) is the conscience of the Palestinian people."[99]

HLF published periodical newsletters such as *S.H.A.R.E.* (i.e., "serve, help, aid, rescue, and educate"), *HLF News,* and *The Holy Land Foundation Newsletter* to increase awareness of the Palestinian and other Islamic causes among the Muslim community in the United States, and thus increase donations. During Ramadan in 1998, for example, HLF included an insert in *HLF News* soliciting check and credit card donations to provide food and medicine to the poor as well as to meet other charitable ends. In this same issue, the foundation presented its partnership with the American Airlines Advantage Program whereby donors could earn American Airlines Advantage miles by donating to HLF.[100]

HLF also relied heavily on advertisements in Islamic publications, in both Arabic and English. Beginning at least as early as October 1988, the charity ran fifteen ads in IAP's Arabic publication *Ila Filastin;* they continued after the paper became *Al Zaitounah* in 1991. Advertisements for HLF— each featuring an address to which donations could be mailed— appeared no fewer than 189 times in *Al Zaitounah* before HLF was named a specially designated global terrorist by the US government in December 2001.

Web Sites and Electronic Mailings

Starting in the late 1990s, HLF maintained a Web site that solicited donations from visitors to help Bosnians, Palestinians, and other Muslims living in impoverished regions of the world.

Islamic advocacy groups such as the Council on American-Islamic Relations (CAIR) and the Islamic Association for Palestine (IAP) also engaged in fund-raising for HLF via the Internet. CAIR sent an e-mail to subscribers on its electronic mailing list in 1996 calling on American Muslims, mosques, and Islamic centers to pray for Palestinians and to demand action from politicians after Israel opened a tunnel below the Temple Mount and Dome of the Rock in Jerusalem. CAIR urged "every mosque [to] ask each person for at least one dollar . . . to be sent to the Holy Land Foundation for Relief and Development."[101] The telephone number, fax number, and address of the foundation were provided.

During the summer of 2000, HLF began to offer on its Web site a link called greatergood.com, which enabled online shoppers to access at least eighty brand-name stores such as Amazon.com and the Gap. HLF would receive up to 15 percent of the value of all sales that were made through its Web site.[102] A "Matching Gift Program" was created around the same time, allowing corporations such as Microsoft, Ericsson, American Express, Home Depot, and Reuters to match their employees' charitable contributions to HLF.[103] While particular organizations may have been or may still be on approved lists of organizations for which a corporation will match donations, this does not mean that said corporations approve of or have full knowledge of a charitable organization's activities. HLF was responsible for the abuse of these programs, not the corporations involved in the matching; however, it is clear that more oversight by corporations in these programs is needed.

HLF took part in the 101 Days Campaign—a fund-raising campaign. Some of the Islamic charitable organizations taking part are suspected or known financiers of terrorism in North America, Europe, the Middle East, and Africa. These included the Al Aqsa Foundation in Germany, Interpal (which ran the campaign's Web site) and Human Appeal in the United Kingdom, and the World Assembly of Muslim Youth (WAMY) in Saudi Arabia.

The names of HLF and another SDGT charity, the Global Relief Foundation, appear when someone wishing to make an online donation visits the US section of the 101 Days Web site.[104] There, money for the Al Aqsa Intifada is collected by GRF through the bank account of HLF.[105]

The 101 Days Campaign was featured as a link on Hamas's official Web site (the Palestine Information Center). The Arabic version of the Internet page offers a link to the personal Web page of the campaign's chairman, the militant Islamist cleric Sheikh Yusuf al-Qaradawi.[106] Other board members include the Grand Mufti of Jerusalem, Sheikh Ikremah Sabri,[107] who has extolled suicide bombings on numerous occasions.[108]

Sources of Financing

Donations from individuals, corporations, and other institutions, foreign and domestic, constitute most of the funding for HLF charity activities.

However, the charity did invest in a variety of stocks and funds through US investment firms over the years. For instance, of the more than $6.6 million that HLF collected in 1999, $6.3 million came from direct and indirect public support and around $250,000 from investments.[109] HLF is believed to have invested some of the funds it raised, resulting in additional profits.[110]

Individuals, including those with ties to terrorism, contributed significant amounts to the foundation. In the late 1980s and early 1990s, as noted earlier, HLF received a $210,000 donation from Musa Abu Marzook, $22,450 from Marzook's personal secretary, Nasser al-Khatib, and other substantial individual donations as well.[111]

HLF received corporate donations.[112] The foundation also received sizable contributions from Islamic charities and organizations. In 1992, ISNA donated at least $14,384 to the Occupied Land Fund.[113] IRO gave $21,980 in 1996 and $1,800 in 1997 to HLF[114] and its parent organization; IIRO may also have donated funds. In 1997, HLF received three Safa Trust checks, in the amounts of $75,000, $87,500, and $162,500, which were all signed by a primary SAAR Network officer, Yaqub Mirza.[115]

In 1999 and 2000, the International Education Trust, a SAAR Network organization whose president was Mohammed Jaghlit, donated a total of $37,200 to HLF.[116] The SAAR Network (discussed in greater depth in chapter 10) was described by US law enforcement agents as "a group of individuals that are suspected of providing material support to terrorist, money laundering, and tax evasion through the use of a variety of related for-profit companies and ostensible charitable entities under their control, most of which are located at 555 Grove Street, Herndon, Virginia."[117] Smaller donations came from Islamic academic institutions, such as an Islamic academy in Michigan, which gave $150 to HLF in 1998.[118]

HLF's fund-raising efforts at Islamic conferences and events were often very productive. Although the groups never published fund-raising results, it is believed that HLF director of endowments Mohammed el-Mezain and others collected nearly $200,000 from attendees at just three conferences in 1999 and 2000.

In addition, as noted in chapter 6, the money that the Islamic Association for Palestine raised during IAP's intifada celebrations in the late 1980s and early 1990s all went to HLF (or the Occupied Land Fund, as it was then known).[119] All the proceeds from IAP's 1996 convention also went to HLF.[120]

HLF got its funds from other sources as well. The Bridgeview Mosque in Illinois, long suspected by federal officials of ties to Hamas, has given the Holy Land Foundation more than $175,000 since 1991.[121] After he was arrested in Israel in 1998 for transferring money to terrorist organizations, Jamal Sarsour implicated members of the Islamic Center of Milwaukee in a fund-raising scheme for HLF.[122] Mohammed al-Hanooti, former director of the Islamic Center of New Jersey and a frequent guest speaker at the Dar Al Hijrah Mosque in Falls Church, Virginia, collected more than $6 million to support Hamas, according to an FBI memo,[123]and some or most of this is believed to have been funneled to the terrorist organization via HLF. Not surprisingly, mosques and Islamic centers in or near Texas, where HLF is headquartered, gave significant donations to HLF and other charities. In one session during Friday prayers at the Islamic Association of North Texas in 1999, $50,000 was raised for HLF and other relief groups that focused on refugees.[124]

Before its assets were frozen, HLF was on USAID's list of private voluntary organizations. However, USAID terminated this relationship in September 2000 after a letter from Thomas R. Pickering, then undersecretary of state for political affairs, was sent to USAID's administrator, J. Brady Anderson, advising that "any financial relationship between USAID and the Holy Land Foundation for Relief and Development would likewise be contrary to the national defense and foreign policy interests of the United States."[125]

Transferring the Money

HLF financed Hamas in at least three ways, according to FBI investigators:

- Direct fund transfers from the HLFRD office in Richardson, Texas, to the HLFRD offices in the West Bank and Gaza
- Transfers of funds from the HLFRD Richardson office to *zakat* (Islamic charity) committees located in the West Bank and Gaza, controlled by HAMAS
- Transfers of funds from the HLFRD Richardson office in Texas to other "charitable" organizations in the Middle East not controlled by but believed to be supporting HAMAS[126]

During the late 1980s and early 1990s, HLF's annual budget in the West Bank and Gaza Strip was about $1 million.[127] Significant amounts of money often moved from HLF headquarters in the United States, mainly to three HLF offices in the West Bank and Gaza Strip. Money was then distributed to Hamas-controlled or -affiliated organizations, and to family members of "martyred" or jailed individuals connected to terrorism. Between 1999 and 2000, the HLF office in Hebron received at least $1,443,983; from 1997 to 2000, the Gaza office received at least $591,084.[128]

In an effort to disguise the ultimate end of donations, HLF often passed money through Hamas-controlled committees in the West Bank and Gaza Strip, including the Ramallah Zakat Committee and the Islamic Charity Society of Hebron. Money would then be moved from these affiliated committees to Hamas operatives or their affiliates. From 1997 until September 1999, the Ramallah Zakat Committee received $244,707, and the Islamic Charitable Society of Hebron received $1,155,386.[129]

HLF channeled money to at least two charity organizations in the Middle East outside Israel, the West Bank, and the Gaza Strip known to have ties to Hamas: the Lebanese-based Sanabil Association for Relief and Development (Sanabil) and the Jordanian-based Human Appeal International (HAI). HLF sent $1,463,345 to Sanabil and $651,696 to HAI from 1997 to September 2000.[130]

BENEVOLENCE INTERNATIONAL FOUNDATION

The Benevolence International Foundation (BIF) began operating in the United States in the early 1990s. After the war in Afghanistan ended, BIF helped al Qaeda establish its presence in Sudan, Bosnia, and Chechnya, providing similar support for the mujahideen in those conflicts as well. On November 19, 2002, the US government named BIF a Specially Designated Global Terrorist. [131]

Background

BIF, headquartered in Palos Hills, Illinois, was incorporated as a nonprofit organization in March 1992.[132] BIF described itself as "a humanitarian organization dedicated to helping those afflicted by wars," providing both emergency short-term relief and work on building the infrastructure for long-term improvements.[133] Visitors to BIF's English-language Web site were informed that the group's mission involved supporting "purely relief" efforts in locations with large Muslim populations.[134] The organization did support numerous charitable programs.[135] However, BIF board members weighed carefully to what degree, and to whom, BIF's agenda to support jihadist endeavors were to be made public.[136]

BIF is an outgrowth of two organizations. The first was Al Bir Al Dawalia (Arabic for "Benevolence International"), which was founded by Saudi Sheikh Adel Abdul Jalil Batterjee in the 1980s.[137] Batterjee originally founded the group to support the mujahideen battling the Soviet forces in Afghanistan, and to help shuttle jihadists in and out of the war zone. Batterjee is also linked to the "Golden Chain"—the group of wealthy donors from the Arabian Gulf area that supplied the bulk of the early financing for al Qaeda.[138] Batterjee is listed as a director on BIF's 1992 Articles of Incorporation[139] and as the president of BIF on its 1993 tax return.[140]

The second organization was another Saudi "relief" organization, Lajnat Al Birr Al Islamiah (LBI) (Arabic for the "Islamic Benevolence Committee"), established in Pakistan and run out of Saudi Arabia.[141] Another BIF principal, Enaam Arnaout, had worked for LBI since 1987.[142]

According to tax forms from 1993 to 2001, BIF raised more than $17.5 million.[143] It was also in 1993, according to the minutes of a BIF board meeting, that Enaam Arnaout, Zakaria Khudeira, and Jamal Nyrbe replaced BIF's original board of directors—Batterjee and two other Saudis. According to the minutes, Arnaout, whose position at the time was coordinator of BIF-USA, was selected to run BIF "since everyone knew, worked with, and trusted Mr. Arnaout." The minutes suggest that BIF had not accomplished much in the way of fund-raising in the United States before Arnaout took control. But despite the change in personnel, internal BIF communications indicate that Batterjee continued to play a significant supervisory role at BIF.[144] It remains unclear what percentage or amount of the total raised was funneled toward support of violent jihadist causes under Arnaout's management of BIF. The foundation has not been accused of raising money specifically for any terrorist attacks on American soil or against American interests abroad.

It is thought, however, that BIF operated as money launderers for al Qaeda, providing an alternative to the financing mechanism of *hawala*. *Hawala* is a method of transferring sums of money without actually physically moving any, usually by utilizing family or regional connections.[145] Set up as a nonprofit charitable corporation, BIF could advertise at mosques, in Arab and Islamic newspapers and periodicals, and in its own newsletters. In all these places, BIF implored Muslims to donate money to aid orphans and widows in war zones such as Bosnia, Chechnya, and Sudan.[146]

In response to the 9/11 attacks, the Justice Department took action against organizations it believed had been involved in the financing of al Qaeda by seizing their assets, raiding their offices, or both.[147] On December 14, 2001, a search warrant was issued for BIF's Illinois headquarters and its assets were frozen.[148] At the time, BIF had ten employees in the United States.[149] The FBI seized, among other items, financial documents and many other files, as well as literature and videos promoting jihad and glorifying "martyrdom."[150] On March 19, 2002, Bosnian law enforcement officials raided BIF's Sarajevo office and found a cache of weapons, false identity documents, and plans for explosives.[151] On November 19, 2002, BIF was named a global terrorist organization.[152] That same day, the United Kingdom froze all BIF assets in British financial institutions, citing the US designation to justify the action.[153]

In addition to the Illinois office, BIF had an office in Newark, New Jersey, and ten foreign offices—in Azerbaijan, Bangladesh, Bosnia, Canada, China, Dagestan, and Yemen.[154]

Mission of BIF

Arnaout worked directly with bin Laden in Afghanistan, often as his driver, and managed the mujahideen military camps. His duties included purchasing supplies such as weapons and food. In 1991, after the leadership of al Qaeda moved from Afghanistan to Sudan, BIF opened an office in Khartoum—according to the US government, "specifically to support al Qaeda and the *mujahideen* in the Sudan."[155] It was in the following year that BIF incorporated in Illinois.

The federal government argued that for years BIF acted in support of violent jihad around the world, remaining consistent in its methods but adapting its organization and outreach as the numbers of terrorists and militants expanded around the globe. BIF's support for such groups encompassed the mujahideen and ultimately al Qaeda. Its leadership collaborated at various times with bin Laden and members of his al Qaeda network and with the Afghan warlord Gulbuddin Hekmatyar and his group, the Hizb al Islami (Islamic Party).[156] BIF lent its support where the Islamic militants fought—in Sudan, in Bosnia-Herzegovina, and in Chechnya.[157]

BIF, through its leadership, conspired with individuals associated with these groups in meetings in Afghanistan and Pakistan from the late 1980s on, for the purpose of exporting violent jihad from Afghanistan. As early as 1992, BIF provided food, clothing, money, and communications equipment to the "Black Swans," an Islamic paramilitary unit in Bosnia.[158]

BIF operated in the same manner as other charities that funded al Qaeda. It solicited funds through advertisements, fund-raisers, and brochures. The money would then be placed in various accounts; as cash was withdrawn, a portion would be used for legitimate relief purposes and another portion diverted to al Qaeda operations. All the money used for the latter would be listed in BIF's books as "expenses for building mosques or schools or feeding the poor or the needy."[159]

In 1995, BIF opened an office in Chechnya and began delivering material support and military equipment, including antimine boots, an x-ray machine, military uniforms, and cash to the Chechen mujahideen. BIF raised the money for this endeavor by claiming that the funds were needed for "winter shoes for Chechen civilians."[160]

Employees of Both BIF and Terrorist Organizations

Saif ul-Islam, an Egyptian lawyer, was both an al Qaeda military commander and the BIF officer in Grozny, Chechnya.[161] Gul Muhammed was a BIF officer in Baku, Azerbaijan, as well as Hizb al Islami's Azeri representative.[162] An al Qaeda operative, Mohamed Bayazid (see below), gave BIF's Illinois address as his residence when he applied for a driver's license.[163]

Members of the BIF leadership, particularly Arnaout, were charged with procuring money and supplies for al Qaeda, as well as bearing various al Qaeda communications. BIF offices held many al Qaeda–related documents, in both electronic and paper form. Now in the possession of law enforcement agencies, these include letters signed by bin Laden that direct payment of the salaries of military commanders from the "charitable" funds. [164]

BIF also had a *Tareekh Osama* (or "Osama's History") file in its possession, apparently made near the end of the Afghan-Soviet conflict, which listed a number of goals. Among them were "holding a mass media event to collect in-kind donations . . . clarifying the Mujahideen's situation in the world and keeping the spirit of Jihad alive . . . , forming a committee to receive donations and maintain an account and the spending . . . , sending some brethren to secure provisions for the Mujahideen."[165] BIF files also contained scanned copies of handwritten documents described by the US government as "chronicling the origins of al Qaeda which were not known to the public."[166] One of these recorded the minutes of a 1988 meeting between the future BIF president Mohamed Loay Bayazid and Osama bin Laden, as they discussed the establishment of al Qaeda and its training camps.[167]

BIF also maintained files on al Qaeda personnel and individual training camps;[168] al Qaeda requests for explosives, weaponry, and communications equipment; and a chart with radio frequencies "assigned to particular individuals."[169] The chart gave contact information for both bin Laden and Mohammed Atef, al Qaeda's senior military commander who was killed by US forces in 2001.[170]

Smaller files included requests for dynamite and bags to carry rocket-propelled grenades (RPGs), bombs, automatic rifles, ammunition magazines, hand grenades and detonators, as well as other "provisions for the front."[171] BIF files also contained receipts, in Arnaout's name, for the purchase of 250 rockets and 108 missiles, as well as a check receipt for the purchase of an additional 52 missiles.[172] The files included another receipt in Arnaout's name for a pickup truck, a price list for missiles, and orders to deliver the truck to the "Islami Khalis Party,"[173] a wing of the Hezb e Islami headed by Yunis Khalis, mentor to Afghan warlord Hekmatyar.[174]

Legal Action against BIF and BIF Employees

On December 14, 2001, the same day that BIF's offices in Palos Hills, Illinois, and Newark, New Jersey, were searched, FBI agents also searched Arnaout's home. They seized personal effects belonging to him and his family (including family photographs, Arnaout's citizenship papers, and a microphone from Arnaout's son's Nintendo game).[175]

On September 13, 2002, Arnaout was charged with knowingly and willfully making "materially false, fictitious, and fraudulent statements and representations," and having "made and used false writings and documents" knowing that those documents contained "materially false, fictitious, and fraudulent statements," in an effort to deceive the judicial branch of the United States.[176] In a sworn declaration made to a federal court in the case of *BIF v. Ashcroft*, Arnaout claimed "BIF has never provided aid or support to people or organizations known to be engaged in violence, terrorist activities, or military operations of any nature."[177]

On August 18, 2003, in Chicago, after Arnaout had pled guilty in February to racketeering conspiracy, Federal District Court judge Suzanne B. Conlon sentenced him to 136 months in prison.[178] Arnaout admitted that he "fraudulently obtained charitable donations in order to provide financial assistance to persons engaged in violent activities overseas." Arnaout also admitted that, for about a decade, BIF had defrauded donors by leading them to believe that all donations were being used strictly for humanitarian purposes, when in fact a "material amount" of the funds was diverted to fighters overseas. Finally, Arnaout specifically admitted to providing items for fighters in Chechnya and Bosnia. In addition to receiving a jail term, Arnaout was ordered to pay $315,000 in restitution to the Office of the United Nations High Commissioner for Refugees, also defrauded by his activities.[179]

In a surprise move, a federal appeals court ordered in December 2005 that Arnaout be resentenced. In a fifteen-page opinion, Judge William J. Bauer concluded that there was insufficient evidence that Arnaout defrauded more than fifty people—a number of people that serves as a specific benchmark or guideline in sentencing for this particular offense. Bauer also concluded, however, that Judge Conlon had erred in sentencing Arnaout, by failing to include the abuse of trust enhancement, which could have prompted a stiffer sentence. The opinion also stated that, while Arnaout was not convicted for a crime of terrorism, the fact that he intended to further a terrorist act should have been considered in the sentencing.[180]

On February 17, 2006, Arnaout was resentenced to a slightly more lenient period of 120 months in prison and was given credit for time he had served so far.[181]

Two other BIF employees, Mohamed Bayazid and Mohammed Jamal Khalifa, also had strong ties to terrorists. Bayazid, having given BIF's address as his own, was detained on December 16, 1994, in San Francisco along with Khalifa, who is Osama bin Laden's brother-in-law, and has been identified as a senior al Qaeda member.[182] A traveling companion who also was briefly detained was Salem bin Laden, brother of Osama. Khalifa was wanted in Jordan for his role in the bombing of the Salwa Cinema in Zarqa, and he also was linked to the 1993 World Trade Center bombing.[183]

Khalifa was convicted in absentia in Jordan. He suddenly agreed to extradition after fighting it for months, and was returned to Jordan where an appeal, conducted in secret, overturned all convictions and ordered his release.[184] Bayazid was released from custody in the United States shortly after his original detention, and immediately left the country.

Authorities believe that Bayazid assisted al Qaeda in its pursuit of uranium to develop a nuclear weapon.[185] Bayazid's whereabouts are unknown.[186] The IIRO branch in the Philippines that Khalifah founded was designated as a terrorist entity by the US Treasury Department in August 2006.[187]

In June 2004, Hassan Faraj, a native Syrian doctor and former employee of BIF in Croatia, was charged with illegally procuring his citizenship by lying about both "his refugee status and medical experience."[188] According to prosecutors, classified evidence reveals Faraj's close ties to bin Laden and bin Laden's "terrorism coordinator." Faraj also was responsible for bringing foreign recruits to Bosnian camps. Those searching his Brooklyn apartment found shredded blueprints of an overpass in the Washington, DC, area; his defense attorney claimed they did not belong to Faraj.[189]

Methods of Funding

BIF relied on a group of wealthy donors from the Persian Gulf, as well as a donor base within the Muslim community in the United States and abroad.[190] Because a member of the Saudi "Golden Chain" (discussed in chapter 10) founded BIF, it also had easy access to the Saudi elite.[191]

Like traditional American charities, BIF produced newsletters that helped raise funds in a number of ways. Soliciting direct donations, they informed the Muslim community of BIF-related and other products, such as Islamic calendars, that could be purchased at a premium, and reported on various projects which donors could "sponsor."

One such endeavor was the "Sponsor a Well" project. BIF told potential donors, "Not only will you reap the reward from Allah for the gift of water and the perpetual rewards from the continued use of the well, but also from the du'as [devotional worship] of the people who are using the well."[192] If a gift was large enough to cover the costs of an entire well, BIF promised that a plaque engraved with the donor's name would be attached to the well. BIF marketed such sponsorships as potential gifts for family members, and enclosed a form for would-be participants in the newsletter.[193]

Like most charities, BIF also urged its donors to see if their employers offered matching gift programs, which could double a donation. The group's literature provided information on how to determine whether a company participated in such a program and, if so, how to take advantage of it.[194]

GLOBAL RELIEF FOUNDATION

The Global Relief Foundation (GRF) began operating in the United States as a tax-exempt, nonprofit charitable organization in 1992 and grew into one of the largest Islamic charities in the United States.[195] The FBI began investigating GRF prior to 9/11 on the basis that GRF supported radical Islamic interests, such as the mujahideen and al Qaeda,[196] and had high-level affiliations with an al Qaeda precursor organization in Pakistan.[197] GRF was one of the few organizations registered with the Taliban (others were BIF and the Canadian Relief Foundation).[198] After 9/11, the US government froze GRF's assets, initiated a criminal investigation into its activities, and arrested and ultimately deported its chief executive, Rabih Haddad.[199]

Background

Based in Bridgeview, Illinois, GRF had an initial budget of about $700,000.[200] By the end of the 1990s, GRF was reporting more than $5 million in annual contributions.[201] GRF's IRS filings indicate that 90 percent of the money donated between 1994 and 2000 was shipped abroad.[202] An FBI memorandum notes that "some materials distributed by GRF glorify 'martyrdom through jihad' and state that donations will be used to buy ammunition, equip 'the raiders' and support the Mujahedin."[203]

GRF had overseas registered offices in Islamabad, Pakistan; Brussels, Belgium; Sarajevo, Bosnia; Zagreb, Croatia; and Baku, Azerbaijan.[204] The US government believes that Rabih Haddad, GRF's cofounder, was previously a member of the Mektab Al Khidmat,[205] an organization cofounded by al Qaeda's spiritual leader, Abdullah Azzam, and Osama bin Laden in the 1980s to recruit mujahideen to fight the Soviet occupation of Afghanistan.[206] This entity (discussed in chapter 12) was later established in the United States as the Al Kifah Refugee Center and was designated as a terrorist organization on September 23, 2001. Although Haddad has denied the charge, he does admit to knowing Abdullah Azzam from "prayer meetings."[207]

The phone records collected by the FBI in its pre-9/11 full-field investigation indicate a link between GRF's executive director and bin Laden. GRF's Belgium office had logs of conversations with bin Laden's former personal secretary, Wadih el-Hage, now serving a life sentence in a US prison for his role in organizing the 1998 embassy bombings in Kenya and Tanzania. The FBI also periodically scoured GRF's trash, and over several years it collected photos of communication gear that the foundation had shipped overseas, including high-tech military-style handheld radios. Agents concluded that the equipment GRF was exporting went far beyond the needs of relief workers, and in fact was much more valuable for the creation of a military communications network. After 9/11, the agents learned that equipment had been sent to Chechnya. Also in GRF's garbage were books and literature that espoused a pro-jihadist message, including works by Abdullah Azzam.[208]

In a January 6, 2000, memo, Chicago FBI agents summarized their findings:

> Although the majority of GRF funding goes toward legitimate relief operations, a significant percentage is diverted to fund extremist causes. Among the terrorist groups known to have links to GRF are the Algerian Armed Islamic Group, the Egyptian Islamic Jihad, Gama'at Al Islamyia, and the Kashmiri Harakat Al Jihad El Islam, as well as the Al Qaeda organization of Usama Bin Laden. . . . In the past, GRF support to terrorists and other transnational mujahideen fighters has taken the form of purchase and shipment of large quantities of sophisticated communications equipment, provision of humanitarian cover documentation to suspected terrorists and fund-raising for terrorist groups under the cover of humanitarian relief.[209]

In another memorandum written January 10, the same group of case agents concluded that Rabih Haddad, in his capacity as GRF chief, "has been and continues to be a supporter of worldwide Islamic extremist activity" and that he "has past and present links and associations with a wide variety of international extremists."[210] At this stage, the FBI did not believe that GRF was formally the "humanitarian wing" of al Qaeda, but rather thought that it was a "freelance" group supporting the "pro-jihad" cause around the world, and that underwriting humanitarian aid was critical to such a mission as well.[211]

The FBI agents also believed there were two types of GRF donors: those who thought they were donating money for humanitarian causes and a select few who clearly knew the purpose of their donations was to support the global jihad. On some checks written to GRF obtained by the FBI, the donors had added "pro-jihad" statements on the memo lines.[212]

After various media outlets reported that GRF was deeply involved in terrorist fund-raising and financing, GRF sued the *New York Times*, the Associated Press, ABC, and the *Boston Globe* for defamation in November 2001. GRF argued there was no proof that it had any connections to terrorism and that the reporting on government investigations had substantially damaged the organization's reputation. The court dismissed the case on summary judgment, finding that the reporting on the governmental investigations into GRF's terrorism ties was "substantially true."[213] On December 1, 2004, a federal appeals court, the Seventh Circuit, agreed that GRF's case against the media companies was without merit, because the reports "were either true or substantially true recitations of the government's suspicions about or actions against GRF."[214]

The Treasury Department ordered GRF's assets frozen on December 14, 2001.[215] On the same day, the FBI raided GRF's Illinois offices, seized its records, and arrested its chairman, Rabih Haddad. The search warrants were executed on the same day that NATO-led peacekeepers and UN police raided GRF's offices in Yugoslavia.[216] On October 18, 2002, the Office of Foreign Assets Control designated GRF as a global terrorist organization.[217]

GRF sought redress in federal court, challenging the government's authority to shut the charity down and seeking a preliminary injunction to stop the seizure of its money and other assets.[218] The district court found in favor of the government, ruling that the Treasury Department was within its rights. One of GRF's arguments was that the International Emergency Economic Powers Act (IEEPA) did not grant the Treasury Department the authority to freeze GRF's assets, since GRF is a domestic entity.

The court disagreed, stating that "the simple act of domestic incorporation is not sufficient to exempt an organization from IEEPA regulation if, as the statute says, a foreign national has 'any interest' in the organization or its funds."[219] The district court also rejected GRF's contention that humanitarian aid was exempt from the executive branch's authority, citing the IEEPA statute granting the president the ability to block donations if he affirmatively determines that the distribution of the GRF's contributions "would seriously impair his ability to deal with any national emergency." In drafting the IEEPA, the court decision continued, "Congress enacted broad, sweeping language which authorized the President to block any and all humanitarian efforts by the targeted entity so long as he declares that the provision of such relief would jeopardize his ability to deal with a national emergency."[220]

GRF appealed the decision to the Seventh Circuit, which also upheld the government's action and solidified the law in this area, declaring:

> The Constitution would indeed be a suicide pact, if the only way to curtail enemies' access to assets were to reveal information that might cost lives. Nor does the Constitution entitle GRF to notice and a pre-seizure hearing, an opportunity that would allow any enemy to spirit assets out of the United States. Although pre-seizure hearing is the constitutional norm, postponement is acceptable in emergencies. [221]

GRF's request for leave to appeal to the US Supreme Court was denied.

The Mission of GRF

GRF described itself as a not-for-profit, nongovernmental organization set up to provide humanitarian and charitable relief to Muslims, especially in conflict zones such as Afghanistan, Bosnia, Chechnya, Kashmir, and Lebanon through a series of overseas offices.[222] In addition to undertaking this charitable work, however, the organization served as a propaganda organ for global jihad, and the federal government believes that GRF funded violent jihadist activity as well.[223]

Al-Thilal (*The Shadow*), a magazine published by GRF, spread not the social welfare messages one might expect from a humanitarian organization but anti-Semitic and anti-American propaganda that called for jihad across the world, especially in Palestine, Bosnia, and Kashmir. For example, the January 1996 issue contains the following statements:

> The sending of American troops to Bosnia has brought up the issue of attacks upon the Mujahideen in Bosnia, particularly those who came from all over the world, most of them having graduated from the school of Jihad in Afghanistan. Those Mujahideen are a nightmare for the American troops in Bosnia. The presence of Al Anssar (Mujahideen) in Bosnia causes the Bosnian nation to stay true to their Islamic values and open their mind to Jihad and the love of martyrdom for Allah. The ethnic cleansing of the war in Bosnia is going to finish the Moslem nation there, so we have to fight (the Jews and the Christian will never be pleased until you follow them). To give your money for Allah is like Jihad fighting for Allah—it is a must for all the Umma of Islam. As Allah

> sends to us his book and the balance, he also gave us the iron because the Dawa (preaching) of Islam needs men for its protection. This protection is by iron (the weapons) the brothers Mujahideen established their association on this base (Jihad & Dawa) that means preach and fight. The Mujhideen have school which graduate hundreds of Mujahideen each month, those fighters win all their battle because thy love of martyrdom for Allah, and their enemy don't want to die.[224]

A pamphlet produced by GRF in 1995 declares, "God equated martyrdom through JIHAD with supplying funds for the JIHAD effort. All contributions should be mailed to: GRF."[225]

Another GRF newsletter similarly requested donations:

> [F]or God's cause—they [the *zakat* funds] are disbursed for equipping the raiders, for the purchase of ammunition and food, and for their [the mujahideen's] transportation so that they can raise God the Almighty's word. . . . [I]t is likely that the most important of disbursement of Zakat in our times is on the jihad for God's cause.[226]

Legal Action Taken against GRF Officials

As noted above, Rabih Haddad, a Lebanese citizen and the founder and chairman of GRF, was arrested on December 14, 2001. He had been originally admitted to the United States in 1998 with a "non-immigrant visitor" visa, which had expired on August 31, 1999.[227] After a series of unsuccessful appeals, Haddad was deported to Lebanon on July 11, 2003.[228] He was determined to be ineligible for asylum because he presented "a substantial risk to the national security of the United States."[229]

After his deportation, the Department of Immigration and Customs Enforcement (ICE) issued a press release that reiterated GRF's ties to Wadih el-Hage and stated again that GRF was a Specially Designated Global Terrorist. Acting assistant secretary for ICE Michael J. Garcia said of Haddad's deportation:

> The removal of individuals like Mr. Haddad highlights the importance of enforcing immigration laws in our ongoing efforts to secure the homeland. . . . This action is also a testament to the cooperation between law enforcement agencies in pursuing and removing those individuals linked to terrorism.[230]

In another case, Alaa al-Sadawi, a GRF fund-raiser, was indicted in July 2002, along with his father, Hassan, on currency-reporting violations.[231] In April 2002, Hassan al-Sadawi was about to board an Egypt-bound flight at New York's John F. Kennedy Airport when federal agents discovered $659,000 in cash crammed into boxes of Ritz crackers, Quaker Oats, and baby wipes in his suitcase. Alaa apparently packed the boxes in his father's luggage.[232]

In July 2003, Alaa al-Sadawi was convicted and Hassan was acquitted.[233] During sentencing, prosecutors asserted that between May 2000 and late 2001, the younger al-Sadawi had raised money for GRF[234] and had even passed $10,000 to a member of GRF under a bathroom stall at Chicago's O'Hare Airport.[235] The federal prosecutor also claimed that he had been heard "thanking God for the loss of American lives in Afghanistan" after 9/11.[236] In December 2003, Alaa al-Sadawi was sentenced to sixty-three months in prison.[237]

Sources of Funding

According to GRF's Form 990 filed with the IRS, GRF collected more than $15.4 million in charitable contributions between 1993 and 2000.[238] GRF solicited donations by advertising in Islamic publications, distributing a quarterly newsletter titled *Global News*, conducting fund-raising sessions at Islamic conferences and mosques,[239] posting a Web site, and directly soliciting affluent individuals. During Ramadan, for example, GRF distributed *zakat* worksheets to help Muslims donate 2.5 percent of their total assets to charity in accordance with Islamic law.[240] GRF encouraged donors to see if they qualified for corporate gift-matching programs, and its Web site lists participating Fortune 500 companies, including American Express, Microsoft, Pfizer, and Polaroid.[241]

GRF accepted funds in a variety of forms including:

- checks payable to GRF and wire transfers deposited in a Chicago bank account
- credit card donations accepted online on the GRF Web site or by stocks donated though Wedgewood Partners, a securities brokerage firm located in Missouri
- automatic electronic contributions of specified dollar amounts charged to donors' credit cards or deducted from their checking accounts on a regular basis.[242]

A number of suspect organizations and individuals gave large amounts of money to GRF. For example, Care International (discussed further in chapter 12) donated a total of $180,384.[243] This charity, not to be confused with CARE International, was founded in April 1993 in Boston, Massachusetts, and arose out of the Al Kifah Refugee Center with the stated purpose of "provid[ing] assistance to war victims and to war refugees around the Muslim world . . . in countries such as Chechnya, Bosnia, Palestine, Afghanistan, Kashmir, Sudan, Bangladesh, and Turkey."[244]

The Islamic Society of Arlington in Texas gave GRF approximately $85,000 under imam Moataz al-Hallak's tenure.[245] For more than a decade, a Syrian-born Salafi cleric headed this organization. In 2000, he was removed as spiritual leader when the governing board of the Arlington mosque declined to renew his contract, apparently disagreeing with his conservative Islamic philosophy.[246] Al-Hallak is listed in the address book of Wadih el-Hage. Although al-Hallak has not been charged with a crime, authorities accuse him of providing "cover" for el-Hage.[247]

Adham Hassoun of Sunrise, Florida, gave about $11,000 to GRF.[248] In 2002, US Immigration and Customs Enforcement detained Hassoun, who was granted permission to enter the United States on a student visa, for failing to attend school.[249] Listed as the registered agent on the Articles of Incorporation for the Benevolence International Foundation filed in Florida in 1993,[250] Hassoun also had ties to Jose Padilla, the "Dirty Bomber" who was arrested at Chicago's O'Hare Airport on May 8, 2002. Hassoun's attorney and other sources confirmed that he had contact with Padilla on several occasions and once gave Padilla several hundred dollars as "an act of charity."[251] Hassoun was indicted on September 16, 2004, on two counts of providing material support for terrorists—supplying financial support and recruiting for al Qaeda, and helping Padilla to attend terrorist training camps in Afghanistan.[252] In the November 2005 indictment against Padilla, Hassoun was included in the eleven-count indictment, which accused them of being part of a terrorist cell conspiring to export jihad overseas.[253]

Hassoun was listed as the North American and US distributor of the Islamic magazine *Nida 'ul Islam* (*The Call of Islam*), a militant publication that has published articles on jihad, the Taliban, and Islamic warriors, as well as interviews with members of the Taliban, Sheikh Omar Abdel Rahman, and officials from Jemaah Islamiyah and Sudan's National Islamic Front.[254]

KINDHEARTS

According to its Web site, KindHearts "is a non-profit charitable organization providing immediate disaster relief and establishing programs to improve the quality of life and foster future independence for those in need." The organization claims that its "program emphasis" is emergency relief; water and general sanitation; sheltering refugees; sponsorship of orphans, widows, and poor families; medical and health care; rehabilitation and renovation; vocational training and education; and independent income generation and economic growth.[255] There is evidence, however, that KindHearts might have been filling the void created by the closure of the Holy Land Foundation (HLF).

KindHearts, incorporated in Toledo, Ohio, in 2002,[256] is registered in a number of other states, including Oklahoma,[257] Nevada,[258] Indiana,[259] Colorado,[260] and Pennsylvania.[261] An assessment of its operations indicates a close business relationship with the Holy Land Foundation network as well as with other charities that have been designated as conduits for terrorist financing. These suspicions were given further credence when the US government froze the assets of KindHearts in February 2006. According to Stuart Levey, the undersecretary for Terrorism and Financial Intelligence at the US Department of the Treasury:

> KindHearts is the progeny of Holy Land Foundation and Global Relief Foundation, which attempted to mask their support for terrorism behind the façade of charitable giving. By utilizing this specialized designation tool, we're able to prevent asset flight in support of terrorist activities while we further investigate the activities of KindHearts.[262]

The Department of the Treasury press release went on to detail the connections between KindHearts, HLF, GRF, and Hamas.[263]

KindHearts Founder and CEO: Links to Global Relief Foundation (GRF) and NAIF

Khaled Smaili, founder[264] and CEO[265] of KindHearts, also served as the public relations representative for the Global Relief Foundation (GRF).[266] In July 2000, Smaili donated $15,000 to a program created and managed by Imam Ismaa'eel H. Hackett, the director of the Wilmington, Delaware–based North American Islamic Foundation (NAIF).[267] Hackett was the spiritual adviser to Abdullah Hameen, a convicted murderer executed in 2001.[268] Prior to Hameen's execution, Hackett and NAIF filed a court motion to postpone it, arguing that Hameen's rights were being violated. Hackett argued that "God states that a Muslim cannot be put to death for killing a disbeliever [non-Muslim]. Based on those premises, we have to say that Abdullah Hameen should not be put to death."[269]

KindHearts, the Islamic Association for Palestine (IAP), and the Holy Land Foundation (HLF)

Following the HLF shutdown, KindHearts appears to have assumed the close relationship with the Islamic Association for Palestine (IAP) that was previously held by HLF. Notably, each group uses the other to assist in raising funds: KindHearts lists the Islamic Association for Palestine as its "Fundraiser Organizer" in its tax exemption filings,[270] while IAP prominently featured a clickable advertisement for KindHearts on its Web site. KindHearts was the only charity advertised on IAP's homepage.[271] IAP used its list serve to distribute KindHearts' messages.[272] In one such instance, IAP's list serve distributed an e-mail from Khaled Smaili that stated:

> It is also with great satisfaction that I am able to report that just prior to the start of Ramadan, we received our 501-C(3) tax exemption status from the U.S. government; therefore, all of your contributions are now tax exempt. Please rush your Zakat and Sadaqa in the return envelope today, or donate online at www.kind-hearts.org.[273]

Meanwhile, HLF director of endowments Mohammed el-Mezain served as one of KindHearts' fund-raisers. According to tax records filed by KindHearts in 2002:

> El Mezain was the sole professional fundraiser that has been utilized by KindHearts. Mr. El Mezain was contacted by KindHearts and was asked to appear at events and conduct fundraising activities. . . . The understanding is that KindHears [*sic*] compensated Mr. El Mezain for his travel, lodging and meal expenses, as well as compensation of 10% of the amounts raised, with a cap of $8,000 per event, and a minimum payment of $2,000 per event.[274]

El-Mezain was indicted for providing material support to Hamas.[275] Additionally, Abdelbaset Hemayel—who has served as IAP's director and secretary-general[276]—is listed as KindHearts' representative in Illinois and Wisconsin on a business card produced in April 2004.[277]

KindHearts and Al Nojoum

As was commonplace at IAP and HLF events, KindHearts' fund-raisers have featured "entertainment" by the Al Nojoum band.[278] Al Nojoum, which was previously known as the Al Sakhra band, frequently performed at IAP conventions. According to the HLF indictment, Al Sakhra's "skits and songs . . . advocated the destruction of the State of Israel and glorified the killing of Jewish people." Mufid Abdulqader, who is a half-brother of Hamas leader Khalid Mishaal, was a member of the Al Sakhra band. Abdulqader, an HLF fund-raiser, was indicted with HLF in July 2004 on material support charges.[279]

KindHearts and the Mosque Foundation

KindHearts has received funds from the Mosque Foundation (MF), one of the largest mosques in the Chicago area, which is linked to Hamas.[280] The mosque's imam and registered agent, Jamal Said,[281] served as the treasurer of the Al Aqsa Educational Fund,[282] an entity identified by the FBI as a Hamas charitable front.[283] The Mosque Foundation also employed Kifah Mustapha, the head of HLF's Chicago office,[284] and donated thousands of dollars to HLF.

According to its spring 2004 newsletter, KindHearts honored the Mosque Foundation with its "Mosque of the Year in recognition of their members' tremendous support." The newsletter noted that "this community as a whole donated $195,000 for KindHearts to fund its relief efforts for the innocent victims of home demolitions in Rafah Refugee Camp, Gaza." KindHearts president Khaled Smaili presented the award to Mosque Foundation president Osama Jammal.[285]

Federal authorities reportedly are investigating the Mosque Foundation and associated individuals for suspected involvement in money laundering related to terror fronts. The Mosque Foundation made sizable donations to other organizations later shut down by the US government for funding terrorism, including the Benevolence International Foundation[286] and the Islamic American Relief Agency (IARA), two al Qaeda fronts; and the Global Relief Foundation (GRF).[287] Furthermore, MF raised thousands of dollars for University of South Florida professor Sami al-Arian.[288]

Other KindHearts Representatives Associated with Radical Muslim Groups in the United States: Omar Shahin and Khalifah Ramadan

Other KindHearts representatives are linked with radical Muslim groups in the United States. According to a business card produced in April 2004, Omar Shahin, a former Tucson imam, is a KindHearts representative.[289] Shahin served as the imam at the Islamic Center of Tucson (ICT) for three years until he "left abruptly" in June 2003.[290] ICT—which hosted IAP conferences and has an extensive history of terror links—raised thousands of dollars for HLF in 2001.

In the mid-1980s, ICT was one of the US satellite offices of the Mektab Al Khidmat (MAK) the precursor organization to al Qaeda. MAK was founded by specially designated global terrorist Wael Julaidan, Osama bin Laden, and Sheikh Abdullah Azzam.[291] Julaidan was ICT's president from 1983 to 1984.[292] ICT was one of the US offices listed on the masthead of *Al Jihad* magazine, a publication edited by al Qaeda cofounder Abdullah Azzam (the other US office listed was the MAK office in Brooklyn). In April 1988, Azzam penned an article titled "The Solid Base (Al Qaeda)," which in effect announced the formation of al Qaeda.[293] Other notable ICT attendees include Wadih el-Hage, convicted for his role in the 1998 East African embassy bombings, and Ghassan Dahduli, the manager of the IAP information office in Tucson.[294]

Khalifah Ramadan, who has served as KindHearts' director of domestic programs,[295] was a training and evaluation consultant for the Council on American-Islamic Relations (CAIR) and the Islamic Society of North America (ISNA).[296] There are a number of significant connections between CAIR and HLF, as well as other Hamas front groups—the Islamic Association for Palestine, the United Association for Studies and Research, the Muslim Arab Youth Association, and the Safa Group. For example, less than two months after CAIR filed its Articles of Incorporation, the organization received a $5,000 wire transfer from HLF.[297] Moreover, CAIR assisted in raising funds for HLF throughout the 1990s and until the government shutdown of HLF.[298] Ghassan Elashi, a founding board member of CAIR-Texas,[299] was also chairman[300] and treasurer[301] of HLF.

Further suggesting that CAIR is in the Hamas-affiliated US network is the fact that it is an offshoot of IAP. Both Omar Ahmad and Nihad Awad—two of CAIR's incorporators—held leadership positions with IAP prior to founding CAIR.[302]

ISNA also has significant links to extremism. Cofounded by Sami al-Arian, [303] ISNA has employed an array of individuals who have been indicted on terrorism-related charges, such as former HLF head Shukri Abu Bakr,[304] and even a terrorist operative—Abdulrahman Alamoudi.[305]

ISNA's funding is highly suspect. ISNA provided $170,000 in start-up capital to the Islamic African Relief Agency (IARA),[306] which the US government shut down in October 2004 for funding Hamas and al Qaeda.[307]

KindHearts and the Sanabil Association for Relief

According to KindHearts' 2002 IRS Form 990, the organization made two cash grants, for $85,000 and $15,000, to the Sanabil Association for Relief in Saida, Lebanon.[308]

On August 22, 2003, the US Treasury Department designated five charities funding Hamas, including the Sanabil Association for Relief and Development and six senior Hamas leaders, as terrorist entities.[309]

According to the accompanying Treasury Department fact sheet, Sanabil

> receives large quantities of funds raised by major HAMAS-affiliated charities in Europe and the Middle East and, in turn, provides funding to HAMAS. For example, Sanabil has received funding from the Al Aqsa Foundation (designated as an SDGT under EO 13224 in May 2003), the Holy Land Foundation for Relief and Development (designated as an SDGT under EO 13224 in December 2001), and Interpal (designated as an SDGT under EO 13224 as part of this tranche). HAMAS recruits permanent members from the religious and the poor by extending charity to them from organizations such as Sanabil.[310]

The Treasury press release added:

> At the request of a HAMAS political leader, Sanabil began opening offices in all of the Palestinian refugee camps in Lebanon in August of 2001 in order to increase the foundation's role inside the camps. After starting by providing basic necessities the charity eventually began asking poor families within the camps to fill out application forms, particularly those who had worked with the Islamic Movement (Al-Haraka al-Islamiyya) and HAMAS. As a result of these efforts, Sanabil has increased its scope of influence within the camps.[311]

Moreover, a November 5, 2001, memorandum written by the assistant director of the FBI's Counterterrorism Division, Dale Watson, states that "the largest HLFRD recipients outside of the West Bank and Gaza are Sanabil Association for Relief and Development in Lebanon and Human Appeal International in Jordan."[312]

THE RADICAL ESTABLISHMENT IN AMERICAN ISLAM AND ITS ACCESS TO GOVERNMENT

With the unwitting support of the US government, a small group of Muslim organizations in the United States that claim to represent mainstream, moderate, and even progressive Muslim views have been able to successfully drown out the truly moderate and diverse voices within the American Muslim community. Most prominently, the Council on American-Islamic Relations (CAIR), the Islamic Society of North America (ISNA), the Muslim Public Affairs Council (MPAC), the Muslim American Society (MAS), and the Islamic Circle of North America (ICNA) have gained access to and now influence top lawmakers, while concealing, even from many of their own members, their origins, true sympathies, and intentions. These organizations embody radical Islamist ideologies originating with the Ikhwan ul Muslimoon (Muslim Brotherhood), a fundamentalist and extremist mass movement founded in Egypt, and the mirror Pakistani Jamaat e Islami movement. When referencing these organizations, this chapter is referring specifically to their leadership.

A rigidly fundamentalist and highly secretive Egyptian-based organization dedicated to implementing Islam, the Muslim Brotherhood was founded by Hassan al-Banna in 1928. According to al-Banna, "[i]t is the nature of Islam to dominate, not to be dominated, to impose its law on all nations and to extend its power to the entire planet."[313] Al-Banna also gave the group the motto it still uses today: "God is our purpose, the Prophet our leader, the Quran our constitution, jihad our way and dying for God our supreme objective."[314]

Al-Banna's successor as the movement's ideological mentor, Sayyid Qutb, asserted that, in accordance with al-Banna's creed, unjust rulers could be considered unbelievers and overthrown or killed. This claim galvanized succeeding generations of Islamic radicals.[315]

As the *9/11 Commission Report* notes, Osama bin Laden's ideological development and that of his followers "relies heavily" on Qutb.[316] Other key brotherhood adherents have included al Qaeda mastermind Khalid

Sheikh Mohammed,[317] bin Laden mentor Abdullah Azzam, and Sudanese hardliner Hassan al-Turabi.

Immigrant Muslim men, many of whom were Muslim Brotherhood members in their native countries,[318] came to America in the late 1960s and laid the groundwork for what is now a large network of Islamic centers, mosques, schools, think tanks, and businesses. Those institutions have shown an unwavering adherence to the brotherhood and, in some instances, the Saudi-centered Wahhabi interpretations of Islam.

As Richard Clarke, former National Coordinator for Security and Infrastructure Protection under Presidents Clinton and Bush, stated in October 2003 testimony before the Senate Committee on Banking:

> [I]t is now widely known that every major Islamist terrorist organization, from HAMAS to Islamic Jihad to Al Qaeda, has leveraged the financial resources and institutions of the United States to build their capabilities. We face a highly developed enemy in our mission to stop terrorist financing. While the overseas operations of Islamist terrorist organizations are generally segregated and distinct, the opposite holds in the United States. The issue of terrorist financing in the United States is a fundamental example of the shared infrastructure levered by HAMAS, Islamic Jihad and Al Qaeda, all of which enjoy a significant degree of cooperation and coordination within our borders. The common link here is the extremist Muslim Brotherhood—all of these organizations are descendants of the membership and ideology of the Muslim Brothers.[319]

Sometimes interconnected with this network, via individuals in leadership and joint events, are the like-minded extremist groups that have established themselves in the United States. Radical outfits like the Islamic Assembly of North American (IANA) and the Al Haramain Foundation (an official Saudi charitable agency) are examples. Al Haramain in the United States has been closed in Ashland, Oregon. Most of these groups have been major players in prison outreach along with the Islamic Society of North America (ISNA) and the Islamic Circle of North America (ICNA). ICNA is tethered to the fundamentalist movement of Jamaat e Islami in Pakistan and Bangladesh, which may be described as the sister movement of the Ikhwan.[320]

Attempt to Redefine the Definition of Mainstream Islam

CAIR, ISNA, and MPAC have lobbied Congress, testified at congressional hearings, and routinely met with Hill staffers and influential persons working in the White House and cabinet agencies. They have held personal meetings with both President Bill Clinton and President George W. Bush. Moreover, these same groups are now frequently enlisted to conduct "sensitivity" training for federal, state, and local law enforcement officers.

Islamist Influence in American Government

Starting in the mid-1990s and persisting after September 11, 2001, various Islamist groups enjoyed high-level political access in both Democratic and Republican administrations to the detriment and exclusion of mainstream US Muslims. [321]

Abdurahman Alamoudi (executive director of the American Muslim Council and terrorist operative), other AMC board members, and other Islamic leaders made multiple visits to the White House during the administration of President Bill Clinton.[322] Alamoudi and the AMC also enjoyed good relations with members of Congress—Republicans and Democrats.

The relationship established in 1995 between the Clinton administration and the radical Islamic community developed over the next year. In May 1996, MPAC hosted First Lady Hillary Clinton at its convention—an event that featured a speech by MPAC senior adviser Dr. Maher Hathout.[323]

The Minaret, an MPAC publication, reported a year later in 1997 on a lecture Maher Hathout delivered at the State Department on emerging Islamic trends, which highlighted the efforts by radicals to redefine "moderate" Muslims. Hathout employed a standard Muslim Brotherhood and Wahhabi tactic: reframing Islamic radicals as "reformists."[324] Describing Hathout's philosophy, the author wrote:

> In his [Hathout's] view the reformists, represented by leaders like Jamaluddin Afghani, Muhammad Abdu, Mohammad Iqbal, Hassan Al Banna and Maududi, Ghannoushi, Erbakan and Turabi, have advocated a pluralistic society that would work for peace and justice for all. They have, however, according to Dr. Hathout, been ignored, despite the fact that "they represent the masses and speak their language."[325]

And who were these "reformist" leaders? As stated earlier, Hassan al-Banna was the founder of the Muslim Brotherhood. Abul Ala Mawdudi was the mentor of the Jamaat e Islami. Hassan al-Turabi of Sudan was a prominent Muslim Brotherhood member[326] and also headed the National Islamic Front (NIF) of Sudan, which the US government has condemned for supporting terrorism, launching a genocidal war in southern Sudan, and for continued human rights violations.[327] Al-Turabi gave bin Laden sanctuary in Sudan.[328]

Secretary of State Madeleine Albright hosted the State Department's first Iftar—an event attended by guests including representatives from AMC, CAIR, MPAC, the Islamic Society of North America (ISNA), and the Muslim American Society (MAS).[329]

In January 2002, MPAC's executive director, Salam al-Marayati, spoke at the State Department, delivering a lecture titled "The Rising Voice of Moderate Muslims,"[330] and between April 2002 and June 2004, Secretary of State Powell met three times with Arab American delegations, each time including a CAIR representative.[331]

On April 5, 2006, the US Senate Committee on Foreign Relations held a three-panel hearing on Islamic extremism in Europe.[332] One of the three officials who testified, current US ambassador to Belgium Tom Korologos, outlined his efforts with the State Department to promote various seemingly laudable initiatives in which American and European Muslim organizations met with US officials, opening a dialogue that, in the ambassador's hopes, would "break stereotypes and foster networking opportunities."[333] As explained on a Web site launched by the US embassy in Brussels, the ambassador's efforts culminated with a two-day conference held in Brussels in November 2005, during which thirty-two American Muslims met with sixty-five Belgian Muslims and various US officials.[334]

"A major part" in facilitating the planning of the conference from the US side was played by the Islamic Society of North America (ISNA), which was represented by its secretary-general, Dr. Sayyid M. Syeed.[335] Other America groups participating were the Council on American Isamic Relations (CAIR, represented by Executive Director Nihad Awad and Legal Director Arsalan Iftikhar),[336] the Muslim Public Affairs Council (MPAC), and the Muslim Students Association of the United States and Canada (MSA).[337] The only European Muslim organization that has been publicly mentioned as a partner in the initiative is the Brussels-based Forum of European Muslim Youth and Student Organisations (FEMYSO).[338]

FEMYSO is the youth branch of the Federation of Islamic Organizations in Europe (FIOE), the umbrella organization for various groups that share the ideology of the Muslim Brotherhood.[339] Its three main founding member organizations are the French UOIF (an organization that the French Council of State has described as "a federation to which are affiliated many extremist movements which reject the essential values of French society"),[340] the German IGD (founded by Muslim Brotherhood leader Said Ramadan and headed for more than twenty years by US Department of the Treasury–designated terrorist financier Ghaleb Himmat),[341] and the British MAB, which is featured in a July 2006 exposé by journalist Martin Bright titled "When Progressives Treat with Reactionaries: The British State's Flirtation with Radical Islamism." This report comes with original source documents that were leaked from the Foreign Office.[342]

FEMYSO is affiliated with the World Assembly of Muslim Youth (discussed in various chapters).[343] FEMYSO's longtime president, Ibrahim el-Zayat, came under investigation in Germany for having funneled more than $2 million to an al Qaeda–linked charity and for other suspected money-laundering activities (no charges have been filed because support for or membership in a foreign terrorist organization was not illegal in Germany at the time the transfers took place).[344]

It is clear that in the United States, as in Europe, many of the groups discussed in this chapter have been attempting to redefine radical Islam as mainstream. That all of these like-minded Islamist groups, mirror images of one another in their respective countries, were the ones chosen to meet in Brussels speaks to a template that has been carefully cultivated by extremists and their apologists for decades. This has resulted in an environment in which official interaction with Islam is now largely dominated by the Muslim Brotherhood and Jamaat e Islami.

The Islamic Free Market Institute

In 1998, Grover Norquist, an economic conservative and powerful Republican known for his lobbying group, Americans for Tax Reform, founded the Islamic Free Market Institute, originally known as the Islamic Institute.[345] The institute received money from Abdurahman Alamoudi with two personal checks in the amount of $10,000 each[346] and a $50,000 check to a lobbying firm associated with Norquist[347] and at least two donations from Safa Trust totaling $20,000.[348] Safa Trust is a prominent Islamist network of groups located in Virginia (IIIT, which was the largest donor to Sami al-Arian's front group WISE,[349] is an important part of this network). The Safa Group, also known as the SAAR Network, is the subject of chapter 10. Norquist selected Khaled Saffuri, Alamoudi's governmental affairs deputy at AMC, to run the institute.

Under Norquist's sponsorship, Saffuri joined the 2000 presidential campaign of George W. Bush in the post of National Adviser on Arab and Muslim Affairs.[350] Bush's subsequent election to the White House gave Saffuri access to the president and the upper tiers of the administration—access that he maintained even as the United States became engaged in the Global War on Terror.[351]

A 2001 article in the *New Republic* quotes one of Norqist's associates as saying that Norquist was "[a]bsolutely . . . central to the White House outreach." Also quoted was conservative activist Paul Weyrich, who agreed: "Just like administration officials ask my advice on inviting religious figures to the White House, they rely on Grover's help with Muslims."[352]

In June 2001, Bush's political adviser, Karl Rove, held a briefing attended by members of the American Muslim Council, which included Sami al-Arian. Al-Arian had visited the White House previously, near the end of the Clinton administration, on June 23, 2000.[353] Both visits are remarkable given the fact that he was at both times under active FBI-INS investigation (see chapter 7). In July 2001, Norquist was given an award by the National Coalition to Protect Political Freedom (NCPPF), a "civil rights" group, for his work on abolishing the use of secret evidence in terrorism cases. Sami al-Arian was president of the NCPPF.[354]

According to an institute publication, Khaled Saffuri met early in 2002 with Justice Department officials.[355] He also met with Treasury Secretary Paul O'Neill about the 2001 government raids on entities in the SAAR Network and other organizations, and with Secretary of State Colin Powell.[356]

AMPAC and Election 2000

In 2000, George W. Bush made the first direct appeal by a presidential candidate to the Muslim American voting constituency.[357] For the first time, Muslim Americans were mentioned in a national presidential debate. Opposing then vice president Al Gore, the Democratic candidate, Bush stated:

> There is [*sic*] other forms of racial profiling that goes [*sic]* on in America. Arab Americans are racially profiled in what's called secret evidence. People are stopped, and we got to do something about that.[358]

The American Muslim Political Action Committee (AMPAC)—created jointly in 1997 by the American Muslim Alliance (AMA), AMC, CAIR, MPAC, and others[359]—praised Bush because he "took the initiative to meet with local and national representatives of the Muslim community. He also promised to address Muslim concerns on domestic and foreign policy issues."[360] That praise was followed by the group's endorsement on October 23, 2000.[361]

Hillary Clinton, then campaigning for the US Senate in New York State, attracted support from the same groups. When it became an issue in the campaign, she announced that she would return $50,000 collected at a fund-raiser held by AMA in Boston. Mrs. Clinton said she did not know that the fund-raiser was associated with AMA and stated that she disagreed with the group's positions.[362] She returned Alamoudi's personal $1,000 contribution.[363]

A Dissenting Voice to CAIR, ISNA, and MPAC

In December 2000, Mustafa Elhussein, secretary of the Ibn Khaldun Society, complained that CAIR and MPAC were inappropriate voices for mainstream Muslims. In an editorial criticizing these so-called advocacy groups, Elhussein wrote:

> [These] self-appointed leaders who spew hatred toward America and the West and yet claim to be legitimate spokespersons for the American Muslim community . . . [should] not only be kept at arm's length from the political process, they should be actively opposed as extremists.[364]

It is unfortunate that political leaders in a democracy leading a global war on terror—and the US media—seem largely to have ignored clearly moderate groups like the Ibn Khaldun Society and the countless others who have spoken out over the years.

Talk of Democratic Values Cloaks Extremist Agenda

Americans value the rights guaranteed by the Constitution. Free speech, free association, the rule of law, political democracy, toleration, and separation of church and state are at the core of how we define ourselves as individuals and as a nation. They are also concepts fundamentally inconsistent with and rejected by the extremist Islamist movements that threaten America and anyone who disagrees with them. In today's United States, phrases such as "hate crime," "secret evidence," "civil and human rights," and "Mideast peace process" have acquired a resonance based in legitimate concerns, and we tend to take for granted that whoever utters them is speaking out of a belief in the Constitution and in democratic values.

This assumption is usually true—but not always. The leadership of the groups discussed in this section have cloaked their deep-seated support for extremist Islam and the often violent actions that it spawns in words that convey respect for and adherence to American democratic values. Cleverly deceptive public relations campaigns, waged over a decade and brought to national attention by 9/11, have given extremists access to the top echelons of government. To be sure, these groups have the right to speak and lobby, protected by the First Amendment, but it should be noted that these groups have acted as the self-appointed spokespersons of "mainstream" Islam and were established in the United States with a very specific political Islamist agenda that is not mainstream. Equally, law enforcement and intelligence agencies with a mandate to protect America have the duty, when individuals or groups are shown to have ties to terrorists, to undertake fair investigations and follow them to their honest conclusions.

POST-9/11 TRENDS OF TERROR FINANCING

The explosion of nontraditional methods of terror financing is a growing concern among law enforcement agencies. While most charity organizations use traditional methods of financing such as donation boxes and the like, terrorist fronts have also implemented more nontraditional methods for moving funds. The ability to make large amounts of money through various illegal schemes, such as retail theft, drug trafficking, and auto theft, has the potential to provide terrorist organizations with noncharity-based financing methods. Several recent cases involving retail theft and drug trafficking highlight the possibilities.

Organized Retail Theft: A Major Conduit for Terrorist Financing

Organized retail theft (ORT) has links to money laundering and the financing of Middle Eastern terrorism. It targets everyday household commodities and consumer items, affecting a variety of retail enterprises, including supermarkets, chain drugstores, independent pharmacies, mass merchandisers, convenience stores, and discount businesses. The supermarket industry alone loses $15 billion annually from ORT, while the loss throughout all retail operations is estimated to run as high as $34 billion.[365] Profits from such illegal activity are funneled to terrorist groups in the Middle East, posing a serious threat to national and international security.

Because there is a lack of effective state and federal law addressing the issue, retail theft is becoming increasingly attractive as a high-profit, low-risk avenue for criminal organizations and terrorist groups. ORT rings operate in almost every region of the United States and several of these rings are led by foreign nationals, many of whom are illegal immigrants.

This black market trade employs two groups of individuals. The first group consists of professional shoplifters or boosters—often illegal immigrants—who steal consumer merchandise through a variety of techniques that include organized shoplifting, armed robbery, cargo theft, and hijacking. Products targeted for theft by these groups include infant formula, cigarettes and smokeless tobacco, health and beauty aids, diabetes test strips, over-the-counter medications, and colognes and perfumes.[366]

The second group of individuals is comprised of fences, or low-level buyers—mostly immigrants from various Middle Eastern and Asian countries—who purchase the stolen merchandise and distribute it back to retail outlets. This group owns a variety of businesses such as convenience stores, grocery stores, gas stations, grocery wholesale businesses, travel agencies, used-car dealerships, shipping companies, bookkeeping firms, and nightclubs. While the main activity of this group focuses on the theft and resale of stolen merchandise, members also engage in a number of side activities that include narcotics trafficking, prostitution, extortion, alien smuggling, organized auto-theft, currency smuggling, credit fraud, bank fraud, and welfare fraud. Proceeds from the aforementioned illegal businesses are frequently used in financing terror-related activities.[367]

In his February 2005 congressional testimony, FBI director Robert Mueller highlighted the strong linkages between organized criminal enterprises operating in the United States and terrorist groups:

> Middle Eastern Criminal Enterprises involved in the organized theft and resale of infant formula pose not only an economic threat, but a public health threat to infants, and a potential source of material support to a terrorist organization.[368]

Recent federal investigations of retail theft rings have resulted in indictments and subsequent arrests of such criminal enterprises throughout the country. The Ghali Family organization is a particularly chilling example in its size, impact, and ability to continue its illicit operations, despite incarceration of leaders.

The Ghali Family Organization

In February 2005, Mohammed Khalil Ghali was sentenced to fourteen years' imprisonment following his April 2004 conviction on fifteen counts charging him and seven other individuals with federal felony violations linked to organized retail theft in North Texas.[369] According to the indictment, Ghali was the organizer and leader of a Palestinian gang known as the "Ghali" organization, which ran one of the nation's most notorious retail theft rings from Fort Worth, Texas.[370] At the direction of Mohammed Ghali, members of his organization purchased stolen property that was held at various metroplex convenience stores by store owners/operators who served as "fences." The stolen goods, including infant formula, pharmaceuticals, cigarettes, health and beauty aids, medicinal products, glucose test strips, nicotine gum and transdermal patches, razors and razor blades, were delivered to warehouses where price tags and antitheft devices were removed. The merchandise was then repackaged and shipped to customers throughout the United States.[371] It has been reported that profits generated from the sale of goods were wired to banks in the Middle East.[372]

Despite incarceration of its top leaders, the "Ghali crime family" continues to operate its illegal business with the aid of unjailed associates. Testimony at the sentencing hearing accused Ghali of making inquiries as to how much it would cost to have the Texas prosecutor and federal agent killed by gang members.[373] According to court transcripts, jailed family leader Mohammed Ghali attempted to hire Crip gang members to arrange the hits for $500.[374] The family also made attempts to bribe US Immigration and Customs Enforcement (ICE) supervisors to get the charges against Ghali dismissed.[375] More recently, federal authorities unraveled a plot targeting Fort Worth police detective Scott Campbell, his family, and ICE agent Scott Springer.[376]

Huge Profits from Thefts of Infant Formula

The Jamal Trading Company (JTC) case demonstrates that large sums of money are generated through the theft of infant formula. A wholesaler in infant formula, the Tempe, Arizona–based company owned and operated by Samih Fadl Jamal was the center of a fencing operation for stolen or fraudulently obtained infant formula, which generated more than $11 million in profits.[377] Stolen infant formula was repackaged at the JTC warehouse and distributed and sold to various retail and wholesale businesses.[378]

Most of the defendants indicted in the case were from Iraq, Jordan, or Lebanon. Of the twenty-seven defendants indicted, twenty-two were located and arrested, seventeen have pleaded guilty, and four have been sentenced and deported. Jamal, a naturalized US citizen born in Lebanon, was convicted in April 2005 on twenty counts of conspiracy to traffic in stolen infant formula, money laundering, and related charges. All counts carried a fine of $250,000. In October 2005, US District Court judge Frederick Martone sentenced Jamal to ten years in prison and ordered him to forfeit $2.6 million in assets.[379]

Similarly, a June 8, 2005, indictment charged Carlos Javier Medina-Castellanos, Mahmoud Bassar, and Jose Franscisco of organized theft of baby formula, over-the-counter medicines, and other items related to personal health and hygiene. According to the indictment, the stolen items were collected from locations in North Carolina and Georgia and delivered to depositories, such as private residences or temporary storage facilities. The stolen merchandise was then transported by passenger vehicles and rented trucks to commercial trucking firms where it was loaded onto larger trucks and shipped to destinations across the country. In some instances, the retail value of the shipments exceeded $50,000.[380] The ease of setting up this type of operation combined with the large sums of money generated suggest that the technique could easily be utilized by terrorist organizations to finance terror.

The Use of Mosques, Bookkeepers, and Law Firms in ORT

The organized retail theft ring is sophisticated not only in its operations but also in its exploitation of resources. Investigators of various organized retail theft rings have reported that mosques often are used as meeting places to discuss logistics for burglaries or shoplifting operations.[381] Surveillance of mosques has proven to be difficult because of the sensitivities involved.

In addition to using mosques for planning operations, many of the rings, which often work together, use the same bookkeeping firms. Of these firms, several have represented individuals suspected of criminal activity and, in some cases, the firms themselves are involved as investors in the schemes. Moreover, many of the individuals involved in ORT operations use the same law firm for their defense, creating conflicts of interest that make it more difficult, if not impossible, for law enforcement to approach individual defendants and use them as cooperating witnesses. Examples of this tactic have been reported in Texas, where the same law firm represented "high profile defendants" over several years and thereby "appear[ed] to be acting as an organizational firm for the criminal enterprise Texas operations."[382]

Illegal Drug Operations by Terrorist Organizations

Illegal drug trafficking continues to be a source of income for various terrorist organizations, including al Qaeda and Hizballah. In June 2005, the Ecuadorian government broke up a drug ring run by a local Lebanese restaurant owner. The bust resulted in multiple arrests, including individuals in the United States. Ecuadorian authorities report that at least 70 percent of the profits from the drug-trafficking operation went to help finance Hizballah[383] (see chapter 6).

Similarly, al Qaeda cells have, in certain instances, relied on drug sales to finance operations. For example, the Moroccan terrorist who financed the attacks in Madrid was a hashish dealer who used the drug profits to purchase the explosives used in the attacks.[384]

In another example, in October 2005, Afghanistan native Baz Mohammed was arrested and extradited to the United States for running an international heroin operation whose proceeds funded the Taliban and other Islamic extremist groups.[385] According to the indictment, Baz Mohammed headed the "Baz Mohammed Organization," which since

1990 has been responsible for manufacturing and distributing over $25 million worth of heroin in Afghanistan and Pakistan. The indictment alleged that the manufactured heroin was then transported to the United States and other areas in suitcases, clothing, and containers. Authorities estimate that they have seized $1.4 million worth of Baz Mohammed heroin within the United States.[386]

According to the indictment, Baz Mohammed told other members of his organization that selling heroin in the United States was "jihad" and that they were taking Americans' money at the same time the heroin that they were paying for was killing them.[387]

Drug Trafficking and the Palestinian Islamic Jihad

Connections were uncovered between indicted drug trafficker Tariq Isa and two of the defendants in the Palestinian Islamic Jihad (PIJ) case in Tampa, Florida. In May 2004, Isa, the imam of the Al Qassam Mosque in Chicago, was indicted for conspiracy to possess a controlled substance, conspiracy to possess narcotics, and illegal transfer of firearms.[388] In February 2003, two other officials from the same mosque,[389] Ghassan Ballut and Hatem Fariz, were indicted in Florida along with Sami al-Arian for their involvement with PIJ, a federally designated terrorist organization (see chapter 7 for more on Ballut and Fariz).[390] In seeking Isa's detention, an assistant United States Attorney from the Northern District of Illinois stated in court on August 10, 2004, that Isa had been photographed with Ramadan Shallah, the secretary-general of PIJ.[391] In addition, Isa, Ballut, and Fariz were identified as the only three individuals to hold signatory authority over the mosque's bank account.[392] This case highlights the strong connections between drug trafficking and terrorism. In January 2006, Isa was sentenced to almost twenty years in prison.[393]

Stored-Value Cards

According to the US Department of the Treasury, "stored-value cards (SVCs) are smart cards with electronic value.... The technology eliminates coin, currency, scrip, vouchers, money orders, and other labor-intensive payment mechanisms."[394] They also permit the movement of large sums of cash across international borders without leaving a money trail. The stored-value cards operate as gift cards and can be obtained and recharged in a variety of different locations, and do not require real identification. Experiments have been conducted showing the ease of obtaining and using these stored-value cards without divulging personal information. More important, using SVCs allows individuals to bypass Department of Treasury Office of Foreign Assets Control (OFAC) monitoring. The OFAC maintains lists of individuals and nations, specially designated by US agencies, that are not allowed to receive funds from the United States. But the agency, however, is unable to monitor SVCs, which poses a challenge in the enforcement of Treasury regulations and provides an easy method of transferring funds internationally.

Stored-value cards, while otherwise a convenient invention, have the potential to inhibit efforts to control money laundering. Their ready use eliminates intermediaries such as financial institutions, allowing for virtually undetected global movement of funds. Although no hard evidence exists that stored-value cards have been used in any terrorist financing schemes, SVCs present an easy method to terrorist organizations for money laundering or transferring large amounts of cash across borders.

Vehicle Theft: A Means of Financing, Money Laundering, and Attack

Vehicle theft is playing a burgeoning role in the financing of terrorist organizations. According to Greg Terp, chairman of the North American Export Committee (NAEC) whose mission is to stem the export of stolen vehicles, auto theft "remains a staple of organized crime groups" and recent investigations have shown a "direct link" between organized crime groups and the funding for terrorist organizations.[395] In an attempt to stem this problem, NAEC and Arizona law enforcement officials came together to discuss how to best combat the exportation of stolen vehicles.[396] Arizona has the highest number of auto thefts per capita in the United States, estimated to be more than fifty-six thousand a year.[397]

More alarming, however, is the potential use of stolen vehicles as part of future terrorist acts. Stolen cars in Arizona have been tracked to seaports outside of Los Angeles, Seattle, and Houston.[398] It would be easy to ship these stolen vehicles to places in the Middle East, where they could be prepped for future suicide attacks and car bombings. Thousands of cheap, secondhand cars from Europe, the Persian Gulf, and Asia, for example, flooded through the Middle East and into Iraq after the US-led occupation began.[399] And in a raid conducted by US troops in Fallujah, soldiers discovered a bomb-making workshop where an SUV registered in Texas was being converted into a car bomb.[400]

Money Laundering through Automobiles

The theft and resale of vehicles by organized crime groups is not the only way autos can be used by terrorist organizations. Legitimate auto dealers have been involved in laundering large amounts of cash through the sale of automobiles. In an ongoing investigation in Chicago, Illinois, four men were arrested for allegedly selling automobiles from their car dealership to drug dealers and gang members in exchange for cash made from drug trafficking.[401] To avoid income reporting rules, the defendants deposited the cash in amounts under $10,000 in separate branches of local banks.[402] Although authorities have made no public statements about connections to terrorist organizations, one of the defendants, Amir Hosseini, who is of Iranian descent, is accused of funneling money back to Iran.[403] Hosseini previously had been arrested on INS violations for lying about his country of origin.[404] Arresting officers also noted that Hosseini's residence was "covered with documents supporting the Ayatollah and his policies."[405]

CONCLUSION

Terrorist organizations have used or set up US-based Islamic charities to finance their activities abroad. Hamas set up the Holy Land Foundation. Al Qaeda used the Global Relief Foundation, the Benevolence International Foundation, and the Islamic African Relief Agency to funnel money to their global network in Bosnia, Sudan, and other areas. Other charities not discussed in this chapter have funneled money to the Palestinian Islamic Jihad, the Taliban, and other groups designated as terrorist. The relationships between charities and the financing of terrorism have yet to be fully uncovered, but clearly concern is warranted. In that vein, US forces raided the Iraqi office of LIFE for Relief and Development in the summer of 2004.[406] The International Relief Organization in Virginia was raided by the FBI in 1997, and the International Islamic Relief Organization, with which it is closely affiliated, has been uncovered as a major source of financing for terrorism abroad.[407]

These charities do not only operate independently, they also work with each other to help support al Qaeda, Hamas, and other Islamic terrorist organizations. As noted at the beginning of this chapter, some of these organizations formed a council specifically designed to increase intercharity relationships and cooperation. HLF, BIF, GRF, IARA, LIFE, and IRO all were involved in joint projects both domestically and internationally. BIF partnered with IARA on a project in Afghanistan and worked with IRO on a project in Chechnya. BIF and GRF partnered with HLF on projects focusing on Palestine. HLF donated money to LIFE, and IRO funneled money to IARA, HLF, and Mercy. The end of 2004 saw four of these charities named as SDGTs by the US Treasury Department.

Efforts by US agencies have helped stem terrorism financing by fund-raising organizations operating in the United States, but have been unable to stop it completely. Such financing is accomplished not by lone individuals, but by groups of like-minded individuals cooperating in sophisticated organizations whose goal is to promote and fund various radical Islamic agendas in unstable regions of the world. The charities, organizations, and nontraditional methods discussed above are only some of those that constitute the US network for financing radical jihad. Many terror-financing organizations are still active, whether openly or behind new fronts. New charities or existing ones suddenly inundated with charitable donations must be carefully scrutinized to ensure that "humanitarian aid" is not permitted to become a cover for jihadi terrorism.

NOTES

1. Center for Studies, Intelligence and Information (CSII), June 1981. This unsigned document was seized in a 1995 raid on Sami al-Arian's home and office in Tampa, Florida. Authorities believe it was authored by al-Arian. The "Center" referred to is thought to be the Islamic think tank that Dr. al-Arian was running in Tampa, Florida, which was operating as a cover for the Palestinian Islamic Jihad.

2. Other organizations involved in the council included Care International, Gulf Medical Relief Fund, Islamic Circle of North America (ICNA) Relief, and Indian Relief. "Historical Meeting of Leading Muslim Charity Organizations Paves the Way for More Cooperation," *Global News* 4, no. 1 (Winter 1997). See also *HLF NEWS* 4, no. 9 (November 1997).

3. 1993 Holy Land Foundation, IRS Form 990; Dale Watson, assistant director FBI Counterterrorism Division, Action Memorandum, "Holy Land Foundation for Relief and Development International Emergency Economic Powers Act," to Richard Newcomb, director of the Office of Foreign Assets Control, Department of the Treasury, November 5, 2001, p. 15.

4. "Shutting Down the Terrorist Financial Network," US Department of

the Treasury, Office of Public Affairs press release, December 4, 2001, http://www.ustreas.gov/press/releases/po841.htm (accessed August 17, 2005).

5. John Mintz, "Muslim Charity, Officials Indicted," *Washington Post*, July 28, 2004.

6. *USA v. Holy Land Foundation for Relief and Development, et al.*, 04-CR-240, indictment (ND TX 2004).

7. Illinois Secretary of State, "Global Relief Foundation Articles of Incorporation," January 10, 1992. See also Global Relief Foundation, Inc., IRS Form 990, 1993.

8. "Overseas Registered Offices," *Global News* 4, no. 1 (Winter 1997): 8.

9. "Recent OFAC Actions: Global Relief Foundation, Inc. Financial Assets Blocked," US Department of the Treasury, Office of Foreign Assets Control (OFAC), December 14, 2001, http://www.treas.gov/offices/enforcement/ofac/actions/20011214a.shtml (accessed August 17, 2005).

10. "Feds Close Two More Muslim Groups," CBS News, December 14, 2001, http://www.cbsnews.com/stories/2001/12/14/terror/main321490.shtml (accessed August 17, 2005).

11. Ibid.

12. *USA v. Arnaout, et al.*, 02-CR-892, government's evidentiary proffer supporting the admissibility of coconspirator statements, p. 18 (ND IL 2003).

13. Illinois Secretary of State, Benevolence International Foundation Articles of Incorporation, March 30, 1992.

14. *USA v. Arnaout, et al.*, 02-CR-892, government's evidentiary proffer supporting the admissibility of coconspirator statements, pp. 17–52 (ND IL 2003).

15. Ibid., p. 17.

16. *USA v. Arnaout, et al.*, 02-CR-892, exhibits to government's response, p. 3 (ND IL 2003).

17. Islamic African Relief Agency, Form 1023, State of Missouri, 1987. See also "Treasury Designates Global Network, Senior Officials of IARA for Supporting bin Laden, Others," US Department of the Treasury, Office of Public Affairs press release, October 12, 2004, http://www.treas.gov/press/releases/js2025.htm (accessed August 17, 2005).

18. Attached to the IARA-USA 1023 form for the year 1987 submitted to the IRS were copies of the corporate bylaws for both IARA in the United States and Kartoum. The letterheads for these bylaws dated 1985–1988 have a distinctive crescent logo identical to that of the Sudanese Islamic Da'wa Organization.

19. Islamic African Relief Agency, Form 1023, State of Missouri, 1987 at Part III, Question 3.

20. Specifically these regional offices are or have been located in Baltimore; Detroit; Houston; Los Angeles; Orlando; Brooklyn; Gainesville, Florida; and Norman, Oklahoma. "IARA-USA Partner Offices," Web archive of the Islamic American Relief Agency, http://web.archive.org/web/20010224070450/www.iara-baltimore.org/partners.html.

21. "Treasury Designates Global Network, Senior Officials of IARA for Supporting bin Laden, Others."

22. "LIFE for Relief and Development," http://www.lifeusa.org/about/capsule.php (accessed April 15, 2005).

23. Ibid.

24. "LIFE for Relief and Development," http://www.lifeusa.org/contact/northamerica.php (accessed August 17, 2004). See also http://www.lifeusa.org/contact/international.php (accessed Aug. 17, 2004).

25. "Life's Financial Report," *LifeLink* (Fall 2003): 7.

26. " LIFE for Relief and Development Annual Report," 2003, http://www.lifeusa.org/fileadmin/pictures/ABOUTLIFE/Annual_Reports/2003_AR.pdf (accessed August 17, 2005).

27. Robert Collier, "Michigan-Based Charity Finds Itself Caught in the Middle; U.S. Troops Raid Group's Offices While Militants Denounce It as a Coalition Tool," *San Francisco Chronicle*, June 17, 2004.

28. Colorado Secretary of State, Human Concern International, Inc., Articles of Incorporation, February 7, 1986.

29. "The Role of the Islamic Associations in the Afghani War," *Al Jihad*, December 1986, p. 26.

30. Michigan Department of Commerce, 1998 Human Concern International, Inc., Articles of Incorporation, September 23, 1988. See also Michigan Department of Commerce, Mercy International USA, Inc., Certificate of Amendment to Articles of Incorporation, September 26, 1989.

31. Abdallah Ibrahim, speech at Muslim Arab Youth Association (MAYA) Sixteenth Annual Conference, Detroit, Michigan, December 1, 1993.

32. *USA v. Soliman Bihieri*, 03-CR-365, declaration in support of pretrial detention, p. 5 (ED VA 2003). See also State of District of Columbia, International Islamic Relief Organization Certificate of Incorporation, February 18, 1992. See also State of Virginia, International Relief Organization Certificate of Incorporation, June 22, 1991. See "In the Matter of the Search of 360 S. Washington Street, Falls Church, Virginia, 3rd Floor," 97-MG-25, affidavit of FBI SA Valerie Anne Donahue, p. 38 (ED VA 1997).

33. "Saudi Arabian Information Resources," http://www.saudinf.com/main/k312.htm (accessed August 17, 2004).

34. *USA v. Arnaout, et al.*, 02-CR-892, government's evidentiary proffer supporting the admissibility of coconspirator statements, p. 25 (ND IL 2003).

35. *In the Matter Involving 555 Grove Street, Herndon, Virginia, and Related Locations*, 02-MG-114, affidavit of SA David Kane, attachment C (ED VA Filed March 2002, unsealed October 17, 2003).

36. Richard Chesnoff, "It's More Than Just Who Plants the Explosives," *New York Daily News*, July 31, 1996.

37. *USA v. Global Chemical Corporation*, 97-M-10, affidavit of FBI Special Agent Valerie Donahue, p. 15 (ND IL 1997).

38. *In the Matter Involving 555 Grove Street, Herndon, Virginia, and Related Locations*, 02-MG-114, affidavit of SA David Kane, attachment C7 (ED VA Filed March 2002, unsealed October 17, 2003).

39. "Records Sought about Tax-Exempt Organizations for Committee's Terror Finance Probe," Senate Finance Committee press release, December 22, 2003.

40. "Treasury Designates Director, Branches of Charity Bankrolling Al Qaeda Network," Treasury Department press release, August 3, 2006, http://www.treas.gov/press/release/hp45.htm (accessed August 10, 2006).

41. Charles Richards, "Crisis in the Gulf: Jordanians Hear Call to Arms Against 'Crusaders,'" *London Independent,* August 11, 1990.

42. Louise Lief et al., "The War Will Reshape the Arab World in Unpredictable Ways," *U.S. News & World Report,* January 28, 1991, p. 26.

43. "News and Activities," *International Relief Monitor* 2 (August 1996): 2I. See also Richards, "Crisis in the Gulf," p. 10. See also Saad G Hattar, "Former Islamist Deputy Released on Bail, Faces Charges," *Jordan Times*, September 29, 1999 (accessed via FBIS).

44. "Free Sami Al Arian," http://www.freesamialarian.com/bio.htm, (accessed August 17, 2005).

45. "Members of the Palestinian Islamic Jihad Arrested, Charged with Racketeering and Conspiracy to Provide Support to Terrorists," US Department of Justice press release, February 20, 2003.

46. *USA v. Sami al Arian*, 8:03-CR-77-T-30TBN (MD FL 2005).

47. Meg Lauglan, "Evidence Is Lacking Al Arain Defense Says," *St. Petersburg Times*, November 10, 2005.

48. *USA v. Al Arian, et al.*, 03-CR-77, plea agreement (MD FL February 28, 2006).

49. *USA v. Al Arian, et al.*, 03-CR-77, judgment in a criminal case (MD FL May 1, 2006).

50. State of Missouri, Islamic African Relief Agency Form 1023, 1987.

51. ISNA and OLF were both located at P.O. Box 38, Plainfield, IN, 46168 (*Ila Filastin*, February 1989). See also *Islamic Horizons*, March–April 1988, p. 55.

52. "1992 Annual Report Islamic Society of North America," ISNA Thirtieth Annual Convention, September 30, 1993.

53. "An Open Thank You Letter from Mousa Abu-Marzook," *Washington Report on Middle East Affairs*, August/September 1997, p. 64.

54. "Freeze on Group's Assets Questioned by U.S. Muslims," ISNA press release, December 4, 2001, Web archive of the Islamic Society of North America, http://web.archive.org/web/20020214200911/www.isna.net/news.asp?id=44&view=detail (accessed August 17, 2005). This statement was coissued by the American Muslim Alliance, AMC, ISNA, ICNA, Muslim American Society, Muslim Public Affairs Council, and Muslim Student Association of USA and Canada.

55. Ibid.

56. Ibid.

57. Dan Eggen and John Mintz, "Muslim Groups' IRS Files Sought," *Washington Post*, January 14, 2004.

58. Senator Chuck Grassley, "Memorandum; Re: Committee Review of Certain Charities," US Senate Committee on Finance, December 6, 2005.

59. Ibid.

60. Robert King, "Indiana-Based Islamic Society Cleared in Senate Investigation," Islamic Society of North America, January 13, 2006.

61. This generosity is not surprising, given that IRO's status as an arm of IIRO, itself affiliated with the MWL, gave the organization access to a significant amount of funding from abroad.

62. State of Virginia, International Relief Organization, Inc., Form 990, 1995–1999.

63. State of Virginia, International Relief Organization, Inc., Form 990, 1992 and 1995–1997. This money may have also been used to finance the 1998 bombings of the American embassies in Africa. Matt Epstein and Ben Schmidt, "Operation Support System Shutdown: Who Paid for the 1998 East African Embassy Bombings?" National Review Online, September 4, 2003.

64. State of Virginia, International Relief Organization, Inc., Form 990, 1995 and 1998.

65. Holy Land Foundation Newsletter, *HLF News*, July 1995, p. 4. Note: many instances of donations from other charities not discussed in this section exist. For instance, Care International, which is an organization that was involved in the formation of CAMC, gave over $180,000 to GRF during the late 1990s/early 2000s. See for example: IRS Form 990 for Global Relief Foundation, Inc., showing donations from Care International, Inc., $24,438—Fiscal Year 1996; $7,563—Fiscal Year 1997; $37,360—Fiscal Year 1998; $22,344—Fiscal Year 1999; $10,679—Fiscal Year 1999; $78,200—Fiscal Year 2000; Total: $180,384. State of Illinois, Global Relief Foundation Form 990, 1996–2000.

66. State of Texas, Holy Land Foundation for Relief and Development Form 990, 1999. See also Kevin Pang and Mike Anton, "Rally Supports Muslim Man Who Was Arrested by FBI," *Los Angeles Times*, July 29, 2004, p. 3.

67. Ibid.

68. "Benevolence Report," *Benevolence International Foundation* 3, no. 1 (April 1997): 6. For example, from April 1994 to April 1996, according to BIF's financial report, 80 percent of BIF's international programs focused on Bosnia, 11 percent on Chechnya.

69. *USA v. Enaam M. Arnaout*, 02-CR-892, government's evidentiary proffer supporting the admissibility of coconspirator statements, pp. 28–29 (ND IL January 31, 2003); *USA v. Benevolence International Foundation, Inc.*, 02-CR-0414, sworn affidavit of FBI special agent Robert Walker, p. 29 (ED IL April 29, 2002).

70. *Benevolence International Foundation, Inc., et al. v. Ashcroft, et al.*, 02-CV-763, declaration of Enaam Arnaout, p. 17 (ND IL 2002).

71. "Human Development," *LifeLink* (Fall 2001): 6.

72. "Benevolence Report," *Benevolence International Foundation* 4, no. 2 (July 1998): 10.

73. "Benevolence Report," *Benevolence International Foundation* 6, no. 4 (December 2000).

74. "GRF Spreads the Blessings of Ramadan Worldwide," *Global News* 5, no. 1 (Summer 1998): 5.

75. Web archive of Interpal, "International Donations," http://web.archive.org/web/20020212020222/http://www.interpal.org/web/usa.htm (accessed August 17, 2005).

76. "U.S. Designated Five Charities Funding Hamas and Six Senior Hamas Leaders as Terrorist Entities," US Treasury, August 22, 2003, http://www.ots.treas .gov/docs/4/48937.html (accessed February 9, 2006).

77. Web archive of Interpal, "International Donations," http://web.archive.org/web/20020212020222/http://www.interpal.org/web/usa.htm (accessed August 17, 2005).

78. State of Michigan, LIFE for Relief and Development (formerly Islamic Relief Association) Form 990, 1994–1998.

79. Dale Watson, November 5, 2001.

80. Ibid.

81. *USA v. Benevolence International Foundation, Inc., et al.*, 02-CR-414, affidavit of FBI SA Robert Walker (ND IL 2002).

82. *USA v. Holy Land Foundation for Relief and Development, et al.*, 04-CR-240, indictment, p. 11 (ND TX July 26, 2004).

83. Web archive of Benevolence International Foundation Web site, http://web.archive.org/web/20000229100744/ http://www.benevolence.org/ (accessed August 17, 2005).

84. Ibid.

85. *USA v. Arnaout, et al.*, 02-CR-892, government's evidentiary proffer supporting the admissibility of coconspirator statements, p. 51 (ND IL 2003).

86. Ibid.

87. *USA v. Holy Land Foundation for Relief and Development, et al.*, 04-CR-240, indictment (ND TX, 2004).

88. State of New Jersey, Islamic Center of Passaic County Articles of Incorporation, September 18, 1989. See also David Koenig, "FBI Links Muslim Charity Figure to Anti-Israel Rally," *Bergen County Record*, December 7, 2001.

89. Dale Watson, Action Memorandum to Richard Newcomb, November 5, 2001.

90. "Speech of Mohammed El-Mezain," *15th Annual MAYA Convention*, VHS (1992, Oklahoma City, OK).

91. State of Texas, Holy Land Foundation for Relief and Development Form 990, 1993, 1998, and 2000.

92. "Interrogation of Muhammad Anati," Government of Israel, Israeli Defense Forces (IDF) Report no. 10/319/98, January 19, 1998.

93. *USA v. Holy Land Foundation for Relief and Development, et al.*, 04-CR-240, indictment, p. 13 (ND TX, 2004).

94. Ibid.

95. Ibid., p. 47.

96. Dale Watson, Action Memorandum to Richard Newcomb, November 5, 2001, p. 14.

97. Ibid. Specifically, HLF sponsored at least five of Sheikh Muhammad Siyam's trips to the United States between April 1992 and March 1994.

98. Occupied Land Fund Advertisement, *Ila Filastin*, November/December 1989, p. 8.

99. Islamic Association for Palestine Communiqué, *Ila Filastin*, November/December 1989, p. 8.

100. "Welcome Aboard to HLF's American Airlines AAdvantage," *HLF News* 5, no. 3 (December 1998): 4.

101. *CAIR Action Alert*, September 27, 1996.

102. *SHARE Newsletter*, August 2000, p. 3.

103. Holy Land Foundation for Relief and Development, http://www.hlf.org/giftmatching.shtml (accessed December 7, 2001).

104. "101 Days," http://web.archive.org/web/20021201091330/http://www.interpal.org/web/usa.htm (accessed August 17, 2005).

105. Ibid.

106. Hamas, http://www.palestine-info.com/arabic/links/links.htm (accessed August 17, 2005).

107. Ibid.

108. "'72 Black Eyed Virgins': A Muslim Debate on the Rewards of Martyrs," *MEMRI: Inquiry and Analysis Series*, no. 74 (October 30, 2004); "Interview of Palestinian Authority Mufti Sheikh 'Ikrima Sabri," *Al Ahram Al Arabi*, October 28, 2001, translated by MEMRI, http://memri.org/bin/articles.cgi?Page=archives&Area=ia&ID=IA7401 (accessed August 17, 2005).

109. State of Texas, Holy Land Foundation for Relief and Development Form 990, 1999.

110. *Boim, et al. v. Quranic Literacy Institute, et al.*, 00-CV-2905, oral disposition of Shukri Abu Bakr, section 128 (ND IL January 20, 2003).

111. State of Texas, Holy Land Foundation for Relief and Development Form 990, 1999.

112. Ibid.

113. "Islamic Society of North America Annual Report," 1992.

114. State of Virginia, International Relief Organization, Inc., Form 990, 1996–1997.

115. State of Virginia, Safa Trust, Inc., Form 990, 1998. See also *In the Matter Involving 555 Grove Street, Herndon, Virginia, and Related Locations*, 02-MG-114, affidavit of SA David Kane, p. 40 (ED VA Filed March 2002, unsealed October 17, 2003).

116. State of Virginia, The International Education Trust, Inc., Form 990, 2000.

117. *In the Matter Involving 555 Grove Street, Herndon, Virginia, and Related Locations*, 02-MG-114, affidavit of SA David Kane, p. 2 (ED VA Filed March 2002, unsealed October 17, 2003).

118. Holy Land Foundation for Relief and Development Newsletter, *HLF News* 4, no. 10 (January 1998).

119. *Boim, et al. v. Quranic Literacy Institute, et al.*, 00-CV-2905, deposition of Rafeeq Jaber, pp. 77–78 (ND IL 2003).

120. Ibid., pp. 253–54.

121. Noreen S. Ahmed-Ullah et al., "Special Report: The Struggle for the Soul of Islam; Hard-liners Won Battle for Bridgeview Mosque," *Chicago Tribune*, February 8, 2004.

122. Dale Watson, Action Memorandum to Richard Newcomb, November 5, 2001, p. 48.

123. Ibid., pp. 10–11.

124. Todd Benson, "Dallas-Area Muslims Join Efforts to Help Kosovo," *Dallas Morning News*, April 20, 1999. The figure of $50,000 was given the center's chairman, Osama Abdullah. The Islamic Association of North Texas is the largest mosque in Richardson.

125. Letter from former undersecretary of state for political affairs, Thomas R. Pickering to USAID's J. Brady Anderson, August 30, 2000.

126. Dale Watson, Action Memorandum to Richard Newcomb, November 5, 2001, p. 18.

127. Ibid., p. 22.

128. Ibid., pp. 25–26.

129. Ibid., pp. 32, 28–29.

130. Ibid., pp. 43–45.

131. "Recent OFAC Actions: Benevolence International Foundation Now Listed as a 'Specially Designated Global Terrorist' (SD GT)" US Department of the Treasury, Office of Foreign Assets Control, November 19, 2002.

132. State of Illinois, Benevolence International Foundation Articles of Incorporation, March 30, 1992. See also State of Illinois, Benevolence International Foundation, Inc., Form 1023, 1992.

133. Web archive of Benevolence International Foundation, http://web.archive.org/web/20000229100744/http://www.benevolence.org/ (accessed August 17, 2005).

134. *USA v. Arnaout, et al.*, 02-CR-892, government's evidentiary proffer supporting the admissibility of coconspirator statements, pp. 51–52 (ND IL 2003).

135. *USA v. Benevolence International Foundation, Inc., et al.*, 02-CR-414, affidavit of FBI SA Robert Walker, p. 4 (ND IL 2002).

136. *USA v. Arnaout, et al.*, 02-CR-892, government's evidentiary proffer supporting the admissibility of coconspirator statements, p. 51 (ND IL 2003).

137. *USA v. Benevolence International Foundation, Inc., et al.*, 02-CR-414, affidavit of FBI SA Robert Walker, p. 4 (ND IL 2002). See also *USA v. Arnaout, et al.*, 02-CR-892, pp. 17–52 (ND IL).

138. Ibid., pp. 19–20.

139. State of Illinois, Benevolence International Foundation Articles of Incorporation, March 30, 1992.

140. State of Illinois, Benevolence International Foundation, Inc., Form 990, 1993.

141. Ibid., p. 28.

142. *USA v. Arnaout, et al.*, 02-CR-892, government's evidentiary proffer supporting the admissibility of coconspirator statements, p. 18 (ND IL 2003).

143. *USA v. Arnaout, et al.*, 02-CR-892, exhibits to government's response (ND IL 2003).

144. *USA v. Arnaout, et al.*, 02-CR-892, government's evidentiary proffer supporting the admissibility of coconspirator statements, p. 49 (ND IL 2003).

145. "The Hawala Alternative Remittance System and Its Role in Money Laundering," Interpol General Secretariat, Lyon, January 2000, http://www.interpol.int/Public/FinancialCrime/MoneyLaundering/hawala/default.asp#2 (accessed August 17, 2005). See also "Benevolence Director Indicted for Racketeering Conspiracy: Providing Material Support to *Al Qaeda* and Other Violent Groups," US Department of Justice press release, October 9, 2002, http://www.usdoj.gov/usao/iln/pr/chicago /2002/pr1009_01.pdf (accessed August 17, 2005).

146. Donation form attached to a Benevolence International Foundation Newsletter, *Benevolence Report* 4, no. 1 (March 1998).

147. "Sources: Feds Raid Islamic Charity Groups," CNN, December 15, 2001.

148. *Benevolence International Foundation, Inc., et al. v. Ashcroft, et al.*, 02-CV-763, plaintiff's memorandum in opposition to defendant's motion to stay proceedings (ND IL 2002).

149. *Benevolence International Foundation, Inc., et al. v. Ashcroft, et al.*, 02-CV-763, declaration of Enaam Arnaout, p. 3 (ND IL 2002).

150. Matthew Levitt, "Combating Terrorist Financing, Despite the Saudis," *Policywatch*, November 1, 2002, http://www.washingtoninstitute.org/templateC05 .php?CID=1551 (accessed August 17, 2005).

151. Ibid.

152. Department of the Treasury Office of Financial Asset Control Designates the Benevolence International Foundation, November 19, 2002.

153. Linus Gegoriadis, "Brown Freezes Assets of Charity Suspected of Backing al-Qaida Bombs," *Guardian*, November 20, 2002.

154. Web archive of Benevolence International Foundation, http://web.archive.org/web/20020802072041/www.benevolence.org/faq.asp (accessed August 17, 2005).

155. *USA v. Arnaout, et al.*, 02-CR-892, government's evidentiary proffer supporting the admissibility of coconspirator statements, pp. 20, 23 (ND IL 2003).

156. Ibid.

157. Ibid., pp. 21–89.

158. Ibid., p. 25.

159. Ibid.

160. Ibid., pp. 26–27.

161. Ibid., p. 27.

162. Ibid.

163. Levitt, "Combating Terrorist Financing, Despite the Saudis."

164. *USA v. Arnaout, et al.*, 02-CR-892, government's evidentiary proffer supporting the admissibility of coconspirator statements, p. 33 (ND IL 2003).

165. Ibid., p. 33.

166. Ibid., p. 35.

167. Ibid.

168. Ibid., p. 38.

169. Ibid., p. 39.

170. Stephen Grey, "How the U.S. Kills Al Qaeda Leaders by Remote Control," *Sunday Times*, November 18, 2001.

171. *USA v. Arnaout, et al.*, 02-CR-892, government's evidentiary proffer supporting the admissibility of coconspirator statements, pp. 45–46 (ND IL 2003).

172. Ibid.

173. Ibid., p. 47.

174. Ibid., p. 20.

175. *Benevolence International Foundation, Inc., et al. v. Ashcroft, et al.*, 02-CV-763, complaint (ND IL 2002).

176. *USA v. Arnaout, et al.*, 02-CR-892, complaint, p. 4 (ND IL 2002).

177. *Benevolence International Foundation, Inc., et al. v. Ashcroft, et al.*, 02-CV-763, declaration of Enaam Arnaout, pp. 3–4 (ND IL 2002).

178. *USA v. Arnaout, et al.*, 02-CR-892, minute order for Arnaout sentencing (ND IL 2003).

179. "Fiscal Year 2003 National Operations Internal Revenue Service Annual Business Report—Criminal Investigations (CI): Benevolence Director Sentenced after Pleading Guilty to Racketeering Conspiracy," Internal Revenue Service (IRS), p. 16.

180. *USA v. Arnaout*, 03-3297, 03-3412, appellate decision (ED IL 2005).

181. *USA v. Arnaout, et al.*, 02-CR-892, amended judgment in a criminal case (ND IL February 17, 2006).

182. Treasury Department press release, "Treasury Designates Director, Branches of Charity Bankrolling Al Qaeda Network."

183. *USA v. Benevolence International Foundation, Inc., et al.*, 02-CR-0414, affidavit in support of complaint against Benevolence International Foundation, Inc., and Enaam Arnaout, a/k/a "Abu Mahmood," a/k/a "Abdel Samia," pp. 17–18 (ED IL 2002).

184. *World Trade Center Properties LLC, et. al. v. Al Baraka Investment and Development Corporation, et. al*, 04-728, complaint, p. 103 (SD NY 2004). See also *In the Matter of Mohammed Jamal Khalifah, Deportation Proceedings* A 29 457 661 (US Dept.

of Justice, Office of the Immigration Judge 1994), p. 103. See also State Department cable from Khalifa FOIA.

185. "FBI Arrests Head of the Chicago Based Int'l Charity Organization," Department of State press release, April 30, 2002.

186. Mohammed Jamal Khalifa was deported to Jordan in 1995 and is now back in Saudi Arabia. Mohamed Bayazid was released by INS authorities in 2002 and his whereabouts are currently unknown. J. M. Berger, "U.S. Secretly Detained Bin Laden Brother-in-Law for Four Months after Purported May 1995 Deportation," Intelwire, September 7, 2004, http://intelwire.egoplex.com/2004_09_07_exclusives.html (accessed August 17, 2005).

187. Treasury Department press release, "Treasury Designates Director, Branches of Charity Bankrolling Al Qaeda Network."

188. Michael Weissenstein, "Prosecutors Allege Brooklyn Doctor's Terror Ties," Associated Press, November 5, 2004.

189. Ibid.

190. *USA v. Arnaout, et al.*, 02-CR-892, government's evidentiary proffer supporting the admissibility of coconspirator statements, pp. 19, 51 (ND IL 2003).

191. Ibid., p. 20.

192. Arabic for "calling" in the Islamic religious sense, or "the act of remembering Allah and calling upon Him." See "About Islam," http://islam.about.com/cs/prayer/a/dua.htm (accessed August 17, 2005).

193. Benevolence International Foundation Newsletter, *Benevolence Report* 7, no. 3 (September 2001): 5.

194. Benevolence International Foundation Newsletter, *Benevolence Report* 7, no. 1 (March 2001): 3.

195. State of Illinois, Global Relief Foundation Form 990, 1993.

196. "Monograph on Terrorism Financing," Staff Report to the Commission, National Commission on Terrorist Attacks upon the United States, August 2004, p. 87.

197. "Treasury Department Fact Sheet on the Global Relief Foundation," Department of State: Washington File, October 18, 2002.

198. Kathy Gannon, "Islamic Aid Groups Now Bake Bread, Build Schools and a Mosque in Afghanistan," Associated Press, September 5, 2001.

199. Sarah Freeman, "Co-Founder of Muslim Charity Deported to Lebanon while Family Remains in the US," Associated Press, July 16, 2003.

200. State of Illinois, Global Relief Foundation, Articles of Incorporation, January 10, 1992.

201. National Commission on Terrorist Attacks upon the United States, "Monograph on Terrorism Financing," p. 89.

202. Ibid.

203. Associated Press, "Feds Claim Muslim Charity Had Contact with Bin Laden Secretary," March 28, 2002.

204. *Global News* 4, no. 1 (Winter 97): 8.

205. "Treasury Department Fact Sheet on the Global Relief Foundation."

206. Ibid.

207. Ann Mullen, "Haddad Breaks His Silence," *Metro Times*, March 17, 2004.

208. National Commission on Terrorist Attacks upon the United States, "Monograph on Terrorism Financing," p. 90.

209. Ibid., p. 91.

210. Ibid.

211. Ibid.

212. Ibid.

213. *Global Relief Foundation, Inc. v. New York Times Company, et al.*, 01-C-8821, memorandum opinion and order, p. 17 (ND IL 2003).

214. *Global Relief Foundation, Inc. v. New York Times Company, et al.*, opinion, endnote 6B (7th Circuit 2004).

215. Executive Order no. 13,224, Pursuant to 50U.S.C. 1641(C) and 50 U.S.C, "Message from the President of the United States Transmitting a 6-Month Periodic Report on the National Emergency with Respect to Persons Who Commit, Threaten to Commit, or Support Terrorism, September 23, 2001," p. 4.

216. "Feds Close Two More Muslim Groups," CBS News, December 14, 2001.

217. "Recent OFAC Actions," US Department of the Treasury, Office of Foreign Assets Control, October 18, 2002.

218. *Global Relief Foundation, Inc. v. O'Neil, et al.*, 02-C-674, memorandum opinion and order (ED IL 2002).

219. Ibid.

220. Ibid.

221. *Global Relief Foundation, Inc. v. O'Neil, et al.*, 02-2536, opinion (7th Circuit 2002).

222. National Commission on Terrorist Attacks upon the United States, "Monograph on Terrorism Financing," p. 89.

223. Ibid., p. 88.

224. *Al Thilal*, January 1996.

225. *USA v. Abdurahman Muhammed Alamoudi*, 03-1009M, supplemental declaration in support of detention (ED VA October 22, 2003).

226. Ibid.

227. "Former President of Global Relief Foundation Loses Immigration Appeal and Is Removed from the United States," Immigration and Customs Enforcement press release, July 11, 2003.

228. Ibid.

229. "Statement of Barbara Comstock, Director of Public Affairs, on the Haddad Asylum Decision," United States Department of Justice press release, November 22, 2002.

230. Ibid.

231. *USA v. Al-Sadawi*, 02-CR-00901, criminal docket (ED NY 2002).

232. Tom Hays, "Alleged Smuggler Ordered Held without Bail," Associated Press, July 29, 2002.

233. "Man Convicted of Smuggling $600,000," Associated Press, July 23, 2003.

234. John Marzulli, "Feds: Cleric Was a Terror Money Man," *New York Daily News*, November 14, 2003.

235. Tom Hays, "Feds Link Money Smuggler to Outlawed Muslim Charity," Associated Press, November 27, 2003.

236. Anthony DeStefano, "I Am Not a Terrorist,' Cleric Says," *Newsday*, December 12, 2003.

237. Associated Press, "Islamic Fund-Raiser Gets 5 Years for Plot to Smuggle Cash in Cracker, Cereal Boxes," December 11, 2003.

238. State of Illinois, Global Relief Foundation Form 990, 1993-2000.

239. *Global News*, 5, no. 2 (Autumn 1998).

240. *Al Zaitounah* 6, no. 157 (December 19,1997) and *Global News* 4 (Winter 1997).

241. Web archive of the Global Relief Foundation, "Donate by Corporate Gift Matching," http://web.archive.org/web/20011127234425/http://www.grf.org/helpnow-corporate.html (accessed August 17, 2005).

242. Web archive of the Global Relief Foundation, http://web.archive.org/web/20011127232518/http://www.grf.org/helpnow-wire.html (accessed August 17, 2005).

243. State of Illinois, IRS Form 990 for Global Relief Foundation, Inc., showing donations from Care International, Inc.: $24,438—Fiscal Year 1996; $7,563—Fiscal Year 1997; $37,160—Fiscal Year 1998; $22,344—Fiscal Year 1999; $10,679—Fiscal Year 1999; $78,200—Fiscal Year 2000; Total: $180,384, Global Relief Foundation Form 990, 1996–2000.

244. Muslim Students Association of the United States and Canada: List of Muslim Relief Organizations in Alphabetical Order, Care International, http://www.msa-natl.org/resources/Relief_Orgs.html (accessed August 17, 2005).

245. State of Illinois, IRS Form 990 for Global Relief Foundation, Inc., showing donations from the Islamic Society of Arlington: $5,780—Fiscal Year 1996; $25,500—Fiscal Year 1997; $25,500—Fiscal Year 1998; $26,521—Fiscal Year 1999; Total: $85,636, Global Relief Foundation Forms 990, 1996–1999.

246. Ben Tinsley, "Muslim Officials Want Imam Banned from Mosque; Supporters Say Leader Should Retain Role," *Dallas Morning News*, March 21, 2000.

247. Ibid.

248. IRS Form 990 for Global Relief Foundation, Inc: $5,100—Fiscal Year 1997; $6,000—Fiscal Year 2000; Total: Approximately $11,100.

249. *USA v. Hassoun*, 04-CR-60001, indictment (SD FL 2004).

250. State of Florida, Benevolence International Foundation Articles of Incorporation, February 12, 1993.

251. David Kidwell, "Bomb Suspect, Broward Man Spoke, FBI Says," *Miami Herald*, June 29, 2002.

252. *USA v. Hassoun, et al.*, 04-60001-CR, second superseding indictment (SD FL 2004). See also Curt Anderson, "Feds Charge 2 with Backing Terrorism," Associated Press, September 17, 2004.

253. *USA v. Hassoun, et al.*, 04-60001-CR, superceding indictment (SD FL 2005).

254. *The Call of Islam*, January–February 1996, December–January 1996–1997, February–March 1997, and April–May 1997, and Call of Islam Web site, November 15, 1996.

255. "Mission Statement and Objectives," KindHearts Web site. http://www.kind-hearts.org/ramadhan/KH_mission.htm.

256. Ohio Secretary of State, KindHearts for Charitable Humanitarian Development Articles of Incorporation, filed January 22, 2002.

257. Oklahoma Secretary of State, KindHearts for Charitable Humanitarian Development Articles of Incorporation, filed September 29, 2003.

258. Nevada Secretary of State, KindHearts for Charitable Humanitarian Development Articles of Incorporation, filed August 18, 2003.

259. Indiana Secretary of State, KindHearts for Charitable Humanitarian Development Articles of Incorporation, filed October 17, 2003.

260. Colorado Secretary of State, KindHearts for Charitable Humanitarian Development Articles of Incorporation, filed September 29, 2003.

261. KindHearts for Charitable Humanitarian Development Unified Registration Statement for Charitable Organizations, filed September 9, 2002.

262. "Treasury Freezes Assets of Organization Tied to Hamas," US Department of the Treasury press release, February 19, 2006.

263. Ibid.

264. Ohio Secretary of State, KindHearts for Charitable Humanitarian Development Articles of Incorporation, filed January 22, 2002.

265. KindHearts newsletter, *Kind Hearts* 2, no. 2 (Fall 2003), http://www.kind-hearts.org/publications/Fall-03.pdf (accessed July 18, 2005).

266. *Global News* (Winter 2000): 10.

267. Crystal Nelson, "Youth Project Starts Up," *News Journal*, August 3, 2000.

268. Randall Chase, "Delaware Executes Killer Who Claimed Rehabilitation," Associated Press, May 25, 2001.

269. Randall Chase, "Death Row Inmate Loses Last-Minute Bid for Commutation," Associated Press, May 24, 2001.

270. 2003 KindHearts Form 990, IRS.

271. Web archive of the Islamic Association for Palestine Web site, http://web.archive.org/web/20021201230251/www.iap.org/index2.html (accessed July 24, 2006) and http://web.archive.org/web/20030602045953/www.iap.org/index2.html (accessed July 24, 2006).

272. See also "Eid Cards from KindHearts," Web archive of the Islamic Association for Palestine Web site, February 10, 2003, http://web.archive.org/web/20030407163035/http://www.iap.org/febmarch2003headlines.htm (accessed July 24, 2006).

273. KindHearts, "Message from KindHearts," November 18, 2002, distributed through iapinfo@iap.org.

274. Unified Registration Statement for Charitable Organizations, Supple-

mental Answers, 2002. According to this document, el-Mezain conducted the fund-raising at a KindHearts event on May 12, 2002, in Toledo, Ohio.

275. "Treasury Freezes Assets of Organization Tied to Hamas," US Treasury Department press release, February 19, 2006, http://www.treas.gov/press/releases/js4058.htm (accessed August 11, 2006).

276. "IAP Board of Directors/Shura Council," Web archive of the Islamic Association for Palestine Web site, http://web.archive.org/web/20030803052043/http://www.iap.org/contactus.htm.

277. Business card of Abdelbaset Hemayel, http://www.sakkal.com/Graphics/logos/kindheart/kindhearts_bc03.html (accessed July 24, 2006).

278. "KindHearts Benefit Dinner for Palestine," Orlando, Florida, October 19, 2002. Flyer available at http://www.sakkal.com/Graphics/logos/kindheart/kindheart_orlando_flyer.html (accessed July 24, 2006). See also "KindHearts Benefit Dinner for Palestine," Fort Lauderdale, Florida, October 20, 2002. Flyer available at http: //www.sakkal.com/Graphics/logos/kindheart/kindheart_lauderdale_flyer .html (accessed July 24, 2006).

279. *USA v. HLFRD, et al.*, 04-CR-240, indictment (ND TX 2004).

280. KindHearts, *KindHearts Newsletter* 2, no. 1 (Spring 2004).

281. Illinois Secretary of State, Mosque Foundation Corporation File Detail Report.

282. 1995 Al Aqsa Educational Fund Form 990, IRS.

283. Watson, Action Memorandum to Richard Newcomb, November 5, 2001, p. 13.

284. "In a beautifully decorated hall, dinner guests participated in a silent auction and fundraising event, graciously led by Sh. Jamal Said and Sh. Kifah Mustapha, both of the Mosque Foundation, Bridgeview," "From the Field—MAS Freedom Foundation—Chicago: Legendary Civil Rights Leader Addresses Annual MAS Chicago Fundraising Dinner," Muslim American Society, http://www .masnet.org/takeaction.asp?id=2455 (accessed July 24, 2006).

285. *KindHearts* 2, no. 1 (Spring 2004), http://www.kind-hearts.org/publications/KHSpring04.pdf (accessed March 31, 2005).

286. Benevolence International Foundation Form 990: Contributions of $5,000 & More, IRS. See also Benevolence International Foundation Form 990: Schedule of Contributor Donating $5,000 or More in Money Securities or Other Property, IRS.

287. 1997 Global Relief Foundation Form 990: Donation of Cash & Property Over 5,000, IRS. See also 1999 Global Relief Foundation Form 990: Donation of Cash & Property Over 5,000, IRS; 2000 Global Relief Foundation, Form 990: Statement of Donors in Excess of $5,000 Each, IRS.

288. Ahmed-Ullah et al., "Struggle for the Soul of Islam."

289. Business card of Omar Shahin, http://www.sakkal.com/Graphics/logos/kindheart/kindhearts_bc03.html (accessed July 24, 2006).

290. Stephanie Innes, "Islamic Center of Tucson Hires Nashville Imam," *Ari-*

zona Daily Star, January 2, 2005, http://www.azstarnet.com/dailystar/related articles/55127.php (accessed February 9, 2006).

291. "PO-3553: Treasury Department Statement Regarding the Designation of the Global Relief Foundation," US Department of the Treasury, Office of Public Affairs, October 18, 2002, http://www.treas.gov/press/releases/po3553.htm (accessed July 24, 2006).

292. Arizona Secretary of State, Islamic Center of Tucson Annual Reports, filed May 21, 1984, and February 12, 1985.

293. Dr. Abdullah Azzam, "Al-Qa'ida," *Al Jihad*, no. 41 (April 1988).

294. *USA v. Bin Laden, et al.*, 98-CR-1023, trial transcripts: day 6, p. 789 (SD NY February 15, 2001).

295. "KindHearts newsletter," 1, no. 2 (Summer 2003), http://www.kind-hearts.org/publications/summer-03.pdf (accessed July 18, 2005).

296. "Biographical Sketch: Khalifah Ramadan," Web archive of the Council on Islamic-American Relations Web site, http://web.archive.org/web/20031017201654/www.cair-nj.org/biokramadan.htm (accessed July 24, 2006).

297. NationsBank Wire Transfer #941031011157000, Federal Reference #9410310014920824, October 31, 1994.

298. See also "CAIR Action Alert: American Muslims Asked to Pray for Palestinians," September 9, 1996.

299. Texas Secretary of State, CAIR Articles of Incorporation, filed September 29, 1998.

300. 1999 Holy Land Foundation Form 990, IRS.

301. 1993 and 1998 Holy Land Foundation Form 990, IRS.

302. Nihad Awad, "Muslim-Americans in Mainstream America," *Link* (February–March 2000). Articles of Incorporation, Council on American-Islamic Relations, September 15, 1994; *Boim v. Quranic Literacy Institute, et al.*, deposition of Rafeeq Jaber (ND IL July 20, 2003 and April 9, 2003).

303. "Bio of Sami Al-Arian," American-Arab Anti-Discrimination Committee (ADC) program of speakers, moderators, and award recipients, Seventeenth National Convention, Arlington, VA, June 8–11, 2000. See also American Muslim Council (AMC) Program, Tenth National Convention, Alexandria, VA, June 21–24, 2001, and Yasmin Mull, "A Shattered Dream," *Egypt Today*, December 10, 2003.

304. Résumé of Abdelrahman Alamoudi: Freedom of Information Act request.

305. *Boim v. Quranic Literacy Institute, et al.*, 00-CV-2905, deposition of Shukri Abu Baker, pp. 13–14 (ND IL January 30, 2003).

306. "1989 Islamic African Relief Agency Form 1023, IRS.

307. "Treasury Designates Global Network, Senior Officials of IARA for Supporting bin Laden, Others."

308. IRS Form 990, KindHearts, 2002.

309. US Department of the Treasury, "U.S. Designates Five Charities Funding Hamas and Six Senior Hamas Leaders as Terrorist Entities," August 22, 2003, http://www.ustreas.gov/press/releases/js672.htm (accessed July 24, 2006).

310. Ibid.

311. Ibid.

312. Watson, Action Memorandum to Newcomb, November 5, 2001.

313. Neil MacFarquhar, "Egyptian Group Patiently Pursues Dream of Islamic State," *New York Times*, January 20, 2002.

314. Muslim Brotherhood homepage, http://www.ummah.org.uk/ikhwan/index.html (accessed August 23, 2004); "Muslim Brothers," Federation of American Scientists Intelligence Research Program, http://www.fas.org/irp/world/para/mb.htm (accessed July 18, 2006).

315. MacFarquhar, "Egyptian Group Patiently Pursues Dream of Islamic State."

316. National Commission on Terrorist Attacks upon the United States, *The 9/11 Commission Report: Final Report of the National Commission on Terrorist Attacks upon the United States* (New York: Norton, 2004), p. 51.

317. Ibid., p. 145.

318. Larry Poston, *Islamic Da'wah in the West, Muslim Missionary Activity and the Dynamics of Conversion to Islam* (New York: Oxford University Press), p. 79.

319. Testimony of Richard Clarke before the Senate Committee on Banking, Housing, and Urban Affairs, October 22, 2003.

320. "Pakistan Symposium Focuses on Contribution of Maududi to Present Islamic Struggle," *Message International*, March 1992, p. 33.

321. For a good article on this topic, see Joseph Braude, "Misled: Moderate Muslims and Their Radical Leaders," *New Republic*, February 16, 2006.

322. "AMC Attends Briefing at the White House on Hate Crimes Legislation," AMC press release, April 26, 2000; article in the newsletter of the American Arab Anti-Discrimination Committee, *ADC Times*, December 1995; *AMC Report*, January 1996; *AMC Report*, March 1996.

323. Islam Online, "Resumé of Maher Hathout," http://www.islamonline.net/live dialogue/english/Guestcv.asp?hGuestID=1ClTGp (accessed September 27, 2004).

324. There are countless examples of this reframing by groups such as the World Assembly of Muslim Youth, the Council on American-Islamic Relations, the Muslim American Society, the Muslim Council of Britain, and many of the other groups discussed in this book. For a recent report that addresses this reframing, see Martin Bright, *When Progressives Treat with Reactionaries* (London: Policy Exchange, 2006).

325. "Washington Hears a Fresh Voice: MPAC Opens New Forums for Dialogue with the Media and Government Officials," *Minaret* (July–August 1997): 20.

326. Jim Landers, "Muslim Extremists Justify Violence on Way to Restoring Divine Law," Knight Ridder, November 3, 2001.

327. US Senate, "H. Concurrent Resolution 75, Condemning the National Islamic Front (NIF)," June 16, 1999, http://thomas.loc.gov/cgi-bin/query/z?c106:H.CON.RES.75.RFS (accessed November 19, 2004).

328. *The 9/11 Commission Report*, p. 57.

329. "State Department Hosts Ramadan Dinner for American Muslims," CAIR, MSANEWS, December 21, 1999.

330. "MPAC's Speech on Moderation at the State Department," MPAC press release, January 28, 2002.

331. "U.S. Muslims Meet with Powell on Foreign Policy; Secretary of State Offers Briefing on Issues, Solicits Muslim Input," US Newswire, June 17, 2004.

332. The list of witnesses and links to their prepared statements are found at http://foreign.senate.gov/hearings/2006/hrg060405p.html.

333. Ambassador Korologos's testimony is available at http://foreign.senate.gov/testimony/2006/KorologosTestimony060405.pdf.

334. While in his testimony Ambassador Korologos presented only some aspects of his initiative, more details can be found on the Web site: http://www.muslimdialogue.be/.

335. "American Muslims and Belgian Muslims in Dialogue," ISNA news release, November 21, 2005, http://www.isna.net/index.php?id=35&backPID=1&tt_news=460.

336. "CAIR Participates in Dialogue with European Muslims," CAIR news release, November 18, 2005, http://www.cair-net.org/default.asp?Page=articleView&id=1878&theType=NR.

337. ISNA, "American Muslims and Belgian Muslims in Dialogue."

338. "Michael Privot, board member of the Forum of European Muslim Youth and Student Organizations (FEMYSO) talks about the youth initiative they are putting together with the Muslim Students Association of the U.S. and Canada," Photo Gallery, Muslim Dialogue, http://www.muslimdialogue.be/gallery/pages/MDC21.htm (accessed August 28, 2006); Michael Privot and Salam al-Marayati, "Muslim Communities Participating in Society," Ecumenical Youth Council in Europe, http://www.ev-jugend.de/eyce/modules.php?op=modload&name=Pag Ed&file=index&topic_id=2&page_id=430 (accessed August 28, 2006).

339. For a list of FIOE's member organizations, see http://www.eu-islam.com/en/templates/Index_en.asp. Robin Niblett Senate Committee on Foreign Relations, Subcommittee on European Affairs, *Islamist Extremism in Europe*, 109th Congress, 1st sess., April 5, 2006; "Forty Shades of Green—Political Islam," *Economist*, February 4, 2006.

340. Decision of the French Council of State, June 7, 1999, as quoted in Fiammetta Venner, "OPA sur l'Islam de France: Les Ambitions de l'UOIF" (OPA on Islam of France: the Ambitions of the OUIF) (Paris: Calmann-Levy, 2005), p. 15.

341. History of the IGD, available at IGD's Web site: http://www.i-g-d.com/uber%20unss2.htm.

342. Martin Bright, "When Progressives Treat with Reactionaries," Policy Exchange Limited, July 2006, http://www.policyexchange.org.uk/Publications.aspx?id=192 (accessed July 19, 2006).

343. Sara Silvestri, "Interacting with Muslim Communities in the EU: Problems and Progress on the Way Towards a Multicultural European Society," Center of International Studies, University of Cambridge, 2003.

344. Report on Ibrahim el-Zayat, Cologne police, August 27, 2003; Ian Johnson, "How Islamic Group's Ties Reveal Europe's Challenge," *Wall Street Journal*, December 29, 2005.

345. "Islamic Institute Accurint Report," www.accurint.com (accessed January 31, 2005).

346. Checks #1000 (2/8/99) and 1102 (4/4/99), signed A. Alamoudi.

347. Frank Gaffney Jr., "A Troubling Influence," *Front Page*, December 9, 2003, p. 3.

348. Checks #2761 (10/27/99) and #3022 (08/24/00).

349. December 11, 1991, letter from Ramadan Abdullah to the University of South Florida on WISE letterhead. Ramadan Abdullah (Shallah) now heads the Palestinian Islamic Jihad in Damascus.

350. "News from Your Community," *Herald Dispatch* (Huntington, WV), May 16, 2002.

351. Steven Greenhut, "It's Time to Flush Dornan's Potty Politics," *Orange County Register*, February 1, 2004.

352. Franklin Foer, "Fevered Pitch: Grover Norquist's Strange Alliance with Radical Islam," *New Republic*, November 12, 2001.

353. "Official: Terrorism Suspect Attended White House Meeting," CNN, February 23, 2003.

354. Mary Jacoby, "Friends in High Places," *St. Petersburg Times*, March 11, 2003.

355. "Department of Justice Discusses Outreach on Civil Rights," *Islamic Institute Friday Brief* 37, no. 3, March 17, 2002.

356. Eunice Moscoso, "Targets of Probe Made Political Contributions," *Atlanta Journal-Constitution*, December 12, 2003.

357. In a March 2000 campaign stop near Tampa, Sami al-Arian and his family were photographed with Bush.

358. "CAMPAIGN 2000: Vice President Gore and Governor Bush Participate in Second Presidential Debate," FDCH Political Transcripts, October 11, 2000, p. 13.

359. Agha Saeed, "Seven Muslim Organizations Establish National Coordination Council," *Washington Report on Middle East Affairs* (March 1998): 56.

360. "American Muslim PAC Endroses George W. Bush for President," MSANEWS Listserve, October 23, 2000.

361. Ibid.

362. United Press International, "Hillary Clinton to Return Muslim Donations," October 25, 2000.

363. "Hillary and Hamas," *WSJ Opinion Journal*, November 3, 2000.

364. Mustafa Elhussein, "Commentary: Misjudged Muslims," *Washington Times*, December 17, 2000.

365. Food Marketing Institute, http://www.fmi.org/loss/ORT/ (accessed August 17, 2005).

366. Testimony of Randy A. Merritt before the United States House of Representatives Committee on Government Reform, Subcommittee on Criminal Jus-

tice, Drug Policy, and Human Resources, titled "National and International Consumer Products Fencing Operation Suspected of Providing Support to Terrorist Organizations," November 10, 2003.

367. Ibid.

368. Testimony of Robert S. Mueller, III, director of the Federal Bureau of Investigation, before the United States Senate Committee on Intelligence, February 16, 2005.

369. "Leader of Organized Retail Theft Ring Sentenced to 14 Years in Federal Prison," US Department of Justice press release, February 2, 2005, http://www.usdoj.gov/usao/txn/PressRel05/Ghali_sen1_amd.pdf (accessed August 17, 2005).

370. *USA v. Mohammed Khalil Ghali, et al.*, 03-CR-212, superceding indictment (ND T December 17, 2003).

371. *USA v. Ghali, et al.*, 03-CR-212, superseding indictment (2003).

372. Mark Clayton, "Is Black-Market Baby Formula Financing Terror?" *Christian Science Monitor*, June 29, 2005.

373. US Department of Justice press release, "Leader of Organized Infant Formula Theft Ring Sentenced to 14 Years in Federal Prison."

374. Benson and Riggs, "Feds Uncover Alleged Plot to Assassinate Fort Worth Cop, Federal Agent."

375. US Department of Justice press release, "Leaders of Organized Retail Theft Ring Sentenced to 14 Years in Federal Prison."

376. Benson and Riggs, "Feds Uncover Alleged Plot to Assassinate Fort Worth Cop, Federal Agent."

377. *USA v. Jamal, et al.*, 03-CR-261, indictment (D AZ 2003).

378. Ibid.

379. Michael Kiefer, "Baby-food Scam Nets 10 Years," *Arizona Republic*, October 8, 2005.

380. *USA v. Medina-Castellanos, et al.*, 05-CR-155, indictment (ED NC 2005).

381. Testimony of Randy A. Merritt, November 10, 2003.

382. Ibid.

383. "'Hezbollah Drugs Ring' Broken Up," BBC News, June 22, 2005.

384. Paul Haven, Associated Press, May 29, 2006.

385. *USA v. Baz Mohammed, et al.*, S14 03-CR 486 (DC), indictment (SD NY 2005).

386. Ibid.

387. Ibid., pp. 4–5.

388. *USA v Isa*, 04-CR-473, superseding indictment (ND IL 2004).

389. Chicago Islamic Center, Inc., Annual Report 2002, introduced as exhibit 1961 in *USA v. Al Arian, et al.*, 03-CR-77.

390. *USA v. Al Arian, et al.*, 03-CR-77, indictment (MD FL 2003).

391. Matt O'Connor, "Mosque Official's Release Denied," *Chicago Tribune*, August 11, 2004.

392. *USA v. Al Arian, et al.*, 03-CR-77, trial exhibits: Al-Qassam Mosque corporation filings (MD FL).

393. Natasha Korecki, "Mosque's Ex-treasurer Gets 20 Years," *Chicago Sun-times*, January 7, 2006.

394. "Stored-Value Cards," US Department of the Treasury, Financial Management Service, http://www.fms.treas.gov/storedvalue/ (accessed August 17, 2005).

395. North American Export Committee, http://www.naec.ws/ (accessed August 17, 2005).

396. North American Export Committee, "Scheduled Meetings," http://www.naec.ws/meetings.asp (accessed August 17, 2005).

397. "Fiscal Year 2006 JLBC Budget: Automobile Theft Authority Report," Arizona State Legislature, http://www.azleg.state.az.us/jlbc/06recbk/ata.pdf (accessed August 17, 2005).

398. "Lupita Murillo Reports: Arizona Auto Thefts Linked to Terrorism," Eyewitness News KVOA Tucson, May 18, 2005.

399. Patrick Quinn, "Iraq Car Bombings Kill 586 Since April," Associated Press, June 24, 2005.

400. Maggie Michael, "U.S. Troops Find Suspected al Zarqawi Command Center; Fallujah Toll Put 51 U.S. Troops Dead, 425 Injured," Associated Press, November 18, 2004.

401. *USA v. Amir Hosseni, et al.*, 05-CR-0254, criminal complaint, p. 9 (ND IL 2005).

402. Ibid.

403. *USA v. Amir Hosseini, et al.*, 05-CR-254, memorandum of the United States in support of its emergency motion to stay and revoke the Magistrate Court's order releasing Amir Hosseini, p. 5 (ND IL June 27, 2005).

404. *USA v. Amir Hosseini, et al.*, 05-CR-254, superseding indictment, p. 20 (ND IL January 19, 2006).

405. *USA v. Amir Hosseini, et al.*, 05-CR-254, government memorandum in support of revoking the release of Amir Hosseini, pp. 1–2 (ND IL 2005).

406. Robert Collier, "Michigan-Based Charity Finds Itself Caught in the Middle," *San Francisco Chronicle*, June 17, 2004.

407. *In the Matter of the Search of 360 S. Washington, 3rd Fl. Falls Church, VA*, 97-MG-25, search warrant (ED VA 1997).

-10-

THE SAAR NETWORK: INVESTING IN TERROR

Biheiri was advised to go to the United States [by Abu Saud, a senior member of the Muslim Brotherhood and the author of the first book on Islamic economics] and establish an Islamic financial corporation to take advantage of both the Islamic money in the United States and the freedom of operation of the U.S. financial market. . . . [Biheiri] gave as an example of the lack of freedom of Saudi Arabian institutions, the fact that [Saudi banks] could not take any specific "new" actions without approval of King Fahd. He related that by establishing an American financial company on U.S. soil, they would have the freedom to do as they pleased regarding business activity; he would just have to follow SEC guidelines.

—Soliman Biheiri, interview at Dulles International Airport, June 15, 2003,
US Customs Service Investigation Report

OVERVIEW

This chapter details the complex corporate web of companies, charities, and not-for-profit corporations that has come to be known as the SAAR Network, alternatively referred to as the Safa Group. The following passages are interspersed with extensive fact citations in an attempt to shed light on a shadowy network. By its complexity, it demonstrates the deliberate attempt by the persons involved to conceal their activities. For years they were successful at operating without much notice, but a series of incidents has drawn government scrutiny into this complex group of entities.

The Virginia-based SAAR Network will prove to be a paradigmatic example of large-scale money laundering by terrorist entities should the accusations, reinforced by trenchant and detailed evidence, made by Special Agent David Kane, then of the Bureau of Immigration and Customs Enforcement, in a 2003 affidavit be validated.[1] These accusations portray a tangle of more than one hundred real and paper companies, nonprofit charities, and social institutions with overlapping financial assets and executive personnel, seemingly deliberately designed to mislead and delude, which may prove to be one of the most sophisticated terror fund-raising mechanisms known to have operated in the United States.

Most SAAR entities in the United States were registered at the same Northern Virginia addresses and had no physical presence. Some were dissolved at the first hint of public scrutiny and later reconstituted under new names by the same people who had operated their previous incarnations. Eventually, funds that were collected and passed through multiple layers of businesses, charities, and accounts were transferred to offshore accounts in places with secretive banking practices. From this point, these funds became exceedingly difficult to trace further.

OPERATION GREEN QUEST

Operation Green Quest, a multiagency task force led first by US Customs and then by US Immigration and Customs Enforcement, investigated the SAAR Network and other suspected terrorist-financing nexuses. Other participating agencies were the IRS, the US Secret Service, the FBI, the Office of Foreign Assets Control, the Financial Crimes Enforcement Network, the US Postal Inspection Service, the Naval Criminal Investigative Service, and the Bureau of Alcohol, Tobacco, and Firearms. Operation Green Quest was charged with "identifying, disrupting, and dismantling the financial infrastructures and sources of terrorist funding."[2] Each agency involved contributed its own particular specialties. For example, the IRS brought its experience in investigating tax holdings and filings. The Financial Crimes Enforcement Network examined bank transactions. The Secret Service has long investigated credit card crime. Customs investigators contributed their expertise in scrutinizing the movement of illegal currency. Every agency was able to contribute something valuable within the context of this multiagency task force.[3]

Operation Green Quest was not seeking a smoking gun. The participants were not necessarily trying to uncover a direct transaction involving someone putting money into the hands of an al Qaeda operative. Their mission was focused on closing down the illicit financial systems and repairing vulnerabilities in legitimate systems that could be used to raise funds for and direct funds to terrorists. The investigations started by Operation Green Quest were not intended to bring about direct charges of material support to terrorists, but instead were aimed at uncovering tax evasion, false statements on tax forms, lying to federal agents, and other white-collar crimes—a strategy similar to that used against Al Capone in 1930 when he was charged with tax evasion rather than murder and bootlegging.

Over the course of two days in March 2002, Operation Green Quest raided over fifteen SAAR Network sites, mostly in and around Herndon, Virginia. The investigating agents seized computer and financial records.[4]

Following the restructuring that accompanied creation of the Department of Homeland Security and pursuant to an agreement between then Secretary of Homeland Security Tom Ridge and then Attorney General John Ashcroft in 2003, Immigration and Customs Enforcement now refers financial cases clearly involving a terrorist nexus to the Joint Terrorism Task Forces under the purview of the FBI. The realignment effectively ended Operation Green Quest, after investigations that had resulted in seventy indictments and $33 million seized by 2003.[5]

WHAT IS SAAR?

The origins of the SAAR Network reside with a group of Muslim scholars, businessmen, and scientists from the Middle East and Asia who gathered in the United States in the early 1980s.[6] The network officially was born with the incorporation of the SAAR Foundation, Inc., in Herndon, Virginia, as a 501(c)(3) nonprofit on July 29, 1983.[7] Though this parent corporation dissolved on December 28, 2000,[8] another group, Safa Trust, run by many of those affiliated with the SAAR Network, took its place. SAAR is believed to have taken its name from Sulaiman Abdul Aziz al-Rajhi, patriarch of the wealthy Saudi Arabian al-Rajhi family.[9] Yaqub Mirza, a primary SAAR Network officer, told a reporter that the al-Rajhi family is the foundation's biggest donor.[10]

What exactly is the SAAR Network? Federal investigations have alleged that it is a network of up to one hundred nonprofit and for-profit organizations that "are interrelated through corporate officers and holding companies—subsidiary relationships, to facilitate the funding of terrorist operations."[11] Most of these organizations have the same individuals at their helms—specifically Middle Eastern nationals in Northern Virginia with known ties to radical Islamist groups that have been accused of fostering radicalism and supporting terrorist goals. A large number of these organizations share the same address in Herndon, Virginia—an address that gives no physical indication of being the headquarters of a vast number of businesses. The Kane affidavit alleges that these facts coupled with information garnered from tax and financial records effectively demonstrate that many of the organizations in the SAAR Network are "phantom" entities established solely to engage in the reverse money-laundering process of layering: one that converts clean money from charities and businesses into illicit money, hidden from oversight, that can be channeled toward illegal activities, whether those activities are white-collar crimes motivated by greed or the crime of supporting terrorism. Special Agent Kane noted that while he did not "know for sure why the labyrinth of organizations and charities that comprise the Safa Group was constructed, there does not appear to be any innocent explanation."[12] He went on to provide possible reasons behind the creation of the Safa Group: "to conceal support for terrorism," "to conceal support for otherwise non-exempt organizations," "to shelter income derived from what actually are personal investments," "to shelter income derived from what actually was someone else's personal investments for which individuals in the United States were trustees," "to shelter income from personal investments in the course of sheltering income for someone else," and "to avoid excise taxes that would otherwise be due and payable on private foundations."[13] Based on what had been discovered about the histories of the individuals who led the various SAAR entities, Kane said, "the most likely reason is to conceal support for terrorism."[14]

Millions of dollars have been shuffled between these organizations in confusing patterns made even more confusing by the frequent dissolution of entities within the network, followed by reconstitution under a different name, with many of the same corporate officers moving into the new entities. Over 70 percent of all the contributions to SAAR charities came from other entities within the SAAR Network.[15] Another 12 percent came from unidentified donors from the "overseas general public."[16] Thirteen percent come from other sources abroad, such as Middle Eastern and Asian entities.[17] These shuffled millions have ended up in offshore accounts in the Bahamas and the Isle of Man where they became, for the most part, impossible to trace.[18] Funds that have been traced have arrived at financial institutions designated by the US Treasury Department as financial conduits for terrorist groups.[19] These particular institutions, Bank Al Taqwa and Akida Bank Private, Ltd., will be covered in more detail later in this chapter. Other funds were traced to a group linked to the terrorist organization Palestinian Islamic Jihad (PIJ) called WISE (see chapter 7). This was one of many factors linking the SAAR Network to Palestinian Islamic Jihad and some of the activities of Sami al-Arian that led to his indictment.

The investigation of this network by Operation Green Quest uncovered evidence of multiple crimes involving false statements on Forms 990 and attachments, false statements regarding relationships to other organizations within the SAAR Network, tax evasion, material support to terrorists, false statements relating to contributions received and grants made, misrepresentations made during an audit, possible income-tax fraud, and failure to disclose foreign bank accounts.[20]

SAAR'S STRUCTURE AND LEADERS

The key players in the SAAR Network are Middle Eastern and, in one case, South Asian. The network's founder is Saudi, and the senior SAAR leadership includes a Saudi, an Iraqi, a Kurd, and a Pakistani. Several of its leaders received degrees from American universities in the early 1970s. All four have multiple affiliations with Islamic businesses and foundations around the world. Below are their abbreviated biographies. These maps of their lives present many different names of individuals and organizations, all of which are explained either after the biographies, addressed in detail in other chapters (largely in chapter 9), or both. The biographies of these men who have formed and guided SAAR, and other individuals who have been associated with the network throughout its history, share the common theme of significant ties to Islamist activity and ideology. Other SAAR main players are M. Omar Ashraf, Muhammad Ashraf, Samir Salah, Cherif Sedky, Hisham al-Talib, Ahmad Totonji, and Iqbal Unus.

Abdulhamid Abusulayman is a Saudi who was born in 1936. After attending the University of Cairo, he worked for the Saudi government in the early 1960s. In the early 1970s, Abusulayman was a founding member of the Association of Muslim Social Scientists (AMSS)[21] and earned his doctorate from the University of Pennsylvania. During most of the decade, he was the secretary-general of the World Assembly of Muslim Youth (WAMY) in Riyadh, an organization sponsored by the

Saudi government with chapters worldwide, which has supported radical causes and distributed literature and materials saturated with virulence directed toward the West and those of the Jewish faith.[22] For instance, *Islamic Views*, a book written by WAMY and printed by the Saudi government's Armed Forces Printing Press, reads, "[T]each our children to love taking revenge on the Jews and the oppressors, and teach them that our youngsters will liberate Palestine and al-Quds when they go back to Islam and make Jihad for the sake of Allah."[23] WAMY's involvement in the SAAR Network is discussed later in this chapter. In 1981, Abusulayman helped found the International Institute of Islamic Thought (IIIT).[24] For the next two years he served as the chairman of the political science department at King Sa'ud University in Riyadh. In the mid-1980s, as SAAR was forming, Abusulayman became president of AMSS, the organization he had helped establish.

In 2002 and 2003, Abusulayman served in a leadership position in at least five SAAR Network organizations. He was president of IIIT, editor in chief of the *American Journal of Islamic Social Scientists,* an academic advisory board member of the Graduate School of Islamic Social Scientists (GSISS), and an officer both of the International Islamic Forum for Science, Technology & Human Resources Development and of the Child Development Foundation.[25]

Taha al-Alwani, an Iraqi born in the 1930s, began studying Islamic law in Cairo in 1959 and earned his doctorate in 1973. During his tenure as a professor of Islamic law at King Sa'ud University over the next decade, he met the future SAAR officers Ismail al-Faruqi and Abdulhamid Abusulayman. By 1981, the three had founded IIIT.[26] In 1986, al-Alwani became a trustee of Safa Trust.[27] He also founded and remains active with the Council of the Muslim World League, an organization headquartered in Mecca that is discussed further below.[28]

In 2002 and 2003, al-Alwani was the president of five SAAR organizations: IIIT, the Fiqh Council of North America, GSISS, Heritage Educational Trust, and Mena Estates, and was a lesser executive officer of Heritage Holdings.[29] Al-Alwani came to the United States in 1984 to help lead the American branch of IIIT.[30]

Jamal Barzinji, a Kurd born in Iraq in the late 1930s,[31] attended college in England in the early 1960s, earning a degree in chemical engineering.[32] In 1963, he became a founding member of the Muslim Students Association

(MSA),[33] and in 1974 he received a master's degree in chemical engineering from Louisiana State University.[34] A few years later, Barzinji became the chairman of the North American Islamic Trust (NAIT) in Fort Wayne, Indiana.[35] In 1981, Barzinji became a founding member of the Islamic Society of North America (ISNA),[36] and he served on SAAR's initial board of trustees in 1983.[37] Barzinji is listed as the CEO of Mar-Jac Poultry in Georgia, another SAAR entity.[38] In addition, he has served as a director of Bank Islam Malaysia and helped found the Center for the Study of Islam and Democracy (CSID).[39]

In 2002 and 2003, Barzinji held a leadership position in at least thirteen SAAR organizations, among them posts as director and vice president for research and publication of IIIT, director of Safa Trust, president and chairman of Mar-Jac Poultry, and member of the board of trustees of Amana Mutual Funds Trust. Barzinji has academic affiliations unrelated to SAAR, which include being editor in chief of *Islamiyat Al Ma'rifah*, a publication linked to IIIT, and dean of the Faculty of Islamic Revealed Knowledge and Social Science at the International Islamic University, Malaysia.[40]

Yaqub Mirza was born in Pakistan in 1946. He moved to Dallas, Texas, in 1970, a year after receiving a science degree from the University of Karachi. By 1975, he had earned a doctorate in physics as well as teaching certification from the University of Texas at Dallas. By 1977, he was president of the Muslim Students Association (MSA).[41]

In the early 1980s, Mirza became involved with Islamic activities at the national level, beginning with his membership in the Association of Muslim Scientists and Engineers (AMSE).[42] In 1983, Mirza was listed as an incorporator in the SAAR Foundation's articles of incorporation.[43] Throughout the 1980s, Mirza continued to work in numerous SAAR Foundation enterprises—as acting general manager of NAIT,[44] as an incorporator of Safa Trust,[45] and as an initial trustee and treasurer of Amana Mutual Funds Trust.[46] Mirza's involvement with Amana lasted from 1987 to 2002, and eventually he became the chairman of the trust.[47] During this time he served in senior leadership positions such as executive vice president and chairman at other SAAR businesses as well, including the Mylex Corporation,[48] Sana-Bell,[49] Mar-Jac Investments,[50] Sterling Management Group,[51] Sterling PTech Fund, and Sterling Advisory Services.[52] Between 2000 and 2004, Mirza also was listed as an incorporator and director of the Muslim World League Foundation of Virginia.[53]

In 2002 and 2003, Mirza held important positions in at least twenty-nine SAAR organizations, including director and vice president for research and publication of IIIT, director of Safa Trust, president and chairman of Mar-Jac Poultry, and member of the board of trustees of Amana Mutual Funds Trust. Like Barzinji, he served both as editor in chief of *Islamiyat Al Ma'rifah* and dean of the Faculty of Islamic Revealed Knowledge and Social Science at the International Islamic University, Malaysia.[54]

SAAR'S TERROR TIES: AL QAEDA, HAMAS, AND THE PALESTINIAN ISLAMIC JIHAD

SAAR's purported ties to several designated terrorist organizations[55] are both individual and institutional. Some of the connections are straightforward while others are more complex.

SAAR Subsidiary: The Muslim World League in Virginia

The Muslim World League (MWL) was set up in 1962 by the royal Saud family and tasked with promoting Islamic unity and propagating Wahhabism. As recently as July 2005, Stuart Levey, the undersecretary for terrorism and financial crimes in the US Department of the Treasury, noted that "Saudi Arabian charities, particularly the International Islamic Relief Organization (IIRO), the World Association [*sic*] of Muslim Youth (WAMY), and the Muslim World League (MWL), continue to cause us concern."[56] The MWL Virginia office, one of two US MWL offices, was raided in March 2002 and again in July 2005. Its current US director, Abdullah al-Noshen, was arrested for immigration fraud and is now awaiting trial. The assistant director of that office, Khalid Fadlalah, was arrested for lying on immigration documents that enabled al-Noshen to work in the United States.[57]

MWL is also connected with the SAAR Network through one of its founders: Taha al-Alwani.[58] The interconnectivity of corporations, charities, and persons connected to MWL in Virginia are convoluted, complex, and difficult to decipher. As discussed previously in chapter 9, MWL has ties to al Qaeda. MWL's Peshawar, Pakistan, office, which was funded by bin Laden,[59] was headed by Wael Jalaidan.[60] In 2000, Jalaidan was appointed to the board of trustees of the Rabita Trust, a Pakistani financial arm of MWL, and served as its director-general.[61] Soon thereafter, in a confidential memo from authorities in the United States to United Nations police forces in southeastern Europe, Jalaidan was identified as an associate of Osama bin Laden who had directly assisted bin Laden's efforts to "move money and men to and from the Balkans."[62]

Moreover, MWL's operational arm, the International Islamic Relief Organization (IIRO) (see chapter 9),[63] is both part of the SAAR Network and linked to al Qaeda. Evidence suggests that funding for six militant training camps in Afghanistan came from IIRO.[64] A document with an IIRO and Muslim World League letterhead seized in a post-9/11 raid shows minutes of a meeting between bin Laden and others. Evidently, those in the meeting discussed the opening of "league offices . . . for the Pakistanis," from where "attacks" of an unspecified nature would be made.[65] Furthermore, Mohammed al-Zawahiri, the leader of Egyptian Islamic Jihad's military wing and the brother of bin Laden's second-in-command, Dr. Ayman al-Zawahiri, worked and traveled around the world on behalf of IIRO. Evidence from a number of court cases also has revealed close links between al Qaeda and the IIRO office in the southern Philippines and an allegation that IIRO "secretly funds terrorism and links between al Qaeda and employees of IIRO in Pakistan"[66] As noted in chapter 9, the Treasury Department validated the alleged connections between certain branches of IIRO and al Qaeda when it designated the Philippine and Indonesian branches of the organization and one individual from the Saudi office as facilitators for fund-raising for al Qaeda and affiliated terrorist groups.[67]

Following the 1998 US embassy bombings in Africa, IIRO's chapter in Nairobi was deregistered and closed by the government of Kenya for its alleged connection to the attacks, but it was reregistered later that year on the order of the Kenyan Supreme Court after strong pressure from the Kenyan Muslim community—particularly the Supreme Council of Kenya Muslims.[68] After the American retaliation for the bombings, Indian police arrested members of a terrorist cell attempting to attack the US consulates in Madras and Calcutta.[69] The cell was led by Sayed Abu Nasir, a Bangladeshi national and IIRO employee who was acting on the orders of Shaykh Ahmed al-Gamdin, the director of IIRO operations in Asia.[70] Nasir later admitted to meeting Osama bin Laden at a training camp in Afghanistan.[71]

Abdurahman Alamoudi's résumé indicates that he served simultaneously as an executive assistant to the president of SAAR[72] and as an officer[73] of the Success Foundation, a sister organization of the International Relief Organization (IRO) in Virginia.[74] Alamoudi is serving a twenty-three-year sentence in federal prison for violating the International Emergency Economic Powers Act (IEEPA),[75] making false statements on his naturalization application, and engaging in a tax scheme to conceal his financial transactions with Libya, his foreign bank accounts, and charity-related transactions.[76] His activities are covered further below. The US branch office of the IIRO, known as the International Relief Organization (IRO), was located in the same Falls Church, Virginia, office as MWL.[77] IRO's Virginia office has contributed to other charities suspected or convicted of financing terror.[78] These contributions included:[79]

- $36,322 in 1992 to the Horn of Africa Relief (HARA)
- $21,980 in 1996 and $1,800 in 1997 to the Holy Land Foundation for Relief and Development (HLF)
- $10,000 in 1992 to the Islamic African Relief Agency (IARA)
- $12,500 in 1995 and $5,000 in 1996 to the Taibah International Aid Association

IIRO's financial affiliate, Sana-Bell,[80] is yet another component of the SAAR Network. Sana-Bell and a US branch of MWL were incorporated in Virginia in 2000[81] by Yaqub Mirza.[82] Sana-Bell was founded to generate and manage the operating budget of the US arm of IIRO.[83] Section VI of Sana-Bell's Articles of Incorporation provide that, upon dissolution, the entity's assets shall be distributed to several Islamic organizations—among them Safa Trust, Inc.[84] Mirza was listed as MWL's initial director[85] and as a founding trustee and first secretary, treasurer, and investment committee member of Sana-Bell.[86] The organizations were incorporated at the same Grove Street address in Herndon, Virginia, as the SAAR Network.

The interrelationships of MWL-Virginia, IIRO, and Sana-Bell are further exemplified by Hassan Bahfzallah, who served as vice president of all three organizations.[87] Bahfzallah also was a member of Sana-Bell's board of trustees in 1998, when it was freshly reconstituted.[88] Through his positions with MWL and IIRO in Saudi Arabia, Bahfzallah both directed the activities of Sana-Bell and was involved in the dispute between Sana-Bell and another corporation suspected of funding terrorism, as explained further in this chapter.[89] During this time period, Bahfzallah also served as executive director of the Benevolence International Foundation (BIF) in Saudi Arabia.[90] The US branch of BIF was designated a financier of terrorism in 2002 under the authority of Executive Order 13224, which cited "the close relationship between Arnaout and Usama bin Laden, dating from the mid-1980s,"[91] and the organization's alleged material support of al Qaeda and its operatives.[92]

The Sana-Bell–BMI Case and Soliman Biheiri

Bait ul Mal, Inc. (BMI), a real estate and financial services firm, was founded in New Jersey in March 1986 as an Islamic investment firm. The activities of Bait ul Mal, whose name translates into "House of Money," consisted of real estate investments and providing leasing services for wealthy Muslims both in the United States and abroad.[93] BMI's original investors included top Hamas official Mousa Abu Marzouk (see chapter 5), who resided in the United States for several years, and Yasin al-Qadi, who later was designated as a Specially Designated Global Terrorist by the Treasury's Office of Foreign Assets Control for his financial support of Hamas, al Qaeda, and Osama bin Laden.[94] BMI, Inc., met with great success for a number of years. By 1992, it reported $25 million in projected revenues and leases.[95]

Soliman Biheiri was born in Egypt and moved to New York in 1985 where he lived with his brother after obtaining an economics degree from a university in Switzerland.[96] According to Biheiri, the idea for this firm was given to him in Luxembourg in 1981 by Mahmoud Abu Saud and Gamal Attia, two known senior members of the Muslim Brotherhood. Attia is also his second cousin. Biheiri described Saud and Attia as "fathers of the modern Islamic banking system."[97] Attia's son worked on Grove Street in Herndon, Virginia, for Ahmad Totonji, Hisham al-Talib, and Jamal Barzinji, the key SAAR Network figures addressed earlier in this chapter. At this Luxembourg meeting, Attia and Saud encouraged Biheiri to start up a financial corporation in the United States in the style of other Islamic financial entities like the Islamic Development Bank, an organization initially conceptualized by Attia that has managed funds known to provide money to the families of Palestinian suicide bombers.[98] Saud and Attia saw the benefits of the open nature of the American financial systems and markets that contrasted sharply with most Middle Eastern countries where many actions were subject to approval by government authorities.[99]

Saud's involvement with BMI did not end at the idea phase. In the mid-1980s, he infused $500,000 of his own money into a subsidiary of BMI called BMI Leasing. When Saud died in the mid-1990s, the $500,000 was returned to his widow by BMI. Additionally, Attia maintained an agreement with Biheiri and BMI which stated that Attia would receive a commission for any business he brought to BMI, establishing another long-term business relationship between BMI and the Muslim Brotherhood. In fact, the US government claimed in the course of its 2003 case against Biheiri that BMI was founded explicitly to provide the Muslim Brotherhood with "an American-based financing vehicle."[100] BMI also was tied to Mercy International, a charity tied, in turn, to Bank Al Taqwa, a funding vehicle for the Muslim Brotherhood[101] in Switzerland and Italy that also allegedly provided services to fundamentalist groups around the world, including al Qaeda[102] (addressed later in this chapter).

Biheiri was also tied directly to Al Taqwa. Investigators established ties between Biheiri and Youssef Nada and Ghaleb Himmat, who headed Bank Al Taqwa and other related financial entities in Europe and the Caribbean through which SAAR funds may have been laundered. The activities of Nada and Himmat are addressed later in this chapter. Special Agent David Kane of ICE asserted in Biheiri's trial, and in filings pertaining to sentencing, that the addresses of Nada and Himmat and documents related to the two were on the hard drive of Biheiri's laptop. One such document was a computer file named "Yn-bmil-offer.ob," which was a letter sent by Biheiri to "Mr. Y. Nada" in Lugano, Switzerland, in May 1996. The same address was under the heading "YN." in the contacts folder of a computer seized from Biheiri. Biheiri indicated that he knew Khaldoun Dia-Eddine, a former Al Taqwa employee and husband to Himmat's daughter.[103] Kane claimed that there were "other indications" of ties between Nada's Bank Al Taqwa and BMI, such as financial transactions, but he was prevented from going into further detail because the information was classified.[104]

BMI was further intertwined with the SAAR Network through Sana-Bell and IIRO, and the proceeds from its real estate and development investment accounts were channeled through terrorist financiers like Marzook (chapter 5) and al-Qadi. Business at BMI was "conducted . . . through a series of limited partnerships . . . which invested in projects developing new housing."[105] Biheiri's and BMI's involvement with Marzook and Hamas went through a BMI company called Mostan established by Biheiri in New Jersey in 1988. In the paperwork for an account at the National Community Bank of New Jersey for Mostan International, the president of Mostan is listed as Mousa Abu Marzook with Biheiri listed as vice president. In May 1991, Marzook met with a confidential informant for US Customs in Louisiana. Marzook disclosed that he had been investing money for a housing development with BMI and provided the informant with BMI's phone number. Mostan was involved in building a housing development in Prince George County, Maryland. During the investigations that led up to Biheiri's trial on immigration charges, Biheiri was consistently misleading and dishonest in disclosing his relationship with Marzook and his knowledge of Marzook's involvement with Hamas, a charge for which he was tried and convicted in October 2004.[106]

Biheiri's activities were in violation of the International Emergency Economic Powers Act (IEEPA). When authorities seized Biheiri's computer, they discovered files that indicated BMI dealings with Hamas and Marzook after they were on the specially designated terrorists list. Marzook's money, which Biheiri managed for Marzook after his deportation in 1995, remains unaccounted for.[107]

Marzook was not the only specially designated terrorist who Biheiri did business with. Yasin al-Qadi, whose business activities in the SAAR Network are discussed later in this chapter, also invested in BMI to the tune of millions of dollars, one million of which went into the same Maryland development invested in by Marzook. Biheiri also was involved with Sami al-Arian, the PIJ leader discussed in chapter 7. In October 1993, al-Arian wrote and sent a $2,500 check to Biheiri. In November 1994, Biheiri and al-Arian discussed a possible business relationship concerning a shopping plaza in Florida that al-Arian partially owned. Biheiri also knew Abdurahman Alamoudi and was a board member of the American Muslim Council, an organization founded and headed by Alamoudi.[108] Biheiri was not forthcoming about the extent of these relationships.[109] While Biheiri has been tried and sentenced twice for immigration violations and misstatements to federal investigators, he was never tried for his business ties with Marzook because the statute of limitations had expired by the time they were fully discovered by investigators.[110] Biheiri is currently serving two prison sentences. He was sentenced to one year for immigration violations and twenty-six months for false official statements and the fraudulent procurement of a US passport.[111]

On December 23, 1998, Sana-Bell sued BMI, alleging breach of contract and fiduciary duty, in addition to civil conspiracy. Sana-Bell sought damages mainly from Sulaiman al-Ali, an IIRO officer, and Soliman Biheiri. Sana-Bell is described in the complaint as a "District of Columbia nonprofit corporation with its principal place of business in Jeddah,

Kingdom of Saudi Arabia." Al-Ali was sued on allegations of falsely stating that he was president and CEO of Sana-Bell. Biheiri, a US citizen, was sued on allegations of breach of fiduciary duty by misusing funds provided by Sana-Bell to BMI meant for investment to generate capital to operate the US arm of IIRO. The crux of the complaint was that Sana-Bell had contributed "at least $3,700,000" to BMI Construction and BMI Leasing, all of which was transferred to BMI Leasing without Sana-Bell's knowledge or permission.[112] In September 2000, Biheiri was held liable for more than $2 million in damages and BMI Leasing was held liable for $5,000.[113]

The lawsuit may have been disingenuous and, like the structure of the SAAR Network, meant to deceive. At the time of the investment in BMI, and for years afterward, Sana-Bell's finances were effectively controlled by al-Ali, while Biheiri managed BMI. Major figures from MWL and IIRO in Saudi Arabia approved al-Ali's decision-making authority at Sana-Bell, and it was later rescinded via a letter from Hassan Bahfzallah or Abdullah al-Obaid (the secretary-general of the Muslim World League) to Biheiri.[114]

However, the dispute between Sana-Bell and BMI and the accompanying rescission of al-Ali's authority arose only shortly after the Kenyan and Tanzanian embassy bombings in the summer of 1998. One of BMI's accountants had expressed concern to the FBI that "funds the accountant was transferring overseas on behalf of [BMI] may have been used to finance the embassy bombings in Africa."[115] The timing of this lawsuit raises troubling questions because the circumstances ultimately claimed as the motivation for the *Sana-Bell v. BMI* suit had already existed for some time.[116] Sana-Bell claimed that the $3.7 million was unlawfully transferred on the order of al-Ali, but Sana-Bell was transferring IIRO's money and al-Ali worked for IIRO. The $3.7 million was part of $10 million transferred from IIRO in Saudi Arabia to its US arm. Sana-Bell was the investment arm of the US arm of IIRO.[117] When all of this is taken into account, it is evident that the alleged victim, Sana-Bell, and the alleged violator, al-Ali, were one and the same—IIRO—and all were within the tangled web of the SAAR Network.

An attempted mediation meeting regarding the Sana-Bell lawsuit occurred at the offices of Mar-Jac Investments at 555 Grove Street in Herndon, which was attended by Biheiri, al-Ali, Dr. Saati (director of the Muslim World League in New York City), Abdallah al-Obaid (secretary-general of the Muslim World League in Saudi Arabia), Hassan Bahfzallah (the director of Sana-Bell al-Kheer in Saudi Arabia), and Yaqub Mirza (who held important positions in at least twenty-nine SAAR organizations and was the US Sana-Bell representative).[118] Interestingly, al-Ali was later dropped from the suit.[119] The case raises the question of whether the sudden desire to show an interest in accounting for Sana-Bell's investment in BMI was designed to distance Sana-Bell from BMI in order to avoid awkward questions that might have been asked as a part of the 1998 embassy-bombing investigations.

Yasin al-Qadi and PTech, Inc.

PTech Inc., a Boston-area software company, was raided as part of Operation Green Quest in December 2002 because of its links with Yasin al-Qadi, a Saudi. Al-Qadi is a member of a mercantile family with much influence in Saudi Arabia. His father-in-law, Jamjoom, was once the finance minister of Saudi Arabia. His mother was once the dean of King Abdul Aziz University in Jeddah. Al Qadi's attorneys maintain he has no ties to terrorism despite his designation by the United States as a terrorist.[120]

In addition to BMI, al-Qadi was connected to the SAAR Network through investments in Global Chemical and PTech. According to the *Boston Globe,* Yasin al-Qadi gave $5 million in start-up funds to Oussama Ziade, who founded PTech, in March 1995. These funds were channeled through BMI. Biheiri introduced al-Qadi to Ziade, starting their business relationship. BMI facilitated the initial $5 million investment, which went through an al-Qadi-controlled company based on the Isle of Man called Saramany, but further investments of about $5 million went directly from al-Qadi to Ziade and into PTech.[121]

Biheiri was on the board of directors of PTech along with Hussein Ibrahim, Biheiri's fellow founder of BMI. Ibrahim remained on the board of PTech until its bankruptcy, but Biheiri left the organization earlier due to what Biheiri identified as a disagreement over the future of the company.[122]

Safa's Yaqub Mirza served on an advisory board of PTech, a position from which he resigned after the Operation Green Quest raids of several of his businesses in March 2002, purportedly "to give [CEO and founder Oussama] Ziade more freedom."[123] Mirza is also director of Sterling Advisory Services, which controlled Sterling PTech Fund, LLC, an entity ostensibly created expressly to invest in PTech.[124]

PTech's technical engineer and vice president of Technology Deployment & Professional Services added another interesting dimension to this software company. These positions were held by Suheil Laher and Muhamed Mubayyid, respectively. Both served as officers of Care International,* a Boston charity that originated from the Boston office of the Al Kifah Refugee Center.[125]

Al Kifah was established by Abdullah Azzam to raise money and recruits for the jihad in Afghanistan against the Soviets in the 1980s. Al Kifah is considered a predecessor to al Qaeda. The blind sheik Omar Abdel Rahman, currently serving a life sentence for conspiring to blow up several New York buildings, bridges, and tunnels (see chapter 1), operated out of Al Kifah.

Laher has written many radical articles about jihad, including an introduction to a Care International press release titled "Sh. Abdullah Azzam on Jihad."[126] To preface his introduction, he put forth the following quote taken from Hadith: "Jihad is ongoing until the Day of Resurrection." He referred to Azzam as "the martyred Shaykh and mujahid" and said that Azzam's fatwas "must be given priority to someone speaking from the outside." Abdullah Azzam was also mentor to Osama bin Laden. His general philosophy was: "Jihad and the rifle alone: no negotiations, no conferences and no dialogues."[127]

PTech's Government Contracts

According to a report from the General Service Administration (GSA), approximately 25 percent of PTech's revenue was derived from sales to the US government. These included sales of software and services totaling $3,119,799 as of August 8, 2002. In order to qualify for such sales, PTech filed documents with the GSA[128] and was supported in its government contracts with personnel who needed to obtain security clearances.[129]

PTech had at least thirty-two contracts with major corporations or government entities. Some of the more sensitive were held with

- the Federal Aviation Administration
- the Federal Bureau of Investigation
- the Internal Revenue Service
- MITRE Corporation
- Naval Air Systems Command (NAVAIR)
- the North Atlantic Treaty Organization

*This is not the same organization as the Atlanta-based relief group CARE Int'l.

- the US Air Force
- the US Department of Agriculture Forest Service
- the US Department of Education
- the US Department of Energy
- the US Department of Veteran Affairs
- the US House of Representatives
- the US Postal Service[130]

As of August 2006, no charges have been brought against the firm or its executives and PTech cofounder, Oussama Ziade, has maintained "those connections are distant and inconsequential. In the start-up world, people simply tend to know each other, so connections aren't surprising."[131] There is also no evidence, whatsoever, that PTech's software poses any sort of threat, yet the confluence of all these individuals involved in PTech, several of whom have been or are being investigated by the US government, is intriguing. Then there is the question of security clearances for many of the government-related projects. On a form filed with the GSA, Ptech stated, "Ptech, Inc. personnel to perform under this contract do have a *security clearance*."[132]

Ptech also specially designed and released a version of its software for sales to the US military. According to Ptech documents filed with the GSA: "Military Information Architecture Accelerator (MIAA) is the military version of the IT Architecture Accelerator (ITAA) that is sold commercially. There are military required components that have been incorporated into the ITAA platform, to create the MIAA, and these features are not generally used in the private sector. Ptech, Inc., has also developed the associated training course, so that users of the MIAA Accelerator can be trained as proficient users of the product, so they can manipulate the features to their desired internal planning and management workflow applications."[133]

The Global Chemical Case

The president of IRO and a notable figure in the Sana-Bell–BMI lawsuit, Sulaiman al-Ali, was a 20 percent shareholder of Global Chemical and served as its vice president.[134] Its facilities in Chicago were searched in early 1997, after the government received information that the chemicals being purchased and stored there appeared appropriate not for manufacturing cleaning supplies (as the business claimed) but rather for "organic synthesis" (such as bomb making).[135] Global Chemical's president, Mohammad Mabrook (aka Mohamed Elharezi),[136] was convicted in August 2001 on charges of fraud and money laundering.[137] Mabrook, who was given a fifty-one-month sentence, had served as a director of Mercy International USA in the early 1990s. Mercy USA appears to be the US branch of the Mercy International Relief Agency.[138] US prosecutors have claimed that Mercy's Kenyan branch provided support for the 1998 East African embassy bombings.[139]

Human Concern International and Mercy International Relief Agency

Individuals associated with SAAR held positions of control at Human Concern International, Inc. (HCI USA). HCI USA's 1988 Articles of Incorporation[140] and 1988 application to the IRS for recognition of tax-exempt status[141] show Sayyid Syeed and Ibrahim Hassaballah, both of whom are connected to SAAR, as initial directors.[142] In 1996, bin Laden described HCI as a significant supporter of al Qaeda,[143] and HCI USA is considered to be the US branch of HCI.[144] It is important to note that there is no indication whether or not Syeed and Hassaballah continued their roles with HCI past its incorporation in 1988.

In 1997, HCI USA became Mercy International U.S.A., Inc. (Mercy USA).[145] Abdurahman Alamoudi was listed in 1998 as a board member of Mercy USA.[146]

HCI in Canada was led by Ahmed Saeed Khadr beginning in the mid-1990s.[147] After the al Qaeda attacks on the US embassies in Kenya and Tanzania, the United Nations ordered Khadr's assets to be frozen. After the 9/11 attacks, the United States and Canada both froze his assets and he was designated as a terrorist by the US Department of the Treasury.[148] In 2002, a federal court in Canada found that Khadr was "a close associate of Bin Laden and is reported to have had contact with Bin Laden in Afghanistan."[149] He supposedly was a bagman for the mujahideen during his time in Afghanistan,[150] delivering money from donors in Saudi Arabia to Afghan fighters.[151] Pakistani authorities have asserted that Khadr fought alongside the mujahideen and was wounded in battle.[152] Khadr has also been linked to the 1995 Egyptian Islamic Jihad suicide car bombing that targeted the Egyptian embassy in Islamabad, Pakistan, and killed seventeen people.[153]

Two of Khadr's sons fought against US forces during the invasion of

Afghanistan.[154] One of them, Omar, is being held at the Guantanamo Bay detention facility.[155] He is known to have killed at least one American soldier, a decorated army medic, in combat. Ahmed Saeed Khadr was released by Pakistani authorities after a three-month detention due to pressure from Canadian Muslim lobby groups, which led to the intervention of then Canadian prime minister Jean Chrétien.[156] In 2003, Khadr was killed by Pakistani police. In December 2005, Canadian authorities disclosed that another son of Khadr, Abdullah, was involved in a plot to assassinate the Pakistani prime minister and was engaged in purchasing missiles for militants in Afghanistan.[157]

The Golden Chain

A document obtained from a computer in a 2002 raid of BIF offices in Bosnia listed twenty major donors to al Qaeda whose financial support network became known as the "Golden Chain." The list dates back to the early days of al Qaeda, before bin Laden had publicly declared the United States to be a target, demonstrating the early relationship that existed between these donors and al Qaeda.[158] It is important to note that it is part of a collection of documents seized in the same raid that demonstrates the existence of what US Attorney Patrick Fitzgerald called "a 15-year, international conspiracy to use ostensibly charitable organizations to support violence overseas on behalf of purportedly Islamic causes."[159]

Two individuals named as participants in the Golden Chain, Saleh Kamel and Ibrahim Afandi,[160] are directly involved with the SAAR Network. According to Sana-Bell's "Minutes of Organization Meeting," Kamel and Afandi joined with Mirza in establishing Sana-Bell in the District of Columbia in 1989,[161] only a year after the Golden Chain list is believed to have been drawn up. Kamel's involvement with Sana-Bell continued as he served as a member of the board of trustees in 1998.[162] Kamel, named by Forbes as one of the world's richest people in 2003, is also the majority shareholder of Dallah Albaraka, a Saudi-based conglomerate involved in the banking, manufacturing, real estate, construction, and media industries.[163] Dallah Albaraka companies have been named in post-9/11 civil suits alleging that they "played direct roles in funding al Qaida, in part, through Defendant al-Haramain, and another terrorist organization, HAMAS,"[164] that "Al Baraka provided Osama bin Ladin with financial infrastructures in Sudan beginning in 1983,"[165] and that two of the 9/11 hijackers received funding from Omar al-Bayoumi, the assistant to the director of finance for an Albaraka company.[166] Both Kamel and Afandi are shown on the list as donating money to Adel Abdul Galil Batterjee, a terrorist associated with al Qaeda, the director of BIF, and former secretary-general of the World Assembly of Muslim Youth.[167] Another donor on the list with an obvious tie to SAAR is Sulaiman Abdul Aziz al-Rajhi, SAAR's namesake,[168] who is specifically named as giving to bin Laden.[169]

Wael Hamza Julaidan, an al Qaeda founder, is listed as a recipient of funds.[170] The name of Mazin M. Bahareth, a joint shareholder with SAAR's Bahfzallah in Triple B Trading GmbH, based in Germany, also appears in the document.[171]

United Association for Studies and Research

United Association for Studies and Research (UASR), based in Springfield, Virginia, has numerous links to Hamas. UASR is directly connected to the SAAR Network through Abdurahman Alamoudi, who has served as a UASR director and officer.[172] Hamas's Mousa Abu Marzook was a cofounder of UASR. The association sponsored conferences and publications with other SAAR entities. For example, in June 1991, IIIT and UASR cosponsored a Gulf War conference in Washington, DC, and afterward published a book titled *The Islamic Movement in the Shadow of International Change and Crisis in the Gulf: The Second Seminar on the Future of Islamic Work*.[173]

Global Chemical's Mohammad Mabrook, who used the alias Mohamed Elharezi, also was a UASR incorporator and board member.[174] UASR amended its Articles of Incorporation in 1992 to provide that on dissolution, all net assets would be distributed to the Islamic Society of North America or to the North American Islamic Trust,[175] a stipulation that is common to many of the interconnected Islamist organizations in the United States promoting the Ikwani and Wahhabi ideology, as shown in their own Forms 1023 and Articles of Incorporation.

UASR's prolific executive director, Ahmed Yousef, aka Yousef Salah, appears to have left Virginia around 2004. He has become an adviser to Hamas's Palestinian prime minister, Ismail Haniyeh, and is about to publish a new book in English called *The End of the Jewish State: Just a Matter of Time*.[176]

World Assembly of Muslim Youth

On June 1, 2004, federal agents raided the US branch of the World Assembly of Muslim Youth (WAMY), based in Northern Virginia.[177] Several prominent SAAR Network officers have once been affiliated with WAMY. Abdulhamid Abusulayman, an officer or director of numerous SAAR organizations, served as secretary-general of WAMY from 1973 to 1979.[178] Other officers of SAAR—Taha al-Alwani, Jamal Barzinji, and Ismail al-Faruqi—have also been tied to WAMY.[179] Soliman Biheiri of BMI told investigators that three members of the bin Laden family had invested in BMI, including Abdullah bin Laden—a nephew of Osama bin Laden—who also was the incorporator of the World Assembly of Muslim Youth (WAMY) in Northern Virginia.[180] WAMY has been suspected of links to terrorism and in 2004 the US Senate solicited an inquiry from the IRS regarding WAMY's US branch.[181] According to Senator Charles E. Schumer (D-NY), "They say that where there's smoke, there's fire. Well there's a lot of smoke coming from WAMY and we need to figure out if this group is part of the terrorist network that threatens our security."[182] In a July 13, 2005, testimony before the Senate Banking Committee, Stuart Levey, undersecretary of the Office of Terrorism and Financial Intelligence of the US Department of the Treasury, stated: "Saudi Arabian charities, particularly the International Islamic Relief Organization (IIRO), the World Association of Muslim Youth (WAMY), and the Muslim World League (MWL) continue to cause us concern."[183] WAMY has numerous members, officers, and leaders who were either members of al Qaeda or closely associated with it. Some of these ties were discussed earlier in this chapter.

In November 2001, in a joint FBI-Pakistani intelligence raid on WAMY's Peshawar office, a WAMY employee was detained and later questioned in connection with hand-delivering a recorded message from Osama bin Laden to local media.[184] Nazir Qureshi, the assistant secretary-general of WAMY, has been accused by the Indian government of supplying money to Kashmiri terrorist groups.[185] A Pakistani newspaper reported that a Pakistani-based WAMY organization called Jamiat Taleba Arabia has been focused on militant jihad for the past two decades.[186] A recent issue of the *Future of Islam*, a monthly WAMY publication, featured an interview with a Saudi cleric who, after asserting that he prays for the destruction of America, exhorted Saudis to fight in Iraq or contribute money to the insurgency.[187] Beyond the Middle East and India, WAMY works to immerse its students in its hateful ideology. For example, Philippine resident Zam Amputan told the *Christian Science Monitor* that WAMY paid for him to attend a madrassah in Peshawar in 1987, where he was exposed to the Wahhabi ideology. Amputan told the *Monitor* that he returned to the Philippines "thinking of ways to create a separate Islamic state in the Southern Philippines."[188]

When Ahmad Ajaj, one of the perpetrators of the 1993 World Trade Center bombing, was arrested in 1992,[189] investigators confiscated his belongings. Among them was an official WAMY envelope printed with the organization's return address in Saudi Arabia.[190] Inside the envelope was a manual titled "Military Lessons in the Jihad against the Tyrants." It was a terrorist manual that gave instructions on how to establish terrorist cells. However, it is unclear if he received the manual itself from WAMY.[191] After serving a six-month prison term for attempting to enter the United States with a false passport, Ajaj was released.[192] He was rearrested and convicted in connection with the 1993 WTC bombing on March 4, 1994, and was sentenced to 240 years in prison.[193]

Taibah International Aid Association

The Bosnian Branch of Taibah International (aka Taibah International Aid Association) was named a Specially Designated Global Terrorist on May 6, 2004, for financing al Qaeda.[194] The SAAR Network is connected to Taibah International Aid Association through three of its officers, Samir Salah, Osama Kandil, and Abdurahman Alamoudi.[195]

Samir Salah has been a current or past officer of at least twelve SAAR Network organizations, including the SAAR Foundation, Safa Trust, Mar-Jac Investments, Piedmont Management, and the All Dulles Area Muslim Society (ADAMS).[196] He served as director and treasurer of Taibah in 1999.[197] Salah's role as a part of the Nada-Nasreddin networks is explored further in this chapter.

Abdurahman Alamoudi was employed as assistant to the president with Mar-Jac Investments from 1985 to 1990. Samir Salah was a director during this period.[198] He is listed as a Safa Group officer in the affidavit of ICE special agent David Kane,[199] and he served as vice president of Taibah for the years 1999 and 2000.[200]

Nada and Nasreddin Networks

Youssef Nada—who freely admits to being a highly placed member of the Muslim Brotherhood[201]—and Ahmed Idris Nasreddin—a devout Eritrean who claims his ancestors were royalty[202]—came to the attention of US and European authorities before the SAAR investigations during an Egyptian investigation in the early 1990s and Italian investigations in the mid-1990s. It was discovered that funds were transferred from some SAAR entities to these two men through two banks in the Bahamas that they controlled—Bank Al Taqwa and Akida Bank Private Limited.[203] While Al Taqwa was legally based in the Bahamas, the financial records for the bank were purportedly kept in Saudi Arabia, although they were not found by Swiss investigators who traveled there.[204] Al Taqwa did substantial business through Banca del Gottardo, a large bank in Ticino, Italy, whose correspondents[205] in the United States are Citibank and the Bank of New York. It was through Banca del Gottardo that Al Taqwa was able to gain direct access to the US financial system. Upon further investigation, Nada was designated as a financier of terrorism by the United States and the United Nations in November 2001. Nasreddin was designated as the same by the Group of Seven (G7) and the United Nations in April 2002.[206]

Nada, born in 1931 in Egypt, founded Bank Al Taqwa, which translates to "fear of God," in the 1980s with backing from the Muslim Brotherhood.[207] It was designed, much like BMI, as a financial institution that would adhere to rigid Islamic laws regarding financial transactions.[208] Upon inspection, Bank Al Taqwa aroused suspicion: it had no offices, and consisted of four men in front of computers in an apartment in Lugano, Switzerland.[209] At its height, Bank Al Taqwa held more than $220 million.[210] It was registered in the Bahamas, taking advantage of the protection provided by the discreet banking laws there.

Douglas Farah's book *Blood from Stones: The Secret Financial Network of Terror* states that Samir Salah and Ibrahim Hassaballah, two members of the Safa Group, "incorporated Bank al-Taqwa in the Bahamas, according to Treasury Department documents. Salah is also a founder of the Safa Trust and is an officer of Amana Mutual Funds Trust, both Safa Group entities. Hasaballah serves on the board of the Islamic Charitable Organization, a Safa-related charity. In 2001, according to Safa lawyers, several Safa Group leaders arranged a personal loan to Nada from a joint bank account. The lawyers would not say how much the loan was for or why Nada approached them for the money."[211] Additionally, being registered in the Bahamas allowed the bank to have correspondent accounts with major European banks, such as Banca del Gottardo. Through these accounts, Bank Al Taqwa was allowed to make veiled transfers using the names of these established banks, avoiding the risk of exposing its involvement openly.[212]

Behind these veils, Bank Al Taqwa funneled money to Hamas and al Qaeda through a close associate of Osama bin Laden.[213] Hamas has transferred $60 million into accounts at Bank Al Taqwa.[214] US intelligence purportedly intercepted telephone calls between Al Taqwa representatives in the Bahamas and al Qaeda operatives.[215] A letter from George Wolfe, deputy general counsel of the US Department of the Treasury, to Swiss authorities asserted that Nada had been assisting Ali bin Mussalim, a figure involved in Al Taqwa operations, in "providing direct investment services for al Qaeda, investing funds for bin Ladin, and making cash deliveries on request to the al Qaeda organization" since the 1980s.[216] Wolfe also claims that Bank Al Taqwa "appeared to be providing a clandestine line of credit for a close associate of Osama bin Ladin" who "had a line of credit with a Middle East financial institution that drew on an identical account number at Bank Al Taqwa."[217] This account was sheltered by security measures unique by the standards of any bank, including Bank Al Taqwa. The account was not listed under or associated with any name, and access to it was limited by the bank's computer system to only those with special privileges.[218]

Early suspicion was thrown onto Bank Al Taqwa when Nasreddin, the bank's director, was investigated by the Egyptians in the 1990s.[219] Nasreddin, born in Eritrea, moved to Kuwait as a young man and initiated a successful business career. In the 1990s, the Kuwaiti government asked Nasreddin, who was in Milan, to serve as honorary consul there. Nasreddin was president of the Islamic Community of the Canton of Ticino.[220] While in Milan, he helped found the Islamic Cultural Institute of Milan (ICI), a mosque with well-documented ties to extremist activity and Islamism.[221] The US Treasury Department has identified it as the focal point of al Qaeda in Europe. Attendants and members of this mosque are known to have been involved in terrorist activities, having first drawn attention from intelligence agencies after the 1993 World Trade Center attack in New York City. Ramzi Yousef, who planned that attack, may have received a forged passport from people involved with ICI.[222] In 1994, Italian law enforcement initiated a criminal racketeering investigation involving ICI. As disturbing ties were uncovered in the course of the investigation, it was expanded into a terrorist investigation and eventually exposed the worldwide links of ICI to Islamist militants. The Italians found that ICI served as the European headquarters of Al Gama'a al-Islamiyya, an Egyptian terrorist group.[223]

ICI played an integral part in recruiting Muslims in Europe to fight in the Bosnian conflict in the early 1990s. In fact, the ICI imam commanded a paramilitary unit composed largely of Arab Afghans. Also, a cell of Tunisian terrorists in Northern Italy used ICI as a meeting point. These are only a few of the many ICI ties to Islamist militants in Europe, the Middle East, Afghanistan, and Northern Africa. For a thorough treatment of the Islamic Cultural Institute of Milan, refer to chapter 8 in Lorenzo Vidino's *Al Qaeda in Europe*.[224]

In 1995, Italian investigators found more evidence of Nasreddin's involvement with radical groups. A phone call between two terrorists was intercepted and, in the course of the conversation, Nasreddin's name was mentioned. At the time, he was paying the rent of ICI and his business activities, composed of imports and exports with no apparent lawful logic, aroused further suspicion. His business bought dates, string beans, and eggplants from poor countries with abysmal human rights records and histories of sponsoring terrorism, such as Libya and Nigeria. He often bought from several companies within the same country, paying higher prices than he needed to. At times, the shipping would cost more than the cargo, and other times he bought goods abroad that he could have bought in Italy or France at a lower price. Often, the cargo would take several months to arrive at its destination, and shuttle back and forth between Italy and Croatia. The linchpin was that many of these goods were shipped to Bosnia while the conflict there was in full swing.[225] It has been speculated that he was not shipping produce, but was smuggling weapons to militants, such as the ICI imam mentioned above who went to Bosnia to command a paramilitary unit composed largely of Arab Afghans.[226]

Equally important to the Nada-Nasreddin networks, despite his lesser press exposure, is Syrian-born Ghaleb Himmat. Himmat is a highly placed Muslim Brotherhood leader who, for almost twenty-five years, headed up the Islamic Society of Germany,[227] which was founded by Muslim Brotherhood luminary Said Ramadan. Himmat was one of the founders of Bank Al Taqwa and played an integral part in coordinating Nada's business entities. He owned 30,573 shares of preferred stock in Bank Al Taqwa, only one share less than Nada.[228] Nasreddin owned 8,697 shares.[229] The shareholder list shows other prominent names, including a member of the Kuwaiti royal family, members of the Khalifeh family—an influential family in the United Arab Emirates—and two sisters in the bin Laden family, as well as several Hamas members.[230]

Aside from his relationship via Bank Al Taqwa, Nada has served on the boards of some of Nasreddin's companies and vice versa. Some of their companies share offices and employees. Both operated import-export businesses, drew on some of the same financial contributors throughout the Middle East and North Africa, were connected to ICI in Milan, and were involved with charities and businesses that "are part of an extensive financial network providing support to Al-Qaida and other terrorist related organizations."[231] The areas in which they operated in Switzerland and Italy had loose financial oversight that afforded them substantial anonymity in their transactions and their activities, providing an ideal environment from which to finance terrorism. A report commissioned by the UN Security Council notes:

> For a long time Nada and Nasreddin resided and worked out of a small Italian enclave, Campione d'Italia, near Lugano, Switzerland. They operated their business ventures from offices in Campione d'Italia, Lugano and Milan. Many of their businesses were registered as offshore companies through local trusts in Liechtenstein. These arrangements were usually made through the auspices of so-called "gatekeepers," in most cases one of two law firms in Lifane, specializing in establishing offshore shell companies. At the time Liechtenstein imposed few requirements on such offshore shells, beyond their use of a local trust agent, in this case Asat Trust. There was no requirement to identify or profile the ownership, beneficial ownership or assets of the company being represented and registered locally. No record was kept of activities or transactions on behalf of the companies.[232]

The same report noted a connection with the Safa Group.[233]

The Nada-Nasreddin networks are connected to the Safa Group through multiple avenues. According to Claude Nicati, the chief prosecutor who investigated Nada and Nasreddin, one of the beneficiaries of Al Taqwa was the World and Islam Studies Enterprise (WISE), the organization run by Sami al-Arian with connections to Palestinian Islamic Jihad (see chapter 7).[234] Additionally, Ahmad Totonji, a key SAAR player who was an executive at IIIT (an organization closely connected to WISE) and Safa Trust, founded a business entity called the Arab Gulf Chamber with Nasreddin and three other individuals—Hael Saeed Abuarrahman, Abdul Hamid al-Awadhi, and Sadoon al-Bunnia.[235] Another Nasreddin organization that evolved from the Arab Gulf Chamber and shared the same address, the Malaysian Swiss Gulf and African Chamber (MIGA), was founded not just by Nasreddin but also by a Baghdad firm called the Al

Bunnia Trading Company, run by Sadoon al-Bunnia.[236] Al-Bunnia Trading Company has been hired by coalition forces in Iraq as the "first Iraqi subcontractor to work on the reconstruction of Iraq's Al Mat bridge."[237] MIGA has been designated by the United States and the United Nations as a financier of al Qaeda,[238] raising questions as to the wisdom of contracting the Al Bunnia Trading Company because of its ties to that organization.

Samir Salah, mentioned earlier in this chapter, is a former manager of an Al Taqwa branch in the Caribbean and joined the board of directors of Amana Mutual Funds Trust, where Jamal Barzinji, a central Safa player also addressed earlier, was a founding trustee and officer.[239] Salah is a former director and treasurer of Bank Al Taqwa's Nassau Branch[240] and is an original incorporator of the SAAR Foundation and Safa Trust.[241] He also directed Dar Al Hijrah, a conservative mosque in Falls Church, Virginia, where numerous SAAR and Hamas figures congregated.[242] In 1994, the SAAR Foundation, a Safa entity, gave $15,100 to Dar Al Hijrah.[243]

Dar Al Hijrah is the same mosque where Ahmed Omar Abu Ali and Ali Tamimi worshipped, and where Anwar Aulaqi served as imam.[244] Abu Ali is the Arab American who was convicted on nine counts related to being an al Qaeda member and conspiring to kill President George W. Bush.[245] Ali Tamimi is a Muslim scholar who was convicted of encouraging his followers to engage in jihad against the United States.[246] Eleven of his followers attempted to do so.[247] According to the 9/11 Commission, Anwar Aulaqi introduced two of the 9/11 hijackers, Nawaf al-Hazmi and Khalid al-Mihdhar, to people who helped them find housing.[248] *The 9/11 Commission Report* notes that al-Hamzi and Aulaqi knew each other from the Rabat Mosque in San Diego.[249] Aulaqi left the United States after the 9/11 attacks.

Other connections between Safa and the Nada-Nasreddin networks include Ibrahim Hassaballah and Hisham al-Talib. Hassaballah is a former secretary of Bank Al Taqwa's Nassau branch[250] and he also served as vice president of the US International Islamic Charitable Organization (IICO), located at 555 Grove Street, Herndon, Virginia.[251] Al-Talib, an officer at a Nada entity in the 1960s, was an officer or director of at least nineteen SAAR Network organizations, including IIIT, Safa Trust, and Mar-Jac Poultry.[252] When all of this is taken into account, it is evident that the entities controlled by Nada and Nasreddin were strongly associated with the Safa Group and facilitated the movement of funds to al Qaeda and other terrorist groups.

Neo-Nazi Connections

One of the more interesting elements of the story of the Nada-Nasreddin network is its relationship with Swiss native Ahmed Huber, formerly Albert Huber. Huber, a celebrity in neo-Nazi circles, is a former government affairs journalist who lost his job at *Schweizer Illustrierte* magazine in 1989 when he supported the fatwa calling for author Salman Rushdie's death upon the publication of *The Satanic Verses*.[253] From his office, decorated with pictures of Adolf Hitler, Osama bin Laden, and Ayatollah Khomeini, he advocates the unification of the causes of all right-wing Christian nationalist groups and Islamists.[254] He has ties with white supremacists in the United States, one of whom is William Pierce, author of the infamous *Turner Diaries*, the work that supposedly served as muse to domestic terrorist Timothy McVeigh, and founder of the racist National Alliance.[255] Huber financially backed a later-cancelled Holocaust denial conference scheduled to take place in Beirut in 2001.[256] Huber has praised al Qaeda as "an honorable organization,"[257] called the 9/11 attacks "counterterror against American-Israeli terror,"[258] and has publicly admitted to having met with al Qaeda representatives in Beirut.[259]

Huber was also on the board of directors of the Al Taqwa Foundation.[260] In late 2001, the US designated Huber as a Specially Designated Global Terrorist.[261] He scoffs at the accusations that he has financially supported terrorists saying that, while he is an ideological partner of militant Islam, neither he nor Al Taqwa has funded terrorist groups.

Setback for the Investigation

The dismantling of the Nada-Nasreddin networks and the prosecution of Nada, Nasreddin, and their associates hit a wall. The Swiss criminal investigation of these men and their business entities was suspended on May 31, 2005. The judge supervising the case had given prosecutors until that day to present their findings to the court or to suspend the case. While this does not mean the investigation is terminated, it is suspended until new evidence comes to light. However, its future resumption seems unlikely given that Swiss authorities had had more than three and a half years to assemble a viable case. Swiss authorities blamed the foundering of the Swiss investigation on a lack of cooperation from authorities in the Bahamas, where Al Taqwa was registered. Claude Nicati, the chief Swiss prosecutor, said, "The Bahamas never gave a usable response to Swiss requests for judicial assistance."[262] Bahamian authorities say they are not at fault, since the bank's financial records were stored in Saudi Arabia, but the Swiss assert that they could have done more to obtain them and provide answers to additional pressing questions. Nicati went to Saudi Arabia on two occasions in search of these records, but he was unable to find them.[263]

The Swiss investigation failed despite significant help and pressure from the United States. It has been reported that the same transatlantic cooperation was not extended to Italian investigators and may have hindered the abilities of authorities there to shut down Nada's and Nasreddin's activities. Despite this, the Italians have frozen the funds of fourteen of Nada's and Nasreddin's organizations.[264]

Notwithstanding the suspension of this investigation, Nada and Nasreddin remain on United States, United Nations, and G-7 sanction lists.[265] Their assets are still frozen and they are restricted from leaving their countries of residence; however, there is evidence that there has been a violation of that travel restriction. On January 28, 2003, Nada left Campione d'Italia and went to Vaduz, the capital of Liechtenstein, where he changed the names of two of his companies, Al Taqwa Trade and Ba Taqwa, to Waldenberg and Hocberg. He then put both companies into liquidation under his name, but the government of Liechtenstein, responding to pressures from the United Nations, removed Nada as the liquidator.[266]

Both Nada and Nasreddin have business interests that are still intact. While their bank accounts remain frozen, no government has shut down or seized their physical business assets. They still control one or more hotels in Milan and other property in Switzerland and Italy. The failure of European governments and the United Nations to locate and shut down these businesses and locate Nada and Nesreddin indicates considerable flaws in the ability of the international community to combat the mechanisms of terrorist financing.[267]

SAAR and the Palestinian Islamic Jihad

SAAR's International Institute of Islamic Thought (IIIT) was a significant contributor to PIJ through the World and Islam Studies Enterprise (WISE). IIIT, a Safa Group entity, was incorporated in 1980 by Abusulayman and the late Ismail al-Faruqi.[268] IIIT's largest donor was the SAAR

Foundation, which in 1993 alone gave the institute $285,720.[269] SAAR and IIIT also shared much of the same leadership, in particular Abdulhamid Abusulayman, Taha Jaber al-Alwani, Jamal M. Barzinji, and Mohammed Jaghlit.[270]

Al-Alwani was a founding member and officer of IIT,[271] established the organization in America,[272] and assumed the IIIT presidency in 2003.[273] Al-Alwani and several alleged PIJ leaders—Sami al-Arian, Ramadan Abdullah Shallah, Sheikh Abdel Aziz Odeh (the spiritual leader and cofounder of PIJ), and Sheikh Omar Abdel Rahman (convicted of terrorist plots in 1995)—spoke together at conferences of the Islamic Committee for Palestine (ICP). ICP was a key funding mechanism for PIJ in the United States, as discussed in chapter 7.

According to Agent Kane's affidavit, IIIT was used as a front to fund and support both Hamas and PIJ. An example is shown in a letter written by al-Alwani of IIIT to al-Arian on November 19, 1991. In that letter, al-Alwani referred to the payment of monies from IIIT to PIJ, and wrote that he and his colleagues, and their organizations, considered themselves to be indistinguishable from al-Arian, Shallah (the current secretary-general of Palestinian Islamic Jihad), and other founders and members of PIJ. Specifically, al-Alwani stated in his letter to al-Arian:

> Honorable brother, I think we do not need to affirm that we consider you as a group, you and brother Mazen [al-Najjar], brother Khalil [Shikaki, brother of PIJ founder Fathi Shikaki], brother Bashir [Nafi], Brother Ramadan [Shallah] and Sheikh Abdel Aziz [Odeh], a part of us and an extension of us. Also, we are part of you and an extension of you. We have had no doubts of this since we've known you and we will continue as such. The matter of financial support was never at any time the basis of our relationship, as our relationship, in addition to being a brotherhood of faith and Islam, is an ideological and cultural concordance with mutual objectives. For us, we deem all of your institutions our own, and they receive widespread attention. I explained to you the circumstances that your brothers' institutions are going through, despite which we can truthfully say that we gave your institutions or our institutions that you manage more attention than institutions we manage by ourselves. Because, without a doubt, you are in an important position, and you deserve from us and our like all cooperation, God willing.
>
> I would like to affirm these feelings to you directly on my behalf, and on the behalf of all my brothers, Drs. Abdel-Hamid [Abusulayman], Jamal [Barzinji], Ahmad [Totonji], and Hisham [al-Talib].[274]

Al-Alwani also noted that it didn't matter to the Safa Group how al-Arian characterized the $45,000 al-Arian received from the Safa Group, as part of its total contribution of $50,000:

> And I would like to affirm these feelings to you directly on my behalf and on the behalf of all my brothers, Dr. Abdel Hamid, Dr. Jamal, Dr. Ahmad, Dr. Hisham, and at the same time, affirm to you that when we make a commitment to you, or we try to offer, we do it for you as a group, regardless of the party or the façade you use the donation for. . . . What is left is to remind you that what is mentioned in your letter is that what you already received is forty thousand, and what we have in the records for you is forty-five thousand. I will inquire about the matter with the brother accountants so I can send you what will complete the amount of fifty thousand, God willing, whether it be five or ten thousand.[275]

In another letter seized during the 1995 raid on WISE, Ramadan Abdallah Shallah, director of admissions at WISE and current secretary-general of PIJ in Syria,[276] identifies IIIT as the organization's primary funding source.[277]

Mohammed Jaghlit also sent two letters accompanying contributions—one $10,000, the other $5,000—from the SAAR Foundation to al-Arian in 1994. In each letter, according to the affidavit, "Jaghlit instructed Al Arian not to disclose the contribution publicly or to the media."[278] In a letter in the early 1990s from al-Arian to SAAR's al-Alwani, al-Arian "solicited more funding and referred to a meeting he had with Totonji where Totonji promised him another $20,000."[279]

In 1994, IIIT gave WISE another $10,000 donation.[280] On November 1, 2001, SAAR's Ahmad Totonji wrote a $10,000 check from IIIT to Sami al-Arian's Tampa Bay Coalition for Justice and Peace.[281]

IIIT and WISE also are tied together by patterns of participation at the radical Islamic conferences sponsored by ICP. Kane's affidavit explains that documents and videotapes obtained by searches of the offices of WISE, ICP, and Sami al-Arian, as well as al-Arian's residence, "show that al-Alwani, the President of IIIT, attended and spoke at ICP conferences with al-Arian, Shallah, Sheik Odeh, and Sheikh Rahman. Inasmuch as ICP conferences were, in essence, PIJ conferences . . . al-Alwani has long been a supporter of PIJ."[282]

Al-Alwani expressed views in synch with those of PIJ when he signed a fatwa regarding the Israeli-Palestinian conflict. "Jihad is the only way to liberate Palestine; that no person may settle the Jews on the land of Palestine or cede to them any part thereof, or recognize any right therein for them."[283]

The two groups also exchanged or mutually hired personnel as well. Bashir Nafi, who worked at IIIT as director of research in 1994,[284] was arrested and deported in 1996 for violating his visa stipulation that WISE would be his employer.[285] Nafi has been identified as a leading member of PIJ.[286] In January 2000, IIIT officer Mohammed Jaghlit told FBI agents that IIIT paid WISE in order to employ Nafi. Kane believes that "Jaghlit told the FBI that IIIT paid WISE for allowing Nafi to work at IIIT in order to conceal the fact that IIIT transferred money to WISE precisely because WISE was a front receiving money for PIJ."[287]

Tarik Hamdi was an employee of WISE who later became an employee of IIIT.[288] Hamdi took delivery at his residence of a battery that was ordered by al Qaeda logistics specialist Ziyad Khaleel. Later, Hamdi personally delivered the battery to bin Laden in Afghanistan, and prosecutors stated that the battery operated "the phone that bin Laden and others will use to carry out their war against the United States."[289] Hamdi also escorted an ABC News team—who had contacted him as instructed by Mohammed Atef, the late al Qaeda military commander—to Afghanistan, where they traveled to interview Osama bin Laden.[290] Supporters of Hamdi have claimed that US intelligence was aware of these contacts between Hamdi and the al Qaeda leadership as they were happening and sanctioned them.

IIIT remains active in the United States today. In October 2004, it published *First Impressions: American Muslim Perspectives on the 9/11 Commission Report,* a collection of essays whose authors include IIIT's research director, Louay M. Safi, and Muzammil Siddiqi. Safi was an acquaintance of Sami al-Arian. In a telephone conversation between Safi and al-Arian on February 6, 1995 (less than a month after President Clinton issued Executive Order 12947, which made support of PIJ and other terrorist groups illegal), al-Arian spoke with Safi about the executive order, decrying it as part of a "Zionist campaign."[291] Al-Arian goes on to accuse Zionists of controlling the White House, the State Department, and the Democratic Party. Safi demonstrated knowledge about the Executive Order and asked if the order would effect al-Arian.[292]

SAAR AND HAMAS

SAAR has supported Hamas through both the Holy Land Foundation and the Al Aqsa Education Fund (AAEF). The Al Aqsa Education Fund has been described as a Hamas fund-raising organization,[293] and Mohammed Jaghlit was the president of its board of trustees from 1993 to 1996.[294] In 1993 and 1995, his address is listed as 555 Grove Street, Herndon, Virginia[295]—the location of most SAAR organizations. Jaghlit is also listed as an officer or director of the International Educational Trust, Heritage Educational Trust, Heritage Holdings, and SAAR Foundation, all organizations affiliated with the SAAR Network.[296]

As discussed in chapter 9, HLF's funds were frozen under Executive Order 13224 precisely because, according to the FBI, it funded Hamas.[297] In 1997, HLF received three Safa Trust checks signed by Mirza, in the amounts of $75,000, $87,500, and $162,500.[298] In 1999 and 2000, the International Education Trust, a SAAR Network organization of which Jaghlit is president, donated a total of $37,200 to HLF.[299]

CONCLUSION

While much of the SAAR Network has been dismantled, entities such as IIIT continue to thrive and segments of the Nada-Nasreddin networks remain untouched by authorities. A number of features from the unraveling of the SAAR Network should be noted. First, the individuals who formed SAAR were able to exploit the American free enterprise and corporate regulatory systems so as to set up and maintain an incredibly complex and sophisticated set of front organizations. SAAR Network business ventures ran the gamut from a poultry company in Georgia (Mar-Jac) to a high-tech software firm in Massachusetts (PTech), with many organizations incorporated or headquartered in Falls Church or Herndon, Virginia. Evidence indicates that this network directed funds to radical Islamic causes for over a decade.

Second, these organizations and their leadership may have supported several terrorist organizations, many of which officially distance themselves from each other in the Middle East. Financial operatives in the United States recognized the value of working together for the overarching goal of supporting radical Islam, even though they differed on the political details. This willingness to make common cause must not be underestimated.

The exception to this coordinated approach appears to be Hizballah, which did not join in this cooperative venture for fund-raising in the United States. Instead it had relied on its own methods of organized crime to raise money (see chapter 6). Whether this is because of traditional Sunni-Shia hostility or whether it is for reasons specific to Hizballah is worth further analysis. This is especially so given developments in Iraq, Lebanon, Syria, and Iran.

Proving that business ventures such as SAAR support terrorist activity abroad is, and will continue to be, inherently difficult. Notwithstanding this, law enforcement, intelligence, and corporate regulatory officials must continue and enhance their efforts to stop the flow of money to extremist and terrorist groups intent on using America as a financial base.

NOTES

1. *In the Matter Involving 555 Grove Street, Herndon, Virginia, and Related Locations,* 02-MG-114, affidavit of SA David Kane, sec. X, ¶ 111 (ED VA March 2002), unsealed October 17, 2003; Douglas Farah and John Mintz, "U.S. Trails VA Muslim Money, Ties; Clues Raise Questions about Terror Funding," *Washington Post,* October 7, 2002; Matt Epstein, "Wanting to Stay Sealed," *National Review,* March 19, 2003.

2. "Green Quest," brochure, US Customs Service Office of Investigations, 2002.

3. Shane Harris, "Disrupt and Dismantle," *Government Executive,* February 1, 2002.

4. Michael Fechter, "Federal Agents Raid 15 Sites Tied to Al-Arian's Think Tank," *Tampa Tribune,* March 21, 2002.

5. "Fact Sheet on Expansion of Operation Green Quest," US Customs and Border Control, Department of Homeland Security, January 9, 2003, http://www.customs.gov/xp/cgov/newsroom/press_releases/archives/cbp_press_releases/012003/01092003,xml (accessed August 8, 2005).

6. *In the Matter Involving 555 Grove Street, Herndon, Virginia, and Related Locations,* 02-MG-114, affidavit of SA David Kane, pp. 49–50 (ED VA March 2002); Tagola Karla Bruner, "Terrorist Hunt Hits Poultry Processor," *Atlanta Journal-Constitution,* March 22, 2002.

7. Virginia Secretary of State, 1983 SAAR Foundation, Inc., Articles of Incorporation, July 29, 1983.

8. Ibid.

9. *In the Matter Involving 555 Grove Street, Herndon, Virginia, and Related Locations,* 02-MG-114, affidavit of SA David Kane, pp. 49–50 (ED VA March 2002).

10. Harry Jaffe, "Unmasking the Mysterious Mohamed Hadid," *Business Dateline*, October 1988; *In the Matter Involving 555 Grove Street, Herndon, Virginia, and Related Locations,* 02-MG-114, affidavit of SA David Kane, p. 50 (ED VA March 2002).

11. Ibid., p. 39.

12. Ibid., p. 41.

13. Ibid., p. 42.

14. Ibid.

15. Ibid., p. 44.

16. Ibid., pp. 44–45.

17. Ibid., p. 45.

18. Ibid.

19. Farah and Mintz, "U.S. Trails VA Muslim Money, Ties."

20. *In the Matter Involving 555 Grove Street, Herndon, Virginia, and Related Locations,* 02-MG-114, affidavit of SA David Kane (ED VA March 2002).

21. University of Southern California Muslim Students Association Web site, "Human Relations in Islam, Crisis in the Muslim Mind, the Author," http://www.usc.edu/dept/MSA/humanrelations/crisis_in_the_muslim_mind/author.html (accessed August 8, 2005).

22. Ibid.; Matthew Epstein, Senate Committee on the Judiciary, *Saudi Support for Islamic Extremism in the United States*, 108th Cong., 2nd sess., September 10, 2003; Steven Emerson, Senate Committee on the Judiciary, *Saudi Arabia: Friend or Foe in the War on Terror?* 109th Cong., 2nd sess., November 8, 2005; *Islamic Views* (Saudi Armed Forces Printing Press).

23. *Islamic Views* (Saudi Armed Forces Printing Press).

24. Pennsylvania Department of State Corporation Bureau, IIIT Articles of Incorporation (PA 1980), November 6, 1980.

25. University of Southern California Muslim Students Association Website, "Human Relations in Islam."

26. CSID Web site, "The CSID Board," http://www.islam-democracy.org/alawani_bio.asp (accessed January 24, 2006). Sa'ud University is known for being one of the most radical universities in Saudi Arabia.

27. Safa Trust, Inc., Articles of Incorporation (DC 1986) (filed with DC Department of Consumer and Regulatory Affairs, October 16, 1986).

28. USC-MSA Compendium on Muslim Texts, "The Ethics of Disagreement in Islam: The Author," http://www.usc.edu/dept/MSA/humanrelations/alalwani_disagreement/author.html (accessed January 24, 2006).

29. See Kane Affidavit, Attachment D, "Officers and Directors & Their Related Businesses and Organizations" for a complete list of SAAR Network individuals.

30. *In the Matter Involving 555 Grove Street, Herndon, Virginia, and Related Locations,* 02-MG-114, affidavit of SA David Kane, p. 37 (ED VA March 2002).

31. Larry Poston, *Islamic Da'wah in the West* (New York: Oxford University Press, 1992), p. 102.

32. World Economic Forum Web site, "Contributers," http://www

.weforum.org/site/knowledgenavigator.nsf/Content/Barzinji%20Jamal (accessed January 24, 2006).

33. Poston, *Islamic Da'wah in the West*, pp. 79, 102.

34. Ibid.

35. "Obituary, Sayyed Sabiq," *Islamic Horizons*, http://64.233.187.104/search?q=cache:hShArEMHgagJ:www.isna.net/Horizons/article.asp%3Fissueid%3D6%26artidworld%3D7%26catworld%3D8+Barzinji+AND+%22North+AMerican+Islamic+Trust%22&hl=en (accessed January 12, 2006),

36. *Forum Monthly* 1, no. 1 (March 1, 2003), http://www .muslimforum.org/www.muslimforum.org/NL/ForumMonthly0301032.pdf.

37. Articles of Incorporation for SAAR Foundation, 1983.

38. Georgia State Corporate Record for Mar-Jac Poultry, Inc.

39. *Muslim Democrat* 2, no. 2 (November 2000): 12.

40. *Forum Monthly* 1, no. 1 (March 1, 2003); World Economic Forum Knowledge Navigator; Corporate Records.

41. Cornerstone Conference 2002, "Biographical Summaries," http://www.cornerstone-global.org/Files/2002Conference/Speaker_Bios.pdf (accessed January 24, 2006) and http://www.cornerstone-global.org/Files/2002 Conference/Mirza_Yaqub_remarks.pdf (accessed January 24, 2006); Sterling Management Group Web site, "Management Team," http://www.sterlingmgmt.com/principals.htm (accessed January 24, 2006); Central Mosque.com Web site, "From the Depth of the Heart in America," http://www.central-mosque.com/fiqh/nadwi2.htm (accessed January 24, 2006).

42. Cornerstone Conference 2002, "Biographical Summaries."

43. Articles of Incorporation for SAAR Foundation, Inc., 1983.

44. "Naziruddin Ali Appointed NAIT General Manager," *Islamic Horizon* (April 1984). Mirza was a leader in both MSA and NAIT for years before leaving for the SAAR Foundation in 1984.

45. Articles of Incorporation for Safa Trust, Inc., 1986.

46. *Islamic Horizons* (May–June 1998): 26; Amana Mutual Funds Trust Advertisement in *Islamic Horizons* (July 1987).

47. Cornerstone Conference 2002, "Biographical Summaries."

48. Sterling Management Group Web site, "Management Team."

49. *Sanabell v. BMI*, government exhibit #17, letter dated July 28, 1998, from al-Obaid to Mizra and English translation of A-1.

50. Sterling Management Group Web site, "Management Team."

51. Ibid. There is some indication that Sterling Management Group has taken over lead operations after the dissolution of the SAAR Foundation in 2000.

52. Ibid.

53. Articles of Incorporation, MWL IN VIRGINIA, State of Virginia Corporate Records, 2001 and 2004.

54. *In the Matter Involving 555 Grove Street, Herndon, Virginia, and Related Locations*, 02-MG-114, affidavit of SA David Kane (ED VA March 2002); *Forum*

Monthly 1, no. 1 (March 1, 2003); World Economic Forum Knowledge Navigator, Public & Corporate Records.

55. Al Qaeda was redesignated as a foreign terrorist organization (FTO) on October 3, 2003, extending travel and financial sanctions on the organization, for two years; Hamas has been a specially designated terrorist (SDT) since 1995 and a designated FTO since 1997; and PIJ has been on the US State Department list of terrorist organizations since 1989, an SDT since 1995, and an FTO since 1997.

56. "Testimony of Stuart Levey, Under Secretary Office of Terrorism and Financial Intelligence, U.S. Department of the Treasury, Before the Senate Committee on Banking, Housing, and Urban Affairs," US Treasury press release JS-2629, July 13, 2005, http://www.treas.gov/press/releases/js2629.htm (accessed October 22, 2005).

57. Mary Beth Sheridan, "Raid Targets Islamic Charity in Falls Church," *Washington Post*, July 26, 2005.

58. Center for Islam and Democracy, "Bio of Taha Jabir al Alwani," http://www.islam-democracy.org/alalwani_bio.asp (accessed June 17, 2004).

59. Basil Muhammad, *Al Ansara l'Arab fi Afghanistan*, May 17, 1993.

60. "Usama Bin Ladin—A Millionar [*sic*] Finances Extremism in Egypt and Saudi Arabia," *Rose Al Yusif*, May 17, 1993.

61. "Treasury Department Statement on the Designation of Wa'el Hamza Julidan," US Treasury Department, September 6, 2002.

62. Cited in news report by BBC, April 3, 2000.

63. *US v. Soliman Biheiri*, 03-3650A, declaration in support of pretrial detention (ED VA August 14, 2003).

64. David E. Kaplan, Monica Ekman, and Aamir Latif, "The Saudi Connection; How Billions in Oil Money Spawned a Global Terror Network," *U.S. News & World Report*, December 15, 2003,

65. Ibid.; "Government's Evidentiary Proffer Supporting the Admissibiilty of Co-Conspirator Statements," *US v. Enaam M. Arnaout*, 02-CR-892, p. 31 (U.S.DCt. N.D. Ill., E. Div, January 31, 2003).

66. The IIRO sworn affidavit of FBI special agent Robert Walker, *United States of America v. Benevolence International Foundation, Inc.*, respondent's (moving party) motion record 02-CR-0414 (ED IL April 29, 2002); The Minister of Citizenship and Immigration and Mahmoud Jaballah, respondent's (moving party) motion record: DES-6-99, June 2, 1999, pp. 10, 61–62 (detailing links between al Qaeda and IIRO); "Official Sources Deny Reports on UAE's Extradition of Islamist," *Al Hayat*, June 9, 2000 (stating that Mohammed al-Zawahiri, leader of Egyptian Islamic Jihad's military wing and brother of top al Qaeda leader Dr. Ayman al-Zawahiri, worked and traveled around the world on behalf of IIRO); "Another Saudi 'Hijacker' Turns Up in Tunis," *Middle East Newsfile*, September 18, 2001 (stating that when leaving home, September 11 hijacker Fayez Ahmed Banihammad told his father he was going to go to work for the IIRO); BBC, "Kenya: NGO Council Official Condemns Deregistration of Islamic NGOs," September 9, 1998 (describing how the government of Kenya deregistered, albeit temporarily,

IIRO's chapter in Nairobi for alleged connections to 1998 bombings of US embassies in East Africa); "Anti-U.S. Plot in India Is Foiled; Militant Islamist Intended to Bomb 2 Consulates, Police Say," *International Herald Tribune*, January 21, 1999.

67. "Treasury Designates Director, Branches of Charity Bankrolling Al Qaida Network," US Department of the Treasury press release, August 3, 2006.

68. BBC, "Kenya: NGO Official Condemns Deregistration of Islamic NGOs"; Agence France Presse, "Kenya Lifts Ban on Saudi-Based Islamic NGOs," December 17, 1998; Agence France Presse, "Crackdown on Muslim NGOs in Kenya Sparks New Protests," September 14, 1998.

69. "Pakistan Denies Role in Plotting Bombings in India," *New York Times*, January 22, 1999.

70. Ibid.; "Anti-U.S. Plot in India Is Foiled."

71. "Anti-U.S. Plot in India Is Foiled."

72. Abdurahman M. Alamoudi curriculum vitae: Freedom of Information request.

73. Success Foundation Forms 990 for 1999 and 2000 (showing Alamoudi as secretary); Success Foundation Form 2758 (Application for Extension of Time to File) signed May 4, 2000 (approved June 22, 2000) for tax year 1999 (signed by Alamoudi and showing him as chairman).

74. See line item 80 of Success Foundation Form 990 for 2000 (showing IRO as related organization); Success Foundation Forms 2758 (Application for Extension of Time to File) for tax years 1998 and 1999 (showing Success Foundation's address as P.O. Box 8125, Falls Church, VA 22041—the same address shown for IRO on its Forms 990 for 1992, 1995–1997).

75. This act empowers the president of the United States to issue executive orders to combat and hinder any "unusual and extraordinary threat, which has its source in whole or substantial part outside the United States, to the national security, foreign policy, or economy of the United States, if the president declares a national emergency with respect to such threat." Pursuant to this act, President Clinton issued Executive Order 12947 in January of 1995, which declared a state of national emergency concerning the terrorist actions in the Middle East intended to thwart the Israeli-Palestinian peace process. Two days later, a list composed of people and groups identified as specially designated terrorists (SDT) was released. Among these groups was Hamas. In accordance with policy, individual members of Hamas were identified and added to the list, including Marzook, who was added in August 1995. According to the terms and policies under the IEEPA, it is illegal to do business with groups and individuals on this list.

76. "Abdurahman Alamoudi Sentenced to Jail in Terrorism Financing Case," Department of Justice press release, October 15, 2004, http://www.usdoj.gov/opa/pr/2004/October/04_crm_698.htm (accessed January 4, 2006).

77. William F. Krebs (counsel for the defendants), "Defendants' Proposed Findings of Fact and Conclusions of Law," *The Sana-Bell, Inc. v. BMI Real Estate*

Development, Inc., et al., 98-CV-4177 (PJM), pp. 3–5 (USDC, District of Maryland February 24, 2000).

78. For a description of the relationship of the listed organizations (other than Mercy International Canada) to terrorism, see notes 71–81 and surrounding text of Testimony of Matthew Epstein with Evan Kohlmann before the House Committee on Financial Services Subcommittee on Oversight and Investigations. "Progress Since 9/11: The Effectiveness of U.S. Anti-Terrorist Financing Efforts, Arabian Gulf Financial Sponsorship of Al-Qaida via U.S.-Based Banks, Corporations and Charities," March 11, 2003.

79. The listed donations for each corresponding year are shown on IRO Forms 990 for 1992 and 1995–1997.

80. Sanabel al Kheer translates into "Seeds of Charity"; the organization also goes by Sana-Bell Al-Kheer, Sanabel Al-Khayr, and the Charity Bonds Project; "Islamic Relief Organization Sets Up Income-Bearing Scheme," *Arab News*, March 8, 1992 (describing IIRO's establishment of Sanabel Al-Kheer). The company was originally called Sana-Bell, Inc. However, this version of the company lapsed out of existence and in 2000 was replaced by Sanabel Al-Kheer, Inc.

81. Articles of Incorporation, MWL IN VIRGINIA, State of Virginia Corporate Records, 2001 and 2004.

82. Mirza may have ended his association with the MWL in Virginia on August 18, 2003.

83. *US v. Soliman Biheiri*, 03-3650A, declaration in support of pretrial detention, p. 5 (ED VA August 14, 2003).

84. Article VI of Sana-Bell's Articles of Incorporation (DC).

85. According to its articles of incorporation, MWL in Virginia was first incorporated as the Muslim World League Foundation, with its only office at 555 Grove Street, Herndon, VA. By articles of amendment dated October 31, 2000, the organization shortened its name to the Muslim World League, and at some point the entity also added a business address at 360 S. Washington Street, Suite 300, Falls Church, VA 22046. These changes are reflected in Virginia Secretary of State Corporate Record for Muslim World League (showing business address at 360 S. Washington Street, Suite 300, Falls Church, VA 22046 and registered office at 555 Grove Street, with name changed shown as occurring on December 6, 2000). They are also reflected in the entity's 2001 Annual Report filed with the Virginia State Corporation Commission (signed by Mirza on August 24, 2001).

86. Sana-Bell's "Minutes of Organization Meeting" dated July 30, 1989, Exhibit B to "Defendant's Opposition to Plaintiff's Motion for Summary Judgment," *The Sana-Bell, Inc. v. BMI Real Estate Development, Inc., et al.*, 98-CV-4177 (PJM) (D MD January 21, 2000); Virginia Secretary of State Corporate Record for Sanabel Al-Kheer, Inc., 555 Grove Street, Suite 116, Herndon, VA 20170, filed August 14, 2000.

87. Virginia State Corporation Commission record for Sana-Bell (filing date 03/07/2000, status date 07/31/2001); Virginia Secretary of State Corporate

Record for Muslim World League, filed August 4, 2000; and Virginia Secretary of State Corporate Record for Sanabel Al Kheer, Inc., filed August 14, 2000.

88. Undated Note from Yamani, "To Whom It May Concern" (purporting to be minutes of April 10, 1998, Sana-Bell Board of Trustees meeting, and showing Bahafzallah as member of board). Document submitted as exhibit L to Sana Bell's Motion for Summary Judgment.

89. Letter dated July 28, 1998, from al-Obaid to Mirza and letter dated August 18, 1998, from Bahafzallah to Biheiri (establishing that Bahafzallah was secretary of the Investment Committee of IIRO in Saudi Arabia). Documents submitted as exhibits A and J (respectively) attached to "Memorandum of Points and Authorities in Support of Defendants' Opposition to Plaintiff's Motion for Summary Judgment," *The Sana-Bell, Inc. v. BMI Real Estate Development, Inc., et al.*, 98-CV-4177 (PJM) (D MD January 21, 2000).

90. Omar Basaddiq, "Islamic Charity Committee Moves to New Premises," *Arab News*, May 22, 1994. The exact nature of the connection between BIF in Saudi Arabia and BIF in the United States still needs to be determined.

91. "Treasury Designates Benevolence International Foundation and Related Entities as Financiers of Terrorism," Department of the Treasury press release, http://www.treas.gov/press/releases/po3632.htm (accessed January 12, 2006).

92. Ibid.

93. Jerry Seper, "N.J. Firm Backed Terrorists Linked to Hamas, al Qaeda; Maryland Housing, Virginia Businesses Involved," *Washington Times*, March 29, 2004.

94. Executive Order 13224, "Blocking Terrorist Property," October 12, 2001.

95. Ibid.

96. Soliman S. Biheiri, interview by David Kane and Brad Romanoff at Dulles Airport, United States Customs Service, June 15, 2003.

97. Ibid.

98. Steven Stalinsky, "Saudi Arabia and the WTO," *New York Sun*, September 21, 2005; Biheiri, interview.

99. Biheiri, interview.

100. *US v. Biheiri*, 03-365-A, government's final memorandum regarding sentencing (ED VA January 7, 2004).

101. Biheiri, interview; *US v. Biheiri*, 03-365-A, government's final memorandum regarding sentencing (ED VA January 7, 2004); Victor Comras, "Al Qaeda Finances and Funding to Affiliated Groups," *Strategic Insights* 1 (January 2005), http://www.ccc.nps.navy.mil/si/2005/Jan/comrasJan05.asp (accessed November 11, 2005); Mark Perelman, "Terror Fund Trail Leads to Alpine Kingdom," *Forward*, October 17, 2003, http://www.forward.com/issues/2003/03.10.17/news4.terror.html (accessed December 13, 2005).

102. Douglas Farah, *Blood from Stones: The Secret Financial Network of Terror* (New York: Broadway Books, 2004), p. 147.

103. Biheiri, interview, p. 9.

104. *US v. Biheiri*, 03-365-A, government's final memorandum regarding sentencing (ED VA January 7, 2004); *US v. Biheiri*, 03-365-A, redacted sentencing declaration and supporting exhibits, p. 17 (ED VA December 11, 2003); Perelman, "Terror Fund Trail Leads to Alpine Kingdom."

105. *US v. Biheiri*, 03-365-A, redacted sentencing declaration and supporting exhibits, p. 17 (ED VA December 11, 2003).

106. Ibid., pp. 17–19; *US v. Biheiri*, 03-365-A, government's final memorandum regarding sentencing, pp. 9–10 (ED VA Janaury 7, 2004); *US v. Biheiri*, 04-CR-201, jury verdict as to Soliman S. Biheiri (ED VA October 12, 2004).

107. *US v. Biheiri*, 03-365-A, government's final memorandum regarding sentencing, pp. 3–4, 19–20 (ED VA January 7, 2004).

108. Biheiri, interview, p. 6.

109. Biheiri, interview.

110. Matthew Barakat, "Egyptian National Gets 12 Months for Immigration fraud, Judge Rejects Connections to Terrorism," Associated Press, January 12, 2004.

111. *US v. Biheiri*, 04-201-A, docket report (ED VA January 13, 2005).

112. *The Sana-Bell, Inc. v. BMI Real Estate Development, Inc.,BMI Leasing Inc., Soliman S. Biheiri, and Suleiman Bin Ali Alali* (PJM), 98-CV-4177, civil action (D MD).

113. Ibid.; orders, September 29, 2000, and September 18, 2000.

114. Letter dated August 18, 1998, from Bahafzallah to Biheiri. Telefax dated March 27, 1998, from Mirza to al-Ali. Undated Note from Yamani, "To Whom It May Concern" (purporting to be minutes of April 10, 1998, Sana-Bell board of trustees meeting), and letter dated April 22, 1998, from Yamani to Mirza. Documents submitted as exhibits J, K, L, and M (respectively) attached to "Memorandum of Points and Authorities in Support of Defendants' Opposition to Plaintiff's Motion for Summary Judgment," *The Sana-Bell, Inc. v. BMI Real Estate Development, Inc., et al.*, 98-CV-4177 (PJM) (USDC MD Southern Division, January 21, 2000).

115. Affidavit of FBI Special Agent Robert G. Wright Jr., March 21, 2000; *United States v. Soliman S. Biheiri*, 03-365-A, declaration in support of pretrial detention, p. 9 (ED VA August 14, 2003).

116. No one at Sana-Bell apparently made any serious prior objection to the lack of accounting for the BMI investment, even though previous inquiries had been ignored. See Telefax dated March 27, 1998, from Mirza to al-Ali; undated note from Yamani "To Whom It May Concern" (purporting to be minutes of April 10, 1998, Sana-Bell Board of Trustees meeting), and letter dated April 22, 1998, from Yamani to Mirza. Documents submitted as exhibits K, L, and M (respectively) attached to "Memorandum of Points and Authorities in Support of Defendants' Opposition to Plaintiff's Motion for Summary Judgment," *The Sana-Bell, Inc. v. BMI Real Estate Development, Inc., et al.*, 98-CV-4177 (PJM) (USDC MD Southern Division, January 21, 2000).

117. *US v. Soliman Biheiri*, 03-3650A, declaration in support of pretrial detention, p. 5 (ED VA August 14, 2003).

118. Biheiri, interview, p. 12.

119. Glenn R. Simpson, "Terror Investigators Followed Funds to a Saudi Businessman," *Wall Street Journal*, November 26, 2002.

120. Anthony Shaid, "US Probe Tests Diplomatic Sensitivity—Saudi Charities, Groups Funded Attract Scrutiny," *Boston Globe*, December 13, 2001.

121. Ibid., pp. 2–3; Thanassis Cambanis and Ross Kerber, "Ptech CEO Says Probe Put Firm on Ropes," *Boston Globe*, December 13, 2002.

122. Biheiri, interview, pp. 3, 5.

123. Justin Pope, "Software Company Tries to Survive Terrorism Investigation," Associated Press, January 3, 2003.

124. Ibid.

125. Documents seized from the Al Kifah office in Brooklyn after the World Trade Center bombing in 1993 indicate that donations to the organization and related funds should be sent to Al Kifah's Boston office at 1085 Commonwealth Ave., Suite 124. Al Kifah letterhead also lists the same address. The Massachusetts Articles of Incorporation for Care International, dated April 1993, lists Care International's mailing address as 1085 Commonwealth Avenue, Suite 124, Boston, MA 02215. After Care International's incorporation, Al Kifah's newsletter in English, *Al Hussam*, was being published by Care International. *Al-Hussam* had two mastheads. One masthead listed Al Kifah as the publisher at 1085 Commonwealth Ave. The other masthead listed Care International as the publisher. All printed copies of *Al Hussam* bore the official Al Kifah logo.

126. Scheil Laher, "Sh. 'Abdullah' Azzam on Jihad," introduction, Care International.

127. Jonathan Fighel, "Sheikh Abdullah Azzam: Bin Laden's Spiritual Mentor," Institute for Counterterrorism, September 27, 2001, http://www.ict.org.il/articles/articledet.cfm?articleid=388 (accessed August 10, 2006).

128. Standard Form 1449, General Services Administration, date unknown.

129. Ibid.

130. PTech Customer List, http://www.ptechinc.com/01/abou/abou.cust.list.asp (accessed August 28, 2002).

131. Pope, "Software Company Tries to Survive Terrorism Investigation."

132. Standard Form 1449, General Services Administration, date unknown, p. 6.

133. Ibid.

134. *US v. Mohammed Mabrook*, 98-CR-271, sworn affidavit of FBI special agent Valerie Donahue," p. 2 (ND IL).

135. Glenn R. Simpson, "Tracing the Money, Terror Investigators Run into Mr. Qadi," *Wall Street Journal*, November 26, 2002.

136. Sworn affidavit of FBI special agent Valerie Anne Donahue, in the matter of the search of 360 W. Washington Street, Falls Church, Virginia, 3rd Floor," 97-25-MG, p. 2 (USDC VA, January 30, 1997).

137. Simpson, "Tracing the Money, Terror Investigators Run into Mr. Qadi."

138. Mercy International U.S.A. Inc., Forms 990 for 1991, 1992 and 1994; Matthew Epstein and Ben Schmidt, "Operation Support-System Shutdown," NROnline, September 4, 2003, http://www.nationalreview.com/comment/comment-epstein-schmidt090403.asp (accessed January 24, 2006).

139. Ibid.

140. Michigan Department of Commerce—Corporation and Securities Bureau, Articles of Incorporation for Human Concern International, Inc., September 23, 1988.

141. HCI USA's 1988 IRS 1023 Form.

142. HCI USA's 1988 Articles of Incorporation (MI) and 1988 1023 filing also show Omar Issa Soubani and Mohammed al-Hanooti as initial directors.

143. "Islamic Financier Bin-Ladin Interviewed on Sudan, Iran Ties," *Rose Al Yusuf*, June 17, 1996 (interview allegedly conducted in London but date of interview unspecified) (translated by FBIS 05/22/1997, Document ID: FTS-199-705-2200-2331).

144. In the 1994 edition of *American Muslim Resource Directory*, on page 32, there are two addresses listed for Human Concern International—Canada: PO Box 3984 Station C Ottawa, Ontario K1Y 4P2 Canada (613) 234-4585. Mohamed Rida Beshir, is listed as the vice president of Human Concern International with the address: PO Box 248 Garden City, MI 48135 313-421-CARE (2273). PO Box 248 Garden City, MI 48135 and 313-421-CARE are the address and phone number of Mercy USA.

145. Michigan Department of Commerce, Certificate of Amendment to the Articles of Incorporation of Human Concern International, Inc. (USA), September 26, 1989.

146. Mercy International USA, Inc.'s IRS Form 990 for 1998.

147. "Statement Summarizing the Information and Evidence Pursuant to Section 78(h) of the Immigration and Refugee Protection Act," *Annex V, The Federal Court of Canada*, December 2, 2002.

148. Stewart Bell, "Al-Qaeda's Canadian Vanguard: Khadr Father Tops List of 75 Suspected bin Laden Operatives," *National Post*, September 6, 2002; "Treasury Department Releases List of 39 Additional Specially Designated Global Terrorists," US Department of the Treasury, October 12, 2001.

149. "Statement Summarizing the Information and Evidence Pursuant to Section 78(h) of the Immigration and Refugee Protection Act."

150. "Americans Are Coming, Get Ready to Kill Them," *National Post*, September 21, 2002.

151. Ibid.

152. Ibid.

153. "Statement Summarizing the Information and Evidence Pursuant to Section 78(h) of the Immigration and Refugee Protection Act."

154. "Two Canadian Brothers Held as al-Qaeda Fighters," *Ottawa Citizen*, September 6, 2002.

155. Michael Friscolanti and Stewart Bell, "Khadr Was Dealing in Missiles; Affidavits: 'Admitted' al-Qaeda ties," *National Post*, December 20, 2005.

156. Randy Boswell, "The Khadrs: A Family on the Run," *Ottawa Citizen*, September 2, 2002.

157. Friscolanti and Bell, "Khadr Was Dealing in Missiles."

158. Glenn R. Simpson, "List of Early Al Qaeda Donors Points to Saudi Elite, Charities," *Wall Street Journal*, March 18, 2003.

159. Patrick Fitzgerald quoted in Simpson, "List of Early Al Qaeda Donors Points to Saudi Elite, Charities."

160. *Euro Brokers, Inc., et al. v. Al Baraka Investment and Development Corporation, et al.*, complaint, p. 10 (SD NY September 10, 2004).

161. *Sana-Bell, Inc. v. BMI Real Estate Development, Inc.*, 98-CV-4177, exhibit B to Sana-Bell's motion for summary judgment (DM SD January 21, 2000).

162. Undated Note from Yamani, "To Whom It May Concern." Document submitted as exhibit L attached to Sana-Bell's motion for summary judgment.

163. "World's Richest People—Saleh Kamel," Forbes.com, http://www.forbes.com/finance/lists/10/2003/LIR.jhtml?passListId=10&passYear=2003&passListType=Person&uniqueId=1FXS&datatype=Person (accessed January 20, 2006).

164. *Estate of John P. O'Neill, Sr., et al v. Al Baraka investment and Development Corporation, et al.*, 04-1923(RCC), first amended complaint," p. 11 (SD NY September 23, 2004).

165. *Burnet v. Al Baraka.* 1:02-CV-01616(JR), third amended complaint, p. 232 (D DC November 22, 2002).

166. Ibid., p. 233.

167. Translation of "TAREEKHOSAMA/41/Tareekh Osama.108" (Golden Chain List); Simpson, "List of Early Al Qaeda Donors Points to Saudi Elite, Charities."

168. Al-Rajhi and Afandi have been members of the Executive Council of IIRO in Saudi Arabia. "New Executive Council of IIRO," *Saudi Gazette*, as reprinted in *Moneyclips, Middle East Newsfile*, October 23, 1998.

169. "Les documents originaux de la GOLDEN CHAIN," *L'Investigateur*, http://www.investigateur,info/zines/textes/176_alqaeda.html (accessed June 21, 2005); translation of "TAREEKHOSAMA/41/Tareekh Osama.108" (Golden Chain List).

170. Ibid.

171. Ibid.

172. See UASR Forms 990 for 1994–98 (showing Alamoudi as director); UASR Annual Reports for 1995 and 1997 filed with the Illinois secretary of state (showing Alamoudi as secretary); IRS Form 8734 (Support Schedule for Advance Ruling Period), dated September 3, 1996, signed December 6, 1996, filed December 13, 1996 (showing, in section 15, Alamoudi as secretary).

173. The inset of this book shows the logos of both UASR and IIIT, along with UASR's phone and fax numbers in Chicago and IIIT's address and contact numbers at 555 Grove Street, Herndon, VA. The back cover of the book also shows

UASR's address: PO Box 528320, Chicago, IL 60652 (and contact numbers). The back cover also displays the name "Ahmed Yousef," apparently as author.

174. UASR Annual Report for 1990 filed with the Illinois secretary of state (showing Elharezi as a director); UASR's Articles of Incorporation (filed September 18, 1989) (showing, in article 3, "Mohamed Elharezi" as one of five directors, and signed by Elharezi as an incorporator).

175. Articles of Amendment to UASR's Articles of Incorporation signed on January 23, 1992, and filed with the Illinois secretary of state on February 24, 1992.

176. Avi Issacharoff and Amos Harel, "Lost Innocents," Haaretz.com, June 23, 2006, http://66.102.7.104/search?q=cache:KJUtZTxnH1AJ:www.haaretz.com/hasen/spages/727532.html+Ahmed+Yousef+haaretz&hl=en&gl=us&ct=clnk&cd=1 (accessed July 28, 2006).

177. Jerry Markon, "FBI Agent Raid Northern Virginia Office of Saudi-Based Charity," June 2, 2004.

178. USC-MSA Compendium of Muslim Texts Web site, "The Author," http://www.usc.edu/dept/MSA/humanrelations/crisis_in_the_muslim_mind/author.html (accessed January 24, 2006).

179. Pennsylvania Department of State Corporation Bureau, IIIT Articles of Incorporation (PA 1980), November 6, 1980.

180. Biheiri, interview, pp. 17–18.

181. "Senators Request Tax Information on Muslim Charities for Probe," Department of State, International Information Program, January 14, 2004, http://usinfo.state.gov/ei/Archive/2004/Jan/15-147062.html (accessed July 28, 2006).

182. "Schumer: Virginia Charity Linked to Hamas and Saudis Has Escaped Federal Charges," Senator Charles E. Schumer press release, September 17, 2003, http://schumer.senate.gov/SchumerWebsite/pressroom/press_releases/PR02034.html (accessed July 28, 2006).

183. Testimony of Stuart Levey, undersecretary, Office of Terrorism and Financial Intelligence, US Department of the Treasury, before the Senate Committee on Banking, Housing, and Urban Affairs, Department of the Treasury, July 13, 2005, http://www.treas.gov/press/releases/js2629.htm (accessed July 28, 2006).

184. Assocated Press, "Pakistan Questions Sudan Man about Tape," December 9, 2002.

185. Press Trust of India, "Two Detained for Passing on Fund to Geelani," June 12, 2002.

186. "By the Book, for the Book," *News*, March 25, 2001.

187. "Terror Alliance Targets US Forces in Iraq," *Scotsman*, June 15, 2003.

188. "The Tenets of Terror," *Christian Science Monitor*, October 18, 2001.

189. "New Suspect Charged in Blast," *New York Times*, May 7, 1993.

190. *United States v. Usama Bin Laden, et al.*, S5-93-CR-180, government exhibit 2800—A (SD NY).

191. "A Sixth Suspect Charged in Blast," *New York Times*, May 7, 1993.

192. "Retracing the Steps of a Terror Suspect; Accused Bomb Builder Tied to Many Plots," *Washington Post*, June 5, 1995.

193. "Trade Center Bombers Sentenced to 240 Yrs," *Chicago Sun-Times*, May 24, 1994.

194. "Treasury Designates Bosnian Charities Funneling Dollars to Al Qaida," US Department of the Treasury press release, May 6, 2004, http://www.ustreas.gov/press/releases/js1527.htm (accessed January 24, 2006).

195. Forms 990 for Taibah International Aid Association, 1999 and 2000.

196. Kane affidavit, attachment D, p. 8.

197. Form 990 for Taibah International Aid Association, 1999.

198. *US v. Alamoudi*, detention and hearing exhibit, September 30, 2002, government exhibit 10; Immigration and Naturalization application, 1995.

199. *In the Matter Involving 555 Grove Street, Herndon, Virginia, and Related Locations*, 02-MG-114, affidavit of special agent David Kane, attachment D, p. 1 (ED VA March 2002).

200. Forms 990 for Taibah International Aid Association, 1999 and 2000.

201. Michael Isikoff and Mark Hosenball, "Terror Watch: Probe Closed," *Newsweek*, June 1, 2005.

202. Ibid.

203. Farah and Mintz, "U.S. Trails VA, Muslim Money, Ties."

204. Balz Bruppacher, "Swiss Authorities Halt Investigation into Firm Suspected by U.S. of al-Qaida Links," Associated Press, June 1, 2005.

205. Correspondent accounts enable banks to conduct business in foreign countries where they may not have branches or offices. A correspondent account is a financial account opened on behalf of a foreign bank to facilitate business and transactions related to that foreign bank. In this case, Banca del Gottardo had correspondent accounts with Citibank and the Bank of New York that enabled it to conduct business in the US financial system through those two American banks. Bank Al Taqwa, in turn, had the same relationship with Banca del Gottardo. It has long been a concern that correspondent accounts could be abused for money laundering and other illicit activity. The PATRIOT Act contains provisions that attempt to tighten controls on correspondent accounts.

206. "The United States and Italy Designate Twenty-five New Financiers of Terror," US Department of the Treasury press release, August 29, 2002.

207. Isikoff and Hosenball, "Terror Watch: Probe Closed."

208. Mark Hosenball, Kevin Peraino, and Catharine Skipp, "Terror's Cash Flow," *Newsweek*, March 25, 2002.

209. Ibid.

210. Ahmed Huber quoted in Ken Dilanian, "2 Tied to al-Qaeda Finances Working Freely in Europe," *Philadelphia Inquirer*, December 5, 2003.

211. Farah, *Blood from Stones*, p. 209.

212. Huber quoted in Dilanian, "2 Tied to al Qaeda Finances Working Freely in Europe."

213. US Department of the Treasury, "The United States and Italy Designate Twenty-Five New Financiers of Terror."

214. George B. Wolfe, deputy general counsel of the US Department of the Treasury, to M. Claude Nicati, substitut du procureur general, Switzerland, January 4, 2002; Hosenball, Peraino, and Skipp, "Terror's Cash Flow."

215. Hosenball, Peraino, and Skipp, "Terror's Cash Flow."

216. Wolfe to Nicati, January 4, 2002.

217. Ibid.

218. Ibid.

219. Hosenball, Peraino, and Skipp, "Terror's Cash Flow."

220. "Accusato di terrorismo il presidente degli islamici del Canton Ticino" (President of the Islamic Community of Ticino Accused of Terrorism), Varese News, http://www2.varesenews.it/articoli/2002/maggio/regione-insubria/6-5islamico.htm (accessed January 23, 2006); Claudia Rosett and George Russell, "Possible Saddam–Al Qaeda Link Seen in U.N. Oil-for-Food Program," FoxNews.com, http://www.foxnews.com/story/0,2933,132682,00.html (accessed January 23, 2006).

221. Ibid.

222. Guido Olimpro, *La Rete del Terrore* (*The Net of Terror*) (Milan: Sperling and Kupfer, 2002), pp. 87, 89.

223. DIGOS (Division of General Investigations and Special Operations) note on ICI, November 9, 1996.

224. Ibid.

225. "Interrogati e rilasciati 2 manager egiziani" (Interrogated and Freed 2 Egyptian Managers), *La Repubblica*, November 7, 2001; "Datteri, fagiolini e melanzane: gli strain traficci dell'eritreo Nasreddin" (Dates, String Beans and Eggplant: The Unusual Traffics of Nasreddin), *Corriere della sera*, November 9, 2001.

226. Ibid.

227. "Islamische Gemeinschaft in Deutschland e,v" (Islamic Community in Germany), http://www.i-g-d.com/uber%20unss2.htm (accessed January 4, 2006).

228. "List of Preference Shareholders at 31/12/1999," Bank Al Taqwa Limited, April 15, 2000.

229. Ibid.

230. Ibid.; "Fueling Terror," Institute for the Analysis of Global Security, 2004, http://www.iags.org/fuelingterror.html (accessed November 14, 2005).

231. US Department of the Treasury, "The United States and Italy Designate Twenty-five New Financiers of Terror."

232. Michael Chandler, *Second Report of the Monitoring Group Established Pursuant to Resolution 1363 (2001) and Extended by Resolutions 1390 (2002) and 1455 (2002), on Sanctions against Al-Qaida, the Taliban and Individuals and Entities Associated with Them* (New York: United Nations Security Council, 2003), p. 21.

233. Ibid., p. 22.

234. Sylvain Besson, *La conquete de l'Occident; Le Projet Secret des Islamistes* (*The Conquest of the West: Secret Project of the Islamists*) (Paris: De Seuil, 2005), p. 22.

235. Italian Gulf Chamber Registration Lugano Form.

236. Laura Rozen, "Strange Bedfellows," *Nation*, November 10, 2003.

237. Ibid.

238. Ibid.

239. "Barzinji, Jamal," Fairfax Institute of the International Institute of Islamic Thought, http://fairfaxinstitute.net/cms/courses,asp?id=140 (accessed January 6, 2006); "Faculty and Administration," Fairfax Institute of the International Institute of Islamic Thought, http://fairfaxinstitute.net/cms/template,asp?id=26 (accessed January 6, 2006); Stephen Schwartz, "Wahhabis in the Old Dominion; What the Federal Raids in Northern Virginia Uncovered," *Weekly Standard*, April 8, 2002.

240. Judith Miller, "U.S. Examines Donations of 2 Saudis to Determine If They Aided Terrorism," *New York Times*, March 25, 2002; Farah and Mintz, "U.S. Trails VA, Muslim Money, Ties."

241. Kane affidavit, attachment D, p. 8; Articles of Incorporations for SAAR Foundation & Safa Trust.

242. Ibid.; Mary Beth Sheridan, "Leader Named at Mosque; Falls Church Site Selects Activist," *Washington Post*, June 11, 2005.

243. SAAR Foundation, IRS Form 990, 1994.

244. Matthew Barakat, "Activist Makes Transition to Imam at Virginia Mosque," Associated Press, July 31, 2005; Anwar Iqbal, "Analyis: Jihad Talks No Longer Kosher," Associated Press, April 28, 2005; Curt Anderson, "9/11 Panel Questions Two Hijackers' Help," Associated Press, June 27, 2004.

245. Barakat, "Activist Makes Transition to Imam at Virginia Mosque"; "Attorney General Alberto R. Gonzales Highlights Success in the War on Terror at the Council on Foreign Relations," Department of Justice press release, December 1, 2005.

246. Iqbal, "Analyis: Jihad Talks No Longer Kosher."

247. Ibid.

248. Anderson, "9/11 Panel Questions Two Hijackers' Help."

249. National Commission on Terrorist Attacks upon the United States, *The 9/11 Commission Report: Final Report of the National Commission on Terrorist Attacks upon the United States* (New York: Norton, 2004), p. 229.

250. Ibid.

251. Virginia Secretary of State Corporate Record for IICO.

252. Kane affidavit, Attachment D, p. 2; Bruce Zagaris, "U.S. Conducts Searches of Muslims in Virginia for Suspected Terrorist Ties," *International Enforcement Law Reporter*, May 2002.

253. Stephen Handelman, "Soviets Admonish West to 'Keep Cool' in 'Satanic Verses' Dispute with Iran," *Toronto Star*, March 2, 1989.

254. Ibid.; Fiona Fleck and Tim Shipman, "BNP in Secret Talks with Arab Terror Network; Nazi Link to bin Laden," *Sunday Express*, May 5, 2002; Ahmed

Huber, interview by Mike Boettcher, *Insight*, CNN, March 2, 2005; Henry Schuster, "An Unholy Alliance," CNN, March 29, 2005.

255. Jim Oliphant, "TheHateWithin," *Legal Times*, May 20, 2002.

256. Ibid.

257. Huber, interview.

258. Ahmed Huber quoted in Dilanian, "2 Tied to al-Qaeda Finances Working Freely in Europe."

259. John Mintz, "U.S. Keeps Close Tabs on Muslim Cleric; Officials Suspect Activist Has Close Ties with Iranian Regime," *Washington Post*, January 1, 2003.

260. Jessica Stern, "Holy Avengers," *Financial Times*, June 12, 2004.

261. "Recent OFAC Actions," Office of Foreign Assets Control, US Treasury Department, November 7, 2001, http://www.treas.gov/offices/enforcement/ofac/actions/20011107.shtml (accessed August 10, 2006).

262. Claude Nicati quoted in Bruppacher, "Swiss Authorities Halt Investigation into Firm Suspected by U.S. of al-Qaida Links."

263. Bruppacher, "Swiss Authorities Halt Investigation into Firm Suspected by U.S. of al-Qaida Links."

264. "Italy Freezes 'Terror' Funds," CNN.com, August 29, 2002, http://archives.cnn.com/2002/WORLD/europe/08129/italy.terror/index.html (accessed November 17, 2006).

265. Isikoff and Hosenball, "Terror Watch: Probe Closed."

266. Chandler, *Second Report of the Monitoring Group*, p. 22.

267. Ibid., pp. 22–23.

268. Corporation Bureau, Department of State of the Commonwealth of Pennsylvania, IIIT Articles of Incorporation, 1980.

269. SAAR Foundation, Inc., Form 990, 1993.

270. Virginia Secretary of State Corporate Records for SAAR Foundation, Inc., and International Institute of Islamic Thought.

271. IIIT Form 1023 (Application for Recognition of Exemption), filed June 4, 1982; IIIT Articles of Incorporation (PA 1980), filed with Pennsylvania Department of State Corporation Bureau, November 6, 1980, showing a "Dr. Taha Jaber" (presumably al-Alwani) as an incorporator.

272. "Interview with Sheikh Taha," *Muslim Democrat* 4, no. 1 (January 2002), http://www.islam-democracy.org/documents/pdf/md_january2002.pdf (accessed January 24, 2006).

273. "The CSID Board, Dr. Taha Jabir al Alwani," Center for the Study of Islam & Democracy, http://www.islam-democracy.org/alawani_bio.asp (accessed January 24, 2006).

274. *USA v. Sami Al-Arian*, 03-CR-77, exhibit 325 (MD FL).

275. Ibid.

276. Matthew Levitt, "Confronting Syrian Support for Terrorist Groups," *Middle East Intelligence Bulletin*, May 2003.

277. Letter dated December 11, 1991, from Ramadan Abdallah Shallah, director of administration of WISE, to Dr. Mark Orr, director of International Affairs Center. Seized by federal officials from the offices of WISE in 1995.

278. *In the Matter Involving 555 Grove Street, Herndon, Virginia, and Related Locations,* 02-MG-114, affidavit of special agent David Kane, pp. 38, 40 (ED VA March 2002).

279. Ibid., p. 39.

280. IIIT Form 990, 1994.

281. Ibid.

282. *In the Matter Involving 555 Grove Street, Herndon, Virginia, and Related Locations,* 02-MG-114, affidavit of special agent David Kane, p. 37 (ED VA March 2002).

283. Ibid.

284. Ibid., pp. 25, 57.

285. Ibid.

286. INS Special Agent William West, affidavit in support of search warrant for the residence of Sami al-Arian and the offices of ICP and WISE, November 1995, p. 8.

287. *In the Matter Involving 555 Grove Street, Herndon, Virginia, and Related Locations,* 02-MG-114, affidavit of SA David Kane, p. 57 (ED VA March 2002).

288. The *Muslim Community Directory of Metropolitan Washington* for 2000 shows Tarik Hamdi as publisher of IIIT publication *Islamiyat Al Ma'rifah* (which in the past was supposedly linked to IIIT's Web site).

289. *USA v. Bin Ladin,* 98-CR-1023, trial transcripts, p. 5287 (SD NY May 21, 2001).

290. *In the Matter of a Search Involving the Townhouse Dwelling at 933 Park Avenue, Herndon, Virginia,* 02-MG-114D, affidavit in support of application for a search warrant, p. 3 (ED VA March 13, 2002).

291. *USA v. Sami Al-Arian,* 03-CR-77, exhibit 924 (MD FL).

292. Ibid.

293. FBI report submitted by Dale Watson, assistant director, Counter Terrorism Division, November 5, 2001.

294. AAEF Form 1023, 1993; Form 990-EZ, 1995; Form 990-EZ, 1996.

295. Ibid.; *In the Matter Involving 555 Grove Street, Herndon, Virginia, and Related Locations,* 02-MG-114, affidavit of SA David Kane, p. 39 (ED VA March 2002).

296. Kane affidavit, attachment D.

297. "Shutting Down the Terrorist Financial Network December 4, 2001," Department of the Treasury press release, December 4, 2001, http://www.treas.gov/press/releases/po841.htm (accessed January 24, 2006).

298. Safa Trust, Inc., IRS Form 990, 1996; Kane affidavit, p. 41.

299. The International Education Trust, Inc., Form 990, for the year 2000.

-11-

EXTREMIST MOSQUES IN AMERICA: PROVIDING COVER

The extremists infiltrated [the West and United States] through immigration or political asylum. They have taken advantage of the democratic and liberal atmosphere to organize and form a nucleus of leadership. From these new bases, they attempt to achieve their political agendas. . . . The quick and immediate transferal of monies has also enhanced the power of the extremists, giving them the opportunity to expand by financing and supporting new members into the inner circle and to hijack established Islamic institutions, or establish new ones.

—Omar Ashmawy, an American Muslim testifying before the US Senate Judiciary Subcommittee on Terrorism, 1998

OVERVIEW

Churches, synagogues, and mosques are viewed as havens of worship, faith, and integrity. Since the founding of the United States, Americans have believed that a house of worship for any faith is a sanctified space. But as Islamic fundamentalism has spread globally, radical Islam, despite nonadherence by most Muslims in America, has increasingly dominated mosques across the United States.

The events at Illinois's Bridgeview Mosque provide a textbook example of a fundamentalist takeover, highlighting the influence and power of Saudi-backed groups and the Muslim Brotherhood.[1] They have been replicated throughout the United States, often in America's largest cities. There is growing concern that mosques such as Al Farouq in Brooklyn, Dar us Salaam in Seattle, Masjid as Sabr in Portland, Oregon, and others have effectively been transformed from places of worship into covers for extremist recruitment, fund-raising, criminal activities, and even planning centers for international terror organizations such as al Qaeda and Hamas.

This chapter will initially examine the growth of radical mosque activity in the United States. This will include a review of the North American Islamic Trust (NAIT), which is the institutional umbrella organization for radical mosques in the United States. The chapter will also look at the Islamic Center of Tucson as the birthplace of the takeover movement.

Additionally, this chapter will focus on illicit fund-raising and recruitment for terrorist organizations such as al Qaeda, Hamas, and the Palestinian Islamic Jihad (PIJ), as well as the use of mosques by individuals to further criminal activity such as immigration fraud, drug trafficking, and acquiring weapons.

THE NORTH AMERICAN ISLAMIC TRUST (NAIT)

Experts estimate that the North American Islamic Trust "has physical control over most mosques in the United States."[2] In addition, NAIT "is reported to own between 50 and 79 percent of the mosques on the North American continent."[3]

NAIT holds more than three hundred deeds to properties—some of them mosques—all across the country.[4] NAIT's Web site describes the organization's purpose:

> The North American Islamic Trust was established in 1971 by the MSA [Muslim Student Association] of U.S. and Canada. NAIT provides protection and safeguarding for the assets of ISNA [Islamic Society of North America]/MSA and other communities by holding their assets and real estate in "waqf" [a trust used for charitable purposes]. It also initiates and manages profitable business ventures in accordance with the Islamic Shari'ah; [and] supports and subsidizes projects beneficial to the cause of Islam and Muslims.[5]

NAIT mosques rank among the most radical in the United States. Two of the 9/11 hijackers, Khalid al-Mihdhar and Nawaf al-Hazmi, had close ties with members of the NAIT-funded Islamic Center of San Diego (ICSD).[6] Khalid Sheikh Mohammed told al-Mihdhar and al-Hazmi, who helped fly American Airlines Flight 77 into the Pentagon, "to pose as newly arrived" in order to acquire assistance in assimilating to the United States.[7] This suggests at least some awareness on Sheikh Mohammed's part of the usefulness of certain mosques for this purpose. A worshiper at the mosque, Omar al-Bayoumi, for instance, helped al-Mihdhar and al-Hazmi find an apartment in San Diego and introduced them to members of the local Muslim community.[8] Bayoumi had been the subject of a terrorism investigation in 1999 that was later dismissed.[9] Some ICSD members also assisted the pair in obtaining Social Security numbers and driver's licenses,[10] and another sold them a 1988 Toyota (ultimately discarded at Dulles International Airport on September 11).[11] When al-Hazmi needed funds and a means to access them, $5,000 was wired from Dubai by Ali Abdul Aziz Ali (Khalid Sheikh Mohammed's nephew), through the ICSD administrator's bank account.[12]

Al-Hazmi visited the NAIT-affiliated Dar Al Hijrah mosque in Falls Church, Virginia,[13] after Anwar Aulaqi, former imam of the Rabat Mosque in San Diego,[14] moved to the Virginia location in 2001.[15] While he was taking flight lessons in Norman, Oklahoma, Zacarias Moussaoui sought and received assistance from the NAIT-owned mosque in town.[16] One member even drove him to Minnesota, where in August 2001 Moussaoui was arrested on immigration charges.[17] Moussouai is awaiting sentencing and a possible death penalty, having fired his lawyers and entered guilty pleas to all charges.[18] In November 2001, Mujahid Abdulqaadir Menepta, an associate of Moussaoui's from the radical mosque in Norman,[19] was charged with being a "felon in possession of a firearm."[20] Menepta later was convicted and sentenced to fifteen months in prison.[21]

NAIT Organization and Structure

NAIT's board of directors and advisory board include individuals linked both directly and indirectly to terrorists and terror-propagating organizations. Current members include Muzammil Siddiqi,[22] a fundamentalist and vocal supporter of jihad who once said, "Those who die on the part of justice are alive, and their place is with the Lord, and they receive the highest position, because this is the highest honor,"[23] and Jamal Sa'id, who operates the notorious Bridgeview Mosque in Chicago.[24] A notable past adviser to NAIT is Siraj Wahhaj,[25] named on the list of unindicted coconspirators in the 1993 World Trade Center bombing that was compiled by the office of then US Attorney Mary Jo White.[26]

NAIT maintains intimate connections with the Quranic Literacy Institute (QLI), which was held liable as a Hamas front in the civil suit brought by the parents of David Boim (the American teenager murdered in the West Bank by two Hamas gunmen in 1996).[27] It also has connections to the Safa Trust, a highly complex financial operation rooted in a network of Muslim entities that remains under federal investigation.

According to Safa Trust's articles of incorporation, NAIT is designated a beneficiary of the organization's assets "in the case of dissolution of the Corporation."[28] The trust is an affiliate of the SAAR network, the subject of chapter 10.

The chairman of NAIT,[29] Bassam Osman, was also a past board member of QLI.[30] The founder of QLI,[31] Ahmad Zaki Hammad, was also a past member of NAIT's board of directors.[32] According to an FBI affidavit, bank records show that Hammad gave three checks to a leading Hamas recruiter, Muhammad Salah.[33] In 1998, the Justice Department seized QLI's assets after establishing that QLI was financing terror,[34] and on September 23, 2001, Salah himself was named as a specially designated terrorist.[35] In August 2004, Salah was indicted on three charges: racketeering; providing material support or resources to terrorists; and attempting to influence, obstruct, and impede the due administration of justice.[36] Salah is scheduled to stand trial in October 2006 at the US District Court in Chicago.[37]

MOSQUES AS SOURCES OF RECRUITS AND AS SAFE HAVENS

The Evolution of Radical Islam in Arizona

September 11 pilot Hani Hanjour first spent time in Tucson in 1991 studying English and then attending flight school in 1996 and 1997. He returned to Arizona in early 2001 to refresh his flying skills.[38] His selection of Arizona was in all likelihood not accidental.

In the mid-1980s, the Islamic Center of Tucson (ICT) was the spiritual headquarters for radical Islamist activity in the United States. Before al Qaeda took shape, the center was the US satellite office of the Mektab Al Khidmat (MAK) or "Mujahideen Services Office," an organization based in Peshawar, Pakistan, that the US government has called "the precursor organization to al Qaeda."[39] MAK was founded by Saudi imam Wael Julaidan, Osama bin Laden, and bin Laden's mentor, Sheikh Abdullah Azzam.[40] The Islamic Center of Tucson's annual report to the Arizona state government showed that Julaidan was its president in 1984.[41]

In the late 1980s, Julaidan fought alongside bin Laden in

Afghanistan.[42] In Pakistan, Julaidan served as an official with the Saudi-based Muslim World League.[43] Bin Laden referred to him while discussing the inception of al Qaeda in a 1999 Al Jazeera interview: "We were all in one boat, as is known to you, including our brother, Wa'el Julaidan."[44] Throughout the 1990s, Julaidan had contacts with al Qaeda's military leaders, Dr. Ayman al-Zawahiri and Abu Zubaydah,[45] and by 2002 he had been named a Specially Designated Global Terrorist (SDGT).[46]

Even after Julaidan left his post as imam of the Islamic Center of Tucson, the radical work of the center continued. It was the US source of *Al Jihad*, the Arabic-language publication of the Peshawar-based Services Office. Abdullah Azzam, who cofounded al Qaeda, served as the publication's editor and, in April 1988, penned an article titled "The Solid Base (Al Qaeda)."[47]

Azzam wrote that the Afghan mujahideen already had established the solid base for an international Islamic society in Afghanistan, and then exhorted his followers:

> America is trying to grab the fruits of this great Jihad and to rule without recourse to God's book. Accordingly the solid base has to face international pressures and temptations from all over the world. But they refused to bow their heads before the storm. They decided to continue their march along a path of sweat and tears and blood.
>
> It is the duty of the children of the Islamic world to firmly stand by this solid base, with their wealth and their lives: "Those who disbelieve are friends to one another. If you do not keep them in check there will be anarchy and big corruption all over."
>
> The final call: We shall continue the Jihad no matter how long the way is till the last breath and the last beating of the pulse or we see the Islamic state established.[48]

The purpose of *Al Jihad* was to make young Muslim men aware of their potential role in the current struggle against the Soviets in Afghanistan, while also finding recruits for the future jihad against the United States. The newsletter offered training opportunities for young men in Afghanistan. Each issue contained news clips honoring "martyrs" who had died in combat with the Soviets. Afghanistan, many stories said, was the prototype for how Islam would fight the West once the Soviets were defeated.[49]

The ICT hosted radical inspirational speakers as well. In 1986, Sheikh Omar bin Ahmad As Saif, a fiery and influential religious cleric from

Yemen, addressed approximately 150 local Muslim youths at the center. His audience cheered him wildly as he urged them to take part in the Afghan jihad.[50]

Bin Laden's personal assistant and financial facilitator in the mid-1990s, Wadih el-Hage, also had been involved with the ICT in the late 1980s. The FBI special agent in Phoenix believes that "El Hage established a bin Laden support network in Arizona while he was living there and that this network is still in place."[51] As mentioned in earlier chapters, federal prosecutors also believe that el-Hage has information about the murder of Rashad Khalifa, a visiting imam at the center, in 1990.[52]

The ICT also funneled money to terrorist front groups. In 2001, the center raised more than $7,000 for the Holy Land Foundation (HLF).[53] Even after HLF was indicted for providing material support to Hamas, the center's imam, Omar Shahin, continued to defend the organization: "The Holy Land Foundation collects funds for widows and orphans and needy people. . . . They raised $20,000 for the victims of (Sept. 11), and they were the first Muslim organization to do this."[54] Shahin's own comments on the 9/11 investigation underscore the ICT's continued radicalism: "I think the investigation is not headed in the right direction. They are focusing on the Arabs, the Muslims. And all the evidence shows that the Muslims are not involved in this terrorist act."[55]

As part of the ICT's development as an extremist hub in the United States, it established a fund-raising division: the Al Kifah Refugee Center. Like the Islamic Center, Al Kifah had a parent organization headquartered in Peshawar. It eventually opened scores of offices worldwide, including several in the United States. Set up in the mid-1980s, the office in Tucson was the first. By 1989, Al Kifah's primary US headquarters had moved to Brooklyn, New York, with a strong presence in Jersey City, New Jersey, while Tucson remained its second-largest office in the United States. Al Kifah began by seeking money and recruits for MAK; after al Qaeda was created in 1989, it soon transformed itself into al Qaeda's operational headquarters in the United States.[56]

In retrospect, Al Kifah's open support for terror operatives was evident as early as 1992, when World Trade Center conspirators Ramzi Yousef and Ahmad Ajaj arrived in the United States. Among the many false identification documents they carried were press badges issued by the Al Bunyan Islamic Information Center in Tucson, Arizona. The post office box number given on their badges for the Al Bunyan Center was the same as that on the letterhead of Tucson's Al Kifah Refugee Center.[57]

The Egyptian "Blind Sheikh," Omar Abdel Rahman, another Al Kifah operative, received a life sentence in 1995 for his part in a plot to blow up New York City tunnels and landmarks.[58] President Bush named Mektab Al Khidmat and Al Kifah as specially designated terrorist organizations on September 23, 2001.[59]

Following the indictments in the World Trade Center and landmark cases, the Brooklyn office shut down, and in April 1993 the Boston Al Kifah office reincorporated under the new name of Care International. The continuity between the two organizations was obvious to anyone who scratched the surface. Like Al Kifah, Care International's fund-raising literature supported the mujahideen and jihad. And after the Al Kifah office shut down, Care resumed publication of Al Kifah's pro-Jihad newsletter, *Al Hussam*.[60]

In April 1992, when the founder of Care International, Emadeddin Muntasser, applied for his legal permanent residency, his affiliation with the "Al Kifah Refugee Center, Boston Chapter," a group founded by Osama bin Laden in the 1980s, attracted the attention of the FBI.[61] Muntasser's legal difficulties exploded in May 2005 when he and Care treasurer Muhamed Mubayyid were indicted on tax fraud charges based on false descriptions supplied to the IRS of the nature of Care's activities and its relationship with the Al Kifah Refugee Centre.[62] According to the indictment, both Muntasser and Mubayyid hid the fact that Care "was an outgrowth of, and successor to, Al Kifah Boston and was engaged in non-charitable activities."[63]

Finally, to complete the New York–Arizona radical nexus, in January 2005 the Islamic Center of Tucson announced the mosque's new imam: Abdulhakim Ali Mohamed,[64] who had previously served as imam at the Al Farouq Mosque in Brooklyn.[65]

Weapons, Recruitment, and Terror Financing in Portland

The Islamic Center of Portland, or Masjid as Sabr, was earlier an affiliate of NAIT.[66] The center's imam, Sheikh Mohamed Abdirahman Kariye, was a founding director of the Global Relief Foundation (1992), although this is discernible only through recognizing aliases and matching street addresses cited in the foundation's Articles of Incorporation.[67] Kariye also is believed to have fought with the mujahideen against the Soviets in Afghanistan in the early 1980s and was subsequently imprisoned in Pakistan.[68] According to an FBI affidavit that cites a conversation recorded by a cooperating witness (hereinafter CW), Kariye spoke out "very strongly" in support of jihad and exhorted his followers to fight Americans.[69] In May 2003, Kariye was sentenced to five years' probation after pleading guilty to one count of making false statements relating to healthcare matters and misuse of a Social Security number.[70]

Federal prosecutors allege that Kariye likely provided money and support to a group of Portland men convicted of trying to fight US soldiers in Afghanistan. On October 1, 2002, during a consensually recorded conversation with a CW, one of those men, Jeffrey Battle, told the CW that clerics at Masjid as Sabr were staunch supporters of jihad. Further, Battle replied in the affirmative when the CW asked whether Kariye told his followers to wage jihad against Americans. Other conversations recorded by the FBI indicated that the total amount provided by Kariye was sufficient to allocate $2,000 to each of the travelers going to Afghanistan. Battle said that Kariye had obtained this money from individuals affiliated with the Masjid as Sabr.[71]

Their investigation of Ali Khaled Steitiye, a regular worshiper at the Islamic Center of Portland,[72] led investigators to the Portland cell described earlier in chapter 4.[73] Steitiye, who had a previous criminal record, including a conviction of felony theft in Oklahoma and another of forgery in Oregon,[74] was indicted in an Oregon district court for attempting to acquire a firearm illegally.[75]

Skamania County sheriff's deputy Mark Mercer came upon Steitiye and five other persons on September 29, 2001, at a gated gravel pit outside Washougal, Washington, where they had been discharging weapons. Mercer's investigation included recording the names of the men and the weapons they had with them. Mercer then passed on the information to Sheriff Chuck Bryan.[76] When, in a separate incident, Steitiye was arrested on federal weapons charges, Bryan contacted the FBI in Portland about the earlier episode involving Steitiye and his companions at the gravel pit.[77]

This ultimately led to the Portland cell investigations and convictions and the confirmation that Steitiye had received military training from Palestinian militants associated with Hamas.[78] Steitiye was convicted of a federal gun charge and sentenced to sixty months in prison in June 2005.[79] Six others eventually were convicted as well, on charges including weapons violations and providing services to the Taliban.[80]

Conspiring to Provide High-Tech Equipment to al Qaeda in Seattle

The FBI arrested Earnest James Ujaama (aka Bilal Ahmed) in Denver, Colorado, on July 22, 2002.[81] Ujaama was charged with conspiracy to provide material support and resources, including computer software, technology, and services, to al Qaeda.[82]

After converting to Islam in the early 1990s, Ujaama became involved in the now-closed Dar us Salaam Mosque in Seattle, where preaching of extremist beliefs was common.[83] His arrest followed an investigation into that mosque, which was cofounded by his brother[84] and others in the Seattle area.[85]

Sometime around 1997, Ujaama left his family and moved to London, where he eventually became friends with Sheikh Abu Hamza al-Masri, a radical imam at the Finsbury Park Mosque[86]—one of the most prominent centers of Islamist extremism in Europe.[87] The US State Department has classified al-Masri as a terrorist,[88] and he has been indicted in the United States in absentia for attempting to set up a terrorist training camp in Oregon, taking hostages in Yemen, conspiring to take hostages, and providing material support to al Qaeda and the Taliban.[89] The Republic of Yemen wants to apprehend al-Masri for his role in the 1998 kidnappings of sixteen Western tourists by the Islamic Army of Aden.[90]

A number of terrorists have frequented Finsbury Park, including Richard Reid and Zacarias Moussaoui.[91] On a Friday visit to Finsbury Park, hundreds of young men from around the world, including many European and American converts, circled through the building.[92] When asked if visitors from the United States often come to see him, al-Masri chuckled and responded, "American converts, many American converts from the army converted to Islam, many."[93]

Finsbury Park was raided by British authorities in January 2003 and Abu Hamza was banned from preaching at the mosque. But attempts by the British government to strip him of his citizenship (acquired after marriage in 1981) and deport him to Yemen have been held up.[93] Al-Masri is in police custody following his arrest and request for extradition to the United States on terrorism-related charges.[94]

Ujaama ran Web sites for al-Masri that solicited money for the Taliban[96] and helped spread al-Masri's beliefs concerning the need to conduct global jihad against the West[97] as well as to attract recruits. Also at al-Masri's direction, Ujaama traveled to Afghanistan to deliver computers to the Taliban[98] and to facilitate jihad training for a British citizen, Feroz Abassi.[99] US troops later captured Abassi in Afghanistan and moved him to Guantanamo Bay.[100]

Federal authorities now believe that Ujaama was trying to set up a jihad training camp in Bly, Oregon. As the Ujaama indictment notes, "[C]onspirators planned to provide training in the United States of America to persons desiring to engage in violent jihad so that such persons would be *bona fide* candidates for further violent jihad training in training camps operated by al Qaeda abroad, including in Afghanistan."[101] Ujaama even faxed al-Masri a report on the possibility of establishing the camp. He compared the Bly terrain to that in Afghanistan; stated that the property was suitable for storing and concealing guns, bunkers, and ammunition; and invited al-Masri to stay there at a safehouse.[102]

Others were involved in this venture. Feroz Abassi told US authorities that he had fought in Afghanistan with someone named "Haroon," who claimed he had traveled to the United States to establish a terrorist training camp. Federal agents have confirmed that al-Masri tasked Rashid Haroon Aswat and Oussama Kassir, a Swedish national, with traveling to Seattle and meeting with Ujaama.[103] A British-born citizen of Indian descent, Aswat is regarded as a possible al Qaeda operative and is also believed to have masterminded the July 7 London explosions. Aswat was arrested in Zambia in July 2005 and deported to Britain.[104] In January 2005, a UK court ordered Aswat's extradition to the United States.[105] Aswat's lawyers are currently appealing the order.[106]

In November 1999, Aswat and Kassir inspected the proposed training camp at the Bly property, met potential candidates for jihad training, established security for the property by instituting guard patrols and passwords, and along with the other candidates undertook training in firearms and viewed a video recording on improvised poisons.[107] While at the site, Kassir identified himself to an accomplice and potential Jihad training recruits as a "hit man" for Osama bin Laden.[108] Kassir, an unindicted coconspirator in the Ujaama prosecution, subsequently was sentenced to ten months in a Swedish jail for illegal weapons possession.[109] Based on a complaint charging him with conspiracy to provide material support to terrorists, Kassir was rearrested in Prague, Czech Republic, in December 2005. He is under detention in Prague, and the United States has sought his extradition.[110] The United States has sought

Kassir's extradition, but a decision by the Czech court on the extradition demand is still pending.[111]

Evidence exists that in October and November 1999, Ujaama led discussions with other coconspirators on acquiring further training in the United States. The purpose of this training was to facilitate attending Afghan jihadi training camps, committing armed robberies, building underground bunkers to hide ammunition and weapons, creating poisonous materials for use against the public, and firebombing vehicles.[112] Notwithstanding this, according to the *Seattle Post-Intelligencer*, officials do not believe that "the Seattle group is a fully trained, full-fledged terrorist 'cell' that has regularly received orders from Al Qaida."[113] In April 2003, Ujaama pled guilty "to conspiracy to provide goods and services to the Taliban"[114] and agreed to cooperate fully with US authorities as well as foreign governments in other terrorism cases,[115] most notably that against al-Masri.[116] He was sentenced to a two-year prison term.[117]

Three other Seattle-area men associated with the Bly camp and the Dar us Salaam Mosque are assisting federal authorities.[118] Semi Osman, a British national and a US Navy reservist[119] who served as Dar us Salaam's imam,[120] was arrested on immigration and weapons charges in May 2002.[121] According to an FBI document cited by the *Los Angeles Times*, Osman "helped coordinate" the Bly camp.[122] The paper also quotes a confidential summary of the search of Osman's home: the authorities discovered papers written by al-Masri, military maps and field manuals, weapons, "instructions on poisoning water sources," and "various other items associated with Islamic radicalism."[123]

More specifically, agents found a Lebanese passport, containing Osman's photo, in the name of Sami Samir el-Kassem, and a book titled *Acquiring New ID*. In it was a Washington birth certificate for "Daniel Anthony McClellan." Another document bearing the name of "Michael McClellan" was discovered in a gun encyclopedia. Moreover, federal agents learned that Osman had twice married US citizens in an attempt to gain citizenship himself. Previously, Osman had claimed to be a naturalized British citizen from Sierra Leone.[124]

Osman initially was accused of filing false immigration papers and owning a gun whose serial numbers had been rubbed off, but he did not face terrorism charges.[125] He eventually pled guilty to a weapons charge in August 2002[126] and in April 2003 was sentenced to eleven months in jail.[127] After agreeing to testify against Abu Hamza al-Masri,[128] he was credited with time served and handed over to immigration authorities.[129]

Osman also testified against Abdul Raheem al-Arshad Ali.[130] Ali, a former US Marine and the onetime imam at the Dar us Salaam Mosque, was arrested in November 2002 for illegally buying a semiautomatic handgun for Osman.[131] Previously, Ali had traveled to London, where he stayed for ten days with Ujaama and lunched with al-Masri.[132] A *Los Angeles Times* piece notes that Ali "greatly admires" al-Masri,[133] while a reporter from the *Seattle Times* calls Ali "unapologetic about the Sept. 11, 2001, attacks."[134] Notwithstanding this, Ali is reported to have decided to cooperate with federal authorities[135] and charges against him were dropped in April 2003.[136] A third man in the mosque probe reportedly also has decided to cooperate.[137]

Dar Al Hijrah: A Center of Support for Islamic Terrorists

Since the Dar Al Hijrah Islamic Center was founded in Falls Church, Virginia, in November 1992, its leadership has been linked with persons connected to Hamas, the Muslim Brotherhood, and other radical Islamic groups. Abdelhaleem al-Ashqar, suspected of being a high-level Hamas financier (discussed in chapter 5), was for a time on Dar Al Hijrah's board of directors,[138] and Ismail Elbarasse, another alleged Hamas fund-raiser (also discussed in chapter 5), is one of its founders.[139]

Musa Abu Marzook

Marzook was a well-known member of the Dar Al Hijrah Islamic Center.[140] A 1995 federal complaint alleged that as head of the political bureau of Hamas, Marzook funded terrorist activities that included attacks against soldiers and civilians in the West Bank and Israel.[141]

Marzook was deported from the United States in May 1997, and his legal permanent residency was revoked.[142] One of those who testified in his support at his extradition trial was Dar Al Hijrah's imam, Mohammed al-Hanooti.[143] Marzook now lives in Damascus, Syria, where he is a senior member of Hamas's apparatus.[144]

Dar Al Hijrah's al-Hanooti

Al-Hanooti served as Dar Al Hijrah's senior imam.[145] Earlier, from 1984 to 1986, he had been the president of the Islamic Association for Palestine.[146] In 1995, federal prosecutors in the Southern District of New York named al-Hanooti as an unindicted coconspirator in the World Trade Center bombing.[147] According to a 2001 FBI report, "Al Hanooti collected over six million U.S. dollars for support of HAMAS in Israel."[148]

With a Hamas poster as a backdrop, al-Hanooti addressed a 1988 Islamic Association for Palestine (IAP) conference:

> Our brothers in Palestine give us great honor in their war by applying jihad. And they are closer to God than us. We are just sitting without applying jihad.
>
> Those brothers [mujahideen in Palestine] create a history that makes us honorable. They are the people who are facing the enemy of Allah—the Jews. They raise the flag of jihad and they keep the jihad alive. And those who are going to be killed are not dead but martyrs, and alive in the eyes of God. [He then mentions Quranic verses referring to martyrs being alive, not dead.]
>
> Those who are fighting to elevate the word of God will achieve victory. God will never give the Americans and Russians the upper hand on us because God will never give the infidels the chance to control us.
>
> People are standing up for the sake of God and we want to raise our flag so as to achieve . . . for our religion or we spill our blood.[149]

Mohamad el-Sheikh

The mosque's current imam, Mohamad Adam el-Sheikh, is a cofounder of both Dar Al Hijrah[150] and the Muslim American Society (MAS).[151] In his native Sudan, el-Sheikh was an active member of the Muslim Brotherhood,[152] and from 1973 to 1977, he sat as a senior judge in a Sharia court.[153] He is a current member of the Fiqh Council of North America and served as chairman of the Islamic Judiciary Council of Sharia Scholars of North America (SSANA).[154]

According to the Web site of the Islamic African Relief Association (IARA), el-Sheikh served as the IARA's regional representative when he was imam at the Islamic Society of Baltimore.[155] In October 2004, the Treasury Department designated the worldwide network of IARA, along with five senior officials, as Specially Designated Global Terrorists (SDGTs), declaring: "Information available to the U.S. indicates that international offices of IARA provided direct financial support for UBL [Osama bin Laden]."[156] The same designation confirmed that IARA has also supported Hamas and Al Ittihad Al Islamiya (AIAI), both SDGTs.[157]

In addition to being involved with the Muslim Brotherhood and a front group for al Qaeda and Hamas, el-Sheikh has argued for the legitimacy of suicide bombings. He declared in September 2004, "If certain Muslims are to be cornered where they cannot defend themselves, except through these kinds of means, and their local religious leaders issued fatwas to permit that, then it becomes acceptable as an exceptional rule, but should not be taken as a principle."[158]

Shaker el-Sayed

Another person of interest in a leadership position at Dar Al Hijrah is Shaker el-Sayed. Currently an imam at the mosque, el-Sayed is the secretary-general of the Muslim American Society.[159] He has written with admiration of Hassan al-Banna, the founder of the Muslim Brotherhood: "I found it personally very enlightening and rewarding to study his life, his work, and his movement. I found his words as the strongest argument for any case he presents."[160]

Moreover, in 2004 el-Sayed told reporters for the *Chicago Tribune* that al-Banna's ideas are "the closest reflection of how Islam should be in this life."[161] It is instructive to look at the ideas and words that el-Sayed finds so inspirational. Al-Banna argued that "it is the nature of Islam to dominate . . . to impose its law on all nations and to extend its power to the entire planet,"[162] and he also gave the Muslim Brotherhood its motto: "Allah is our objective, the messenger is our leader, Quran is our law, jihad is our way, and dying in the way of Allah is our highest hope."[163]

El-Sayed has also lauded Mustafa Mashour, the supreme guide of the Muslim Brotherhood, calling his death in November 2002 "a grave loss for the Muslim World and the Islamic movement everywhere."[164] The press release from MAS on this occasion, which lists el-Sayed as the contact, noted that Mashour "made tremendous sacrifices for the sake of spreading the moderate and balanced understanding of Islam that has been the trademark of his movement."[165]

Like his colleague Mohamad el-Sheikh, el-Sayed refuses to condemn suicide bombings. In fact, he has openly supported them. When asked at a June 5, 2001, press conference and sit-in at the State Department, "Do you condemn the terrorist attacks from Hamas and the suicide bombings?" he replied:

> I made a statement that we do support the Palestinian resistance. . . . The so-called Israeli settlers are not civilian population. They are military reserves; they are armed, trained and dangerous. They invade the Pales-

> tinian neighborhoods at night and squander everything. They kill, maim, and destroy homes. . . . If I were there, I would use every power in my hand to defend my family.
>
> . . . We say to the Palestinian people, "Go ahead. Continue your fight against occupation no matter what name they give you because we give you the name of courageous people who stand for the rights and we're standing with you."[166]

Similarly, at the December 2002 Islamic Circle of North America (ICNA)–MAS conference, el-Sayed was asked, "If killing people is *haram* [evil], what is happening in Palestine?" He responded:

> about the subject unfairly named suicide bomber, homicide bomber, murderers, or killers. Our answer to this issue is simple. . . . The Islamic scholars said whenever there is an attack on an Islamic state or occupation, or the honor of the Muslims has been violated, the Jihad is a must for everyone, a child, a lady and a man. They have to make Jihad with every tool that they can get in their hand. Anything that they can get in their hand, and if they don't have anything in their hand, then they can fight with their hand without weapons."[167]

Al Qaeda Recruitment Using Religious "Instruction"

A clear example of religion as a recruiting tool for terrorism is the "Lackawanna Six" case, in which local Muslim Americans were inspired to attend an al Qaeda training camp through the initial "religious" instruction of two men, Juma al-Dosari and Kamal Derwish. Both had fought in the Bosnian war.[168]

Derwish was born in Lackawanna, New York, but left the city as a child in 1973 with his parents to return to Yemen. He grew up in Saudi Arabia and was later deported from the country for his radical views. Derwish returned to Lackawanna, which has a relatively large Yemeni population, and integrated quickly into the local Muslim community. Over time, he established a loyal following of teenagers and young adults, to whom he preached an extremely radical view of Islam, encouraging violent jihad and armed training.[169]

In the spring of 2001, Derwish guided six of his followers—all young American men—from upstate New York through Pakistan to Al Faruq, Osama bin Laden's most notorious terror training camp in Afghanistan. Here the group engaged in training for violent jihad and allegedly met with bin Laden.[170]

In October 2003, PBS *Frontline* produced a detailed program on the Lackawanna Six. The program's Web site posted an FBI profile that describes how al-Dosari and Derwish were believed to have used religion as the entrée for jihadi recruitment.

The FBI has determined that the following tactics were used in the Lackawanna cell, and they appear to be a template for jihadi recruitment, especially in the West:

- Locating an Islamic center and identifying young men who seek knowledge of Islam.
- Developing a friendship with individuals and recognizing individual interests, emotional states, strengths, and weaknesses.
- Bringing young people to an apartment or house to socialize and learn more about Islam. The discussions/meetings usually occur after evening prayers, which would be after 10 PM, and last until 2 AM to 3 AM.
- Emphasizing historical Muslim conflicts, detailing individuals who fought for Islam, winning honor and fame for themselves and God.
- Evaluating the reaction of individuals as the discussion moves to suffering of Muslims in the world. Emphasis on how Muslims are being prosecuted; Muslim women are being raped, tortured, and killed; and how true Muslims are fighting for their faith. Stressing the duty to fight in Jihad and how martyrdom is justified.

Eventually, the individual members identified as suitable are approached and recruited to fight for jihad, the arrangement for which the operatives can provide.[171]

This pattern of recruitment unfolded for the Lackawanna group who were apprehended on their return to the United States. Six of the men pled guilty and were sentenced to prison terms, ranging between seven and ten years, on charges of providing material support to a designated foreign terrorist organization, because they attended an al Qaeda training camp.[172] For Attorney General John Ashcroft the conviction of the Lackawanna Six was critical to the United States' war on terror:

> Several important objectives in the war on terrorism have been achieved as a result of the convictions and sentences in the Buffalo case. . . . The defendants in this case received strong sentences for providing material support to our terrorist enemies. At the same time, the government is

> gaining valuable assistance from these cooperating defendants, who traveled to the al Farooq camp and trained side-by-side with Al Qaeda terrorists.[173]

Derwish is believed to have been killed in November 2002 in a targeted air strike by the CIA as he was traveling in an SUV through a desolate desert region of Yemen with five other suspected al Qaeda members.[174]

MOSQUES AS A FOUNDATION FOR TERROR FINANCING

Over the past fifteen years, radical mosques have been sites where millions of dollars have been raised for terrorists. Earlier chapters have detailed some of these examples, including:

- New Jersey imam Alaa al-Sadawi's aborted attempt to export $659,000 in cash in suitcases on a trip to Egypt in July 2002. The El Tawheed Islamic Center's "religious" leader had raised money for the Global Relief Foundation (GRF),[175] designated a Specially Designated Global Terrorist in September 2001 for providing financial support to al Qaeda.[176]
- Imam Mohammed el-Mezain of the Islamic Center of Passaic County, New Jersey, served as director of endowments for the Holy Land Foundation, set up to fund Hamas.[177]
- Imam Yassin Aref of the NAIT-owned Masjid as Salam Mosque in Albany, New York, and Mohammed Hossain, the mosque's founder, were both indicted in August 2004 on charges of money laundering and supporting terrorism.[178] The indictment followed a yearlong FBI sting, in which an undercover informant, a Pakistani immigrant and Muslim, convinced Aref and Hossain to take part in a plot to make money from the sale of a shoulder-fired missile that was to be used to assassinate a Pakistani diplomat in New York City.[179] A superseding indictment in September 2005 charged the Albany mosque leaders with conspiracy to provide material support to Jaish e Mohammed (JeM), a Pakistan-based Islamic extremist group that was declared a terrorist organization by the US Department of State in May 2002.[180] The indictment accused Aref of lying to FBI agents when he denied having ties to foreign

> political groups. Aref has, in fact, been an active member of a terrorist militant group—Islamic Movement in Kurdistan—that seeks to establish an Islamic government in Iraq. The indictment further alleged that Aref knew Mullah Krekar, the purported founder of Ansar al-Islam, a radical Islamist fundamentalist group.[181] In addition, a forty-eight-page memorandum filed by federal prosecutors included references to an incendiary poem, allegedly written by Aref in December 3, 1999: "Raise the Jihad sword/Raise the Koran with blood/So we bring back the freedom for ourselves and the entire people of this Earth."[182] Both Aref and Hossain are scheduled to stand trial in US District Court in Albany in September 2006.[183]

Other examples abound.

Brooklyn-Area Mosques and Fund-Raising for al Qaeda

The involvement of Brooklyn-area mosques in al Qaeda fund-raising was exposed during the FBI investigation of Mohammed Ali Hasan al-Moayad and Mohammed Mohshen Yahya Zayed. In March 2003 the two men were arrested after an extensive FBI undercover operation. They were charged with conspiring to provide material support to al Qaeda and Hamas through al-Moayad's worldwide fund-raising operation.[184]

According to the affidavit filed in support of the arrest warrant for al-Moayad, he "received money for the *jihad* that was collected at the Al Farouq Mosque in Brooklyn."[185] Further, the Department of Justice released a statement in the case explaining,

> According to the charges filed against Al Moayad and Zayed, a confidential informant working with the FBI met with Al Moayad in January 2002 and was told by Al Moayad in subsequent conversations that he regularly provides money to support mujahideen fighters in Afghanistan, Chechnya and Kashmir. Al Moayad also allegedly stated during this and other conversations with the informant that he had supplied Al Qaeda with arms and communications equipment in the past, delivering more than $20 million to Al Qaeda prior to Sept. 11, 2001. Al Moayad even boasted of several meetings with Osama Bin Laden, and said he personally delivered the $20 million to Bin Laden, with much of this money coming from contributors in the United States, including Brooklyn.[186]

In November 2001, the FBI's International Terrorism squad began working with a confidential informant who had known al-Moayad for more than six years. During several meetings with the FBI informant, al-Moayad boasted that "jihad" was his field; trumpeted his involvement in providing money, recruits, and supplies to al Qaeda, Hamas, and other terrorist groups; and said he received money for jihad from collections at the Al Farouq Mosque in Brooklyn. The investigation also revealed that al-Moayad had "substantial and direct ties to" al Qaeda and bin Laden.[187]

As the trial began, Assistant US Attorney Kelly Moore characterized al-Moayad's address book as a "Who's Who of terrorist organizations."[188] In a tape played during his trial, al-Moayad prayed for the death of Jews and Americans,[189] proclaiming, "Dear God strike them with earthquakes, put them in their coffins, abandon them and defeat them."[190]

Al-Moayad and his assistant, Mohammed Moshen Yahya Zayed, were convicted on all charges on March 10, 2005.[191]

Sheikh Abdullah Satar and Imam Numan Maflahi

In early 2000, Sheikh Abdullah Satar, a prominent Yemeni cleric and politician, came to New York to raise funds, visiting several mosques in Brooklyn including the Al Farouq Mosque in Boerum Hill, the Institute of Islam in downtown Brooklyn, the Islamic Center of Canarsie, and the Bay Ridge Islamic Center.[192]

Satar also spent time at the Charitable Society for Social Welfare (CSSW) in Park Slope, which FBI special agent Brian Murphy called a "front organization to funnel money to terrorists."[193] Anwar Aulaqi, who mentored two of the 9/11 hijackers, was the CSSW's vice president/treasurer in 1998.[194] He is known to have worked closely with Numan Maflahi, the head of CSSW Brooklyn.[195] Federal prosecutors insisted that Maflahi "could not have been unaware of the true nature of that organization or its involvement with and support of Al Qaeda."[196]

Satar remains in Yemen.[197] Maflahi was convicted and sentenced to five years in prison in February 2004[198] for lying to investigators about his ties to Satar. He told agents that he had only limited contact with Satar and no involvement in Satar's fund-raising for al Qaeda and Osama bin Laden.[199]

According to US authorities, after leaving New York, Satar met with a top al Qaeda operative in Italy.[200] In a speech in Italy, Satar accused the United States of persecuting Maflahi "to curry favor with the Jewish population and to project hatred upon Muslims."[201]

Imam Mazen Mokhtar, the Masjid Al Huda, and Internet Solicitation

In 2004, the Friday prayers at Masjid Al Huda in New Brunswick, New Jersey, occasionally were led by Mazen Mokhtar.[202] Mokhtar, a naturalized American who was born in Egypt, is also listed in Internet directories as the registrant and the administrative and technical contact for the Web site http://www.minna.com.[203] The site is an exact duplicate of one run by Babar Ahmad, a British man arrested in London and charged with aiding terrorists.[204] The site, which solicited funds for the Taliban and for terrorists in Chechnya, contained a section on how to train oneself for armed jihad.[205] Other sections discuss such topics as the permissibility of executing prisoners of war and—as illustrated below—of martyrdom:

> Martyrdom or self-sacrifice operations are those performed by one or more people, against enemies far outstripping them in numbers and equipment, with prior knowledge that the operations will almost inevitably lead to death.
>
> The form this usually takes nowadays is to wire up one's body, or a vehicle or suitcase with explosives, and then to enter amongst a conglomeration of the enemy, or in their vital facilities, and to detonate in an appropriate place there in order to cause the maximum losses in the enemy ranks, taking advantage of the element of surprise and penetration. Naturally, the enactor of the operation will usually be the first to die.
>
> The name "suicide-operations" used by some is inaccurate, and in fact this name was chosen by the Jews to discourage people from such endeavors. How great is the difference between one who commits suicide—because of his unhappiness, lack of patience and weakness or absence of iman [faith] and has been threatened with Hell-Fire—and between the self-sacrificer who embarks on the operation out of strength of faith and conviction, and to bring victory to Islam, by sacrificing his life for the upliftment of Allah's word![206]

Jihad is described as a requirement:

> According to the verse "*And prepare against them all you can of power . . . ,*" military training is an obligation in Islam upon every sane, male, mature Muslim, whether rich or poor, whether studying or working and whether living in a Muslim or non-Muslim country.
>
> In other countries, e.g. some states of USA, South Africa, it is per-

> fectly legal for members of the public to own certain types of firearms. If you live in such a country, obtain an assault rifle legally, preferably AK-47 or variations, learn how to use it properly and go and practice in the areas allowed for such training.[207]

The site even recommends obtaining US Army training manuals to prepare for armed jihad:

> The US Army has produced a number of military field manuals on CD on all topics from light weapons, tanks and artillery to mines, military fieldcraft and combat medicine. The full set is available on CD for less than US$100 and many field manuals are also available on the Internet. . . . Even though the US Army Field Manuals contain information specific to US Weapons, they still contain a large amount of useful information applicable in all circumstances. It is useful to get a full set of CDs for your mosque or Islamic society that everyone can use.[208]

In October 2004, Babar Ahmad was arrested in the UK, based on a four-count US indictment charging conspiracy to provide material support to terrorists (in particular the Taliban and the Chechen mujahideen), providing material support to terrorists, conspiring to kill persons in a foreign country, and money laundering.[209] In November 2005, British Home Secretary Charles Clarke authorized Babar Ahmad's extradition to the United States to face terrorism charges.[210] Investigators have searched Mokhtar's Web site business and investigations into his culpability are continuing.[211]

Imam Majeed Sharif, the United Muslim Mosque, and the IARA

As noted earlier in this chapter, the US Department of the Treasury designated the worldwide network of IARA and five of its senior officials as SDGTs in October 2004, accusing them of directly financing Osama bin Laden as well as the terrorist organizations Hamas and Al Ittihad Al Islamiya. Shortly after this announcement, FBI agents raided the home of Majeed Sharif, the president of the United Muslim Mosque in Waterbury, Connecticut,[212] and seized financial and other records.[213]

In 1999, Sharif had been invited to become IARA's volunteer representative in the US Northeast,[214] and later worked for IARA in Africa.[215] Members of his family have made charitable contributions to IARA[216] and according to the mosque's vice president, Magdy Galal, the United

Muslim Mosque has distributed IARA's literature and received donations for the organization.[217] To date, no charges have been filed and documents related to the search are sealed.[218]

Abdel Jabbar Hamdan and the West Coast Islamic Society

Abdel Jabbar Hamdan is the founding CEO of the West Coast Islamic Society located in Anaheim, California.[219] He also has been intimately involved with other groups connected to terrorism operating in America. In 1993, Hamdan attended a conference in Philadelphia where senior Holy Land officials met with high-ranking representatives of Hamas (see chapter 6).[220] He also served as a member of the Islamic Association of Palestine[221] and was a top Holy Land Foundation fund-raiser (see chapters 5 and 9).[222]

On the same day that the indictment alleging that HLF had funneled millions of dollars to Hamas was unsealed, Hamdan was arrested on immigration charges.[223] While acknowledging that he had indeed raised money for HLF, Hamdan claimed that the donations went to legitimate charities.[224] On April 7, 2006, an appeals board ruled that Hamdan should be deported to Jordan; his attorneys said they would appeal the ruling.[225]

MOSQUES AS A COVER FOR LOW-LEVEL CRIME

Cases of radical mosques recruiting terrorists and financing terrorism have received widespread media coverage. Less well known are those mosques connected to individuals committing crimes involving immigration fraud, weapons acquisition, and drug trafficking. A few of the most egregious examples are considered below.

Ghassan Zayed Ballut, Hatem Fariz, and the Chicago Islamic Center—Fraud, Money Laundering, Illicit Drug Production, and Palestinian Islamic Jihad

The martyr Izzedine al-Qassam, a beloved Hamas icon killed by the British in 1935, has at least two namesakes: the military wing of Hamas[226] and the Al Qassam Mosque in Chicago, more widely known as the Chicago Islamic Center. The mosque's three leaders all have been indicted on a variety of charges, including illicit drug distribution, money laundering, food stamp fraud, and membership in the Palestinian Islamic Jihad, a US-designated terrorist group.

In February 2003, Ghassan Zayed Ballut and Hatem Fariz, two of the three officials in the Chicago mosque who have authority over its bank account, were indicted in Florida along with Sami al-Arian for their involvement with PIJ.[227] In December 2005, Ballut was acquitted on all charges; Fariz was acquitted on twenty-four charges and the jury deadlocked on the remaining eight.[228] Furthermore, in July 2006, as part of a plea deal with federal prosecutors, the government dismissed seven other charges against Fariz. Fariz was sentenced to thirty-seven months in prison after he agreed to plead guilty to charges of making or receiving contributions for PIJ.[229]

In July 2004, Fariz also was charged with money laundering and defrauding the federal food stamp program from May 1999 to December 2000. Federal prosecutors allege that Fariz "knowingly devised, intended to devise and participated in a scheme to defraud and to obtain money and property from the USDA by means of materially false and fraudulent pretenses, representations, and promises."[230] By illegally exchanging cash for food stamp benefits, Fariz is accused of laundering money through the account of T & T Foods, a corporation of which he is president. In one instance, he wire-transferred approximately $1.7 million to the T & T Foods account at La Salle Bank.[231]

In June 2006, Fariz pled guilty to fraud and money laundering charges.[232]

In August 2004, the Chicago Islamic Center's longtime treasurer, Tariq Isa, was arrested and charged with distributing more than 1.7 million tablets of pseudoephedrine, a chemical used in the manufacture of methamphetamine. As the *Chicago Tribune* reported, prosecutors seeking Isa's detention said that he had been photographed with Ramadan Shallah, the worldwide head of PIJ.[233]

Isa was convicted on drug charges and sentenced to twenty years in prison in January 2006.[234]

Court proceedings involving Isa, Ballut, and Fariz have confirmed that the trio are the only officers of the Chicago mosque with signatory authority over its bank account.[235]

Imam Saleh Nawash and the Islamic Mosque of Cleveland—Arson, Money Laundering, and Contract Murder

In 2002, the Cuyahoga County Common Pleas Court sentenced Saleh Nawash, a religious leader at the Islamic Mosque of Cleveland, to nine years in prison for attempting to have his meat shop, Halal Products, burned down so that he could collect the insurance money.[236] The court also sentenced Nawash's friend, Ahmed Jaffal, to eight years in prison for helping to arrange the arson as well as for hiring a contract killer to rob and kill two of Jaffal's former business partners.[237]

An FBI undercover agent posing as a hit man agreed to burn down the business as well as rob and murder Jaffal's former business associates. The agent was promised $1,000 for the arson and a share of the money from the men he robbed and killed.[238] According to Assistant County Prosecutor Steve Dever, Nawash scrawled anti-Palestinian messages on the windows of his store to make the arson appear as a hate crime.[239] Dever further alleged that Nawash left kerosene inside the building and gave the go-ahead signal for the arson.[240]

The Cleveland mosque was the subject of another recent crime-related investigation. On February 3, 2005, the FBI conducted a raid on Abrar Haque's home, office, and mosque in the West Park section of Cleveland, Ohio. Haque, a certified public accountant, founded the Islamic Mosque of Cleveland. While authorities have yet to release information about the raid or the FBI's warrant, neighbors report that two trailers full of materials were seized by law enforcement agents.[241] In February 2006, a federal grand jury in Cleveland returned a seventy-nine-count superseding indictment, charging Haque and fourteen others for offenses including money laundering, bank fraud, and immigration fraud, among other charges.[242] Antiterrorism officials are leading the ongoing investigation.[243]

CONCLUSION

Both before and after 9/11, some mosques have been conduits for supporting terrorism. Saudi petrodollars have unquestionably helped deepen the hold of the radical Wahhabi branch of Islam in mosques throughout the United States. This relationship fostered by NAIT's continuing ties to fundamentalist mosques underscores the connection between the Saudi-inspired spread of Islamic extremism and terror in North America.

In the months and years leading up to 9/11, many would-be terrorists sought safe harbor and assistance from American mosques. Some mosques have acted as recruiting grounds and sanctuaries for terrorist organizations. Others have been gulled by charity fronts into raising funds for terrorist organizations.

US authorities clearly face a delicate task in ensuring respect for places of worship while remaining effective against those who exploit that respect by hiding behind mosques and religious learning centers. A combination of continuing law enforcement vigilance and insistence by Muslims themselves that their mosques not be abused by extremists is likely the only solution to this continuing problem.

NOTES

1. For a comprehensive narrative of the radical Islamic takeover of the Bridgeview Mosque, see Noreen Ahmed-Ullah et al., "Struggle for the Soul of Islam: Hard-Liners Won Battle for Bridgeview Mosque," *Chicago Tribune*, February 8, 2004.

2. Testimony of Michael Waller before the Senate Judiciary Subcommittee on Terrorism, Technology, and Homeland Security, "Terrorist Recruitment and Infiltration in the United States: Prisons and Military as an Operational Base," October 14, 2003.

3. Ibid.

4. North American Islamic Trust, http://www.nait.net/ (accessed April 6, 2006).

5. North American Islamic Trust, http://www.nait.net/nait.html (accessed December 21, 2004).

6. Sarah Downey and Michael Hirsh, "A Safe Haven?" *Newsweek*, September 30, 2002.

7. National Commission on Terrorist Attacks upon the United States, *The 9/11 Commission Report: Final Report of the National Commission on Terrorist Attacks upon the United States* (New York: Norton, 2004), pp. 215–16.

8. Ibid., p. 219.

9. Ibid., chap. 7, n. 19.

10. Downey and Hirsh, "A Safe Haven?"

11. Ibid. See also *The 9/11 Commission Report*, chap. 7, n. 29.

12. *The 9/11 Commission Report*, p. 220.

13. Dar Al Hijrah Web site, http://www.hijrah.org/constitution.html (accessed April 6, 2006).

14. *The 9/11 Commission Report*, p. 221.

15. Ibid.

16. Downey and Hirsh, "A Safe Haven?" Moussaoui was considered for replacement of pilot Ziad Jarrah in the 9/11 plot when Mohamed Atta and Jarrah were suffering from disagreements in the summer of 2001. See *The 9/11 Commission Report,* pp. 245–47.

17. Ibid.

18. *USA v. Moussaoui*, 01-CR-455, plea (ED VA April 22, 2005). See also Pete Yost, "Moussaoui Pleads to Conspiring with Sept. 11 Hijackers, Could Be Put to Death," Associated Press, April 22, 2005.

19. William F. Jasper, "Al-Qaeda's OKC-9/11 Ties," *New American*, July 26, 2004.

20. *USA v. Menepta*, 01-CR-207, complaint (WD OK October 26, 2001).

21. *Menepta*, 01-CR-207, sentencing courtroom minutes.

22. Islamic Society of North America (ISNA), http://www.isna.net/majlis/Muzammil_Siddiqi.asp (accessed December 21, 2004). See also Dow Jones Islamic Index Fund Web site, http://www.investaaa .com/pdfs/dow_Board_of_Directors.pdf (accessed January 31, 2005). The Dow Jones Islamic Fund is offered by Allied Asset Advisors, a subsidiary of the North American Islamic Trust (NAIT).

23. Helen T. Gray, "Contradictory to the Faith: American Muslims Say Terrorists Aren't Following Religious Teachings," *Kansas City Star*, January 28, 1995.

24. Dow Jones Islamic Index Fund Web site.

25. "First Woman Elected to ISNA Majlis Shura," ISNA press release, May 4, 1997.

26. *USA v. Rahman, et al.*, 93-CR-181, Mary Jo White's list of unindicted coconspirators (SD NY February 2, 2005).

27. *Boim, et al. v. QLI, et al.*, 00-C-2905, complaint (ND IL June 8, 1998).

28. District of Columbia Secretary of State, Articles of Incorporation of Safa Trust, September 30, 1986, at article 6.

29. Dow Jones Islamic Index Fund Web site.

30. *Boim, et al. v. QLI, et al.*, 00-C-2905, deposition of Amer Haleem (ND IL February 12, 2003).

31. Ibid. See also William Gains and Andrew Martin, "Terror-Funding Probe Touches Suburban Group; The FBI Is Investigating an Oak Lawn Organization Suspected of Investing in Real Estate to Launder Money for Hamas," *Chicago Tribune*, September 8, 1998.

32. Gains and Martin, "Terror-Funding Probe Touches Suburban Group."

33. *USA v. 1997 E35 Ford Van, et al.*, 98-CV-3548, verified complaint for forfeiture (ND IL June 9, 1998).

34. Ibid.

35. Executive Order no. 13224, *Code of Federal Regulations*, title 31, secs. 595–97 (September 23, 2001).

36. *USA v. Marzook, et al.*, 03-CR-978, second superseding indictment (ND IL August 19, 2004).

37. Mike Robinson, "Lawyer in Hamas Case Asks for New Hearing on Secret Evidence," Associated Press, July 19, 2006.

38. *The 9/11 Commission Report*, pp. 225–26.

39. US Department of the Treasury, Office of Public Affairs, *PO-3553: Treasury Department Statement Regarding the Designation of the Global Relief Foundation*, October 18, 2002.

40. Ibid.

41. State of Arizona, Islamic Center of Tucson Annual Report and Certificate of Disclosure, February 7, 1985.

42. US Department of the Treasury, Office of Public Affairs, *PO-3397: Treasury Department Statement on the Designation of Wa'el Hamza Julidan*, September 6, 2002.

43. Nabil Sharaf-ad-din, "Usama Bin Laden—A Millionaire [*sic*] Finances Extremism in Egypt and Saudi Arabia," *Rose Al Yusif*, no. 3388, May 17, 1993.

44. US Department of the Treasury, *PO-3397*.

45. Ibid.

46. Ibid. The designation occurred in conjunction with the Saudi government. President Bush's Executive Order 13224 designates Julaidan "as a person who supports terror." The designation also named the Rabita Trust "as an organization that provided logistical and financial support to al-Qaida."

47. Dr. Abdullah Azzam, "Al-Qa'ida," *Al Jihad*, no. 41, April 1988.

48. Ibid.

49. See past issues of *Al Jihad* (1988–1990).

50. "Videotape Lecture by Shaikh Omar Bin Ahmad As Saif," VHS, (Tucson, AZ: Islamic Center of Tucson, March 17, 1986). Shaikh Omar Saif is an influential veteran of the Arab Afghan mujahideen. In Yemen in 2000, Saif declared a fatwa stating that "shaking hands with the Jews is a great treachery." See "Law & Diplomacy," *Yemen Times* 10, no, 15, April 10–16, 2000.

51. Eleanor Hill speaking for the Senate Select Committee on Intelligence, *The FBI's Handling of the Phoenix Electronic Communication and Investigation of Zacarias Moussaoui Prior to Sept. 11, 2001*, September 24, 2002.

52. Blake Morlock, "Key Bin Laden Aides Met Here in Late '80s," *Tucson Citizen*, July 23, 2004.

53. Associated Press, "Tucson Islamic Center Won't Raise Money for Accused Agency," December 5, 2001.

54. Ibid.

55. Dennis Wagner and Tom Zoellner, "U.S. Muslims Torn between Love of Islam and America," *Arizona Republic*, November 4, 2001.

56. According to the indictment (*USA v. Bin Laden, et al.*, 98-CR-1023, indictment [SD NY November 4, 1998]) against bin Laden and others for their role in the bombing of the United States embassies in Kenya and Tanzania in August 1998, the al Qaeda "grew out of the 'mekhtab al khidemat' (the 'Services Office') organization which had maintained (and continues to maintain) offices in various parts of the world, including Afghanistan, Pakistan (particularly in

Peshawar) and the United States, particularly at the Alkifah Refugee Center in Brooklyn."

57. *United States v. Yousef,* 93-CR-180, government exhibit W2799-1. Address from official Al Kifah Refugee Center document is noted as "P.O. Box 44149, Tucson, AZ 85733."

58. "Sheik Gets Life Sentence in Terror Trial," CNN, January 17, 1996. See also Andrew Marshall, "Terror 'Blowback' Burns CIA," *Independent*, November 1, 1998.

59. Executive Order 13224, US Department of State, December 20, 2002.

60. *USA v. Mubayyid, et al.*, 05-CR-40026, indictment (D MA May 11, 2005).

61. Denise Lavoie, "Judge Delays Citizenship Hearing for Islamic Charity Leader," Associated Press, January 6, 2005.

62. *USA v. Mubayyid, et al.*, 05-CR-40026, indictment (D MA May 11, 2005). See also "Former Officers of Care International, Inc. Indicted," US Department of Justice press release, May 12, 2005.

63. "Former Officers of Care International, Inc. Indicted."

64. Stephanie Innes, "Islamic Center of Tucson Hires Nashville Imam," *Arizona Daily Star*, January 2, 2005.

65. The Islamic Center of Nasvile [*sic*], http://www.muslimeen.org/sheikh.htm (accessed January 28, 2005).

66. Downey and Hirsh, "A Safe Haven?"

67. Illinois Secretary of State, Articles of Incorporation of Global Relief Foundation, January 10, 1992. Kariye's name was given as "Muhamed Abdirahman," a variation of one of several names he used. The address listed in the papers is in a Southwest Alfred Street complex where Kariye lives.

68. *USA v. Kariye*, 02-CR-399-02-JO, affidavit of FBI SA Mark A. McBryde (D OR August 2003).

69. Ibid.

70. *USA v. Kariye*, 02-CR-366, minutes of proceedings (D OR May 29, 2003). See also *Kariye*, 02-CR-366, judgment (D OR 2003).

71. *Kariye*, 02-CR-399-02-JO, affidavit of FBI SA Mark A. McBryde.

72. Mark Larabee, "Man Guilty in Gun, Fraud Case," *Oregonian*, June 18, 2002.

73. Les Zaitz, "Palestinian Faces Weapons Charges in Portland Terror Case," *Oregonian*, June 10, 2004.

74. *USA v. Steitiye*, 01-CR-396, indictment (D OR October 17, 2001).

75. Ibid.

76. Zaitz, "Palestinian Faces Weapons Charges in Portland Terror Case."

77. Ibid.

78. Larabee, "Man Guilty in Gun, Fraud Case."

79. *USA v. Steitiye*, 04-CR-110, judgment (D OR May 31, 2005).

80. *USA v. Battle*, 02-399-01-JO, plea agreement (D OR October 16, 2003); *USA v. Ahmed Bilal*, 02-CR-399-03-JO, plea agreement (D OR September 2003); *USA v. Muhammad Bilal*, 02-CR-399-04-JO, plea agreement (D OR September

2003); *USA v. Hawash*, 02-CR-399-07-JO, plea agreement (D OR August 6, 2003); *USA v. Lewis*, 02-399-06-JO, plea agreement (D OR September 26, 2003).

81. Christopher Newton, "Seattle Man Arrested in Denver in Terrorism Probe," Associated Press, July 23, 2002.

82. *USA v. Ujaama*, 02-CR-283, indictment (WD WA August 28, 2002).

83. Gene Johnson, "Ujaama Sentencing Set for Aiding Taliban," Associated Press, February 13, 2004.

84. "Muslim Author Arrested for Al Qaeda Ties," *Philadelphia Daily News*, July 24, 2002.

85. Ibid. See also Patrick McDonnell, "FBI Focuses on Black Muslims in Seattle," *Los Angeles Times*, July 20, 2002.

86. Johnson, "Ujaama Sentencing Set for Aiding Taliban."

87. Congressional International Relations Subcommittee on International Terrorism, Nonproliferation, and Human Rights, *Hearing on Visa Waiver Program and the Screening of Potential Terrorists*, 108th Cong., 2nd sess., June 16, 2004.

88. "Executive Order no. 13224, *Blocking Property and Prohibiting Transactions with Persons Who Commit, Threaten to Commit, or Support Terrorism*, Title 31, secs. 595–97 (designated on April 19, 2002).

89. *USA v. Mustafa*, 04-CR-356, indictment (SD NY April 19, 2004).

90. Johnson, "Ujaama Sentencing Set for Aiding Taliban."

91. Jill Lawless, "Radical Cleric Abu Hamza Al Masri Makes Court Appearance in Britain," Associated Press, August 20, 2004.

92. Eyewitness reports and taped personal interview with Abu Hamza al-Masri, Finsbury Park Mosque, London, June 2002.

93. Sheikh Abu Hamza al-Masri, interviewed by the Investigative Project, June 28, 2002.

94. "Hamza Faces 11 US Terror Charges," BBC News, May 27, 2004, http://news.bbc.co.uk/1/hi/england/london/3752257.stm (accessed August 9, 2005).

95. Lawless, "Radical Cleric Abu Hamza Al Masri Makes Court Appearance in Britain."

96. Mike Carter and Steve Miletich, "Ujaama's Guilty Plea Part of Deal to Testify against Radical Cleric," *Seattle Times*, April 15, 2003.

97. *USA v. Ujaama*, 02-CR-283, indictment (WD WA August 28, 2002).

98. Patrick McDonnell, "The Entrepreneur Who Saw Road to Profit in Al Qaeda," *Los Angeles Times*, September 22, 2002.

99. Carter and Miletich, "Ujaama's Guilty Plea Part of Deal to Testify against Radical Cleric."

100. Ibid.

101. *USA v. Ujaama*, 02-CR-283, indictment (WD WA August 28, 2002).

102. Ibid.

103. Carter and Miletich, "Ujaama's Guilty Plea Part of Deal to Testify against Radical Cleric."

104. "Terrorism Suspect Arrives in Britain," http://www.telegraph.co.uk/

news/main.jhtml?xml=/news/2005/08/08/nextrem308.xml (accessed August 8, 2005).

105. Daniel McGrory, "Al Qaeda Suspect Fears Torture after Extradition Order," *London Times*, January 6, 2006.

106. Jill Lawless, "2 Britons Appeal Extradition to US on Terrorism Charges," Associated Press, July 11, 2006.

107. *USA v. Ujaama*, 02-CR-283, indictment (WD WA August 28, 2002).

108. Ibid. See also Andrew Norfolk, "Hijack Case Swede 'Linked to al-Qaeda,'" *Times of London*, September 2, 2002. Kassir served as a mentor to Kerim Chatty, a Swedish Muslim who tried to carry a loaded gun aboard a London-bound flight from Sweden. Investigators feared that Chatty, who received flight training in South Carolina in 1996, may have been plotting a 9/11-style hijacking days before the first anniversary of September 11. See also Douglas Frantz and Desmond Butler, "Traces of Terror: Radical Cells," *New York Times*, September 4, 2002.

109. Associated Press, "In Sweden, a Former Terror Suspect Goes to Jail for Illegal Weapons Possession," November 17, 2003.

110. "United States Unseals Complaint against Terrorism Suspect Arrested in Czech Republic," US Department of Justice press release, December 13, 2005. See also *USA v. Kassir* 04-MJ-898, complaint (SD NY 2004).

111. Agence France Presse, "Czech-US Extradition Agreements Signed," May 16, 2006.

112. *USA v. Ujaama*, 02-CR-283, indictment (WD WA 2002).

113. Sam Skolnik, Chris McGann, and Daikha Dridi, "Mosque Members under Investigation," *Seattle Post-Intelligencer*, July 13, 2002.

114. "Earnest James Ujaama Pleads Guilty to Conspiracy to Supply Goods and Services to the Taliban,"US Department of Justice press release, April 14, 2003.

115. Ibid.

116. Carter and Miletich, "Ujaama's Guilty Plea Part of Deal to Testify against Radical Cleric."

117. McDonnell, "The Entrepreneur Who Saw Road to Profit in Al Qaeda."

118. Ibid.

119. McDonnell, "FBI Focuses on Black Muslims in Seattle." See also Robert Jamieson, "Seattleite Accused of Ties to Terror in Custody," *Seattle Post-Intelligence*, July 23, 2002.

120. McDonnell, "The Entrepreneur Who Saw Road to Profit in Al Qaeda."

121. *USA v. Osman, et al.*, 02-CR-175, complaint (WD WA May 23, 2002).

122. Ibid.

123. Ibid.

124. Mike Carter, "Man's Links to Mideast Probed," *Seattle Times*, May 25, 2002.

125. Associated Press, "Terrorism Ties Cited in Immigration Case," June 6, 2002.

126. Associated Press, "Man Pleads Guilty in Al-Qaida Probe," August 2, 2002.

127. Melanthia Mitchell, "Man Arrested in Terrorism-Related Probe Sentenced to 11 Months," Associated Press, April 26, 2003.

128. Paul Shukovsky, "Former Prayer Leader Sentenced," *Seattle Post-Intelligencer*, April 26, 2003.

129. Mitchell, "Man Arrested in Terrorism-Related Probe Sentenced to 11 Months."

130. Sam Skolnik and Daikha Dridi, "Ex-Mosque Leader Arrested," *Seattle Post-Intelligencer*, November 6, 2002.

131. Ibid.

132. McDonnell, "The Entrepreneur Who Saw Road to Profit in Al Qaeda."

133. Ibid.

134. Laura Sullivan, "Al-Qaida Targets 'Captive Audience,'" *Seattle Times*, November 30, 2002.

135. Carter and Miletich, "Ujaama's Guilty Plea Part of Deal to Testify against Radical Cleric."

136. *USA v. Ali*, 02-CR-411, government's motion to dismiss indictment without prejudice (WD WA April 25, 2003).

137. Carter and Miletich, "Ujaama's Guilty Plea Part of Deal to Testify against Radical Cleric."

138. Caryle Murphy, "In Washington, Muslims and Jews Despair over Mideast Violence," *Washington Post*, October 13, 2000.

139. Caryle Murphy, "Facing New Realities as Islamic Americans," *Washington Post*, September 12, 2004.

140. *Marzook v. Christopher, et al.*, 96-CV-4107, memorandum in support of application for bail, pp. 15–16 (SD NY).

141. Ibid., p. 18.

142. US Department of Justice and Federal Bureau of Investigation, *Terrorism in the United States 1997*, p. 6.

143. *Marzook v. Christopher, et al.*, 96-CV-4107, testimony of Imam Mohammed al-Hanooti (SD NY April 24, 1996).

144. John Ashcroft, "Prepared Remarks of Attorney General John Ashcroft Regarding the Indictment of Hamas," August 20, 2004.

145. *Marzook v. Christopher, et al.*, 96-CV-4107, testimony of Imam Mohammed Al-Hanooti (SD NY April 24, 1996).

146. *Ila Filastin*, February 1990, p. 70.

147. *USA v. Omar Ahmad Ali Abdel Rahman, et al.*, 93-CR-181, list of 173 possible coconspirators submitted by Mary Jo White (SD NY 1995).

148. Dale Watson, Assistant Director Counterterrorism Division FBI, Memo to Mr. R. Richard Newcomb, Director Office of Foreign Assets Control Department of Treasury, *Holy Land Foundation for Relief and Development International Emergency Economic Powers Act*, November 5, 2001.

149. IAP Conference in Jersey City, NJ, as reported by the Investigative Project, November 26, 1998.

150. Dar Al Hijrah Islamic Center, http://www.hijrah.org/imam.html (accessed August 7, 2005).

151. Murphy, "Facing New Realities as Muslim Americans."

152. Ibid.

153. Dar Al Hijrah Islamic Center, http://www.hijrah.org/imam.html.

154. Ibid.

155. Web archive of IARA-Baltimore, http://web.archive.org/web/20010224070450/www.iara-baltimore.org/partners.html (accessed August 11, 2005).

156. US Department of the Treasury, *Treasury Designates Global Network, Senior Officials of IARA for Supporting bin Laden, Others*, October 13, 2004.

157. Ibid.

158. Murphy, "Facing New Realities as Muslim Americans."

159. Mary Beth Sheridan, "Leader Named at Mosque," *Washington Post*, June 11, 2005.

160. Shaker el-Sayed, "Hassan Al-Banna: The Leader and the Movement," *Muslim American Society*, http://www.maschicago.org/library/misc_articles/hassan_banna.htm (accessed September 14, 2004).

161. Noreen Ahmed-Ullah, Sam Roe, and Laurie Cohen, "A Rare Look at Secretive Brotherhood in America," *Chicago Tribune*, September 19, 2004.

162. Neil MacFarquhar, "Egyptian Group Patiently Pursues Dream of Islamic State," *New York Times*, January 20, 2002.

163. Muslim Brotherhood Movement, http://www.ummah.org.uk/ikhwan/index.html (accessed August 23, 2004).

164. "MAS Mourns Loss of Sheikh Mustafa Mashour," MAS press release, November 14, 2002, http://web.archive.org/web/20021207171137/masnet.org/news_and_releases /Nov._14_2002.htm (accessed September 23, 2004).

165. Ibid.

166. Press conference and sit-in, US Department of State, Washington, DC, June 5, 2001.

167. Shaker el-Sayed, Speech at ICNA-MAS Annual Convention, Chicago, IL, December 25–29, 2002.

168. Michael Powell, "No Choice but Guilty," *Washington Post*, July 29, 2003.

169. James Sandler, "Kamal Derwish: The Life and Death of an American Terrorist," *PBS Frontline*, October 16, 2003.

170. Ibid.

171. Juma Al Doseri recruitment profile, http://www.pbs.org/wgbh/pages/frontline/shows/sleeper/inside/jumafbi.html (accessed January 28, 2005).

172. "Sahim Alwan Sentenced for Providing Material Support to Al Qaeda," US Department of Justice press release, December 17, 2003.

173. Ibid.

174. "CIA's License to Kill," CBS News, December 4, 2002.

175. John Marzulli, "Feds: Cleric Was a Terror Money Man," *New York Daily News*, November 14, 2003.

176. "Treasury Department Statement Regarding the Designation of the Global Relief Foundation," US Department of the Treasury, October 18, 2002.

177. *USA v. Holy Land Foundation for Relief and Development, et. al.*, 04-CR-240, indictment (ND TX July 26, 2004).

178. *USA v. Aref, et al.*, 04-CR-402, indictment (ND NY August 6, 2004).

179. *USA v. Aref, et al.*, 04-CR-402, criminal complaint (ND NY August 5, 2004).

180. *USA v. Aref, et al.*, 04-CR-402, superseding indictment (ND NY September 29, 2005).

181. Ibid.

182. *USA v. Aref, et al.*, 04-CR-402, government's memorandum in support of motion (ND NY September 29, 2005).

183. Brendan Lyons, "Release Denied for Mosque Leader," *Times Union*, July 14, 2006.

184. *USA v. Al-Moayad, et al.*, 03-CR-016, indictment (ED NY December 15, 2003).

185. *USA v. Al-Moayad*, 03-MJ-16, affidavit in support of arrest warrant (ED NY January 5, 2003).

186. "Yemeni Citizens Charged with Material Support to Al Qaeda Extradited to the United States," US Department of Justice press release, November 17, 2003.

187. Ibid.

188. William Glaberson, "Sheik Prayed for Death of Jews, Prosecutor Claims," *New York Times*, January 29, 2005.

189. Ibid.

190. Michael Weissenstein, "Surveillance Tapes Offer Damaging Evidence against Sheik in Terror-Funding Trial," Associated Press, February 5, 2005.

191. "Statement of United States Attorney Roslynn R. Mauskopf on Verdict in United States v. Mohammed Al Hassan Al Moayad and Mohammed Mohsen Yahya Zayed," US Department of Justice press release, March 10, 2005.

192. John Marzulli, "Yemeni Cleric Suspected of Raising Terrorist Funds in Brooklyn," *Daily News*, February 12, 2004.

193. Tom Hays, "New York City–Based 'Charity' Eyed in Terror Money Probe," Associated Press, February 26, 2004.

194. Charitable Society for Social Welfare, IRS Form 990, 1998.

195. Hays, "New York City–Based 'Charity' Eyed in Terror Money Probe."

196. Tom Hays, "Feds Demand Stiff Prison Term for Gas Station Owner Linked to Terror Money Scheme," Associated Press, May 5, 2004.

197. Ibid. See also "Fed Detail Alleged Terror Money Scheme," CNN, February 12, 2004.

198. *USA v. Maflahi*, 03-CR-412, jury verdict (ED NY February 18, 2004).

199. William Glaberson, "Man Gets 5 Years for Lying in Terror Inquiry," *New York Times*, July 10, 2004.

200. William Glaberson, "U.S. Traces Financial Roots of Terror Network to Brooklyn," *New York Times*, February 12, 2004.

201. Ibid.

202. Susan Schmidt and Michelle Garcia, "N.J. Man Accused of Aiding Terrorists Called 'Moderate,'" *Washington Post*, August 12, 2004.

203. Whois.com, http://whois.com/EasyDomainSearch.aspx?isavailable=no (accessed March 2, 2004).

204. *USA v. Ahmad*, 04-M-240, criminal complaint (CT 2004).

205. Ibid.

206. Web Archive Jihad in Chechnya Web site, http://web.archive.org/web/20010405150852/http://minna.com/ (accessed January 25, 2005).

207. Ibid.

208. Ibid.

209. *USA v. Ahmad, et al.*, 04-CR-301, indictment (D CT October 6, 2004).

210. "The Battle to Banish Babar Ahmad," BBC News, November 16, 2005.

211. Karen McVeigh, "British Terror Suspect Facing Extradition to U.S.," *Scotsman*, May 18, 2005.

212. Matt Apuzzo, "FBI Raids Connecticut Mosque Leader's Home in Terror Probe," Associated Press, October 14, 2004.

213. Edmund Mahony, "FBI Targets Wolcott Home," *Hartford Courant*, October 15, 2004.

214. Mark Azzara, "Desperate Poor of Africa Move Wolcott Couple," *Republican-American*, January 23, 2003.

215. Associated Press, "Islamic Charity Denies Terrorism Support Accusations," October 21, 2004.

216. Edmund Mahony, "FBI Targets Wolcott Home," *Hartford Courant*, October 15, 2004.

217. Laura Walsh, "Mosque Officials Says Leader Not Involved in Terror Funding," Associated Press, October 15, 2004.

218. Apuzzo, "FBI Raids Connecticut Mosque Leader's Home in Terror Probe."

219. West Coast Islamic Society, IRS Form 990, 1999.

220. H. G. Reza, "Man Tied to Charity Stays in Jail," *Los Angeles Times*, December 3, 2004.

221. Ibid.

222. Holy Land Foundation, IRS Form 990, 1999.

223. Kevin Pang and Mike Anton, "Rally Supports Muslim Man Who Was Arrested by FBI," *Los Angeles Times*, July 29, 2004.

224. Ben Fox, "Mosque Founder Denies Terrorism Link," Associated Press, August 24, 2004.

225. H. G. Reza, "Muslim Should Be Deported, Board Rules," *Los Angeles Times*, April 12, 2006.

226. Ibrahim Barzak, "Abbas Pays Tribute to Palestinians Killed Fighting Israel," Associated Press, December 31, 2004.

227. *USA v. Al Arian, et al.*, 03-CR-77, indictment (MD FL February 19, 2003).

228. *USA v. Al Arian, et al.*, 03-CR-77, verdict form of Ghassan Ballut (MD FL December 5, 2005) and *USA v. Al Arian, et al.*, 03-CR-77, verdict form of Hatem Fariz (MD FL December 5, 2005).

229. *USA v. Fariz*, 03-CR-77, plea agreement (MD FL July 25, 2006).

230. *USA v. Hatem Fariz*, 04-CR-663, indictment (ND IL July 7, 2004).

231. Ibid.

232. *USA v. Fariz*, 03-CR-633, plea agreement (ND IL June 16, 2006).

233. Matt O'Connor, "Mosque Official's Release Denied," *Chicago Tribune*, August 11, 2004.

234. *USA v. Isa*, 04-CR-473, judgment (ND IL January 6, 2006).

235. Ibid.

236. Karl Turner, "2 Jailed for Recruiting Arsonist, Killer in Scheme to Collect Insurance on Shop," *Cleveland Plain Dealer*, August 29, 2002.

237. Ibid.

238. Ibid.

239. Karl Turner, "Grocer Pleads Guilty in Arson Plot; Fire Was to Look Like a Hate Crime," *Cleveland Plain Dealer*, July 30, 2002.

240. Ibid.

241. Amanda Garrett and John Caniglia, "CPA, Mosque Raided by FBI," *Cleveland Plain Dealer*, February 5, 2005.

242. *USA v. Haque, et al.*, 05-CR-182, superseding indictment (ND OH February 2, 2006).

243. US Department of Justice press release, February 2, 2006.

-12-

JIHADI WEBMASTERS

The semester begins in three more weeks. We've obtained 19 confirmations for studies in the faculty of law, the faculty of urban planning, the faculty of fine arts, and the faculty of engineering.

—Mohamed Atta's last correspondence with the other 9/11 hijackers; the "faculties" are thought to refer to the buildings targeted in the attacks

OVERVIEW

Since the Internet obtained almost universal usage in the 1990s, Islamic extremists have frequently exploited its rich, multifaceted resources. Islamist propaganda and recruitment activity are prevalent in cyberspace, which allows radical Islamists to easily spread their violent message to every corner of the globe—including the United States. By simply logging online, Islamic militants from Indonesia to Indiana are able to post articles, exchange information, and debate ideas on radical Web sites and in chat rooms. The Internet has become an operational tool for terrorists as they use the Web to communicate with each other, buy travel tickets and equipment, and obtain information on potential targets. The Internet is also used to recruit, train, and fund-raise.

In addition to these valid concerns about terrorist infiltration on the Internet, the greatest cyberworry is the use of the Internet by terrorists to hack into critical US infrastructures, either from inside or outside the country's borders. Computer-dominated sectors such as banking, communications, and the Internet itself are all potential targets of a cyberattack that could cause enormous disruption and expense. Another Internet tactic that has raised attention is the use of steganography—the hiding of messages in digital photographs or music files with no outward trace that they have been altered, thus making it possible to convey a private message to a knowing recipient via a publicly available image or sound.[1]

The US government has alleged that "al Qaeda uses prearranged phrases and symbols to direct its agents." For example, they may use an image of an AK-47 next to a picture of Osama bin Laden one day and reverse the images the next. They have also been known to change the color of icons. Similarly, they have used chat rooms to relay information.[2]

Computer software programs enable terrorists to create and store both real and false identification and travel documents that are used to facilitate travel, open bank accounts and credit cards, and carry out operations. By using the Internet and creating false documentation, terrorists and their organizations can acquire the anonymity essential for their clandestine activities. Computer technology is thus a vital tool for terror organizations seeking to strike at US interests. It facilitates passing information through e-mail and chat rooms and indirectly through Web sites to members already embedded in the United States or to those poised to attack American interests abroad. The use of Arabic Web sites provides further cover from law enforcement and intelligence agencies that are already playing linguistic catch up and do not possess the ability to provide real-time translation of scores of Web sites.

Although terrorist Web sites often change URLs or are inaccessible due to "technical difficulties," the Internet generally provides a steady, censorship-free venue for those who wish to spew hatred and preach violence. Terrorist groups use Web sites to laud their own accomplishments, conduct fund-raising, threaten their enemies (invariably Israel, the West, and Western-friendly Arab governments), and provide a public organizational face by posting their leaders' biographies as well as their ideology. Terrorist groups also frequently post the number of attacks they have committed on their Web sites, not only to boast about their capabilities and inspire sympathetic Web surfers, but also to taunt counterterrorism officials and other opponents. Because of the audio and visual capacities of this digital medium, terrorist groups can enhance and intensify the indoctrination experienced by new recruits. Moreover, these sites can be hosted on servers located in other countries (beyond US jurisdiction), use fast-emerging technologies such as instant-relay chat rooms, manipulate free speech protections afforded by US law, and employ sophisticated encryption techniques.[3]

Cheap, difficult to track, and easy to use, the Internet is indispensible to the international terror networks. While terrorists' uses for the Internet are expanding, so are the number of radical Islamist sites, which have increased significantly since 1997.[4]

THE INTERNET AS A TOOL

Operational Communications

Prior to 9/11, e-mails and instant messaging enabled terrorists to give and receive operational instructions for surveillance and attacks when physical or even phone contact proved too risky. A wealth of evidence emerged in late 2001 when Allan Cullison, a *Wall Street Journal* reporter in Afghanistan, purchased two computers that had been used by Osama bin Laden and his associates. US intelligence quickly took possession of both, but not before Cullison managed to copy the hard drive of one; the other was eventually returned to him. Both contained a variety of communications between al Qaeda members.

Although the saved e-mail discussions do not appear to have addressed a pending operation against the United States, they nonetheless could have included coded instructions for a future operation elsewhere. Al Qaeda's concern for operational secrecy led to the use of heavily coded language even in messages that were not encrypted. Cullison notes,

> As Al Qaeda established itself in Afghanistan in the late 1990s and began managing international operations of ever increasing complexity and audacity, the group focused on ensuring the secrecy of its communications. It discouraged the use of e-mail and the telephone and recommended faxes and couriers. The electronic files reflect the global nature of the work being done; much of the correspondence was neatly filed by country name. Messages were usually encrypted and often couched in language mimicking that of a multinational corporation; thus Osama Bin Laden was sometimes "the contractor," acts of terrorism became "trade," Mullah Omar and the Taliban became the "Omar Brothers Company," the security services of the United States and Great Britain became "foreign competitors," and so on. Especially sensitive messages were encoded with a simple but reliable cryptographic system that had been used by both Allied and Axis powers during World War II.[5]

An example of this is shown in a February 1, 1999, e-mail from Ayman al-Zawahiri, bin Laden's chief deputy and the former leader of the Egyptian Al Jihad terrorist organization, to al Qaeda members in Yemen where the word *birthday* refers to an attack:

I would like to clarify the following with relation to the birthday:

a) Don't think of showering as it may harm your health.
b) We can't make a hotel reservation for you, but they usually don't mind making reservations for guests. Those who wish to make a reservation should go to Quwedar [a famous pastry shop in Cairo].
c) I suggest that each of you takes a recipient to Quwedar to buy sweets, then make the hotel reservation. It is easy. After you check in, walk to Nut. After you attend the birthday go from Quwedar to Bushra St., where you should buy movie tickets to the Za'bolla movie theater.
d) The birthday will begin the third month. How do you want to celebrate it in the seventh? Do you want us to change the boy's birth date? There are guests awaiting the real date to get back to their work.
e) I don't have any gravel [probably ammunition or bomb-making material].[6]

Gathering Cyber and Physical Target Information

The Internet has provided terrorists with everything from logistical information about targets to manuals on creating explosives. The 9/11 hijackers, for instance, relied heavily on the Internet, using it to achieve such tasks as finding information relating to US flight schools, training for the actual attack, and purchasing the tickets for the fortuitous flights. Another group, the Muslim Hackers Club, ran a Web site that specialized in teaching advanced hacking and digital security skills to hackers and would-be hackers worldwide. The site featured links to US Secret Service hidden locations as well as detailed instructions on how to hack into "Milnet," the computer network used by the US Air Force. In e-mails sent in 1997, the club's founders urged supporters to gain computer expertise in order to "protect your own side and infect the other side."[7] In addition to offering instructions on hacking and spreading computer viruses, the Muslim Hacker's Club also posted a version of *The Anarchist Cookbook*, which contains a great deal of information on explosives.[8] Visitors to the site could learn how to make napalm and bombs, perfect electronic terrorism, and "How to Kill Someone with Your Bare Hands."[9] An archival version of the manual can still be found online, free of charge, although not in its original version.

Psychological Warfare

A common method used by Islamist terrorists since 9/11 has been the dissemination on the Internet of graphic images of violence, which encourage sympathizers to do the same. Beginning with the savage May 2004 beheading of American contractor Nicholas Berg in Iraq by al Qaeda's late leader in Iraq, Abu Musab al-Zarqawi, beheadings by Islamist terrorists have become increasingly common. While print and television media outlets usually censor such footage, Islamist Web sites show the gruesome images in their entirety. These Internet postings can have far-reaching effects. One disturbing illustration of this was the subsequent "reenactment" video of Berg's beheading created by four Muslim children—each no older than twelve—that was then posted on the Internet shortly after his murder.[10]

Terror Financing

Terrorists often raise funds via the Internet simply by making online pleas for donations. According to Professor Gabriel Weimann of the University of Haifa in Israel, an expert on terrorists' use of the Internet, "Al Qaeda . . . has always depended heavily on donations, and its global fund-raising network is built upon a foundation of charities, nongovernmental organizations, and other financial institutions that use websites and Internet-based chat rooms and forums."[11]

In an attempt to compete with Hamas's considerable success in soliciting funds for terror both domestically and internationally, the terrorist group Palestinian Islamic Jihad (PIJ) created the Elehssan Society. On May 4, 2005, the Elehssan Society was designated by the US Department of the Treasury as a charitable front for the Palestinian Islamic Jihad. Stuart Levey, the US Department of the Treasury's undersecretary for the Office of Terrorism and Financial Intelligence (TFI), stated, "Elehssan masquerades as a charity, while actually helping to finance Palestinian Islamic Jihad's acts of terror against the Israeli people and other innocents."[12] The charity has used Internet Web sites not only to solicit funds but also to post its claims of responsibility for terrorist attacks.[13] The Elehssan Society Web site justified its financial appeals by citing the Hadith: "Who ever finances a fighter for Allah or supported his family, then it is as he was a fighter."[14]

Donation appeals on terrorist Web sites are often published in multiple languages in order to reach the largest possible audience. Charities such as the Holy Land Foundation (Hamas), the Global Relief Foundation (Hamas and al Qaeda), the Benevolence International Foundation (al Qaeda), and the Elehssan Society (PIJ), all of which have been identified as terrorist financiers by the US government, address potential donors in English. In an August 2000 posting, for instance, the Benevolence International Foundation (BIF) instructed its visitors on the different methods available for making donations.[15]

Terrorist financing can also be accomplished over the Internet via traditional criminal schemes, such as identity theft, fraud, trading of Social Security numbers, and "phishing" scams. According to the Federal Trade Commission, phishing "involves Internet fraudsters who send spam or pop-up messages to lure personal information (credit card numbers, bank account information, Social Security number, passwords, or other sensitive information) from unsuspecting victims."[16] Just as criminal groups in Russia have used the Internet for these activities, so can terrorist groups.

Providing Jihad Training via the Internet

One example of how the Internet is utilized by radical Islamists for training purposes is a Web site run by a London-based Saudi militant named Muhammad al-Massari. The al-Massari site is www.tajdeed.net/ and has remained active since the end of August 2005, even after the July 7 and July 21, 2005, attacks in London. Al-Massari only closed down the site after the Home Office, "the government department responsible for internal affairs in England and Wales,"[17] began to compile a list of extremists it planned to deport.[18] The site, which is mostly in Arabic, calls for attacks on coalition troops in Iraq and presents video and audio clips providing detailed advice on physical training, surveillance of targets, and various operational tactics. There is also a segment on the selection of knives, which recommends one that is better for stabbing and "not suitable or good for beheadings."[19]

This site recommended that would-be mujahideen seek advice from the late Abu Musab al-Zarqawi on the topic of the "proper" manner of conducting beheadings, since al-Zarqawi was so experienced in such matters. The site provides advice on the use of night-vision equipment, how to set up and operate terror cells, and posts various videos of insurgent terrorist operations against US and coalition troops in Iraq, as well as radical Islamic propaganda slogans.[20]

AL QAEDA'S USE OF THE INTERNET

Al Qaeda has long understood the value of computers, using them to provide coded instructions to operatives, store data, communicate, obtain information, create false documents, and set up Web sites for a wide range of uses.

In July 2004, there were reports of increased and better-organized online postings of military materials by supporters of al Qaeda. These included Arabic translations of Western materials as well as more effective distribution of two Saudi-published, al Qaeda virtual magazines, *Sawt Al Jihad* (*The Voice of the Jihad*), *Al Battar* (al Qaeda's military manual),[21] and *Al Khansaa* (al Qaeda's women's magazine).[22] In October 2004, the following call to arms appeared in *Sawt Al Jihad*:

> Muslims! Go out to [fight] Jihad for the sake of Allah! Paradise has already flung open its gates and the virgins of paradise are already decked out in anticipation of their grooms—this is Allah's promise. No man of heart can allow himself tranquility and peace of mind until he goes out to fight against Allah's enemies, as he was commanded by Allah. He who does not act [i.e., fight the jihad] out of obedience to Allah's command, and out of zeal for the honor of the Muslim women which was defiled at Abu Ghraib and in the other prisons of the leaders of unbelief, and out of fervor, and out of mortification at [the thought of] shirking [battle]—what else could arouse him [to go to battle] other than all of these?[23]

The *Al Khansaa* site features articles offering advice for female suicide bombers, including tips on how to "dominate the passions" before blowing oneself up.[24] The emergence of *Al Khansaa* has led some analysts to conclude that al Qaeda now sanctions the use of female suicide bombers, a phenomenon previously seen only in Chechnya and the Palestinian territories, but has materialized in at least two instances. First, the attempted suicide bombing by Saijida Mubarak Atrous al-Rishawi, along with the successful attack by her husband and two other Iraqis of hotels in Amman, Jordan[25] (see chapter 4), and the "martyrdom" of the Belgian female suicide bomber Muriel Degauque. In November 2005, Degauque, a Muslim convert, blew herself up in Iraq when targeting an American patrol.[26]

The Italian newspaper *La Stampa* quoted an Italian intelligence analyst's comment about *Al Khansaa:* "[Y]ou won't find the usual fashion features that fill the pages of ladies' magazines the world over, except for a section dedicated to fitness with advice on diet and training to follow so as to acquire not a catwalk waistline, but martyrdom in the holy war."[27]

Al Qaeda has also received online recruitment assistance from a radical, Syrian-born London cleric, Sheikh Omar Bakri Mohammed. Mohammed, who has openly pledged allegiance to Osama bin Laden, has used nightly live broadcasts through an Internet chat room to recruit for al Qaeda. During one Webcast, Mohammed told his listeners: "Al Qaeda and all its branches and organizations of the world, that is the victorious group and they have the emir and you are obliged to join."[28] During another, he announced that the voices of dead mujahideen were calling young Britons to fight: "These people are calling to you and shouting to you from far distant places: al jihad, al jihad. They say to you my dear Muslim brothers, 'Where is your weapon, where is your weapon? Come on to the jihad.'"[29]

By the late 1990s, terrorist organizations had a significant online presence, and experts were warning of the danger posed by terrorist access to the Internet. In 1998, Michael Whine, director of the Defence and Group Relations Division of the Board of Deputies of British Jews, warned of the emerging dangers of Islamist organizations that had taken their campaigns to cyberspace: "That Internet usage by Islamists is growing is obvious. What is also obvious is that they will use it to promote their views, advance the strategies of the 'global Islamic movement' and organize their activities. . . . This poses clear dangers to the west in general and to Jewish communities in particular."[30]

Indeed, during the two years spent preparing for 9/11, Mohamed Atta and his fellow hijackers used a password-protected section of an extremist Islamic Web site to send thousands of messages to each other. It is also now known that they used the Web to research and inquire into US flight schools and make flight reservations.[31]

Around the same time, at least two accused al Qaeda–related Webmasters were reaching American Internet users. Babar Ahmad and Sami Omar al-Hussayen, two computer technicians, created Web sites whose purpose was to recruit for jihad.

Babar Ahmad

In August 2004, authorities in the United Kingdom arrested British citizen and computer expert Babar Ahmad on a criminal complaint issued in Connecticut. He was charged with conspiring to provide material support to terrorists—such as the Chechen mujahideen and the Afghan Taliban regime—and on a money-laundering charge.[32] On November 15, 2005, the UK agreed to extradite Ahmad to the United States.[33] Ahmad is the cousin of Mohammed Naeem Noor Khan (also mentioned in chapter 4 as tied to some of the 7/7 bombers), who was arrested in the summer of 2004 in Pakistan. Khan's computers contained information on financial buildings in New York, Newark, and Washington, DC.[34]

Ahmad's role as a Webmaster was to help create, operate, and maintain various Internet Web sites and e-mail accounts.[35] He also provided communications equipment, military items, lodging, training, false documentation, transportation, funding, personnel, and other assistance to the Chechen mujahideen, the Taliban, and associated groups, and he used the Web sites he maintained to support and justify violent jihad in Chechnya, Afghanistan, and elsewhere.[36]

One of Ahmad's primary conduits for inciting jihad was an entity known as Azzam Publications, a series of pro-jihad Web sites that was self-identified as the official source for news about the "Jihad and the Mujahideen Everywhere."[37] Its name is taken from a prominent figure in jihadi culture. Sheikh Abdullah Azzam, widely acknowledged as bin Laden's spiritual mentor, was born in Palestine but later relocated to the Peshawar region in Pakistan, where he helped to create an infrastructure for recruitment of fighters from throughout the Islamic world to lead the Arab and Afghan jihad against the Soviet Union in the 1980s.

Between 1997 and 2003, the Azzam Publications Web sites—including azzam.com, azzam.co.uk, qoqaz.net, qoqaz.co.uk, web storage .com/~azzam, and waaqiah.com—were hosted by an Internet service provider headquartered in Connecticut.[38] The two main Azzam Publications Web sites were azzam.com and qoqaz.net.[39] The latter was al Qaeda's primary English language Web site, and helped raise funds for the jihad in Chechnya. A quote featured prominently on Qoqaz.net's homepage is telling: "Jihad and the rifle alone. NO negotiations, NO conferences and NO dialogue."[40]

Although Azzam Publications stated that it personally took no financial donations, it told visitors how to donate to the Chechen jihad. On March 16, 2000, qoqaz.net posted directions: "How to Donate to Chechnya through Omega Relief Foundation."[41] Azzam Publications attempted to legitimize this appeal by asserting, "It is an obligation upon the Muslims all over the World to help their Muslim brothers and sisters in Chechnya, with their duas [prayers of support], wealth, actions and all other means at their disposal."[42]

From February 29, 2000, through December 17, 2001, in the "Frequently Asked Questions" section of both azzam.com and qoqaz.net, Muslims were explicitly instructed on joining the Chechen jihad. For example, the first FAQ asked: "I want to go and fight in Chechnya. How do I get there?" One answer recommends: "Anyone interested in going to fight (if they are trained) or in going to train should contact members of their own communities and countries who are known to have been for Jihad. You will know these people and they will know you. In these cases, you should only speak in confidence to those whom you trust, rather than speaking to everyone."[43]

In addition, on March 4, 2000, qoqaz.net contained a page titled "How Can I Train Myself for Jihad," along with a question-and-answer section that offered advice on physical training, survival, and outdoors and firearms training.[44] Similarly, an entry on azzam.com's FAQ included a question regarding finding information on homemade explosives on the Internet.[45]

In July 2004, a criminal complaint filed in the US District Court for the District of Connecticut stated that through azzam.com, Babar Ahmad "instructed individuals applying for a visa to provide a false reason for travel."[46] In addition, the subsequent indictment filed against him notes that Ahmad provided support to terrorists seeking temporary residence in London, England, and helped procure camouflage suits and global positioning system equipment.[47]

Ahmad was also communicating with at least one US military officer serving on the US guided-missile destroyer *Benfold* in the Middle East in 2000 and 2001. According to court documents and media reports, Hassan Abujihaad, a crewman on that ship, sent e-mails to Ahmad expressing anti-American sentiment and expressing admiration for the mujahideen. Abujihaad praised the attack of the USS *Cole*, and the "men who have brought honor . . . to the ummah in the lands of Jihad Afghanistan, Bosnia, Chechnya, etc."[48] In response, Ahmad encouraged the enlistee to "keep up with the Dawah the psychological warefare [*sic*]."[49] When British law enforcement authorities executed several search warrants at locations connected to Ahmad, they seized a document that "set forth plans for a U.S. naval battle-group operating in the Straits of Hormuz in April 2001."[50] The document also discussed the vulnerabilities of the naval group to a terrorist attack.[51]

As of July 2006, Ahmad appealed the order of his extradition to the

United States, where he has been indicted, and is currently awaiting the decision in the United Kingdom.[52]

Sami Omar al-Hussayen

In February 2003, Sami Omar al-Hussayen, a Saudi graduate student, was indicted on charges that included using the Internet to recruit and raise money for violent jihad in Israel, Chechnya, and elsewhere. Al-Hussayen served as the Webmaster, official registered agent, and business associate of the Islamic Assembly of North America (IANA), an organization based in Michigan.[53] "IANA's Internet web sites contain messages calculated to raise funds and recruit persons for anti-U.S. violence and jihad," according to the Department of the Treasury's "2003 National Money Laundering Strategy" report.[54] The investigation of al-Hussayen was a coordinated effort between law enforcement officers in Idaho and New York and produced what is believed to have been the most paper-intensive case to date in the post-9/11 era. Much to the disappointment of counterterrorism officials, the government was unable to use certain classified information in open court against al-Hussayen, and he was acquitted of three terrorism-related charges and two immigration charges.[55] On July 22, 2004, al-Hussayen was deported to Saudi Arabia.[56]

Al-Hussayen created and operated more than a dozen Web sites on behalf of IANA, one of which he established as Islamway.com, in August 1998. The site offered a link to qoqaz.net (see earlier discussion) and the Holy Land Foundation, accused of funneling money to Hamas.[57] On a link from Islamway.com to a "Palestine" Webpage is a section titled "What Is Your Role?" which contained specific instructions on how to aid the Palestinian jihad. The third step encouraged the reader, "Participation through Money—The Palestine Information Center—(The official communications entity for the Islamic Resistance Movement–Hamas) opens the doors for donations for all the Muslims so they can help the brothers in their noble Jihad against the dictatorial Zionist Jewish enemy."[58] Would-be donors could select a link, directly below the plea for financial assistance to Hamas, to www.palestine-info.org.[59]

Until January 2002, Islamway.com visitors could download two Arabic-language videos from the site about al Qaeda's role in Bosnia. One of them, *The Martyrs of Bosnia,* is a two-hour video documentary[60] depicting the 1992–93 civil war in the Balkans from the point of view of Arab and Afghan mujahideen acting under an al Qaeda and an Al

Islamiyya commander. The al Qaeda commander was Abdelrahman al-Dosari, aka Shaykh Abu Abdel Aziz "Barbaros," and the Al Islamiyya commander was Anwar Shaaban. The other video, *Operation Badr*—produced by the Arab-Afghan Mujahideen Battalion in Bosnia—features several suspected al Qaeda members and eulogizes the fall of the same Al Islamiyya commander featured in *The Martyrs of Bosnia.* The videos are still available for downloading and viewing in the Web archive of Islamway.com.[61]

Beginning in early 2000, al-Hussayen maintained and moderated an e-mail group on behalf of IANA. Because as moderator he approved all messages that were posted, he necessarily was aware of their radical nature. One particularly troubling posting was a February 25, 2003, message that contained an "urgent appeal" to Muslims in the American military to provide information on key targets and logistical support. Al-Hussayen also sent subscribers a monthly reminder appealing for financial support for the jihadi cause.[62]

As stated earlier, despite al-Hussayen's activities in setting up these Web sites and facilitating fund-raising efforts for Islamist groups worldwide while also disseminating their propaganda, al-Hussayen was acquitted of all charges that he provided material support or resources to a terrorist organization.

HAMAS'S USE OF THE INTERNET

Similar to al Qaeda, Hamas has effectively used the Internet to spread its message throughout the globe. Hamas Web sites promote the organization's leaders as cultural icons and glorify "martyrs" (suicide bombers or those killed by the Israeli army) by posting their pictures and biographies. The sites take such pride in the group's murderous record that they provide links to each martyr, listed in reverse chronological order dating back to the beginning of the Al Aqsa Intifada, the Palestinian armed uprising that commenced in September 2000.[63] Palestinian prisoners receive similar veneration and support.

Hamas's official Web site, housed on the Web site of the Palestine Information Center (www.palestine-info.com), is in Arabic; however, readers are offered sites in six other languages: French, English, Urdu, Russian, Farsi, and Melayu (Malaysian).[64] Although the site—both in name and appearance—presents itself as a media outlet, among the six sites, several contain hyperlinks to official Hamas news and statements.[65] As of August 2006, the hyperlink to Hamas provided a disclaimer: "This site is not the official site for Islamic Resistance Movement 'Hamas' but is a special division for the studying of the movement and its ideologies and the opinions that are distributed on this site do not reflect the opinions of the movement."[66] The creators of Islamist Web sites may use such disclaimers in hopes of preventing their sites from being shut down.

From the main Palestine Information Center site, a link is provided to the Web site of the Izz Al Din Al Qassam Brigades, Hamas's military wing.[67] Like www.palestine-info.com, this site glorifies "martyrs," prisoners, and terrorist operations. It is also notorious for posting videos of suicide bombers' final statements, or *shahadas* (testimonies to Allah), and even produces videos of actual terrorist operations against Israeli targets. On May 12, 2004, after six Israeli soldiers were killed in an operation in Gaza, members of the Al Qassam Brigades videotaped themselves with the soldiers' body parts and posted the footage online in order to taunt the soldiers' families.[68]

Hamas uses the Internet to recruit members from all age groups, using sites designed specifically for children (www.al-fateh.net) and for students (www.alkotla.com).[69] The children's site features snapshots of Palestinian children and toddlers dressed in Hamas military insignia and holding automatic weapons. In addition to bedtime stories and games, the site showcases a Hamas "Featured Martyr."[70] A number of graphic poems also appear on the site. One of them, titled "Palestine," includes the phrase, "I walked toward my destiny as a martyr covered in blood."[71]

Hamas has long courted individuals in these age groups in order to groom them for either future leadership positions within the organization or as volunteers for operations. To that end, members of Hamas's student movement, Al Kutla Al Islamiyya, founded www.alkotla.com to encourage Palestinian teenagers to join the group and carry out suicide operations against Israel.

Hamas operatives in the United States, based in Richardson, Texas, began an Internet and Web hosting company, Infocom Corp. Infocom and its officers have been convicted for money laundering in connection with Hamas as well as violating sanctions against state sponsors of terrorism.[72] Although Infocom did not host any actual Hamas Web sites, it was the Web hosting company for a variety of radical sites. (For a full discussion of the Infocom case, see chapter 5.)

PASSIVE RECRUITMENT AND COVERT COMMUNICATIONS

Many jihadist Web sites engage "passive recruitment," accomplished by the pervasive spread of radical Islamic propaganda. Jihadist cells are evolving into smaller and more operationally independent units, remaining ideologically linked to their global brethren via Internet communication. The potential for "virtual" recruitment, training, and other "management functions" controlled from one part of the world while the attackers operate and plan in another, without ever physically meeting, becomes quite real. This may be a critical factor in the growing threat of the so-called homegrown jihadi cells in western Europe and the United States.

A technology that has increasingly become the focus of law enforcement and counterterrorism officials is steganography. Steganography, as described by Gary Kessler, a professor of computer and digital forensics at Champlain College in Vermont, is "the art of covered or hidden writing. The purpose of steganography is covert communication—to hide the existence of a message from a third party."[73]

One example of the use of steganography is the transmission of a message via the Internet that is embedded into a photograph. When the recipient receives the photo message, the photo "background" is electronically removed or dissolved, leaving the written message. Despite the different methods of hiding messages in movies, photographs, and text files, the actual use of steganography by terrorists is unknown. According to Kessler, "[t]he use of steganography is certain to increase and will be a growing hurdle for law enforcement and counterterrorism activities."[74]

CONCLUSION

The Internet is a global communication medium that provides terrorist operatives and their organizations an often anonymous and instantaneous method of sending messages, images, intelligence, financial transactions, operational orders, training material, and any variety of other information to further their goals. Within the past decade, terrorist organizations, particularly radical Islamic terror groups, have become especially expert at manipulating the Internet to their advantage. There is every reason to believe this trend will continue. Western governments and others involved in counterterrorism efforts will need to become at least as innovative, aggressive, and progressive in their approach to the Internet in order to counter the enemy who fully intends to employ this medium against us.

Although US authorities have cracked down on Islamic militants who use the Internet to recruit, preach, and raise funds, they still face enormous obstacles in attempting to eliminate Islamist Web sites. Radical Islamists have become adept at the hide-and-seek game of moving constantly from one service provider to another to avoid detection. In addition, security measures such as commercial encryption are making their online communications increasingly immune to interception.

The arrest of Web-savvy Islamists such as Babar Ahmad and Sami Omar al-Hussayen are welcome developments, but foreign-based jihadists continue to post material that is readily available to computer users in the United States. Identifying and locating the purveyors remain difficult tasks. For example, "Internet cafés" in even the poorest countries in the Middle East provide affordable Internet access to radical Islamists and terrorists who do not own computers, enabling them to post inflammatory material online for a global audience. Despite the dogged efforts of the United States and its allies, the continued ability of radical Islamists to spread propaganda, recruit, and communicate via the Internet ensures that over the next several years much of the battle for the hearts and minds of Muslims in the United States and around the world will be waged in cyberspace.

NOTES

1. 7-Seas Global Intelligence, http://www.7-seas.net/METHODS.HTM (accessed August 10, 2005).

2. Colin Soloway, Rod Nordland, and Barbie Nadeau, "Hiding (and Seeking) Messages on the Web," *Newsweek*, June 17, 2004.

3. Ariana Eunjung Cha, "From a Virtual Shadow, Messages of Terror," *Washington Post*, October 2, 2004.

4. Luis Miguel Ariza, "Virtual Jihad," *Scientific American*, January 2006, p. 18.

5. Alan Cullison, "Inside Al Qaeda's Hard Drive," *Atlantic Monthly* 294, no. 2, September 2004, http://www.theatlantic.com/doc/200409/cullison (accessed August 1, 2005).

6. Ibid.

7. Mohammad Sohail (SMohammed@shl.com), "Subject: Muslims and Hacking," Newsgroup: Soc.religion.islam, March 17, 1997.

8. Web archive of Muslim Hackers Club, http://web.archive.org/web/20000930155126/www.ummah.net/mhc/hackinghtml (accessed August 10, 2005).

9. Web Archive of Muslim Hackers Club, http://web.archive.org/web/20050810134918/http://www.ummah.net/mhc/download/anarcook.zip (accessed December 7, 2004).

10. Derek Rose, "These Tots Are Terrors; Kids Parody Grisly Real-Life Killings in Web Video," *New York Daily News*, June 24, 2004.

11. Gabriel Weimann, "Terrorists and Their Tools-Part II," *Yale Global*, April 26, 2004, http://yaleglobal.yale.edu/display.article?id=3768 (accessed August 1, 2005).

12. "Treasury Designates Charity Funneling Money to Palestinian Islamic Jihad," Department of the Treasury, May 4, 2005, http://www.treas.gov/press/releases/js2426.htm (accessed December 13, 2005).

13. *USA v. Al-Arian, et al.*, 03-CR-77, superseding indictment, ¶ 20 (MD FL September 21, 2004).

14. Web archive of the Elehssan Society, http://web.archive.org/web/20010606171327/www.elehssan.com/index3.html (accessed August 10, 2005).

15. Web archive of the Benevolence International Foundation, http://web.archive.org/web/20000819023225/www.benevolence.org/donate.htm (accessed February 28, 2006).

16. "How Not to Get Hooked by a ' Phishing' Scam," *Federal Trade Commission Consumer Alert*, http://www.ftc.gov/bcp/conline/pubs/alerts/phishingalrt.htm (accessed December 14, 2005).

17. Web site of the Home Office of United Kingdom, http://www.homeoffice.gov.uk/ (accessed February 28, 2006).

18. "Saudi Dissident Shuts Down Site," BBC.com, August 27, 2005, http://news.bbc.co.uk/1/hi/uk/4191396.stm (accessed August 27, 2005).

19. Dipesh Gadher and Hala Jaber, "Saudi Exile Runs Urban Warfare Website in UK," *London Sunday Times*, August 14, 2005, http://www.timesonline.co.uk/article/0,,2087-1734147,00.html (accessed August 14, 2005).

20. Ibid. See also Philip Johnston, "Calls to Deport 'The Voice of al-Qa'eda,'" *London Daily Telegraph*, July 27, 2005, http://www.telegraph.co.uk/news/main.jhtml?xml=/news/2005/07/27/nmass27.xml (accessed July 28, 2005).

21. Reuven Paz, ed., "Who Wants to Email Al Qaeda?" *Project for the Research of Islamist movements (PRISM)*, vol. 2, no. 2, July 2004, http://www.e-prism.org/images/PRISM_no_2_vol_2_-_Who_Wants_to_Email_Al-Qaeda.pdf (accessed August 10, 2005).

22. Sebastian Usher, "'Jihad' Magazine for Women on Web," BBC News, August 24, 2004, http://news.bbc.co.uk/2/hi/middle_east/3594982.stm (accessed December 21, 2005).

23. Sa'ud bin Hamoud al-Utaybi, as quoted in the al Qaeda–linked *Sawt Al*

Jihad Internet magazine as translated by MEMRI, "Al-Qa'ida Internet Magazine Sawt Al-Jihad Calls to Intensify Fighting during Ramadan—'The Month of Jihad,'" October 22, 2004: Special Dispatch Series-no. 804, http://memri.org/bin/articles.cgi?Page=archives&Area=sd&ID=SP80404 (accessed August 10, 2005).

24. John Phillips, "Women's Magazine Offers Tips to Terrorists," *Washington Times*, January 17, 2005, http://www.washtimes.com/world/20050117-122001-8417r.htm (accessed August 1, 2005).

25. "'Bomber Confession' Shocks Jordan," CNN, November 14, 2005, http://www.cnn.com/2005/WORLD/meast/11/14/jordan.blasts/ (accessed December 21, 2005).

26. "Belgian Paper IDs 'Suicide Bomber,'" CNN, December 1, 2005, http://www.cnn.com/2005/WORLD/europe/12/01/belgium.iraq/?eref=yahoo (accessed December 21, 2005).

27. Ibid.

28. Sean O'Neil and Yaakov Lappin, "Britain's Online Imam Declares War as He Calls Young to Jihad: Omar Bakri Mohammed, Banned from Many British Mosques, Is Issuing a Call to Arms to a Committed Audience," *Times Online*, January 17, 2005, http://www.timesonline.co.uk/article/0,,2-1443903,00.html (accessed August 1, 2005).

29. Ibid.

30. Michael Whine, "Islamist Organizations on the Internet," *International Policy Institute for Counter-Terrorism*, April 1998, http://www.ict.org.il/articles/islamnet.htm (accessed August 10, 2005).

31. National Commission on Terrorist Attacks upon the United States, *The 9/11 Commission Report: Final Report of the National Commission on Terrorist Attacks upon the United States* (New York: Norton, 2004), p. 157.

32. "Babar Ahmad Indicted on Terrorism Charges in Connection with Support to Chechen Mujahideen, the Taliban, Other Groups: Charges Follow Three-Year Investigation by ICE," US Immigration and Customs Enforcement (ICE) news release, October 6, 2004, http://www.ice.gov/graphics/news/newsreleases/articles/ahmad100604.htm (accessed August 10, 2005).

33. "U.K. Agrees to Extradite Terror Suspect to U.S," MSNBC, November 16, 2005, http://msnbc.msn.com/id/10064015/ (accessed December 14, 2005).

34. Dana Priest and Susan Schmidt, "Terror Suspect's Arrest Opens New Inquiries," *Washington Post*, August 8, 2004.

35. *USA v. Ahmad, et al.*, 04-CR-301, indictment (D CT October 6, 2004).

36. Ibid.

37. Web archive of Azzam Publications, http://web.archive.org/web/20001014014638/azzam.com/home.htm (accessed August 10, 2005).

38. *USA v. Ahmad, et al.*, 04-CR-301, indictment (D CT October 6, 2004).

39. Ibid.

40. Web archive of Azzam Publications, http://web.archive.org/web/20000621135807/www.qoqaz.net/ (accessed August 10, 2005).

41. Web archive of Azzam Publications, http://web.archive.org/web/20000818175151/63.249.218.164/html/chechnyafacts.htm (accessed February 28, 2006).

42. Ibid.

43. Web archive of Azzam Publications, http://web.archive.org/web/20000818175151/http://63.249.218.164/html/chechnyafacts.htm#faqs (accessed February 28, 2006).

44. Web Archive of Azzam Publications, http://web.archive.org/web/20000816204345/63.249.218.164/html/chechnyajihadtrain.htm (accessed August 10, 2005).

45. Web archive of Azzam Publications, http://web.archive.org/web/20000929092759/www.azzam.com/html/faqsazzam.htm (accessed February 28, 2006).

46. *USA v. Ahmad, et al.*, 04-CR-301, criminal complaint (D CT July 28, 2004).

47. *USA v. Ahmad, et al.*, 04-CR-301, indictment (D CT October 6, 2004).

48. "British Man Arrested on Several Terrorism-Related Charges," US Department of Justice, United States Attorney's Office District of Connecticut press release, August 6, 2004, http://www.usdoj.gov/usao/ct/Press2004/20040806.html (accessed August 10, 2005). See also H. G. Reza and Richard B. Schmitt, "Arizona Man Was Sailor Who Wrote Radicals," *Los Angeles Times*, August 14, 2004.

49. *USA v. Ahmad, et al.*, 04-M-240, affidavit in support of request for extradition of Babar Ahmad, p. 26 (D CT 2004).

50. US Department of Justice, "British Man Arrested on Several Terrorism-Related Charges."

51. Ibid.

52. "'Terror Charges' Man Takes Case to Court of Appeal," IC South London, February 23, 2006, http://icsouthlondon.icnetwork.co.uk/0100news/merton/tm_objectid=16739675&method=full&siteid=50100&headline=-terror-charges—man-takes-case-to-court-of-appeal-name_page.html (accessed February 28, 2006); "Briton Indicted on U.S. Terror Charges," CNN.com, July 19, 2006, http://www.cnn.com/2006/LAW/07/19/terror.indictment.ap/index.html (accessed August 10, 2006).

53. *USA v. Al Hussayen*, 03-CR-048, indictment, p. 17 (D ID 2003).

54. US Department of Treasury, "2003 National Money Laundering Strategy," September 22, 2003, p. 34, http://www.treas.gov/press/releases/reports/js10102.pdf (accessed August 10, 2005).

55. *USA v. Al Hussayen*, 03-CR-048, verdict (D ID June 10, 2004).

56. Patrick Orr, "Al-Hussayen Finally Heads Home; Saudi Deported 5 Weeks after He Was Acquitted," *Idaho Statesman*, July 22, 2004.

57. Web archive of Islamway, http://web.archive.org/web/20000407183941/http://www.islamway.com/ (accessed August 10, 2005).

58. Web archive of Islamway (Arabic), http://web.archive.org/web/20010507084858/64.224.26.35/palestine/rule.htm (accessed August 10, 2005).

59. Ibid. See also Hamas (The Palestine Information Center), http://www.palestine-info.com/ and http://www.palestine-info.com/arabic/hamas/index.htm (accessed August 10, 2005).

60. Web archive of Islamway (Arabic), http://web.archive.org/web/20020205130422/www.islamway.com/ara/vidoes.php (accessed February 28, 2006).

61. Ibid.

62. *USA v. Al Hussayen*, 03-CR-048, superseding indictment, pp. 6–7 (D ID 2004).

63. Hamas Web site (Arabic), http://www.palestine-info.com/arabic/hamas/shuhda/shuhda.htm (accessed August 10, 2005).

64. Hamas Web site, http://www.palestine-info.com/ (accessed August 10, 2005).

65. The Arabic (http://www.palestine-info.com/arabic/hamas/index.htm), Farsi (http://www.palestine-persian.info/jonbesh-e-hemas/index.html), Urdu (http://www.palestine-info-urdu.com/urdu/hamas/index.shtml), and Melayu (http://www.infopalestina.com/hamas/) versions of the Web site all provide hyperlinks to official Hamas Web pages. The link is titled "HAMAS Movement" (Harakat al Moqawama al-Islamiyya).

66. Hamas Web site, http://www.palestine-info.com/arabic/hamas/index.htm (accessed December 21, 2005).

67. Izz al Din al Qassam (Arabic), http://www.alqassam.ws/arabic/ (accessed August 10, 2005). See also Izz al Din al Qassam (English), http://www.alqassam.ws/english/ (accessed August 10, 2005).

68. The video was featured on Izz al Din al Qassam's former Web site, www.ezzedeen.net (video in possession of author).

69. Hamas Web site, http://www.palestine-info.info/arabic/index.shtml (accessed August 10, 2005).

70. Web archive of Hamas' Children's, http://web.archive.org/web/20041229085909/http://www.al-fateh.net/fa-22/shahid.htm (accessed August 10, 2005).

71. Web archive of Hamas' Children's, http://web.archive.org/web/20040220142614/www.al-fateh.net/site/musharacat-falastine.htm (accessed August 10, 2005).

72. "More Federal Convictions for Elashi Brothers and Infocom Corporation at Second Trial," US Department of Justice United States Attorney Northern District of Texas, April 14, 2005.

73. Gary C. Kessler, "An Overview of Steganography for the Computer Forensics Examiner," *Forensic Science Communications* 6, no. 3, July 2004, http://www.fbi.gov/hq/lab/fsc/backissu/july2004/research/2004_03_research01.htm (accessed December 14, 2005).

74. Ibid.

CONCLUSION

Militant Islamism continues to present a grave threat to America and to the world. Given that indisputable fact, it becomes vital for the American public to gain the greatest possible awareness of the face of the enemy. Clearly, the task of ferreting out and combating the ever-shifting terrorist threat falls primarily to our law enforcement agencies and intelligence community, who remain vigilant in that pursuit. But an informed and supportive citizenry is also a vital factor.

Al Qaeda brought terrorism home to the majority of Americans who had previously perceived militant Islam as an external, overseas problem. On September 11, 2001, the country awoke to a violent reality. However, as the material in this book has demonstrated, al Qaeda, while perhaps the most notable, is not the only terrorist group seeking to harm the United States. Varioius groups that have waged jihad in South Asia, the Middle East, North Africa, and beyond have infiltrated our society. They have hatched plots from within our borders to execute attacks domestically and to raise funds for their terror campaigns abroad.

These groups have not only created physical networks on the ground for these campaigns dating back to the early 1980s but they have also graduated to the use of modern-day technology, creating a virtual world on the Internet where extremists, planners, and operatives can communicate via chat rooms, e-mail, and messaging software.

Fervent and fiery imams propogate the necessity of jihad to young men and women from Karachi to Chicago. With minimal effort, manuals on terrorism that contain knowledge on subjects such as explosives, chemical weaponry, and guerrilla tactics are disseminated secretly across the globe from training camps on the Pakistani-Afghani border to populated Western metropolises. In the age of cyberspace, the enemy has become ethereal and elusive—connected by an ideology that spreads with an ease that is not yet matched by our ability to track and defeat it.

The Internet's role in dissemination coupled with the decentralization of major terrorist groups—particularly al Qaeda—has led to the increasing threat from homegrown groups, consisting of American citizens who have turned against their own country to wage jihad. The 7/7 bombings in London and the arrests of seventeen terrorist suspects in Canada may come to mind as the primary examples of indigenous threats, but such plotters have been active in America as well. Among the most recent examples are the cell at California's Folsom Prison that allegedly conspired to attack US military facilities and Jewish targets; the Portland Seven; the Toledo cell; and the Virginia "paintball jihad" network. Homegrown groups will undoubtedly continue to be a major focus of our War on Terror.

While militant Islamism is just the latest in a series of threats that our nation has faced, its uniqueness and malevolence cannot be understated. Determined to combat whatever it sees as divergent, different, or unholy, this zealous strain of Islam will settle for nothing less than our total subjugation or destruction. It couples its zealotry in pursuit of its goals with patience as to achieving them.

Homegrown plotters, sleeper cells, intolerant and hateful imams, and their domestic apologists all seek to undermine the foundations of this country through a variety of means: rhetoric, fund-raising, and violence. Intricate webs of interconnected groups and organizations have been established to pursue—and often to obfuscate—the zealots' destructive objectives.

The makeup of those webs keeps shifting, the face of the enemy keeps changing, but the danger posed remains constant and real. An informed American public can confront this threat—not with anxiety and dread—but with intelligence, honesty, and courage. The goal of this book, then, is to provide the public with the best and most up-to-date snapshot that diligent research can assemble of the ever-changing face of the terrorist organizations, and their support groups, that make up Jihad Incorporated.

ACKNOWLEDGMENTS

First and foremost, I would like to publicly recognize the past and current analysts at the Investigative Project on Terrorism, as well as outside experts, who, through their tireless efforts and exemplary dedication, applied their expertise and passion to the production and completion of this book. I would like to take this opportunity to name them: Olivia Gillig, Ryan Evans, Brian Hecht, Cynthia Dachowitz, Michal Khayat, Tamar Tesler, Abha Shankar, Scott Rosenbaum, Lorenzo Vidino, Steven Helman, Jason AbuAliza, S. Walter Jones, Tally Aharony, William D. West, Joseph Perry, Denise Katz, Bryan Wheeler, Scott Newark, Jacob Wallace, Jeremiah Baronberg, Aaron Aft, Daveed Gartenstein-Ross, Erick Stakelbeck, Dov Gardin, Dana Leseman, and Max Sicherman. A special thanks to Janice Kephart who helped manage the project for a critical period of time. Kim Perkins has been a godsend. The book is dedicated to the memory of Jason Korsower whose death denied the world of a brilliant thinker and a warrior in the war on terrorism. Thank you all for your research, analysis, and writing.

There are many more to thank, and should I forget anyone, I assure you the lapse is entirely unintentional. The supporters of the Investigative Project on Terrorism have ensured our survival and allowed us the privilege of playing a role in the war on Islamic extremism.

The efforts of Richard Horowitz were vital in the completion of this volume. Last, and perhaps most important, I would like to thank everyone at Prometheus Books for their boundless patience, especially Steven L. Mitchell, Mary A. Read, and Christine Kramer.

INDEX